The Who on Record

The Who on Record

A Critical History, 1963–1998

by
JOHN ATKINS

McFarland & Company, Inc., Publishers
Jefferson, North Carolina, and London

The present work is a reprint of the library bound edition of The Who on Record: A Critical History, 1963–1998, *first published in 2000 by McFarland.*

LIBRARY OF CONGRESS CATALOGUING-IN-PUBLICATION DATA

Atkins, John, 1961–
    The Who on record : a critical history, 1963–1998 / by John Atkins.
        p.   cm.
    Discography: p.
    Includes bibliographical references and indexes.

    ISBN 978-0-7864-4097-9
    softcover : 50# alkaline paper ∞

    1. Who (Musical group)   2. Who (Musical group)—Discography.
I. Title.
ML421.W5 A9   2009   99-87872
782.42166'092'2—dc21

British Library cataloguing data are available

©2000 John Atkins. All rights reserved

No part of this book may be reproduced or transmitted in any form or by any means, electronic or mechanical, including photocopying or recording, or by any information storage and retrieval system, without permission in writing from the publisher.

Cover images ©2009 Shutterstock

Manufactured in the United States of America

McFarland & Company, Inc., Publishers
  Box 611, Jefferson, North Carolina 28640
  www.mcfarlandpub.com

To Elaine,
and the memory of
our beloved Paddy

Contents

Preface   1

1. Art, Rock and Roll, and the Who   5
2. Maximum Reaction (1963–1965)   29
3. Art Pop (1966–1967)   63
4. High Energy, Deep Mysticism (1968–1970)   100
5. To the Lifehouse (1971–1972)   139
6. Rockers and Mods (1973–1974)   177
7. Beating the Retreat (1975–1978)   216
8. Second Generation (1979–1998)   245

Notes   273
Appendix 1: Essential LP and CD Releases (1965–1998)   281
Appendix 2: Index of Who Songs and Recorded Performances (1963–1991)   289
Index   331

Preface

The main text of this book constitutes an attempt to offer a critical analysis and assessment of the recorded music of the British rock-and-roll band the Who. Its chronology begins with the day in 1963 when the young band (probably under a different name) first entered a recording studio in London to complete a test acetate disk, and concludes with the 1998 CD release of previously unreleased music. These are the catchall extremes of the thirty-five-year time period involved in the Who's history of making and releasing records. However, the band really only had an active recording life of seventeen years, from 1965 to 1982, and the last decade of this period was less than prolific. The Who did not make anywhere near as many records as the Beatles, the Rolling Stones, the Kinks or Bob Dylan, and the records that they did release trailed behind these acts in terms of sales. Yet the Who's achievement on record was (and is) substantial and forms one of the most powerful and definitive rock-and-roll statements of all time.

By a general consensus, the concert stage—rather than the recording studio—was the Who's natural environment. They functioned at their best as a live act and deservedly gained the reputation as the greatest live rock-and-roll band in the world, a phenomenal epithet by which they are most often remembered today. Implicit in the logic of this line of argument, however, could be the belief that their records should be written off as somehow being weak, flawed, pale, and less exciting representations of the band's music, which is a judgement that does not bear up to any analysis. Today, the recordings are all we have of the Who, and for the large part they have taken on a form of their own that is comfortably detached from what the band were on stage. On record, the Who functioned differently and exploited the different medium for its own qualities; they never tried to be the same band on stage as they were in the studio and vice versa. The records remain; the concerts become a distant, albeit glorious, memory.

The narrative of this book deals with the Who's recordings in chronological order, that is, the order in which the band recorded the material. It also details the Who's record releases in a similarly historical order, although the recording chronology and the release chronology may well not adhere in a linear fashion. A recent reissue program of Who material on CD has made available (legally) for the first time much material from the band's past; indeed, the latest Who CD to appear conversely contains two tracks from 1964 that have never been heard before. I discuss each recording in its rightful historical place, irrespective of its discographical position. The discographical elements of this work, I should point out, do not include bootleg or underground releases, although I do draw upon a considerable quantity of unreleased material for discussion where relevant in the text.

In discussing the music of the Who, I refer to the band's activities and the background details of their work in the past tense, as befits any historical text; but in discussing their actual records, I revert to the present tense. The music one hears from a record or CD is part of the present, and it remains so each time one listens. So it seems to me that this is the correct approach to take in a book of this sort. I must apologize in advance if the tense shifts prove disconcerting to the reader, but the logic of such a method should soon become apparent. I describe the Who quite simply as a "rock-and-roll band," and reserve the shortened "rock 'n' roll" epithet very specifically for the music's 1950s progenitors. This distinction has evolved over thirty years of serious rock writing, and I see no reason here to depart from it. Whether it is adequate, accurate or appropriate to consider the Who as nothing more and nothing less than a rock-and-roll band is open to question, but it is the only description I wish to apply.

One important point is implicit in the title of this book: This is a study of the Who's records, which largely means music created in a recording studio. I necessarily limit any analysis of the Who's live work to those concert excerpts that have been released on record. I am aware that a massive quantity of unreleased live material exists in the Who's archives, but this forms a different subject entirely. I feel the Who's live performance career has been more than adequately covered in *The Who Concert File* (Omnibus, 1997) by Joe McMichael and Irish Jack Lyons, a publication to which I also contributed. I unhesitatingly direct to this work readers who want to explore this aspect of the band's career. A similar restriction is necessitated in the discussion of the solo careers of Roger Daltrey, John Entwistle, Keith Moon, and Pete Townshend. If the solo work of the band members had been intimately linked with (or shed important light upon) the work of the band as a whole, then it might have warranted due attention; for the large part this was not the case. Solo work was often entirely peripheral to the band and I thus largely disregard it.

The music critic or biographer has gained an indirect advantage with the advent of the compact disc because of the way the music on a CD has an encoded elapsed time index in minutes and seconds. Reviewers of classical music have found it accurate and satisfactory to pinpoint for readers certain moments by simply quoting the time index on the CD at any given place, where in the past they would have had to quote the printed musical score or use extremely precise terms of description. I utilize the same method, and the CD time index is liberally quoted throughout the main text of this book within square brackets, for example, [2.05].

I sincerely hope that this book will enhance people's enjoyment of the Who's music and offer some understanding of the context from which it came. *The Who on Record* is the result of twenty-five years of listening to Who music—sometimes in awe, sometimes in doubt, but mostly in respect and enjoyment. It is perhaps only right for me to declare my appreciation of the band right at the beginning, although I certainly hope that this narrative avoids any blind allegiance or uncritical perspective. I enjoy many kinds of music, including that of a handful of rock-and-roll bands (the Smiths, the Byrds, the Kinks, R.E.M., the Clash, Wire) among whom I rate the Who the finest. This is not a biography or a discography (although it includes elements of both); it is a critical study that addresses the central body of the band's recorded work as a substantive aesthetic entity in its own right. I found there was a great deal to say about the Who's music, and I hope readers gain an equally positive response.

I should mention that some of the material included was published previously in the British Who magazine *Generations* from 1988 to 1997. However, I have extensively revised and updated this material and woven it into a complete historical narrative that represents my final response to the Who's music. The original sources of all the quotations from newspapers, magazines, journals, letters and broadcasts are acknowledged in the footnotes. Mindful of the laborious overuse of the same comments from band members in many previous books, I have tried to include here quotations that have never appeared before in book form. More general acknowledgments must go to the following books: *Classic Albums: Interviews from the Radio One Series* (BBC Books, 1991) compiled by John Pidgeon; *The Lamberts* (Chatto & Windus, 1986) by Andrew Motion; *The Who: Before I Get Old* (Plexus, 1983) by Dave Marsh; *The Who: An Illustrated Discography* (Omnibus, 1983) by Ed Hanel; *The Who: Maximum R&B* (Eel Pie, 1982) by Richard Barnes; *The Complete Guide to the Music of the Who* (Omnibus, 1995) by Chris Charlesworth; *The Who Concert File* (Omnibus, 1997) by Joe McMichael and Irish Jack Lyons; and finally the booklet notes (by various authors) produced for the CD reissue program by Polydor and MCA (1994–1998). Also, *The Who in Print* (McFarland, 1992) by Stephen Wolter and Karen Kimber has been an invaluable help.

I would like to thank the following people who directly or indirectly have helped to make this book possible: Jon Astley, Elaine Atkins, Scott Campbell, Chris Charlesworth, Richard Evans, Phil Hopkins, Tim Joseph, Bruce

Kawakami, Andy Macpherson, Joe McMichael, Brian Parrott, Jan Reynaert, Nick Ryle, Rod Wilson and readers of the Who magazine *Generations* who have offered comment and support. I should also thank Polydor in London for supplying me with CDs at various times in the past. Finally, thanks to the members of the Who for being themselves in the first place and doing it the way they did!

John Atkins
Fall 1999

1

Art, Rock and Roll, and the Who

1963: London breathes in the optimism of a new decade. Youth emerges from the submersion of a dull few years during which rock and roll erupts with a rebel yell from the gutter and throws a lifeline to anyone in the restless state of adolescence. The salvation of the young explodes across the streets, and an exciting new music is embraced: rock and roll, skiffle, folk, bop, beat, rhythm and blues. The scent of fresh cappuccino mingles with the smoky aroma of dope in espresso coffee bars where a new altar of worship is to be found in the jukebox. New possibilities are staring teenagers in the face, but time seems to be running out. Bertrand Russell tells thousands of young people at a Campaign for Nuclear Disarmament demonstration that the world will come to an end within a few years unless something is done now. One still-insignificant young man amongst thousands is Peter Townshend, a member of CND and would-be graphics artist in the making. He hears Russell's appeal to the new generation at a rally in Trafalgar Square, returns to Ealing Art College, determines to change the world, smokes some dope, listens to some Mose Allison and Jimmy Reed, smokes more dope, and emerges from his world with a vision. He then picks up his guitar and starts to play...

"Pop music is crucial to today's art," Pete Townshend asserted in 1968, speaking to the world on a serious national television program, "and it's crucial that it should remain art, and it's crucial that it should progress as art."[1] Ostensibly, however, rock and roll and art don't mix. Art has traditionally sought and been accorded an aesthetic level well above and beyond that of anything as populist as rock, and in turn rock has so often had at the heart of its very purpose and appeal a contemptuous and self-conscious rebuke and debunk of art's pretensions. Rock-and-roll music has, however, since the mid–1950s, staked a claim towards being recognized as a legitimate part of Western culture. As a sociological phenomenon, some would say that it initially found its way into the textbooks and theses under the "youth subculture" entry (alongside the Beatnik) when it was perceived that teddy boys, boppers and greasers had become too numerous to be written off as a bizarre fad. Musicologists would claim rock and roll to be a direct development and debasement of jazz, blues, bebop, doo-wop or whatever form of semimusical sound a society dominated by commercial vulgarity could throw up to give the otherwise inarticulate a kind of voice.

It was first called *rock 'n' roll*: a name that evoked the forbidden sexual delights of black Americana and fulfilled the demands of the nascent postwar youth for a personal argot to which adults couldn't relate. It was embodied by Elvis Presley, Chuck Berry, Little Richard, Jerry Lee Lewis, Bill Haley and others. By the early 1960s, it was referred to as *rock and roll*, *pop* or plain *rock*, depending on whom you listened to (not to mention the burgeoning substrata of soul, beat, R&B and so forth). Only in the late 1960s did it become clear that rock and roll would have a longevity beyond that of the couple of years predicted by the cynics and would find a context and social position that would go beyond the jukebox, coffee bar and discotheque. And at this point—rightly or wrongly—people began taking rock seriously. Whether rock had matured and proved itself worthy of artistic recognition, or its sudden pre-eminence merely indicated a crisis within Western culture remains debatable.

Rock's progress toward establishing itself as a commercial force was much more rapid, in a capitalist system and consumer society it found an easy niche and gained a market respectability almost immediately—after all, you didn't have to like the product to market it and enjoy the profits it could yield. The mainstream light entertainment establishment of the 1950s (radio, cinema, variety and musical theater, the record industry) went some way toward embracing rock 'n' roll and managed to process and incorporate it without any great adjustment or culture shock to itself—although purists have claimed the music suffered a dilution from which it never really recovered. The individuals within rock 'n' roll were rebels on the stage only: a small overspill of aggression and wildness into their real lives didn't disguise the fact that they were invariably showmen of the old school, businessmen and showbiz professionals.

Rock's bid for recognition as a *bonafide* art form has been more troubled. In the 1990s Frank Zappa, Jimi Hendrix, Eric Clapton and the Beatles only very occasionally rub shoulders with Stravinsky, Sibelius and Harrison Birtwistle on the BBC's largely all-classical Radio 3 (the sacred British touchstone of high culture), and rock artists are given begrudgingly short reviews in the Sunday newspapers. Rock and roll has barely scraped a reputation as anything other than at worst an exploitation of teenage gullibility and at best a loud form of light entertainment. The debate doesn't rage as hard as it once did; most popular musicians don't much care for artistic recognition anyway. Very little "popular" music aspires toward anything greater than commercial success or, failing that, a vague and largely illusory quality of street credibility (in other words, the regard of one's peers and the approval of those who seek to define what is and what is not fashion).

Also, the diversification of form in popular music hasn't helped its cause for recognition as art. Where once in the 1960s "pop music" as a whole (with the Beatles at its forefront with their *Rubber Soul* and *Revolver* albums) was less readily dismissed and somewhat easier to comprehend as a substantive musical entity, we now have a multitude of strands that share no collective identity. Division and diversification have led to a less focused and more incoherent whole. The vast array of different types of music that congregate under the generic term *popular* often bear no real resemblance to one another. Yet they exist within their own closed world in which they hold a definition, a status and a place in a hierarchy. It is a world encapsulated by the breadth of coverage in *New Musical Express, Rolling Stone, Mojo, Smash Hits, Q* or *Melody Maker* and the playlists of FM radio stations. Contemporary popular music remains a force year after year for two simple reasons: first, its fans and followers are numerically great, and second, its power to generate money is phenomenal. If rock had to survive on its cultural kudos alone it would have long ago all but diminished into a cultish outer fringe of musical form.

Rock in Britain initially gained its status when a small number of performers saw making records and playing concerts as their only expressive outlet, using their music as a means of liberation from a life of conventional labor. These men (few women, alas) took rock 'n' roll—as initially imported from the U.S.—as a lifeline to something better. It was the only option they had. Their talents would not lend themselves to classical musicianship, composition, writing or the visual arts. In the end, expedience and pragmatism dictated their function as entertainers. They played their music through the economic necessity to aspire toward a higher standard of living and to become "a name," rather than being driven by creative urges.

However, to compound this trend, a newer generation of talented individuals *chose* rock and roll as their means of expression *instead* of pursuing an alternative and more conventional artistic outlet. Ray Davies (of the Kinks), John Lennon (of the Beatles) and Pete Townshend (among many others), it has often been pointed out, all hailed from the same type of art college background and *abandoned* the more formal disciplines that they were learning in favor of singing, playing and songwriting. They had options available to them and a choice of media. Hence for the first time, the generation of pop musicians from the early 1960s considered themselves to be artists. It was but a short step before others recognized the concept of the pop artist. Before the end of the decade, perceptive social commentator (and jazz performer) George Melly had written that the Who "were extremely important in their *conscious* exploration of the potentials of pop as an art form. They succeeded, temporarily at any rate, in making the Beatles sound precious and the Stones old hat."[2]

Pete Townshend (guitarist, keyboard player and singer), Roger Daltrey (singer), Keith Moon (drummer) and John Entwistle (bass guitarist and singer) were the four individual musicians who happened to congregate in London as the Who. Their story has been often told and their names are familiar, but the essence of the Who—the result of their combined genius—remains more remote, more precious and rarefied. More than any other group, the Who worked as a collective whole and were much more than the sum of the four parts *despite* the fact that they had essentially only one songwriter. Their sound, attitude, style, and reason for existence was an ensemble collusion of four diverse personalities. The numerous British groups who were the Who's contemporaries in the 1960s were essentially generic, and the individuals within them often seemed interchangeable. In our memory now and even in the public consciousness of the time, the bass player in the Dave Clark Five was no different in ability and persona to his counterpart in, say, the Hollies; the drummer in the Animals didn't seem differentiated from the drummer of the Yardbirds. The "pop star" who was a member of the Tremeloes, Unit 4 + 2, Gerry and the Pacemakers, the Mindbenders, Amen Corner or the Searchers, for example, could quite easily have been reproduced from a mop-topped guitar-wielding archetypal mold. This isn't to say that the individuals involved in these pop acts lacked any personality, character or musical identity but simply illustrates the conformity of the scene and the limitations that prevailed. Only the really big groups (Beatles, Rolling Stones, Kinks, Small Faces) gained enough media exposure to delineate individual group members in the public eye. Even among the four exceptions named above, the Who was markedly different from all its contemporaries, seemingly being more detached and aloof and more willing to ignore the rules or exceed the limits. It was because the Who occupied a unique musical terrain and was vividly individualistic that its music was of such significance.

The Who was a *rock* band at a time when that four-letter word meant something. The term *rock music* is no longer the expansive musical label that it once was. It has somehow become debased through the 1980s into synonymy (and, indeed, anonymity) with heavy metal and its more obscure and grisly subgenres; at best it has come to denote a kind of old-wave, yuppie-friendly ultrarespectable coffee-table CD mainstream (Eric Clapton, Pink Floyd, Dire Straits, Rolling Stones, Bruce Springsteen). To refer to more vital musical forms such as R.E.M., the ill-fated Nirvana, current British guitar band favorites Blur and Oasis, or eccentrics like Morrissey or P. J. Harvey as rock seems to now mislead and devalue these artists—yet all are undoubtedly creators of rock in its purest form (exemplified by the Sex Pistols, the Velvet Underground, the Clash, the Ramones, MC5, Patti Smith, the Stooges and a long list of like-minded groups in the same tradition who have honed revelatory melody and the poetry of angst and cynicism from adrenalin, amplifiers, drums, distortion, screams and noise). *Indie* and *Grunge* are also

1980s terms for what in essence would previously have been considered simply to be rock music, and no less valuable or artistically valid for it—likewise *punk* and *new wave* in the late 1970s and the current vogue of *Brit–pop*. All these strands of classic rock and roll are labeled with varying degrees of accuracy by the media to give reference points to the uninitiated.

The Who were, in essence, a rock-and-roll band without a label other than the polymorphic *rock* (or *Rock*, with the capital *R*, as Pete Townshend used to grandly espouse), but this bears little connection with what is considered "rock" today. Indeed, the phrase only diminishes the value of The Who's music to those whose uninitiated conception of rock equates only with Guns N' Roses, Metallica, Aerosmith, Bon Jovi, Def Leppard and their ilk. In many ways, the Who were the R.E.M. and the Nirvana of their era, (as well as the Oasis and the Blur): it was exploratory, disciplined, powerful, diffuse, and able to mix experimentation with mass appeal—but most important. They were not strictured by a category. The Who weathered many prevailing trends within the changing domain of rock and roll—R&B, beat, pop, mod, psychedelia, heavy metal, progressive, glam/glitter, punk and new wave—without feeling any need to adapt or conform to a musical label. Definitions can become limitations, and limitations stifle creativity.

In this book, the term *rock and roll* is used in its strictest sense to evoke the spirit of the Who's music without tainting it with a name shared with much lesser forms of entertainment. It also remains contentious whether it is meaningful to regard pop music as an art form *per se,* as the vast majority of it seems to have merely an ephemeral and commercial value. As entertainment it has its place in our lives and we can choose to take it or leave it. But when under the gaze of a contemporary critic of Western culture, from whatever viewpoint, philosophical, sociological or political, the question most likely to be asked is not whether rock and roll is art but whether it is even *music*. That particular issue must, in this work at least, go unanswered.

This does raise the question whether the Who's music can be truly called art either; although, if it cannot, it must at least be recognized as belonging to a precious rare strain of rock and roll that has the ability to evoke thought and express vital emotions that are relevant to modern life. At its very least, Who music communicates, which is a great deal more than what much of what we hear on the radio, in the pop charts or in nightclubs manages to achieve. Undoubtedly, Pete Townshend—in particular among rock musicians—possesses the sensibilities of a creative artist, which may or may not amount to the same thing. Within the closed quarter of pop music culture, the Who held and still holds a great significance. They were considered among their peers to possess a rare artistic integrity. Outside of the pop music sphere, they gained a small reputation for their music—as very few groups have done—within the arts mainstream. To overstate the value of rock and roll within the global cultural continuum of the past few millennia would be intellectually risible. It is timely, however, to assert the Who's standing in a world of constantly shifting values. Pete Townshend, particularly, evokes the aura of the tortured creative genius, fighting for his place in the pantheon but willingly accepting his own mortality and lack of potency. Yet Townshend's achievement among the Western intellectual and cultural coterie is notable because, ultimately, rock-and-roll musicians are (still) not expected to be thinking, caring, or intelligent people.

Pete Townshend talked about the Who's music as art almost from their first single release in 1965. He called it "pop art," a very familiar concept at the time but one normally associated with the visual arts rather than with music. Townshend knew that the Who's music could never compete on a conventional artistic level with classical music or even jazz and folk, but he also recognized (as few others did at this time) that rock had something vital of its own that the more respectable forms of music lacked. He specifically set out to eschew (and even directly confront) the prevailing norm in pop music, which was ostensibly bland and conformist and had much to do with traditional family entertainment values (Cliff Richard, Dave Clark Five, Freddie and the Dreamers, Herman's Hermits) and nothing to do with changing the world. However, the Who couldn't escape the machinery that made and sustained these pop acts: their singles stepped up and down the same sales charts and were played by the same disc jockeys, and the Who performed alongside them on *Top of the Pops* and *Ready Steady Go!* without much compunction in search of the all-empowering hit single. But Townshend lost no opportunity to emphasize just how different was the Who's approach, once saying, "There is no suppression within the group... We play how we feel... Pop-art is something society accepts, but we represent it to them in a different form."[3]

Pete Townshend was born on 19 May 1945 and educated at Acton County Grammar School and Ealing Art College. He played guitar from an early age and while at art college found that his latent talents were in fact largely musical, having played in various bands since his early teens alongside Roger Daltrey and John Entwistle. Townshend adopted a nonconformist approach to life right after leaving school, rejecting conventional employment and immersing himself in jazz, blues, folk, R&B, pot smoking and the general dissolution surrounding college-bound teenagers during the first phase of the CND protest movement. Admittedly, Townshend adopted a ready-made persona of art student at a time when rebellion was prescribed by fashion. While his formal artistic accomplishments remain untested (he was studying graphic arts), Pete Townshend absorbed important theories of art, in particular those of "auto-destructive" artist Gustav Metzker.[4]

While at Acton County Grammar School, Townshend met and began to make music in groups with fellow pupils Roger Daltrey and John Entwistle, enjoying the kind of early grounding in ensemble musicianship that very few other groups manage to achieve. Daltrey (born on 1 March 1944) was also a rebellious teenager, although along more traditional delinquent lines than was Townshend. He took a tough, practical attitude to life and saw singing in a group to be a better alternative to conventional work. Entwistle (born 9 October 1944) had a much less volatile personality and was more conventionally trained in music (having studied the French horn and piano). However, the quartet of the Who was only really formed in May 1964 when Keith Moon (born 23 August 1946), a hugely talented drummer, natural comedian and mercurial character, finalized the lineup for good. Moon seemed born to play drums with the Who; his style and personality were so uncannily right—frantic, eccentric and flamboyant.

The members of the Who, significantly enough, never saw themselves as a pop group. They were originally known as the Detours, and played extensively on the West London club circuit (centered around Ealing, Acton and Shepherd's Bush). Their original repertoire was dictated by the demands of the audience: it was a mixture of Shadows instrumentals, pop hits, a little traditional jazz and—when they could get away with it—some raw rhythm and blues. As the Beatles became the big new phenomenon through 1963, the Detours even veered toward Merseybeat. But at the time R&B seemed to be the coolest option and the form of music with which they felt most likely to succeed.

In the early 1960s, R&B was the most significant alternative to pop. This music was very credible among a more discerning young audience and was not overtly commercial, based as it was on live performances in intimate surroundings rather than 45 rpm disks and variety theaters. But R&B was musically limited and rooted in an established tradition that didn't allow for much creativity. Inevitably (and even before they had signed a recording contract), the Who outgrew R&B. The Beatles (and slightly later the Rolling Stones and the Kinks) had established a precedent for writing original songs and in the process had thrown down a challenge for all British groups to come out from behind the shield of R&B and pop cover versions and prove their worth. The Who, and Pete Townshend in particular, seized this chance and made an indelible impact on the music scene.

Richard Barnes has extensively chronicled the early career of the Who in his authorized biography *Maximum R&B*.[5] Barnes was a contemporary and colleague of Townshend who had first-hand knowledge of the group's formative years. Further coverage has been provided by American rock critic and author Dave Marsh in *Before I Get Old*, for which Marsh undertook exhaustive field research.[6] More recently the band's concert career has been painstakingly documented by Joe McMichael and Irish Jack Lyons in *The Who Concert File*, a work that is unlikely to be surpassed in terms of recording the fine detail of Who performances.[7] But the fact remains that the early work of the Who—also under the names the Detours and the High Numbers—was often indistinguishable from that of countless other bands in West London in the early 1960s, many of whom are now forgotten.

Since the Who only really became a fully fledged recording act in 1965, the preceding years have left scant recorded evidence upon which a judgement can be formed. These were the years of apprenticeship, where the members of the band learned their trade on the sweaty stages of London's pubs and clubs while their abilities and inspiration evolved and matured. As the Detours, they never released any records; the High Numbers managed one solitary single. Hardly any test recordings, demo acetates or audition and rehearsal tapes from 1963 and 1964 have survived. The band rarely visited a recording studio during 1964, and only a handful of songs can be confidently identified as having hailed from this year. Nineteen sixty-five is a different story altogether, of course, but the Who's formative years can have little place in a work devoted to their recorded works.

In fact, from all accounts, the early music of the Detours gave few hints of what would follow, and it was only during 1964—after Keith Moon had completed the lineup—that the band began to display any indication that it would so gloriously transcend the rhythm and blues music that had found a growing audience from the beginning of the 1960s. Even in later years, the Who's musical roots would be less easily identifiable than those of, say, the Beatles or the Rolling Stones. The early incarnations of the band played everything that was expected of them in an environment led by audience demand. They played high-powered R&B from a standard stock of songs that almost every group drew upon ("Plum Nellie," "Smokestack Lightning," "Spoonful"), covers of recent pop hits, and various Shadows/Ventures-style instrumentals. By 1964, however, the R&B element of the set had begun to be displaced by cover versions of Tamla Motown and Soul, a new departure for a white rock-and-roll act. The Who became notable as unique interpreters of this material. (Despite the influx of black music into their repertoire, it should be stressed, however, that at no stage did the Who ever sound remotely like what we now think of as a soul act—what they offered was Tamla material played as high-energy rock and roll.)

Various people have attempted to analize the Who's musical roots, but the fact remains that, although the band initially drew from a wide variety of styles, they are notoriously difficult to define. In terms of the Who's choice of other artists' material during their formative years, they encompassed blues (Jimmy Reed, Howlin' Wolf, Muddy Waters), jazz (Mose Allison), R&B (Bo Diddley, Otis Blackwell, Arthur Alexander, Chuck Berry), pop/surf (Everly Brothers, Beach Boys), rockabilly (Eddie Cochran, Larry Williams), instrumental (Link Wray, Duane Eddy, Shadows), soul (Marvin Gaye, James Brown, Martha and the Vandellas) and more recent British pop (the Kinks, the Beatles, Johnny Kidd and the Pirates). The Who evolved a sound and style that went far beyond the sum of these influences, and also the sheer eclectic range of this band makes any idea of a composite sound very difficult to imagine. By 1965, a number of nonmusical influences had also begun to play an important part: modern art, classical music forms, and nihilism.

As the Detours, the band was originally managed by Helmut Gorden and regularly performed on a circuit of West London venues run by Bob Druce, a chain at which it eventually rose to enjoy premier billing. However, by the beginning of 1964 the Detours had thus far failed to attract the crucial interest of a record company. Nor had they managed to crack the larger venues in London's West End. The situation remained static for a while, and the members of the band realized that they would need a significant boost to break through into the front rank of the music scene. Shedding the name the Detours and adopting the name the Who was the start of this process.

The change of name from the Detours to the Who was ostensibly because another group called the Detours appeared on television. From February 1964, the band was billed for the first time the Who. Richard Barnes was instrumental in coining the new name. The name the Who was (and is still) an abstract, unspecific, mystical and commanding name. It was short (and came out large on posters) and gimmicky enough to initially provoke mild amusement, though as the stature and reputation of the band increased, the name seemed to become more profound and omnipotent. It was timeless and universally relevant, and it suited the band's future music perfectly. What they probably didn't know was that a five-piece beat group from Sheffield had called themselves the Who a few years previously, although it seems likely that this (original) Who were by 1964 defunct.

For quite a while the Detours had played as a five-piece lineup with Colin Dawson on lead vocals, Pete Townshend on rhythm guitar, Roger Daltrey on lead guitar, Doug Sandom on drums and John Entwistle on bass guitar. Dawson quit and Daltrey moved over to lead vocals. After a while drummer Sandom was ousted, deemed to be too old and unsuitable; while a replacement was sought, various temporary drummers were used to fulfil engagements. In May of 1964 Keith Moon was recruited as drummer. Moon's becoming part of the Who was one of the most fortuitous and significant changes of all, and it sealed the musical combination for good.

One of the most startlingly original aspects of the band was its live sound. This is a factor not generally appreciated today. Most groups of the era had either two guitarists or a guitarist and a keyboard player, as well as a vocalist and bass/drums rhythm section. The only prominent four-piece lineup of singer, guitarist, and rhythm section was Johnny Kidd and the Pirates, on whom the Detours had loosely modeled themselves and whose "Shakin' All Over" and "Please Don't Touch" had featured in the Detours' live set. Instrument and equipment technology had not progressed a great deal beyond what it had been the mid–1950s, and the Who had to gradually develop their sound beyond the accepted format of the time. (One factor that should be borne in mind is that in concert many bands sounded much poorer than on record—the reverse of which was always true of the Who.)

Both Pete Townshend and John Entwistle were interested not only in innovations of playing technique but also in the attendant amplification and development of technology. The marketplace didn't always offer what groups wanted, and even when it did, the price of amplifiers and guitars was prohibitive. Both these factors prompted the band to improvise, build homemade instruments and construct speakers from scratch. The main motivation within the band was to develop the overall volume of sound. This was a distinctive trademark: the Who used twice as much equipment as was customary and played exceptionally loudly. The volume itself was like a fifth instrument, delivering a sonic punch that greatly enhanced and fortified the structure of its music.

As instrumentalists, Townshend, Entwistle and Moon each had an individual style that set them apart from (and above) the average of the time. Townshend favored full, thrashed chord patterns, utilizing unusual open chord shapes—he had little time for barré chords, arpeggios or lead melody lines—and his style blurred the traditional roles of rhythm and lead guitar. Being the only guitarist, Townshend had to develop a technique to play both lead and rhythm parts, as had Mick Green (of Johnny Kidd and the Pirates) before him. His playing bore more in common with Link Wray than with Hank Marvin. His solos were a distinctive combination of individual picked notes and thrashed, highlighted chords. Townshend developed the concept of the *power chord* as a startling musical effect that was used to give a crashing, dramatic edge to a song. Also, by his hitting the strings hard and utilizing overamplification, the guitar notes would distort into a thick block of noise. At this time the newly introduced fuzz boxes were crude and somewhat unstable, but Townshend discovered (along with Dave Davies of the Kinks and some others) that distortion could be achieved by playing through an overdriven valve amplifier.

John Entwistle was a bass player of exceptional talent and style. The bass guitar at the time fulfilled a mostly perfunctory role in rock, and Entwistle almost single-handedly turned the bass into a melodic, expressive instrument. The lack of a second guitar in the lineup was partly compensated by John's development of a bass sound that was thick and dirty, rather than tame and muted. Entwistle also used an equal level of volume and distortion as Pete, and his speaker cabinets often emitted a sound likened to thunder. A great deal of the band's dexterity can be ascribed to John Entwistle's growing musical skill—over the next thirty years his bass playing would be unsurpassed in sheer technical accomplishment and creative drive.

Keith Moon was simply the most talented, tireless, inventive drummer of his generation; he was as unconventional as Townshend and Entwistle and had a very unusual and distinct ability to not only lay down a solid beat but also weave around it with fills, giving the impression that two drums kits were being played at once. The amazing and crucial fact about these three musicians was that their respective individual styles fitted together perfectly. They coalesced at a stage in their careers when they could develop and grow alongside one another, fusing the Who sound into an organic whole. The final element was Roger Daltrey. He had a commanding stage presence and a powerful voice, but his singing during the early years had yet to develop into anything more distinctive, and the band's material did not yet extend his range as it was later to do. Daltrey was also a fine harmonica player, but as the Who abandoned R&B, this became a redundant skill, certainly in the studio.

This band nurtured no star player or featured instrumentalist, no virtuoso soloist or vocalist—there was no Hank Marvin, Eric Clapton, Brian Jones, Rod Stewart, Jeff Beck, Manfred Mann or Brian Auger. The music developed with genuine ensemble unity and an almost competitive four-way tension. The members of the Who *were* rivals, in a sense, and each was determined to hold his own, if not dominate the remaining three. Whether through deliberation or chance, they found a musical balance that fused into a singular Who identity. Extra instruments were occasionally added in the studio—usually a keyboard or horn arrangement—but the basic four-part composition of personality and instrumental force remained in place and developed intact because they were lucky to not suffer any personnel changes.

In addition to the sheer force of personality that gave the band its identity, there were technical advantages that characterized their sound. Even as early as August 1963, the Detours had begun to use Marshall amplification equipment. John Entwistle had initially commissioned a speaker cabinet from Marshall's music shop in London, specifying that it should comprise four-by-twelve-inch speaker cones. This was much more powerful than those otherwise available at the time, and Entwistle soon after ordered a second four-by-twelve-inch cabinet. Thus was born the next generation of group amplifiers and speakers that superseded the less powerful Peavey, Vox and Fender equipment that had prevailed up to that point. Pete Townshend liked these custom-built speakers and ordered some for himself. While setting up at one concert at the Oldfield Tavern in 1964, Pete placed his speaker cabinet on a piano at waist height and immediately produced a screeching feedback noise that guitarists usually tried to avoid. The Rickenbacker semiacoustic guitars that Townshend favored at the time were particularly susceptible to this kind of aural manipulation. Pete liked the sound and soon learned to control and channel it through the use of the guitar volume knob and the pickup selector switch. This was a revolutionary development, and it very soon became an integral part of Townshend's sound. Other guitarists harnessed feedback soon afterward, but usually in a much more restrained way. Feedback soon crept onto records, like the beginning of the Beatles' "I Feel Fine" (recorded in October 1964), and was later incorporated into the playing of Jeff Beck (the Yardbirds) and Eddie Phillips (the Creation), but none utilized it in such an unrestrained manner as Townshend.

With the later popularity of much more sophisticated fuzz boxes, feedback became a more tangible and commonplace musical effect when used to produce an infinite sustain on a particular note, which became one of Jimi Hendrix's trademarks. But Townshend generated a more anarchic form of acoustic feedback that was more difficult to control and that jarred intensely on the ear. Certainly the use of the pickup switch to give an intermittent Morse code effect was completely and radically original. With the later introduction of onstage guitar smashing, the feedback would grow to even more dramatic and chaotic proportions. By 1964, Pete Townshend had commissioned a custom-made 100-watt "stack" from Marshall's, in a move that confirmed the direction in which hard rock and roll was to go onstage, increasing volume and distortion to what would hitherto have been considered painful levels. (By 1965 both John Entwistle and Pete Townshend would be using 2 x 100-watt amplifiers and 16 x 12-inch speakers each on stage.) The high level of feedback from Townshend's guitar was to remain unique to the Who until utilized in 1967 by the Velvet Underground (especially on their *White Light/White Heat* LP) and a handful of psychedelic and garage bands hungry for access to weird sounds.

Another change during early 1964 came about when manager Helmut Gorden made contact with a freelance publicist named Peter Meaden, who had his finger on the pulse of all things mod. Mods were dapper, clean-cut teenagers who had forged an alternate perspective on the early 1960s by eschewing the prevailing teddy boy/rocker image of the previous decade and by developing an obsessive penchant for obscure soul and R&B music, Italian motor scooters, a rigid dress code and gang hierarchies. In 1964 it was a scene ripe for a pop group to break through representing mod tastes and fashions. So Meaden promoted the Who as the first "authentic" mod band. They had already played at some of the "in" mod venues, but Meaden immediately thrust the band into the hub of mod activity at the Scene Club in Soho, in the West End of London. As a direct result of Meadon's influence, the band's image was sharpened and the name was changed from the Who to the High Numbers.

Meaden recalled, "I had this dream of getting a group together that would be the focus, the entertainers for the mods... The name was perfect... There was a hierarchy situation with the mods and the High Numbers gave them a step up the hierarchy."[8] Much has been written regarding the band's status as mods and about the circumstances that brought about this fashion-conscious youth cult.[9] Essentially, the band found that the mods formed their primary audience, demanding music to which they could dance, venues that were "in," and a lifestyle that was "cool." Mod was nihilistic and ultimately ephemeral—the High Numbers just happened to correspond most directly to the music the mods liked, which reflected a move away from traditional R&B toward soul, imported and not widely heard records from the heart of young black America. While the music sprang naturally from the tastes of the members of the group, the image of the High Numbers was deliberately tailored to reflect mod consciousness under the direction of Peter Meaden. We can now see that this packaging of the band was to have a lasting influence on much of what they did for the following year.

The real story of the High Numbers and the Who is not the history of mod. Modism was a sociological phenomenon in which the group played a part largely because of the time and place of their activities. Mod purists have sometimes emphasized the fact that no U.K. rock-and-roll group truly encapsulated the scene, that as individuals the Small Faces (a contemporary group from the East End of London) were more representative of the "in crowd" than were the Who and that the Action (another London group) offered a more faithful "blue-eyed soul" sound. The sounds, styles, trends and ideas of mod reverberated outward and touched—in a diluted form—almost every aspect of pop culture. Mod soon held a place as part of a larger movement that influenced the rest of the world. The pop scene was at the heart of the Swinging London mythology, within which mod formed an inner cult. That the Who courted this cult for a short time matters but little now. After the Meaden period, the band made few overt concessions to mod for the sake of gaining credibility. They shared certain common elements of mod but during the early months of 1965 had forged a unique style on their own terms, a style that was accessible and meaningful to young people everywhere. Partly because of mod and partly because of the Pop Art philosophy and auto-destruction, the Who remained a voguish group through 1965 and 1966.

Mod can be easily criticized for its self-indulgence, its irrationality and divisiveness (a hatred of rockers), its gang mentality and its predilection for violence and thuggery. But it had a deep influence on Pete Townshend, who embraced the mod ethos most completely and referred to it throughout the years to come as a direct connection with his roots and youth. Even with the grand cerebral works of the Who's future, it often seemed as if he were constantly asking himself,: What does this mean in terms of mod? or, perhaps in times of doubt, Does this maintain a fidelity to my original roots? Irish Jack Lyons, the archetypal mod Who fan whom Townshend met in 1964 and thereafter remained in touch, sometimes personified these roots. For Townshend, mod was a pure ideal; despite offering many criticisms over the years, he stayed faithful to the original cause, an involvement that led to the conception of *Quadrophenia* in 1973.

The High Numbers were an essentially live band and their solitary attempt at recording ("I'm the Face") failed to secure a hit. The most dynamic aspect of the band was its onstage energy—an energy that was expressed through a combination of sound, clothes, imagery, showmanship, and an aggressive performance style. Meaden's plan for a mod domination of the charts failed, it could be argued, because the band were simply unable to capture their onstage sound and visual style on a record (the days when acts were made through the use of promotional videos was almost twenty years ahead). The R&B and soul sounds that meant so much in the clubs could not compete in the charts with the pristine pop of the Merseybeat groups, and even the bands that had broken through with straight R&B (Rolling Stones, Yardbirds, Animals) had by 1964 progressed onto more pop-oriented and usually self-written material. While the High Numbers' only single might have meant something to a few hardcore mods, it was obviously indistinct to the majority of record buyers, who were beginning to expect more sophisticated material. "I'm the Face" and its B side "Zoot Suit" are no less accomplished or exciting than other debut singles (the Beatles' "Love Me Do," the Rolling Stones' "Come On," or the Kinks' "Long Tall Sally"); they were just released a year or two years too late to be appreciated on the same level.

Two ex–film industry mavericks, Kit Lambert and Chris Stamp, stumbled on the Who at the Harrow and Wealdstone Railway Hotel and became their managers. The pair were looking for a subject around which to create a feature film and stopped their search instantly after hearing the band. They soon after also abandoned the film in favor of full-time management. Lambert and Stamp formed a dynamic partnership: they were chaotic, inspired, naive, opportunistic and seemed to have a magic touch in an alien world, despite being very different from one another.[10] They were perhaps the only people capable of taking the Who and encouraging their idiosyncrasies to work to commercial advantage. Lambert and Stamp were part of a new breed in the 1960s who snatched pop management away from the traditional agents and promoters and acted in collaboration with the groups. To Lambert in particular Townshend ascribed many of his classical musical influences and artistic theories.

Lambert and Stamp—like the many thousands of people who saw the Who for the first time during the 1964–1965 period—responded to the tangible edge of anarchy in the Who. Said Lambert, "As soon as I saw them I felt a total conviction that this was it... They're really a new form of crime—armed against the bourgeois."[11] And Chris Stamp was equally knocked out; he said, "To my mind their act creates emotions of anger and violence, and a thousand other things I don't really understand myself."[12] Not all of their moves on behalf of the Who were astute, and their cut of the income was said to be disproportionately high, but generally this team—in the 1960s at least—provided an essential focus for the band. They had a vital determination to succeed.

More than any of their contemporaries, the Who seemed organically suited to be primarily a live performance act. Yet the band soon learned to overcome the limitations of the studio to produce a substantial canon of recorded works. However, the stage accommodated the Who's presence, energy and uncompromising vision of rock and roll more readily than did the studio. But during 1964–1965 the Who were establishing their territory and breaking new ground as an inevitable means of growth—in different ways both onstage and in the studio. The mod movement had seemed to happen around them in an uncontrived and spontaneous manner and represented a spirit that would become impossible to re-create later under altered circumstances. Perhaps the group took such empathy and closeness to their audience for granted; it was the kind of precious commodity that they maybe valued only later when it became noticeable by its absence.

One famous and important aspect of the Who's concert act that is not represented on record is the destruction of guitars, amplifiers and drums. This anarchic trademark was strikingly original and remains unsurpassed as a means of encapsulating the frustrations and anger of the audience. Townshend began smashing guitars in late 1964 and retained the habit (with decreasing frequency) into the 1980s. By mid–1966, Keith Moon had joined in the frenzy by dismembering his drum kit. Although the sound (simulated or otherwise) of a guitar being smashed was represented on record on occasion ("My Generation," "The Ox"), the full effect of this disturbing and radical form of performance art could be witnessed to full effect only in person. (A handful of film clips give some flavor of this, mostly collected in the Who documentary film *The Kids Are Alright* from 1979.)

When the Who smashed their equipment, Townshend was always ready to bamboozle disapproving onlookers and critics with his theory of auto-destruction. It served a grand purpose over and above its shock gimmick value as a theatrical, cathartic tool. It was a very clear expression of anger that jarred against the materialist sensibilities of the mainstream of society. Guitars, amplifiers and drums were hugely expensive items (and usually protected and coveted by musicians), and their violent destruction was a nihilistic defiance of the traditional concept of musical instruments' being sacred. Smashing instruments was akin to burning books, a cultural heresy. But Townshend's artistic theory was unequivocal, and his usual summary ran as follows: "When I was in art school I got wind of an auto-destructive artist named Gustav Metzker. That really blew my mind! So I introduced the idea of breaking up the instruments as part of the finale of the show... You see it's a whole pattern of apprehension and tension, then relief and then remorse. The whole process of life. The current big, imperishable, holy art is pop music, and the break-up routine really says something about it. The ideal, of course, would be for me to get killed in an airplane crash right after a really stupendous performance."[13]

A devastating stage act, a sharp but slightly surreal image and an unusual approach to their work placed the Who in late 1964 on the brink of a breakthrough. The only missing ingredient at this stage was original material. For Townshend, it wasn't just a case of writing songs; it was an opportunity for noise exploration and sonic experimentation. What the Who had been doing on the concert stage was now possible in a recording studio and on a record, however alien its sound might initially have been. But as if to prove that the Who really did represent a more demanding post–Beatles, post-pop audience, they struck commercial success immediately with the help of a manipulation of the existing pop machinery of the time and an exploitation of their visual strengths on television. Ultimately, however, the sheer forcefulness and inspiration of their records was enough.

The first three Who singles, "I Can't Explain," "Anyway Anyhow Anywhere" and "My Generation" (all 1965) were angry, defiant, aggressive and exciting without being crude or simpleminded. They were also big hits. "My Generation" in particular was the Who's statement of noise as art—their manifesto of ear-jarring chaos that connected so directly with the dissident youth consciousness of the times. Under the guise of Pop Art, the band aggressively manipulated the totems of an art form, very much with the emphasis on art rather than pop. This formed a general credo for the band until Townshend grew tired of the tag in 1966 and moved onto something else. The wild smashing of guitars and drums remained for some years, however, always tagged *auto-destruction*. But whatever was the most descriptive phrase, the Who produced rock music in a pure form, amplified and distorted into a frenzy of aural sensation despite the melody, wit and intelligence of Townshend's songs. All the essential elements of the Who were intact and fully developed from "I Can't Explain" onwards. They later matured and improved yet retained their vitality into the mid–1970s and only really lost their creative spark with Keith Moon's death in 1978.

In comparison with the prevailing norm in the 1960s pop scene (the commercial machine that sustained the Beatles/Rolling Stones axis), the Who tended toward nihilism. The guitar and drum smashing was undoubtedly a powerful and original antimaterialism statement, although it was more often clearly seen in this light from a Continental perspective. (The British establishment saw no art in destruction and could only condemn what it considered to be vandalism.) Conversely, European filmmakers were attracted to the Who for the very qualities that brought them popular-press criticism in their homeland. The French film producer Alain de Seduoy (making a documentary about the London scene) described the Who as "a logical musical expression of bewilderment and anarchy of London's teenagers."[14] The Italian director Michelangelo Antonioni (who first saw the Who at the Goldhawk club in November 1965) wanted the band in his film *Blow-Up* (1966) but for various reasons ended up with the Yardbirds imitating the Who's auto-destruction. However, despite such attention during the 1960s, they appeared only briefly on the big screen in documentary films (such as *Monterey Pop* and *Woodstock*) and early plans for a Who feature film never materialized.

Nevertheless, the Who were very prominent on television and had a natural flair for arresting visual presentation. During the 1965–1967 period, they appeared on—among others—such British programs as *Ready Steady Go!* (many times), *Top of the Pops* (many times), *Beat Club* (a German version of *Top of the Pops*), *A Whole Scene Going*, *Twice a Fortnight,* and the American shows *Smothers Brothers Comedy Hour* and *Shindig*. All were memorable occasions within the confines of their specific genre, but television was limiting at the time in both form and content: pictures were in black and white, sound was in mono and often of poor quality, time allocation was very brief, artists generally had to mime to prerecordings and artistic freedom was constrained by a prevailing adherence to the very showbiz values of good taste that groups like the Who abhorred.

Many believed that feature films offered artists greater freedom than television, although on the evidence of the pattern set with the British film industry's lamentable efforts in the pop field such as *Live It Up* (1963), *Every Day's a Holiday* (1964), *Wonderful Life* (1964), *Gonks Go Beat* (1965), *Out Of Sight* (1966), and *Hold On!* (1966), this can hardly be true. Even where an attempt to break the mold was attempted, such as the Beatles' *A Hard Day's Night* (1964) and the Dave Clark Five's *Catch Us If You Can* (1965), the results were hardly overwhelming. In such films, the music was still as neatly packaged and compromised as it had been on the television variety shows. Even on the few occasions when television cameras found their way into the club or concert hall to record a live performance of a rock group in front of their own audience, they invariably failed to capture the excitement of the music and the event. This was mostly due to the limitations of the technology and the unsympathetic approach of production teams trained on *Sunday Night at the London Palladium* or *The Billy Cotton Band Show*, two shows that represented the norm of British popular entertainment on television at the time.

The Who had wanted to make a film (and Lambert and Stamp's film background led them to think in this direction), but finding a company willing to put up sufficient funds was no easy thing. On two occasions (in late 1966 and early 1968), the members of the band even toyed with the idea of a Who TV series, which could hardly have given them the format they wanted. Then during the recording of *Tommy* (during 1968–1969) they found the obvious answer: a Who rock film that would be a visual presentation of the album—something that no one had done before. For various reasons this film plan also foundered at the time: the *Tommy* film that eventually appeared in 1975 was a vastly different artifact.

Also remember that the 1960s was an era when the commercial pressures of the music industry could often be blamed for the creative visions of artists becoming garbled, dissipated or prematurely bathed in cynicism. Onerous contracts were generally signed at the start of careers when groups held no bargaining power. During a time when independent record labels didn't exist, when group autonomy was unheard of and when all the established companies recognized only the hit single, artistic freedom was largely an illusory quality. Managers, record producers, promoters and agents were all-powerful and often would brook no deviation from their perceived norm of showbiz entertainment values. Consequently, very few rock-and-roll artists of any individuality or vision managed to escape an inevitable internecine court struggle over contracts and agreements that had turned sour with management, producers and record companies. The Beatles, the Rolling Stones, Bob Dylan, the Kinks, the Yardbirds, the Small Faces and the Who were all involved in such disputes.

In the Who's case, the legal battle came during the early part of 1966 and involved the band's first producer Shel Talmy and the Brunswick record label, with whom they had recorded three singles and the *My Generation* debut album. The final outcome (where the Who had recorded for a different label and breached a contract) cost the band much financially but gained them a very precious artistic freedom, which—in Britain at least—meant they could record what and where the band members liked without pressures to compromise. Lambert and Stamp promptly founded their own label, Track Records, to accommodate the Who (and other acts), a move toward independence that preempted even the Beatles' Apple label. Kit Lambert proved to be an imaginative producer who was entirely sympathetic to Pete Townshend's ideas. As early as mid–1966 Townshend was planning an opera of sorts called *Quads*, and Lambert encouraged the "bigger, louder, better, artier" approach to sound and songwriting that characterized the band's progression through 1966 and beyond. Their second album *A Quick One* featured a "mini-opera" title track, and this was followed by *Sell Out*, which included a second lengthy narrative song "Rael." This quest for a new form and a wider context in which rock and roll could function, led to *Tommy*, *Lifehouse* and *Quadrophenia* in the golden period of Who achievement, 1969–1973.

The steps toward this period of breakthrough were noteworthy in their own right. The Who's manifesto—that spontaneous explosion of noise, anger, smoke bombs, and fragments of shattered guitars—was for rock and roll to be bigger, louder, more substantial and longer lasting, and they found themselves at odds with the pop music establishment all the way. It was on the stage, however, that much of the Who's progress and achievement was made. All the early anger and musical explosiveness was contained in a dense, scabrous concert act that shifted the focus away from the hits and recordings and established its own rules and conventions based on huge amplified sound, an inherent sense of character projection, a frenetic musical drive and an infectious enthusiasm that made the band sound like they were ecstatically playing their material for the first glorious time.

The Who made a transition from being an act compatible with a consistent string of Top Ten hits to becoming—simultaneously—the darlings of the serious music press and heroes of the underground sometime toward the end of 1966. Later, in 1967, the Who launched an all-out assault on the United States at the Monterey Pop Festival, one of the watersheds of American hippie activity. The Who spent the latter half of 1967 and almost all of 1968 touring the U.S. The band did this the hard way, at first supporting Herman's Hermits (a laughably undignified and inappropriate pairing), then later headlining their own shows at theaters and concert halls across the United States.

Then, in 1969, the Who finally succeeded in smashing the conventions for good with *Tommy*, a double album and so-called rock opera that told a mystical and fantastic story in a series of connected songs. Despite its reputation *Tommy* remained pure rock and roll in the Who's hands; no attempt was made to give it an operatic, musical or theatrical treatment; indeed, it was never very satisfying as a story. However, the critics and the rock public (over and above the regular Who audience) responded warmly to the work. In short, *Tommy* brought fame, adulation, wealth, and critical acclaim and put the final touch to the Who's growing aura of mystery and superiority.

The alleged operatic pretensions of *Tommy*—like "A Quick One While He's Away" and "Rael" before it—are generally ascribed to the influence of Kit Lambert, who produced all Who records between 1966 and 1969. Lambert was well versed in opera and classical music, courtesy of his father Constant, and by introducing this sensibility of *bona fide* mainstream art, the Who acquired a unique, though not always comfortable, perspective. Lambert often thought in terms of narrative structures and major form (as applicable to opera or even film) and didn't see why rock music couldn't draw from the traditions known to his father.[15]

It is probably fair to say that the attention given to *Tommy* surprised even the Who. And the critical interpretation to which it was subjected was relentless. The exegesis that *Tommy* suffered during 1969–1970 was unprecedented (despite the critical scrutiny given to the Beatles' work). *Tommy* was embraced by the underground youth culture, which wanted to establish a kind of standard repertoire and, indeed, felt a desperate need to convince the arts establishment that it too could produce substantial works of creative integrity. Even more amazing, perhaps, was the fact that the British underground press (which adopted a fiercely subversive though sometimes incoherent standpoint that was anarchist in complexion and who therefore might have been expected to sneer at *Tommy*'s commercial appeal) took the work to heart—particularly *Friends* and *It*. Maybe the Underground movement had too few genuine artists, writers and musicians producing work that would withstand analysis and wanted some tangible landmarks or totems around which to base their short-lived credo of drugs, sex, rock and revolution.

The inspiration behind the theme of *Tommy*, however, was less identifiable. "Avatar" Meher Baba was mentioned on the sleeve, and it was clear that Baba's philosophy had influenced the whole conception. Townshend was introduced to Baba's works in late 1967 and over the next few months began to immerse his life in the teachings of this Indian mystic to the extent that almost all of his lyrical themes and perspectives thereafter were the result of his obvious devotion. Meher Baba's philosophy was esoteric: it was compatible with conventional Christianity and reflected a belief in a universal God and reincarnation rather than drugs and meditation. In an era when the rich and famous flocked to trendy Eastern gurus to alleviate their Western anxieties, Baba was markedly different. He and his followers didn't proselytize, seek publicity or travel in search of money or converts. In fact, Baba had taken a vow of silence earlier in his life that he maintained up until his death on 31 January 1969. Although Townshend never met Baba and the other members of the band had no great sympathy with his teachings, Who records reflected his philosophy and symbolism in greater and lesser degrees from this point on.

The momentum of *Tommy* sustained the Who throughout 1969 and 1970, a period that included some of their biggest concerts, at Woodstock and two Isle of Wight festivals. More than any other rock work of the era—with the dubious exception of Beatles LPs—*Tommy* was seen by the cultural mainstream as a work of art. It was played at the Concertgebouw in Amsterdam, the Theatre Des Champs Elysees in Paris, the Coliseum in London, the Metropolitan Opera in New York, and at Tanglewood in Massachusetts. On a cultural level and in terms of mainstream critical regard, the Who seemed to have reached a high plateau of achievement. They weren't complacent about success, however, and they all knew—despite Kit Lambert's cultural posturing—that as high art, *Tommy* was a bit of a fraud. As if to prove the point, they unleashed *Live at Leeds* (1970)—perhaps the loudest, most visceral rock music released by any group at that time—which challenged the view of the Who as opera stars in the most fundamental way possible. As *Tommy* had indicated just what could be done and had rewarded the Who plentifully, the stocks were cleared for Townshend's master plan *Lifehouse*. This was to be a film-and-music project that would be not only the Who's pièce de résistance but the work that would show rock and roll the true pathway into a better future.

But to the listening public, *Lifehouse* now means almost nothing, for it never materialized. What was issued in its place in 1971, *Who's Next*, superficially appeared to be a simple, straightforward "supergroup" classic album. The glittery but tattered landscape of rock and roll is littered with the remnants of uncompleted projects, unreleased albums and failed dreams aplenty, alongside the towering achievements and landmarks. For every *Sgt Pepper's Lonely Hearts Club Band* there's a *Get Back* (the Beatles' last-gasp attempt at revitalization during 1969), a *Smile* (the Beach Boys' abortive masterwork from 1967) and a *First Rays of the New Rising Sun* (Jimi Hendrix's work in progress at the time of his death in 1970). These disparate musical enigmas, all examples of desultory creative energy's exceeding practical reality, retain a strange and enduring fascination for fans and provide a broad canvas for enterprising bootleggers to belatedly attempt to fill the gaps with illicit releases lovingly pieced together from tapes that have gone astray. *Lifehouse* can join these great lost works, although typically the Who's abandoned project exceeded almost all in its sheer complication, ambition and frustration.

From the failure came a more conventional kind of triumph, for many now regard the 1971 *Who's Next* album as the Who's greatest achievement, while a smaller number of people (including its creator, Pete Townshend) lament the fact that its starting point, the *Lifehouse* film and show, didn't manage to overwhelm the whole rock scene of the early 1970s with its visionary magnitude. And while *Who's Next* remains a classic rock-and-roll album, a back-catalog CD perennial and FM radio favorite in the U.S., *Lifehouse* has now receded into the distant past, mentioned only as a vague footnote in rock history and, in the fertile imaginations of Who fans worldwide, as a legendary suggestion of what could have been.

A twisted saga unfolded around *Lifehouse*, and eventually Who fans (and perhaps the band themselves) came to regard the Who's activities in 1971 as being their creative peak. But having reached a transcendent level of inspiration, they didn't slip for quite a while. The band had reached a musical pinnacle that was substantial enough to sustain them both artistically and commercially for the next few years. With a long-term financial security and widespread acclaim, the band's activity slackened and the group members diversified their interests into solo work and films. However, all such activity was regarded as little more than a hobby by the band members, and it never managed to destabilize the group (as happened with Rod Stewart and the Faces).

The nonmusical reputation that the Who had acquired by the late 1960s was curiously ambivalent. They were both the good guys and the bad guys. Apart from fitness fanatic Roger Daltrey, the band members were known to be heavy drinkers, prone to destroying hotel rooms, difficult to work with and so liable to indulge in infighting as to frighten off outsiders. Apart from Keith Moon, they never really embraced the superstar lifestyle: Daltrey and Entwistle had large country homes and for the most part kept out of the public eye; Townshend remained in West London and occupied himself with music making and good causes; Keith Moon alone took an extrovert approach to his fame, often in cahoots with celebrity friends and drinking companions.

Members of the group took drugs at various periods, Moon sustained a cocaine habit over several years, and Townshend belatedly succumbed to heroin dependency in 1981. Additionally, Entwistle, Moon and Townshend at various stages battled with drinking problems.

Yet despite these traits—which were very public knowledge—the Who band members were respected for their honesty, lack of pretension, sincerity and dependability. In the rock industry, more populated with gangsters, sharks, and wheeler-dealers than even the film industry, the band members were decent, fair-minded, compassionate and self-effacing. They customarily donated large sums of money to worthy causes (such as the Chiswick Battered Wives' Rescue in London) long before it became the trendy conscience-easing and publicity-gaining gesture of the Band Aid/Live Aid ilk. Even the band's music was scrupulously nonsexist in an environment where attitudes of male domination and female subjugation were endemic, and indeed, the standard fare of almost all their contemporaries. The Who was politically correct by instinct long before it became a deliberate ideology.

The level of excellence that had been established with *Who's Next* was maintained with the Who's next album, *Quadrophenia*, in 1973. This was a more modest concept work in form—simply a double album with a loose though workable story—but musically it hit such a sustained level of inspiration that it at least equaled *Who's Next*. In it the fantasy elements of *Tommy* and *Lifehouse* were replaced by Townshend's more mature concerns: an obsession with the Who's roots, a fascination of the nature of fan worship and the status of rock-and-roll heroes, all expressed in music and lyrics that were suffused in a kind of ecstatic desperation and chilling isolation from the world. *Quadrophenia*'s themes were insecurity, self-doubt and the fickle nature of youth culture. In almost every way, *Quadrophenia* was a substantial hit. Unlike *Lifehouse*, it worked as a concept on record and fully justified its great length over two albums, although it was less cohesive as a live piece. Townshend's lyrics were honed to perfection because his subject was as basic as possible (the Who's roots and the consciousness of their early fans), and it never strayed outside of its own terms of reference, it seemed Pete had learned some lessons from the *Lifehouse* experience. *Quadrophenia* also became a successful film in 1979, realizing much of what *Lifehouse* failed to even suggest.

However, *Quadrophenia* had to wait six years before it was adapted for the screen, and *Tommy* took its place as the first Who film project in 1974. Following the release of the *Tommy* film in 1975, the Who recorded their first straight album for years, *The Who by Numbers*. Once more a crisis had enveloped the band, and it was to prove largely insoluble. Townshend—now thirty—was beginning to harbor serious doubts about the integrity and value of his role as a street-credible rocker. He poured out his feelings in a set of personal songs that didn't spare him or the other members of the band from his scabrous analysis of hypocrisy, wealth, fame and the meaninglessness of modern life. Indeed, we can now see the crisis within the Who as being symptomatic of a wider crisis within rock and roll.

The Who by Numbers signaled the end of Townshend's faith in the rock-and-roll dream, and it coincided with his first serious ruminations about quitting. But he procrastinated. The rock movement was in the doldrums in the mid–1970s, and Townshend was acutely aware of the sorry state of the situation. It would be gratifying but delusory to think that he kept the Who going until a real rock-and-roll movement based on a purer vision (punk) could relieve them. But in reality the Who carried on regardless after the first punk bands had arrived (on a tremendous wave of excitement), unsure whether or not their music would continue to hold any relevance. The Who's first postpunk album, *Who Are You* (1978), was lacking a vital edge of excitement and a true sense of purpose. It was the Who marking time. It had a fair share of good songs, like "Music Must Change" and the epic title track (itself a *Lifehouse* remnant), but in an essential sense *Who Are You* failed to deliver the uncompromising and revelatory goods upon which the Who had built their career. Townshend knew that something was lost, but he couldn't find an easy solution. The Who didn't play live during 1977 and 1978, even though the album was a commercial hit. Townshend—for a short while at least—refused to drag his musical past round the world one more time.

Soon after the release of *Who Are You*, Keith Moon died. And with Moon gone, Townshend and the other band members realized the original Who vision was now all but irrevocably lost. However, Moon's death made the band search inwardly for some semblance of meaning and purpose and, against all odds, they decided to continue. Keith's absence forced the Who to adopt a new direction, and for a while it seemed that something could be salvaged. Kenney Jones joined on drums, and John "Rabbit" Bundrick came into the lineup on keyboards. However, despite some fine concerts, during which they managed to stretch some of their original inspiration into extra time, the band's real efforts throughout this period were in filmmaking.

The two post–Moon studio albums *Face Dances* (1981) and *It's Hard* (1982) still sold well. The Who was a legendary name, and people bought their records and concert tickets to secure their own personal part of that legend. On these records, for the first time, the band achieved no kind of musical voice to do any justice to the songs, which in themselves were, at best, variable. John Entwistle contributed five hard rock songs to these two albums, in a self-conscious attempt to retain a "classic Who" sound. The remainder of Pete Townshend's material was an equally self-conscious attempt to avoid a classic Who sound. Unsurprisingly, both albums sounded uninspired, noncommittal and insubstantial. *Face Dances* had a few idiosyncratic melodies and lyrical flourishes and no significant guitar work, while *It's Hard* sounded like a rushed selection of left-overs. Together, these albums damaged the Who's reputation: Keith Moon, *Lifehouse* and idealism seemed a long way away.

As it was composed of elder statesmen on the rock scene of the 1980s, the band retained respect and fans, even though the band members' creative drives were now channeled largely into solo projects and films. The Who were now businessmen, investors, employers, charity workers, film producers and philanthropists as well as musicians. Pete Townshend's personal struggle against drink and heroin addiction in 1981–1982 often became more newsworthy than his music making, despite his solo album, *Empty Glass* (1980), being warmly received. A follow-up, *All the Best Cowboys Have Chinese Eyes* (1982), fared less well but still showed a vivid streak of originality and a willingness to take risks. John Entwistle recorded one glossy hard rock album, *Too Late the Hero* (1981), then disappeared from the scene for several years. Roger Daltrey established himself as an actor of considerable versatility and recorded music when the urge took him, a handful of albums in the mid–1980s, the best of which is generally considered to be *Under a Raging Moon* (1985).

Despite rumors of imminent retirement and lack of commitment from the inside, the band still toured in the early 1980s: U.S. in 1980, U.K. in 1981 and U.S. in 1982 (breaking all records). Finally in a gesture of pure commercial revivalism, the Who toured the U.S. in 1989 (breaking all records once more.) During this period, the Who's critical standing slipped away. An ill-advised appearance at Live Aid in London on 13 July 1985 did little to rekindle their flame. Repackaging of the Who's work became patchy and less inspired. The 1982 and 1989 tours each spawned a live album (a double and a triple, respectively) that were a complete negation of everything for which *Live at Leeds* had valiantly stood. It seemed that the Who's cause needed urgent attention, as there was a danger that their real years of achievement would become eclipsed by recent events.

Against all odds, and simply because their music deserved it, the renaissance came. Fans had kept the faith, and fanzines had sprung up—*Anyway Anyhow*, *The Relay*, *Generations*, *Sparks*, *Naked Eye*—all put together by younger fans, passionate about The Who simply because contemporary music could offer little that was comparable. A younger generation of musicians also recognized the Who's true worth and their influence spread across dozens of successful acts who formed the grunge and Brit–pop movements. Eventually, after many years of apathy and misunderstanding, not to mention campaigning by fans, something was done to reestablish the Who's back-catalog. Older compatriots like Chris Charlesworth brought some influence to bear, and in 1994 a CD boxed set *30 Years of Maximum R&B* was released to great acclaim. This was followed by a video and then a further CD reissue program that reproduced the whole Who canon with improved sound quality and previously unreleased and uncollected tracks. This program accorded the Who the kind of high quality and intelligent packaging that their music deserved.

And here the story begins again…

2

Maximum Reaction (1963–1965)

The beginnings of any great rock-and-roll band can be viewed in retrospect as being especially significant and worthy of detailed investigation. Facts can be examined in hindsight and placed in a position of supposed relevance in the threads of a particular history that they may not necessarily deserve. But history, being subject to interpretation, is not merely a collation of static facts, and music—that most ethereal of art forms—can seldom be satisfactorily represented as mere history. Just where does a musical heritage start? And while the music of the past is still with us, does it ever cease? The standard biographical accounts of how rock-and-roll music came about almost always identify social conditions as being the factor that dictates the form of the resulting sounds. Yet this does not render the music incomprehensible to those ignorant of such social conditions. The music must have a quality that stands in isolation from the environment in which it is created.

Almost all the early rock-and-roll stars embraced a rags-to-riches biography that was often the product of an audacious publicist's imagination. The "guttersnipe makes good" scenario is a familiar and largely hollow myth that no longer sustains analysis; in the 1990s we are much less willing to accept the sanitized, authorized versions of events that were customarily offered in more innocent times. The entertainment industry was rife with romanticized tales of the histories of personalities, indeed, big-budget feature films were made of such stuff, as anyone who has seen *The Tommy Steele Story* (1957) or Joe Brown in *What a Crazy World* (1963) will testify. Sometimes artists have suffered from an overkill of journalistic myth making at the expense of attention being given to their music. Such myths are ultimately dismissed as nothing but a cynical fabrication of contrived postures; the double-edged sword of the publicist can make or break with equal force.

For any young rock band in the early 1960s, the publicity machinery was a component of the entertainment industry that could be neither avoided or ignored, especially in England where there was only one place where any kind of success could be sustained: London. Public relations was deemed to be a necessary tool in the progress from obscurity to fame that all pop musicians craved. But since rock and roll was supposed only to be the domain of "bad boys," not all the first generation of British would-be rockers had quite the required rebel credentials. For some a change of name was enough (Ronald Wycherly to Billy Fury, Reginald Smith to Marty Wilde); Cliff Richard needed to perpetually make a theatrical sneer at the camera as well as a new name; Johnny Kidd wore a sinister black pirate patch over the eye. The British acts often required a smokescreen of fabricated biography to fit the part; fame often needed notoriety of sorts. Not everyone had such ready-made infamy as Jerry Lee Lewis's underaged wife, Chuck Berry's prison record, Elvis Presley's pelvic gyrations and untimely conscription, or Little Richard's camp flamboyance to satiate the media.

So publicists customarily lied about acts: Peter Meaden lied about the High Numbers, Kit Lambert and Chris Stamp lied about the Who. It was part of the game, a petty-minded exercise to catch the attention of the squalid-minded press. This was, however, a short-lived practice, as the second generation of British rock-and-roll acts (Who, Rolling Stones, Kinks, Beatles) before long produced music vibrant and real enough to not require any hype. It later took a much more intelligent publicist named Keith Altham to realize that in the Who's case at least, the truth was better than any exaggeration or mythology. When we approach the Who we can now discard much of the hyperbole with ease—after all, no publicist can make a record sound better than it actually is.

While the standard discography of the Who necessarily begins with the High Numbers' "I'm the Face" single, any comprehensive study of the band's recorded works must delve back even further. Predating the debut single was the band's very first recording session, which dates from late 1963 or early 1964. As the Detours, and with Doug Sandom on drums, the band made the first and only recording with this lineup on a Sunday evening at the home of Barry Gray. Gray was a composer and arranger who worked mainly in British television and whose memorable theme music was to be heard throughout 1963 with the children's sci-fi animation program *Fireball XL5*, and later on *Stingray* (1964) and *Thunderbirds* (1965). More important, Gray had a recording studio built into his London home. As Townshend's father Cliff was also a professional musician and an acquaintance of Gray, he was able to arrange for the young band members to have a taste of a professional working environment. They must have been excited by this first visit to a recording studio, presumably with the added bonus of not having to pay professional rates for the time. This session was either prompted by or coincidental to the completion of Pete Townshend's very first batch of songs, among which only one title has since been identified, "It Was You," for this was the song chosen to be recorded.

This early attempt at composition was not, it would seem, the true genesis of Pete Townshend's creative urges. It was an initial foray that provided the band with some indigenous material, Pete later describing his work as comprising some "odd little love songs, a couple of which the group used to play on stage."[1] Almost a year was to pass before he resumed songwriting; it would seem that he had yet to find his muse or maybe simply lacked confidence, and "It Was You" was merely written to order. The Detours' recording of "It Was You" has not been publicly heard, and it is most likely that the master tape is now lost. The recording by all accounts did not really reflect the direction in which the Detours' music was heading, and it was described by Dave Marsh as a "light harmony number in the Mersey style."[2] Richard Barnes recalled that it was "very powerful for a first recording but sounded too much like a Beatles song."[3] The conventional romantic nature of the song is exemplified by the lyrics "It was you, who set my heart a-beating / I never knew, that love would come with our meeting." (This suggestion of lack of originality is compounded by the fact that James Brown had already released a song called "It Was You" as a single B side in October 1959. Given their thorough knowledge of the James Brown repertoire, the band members must have known that Townshend's title was secondhand.)

But Townshend had to start somewhere, and although the Detours chose to take the song no further, "It Was You" did the rounds of the London music publishers and eventually found a taker. It appeared as the A side of a single by British group the Naturals in late 1964 and became Townshend's first published song, beating "I Can't Explain" by a whisker. Although the Naturals enjoyed several moderate hits, their take of "It Was You" failed to make the chart, and the song has been quietly forgotten in Who circles—Townshend customarily cites "I Can't Explain" as his first song. Although the song was deemed competent enough by the band members, Townshend didn't press further material forward until it became critical for the Who to have original songs. For the time being, Townshend was content to play old standards, commenting, "We tended to sandwich Jimmy Reed tunes in between our latest carbon copies of Top 20 hits. I remember the buzz I would get as we launched into 'Plum Nellie' and my arm would leave the guitar I was getting off so well..."[4]

Relaunching as the High Numbers in mid–1964, Peter Meaden managed to convince Fontana Records that his new mod band were a potential hit act, and he arranged for a one-time single deal to test the market. The band did not have any original material prepared and probably intended to fall back on their successful stage numbers, but Meaden intervened and introduced two "original" songs that expressed the mod ethic more precisely. Meaden was perhaps correct in dissuading the band members from releasing a straight cover version as their first disk—but if they had it could hardly have been less successful than the songs that *were* released. Up until around 1964, cover versions had been the standard approach for bands to take on a debut disk, as evidenced by the first singles by the Rolling Stones, the Kinks, the Animals and the Yardbirds. But the Beatles had set a healthy precedent with their own songs, and by 1965 for a band who wanted to penetrate the chart with some effect, cover versions were passé.

In June 1964, the High Numbers entered Fontana Studios in London under the supervision of recording manager Jack Baverstock, although the production credit on the resulting single went to Peter Meaden and Chris Parmeinter. A few friends joined them and added hand claps: Jack the Barber (a mod hairstyling trendsetter!), manager Helmut Gorden, and Richard Barnes (who handled the maracas). It has also been suggested that Fontana session singers may have added the backing vocals at this session. Studio time allowed for several takes and overdubs for four songs: "I'm the Face" and "Zoot Suit" were Meaden's rescored and ready-made mod anthems, while "Here 'Tis" and "Leaving Here" were stage favorites. The latter two remained unreleased despite the quality of the band's performances.

The two songs chosen for the single constituted the High Numbers' attempt to catch the imagination of the record-buying public with two ultra-hip odes to modism. In retrospect, both songs are pleasantly entertaining, but one cannot escape the fact that the band was blatantly shaped by the ideas of Meaden and the songs themselves were very contrived and forced. Without any credit to the originals, Meaden had merely rewritten Slim Harpo's blues standard "Got Love If You Want It" as "I'm the Face" and the Showmen's 1961 single "Country Fool" as "Zoot Suit." He had added lyrics that exploited the superficial aspects of mod and went on a publicity spree that probably owed more to his alleged intake of amphetamine drugs than to a studied promotional strategy. The record failed to convince even Fontana, whose initial pressing was of a very moderate one thousand copies. Lack of any kind of movement of the single in its first few weeks in the marketplace prompted Fontana to reverse the A and B sides, but to little avail. Its failure to sell prompted the cancelation of a proposed second High Numbers' single.

The straight R&B structure of "I'm the Face" was too conservative and traditional and somewhat at odds with the supposedly up-to-the-minute lyrics, which formed little more than a roll call of hip mod clichés. It is built on a rudimentary repeated riff sequence that involves no more than three chords. A session keyboard player (unidentified) was added to fill out the sound, and the most interesting aspect of the song are John Entwistle's overdubbed and reverbed bass "zoops" (as Townshend later described them when the song appeared on the *Odds and Sods* LP in 1974). The song is led by a effective harmonica melody by Roger Daltrey—the harmonica was a staple tool of R&B groups at this time but was only infrequently used on future Who recordings despite Daltrey's obvious skill as a player. "Zoot Suit" is more uptempo and pop oriented and has at least a taut and dramatic melody line. It is probably the superior of the two songs, but again the mod references "tickets" and "two-tone brogues" were too obvious. Townshend overdubbed a lead guitar line that followed through the melody, but the result was a performance tame enough to have been by Cliff Richard and the Shadows and five years earlier at that. It might have set the kids' feet tapping along to the coffee-bar jukebox, but it would hardly have caused a riot among the scooter boys on the Margate sea front. The wild aggression of the stage shows was not present, although Townshend did contribute a skillful, if restrained, jazzy guitar solo to each number.

Bo Diddley's R&B song "Here 'Tis" had been recently released in a (somewhat weaker) version by the Yardbirds, and the High Numbers give it a tight, bouncy arrangement with basic slashing guitar chords and an energetic, pumping bass line. Daltrey contributes two obligatory harmonica solos, and in general the song more readily attains the feel of the band's live sound. Eddie Holland's upbeat "Leaving Here" is a lighter, faster and more dynamic song, a mild protest against the abuse of women; it's propelled by a superb drum beat from Keith Moon and heralded by a crisp and catchy intro guitar riff. Roger Daltrey provides a raw but committed vocal, and overall this song certainly would have justified a release at the time.

On all four recordings, however, the performances were rendered a little innocuous because of the clean guitar sound. Townshend's onstage distortion was nowhere in evidence. Perhaps the record company insisted on this change for fear of jeopardizing the commercial appeal of the single, or possibly it was the insistence of the recording engineer whose reputation and expertise would be judged on the clarity and translucence of his or her work. The two songs here selected as their bid for the charts were uncluttered and simple in execution but ultimately sounded too routine. They clearly failed in their intention of encapsulating a scene where the routine and the normal were something against which to rebel. Meaden's hype was also somewhat at odds with the tameness of the record, and he claimed in a press release that accompanied the single that the High Numbers were "the most potentially exciting and powerful group in the field of beat music today. The things expressed on this, their first record, cause an immediate rapport between them and thousands of young people like themselves."[5] On the strength of the sales of the single, the "rapport" was limited to a mere couple of hundred rather than thousands! Demand did not warrant a further pressing.

The few brief reviews that the single received were lukewarm. Singles reviews at the time, in any case, were cursory and largely blind attempts to predict whether a disk would be a hit or a miss. The fashion references actually gained more attention that the musical content of the disk, and one reviewer at *Boyfriend*—undoubtedly influenced by Meaden's hustling, paraphrasing his press sheet almost word for word—wrote that "the two sides of their first record ... expresses [the mod ethos] perfectly, and builds up an immediate link between them and the thousands of young people like themselves."[6] "I'm the Face" simply didn't compare with the best in a year that included the Kinks' "You Really Got Me," the Animals' "House of the Rising Sun," and the Beatles' "Hard Day's Night." If every song has a message, then both "I'm the Face" and "Zoot Suit" communicated a kind of naïve braggadocio that asserted mod superiority over those uncool enough to be outside of the cult. Unfortunately, both overloaded the glib imagery of mod fashion so much as to be almost incomprehensible to the general listener. The songs referred to the *face* (the elite, the leader and trendsetter) and the *ticket* (the follower, the underling) and stressed the need to keep to a predetermined standard of dress, behavior and code of social activity and to recognize the superiority of the *face* (in this case the singer). It remains a novelty record of its time but can now at least be listened to in a more meaningful context.

Given its modest pressing, "I'm the Face" became a sought-after collectors' item when the Who became more successful in 1965. Copies began changing hands for inflated sums, but the vast majority of Who converts during the 1960s and early 1970s knew of but had never heard the disk. When John Entwistle put together *Odds and Sods* in 1974, he included "I'm the Face" for the first time on LP. "Zoot Suit" then found its way onto a Polydor Records various artists compilation titled *Rare Tracks* in 1975. The first Who album to bear "Zoot Suit" was the *Quadrophenia* soundtrack LP from 1979. The single was rereleased in both the U.K. (on Backdoor) and the U.S. (on Mercury) in March 1980, prompted by a current mod revival (especially in the U.K.), and finally, both songs appeared together (in their original mono mixes) on the *Quadrophenia* soundtrack CD.

When Jon Astley came to remix and remaster all four High Numbers songs for the CD boxed set of 1994, he found the tapes had been very well preserved. Once mixed into stereo and mastered onto CD, the sound quality was truly astounding and the material exuded a vitality and depth that was not present on the original mono single. Astley commented that the sound quality was "fantastic ... I couldn't believe it. When I was doing the transfers from 4-track to the 32-track digital machine I was using they just leaped off the tape. I thought 'Christ! I've never heard them sound like this before!' They were quite easy to mix ... It was good fun."[7] So *30 Years of Maximum R&B* remains the most extensive source of the remixed High Numbers material, although the *Odds and Sods* CD offers a slightly longer version of the remixed "I'm the Face."

Whatever Fontana's expectations for the High Numbers, tentative plans were in place for further singles to follow, with Fontana retaining an option on the group. It has been rumored that the band recorded demo versions of further songs for a potential follow-up single. An acetate disk apparently exists in the hands of a private collector that contains a reprise of "It Was You," together with early versions of Townshend's next two songs, "I Can't Explain" and "The Kids Are Alright." This material has not been generally heard, even among Who collectors, so I cannot offer detailed comment. (It has been suggested that Fontana pressed a version of "The Kids Are Alright" during late 1964 and that promo copies of it are listed in record collectors' guides. However, since Pete Townshend stated in the sleeve notes for *Another Scoop* that the song was written during winter 1965 and no one has ever confirmed that they have heard such an early recording, there is some doubt that this High Numbers version of the song does in fact exist.)

The arrival of Kit Lambert and Chris Stamp around this time certainly intensified the hunt for a future record deal. They approached many record companies and recorded a number of test sessions and auditions, and this acetate could hail—if not from Fontana—from one of these. It is a period of their career shrouded in some uncertainty, and only three record company auditions can be confirmed to have taken place: with Pye Records, an acetate of which does still exist; with Decca, and with EMI, who rejected the band on 22 October 1964. It is reported that both Decca and EMI were offered—among others—versions of "Smokestack Lightning," a choice of song hardly likely to impress upon the A&R staff that here was a band brimming full of new ideas.

The Pye session hails from late 1964 (exact date unknown) and consists of two songs: a second version of "Leaving Here" and a rigorous treatment of Marvin Gaye's then recently released "Baby Don't You Do It." (The presence of this latter selection confirms that this session is dated no earlier than the U.S. release date of the song on 2 September 1964. The soonest the band could have heard it—allowing for imported copies of the original single to reach Britain—is likely to be about a month later. The Gaye single was not given a U.K. release at all even though it was a moderate U.S. hit). "Leaving Here" has an identical arrangement to the High Numbers take and is the more melodic of the songs, with somewhat bland backing vocals. The main point of divergence with the earlier recording comes with the guitar breaks, which are completely different. The drumming—suitably prominent in the mix—is very dynamic, and Moon emerges for the first time on a recording as a leading musical force within the band, rather than a mere component in the rhythm section. It isn't known who produced or engineered the session, but unlike the staff at Fontana Studios, they seemed to have understood just how important was Keith Moon's contribution. In fact, even more than on "Leaving Here," "Baby Don't You Do It" is built around his powerful, idiosyncratic drum style.

"Baby Don't You Do It" is a more radical performance overall. Starting with a brilliant, exuberant drum beat that carries the song to inspiring heights, no one listening could fail to be knocked out by Moon's extraordinary abilities.

Roger Daltrey's vocals are also noteworthy, sounding semi-improvised (though obviously not). His singing here allows for more subtleties and expressiveness than he was given the opportunity to add to "Leaving Here" and a lot of the band's other material at the time. The guitar and bass work are more pedestrian, however, following a repetitive two-chord shuffle and adding no further embellishments until the guitar solo [1.40]. This is extraordinary: Townshend cranks up his amp and treats the listener to a twenty-second power chord/feedback solo with the Morse code tapping effect from the pickup switch. It is wonderfully exciting (and very similar to the middle section of the later "Anyway Anyhow Anywhere.") It would seem that this must have been the first time that this effect had been recorded (coming here maybe six months in advance of "Anyway Anyhow Anywhere") and would have been even more startling for this reason. So startling, indeed, that the Pye A&R staff might have been frightened off, for this audition, we should not forget, was a failure!.

Hardened-up Tamla Motown mingled with an avant-garde sonic freak-out obviously wasn't as easy on the ears as the neat, controlled and smoothly honed beat music that the record companies obviously preferred. It is now difficult to imagine how the Pye staff viewed the Who. Maybe they felt the combination of Tamla Motown and the Who's amphetamined, distorted sound (with its electronic craziness) was incompatible. The Beatles were still the model for what British beat groups should be, with self-written pop tunes, vocal harmonies and easygoing melodies—all of which both these recordings lacked. Also, Pye had acquired the Kinks early in 1964 and its staff may have felt one noisy bunch of London rowdies was more than enough. It can now be seen, however, that these two recordings were very close to the Who's roots, to their live performances and to a mod idealism, to a much greater extent than the more self-conscious High Numbers single. The two performances can be taken as representing the Who's first real recording work—not their own songs, obviously, but songs that meant a great deal to them and to their audience and that were inexorably connected with their roots.

The Pye audition acetate has only recently surfaced. Neither the master tapes nor even a copy of the disk had been retained in the Who tape archives, and seemingly everyone had forgotten that the recordings ever took place. Phil Hopkins, co-editor of the British Who magazine *Generations*, was lucky enough to obtain the only known acetate copy and deliver it to Jon Astley at Revolution Studios in 1994. Astley subsequently made a digital copy and cleaned up the extraneous surface noise (acetate discs have a limited playing life and become susceptible to crackles and scratches). The versions of "Leaving Here" and "Baby Don't You Do It" finally appeared on CD as part of the revamped *Odds and Sods* in March 1998. These two songs represent a major find and add a great deal to our understanding and appreciation of the kind of band the Who were during their "maximum R&B" period.

In August 1964 Kit Lambert and Chris Stamp adopted management control of the band and cast off most (but not all) of Meaden's mod vestiges. Their first aims were to revert the name to the Who, consolidate a growing live following and secure not only a recording deal but also a hit record. Within a few months all of this had happened. The band's live profile was boosted by a residency of shows at the Marquee Club in Soho, London. This series of concerts was a vitally important event in the band's development. The six-month Tuesday night residency commenced on 24 November 1964, and at these concerts more than any others the band found a sense of vocation and a much-increased audience.

Throughout these heady few months, Lambert and Stamp built the Who in stature and confidence, introducing distinctive group graphics (namely the famous black "maximum R&B" bill for the Marquee shows), attracting record company interest and finally gaining the rewards of a hit single and attendant television appearances. Within six months the band had become a hit act, a status they then maintained against all the odds for the next twenty years. Lambert particularly nurtured Townshend's songwriting potential and applied the more highbrow aesthetic principles of his background to the music and image of a band already displaying a strange mixture of working-class vigor and strength with avant-garde sensibilities and nihilistic verve. Lambert and Stamp made a significant contribution to the way the band members saw themselves and instilled into them an "anything is possible" spirit.

Personal relationships within the Who, however, were often strained, and tensions had developed regarding the direction the music should take. Roger Daltrey didn't want the band to compromise its R&B roots. He fully supported the incorporation of soul and Tamla material, but he initially felt that Townshend's songs might steer the Who into more shallow, pop-oriented territory. Throughout this period, indeed, the band was seriously questioning the validity of R&B, and the success of Townshend's new songs confirmed a future direction that could not be ignored—but for a while the situation was uneasy. Daltrey's forceful personality made any new suggestion a difficult battle of wills. As Townshend, Daltrey, Moon and Entwistle were naturally abrasive individuals, disagreements abounded, not just during the unsettled period of adjustment while becoming a chart act, but for the remainder of their careers. Townshend actually admitted on British television that "offstage, the group get on terribly badly.... The singer is a Shepherd's Bush geezer who wants everything to be a big laugh, and when it isn't, he thinks something's going wrong, terribly wrong. The drummer is a sort of completely different person to anyone else I've ever met. The bass player, he just doesn't seem to be interested in anything, which makes it all very difficult."[8]

Success with Lambert and Stamp didn't come without some considerable effort being expended. The new management team bought out Helmut Gorden and Peter Meaden, and in many ways the band was reluctant to see

Meaden go. His influence, although brief, had had its advantages, but Lambert and Stamp harbored altogether more ambitious and elaborate plans. As one would expect from their backgrounds, they initially produced a short film of the band that stressed their visual elements and the cult of their audience.[9] The failure of "I'm the Face" was an essential part of the process that spurred the band into developing a more distinctive style of their own with original material.

Kit Lambert was the catalyst who ensured that the Who moved a step ahead of the mod/High Numbers theme almost as soon as he took over, leaving the audiences and other groups to catch up. The key to this change was Pete Townshend's songs. They were fresh, bright and uncommonly good, and they benefited from Lambert's critical ear. The Who had been inherited by Lambert and Stamp with a strong but ephemeral image, a great ensemble live sound and a fanatical though limited following in West London. Lambert cultivated the Who's most durable and vital asset: Townshend's songwriting ability. From this point onward the band would progressively break through to new territories into which other bands couldn't follow without seeming like imitators: auto-destruction, pop art and later rock opera.

Auto-destruction was very much an activity nurtured by Lambert. Because of the low ceiling of the Harrow & Wealdstone Railway Hotel, Pete Townshend had a mishap one evening in late 1964, snapping the neck of his fragile Rickenbacker guitar. He then smashed the whole guitar in a more willful manner, evoking a strong response from the audience. This was a sensational, though expensive, gimmick, and it attracted much criticism and derision, but in terms of audience impact it was sensational. When Townshend bashed his guitar on the stage—still amplified—it created discordant screeches and feedback, becoming a perfect theatrical tool, an electronic noise machine. This destruction was incorporated into the act: later on, Keith Moon would simultaneously break up his drum kit, Daltrey would bash cymbals with a microphone, and Entwistle alone would provide a random noise with this bass while smoke bombs would cloud the stage in a surrealistic finale that would, by the end of 1965, have become the scary climax of "My Generation." (This should be considered in the context of the members of the Beatles'—whom many people viewed as rebellious and subversive—finishing their performances at this time by standing in line in neatly matching suits and ties and actually bowing to the audience!)

Not wishing to be labeled a thug or vandal (which he was anyway), Townshend tied in the guitar smashing with the art form auto-destruction, on which subject he had been lectured at Ealing Art College by Gustav Metzker. The auto-destructive theory of art is based on the post–Dadaist premise that the material world is worthless and ultimately brings about its own decay and demise. Art forms developed under this theory, therefore, should reflect the inevitability of this destruction. Metzger's work reportedly consisted of mechanical sculpture forms that were preprogrammed to disintegrate. The band also introduced the concept of pop art into music, by so classifying the feedback as reflecting this recent school of art that had taken the early sixties by storm. Essentially, however, aside from the showmanship and intellectual posturing, destruction was an act of pure frustration that seemed to purge both performer and audience of negative aggressive energies. It remains an antimaterialist statement and (in the pop world at least) an unsurpassed expression of anger. Kit Lambert characteristically joined in the debate, attempting, like Townshend, to give the destruction an artistic context. But ultimately people enjoyed watching the band members smash their equipment not as an artistic statement: it was pure performance theater, musical anarchy, both disturbing and exhilarating and one of the most effective forms of catharsis ever seen in rock music.

In general, Townshend's handling of his guitar attracted a great deal of attention. He used it in ways that had never before been seen in ways beyond its musical use. He wasn't restricted or hampered by it on stage, not rooted to a spot or rendered immobile. He found the guitar could be a means of constant visual expression. Townshend was part matador, part ballet dancer, part Luddite and part martial artist. One early trick was to extend his arms outward in a "flying" posture when feedback was screeching from his speakers, as if to say "Look—no hands!" This earned him the nickname Birdman, which was later inaccurately assumed to have arisen due to his jumps. With the later solid-bodied guitars, Pete would often hold the instrument aloft with his arms fully extended upward, like a rock-and-roll Moses delivering the gospel of feedback on a tablet of guitar-shaped stone.

But the history of the Who onstage, as previously mentioned, is a different story. The progress the band had made with their concert performances during 1964 raised a new question: How could the band equal that impact on a record, where listeners couldn't see guitars being smashed? Some of the noise and feedback could be recorded, but the actual destruction of guitars and equipment worked only when it could be seen by audiences. Here lie the roots of a dichotomy that characterized the Who for the remainder of their career: their concert work was of a different nature to their studio recordings. In practice, this meant that if you saw the Who in concert they would sound different (arguably much better) than their records, and often concert performances would include material not issued on disks. Likewise, many of the songs recorded were never played onstage. This was a complex approach that sometimes caused confusion and disappointment or delight, depending upon expectations. But the Who were one of the first bands to forge a duality of identity without one aspect of their work suffering by comparison with the other. The Beatles (to use the most obvious example) paled as a live act in comparison with their records, ditto the Byrds, the Kinks and the Beach Boys. The early Pink Floyd, Led Zeppelin and Crazy World of

Arthur Brown, however, turned in concert acts that far surpassed their recordings. The Who certainly tended to fall into the latter category, but their records have great value in their own right because the band usually took a different, though equally valid, approach in the recording studio.

Through perseverance, Lambert and Stamp gained the attention of American record producer Shel Talmy, who was based in London and whose work on the early Kinks records was much admired and very commercially successful. (After a couple of false starts, the Kinks had released "You Really Got Me" in August 1964, capturing the hardest and toughest guitar sound of any of the British groups *and* scoring a number 1 hit.) Some claim that Talmy listened to a demo of "I Can't Explain" over the telephone, liked it immediately and agreed to record the Who. No one in the Who camp could have faulted Talmy's track record and reputation as a producer of hit records, and all lacked the experience to foresee that the contract terms agreed to with him were unfavorable to the Who. Talmy contracted the Who to his own production company, which gave him the freedom to license his acts to record companies. In the Who's case, he arranged for a deal with Decca (U.S.) and its U.K. subsidiary Brunswick Records.

Talmy contracted the Who to a six-year production deal, giving the band a meager royalty rate of 2.5 percent. Although this was raised to 4 percent following the first hit, Talmy was allowed a wide degree of commercial and artistic control, and these factors became problematic as 1965 progressed. As a basis for comparison, bear in mind that a major label record deal for a new hot property in the 1990s would typically offer a royalty rate in excess of 10 percent. The band members' ultimate discontentment came to a head in early 1966, and their ensuing legal battle with Talmy was to have catastrophic financial consequences over the next few years. However, Talmy's work with the band is musically important, and he must be given due credit for getting the Who sound first onto vinyl and second, onto the charts.

"I Can't Explain" proved to be the song that really represented the Who's arrival and forged a unique direction away from R&B and into the future. Kit Lambert had encouraged Pete Townshend to write songs for the group, being the only member of the band who had previously shown any interest in composition. Townshend's early efforts were somewhat at odds with the band's prevailing style, but it was accepted that—for singles releases at least— such original songs were required. The strength of Townshend's songs was before long to provoke a reassessment of the band's style and direction, but even after the success of "I Can't Explain" and the follow-up single "Anyway Anyhow Anywhere," it was not assumed that Pete Townshend material would displace the soul and R&B music from the core of the Who's repertoire.

Townshend had begun writing songs in earnest in 1964 when Kit Lambert equipped him with two Vortexion tape recorders—compact and robust machines usually used by film crews—and a single microphone. Pete's first makeshift studio was at his flat situated above his parents' home in Ealing, which he shared with Richard Barnes. With the two tape machines, Townshend could overdub guitars and vocal parts to approximate a group arrangement of a song. The resulting demo recordings, although rudimentary in arrangement and detail, were of a sufficiently high quality to prove worthy of release on CD twenty years later. The first songs had a bouncy, echoey, innocent quality that was very appealing, and when the band members began to record these songs in earnest they rarely needed to alter either the music or lyrics. Apart from the aforementioned "It Was You," "The Kids are Alright" and "I Can't Explain," Townshend's early songs included "Call Me Lightning," "You Don't Have to Jerk," and "You're Going to Know Me" (later retitled "Out in the Street"). During 1965, Townshend moved into a flat in Belgravia, and expanded his studio with the installation of a Vortexion CBL two-track recorder. Recording demos of his compositions was Pete's abiding interest during this period, and his equipment was updated and expanded as regularly as funds would allow.

Townshend attempted to supply songs to order but soon found that tailoring material to please everyone in the band and the management had its difficulties. An example of this is indicated by Pete's comments on "Call Me Lightning," the lyrics of which portray a rather crude and exaggerated sexist's posturing and bragging references to Jaguar sports cars: "The song is a very clear example of how difficult it was for me to reconcile what I took to be Roger's need for macho, chauvinist lyrics and Keith Moon's appetite for surf music and fantasy sports car love affairs."[10] Some may have resented that Townshend was able to so influence the musical direction of the group, and the fact that a different member of the group sang his lyrics placed him in an unusual and in some ways uncomfortable position.

In general, however, Townshend managed to hit an original theme in most of his songs. Although he occasionally adhered to the conventions of pop at the time in singing about love, girls, romance and relationships, he managed to reflect the frustrations and difficulties of teenage life very succinctly without resorting to cliché. Songs such as "The Kids Are Alright" assessed situations from an unusual angle that was direct and uncontrived. Chris Charlesworth recently wrote that in comparison with the Beatles, Rolling Stones, Kinks and so on, the Who presented "a different kind of pop song ... one that's real, that deals with unpleasant truths with which real teenage boys, not just those lucky enough to have a girlfriend, can identify."[11] Yet at this stage Townshend's characteristic anger and studied rebellion wasn't apparent.

He had a natural lyrical skill that developed and matured and along with Ray Davies of the Kinks became probably the most noted rock lyricist of the era. The lyric writing of both Davies and Townshend far exceeded anything done by the Beatles or the Rolling Stones and certainly equaled Bob Dylan, then considered the master. This assertion might surprise those readers who are only moderately familiar with the Who's music, but the evidence cannot be denied. If we are unused to classifying Pete Townshend along with the more celebrated exponents of rock-and-roll lyric writing, then we can only point to Townshend's own wariness of his lyrics' being reprinted, anthologized, examined out of context or treated as poetry. He has resisted all temptations to produce a book of his song lyrics, a volume of which would undoubtedly form a formidable collection of work. This tacit discouragement (and maybe modesty on his part) has arguably dissuaded those who might otherwise have made his work the subject of literary analysis. (In this book I have no such purpose in mind either, though I hope to offer some insights into Who lyrical themes that have previously been passed by.)

Shel Talmy arranged the first recording session for the Who sometime during December 1964, at Pye Studios in London. They recorded "I Can't Explain" and "Bald Headed Woman," the two sides of what was to be the Who's debut single, and Talmy was aided by engineer Glyn Johns, who was later to collaborate with the band as a top producer in his own name. The band's enthusiasm for their new producer was somewhat dampened, however, by the fact that Talmy had also booked the Ivy League (soon to become a hit pop act in the U.K. in their own right) to sing the vocal backings for the Who, and Jimmy Page (future Yardbirds and Led Zeppelin mainstay) to play guitar. Talmy was a slick professional and making records was his forte: he wasn't about to waste time tutoring Daltrey, Townshend and Entwistle in the rudiments of vocal harmony. As for Page's presence, Talmy was simply unsure whether Townshend could deliver what was needed to produce a guitar-dominant recorded sound. Townshend was, of course, more than competent. The backing singers prevailed, but Townshend didn't need Page to play guitar, although some outtakes of "I Can't Explain" (presumably discarded after the session) featured both guitarists. The released version of "I Can't Explain" on the A side of the single features only Townshend, as is clear from the two very distinctive and unusual guitar solos. Page did, however, play on "Bald Headed Woman"—a one-chord strum that required a fuzz box, a piece of equipment that Townshend didn't possess. Talmy apparently foisted this song onto the Who (as he had also done with the Kinks three months earlier on their debut album) to earn himself an extra royalty. Despite being recorded by two such distinguished bands, "Bald Headed Woman" remains an almost unlistenably bad song, a bluesy dirge that lacks melody and dynamics of any kind and has ludicrous lyrics. A sudden surge in tempo [1.18] sees the introduction of a Daltrey harmonica break that brings the Who perhaps as close as they ever would come on record to the souped-up Delta blues feel extolled by the early Rolling Stones and Yardbirds; it remains the most conventional R&B moment the Who ever released.

In vivid contrast was "I Can't Explain," which reflects the band at its best. It is a short, sharp, jagged, four-chord burst of energy that transcends beat music and became a definitive statement of teenage insecurity that had a universal application far beyond merely expounding the mod ethos. Townshend offers a toughened-up guitar tone, which, although still falling short of his stage sound, is at least more characteristic than the earlier High Numbers recordings. The hard mono sound of the original single (retained on subsequent CD masterings) punches out of the speakers with its theme of the confusion of youthful emotions and paradoxically voices the significance of inarticulate youth needing to express feelings to address a more wide-reaching situation, beyond self-consciousness.

In retrospect, "I Can't Explain" is not only the epitome of perfect pop but is an encapsulation of primal rock and roll—exciting, lively and fresh. It has wonderfully emphatic drumming from Moon and the two jerky, wholly original Townshend guitar solos. The only negative aspect of the record lies in the backing vocals, which sound a little too smooth and conventional, at odds with the slabs of metallic guitar chording that power the beat forward. "I Can't Explain" wasn't an immediate hit, taking some time (and television exposure) before attaining the U.K. chart position of number 8 on 17 April 1965. It spent over three months in the chart, as if to affirm the arrival of the Who in the higher echelon of the British pop scene, but its performance in the U.S. was disappointing. With relief and astonishment that the first Who single had scored a hit, Townshend commented at the time, "I hoped I'd written something that would prove to be a steady climber and fortunately I did. I was trying for a good contrast between singer and backing in the song. We got a heavyish surf-type sound in the backing, mostly on account of the boys liking the surf group sound."[12] Although the band members might not have believed it at the time, "I Can't Explain" retained its timeless freshness through years of subsequent stage performances—over the next twenty years or so, they would never tire of playing it.

With "I Can't Explain" in the charts, Pete Townshend had proved himself capable of writing a hit song—not just a successful melody but a lyrical statement to which the record-buying public had made a positive response. By using the first-person singular, *I*, Townshend set a lyrical pattern that would follow through for the remainder of the Who's work. The reason this point is noteworthy lies in the Who's *modus operandi*, where the singer is not the lyricist and vice versa. The *I* in Who songs is the character who speaks through the lyrics, and one cannot, therefore, ascribe what is directly expressed in a song as being personal to either the writer (Townshend) or the singer (Daltrey). The overall meaning of a Who song is consciously or unconsciously the product of the writer and the environment in which he lives and works, and the use of *I* is largely an abstract method of expression. Although Daltrey generally sings words written by Pete Townshend, Daltrey is not merely the mouthpiece for Townshend. First, in singing the lyrics, Daltrey attaches an interpretation, however subtle, through inflexion and nuance, that is not Townshend's; second, we cannot discount the possibility that Daltrey is singing "in character." In later works this is certain because the characters are clearly delineated (Tommy, and Jimmy in *Quadrophenia*), but the idea of "character" is no less relevant in early Who songs as well.

"I Can't Explain" addresses a relationship between the "singer" or the character who speaks and another person or thing. The song strongly emphasizes a feeling of confusion about changing emotions (common in teenagers) and also an inability to account for and express this turmoil. But via the words projected in the song, the inarticulate character here becomes, paradoxically, articulate by expressing the fact that he (or she) "can't explain." Indeed, the symptoms of the malaise are actually stated as being physical: "dizzy in the head," and, suggesting a loss of control, "I'm going out of my mind..." No firm conclusion is reached, no love is proclaimed and the confusion remains. The only positive line is a mere "I think it's love," but, of course, it might not be. Where 99 percent of pop songs at the time were positive in their uncomplicated proclamation of love, in Townshend's song—just as in real life— absolutes become uncertainties.

Further recording sessions followed in March 1965, with plans for a follow-up single and album. Talmy and the band realized that the Who's time had arrived and must be exploited in an environment where a year was often the average trajectory of a hit act before it fell from public favor. Townshend sensed this at the time and had set his ambitions on scoring one huge hit single, saying, "I figure that we will probably have about a year as a popular group. Could be less. Maybe more. But we have to make the most of the time we have. We would also like to get a No. 1. I hope we make it with our next disc."[13] But the future held just the opposite: the Who lasted a further sixteen years as a popular group but never achieved the much-hoped-for number 1 hit single!

In those days sessions were delineated as being for singles or for album tracks, although initially the Who simply recorded a bulk of its stage material for the album, setting Pete to work on singles material. An early contender for the next single was "You Don't Have to Jerk." The dance craze the Jerk had been celebrated in a number of American soul records, which, although they hadn't become hits in the U.K. charts, were very much the in thing on the mod dance floors in London. Pete Townshend recorded a demo version of "You Don't Have to Jerk," but it isn't known whether the band completed a full version for Talmy at these sessions. At some point the song was rejected; maybe it was deemed musically inferior or, more likely, destined to become dated too quickly, cashing in as it did on a passing trend.

Other initial recordings consisted of "Shout and Shimmy," "I Don't

Mind" and "Please Please Please" (all by James Brown); "Anytime You Want Me" (by Garnet Mimms); "Daddy Rolling Stone" (by Otis Blackwell); "Heat Wave" and "Motoring" (both Martha and the Vandellas); "Lubie (Come Back Home)" (by Paul Revere and the Raiders); and "I'm a Man" (by Bo Diddley). The only other Townshend song attempted was "You're Going to Know Me" (later retitled "Out in the Street"), which was much less melodic than "I Can't Explain" and not really suitable for a single release. Nicky Hopkins was drafted by Talmy to play piano at these sessions, and those involved felt that these songs—along with the resurrected High Numbers take of "Leaving Here"— would be suitable for a hastily assembled album to catch the market broached with "I Can't Explain." Roger Daltrey's concern that Townshend's songs would steer the group too far away from the R&B and soul music of their roots persisted. But the success of "I Can't Explain" really acted as a catalyst in changing the musical policy of the band.

This new direction was further confirmed by the April 1965 recording of the second Who single, "Anyway Anyhow Anywhere," a collaboration between Townshend and Roger Daltrey. This song was a bold departure from "I Can't Explain", although less a crafted song and more a sonic assault. It was a groundbreaking composition that was aggressive and arrogant but entirely successful in its experimentation, an audacious choice for a follow-up hit. Yet "Anyway Anyhow Anywhere" retained the pure pop sensibilities of all of Townshend's work during this era. Starting with a slower three-chord strum than "I Can't Explain" (a figure borrowed from the temporarily discarded "You're Going to Know Me"), the song dispenses with the verse-chorus-verse-chorus structure. This willingness to take chances paid off, as "Anyway Anyhow Anywhere" moved up the U.K. charts, reaching number 10 on 3 July 1965. The highlight of the performance is the guitar solo [1.10]— a profound innovation—that duplicated Townshend's onstage feedback routine, similar to that previously recorded only on "Baby Don't You Do It" from the Pye audition. The closing backing vocals and Nicky Hopkins's piano bring the song to a perfectly controlled climax.

On the B side, "Daddy Rolling Stone" was, in comparison, a more pedestrian performance, being a straight run-through of the R&B standard. It has one shot of Who individuality with the power chord guitar solo [1.29], a technique further developed by Townshend on recordings later in the year. In America, however, where the single failed to chart, "Anytime You Want Me" was placed on the reverse. This recording is a ballad with Ivy League backing vocals and Hopkins's piano to the fore and a performance so laid back that it could be by a different group. This was Roger Daltrey's first attempt at a more controlled ballad vocal, and I admit that he copes well with the change of pace, although no musical element of the performance belies this as a Who recording. Confusion over master tapes led to an EP's being released in France on which a version of "Anyway Anyhow Anywhere" with an alternate lead vocal appears. Decca in the States returned the master tape of "Anyway Anyhow Anywhere," believing the feedback to be an engineering fault. This incident has about it something of the apocryphal.

The feedback was crucial to Townshend's conception of the song, on which, he stated, the band members "were trying to achieve the sound which we get on the stage at present, all in a commercial record which will sell."[14] Arrogance and aggression, the other side of the coin of teenage insecurity, had replaced some of the innocent confusion of "I Can't Explain." This pose was the one most identified with the early image of the Who (irresponsible, violent and anarchic), and the Roger Daltrey's blunt approach emphasized these qualities on "Anyway Anyhow Anywhere" for the first time. This persona was that of a character in opposition, in conflict, and using aggressive means of achieving results. But the character can also be seen to be a braggart, attempting to cover up inadequacies and deficiencies in himself with outward displays of machismo and unfocused antagonism. On the later "My Generation," however, this spirit reached a higher plane and formed a critique of a whole older generation and its world. Positions are not resolved here, as indeed they are often not in reality, and continued frustration is the outcome.

Arrogance comes to the fore in overkill proportions in "Anyway Anyhow Anywhere," resulting in an attitude of nihilism and possibly the abuse of freedom. If the character follows through his sentiment to a far extreme, a shadow of amorality falls. But in reality, we can sense that the song's overt rebellion is merely wishful thinking. Yet the forcefulness and single-mindedness of the character make an impact that the musical explosiveness backs up. The division of compositional labor between Townshend and Daltrey has never been identified in any detail, though the lyrics certainly seem more reflective of Daltrey's pragmatic approach to life.

The power of "Anyway Anyhow Anywhere" was also enshrined by a groundbreaking appearance on U.K. television's *Ready Steady Goes Live!* (broadcast on 21 May 1965), which was later preserved in the *The Kids Are Alright* film and soundtrack album. Playing live, the band pushed the song to its limit on this occasion, and the feedback break was a revelation, with Townshend slashing away at his guitar and producing a distorted, chaotic sound that even exceeded that which had been committed to the record—a defining moment in rock television history that put the revolutionary feedback sound into millions of homes in the U.K. early on a Friday evening. The release on record (and later CD) of this TV performance, although in compressed and boxy mono, retains all the explosive power of that remarkable moment and is a good alternate means of experiencing "Anyway Anyhow Anywhere" in its raw state, unembellished by the piano and studio singers. Although technically flawed in terms of sound quality—the drums are almost inaudible—the feedback solo of this performance is simply astounding and alone justifies the release of an otherwise deficient recording. On this same *Ready Steady Go!* appearance, the Who also turned in a version of "Shout and Shimmy," which at the time had been recorded but was still unreleased. This performance attained a more concentrated feel of the song than the studio take, with Townshend's fast, choppy, rhythmic guitar chording to the fore and with a characteristic explosion of drums [1.14], almost a solo. Although retained in the *Ready Steady Go!* archives, this recording has not been released.

Collecting the songs recorded at that point, Talmy put together a rough assembly of the debut Who album that would form a direct reflection of their stage act. Already there were doubts as to whether this would be adequate for the band's first major sustained statement on record. The dilemma facing them was either to issue the record in July 1965, capitalizing on the success of the two singles, or defer it until better material could be recorded but risking a loss of interest in the interim. As if unsure of its reception, an acetate pressing of nine songs was played by Shel Talmy for writer John Emery, who made the obvious comment that if released the record would "lack originality in choice of material." He went on to say, "True, they are given that distinctive Who treatment but that might not be enough if they want to make a big impression with the album ... they have not used their electronic effects as extensively as one might have expected."[15]

Emery's sympathetic but critical appraisal can only have been the result of a feeling of anticlimax when comparing the material on the acetate to "Anyway Anyhow Anywhere"—which both was original *and* possessed "electronic effects" aplenty. According to the article, the acetate had sequenced the following songs: "I'm a Man," "Heat Wave," "I Don't Mind," "Lubie (Come Back Home)," "You're Going to Know Me," "Please, Please, Please," "Leaving Here" and "Motoring." Although referred to as comprising nine tracks, only the eight titles above are detailed, and a complete album would have needed at least three more songs. One can only speculate that some of the missing tracks would have been "Shout And Shimmy," "Anytime You Want Me" and maybe "You Don't Have to Jerk," if it hadn't been completely discarded by then.

Emery's comment added fuel to a debate that was already raging internally—certainly between Townshend and Daltrey—regarding the band's direction, and the fact that this version of the album was scrapped was really the death knell for Daltrey's pure R&B version of the Who. Soon after Emery had heard the acetate, the band members made a decision to rethink the nature of their debut album and issued a statement to the press to this effect. "Who make drastic policy changes," stated *Melody Maker*. "Re-recording holds up first LP ... Says Who manager Kit Lambert: 'The Who are having serious doubts about the state of R&B. Now the LP material will consist of hard pop. They've finished with "Smokestack Lightning!"' The main contents of the album will now be originals written by guitarist Pete Townshend, and singer Roger Daltrey..."[16] The prospect of starting an LP again from scratch, as this dramatic report suggested the Who would be doing, was an expensive and time-consuming job. An album of all-original material sounds very appealing to us now, but at the time those involved reached a compromise in order to expedite release of an already delayed work. Talmy may well have forced the matter by accepting the need for some new material but insisting that a few of the completed recordings be retained. But, the band did not return to the studio again until October, by which time further pressure was mounting to get an LP into the shops by Christmas.

Aside from "Leaving Here," three of the tracks on this acetate were completely abandoned, while the remaining four appeared on the eventual debut LP. Of the rejects, "Heat Wave" was a successful performance of a pristine Tamla Motown standard, although the Who's version lacks the slickness and fluidity of the Martha and the Vandellas original. The minor chords and soulful backing vocals are effective, if a little clumsy, and the drums weave around the rhythm with real purpose. (The band returned to this song a year later and produced a much tighter and more compact recording for their second album). "Lubie (Come Back Home)" is patently inferior to the other material, being a routine version of an inane and uncomplicated pop song, and much less distinctive than most Who cover versions. Being a lengthy interplay between lead and backing vocals, it passes over the band's true instrumental strengths. The third Motown selection, "Motoring," also fails to achieve the quality of "Leaving Here" or "Heat Wave," although it was an uncommon choice of song. It is a high-energy one-chord workout with one defining moment [1.50] where the drums play a brief solo passage. Daltrey's vocals here sound monotonous and almost lack any kind of melodic value. (All four of these tracks were given a belated and unexpected first release on the archive albums *Who's Missing* and *Two's Missing* in the mid-1980s.)

The realization that the band would be expected to produce an album more substantial in new ideas spurred Townshend into writing a bulk of fresh material that continued in the direction taken with its first two singles. Certainly Lambert and Stamp were behind this move, while Daltrey publicly expressed his dislike for the hit singles, which he considered to be too commercial. A few months passed during which the new material was prepared, but lack of a new single during the summer of 1965 was partly assuaged by the band's constant gigging schedule and radio and television appearances.

In common with most of the major artists of the 1960s, the Who also enjoyed a parallel career recording for BBC radio. At the time, the Musician's Union had an arrangement with the BBC that sought to limit the broadcasting of commercially issued records in order to protect the demand for live or specially commissioned performances by musicians. The agreed restriction on *needletime*, as it was called, meant that all the BBC Light Programme's pop-oriented shows broadcast a fair proportion of exclusive recordings and live broadcasts. These appearances were often a valuable way of getting new music onto the air waves, and the BBC has retained some of the recordings in its archives. In later years, this material was commercially issued, although at the time of this writing no material recorded by the Who has gained an official release. As early as 9 April 1964, the band had auditioned with the BBC in the hope of becoming "employable" on its programs, but on that occasion the stiff panel of BBC personnel was not impressed and judged them unsuitable and substandard for radio bookings.

A second audition took place on 12 February 1965 and was successful, despite some remaining doubts from the selection panel. The band was booked initially on the rather sedate *Joe Loss Pop Show*, which was broadcast live on Fridays at lunchtime. This debut performance wasn't recorded, but a second appearance on the more influential *Saturday Club* was. Recorded on 24 May 1965, this broadcast featured four songs: a tight performance of "Leaving Here," which lacks the three bars of guitar intro of the High Numbers version; an obligatory retread of "Anyway Anyhow Anywhere"—the current hit single—which is slightly more laid back, minus the piano part of the single and with the overdubbed feedback guitar part; "Good Lovin'," a short and breezy vocal harmony workout; and James Brown's "Just You and Me, Darling," the weakest performance of the four, enlivened only by two guitar solos. These latter two songs were not recorded in any other form by the Who, making this session a valuable performance. The technical quality of the BBC's 4-track recordings (all in mono) arguably surpasses the Brunswick record releases, although these recordings lack Shel Talmy's hard-edged production and compactness.

Although following the Beatles and the Kinks, both of which also worked on similarly innovative styles and sounds during the 1964–1965 era, the Who were considered to be the true avant-garde of British rock: their conception of their act was unrestricted by convention and their music was the subversive result of a healthy disregard of the commercial forces of capitalist society, of the so-called normal and respectable, and of the middle-class derived notions of good taste and acceptability. This attitude wasn't politically motivated, and the band had no ideological ax to grind (the era of politically aware rock music had yet to come and at this stage was present only in the folk/protest movement). The Who's reaction and response to the world in which they found themselves was merely intuitive and emotional. In truth, the pop world was cynical, greedy, and artistically negligible—its gestures and images were largely tame. The Beatles were the biggest band in the world, and while they flirted with ideas of rebellion and high art, they were in reality the epitome of good show business conformity, the result of entrepreneurial capitalism. All the other groups fell into line behind them; the system in which they functioned was rigid and harsh.

For their part, the Who were engulfed as part of the same pop music industry machine—they had little choice. No record label was free from corporate control, and all the outlets for pop music (records, sheet music, concerts, films) fell under the control of a web of agents, producers and managers who all, ultimately, represented the same thing. Within this structure, the Who worked to achieve a musical subversion as far as they were allowed. Luckily, the results of their efforts coincided with a strain of popular taste (they had at this time enjoyed two hits sizeable enough for the band to be taken seriously), otherwise they might have been destined always to miss that critical first wave of success, with the result of retiring early from the fray to be remembered in later years only as an obscure, freakish, experimental art-school rock act that had taken its music too far out into the creative twilight zone for it to retain an audience. That this did not happen, we have to thank the people who bought the Who's first two singles; many of their contemporaries (the Eyes, the Action, Creation, the Birds) found themselves in the position of never quite engaging public taste after releasing worthy but uncommercial music, only to be rediscovered by obsessive record collectors twenty or thirty years later in search of prepsychedelic gems latterly dubbed *freakbeat*. To the endless good fortune of bands such as the Who and the Kinks, this was one era in rock history when the fans were sometimes prepared to travel the distance along with the new music and were willing to allow their preconceptions of the sounds a pop group should make to be reshaped along the way.

With the two hit singles behind them, the Who had achieved a greater prominence on the U.K. pop scene and had attracted many new admirers across the country, especially with their stage act, now that concert appearances were radiating out from the West London stronghold. Concert bookings filled in almost every night in their schedule. While the country at large now embraced mod as a more diluted and marketable commodity, the Who extricated themselves from their association with it. With the release of "Anyway Anyhow Anywhere" and its tenuous but publicity-catching association with pop art, the band concentrated on this new image and gradually shed its connections with mod. The heyday of mod had passed by early 1965, although mods abounded in Who audiences throughout the year and beyond, especially at summer concerts at seaside venues such as the Brighton Aquarium Ballroom. The clothing and symbolism of pop art was a subtle progression from mod ideas, now suffused with surrealism. The Who attained this image through a variety of means, including the use of the British flag, the Jack, subversively cut into a jacket or draped over speakers and the wearing of medals and military insignia. The trend of wearing Victorian militaria really took hold of the fashion world in 1966 and became one of the most characteristic aspects of Swinging London. In the world in which the Who worked, pop art was still ahead of its time and gave the group an extra aura of visionary mystique.

The strained relationships within the band—which apparently came to physical blows on many occasions—were to reach a crisis point just prior to the release of the "My Generation" single. Roger Daltrey, still unhappy about the band's musical direction, was "invited" to leave the band, his behavior being considered unreasonable. With the potential huge hit in "My Generation," Daltrey thought better of his former approach and moderated his behavior from that point onward. However, internal disagreements were to dog the Who for many years to come, and this friction may well have been part of the creative spark that generated the band's vitality and drive.

The change of direction away from R&B, combined with Daltrey's more diplomatic approach to group politics, allowed for a bigger priority being accorded to Townshend's songs. Townshend recorded demos alone at his home, Kit Lambert would assess them and the band would select the most suitable for use by the Who. Through the summer of 1965, Pete had written "It's Not True," "The Good's Gone," " Do the Strip," "La-La-La-Lies," "Things Have Changed," "Much Too Much," "Kill My Appetite," "A Legal Matter," "Circles," and, most important, "My Generation." Enough good material now existed for an album, although "Things Must Change" was deemed too lightweight, being an uptempo country & western–styled song that it is hard to imagine the Who recording with any conviction. "Do the Strip" was a Motown-inspired mock dance-craze song that could never have been a serious contender as Who material, while "Kill My Appetite"—a simplistic pop song—similarly failed to make the grade.

"My Generation," which was most likely written in May 1965, was the most important new song. The qualities of this number were immediately apparent to neither Townshend nor the remainder of the band. Pete had been influenced by Jimmy Reed and the talking blues style and was heeding demands from his managers to make a provocative statement rather than express personal and individual dilemmas, as he had in his other songs. Pete recorded at least two demo versions of "My Generation," the first of which was given a slow, plodding blues rhythm and on which the vocal delivery that rendered the lyrics ironic and cynical, rather than angry and demonstrative. This demo generated little interest from a band that had just turned their backs on R&B, but Chris Stamp asked Townshend to record another version. The second demo was much faster and more intense and included a bass solo, and this was presented to the band as a much more viable proposition for a Who hit. The song slowly developed onstage but it was not until the final recording that it became the classic anthem that was to be one of the Who's biggest hits and most celebrated statements.

Working in a variety of London recording studios (IBC, City of London, Marquee, Landsdowne), an alledged five versions of "My Generation" were completed before the final take was selected. It has been said that each version was quite different from the others, but since the outtakes have not been heard, we are not able to compare them. The first attempt at capturing the song was at the Marquee Studios (probably during September 1965), where two versions were completed. These lacked both the bass solo and Daltrey's stuttered vocals. After these were rejected, the song was restructured, with upward key changes to heighten the dramatic edge of the lyrics and the bass solo was added. At IBC Studios some days later, the band made a second attempt at recording the song. John Entwistle, wishing to make the most of his solo spot, purchased a Danelectro bass to give a trebly, prominent sound. A famous story relates his frustrating experiences as he broke the strings, couldn't replace them without buying another bass guitar, had the same thing happen, and ended up owning three or four identical Danelectro basses, each with broken strings. The band provided the backing vocals now, and although Nicky Hopkins was still on call to add piano, he wasn't present at the session that produced the electrifying best take.

The final version of "My Generation" as released is breathtakingly good; the band's persistence with this song paid off admirably. Not only is the composition brilliant, but the Who's performance is razor-edged and charged with adrenalin and Talmy's production is as hard and gut-wrenching as anything he did with the Kinks. "My Generation"—recorded on 13 October 1965—is a song and a performance that simply exploded from the four walls of the studio into the ether of the national consciousness. It was the ultimate statement of the time, and it remains a wholly satisfying rock song on every level. The sharp performance adds to the musical structure to form a tour-de-force of focused rebellious energy. The amazingly hard two-chord riff, driven over on- and off-beats, combines with the drumming, bass solo, feedback, and upward key changes to elevate noise to an aesthetic form that supersedes closed definitions of pop and rock. Aside from the formal significance of this definitive British rock-and-roll song, "My Generation" is a remarkably catchy and accessible record that cumulates in the aural equivalent of auto-destruction and controlled electronic chaos. It charts the internecine anger and disaffection of modern youth with alarming clarity: it is a nihilistic, bitter, cynical and angry tirade that develops the milder sentiment of youth disaffection in Eddie Cochran's "Summertime Blues" to a disturbing extreme. In 1965 the single reflected everything that was vital about youthful arrogance and gave an impression of subversive violence that had been channeled into a positive and tangible form. Remarkably, although it caused concern in many Establishment quarters, "My Generation" didn't alienate the record buyer, reaching number 2 in the U.K. charts on 14 December.

Daltrey's stuttered vocals give an impression of a man fighting to put his message across, and while this may have initially puzzled some listeners, it actually has a more substantial purpose: stuttering is a side-effect of overusing amphetamine drugs (*blocked* in underground parlance), a common condition among the mods. Pete Townshend explained, "The guy who's singing is supposed to be blocked.... No, he's not blocked, he just can't form his words. The ending is a natural progression of what's come before. It's the way it happens on stage."[17] The feedback climax to the performance was the simulation of auto-destruction in purely aural terms. This was the logical follow-through from what had been established on stage and on "Anyway Anyhow Anywhere." Moon's drumming reaches a true fever pitch at the zenith of the song's final apocalyptic passage, where the Who establishes the apogean limit of their sound and vision—a place where no other group had ever dwelled.

As a lyrical statement, "My Generation" is the Who's most discussed work, containing what have become Pete Townshend's most famous lines. It is a short, sharp, incisive attack on the older generation (the generation in power at every level, the Establishment), who represent society at large. "I hope I die before I get old" is usually taken as a literal wish to die young rather than join the Establishment. What it really means is "death would preferable to becoming like you," a rebuke to an older order. This theme is almost universal and a precursor of Townshend's line can be found in an earlier British novel, *Sisters by a River* (1947) by Barbara Comyns, in which the young narrator says, "I do hope I am dead before I'm old." Whatever the interpretation of "My Generation," this is an ultimate negation of what are seen to be corrupting values in society. The voice here would prefer the ultimate opt-out over accepting conformism. The first-person singular *I* of Townshend's other songs becomes here a more collective voice with the use of the plural *we*—giving the song a spirit of solidarity. The rebellion of youth is easy to dismiss—it is often unfocused, confused and ultimately empty—but "My Generation" really holds the conviction that "us" and "them" are stuck in an incompatible and intractable relationship of antagonism.

On the B side in the U.K. was "Shout and Shimmy," the James Brown song recorded back in March. Ostensibly the same song as "Shout"—a hit for Lulu and the Luvvers in mid–1964—this performance was a brisk jaunt through the dance number, with an annoying gimmicky talk-back response to Daltrey's overemphatic "Do you feel all right?" The tempo cools a little midstream but lacks the drum solo passage that made the live performances of this song so memorable. (You might note that this track incorporates some very ineffective handclaps!) In the U.S., "Shout and Shimmy" was discarded and replaced with "Out in the Street," discussed later as part of the *My Generation* album. The choices of alternate B sides for the U.S. market is not easily explained. The Who was perceived in a slightly different way in the States, and the function of albums and singles in the pop marketplace differed somewhat, but Decca's decisions (or maybe Shel Talmy's) as to what to release cannot be readily accounted for. The net result of the choices simply deprived U.K. fans of hearing "Anytime You Want Me" and U.S. fans of hearing "Daddy Rolling Stone" and "Shout and Shimmy." (Differences between the *My Generation* album in the two countries later had a similar effect).

The sessions that produced "My Generation" also saw the Who completing material for their much-delayed and much-anticipated debut LP. The best of Townshend's new songs were selected and recorded during October and November 1965, but problems still persisted among the band members themselves and between the band and Shel Talmy. Talmy's working methods had begun to seriously aggrieve the band members and, inevitably, they felt their contract with him offered them poor remuneration. Kit Lambert and Talmy apparently felt very antipathetic toward each other. The three hit singles had made it clear that the band's rewards were not what the band members felt they should be earning at their current level of success. Roger Daltrey indicated some of these problems when he commented, "We are all so different and we've all got different points of view.... We find friction in the group helps anyway because we play emotional music. We might take a month arguing about 20 new numbers and end up with four. But we are so busy now we don't get much time for rehearsals. We feel very pleased about our success but wary."[18]

One idea that was under serious consideration for the debut album was to present it as a "party in progress," with each track linked with the appropriate sound effects of people chatting, clapping, dancing, clinking glasses and shouting. "We wanted to create the sound of a studio party," Pete recalled.[19] This had been inspired by the Everly Brothers' *Instant Party* album (1962), and it seemed that this title was to be retained by the Who. In many ways this would have been a development of the background voices that were added to "Shout and Shimmy." This idea had been exploited by a number of American pop acts as well and was therefore not original. It is fortunate that this concept was not used, as it would have been a gimmick that would have become tiresome after the novelty had worn off and would have ultimately served only to trivialize the songs.

Working close to Townshend's home demos, the Who recorded "The Kids Are Alright," "It's Not True," "Much Too Much," "A Legal Matter," "La-La-La-Lies," "The Good's Gone" and "Circles." An all-instrumental number, "The Ox," was developed from a jam including Townshend, Moon, Entwistle and Nicky Hopkins, and the writing credit reflects this coauthorship. "Circles" was a particularly melodic song that was considered suitable for the Who's next single, and Talmy held this back from the album lineup with the intention of its gaining an early–1966 single release. "I Don't Mind," "Please, Please, Please," "I'm a Man," and "You're Going to Know Me," now retitled "Out in the Street," were selected from the earlier sessions in March. Although there was a strong tradition of not including songs previously released on single albums in the U.K. "My Generation" was considered too powerful as both a song and defining statement to be excluded. Logically, the album itself was entitled *My Generation* and released on 4 December 1965.

Despite the fact that the material was recorded in two separate bouts months apart, the album has a cohesive sound. Talmy had done good work in achieving a hard, punchy mono sound scheme, which—despite sonic limitations—buzzes with energy and fulsome volume. But the fact cannot be denied that the inclusion of the cover versions—maybe at Talmy's insistence—weakens the effect of the album as a whole. Townshend's songs range from good to great but are inevitably somewhat one-dimensional compared to his later work. More important, the album managed to please fans of the band's singles, gain critical praise, and reach number 5 in the U.K. album charts. (Remember, however, that albums were considered at this time to be much less important than singles, although the band had at least maintained a consistent quality).

The opening song "Out in the Street" rings out the familiar three-chord strum of "Anyway Anyhow Anywhere" before bursting into an uptempo rhythm. This is a simple but effective performance in which Townshend tries to imitate the R&B and soul elements of the band's earlier repertoire. As one of the oldest songs, predating "Anyway Anyhow Anywhere," it is the least sophisticated original on the album, a spurt of energy that holds little in terms of melody. The overdubbed feedback solo is tame in comparison with the second single and "My Generation" itself, and lyrically the song is crude. The oft-repeated line "you're gonna know me" is said by a character determined to force his personality on women through sheer aggressiveness. A sexist and juvenile predicament, this merely imitates the clichéd lyrical content of much R&B. The title is taken from the first line, evocative and strong but suggesting a kind of celebration of the vitality of urban activity that the song fails to deliver.

"I Don't Mind" is a competent interpretation of a James Brown song, much slower than the rest of the record and featuring some conventional piano fills from Hopkins. It sounds somewhat ungainly but is effective enough without adding anything further to the song. Townshend's guitar solo [1.19] is done in a conventional manner rather than having the power chord effect, and a second guitar solo takes the track to its fade-out without gaining much. The progress of the record is, thankfully, instantly redeemed by "The Good's Gone," a medium-paced and solid Townshend composition that utilizes an unusual arpeggio guitar figure and moves through some dramatic chord changes before returning to the insidious initial guitar phrase. Although he sounds very mannered on the James Brown material, Daltrey here (double-tracked) sounds suitably malevolent and gives the song an extra dimension of emotional charge, supported by Townshend and Entwistle's harmonic vocal backings. However, the highlight of this exceptional song is the power-chord guitar solo [1.55]—a chopping, rhythmic break that reflects the early Townshend at his most inventive. Pete here chronicles a love gone sour and a character who wants out. But does his lover reach the same conclusion? It's a song of persuasion—"You know it's wrong"—and an unfavorable comparison with earlier times when "we used to love as one." The desire to jilt overwhelms all.

"La-La-La-Lies" is a straight pop song, light in comparison and maybe suited to a more conventional pop outfit than the Who. It fails to bring any substance to the album as a whole and now sounds like a filler. The song that follows, "Much Too Much," effectively combines the heavy chordal power of the band with its R&B roots, transcending the pop idiom with a thunderous depth of sound that almost completely submerges the conventional R&B piano part. Both of these songs are lyrically slight: the protagonist in the former faces the medacity of a former lover; while the latter details a character backing out of a relationship that he feels has become too serious. The inclusion at the close of side one of "My Generation"—the same take as the single—is somewhat questionable. The vinyl LP pressing sounds inferior to the single version, with a slightly muted, less explosive sound. (Indeed, during this era of the 45 rpm mono single and songs under four minutes in length, pressings were cut at "gorge" level, which gave all the early Who singles a terrific volume and bite. Purists would argue that this is the format in which the songs should be heard and for which they were originally conceived and engineered. Anyone returning to original copies of the singles might be surprised at just how startlingly vivid the sound is in comparison with later LP reissues of the same material.) However, the inclusion of "My Generation" (as previously mentioned) gives the record its era-defining title, and it encapsulates the imagery and themes of the Who at the time better than any other track. It is a pity, therefore, that an alternate version could not have been used instead, as everyone who bought the LP would have had the single already. (However, any alternate take must surely have been inferior). What cannot be denied is that this was Townshend's strongest song to date, and the version released on the single was a leviathan of sound that couldn't be disregarded.

The second side of *My Generation* offers "The Kids Are Alright," which actually presents the best elements of Townshend's songwriting, although a passing melodic resemblance to the Beatles' "All My Loving" gives the song an unwelcome (and, indeed, misplaced) Merseybeat slant. The crashing guitar chords, propeled by Entwistle's bass and Moon's drums, carry the soaring vocal harmonies to make this one of the best examples of the Who's melodic and lyrical power: it is the archetypal Who performance of the era, more representative than "My Generation" and more mature than "I Can't Explain." The middle section is very well achieved, culminating in one of the best recorded examples of Townshend's revolutionary power-chord solo technique—a ringing, cascading succession of distorted riffs and variations—before the song returns to a repeat of the first verse.

The song reflects one of Townshend's main lyrical themes of isolation and insecurity. It presents a social scene in which a character has assimilated his environment and feels a strong need to break away to new experiences but finds the practicalities of achieving such freedom difficult to surmount. The character's relationship with his girl is failing and he is ready to accept that she should find another man: "I don't mind other guys dancing with my girl." He later blames her parents, maybe seeking a scapegoat, as if he wanted to leave anyway and needed an excuse. "I know sometimes I must get out in the light" is the key line that sums up the restlessness and lack of satisfaction to be found in life. The man is full of talk of change, but since it isn't indicated how he will bring this about, no conclusion is reached.

The version of James Brown's "Please, Please, Please" pales in comparison, for the same reasons as "I Don't Mind" did. It is too one-dimensional, and instrumentally the band sounds too stiff. Additionally, Daltrey's voice lacks real clarity and feel, sounding merely imitative. Soul music (or the R&B–derived soul of James Brown) requires a musical fluidity and looseness that the Who cannot provide. The guitar solo [1.07] is again very conventional, but toward the end Pete throws in a slight Morse code effect. Different problems are presented with "I'm a Man." The song begins in a conventional fashion, with Daltrey attempting to sound like a deep-voiced blues oracle over the repeated riff pattern. Roger's enunciation is almost like a parody, and the instrumentation is so deadpan that it comes close to unintentionally providing a comical effect. Thankfully, the structure breaks down and free-form elements are unleashed [1.06]. Hopkins's jazzy piano fills surge forward, while John Entwistle adds some fine bass variations, intermingling with Moon's drum fills. Townshend uses the change of mood to inject some noise and discord before another lapse where Hopkins's piano comes to the fore [2.32] to close the song. "I'm a Man" therefore combines both good and bad elements in one song. (On release of the LP, Townshend stated that he "hated" the version of "I'm a Man" despite the fact that it contained "probably our best recorded feedback."[20])

The two remaining Pete Townshend songs are excellent: "A Legal Matter" and "It's Not True" both employ the short, jolting rhythm of "My Generation," and both display an ironic humor that was an important though often-overlooked part of the band's persona. For the first time on a Who recording, Pete Townshend sings the lead vocals, which contrast Daltrey's, Pete's voice being of a higher register and less abrasive in tone. The introductory two-note guitar figure is memorable and catchy, and Hopkins's piano plows into the rhythm with gusto. (I must admit, however, that on this song alone, the Who evokes the upbeat Chicago blues of the early work of the Rolling Stones.) A failed relationship is settled in "A Legal Matter" in strictly legal terms: divorce. The character (an office worker) feels swamped by domesticity and decides to break free. The marital strings don't hold him, and revenge (and freedom) comes in the form of a separation, undoubtedly expressed in sexist terms. "It's Not True" is a reflection of frustration in the face of gross misrepresentation given a more comical treatment than any of the other songs. This involves a character desperate to achieve vindication, and the loss of love is clearly at stake. The same theme had been broached already in "La-La-La-Lies" but is expressed here much more effectively. Musically, the chugging verse of "It's Not True" owes something to the melody and rhythm of Chuck Berry's "Memphis Tennessee."

The final track, "The Ox," (named for John Entwistle's nickname) was put together in the studio as an instrumental blowout. Every instrumental and surf artist from the Ventures to Sandy Nelson and Link Wray are simultaneously acknowledged and overpowered by the unrelenting barrage of heavy riffing, machine-gun drumming, distortion and feedback. The song features probably the heaviest and most powerful guitar and bass sound captured on vinyl at the time and one of the most exhilarating drum performances ever played. Keith Moon, although his kit is not too well recorded (probably with one suspended microphone), turns in an astounding performance that has to be heard to be believed.

"The Ox" is a primal, gut-wrench fusion of distortion and frenzy that lays out the Who's bottom-line theory of rock and roll as explosive anarchic noise, a sonic pop art sound sculpture, the shock of auto-destruction. It is ugly, disturbing and devoid of structure and melody, and apparently Townshend wrecked a guitar in the studio to produce the screeching final bars of the riff, which capture the death-throes of an abused instrument. We hear not only acoustic feedback but the crackle and buzz of the guitar lead shorting, a sound no engineer had ever before permitted on a record. The title, "The Ox," may seem a little bizarre, despite its associations with Entwistle, until we consider it alongside other instrumentals of the 1960s that also utilized the names of creatures: "Beatnik Fly" (Tune Rockers), "Albatross" (Fleetwood Mac), "Mad Goose" (The Beachcombers) and "The Green Mosquito" (Johnny and the Hurricanes). In the context of such creature-titles, "The Ox" seems comparatively appropriate for the music offered here.

Despite its faults, *My Generation* is an LP that has been consistently highly regarded over the years, although in the U.K. it was for a long time deleted throughout the late 1960s and all of the 1970s, during which time (in its absence) its reputation grew somewhat to exceed its merits. David Wedgbury's cover photograph—with a priceless cynical expression from Townshend so attuned to the sentiment of the songs—is a classic pop art image, and the music it represents is the cumulation of two or three years' work by the Who, a summation of mod, a suggestion of pop art, and a new definition of pop and maximum R&B. It's pure rock and roll of a new kind, which owed nothing to either of the twin frontiers forged by the Beatles and the Rolling Stones. People have commented that Roger Daltrey's singing is somewhat limited in range and that Nicky Hopkins's piano is largely superfluous. Indeed, in the light of the above-stated factors, what is arguably the best track on the album (after "My Generation") is "The Ox," which doesn't feature Daltrey at all, and Hopkins (despite a composing credit) battles in vain to make an impression above the power trio. If nothing else, this song was a triumph for Townshend, Entwistle and Moon as instrumentalists. Nicky Hopkins's overall contribution (he plays on eight out of the twelve tracks) is to bring a very conventional approach to material that often wins through its lack of adherence to convention, and his piano work tends to dampen the abrasive edge of some of the songs, although on "It's Not True" and "The Ox" he takes a suitably unorthodox approach.

Typically idiosyncratic, the band members hated the finished record on its release. Daltrey thought that it failed to reflect enough of the band's stage act, while Moon claimed in an interview that he disliked Daltrey's singing.[21] However, Daltrey wasn't—as is sometimes believed—so keen on the James Brown material. He commented less than a year later that the *My Generation* LP "was so rushed it was ridiculous. The instrumental parts were really rushed and they put out all those James Brown things, which weren't intended for it."[22] Townshend was particularly dismissive of the work in general and even conducted an interview with Richard Green in *Record Mirror* in which he offered a track-by-track repudiation. Only with "The Ox" did Pete express any satisfaction, commenting, "I got out of this something I've always wanted to get out of a piece of music," while Green agreed, concluding, "Not until 'The Ox' do we get the type of sound that sends Who addicts into a frenzy of pop art. But it is bound to be a best seller...."[23]

It is reasonable now to speculate upon what *My Generation* might so easily have been with "Circles," "Heatwave" and "Leaving Here" replacing "Please, Please, Please," "I'm a Man," and "I Don't Mind." This would certainly have rendered the whole album more uptempo, more radical and exciting, but back in 1965 it was an accepted function of a long player to attempt to display the *widest range* of an artist's repertoire and present even rock-and-roll bands as all-around entertainers. This usually meant that an album would include ballads alongside the rockers, and by Who standards "I Don't Mind" and maybe even "I'm a Man" *were* ballads. Given the band's comments on the album and the fact that they all but disowned it immediately, it seems likely that Shel Talmy was responsible for the song selection. That the band members had more or less decided at this stage that they didn't wish to work with Talmy again, it was inevitable that he should receive the blame. In retrospect, of course, *My Generation* could have been a better album with these slight adjustments, but the past, as they say, is another country, and the album as it stands is not so bad as to rankle about what could have been.

On 22 November 1965, after the album had been completed, the Who returned to the BBC's studios to record another session for *Saturday Club* (broadcast 27 November 1965). On this occasion they taped a less fierce version of "My Generation" and gave a taste of their newer album material with

"La-La-La-Lies" and "The Good's Gone," the latter of which features an additional fuzz-tone guitar solo. These versions were all less effective than the records, perhaps softer and less dramatic on the ears. Pete Townshend told the BBC's Brian Matthew at the recording session that "My Generation" was "aimed at trying to create a feeling more and the actual idea is of a kid, you know, who's not really satisfied with his life and is trying to complain, but can't."[24]

The American version of the album, *The Who Sings My Generation*, was released in April of 1966 and bore several significant changes. The Wedgbury photograph had been replaced by a shot of the Who (admittedly with equally sullen expressions) in front of the Westminster Clock Tower—a rather more conventional Swinging London image. "The Kids Are Alright" had a crucial twenty-one seconds edited out of the power-chord solo, an utterly pointless and unfathomable deletion by Decca. "I'm a Man" was deleted entirely in favor of "Circles" (titled "Instant Party," for reasons detailed in the next chapter). By the time this U.S. version of the album was released, the Who had ceased their partnership with Shel Talmy, they had issued "Substitute" as their next single, and "Circles" had been rendered surplus to requirements. Despite the fact that *The Who Sings My Generation* was inferior to its British counterpart on Brunswick, "Circles" was a worthy addition.

Coming at the end of side two, "Circles" seemed to point to the future and is by far the most sophisticated and ambitious track the Who ever completed with Talmy (although the sound is somewhat rough). The arrangement shows a willingness to progress and take chances with a new musical vocabulary. The soaring melody is contained within the guitar figures and (for the first time) a counter melody from John Entwistle on the French horn. A dramatic rising second melody forms a bridge section [1.42], where Townshend's voice alternates with Daltrey's to give a fascinating contrast. The most surprising aspect of this recording, however, comes after the bridge: a chaotic, atonal freak-out [1.58] that lasts 43 seconds. This is not based on feedback but on actual discordant guitar figures, in the manner of some modern jazz performers (notably John Coltrane). This short section of free-form chaos was extremely prescient in late 1965, anticipating psychedelia by a year. This fact has not been previously appreciated (after all, 43 seconds of an obscure track is indistinct), and the Who can belatedly be cited as a pioneer. Interesting enough, this sound invites comparison with the atonal, raga-influenced guitar work of "Eight Miles High" and "Why" by the Byrds, both of which were recorded initially on 22 December 1965—around the same time. A 1960s pop song of the purest vintage, this version of "Circles" also shows the radical and avant-garde edge of the Who still intact. (The Who rerecorded "Circles" in January 1966 without Talmy and, although they produced a more slick reading, the instrumental break was much less radical, weakening the whole impact of the song.)

A song of frustration and confusion, "Circles" is a clear expression of doubt expressed with the metaphor of a whirlpool, a vortex of engulfing emotion leading to catastrophe, and prompted by a broken relationship, the loss of love. The turmoil is cyclic and ever descending, using the image of the whirlpool as a force that is "dragging me down." Like "I Can't Explain" before it (and to which it bears a close lyrical connection) the matter is not resolved and remains desperate, but also like the earlier song, we are aware of an innocent longing that doesn't subside. The atonal solo musically depicts this vortex aspect.

Rumours persist that the Who completed an early version of their next single "Substitute" during their final recording sessions with Shel Talmy early in 1966. This has not been confirmed, but it has been reported that Talmy's Who archive comprises of twenty-four master recordings. Taking into account all the output as released, one song does indeed remain unaccounted for, suggesting that Talmy *may* possess a version of "Substitute" or possibly "You Don't Have to Jerk," the single discarded earlier during 1965. This remains speculation, however, and it may be some time before the true extent of Talmy's archives can be established.

When the Who came to reactivate their entire back catalogue on compact disc, their long-standing dispute with Shel Talmy prevented the multitrack master tapes of all their 1965 recordings being made available for remixing and remastering. Today, negotiations are still in progress between Talmy, the Who's management, MCA and Polydor to deliver a definitive CD remaster of the *My Generation* album. The Who's back-catalogue producer Jon Astley had hoped to remix the material into true stereo, although much of the distortion of Talmy's recordings has become a legitimate part of their appeal, and stereo separation can sometimes soften the edges to the point of dismembering the structure of the sound. Astley is fully aware of such problems, of course, and his work on the High Numbers material (as mentioned earlier) shows just what wonders can be achieved. That said, it is very difficult to envisage hearing this material in genuine stereo.

A stereo mix had, in fact, been prepared in 1966 and released as an optional U.S. version of the album, but this was crude and tended to merely separate a few components of the sound without adding any tangible advantage. Many listeners have expressed a preference for the mono mix because this is the one on which Talmy did the most work and that gained the band's approval. I should mention that MCA's current CD (U.S. only) pressing of *The Who Sings My Generation* is a decent transfer of the mono mix of the original U.S. version of the LP. The sound gains some clarity over the vinyl pressings and should not be dismissed by those frustrated that a properly authorized U.K. edition has failed to materialize. (Note that this CD is currently the only available source of the superior first version of "Circles," or "Instant Party" as it is still called.) Without the use of Talmy's master tapes, the most accurate and successful remasterings of the early Who material available are to be found on the boxed set *30 Years of Maximum R&B*, which offers all three singles plus "Daddy Rolling Stone," "The Kids Are Alright," "The Ox" and "A Legal Matter." (Present-day listeners should note that a degree of upper range distortion is endemic to all Talmy's Who productions, and modern remastering techniques are unlikely to improve the situation. It is most likely that the distortion was gained with the recording levels being at the top of the limit during the actual sessions, rather than at a subsequent mixing or cutting stage.)

Nineteen sixty-five was a year full of activity and achievement for the Who. They had scaled the heights of the U.K. pop scene more rapidly than perhaps the band members themselves had expected. During the year, they had to shout to be heard and fought for their space on the music platform. They had arrived, quite literally, with a flash and a bang. All the work during the year indicates a band pushing at the limits and trying to state their case with the kind of desperation and lack of restraint that can only be countenanced by those with nothing to lose. The Who penetrated the marketplace by making anger (as opposed to mere aggression) a legitimate form of musical dialogue, establishing a new Zeitgeist for the 1960s.

3

Art Pop (1966–1967)

The impact and implication of "My Generation" was to linger with the band for the remainder of its career. Journalists would repeatedly ask Pete Townshend whether he meant it when he had said he wanted to die before he got old (and later on they would ask him if he regretted writing a line that had patently proved to be untrue). His responses to such simpleminded queries would vary with his moods. But the fact remained that "My Generation" was a statement on which there could be no going back. Townshend never repudiated a word of the song, nor did he seek to qualify it. Whatever the controversy, the Who's hit status was confirmed, and many people (including a good number of influential journalists) looked to the band at the beginning of 1966 as representing the new future of rock, the exciting sound of the moment. The question was, How long would the moment last? The year of success that Townshend had predicted in April 1965 was nearly up. There were pressures on the band that probably hadn't been anticipated, and Pete Townshend especially—as songwriter—felt the burden of responsibility to maintain the level of success and to produce something radically new each time. Yet however tumultuous the situation became, the band members continued to work at an intense pace, taking concerts and recording sessions in their stride and without once appearing to fracture or founder, although internally the band seemed always to be on the brink of disintegration—the arguments and rows within hardly abated.

The biggest crisis that faced the Who during the first months of 1966, potentially the most damaging to their future, was this: they needed to break their links with Shel Talmy and Brunswick to achieve artistic autonomy and financial buoyancy, and Talmy—armed with a watertight contract that the band members had innocently signed a year earlier—wasn't willing to let them go. Bloodthirsty legal wrangling, prolonged litigation, financial impropriety and acrimonious splits among artists, their managers, record companies, promoters or producers were commonplace in the pop world at the time, and these events often blighted or extinguished promising careers. The Who suffered both long- and short-term damage from their dispute. Since their financial solvency was already unstable, it is surprising that the band's music or enthusiasm remained intact. Also, the sum total of New Action (Lambert and Stamp's management company) and the Who's earnings from a year of continued success was depleted by repair bills, low record company returns and other expenses. Working flat out in Europe did not bring just financial rewards, and it became clear during 1966 that success in America was the only way for the Who to survive.

If nothing else, the legal dispute gained the band a lot of publicity and much space in the music papers. Despite this dubious coverage, Lambert and Stamp were always still looking for new ways to promote them. One successful instance of this was their getting the band onto the glossy front cover of the *Observer Colour Magazine* (20 March 1966) with a much-admired photograph by Colin Jones. Lambert and Stamp arranged for an in-depth article about the Who by John Heilpern, who spent several days with the band and the management, even with Chris Stamp in the United States, as he tried to push the "My Generation" single. The quality Sunday newspapers in the U.K. carried a great level of highbrow prestige, and the image of Pete Townshend in his Union Jack jacket nosing its way onto thousands of middle-class breakfast tables was a major coup. However, new recordings (done without Talmy) remained at the center of the Who's public profile. "Circles" had been scheduled for release by Brunswick on 18 February, but its withdrawal was announced a week beforehand.

Overall, 1966 was a year in which pop music overstretched itself into new areas of meaning and significance. The best groups of the era, Byrds, Beatles, Rolling Stones, Yardbirds, Kinks, as well as the Who, all produced outstanding and groundbreaking singles, yet toward the end of the year the LP had gained a greater prominence than the single as the format by which groups would be judged. Many groups really found their feet during this year and turned out classic albums such as *Face to Face* (Kinks), *Fifth Dimension* (Byrds), *Revolver* (Beatles), *Pet Sounds* (Beach Boys) and *Aftermath* (Rolling Stones). And so too did the Who with *A Quick One*, which I unhesitatingly add to this list. But singles still held supreme importance, and generally the best rock music still appeared in this form. Accordingly, the Who's three hit singles from this year didn't appear on their LP at all, an adherence to the British tradition of the two formats being regarded as separate entities.

It was during the last week of January 1966 that the Who set about making a record without Shel Talmy. In fact, no formal producer had been drafted, and Pete Townshend supervised the session at Olympic Studios. This was an unconventional move for the time, when very few records were self-produced by the artists. Although "Circles" had been lined up as the next single, the band members favored a new Townshend song that was potentially superior: "Substitute." Pete took the opportunity on this occasion to use an acoustic guitar in a Who session for the first time. This wasn't to be taken as a portent that the band members wanted to soften the Who's sound, however. The acoustic guitar merely instigated a more imaginative and subtle approach: *power pop*, as Townshend was later to describe Who music of this era. The same session also saw a rerecording of "Circles" that despite the strength of the song, was relegated to the B side. Both songs were released on single on 4 March 1966—the first New Action Production, as the label stated. Gaining the instant approval of Australian impresario Robert Stigwood, the song was released on his new Reaction record label in direct contravention of the Talmy contract.

"Substitute" is a more sophisticated and willfully structured song than the band's previous efforts, with dominant bass lines and a bouncy guitar rhythm. The song has none of the innocence of "I Can't Explain," the arrogance of "Anyway Anyhow Anywhere" or the anger of "My Generation," but rather has a cynical kind of subtlety that can be seen as evidence of a new maturity. Musically, the record is springy, sprightly and overflowing with energy and invention. Daltrey's singing hits exactly the right tone on a vocal line brimming with malevolent melody, and his vocal performance is a large leap forward from the previous year's work. Roger delivers—with just the right balance of force and vulnerability—the lyrics that tease the listener with contradictions and witticisms in a wry examination of an identity in crisis. The song has a beautiful catchy chorus based upon a truly inspired (though apparently "adapted") guitar riff. The prominent bass guitar lines mark a real triumph for John Entwistle, as the bass here carries so much of the work—both rhythmic and melodic—even breaking into a solo [1.50] before an extremely effective return to the second part of the verse "I'm a substitute for another guy...." The omnipresent acoustic guitar rings out with a bright tone and takes the second solo spot, where Townshend runs through several variations on the main riff. A powerful and intelligent record, "Substitute" reached the number 5 position in the charts on 16 April.

The progress in evidence here was not all musical. Townshend's lyrics formed a classic examination of an identity crisis, dealt with in witty and telling lines such as "I was born with a plastic spoon in my mouth." This gives a full impression of a character out of sync with the rest of the world and possibly with an inferiority complex. In this case the resulting isolation produces an almost aggressive plea for change and correction, as in the chorus, where change for the sake of it is demanded. The protagonist merely wants to be someone else. Fact and illusion combine to confuse the character, and the objectivity of the listener is questioned with lines such as "I look all white but my dad was black." The problem is unresolved, but the articulation of the crisis by the character gives depth and understanding to the matter. The song forms a psychological case history of the kind that only Bob Dylan and Ray Davies were attempting at this time.

The second recording of "Circles" gave the song a less harsh sound that emphasized the pop elements of the composition. The lead vocal was a little muted, and the horn work was slightly less strident. Other aspects of the melody were made sharper with the clearer guitar work, but the solo passage [1.27] fails to deliver the innovative edge of that of the earlier take. Due to Shel Talmy's legal action, the name was changed on the second pressing to "Instant Party"; this title is fairly meaningless in that it bears no connection with the lyrics of the song. As mentioned in the last chapter, it was taken from the title of a 1962 Everly Brothers' LP. A third pressing of the single (by far the most common) left off "Circles" entirely in favor of "Waltz for a Pig," credited to the Who Orchestra but which turned out to be an instrumental by the Graham Bond Organisation (a group managed by Stigwood). The fact that an alternative Who song couldn't be used on the B side suggests that the band had recorded no more than these two tracks since their split with Talmy. "Circles" had, in fact, already been premiered on U.K. television's *Ready Steady Go!* broadcast on 28 January 1966.

A couple of weeks after "Substitute" had been released, the band could be heard on BBC radio's *Saturday Club* (19 March 1966) featuring three tracks that had been recorded six days earlier. The main point of interest at this session was a rerecording of "Substitute" in which Townshend more conventionally played an electric guitar. This take of "Substitute" is strong and sharp-edged but lacks the subtle depth of the single. Pete employs a clean, slightly echoey guitar sound that could perhaps have been thickened with some distortion (as he would have played it on stage). The level of energy in the Who's attack is also slightly muted, but the recording makes a fine alternate interpretation of the song.

Accompanying "Substitute" were two songs that had been played on stage: Martha and the Vandellas' "Dancing in the Street" and the Everly Brothers' "Man with Money." For the Who at this time, the Everly Brothers seemed to represent the most pure face of American pop, and the Who also included "Love Hurts" in their stage act. "Man with Money" is a very impressive reading and is given a lilting and well-structured arrangement. The band's voices work very smoothly on a song full of graceful harmonies and dramatic pace. An even better version was recorded later in the year, although it was not released until 1995 (and is discussed later).

"Dancing in the Street," however, was an ambitious choice, but the Who's performance here falls far short of the original. The main problem is that it lacks the confident brass riff—one of Tamla Motown's very best—that carries the song and gives it its distinctive swagger. John Entwistle could have overdubbed this, but the BBC session probably didn't allow time for such an arrangement to be worked out. Since the brass is the main component that establishes the strong beat of the song as originally recorded, the Who struggles here to find enough musical color with which to work. Although the song is treated with some degree of reverence, the interpretation remains worthy but dull. Toward the end, Townshend adds a fuzztone guitar solo, but the excitement level doesn't lift significantly. As far as is known, the Who never attempted this in the studio on any other occasion, although in 1979 they revived the song onstage with remarkable success (with the brass section intact!)

The band's battle with Shel Talmy was one of the more publicized legal disputes in the music business of the time, and it would be laborious to repeat all the details here. In short, the Who gained its freedom from the original contract, but Talmy won a 5 percent cut of all the band's future profits from recording work up to 1971. Chris Charlesworth has observed that this ruling allowed Talmy to "earn considerably more in royalties from The Who's record sales than the individual members of the band ever did ... without so much as lifting a finger.... The Who, like so many others, signed away a big chunk of what was rightfully theirs in the adrenaline rush to get into the recording studio. It doesn't take a great leap of imagination, therefore, to realise that The Who have never received a just reward from their best selling work, and that the only way for them to survive was to work hard, performing live as often as possible...."[1]

In practical terms, the dispute with Talmy resulted in "Substitute" being temporarily withdrawn and "Circles" being retitled "Instant Party" in a ploy to deflect some of Talmy's case. When it became clear that the title change would have little effect on Talmy's action, they withdrew the song altogether. The availability of "Substitute" was, for a while, intermittent, but Talmy couldn't prevent the single remaining on sale. While litigation was in progress the Who were prevented from issuing further records for a period, and when they resumed during the summer of 1966, Talmy replied in kind by issuing tracks from the *My Generation* album as singles on Brunswick ("A Legal Matter," "The Kids Are Alright" and "La-La-La-Lies"), which the band understandably disowned. Talmy might have preferred to release some of the then unreleased songs on single to generate extra sales, but he probably required the band's permission for this, which would have been declined.

With the freedoms gained by the new Reaction deal, the Who embarked upon a fresh surge of activity—although during the interim they had never stopped performing concerts or television or radio engagements. The vogue for Swinging London probably reached its peak during the summer of 1966, and the identity of the Who fitted well with the times, despite their being considered a unique one-shot act. By now mod had been further exploited as a commodity of fashion and had lost its cohesive identity, and the Who no longer had any tangible connection with it. The Who even played down their connection to pop art in an attempt to avoid being caught in a passing phase. Indeed, the Who's bold and striking use of the British flag (which use had no nationalist or patriotic connotations) had by 1966 permeated into the lower echelons of graphic design and marketing, and soon enough it was usual for tourists in London to be seen carrying their purchases in a plastic Union Jack bag! During this period "serious" rock music became more prevalent (Cream, Jimi Hendrix, Pink Floyd, Soft Machine), and a clear divide was soon discernible between such underground (or counterculture) acts and the more established pop groups that worked to maintain hit singles and a largely teenybopper audience. The members of the Who probably felt that the rest of the world had finally caught up to them, and they uneasily stood their ground in the U.K. as both a solid chart act *and* an underground concert attraction. Gradually over the next few years, the Who would establish an identity that would make these two factors compatible and workable, without compromise of either.

One of the advantages of the new arrangement was that Pete Townshend's songwriting skills became recognized as a much more viable potential hit-making entity, and his songs were picked up by other acts hoping for that elusive initial success. With "Circles" being quickly withdrawn from the flipside of "Substitute," its chart potential was seized upon by the Fleur-De-Lys, who released a version on the Immediate label in March 1966. Also in March another Townshend song, "It's Alright," was recorded by the Rockin' Vicars for CBS. This song was a partial rewrite of "The Kids Are Alright," but with a different chorus. It is given a fierce Who–like power-chord treatment by the Rockin' Vicars, but both these songs failed to reach the chart, and "It's Alright" was obviously not considered substantial enough for the Who to record. It remains one of the least heard Townshend songs of the era.

Audiences looked forward to the Who's second album with much anticipation and many questions about what sort of material it would contain. The sheer quality attained with "Substitute," had proved that the band could survive the impact of (and progress from) "My Generation." Also, with the band members' being very public about their low opinion of the *My Generation* album, expectations began to rise that the next Who LP would be significantly better than their debut. Plans were being made for the new album in April 1966 when the Who's fan club published a newsletter that reported that Townshend was currently working on songs for the new work. However, when questioned by Richard Green of *Record Mirror* as to how much he had written, Pete had elusively commented, "Nothing yet. We'll do a few more instrumentals." Meanwhile John Entwistle stated in the same article that the album would "consist largely of Pete Townshend numbers, a couple associated with the Everly Brothers and maybe two Moon-Entwistle things."[2] This was the first indication that other band members were working on songs as well as Pete, although the Moon–Entwistle partnership never developed beyond one song.

The Everly Brothers material was almost certainly "Man with Money" and "Love Hurts." Concert goers to Who shows during this period would also likely have heard "Heat Wave" and "Runaround Sue" (Dion), "Dancing in the Street" and "Uptight" (Stevie Wonder), "On the Road Again" (Lovin' Spoonful) and "Barbara Ann" (Beach Boys) rather than any new Townshend songs. In spite of the Who's constant activity, Pete had also found time in April to work with a new British group called the Cat, which he had agreed to produce for the Reaction label. This was Pete's first attempt to produce another group, and he also offered them one of his newest songs, "Run Run Run," a fairly straightforward rocker with a repetitive riff pattern. The Cat failed to make the chart with "Run Run Run," which was released in May 1966.

The band gave a taste, however, of a more significant new song when they appeared on BBC television's *A Whole Scene Going* on 15 June. The band performed "Disguises," and speculation grew that this would be its next single. It had been recorded the day before the broadcast but release was subsequently postponed in favor of "I'm a Boy". "Disguises" was actually a most inventive song and was based on a droning guitar figure and drenched in reverb, suggestive of the Eastern raga influences that characterized the psychedelia of the near future. This was a novel departure for the Who but a successful experiment, perhaps influenced by the Kinks' "See My Friend," a hit in August of the previous year. We should also, indeed, consider that by this time Townshend would have been familiar with the Byrds' seminal "Eight Miles High"—perhaps the definitive blend of pop sensibilities with raga atonality. "Disguises" seemed to point toward a new direction in which rock music would be taken by the psychedelic groups (and indeed, the Beatles). Other material was being gathered under a new song-publishing deal that Kit Lambert had negotiated for the band members, which netted each of them £500 if they came up with two songs each. So Moon, Entwistle and Daltrey were at work on the first proper compositions of their careers.

The members of the group the Merseys (formerly the Merseybeats) were friendly with the members of the Who and had toured with them. This group became the next recipient of a new Townshend song when they recorded "So Sad About Us," released on the Fontana label in July. A solid, majestic pop song, this was perhaps the most likely candidate for chart success out of all Pete's new songs, but, like the Rockin' Vicars, Cat, and Fleur-De-Lys before them, the Merseys failed to score a hit. The magic of Townshend's songwriting really only came over in Who performances, as this succession of failed singles by other bands obviously demonstrated. (In the following year, another Townshend song unrecorded by the Who appeared in the form of "Lazy Fat People" by the Barron Knights; this single also failed to make the chart. Another further song attributed to Pete Townshend in 1967 was "Kensington High Street" by Dead Sea Fruit, but this was a case of mistaken identity—the "Townsend" to whom the song is credited is a different person.)

Finally, on 1 August 1966, the Who completed the recording of "I'm a Boy" at IBC Studios in London, and they released it a couple of weeks later. Despite the song being considerably softer than the established Who style and in spite of the recording ban imposed during the Talmy litigation that had held it up for five months, the Who's fifth single became their most successful to date. Kit Lambert had taken on the role of producer of the band, a task he approached with enthusiasm and verve but without great technical expertise. He left this aspect of recording to house engineers and concentrated more on musical ideas and song structures and generally set about providing a more creative environment for the band. "I'm a Boy" (as a composition) bears all the hallmarks of his influence. For good measure, the Who's fan club newsletter had given somewhat misleadingly advance information about the single "I'm a Boy"; as "a hard driving number with an intensive beat and certainly must be the best number Pete has written so far. The Who have broadened their following by offering the teenagers refreshingly new and different types of recordings clearly displaying their versatility and talent...."[3]

"I'm a Boy" is really a song that stands out from Townshend's demo pile as a fascinating oddity. It certainly doesn't conform to any established Who style, having a novelty theme and a sophistication that goes against the customary Who grain. The energy level of "My Generation" and "Substitute" is considerably diluted on this recording, and it took the Who's music in a new direction, away from their prevailing stage act and into the realms of more delicate, studio-oriented pop. It is a self-contained vignette without any kind of roots in the stage act, and it creates its own strange world. The recording does, however, have a recognizable Who sound. The guitar chords, harmonies and drumming still have a rough-edged and vigorous quality to them, and the elaboration of the arrangement (some lines sung by Pete, some by Roger; some harmonies and a choral middle-eight) was a real leap forward. The song clearly lacks the dynamism and instant appeal of the previous four singles, as well as their uncompromising lyrical attack. "I'm a Boy" was the most complex song the band had attempted to date, emanating a wry cleverness and craftsmanship that compromised some of their explosive energy.

Perhaps the most interesting aspect of the song is the middle section: four bars of staccato guitar riffs [1.26] (the nearest Townshend comes to playing any power chords) usher in the passage [1.33] where the guitar follows an unusual progression of chords, giving an almost melodramatic effect as it twists through a melancholic, minor-key, wordless chorus. In fact, the unison guitar chords and echoed vocal harmonies are perhaps the most radical element in the production, sounding most unlike the kind of thing any other pop group would have attempted. This has been compared to the music of Henry Purcell (the seventeenth century English composer), and it does bear a stylistic similarity (allowing for a faster tempo) to, say, *Funeral Music for Queen Mary*. (Pete ascribed much of his characteristic suspended chord work in songs from this period to the influence of Purcell). Following a pattern set with the arrangement of "Circles," the vocals here are similarly shared between Pete (first four lines of the first verse) and Roger (remainder). Despite the complex approach, however, "I'm a Boy" proved to be ideal for the chart, climbing to number 2 by 1 October 1966.

A second version of the song was later recorded during the sessions for the band's next album—for which it was originally scheduled—and this take is over a minute longer and less harsh than the original single and has a slightly cleaner and less distorted guitar sound. It is notable for Entwistle's tuba playing, and in place of the choral central section, it offers a succession of moody chord changes with the tuba highlighted. This is followed by an additional verse (about washing up), but otherwise its effect is very similar to the single's. This was first released in 1971 on the *Meaty Beaty Big & Bouncy* LP. One of the backing tracks of "I'm a Boy" was given an experimental horn arrangement by John Entwistle in place of the vocal lines. This may also have been intended for the upcoming album but has never been released.

Keith Moon and John Entwistle's first and only songwriting collaboration, "In the City," was used as the B side of both the U.K. and U.S. versions of the single. Perhaps daunted by Pete Townshend's reputation as a hit songwriter, Moon and Entwistle allegedly recorded this modest contribution without Daltrey and Townshend's being present. It is a weak Beach Boys–Jan and Dean pastiche of "Surf City"/"Drag City" ilk, with Entwistle providing a simplistic guitar progression and horn overdubs. The harmony singing is actually quite passable, despite the shortcomings of the song. (Both the title and part of the melody line of "In the City" were to inspire the British group the Jam to write another song of the same name, which was released in 1977. This was an act of homage rather than plagiarism, the Jam at this time being very much modeled after the early Who.) The pairing of "I'm a Boy" with "In the City" began a string of John Entwistle–written B sides that continued through to the 1980s, a Who tradition that on occasion submerged a fine song into a relegated and neglected position.

The assertion of gender in the title "I'm a Boy" is clearly a sardonic riposte to Bo Diddley's "I'm a Man." The themes of the song are quite different, however. "I'm a Boy" is a plea for the recognition of truth, without any facade, illusion or hypocrisy, and the song sketches a condition that, although amusing in presentation, is a real nightmare. To be denied one's gender and sexual identity must have catastrophic effects. The corrupting influence of parents is here held under scrutiny, with a mother who wants a girl rather than a boy. (This obviously happens in real life, although few mothers go as far as to dress their sons as girls.) The denial of masculinity is seen to produce a boy who then wishes to overcompensate: "cut myself and see my blood, I wanna come home all covered in mud." For Bill (the character), the isolation and repression of his instincts and inclinations is a form of hell—a

Freudian dilemma, no less. "I'm a Boy" is the first Who song to have a defined, named character, Bill. Superficially hailed as the first chart hit to embrace transvestism, "I'm a Boy" is a case study akin to "Substitute."

Townshend later stated that "I'm a Boy" was in fact a segment from an "opera" titled *Quads*, which linked together several pop songs with characters and narrative development. The theme of the opera was a world set in a future where couples could choose the sex of their children. Bill was an error, born to a family who wanted a girl instead of a boy—hence his enforced gender change. Much of this project reveals the influence of Kit Lambert, who was pushing Townshend to expand the scope of pop songwriting into a larger, quasi-classical framework. One response from Pete to this suggestion was a piece called "Gratis Amatis," a mock oratorio that Richard Barnes described as a "10 minute Aria consisting of high pitched Goon Show voices singing 'Gratis Amatis' over and over for what seemed like an hour."[4] Townshend had developed this piece with Ray Tolliday and had presented the tape to Kit Lambert for his birthday on 11 May. Townshend later called it "a kind of joke Gilbert & Sullivan opera."[5] Another Pete Townshend song that can be seen as a companion piece to "I'm a Boy" is "Join My Gang," which was not recorded by the Who but by a singer called Oscar. His version was released on Reaction in September 1966. In many ways "Join My Gang" is closely related to "I'm a Boy": it is about a *girl* joining an all-*male* environment. It is highly likely, though unconfirmed, that "Join My Gang" also originated as part of the *Quads* idea. Pete Townshend held "Join My Gang" in high regard, describing it as "a fucking good song ... I really like it."[6] He played it at a solo concert at the Roundhouse in London in 1974, and also—uncharacteristically—allowed the lyrics to be printed in a magazine.[7] However, the Who probably felt it to be too gentle a pop melody and too similar to "I'm a Boy" to warrant release, and in recent years it has become all but forgotten.

At this stage in mid-1966, the Who were in the precarious position of having released three new Townshend songs during the year, while other groups had released five written by him. As the summer drew to a close, the new Who LP still had not materialized. Some respite was given to the growing numbers of Who fans with another BBC radio session recorded on 13 September. This *Saturday Club* appearance (broadcast on 17 September) offered an alternative version of "I'm a Boy", a dazzlingly spontaneous and energetic "Disguises" and the premier airing of the Who's interpretation of "So Sad About Us." However, the group was recording in fits and starts for the album, and Roger Daltrey gave an interim report to Norman Jopling of *Record Mirror*. He confirmed that they had recorded "Barbara Ann," "So Sad About Us" and "Heat Wave" for the album, and he said, "but the track I like best so far is Pete's 'Disguises.'"[8] Daltrey also mentioned that he thought some of the new songs didn't work so well on stage but were fine for the record—reflecting a new policy that had been recently adopted whereby some songs were not introduced to the live act at all and played only in the studio.

A few weeks later, Keith Moon gave a characteristically exaggerated account of how the recording sessions were going to Keith Altham of *New Musical Express*: "Our next album has the kind of progressive material which should enable us to break into America within the next six months.... This LP is much more of a group effort and includes a few surprises. I play zither on one track and John plays 'double track tuba,' French horn, bass and nose flute on another...."9 Moon was obviously in a playful mood, and when he mentioned that the band was working on such songs as "Boris the Spider," "Whiskey Man," "Cobweb Strange" [sic] and "I Need You (Like I Need a Hole in the Head)," Altham might have doubted that such unlikely titles would really materialize. However, materialize they did. This full title of Moon's "I Need You" gave what later appeared to be a simple love song a savagely ironic twist. Moon's description of the extra instruments played certainly sounds like a send-up, but John Entwistle gave a similar account in *Beat Instrumental*: "I'll be using [a tuba] on some tracks but I'm going to play French horn, euphonium and flugelhorn on this LP. We'll probably re-record 'I'm A Boy' and there's this one I've written called 'Whiskey Man,' that'll sound good with French horn."10 Certainly, the extensive horn work on the new Who recordings was sufficiently unusual to generate a lot of interest— few groups had a bassist who would double as a horn player, and the Beatles, Rolling Stones and Kinks rarely featured such instruments. Groups sometimes used brass sections, but these were mostly saxophones and trumpets. Entwistle's French horn and tuba work was perhaps unique in rock music.

Because of these elaborate musical arrangements, many of the newer songs were deemed too difficult to reproduce on stage. All the horn and keyboard parts were entirely lost in the live environment, and for the first time the band didn't even attempt some of the newer songs in concert. The live act remained rooted in the high-energy sound that concentrated their musical power, while the recordings became more expansive and multilayered— the result of the growing practice within the industry of multitracking. This dichotomy did not worry the band members too much, and their dogged adherence to the basic essence of the live performance meant that they retained all their early inspiration and excitement as a concert act. The Beatles, in comparison, simply lost their way as a live act during 1965 and 1966 because they failed to accommodate the complexity and elaboration of their later material into their concert performances, and at the same time they had become tired of playing their older songs. The Who recognized the essential differences between the two disciplines and never attempted to record their explosive concert sound in a recording studio; conversely, they never contemplated adding extra musicians to their live lineup in order to reproduce what they had recorded. Their dual approach enabled them to successfully maintain a musical validity in both environments.

Before the album was completed, the Who were booked to record a special edition of the *Ready Steady Go!* TV show, which was broadcast on 21 October 1966. This was to be accompanied by an EP of live soundtrack recordings from the show. This plan became untenable when negotiations with the television company, Associated-Rediffusion, failed to secure the rights for the material to be released on record. Rather than cancel what was to be one of their more unusual ventures, the Who decided to release an EP, *Ready Steady Who!*, as scheduled, but with different tracks. This collected the recording of "Disguises" from June, a reprise of "Circles" from the B side of "Substitute," and three cover versions of some of Keith Moon's favorite material that had been recorded in August: "Batman," "Bucket T" and "Barbara Ann." The impression was given at the time, and has persisted, that this *was* still the material that had been played in the television special. (However, it is possible that the broadcast featured "Batman," "Man with Money," "Happy Jack," "In the City," "Disguises" and "My Generation/Land of Hope and Glory"—all of which exist on a master tape in the Who archives.)

The program was hyped by Kit Lambert this way: "Theatre of the Absurd. It will be a Who happening." But the resulting EP released on 11 November 1966 was more lightweight and unpretentious. "Disguises" was the lead track, a fine example of the Who's exploration into new areas, with many overdubs of percussion giving the impression of a psychedelic sound collage (clanging metal, sawing wood) and incorporating a fine horn arrangement [1.33]. The song has no chorus as such and is notable for its shuffling, insidious rhythm that culminates in the dramatic stop-dead chord at the end of each verse. The drums are slightly masked and the instrumental melody is largely carried by the solid bass guitar pattern. The drones and metallic crashes render "Disguises" a radical and fully realized experiment that offers further evidence of the Who's willingness of the time to take chances with their sound. The superb remix of "Disguises" that was prepared for *30 Years of Maximum R&B* presented the song in stereo for the first time, emphasizing the sheer imagination and innovation of the work, although I must say that the BBC recording of the song previously mentioned is more spontaneous in feel.

"Disguises"—like "Circles" and "I Can't Explain"—takes confusion as its subject, but in a more literal sense. The confusion here is actual mistaken identity and lack of recognition ("suddenly a girl surprises me when she turns out to be you—wearing disguises") and the difficulty this presents for the character. But the spontaneous and unpredictable nature of the girl who plays tricks provides a thrill with the *surprise*, a word that also rhymes very strongly with *disguise*. A question is posed: Who, as a result of this confusion, has the identity crisis—the boy or the girl? The lack of recognition of the appearance of one so close also suggests a recurring theme in dreams (and nightmares) and is an established Freudian motif.

The campy television series *Batman* was a hit in Britain in mid–1966, and the Who's riotous rendering of the theme song greatly adds to the party atmosphere of the EP. The unison bass and guitar riffs are powerful and vibrant, and the bass comes to the fore with a vengeance [0.48] in a few bars that can still test the mettle of the sturdiest of hi-fi speakers. "Barbara Ann" and "Bucket T" are entertaining romps of a deliberately lightweight kind on which the band even allowed Keith Moon to sing. Keith's vocals are by no means bad, although both songs rely upon extensive backing vocals. Moon's efforts cannot be considered solo performances in any way; that said, his falsetto vocals on "Barbara Ann" are verging on the ridiculous. This was the surf material that Keith loved, and the Who's treatment is brusque but affectionate. The guitar solo in "Barbara Ann" [0.52] is an interesting diversion, played in an arpeggio style, with Pete resisting the temptation to apply a heavy power-chord approach; someone can be heard whistling in the background at this point. John Entwistle contributes a jolly and comical trumpet melody line in "Bucket T" [0.24] that is repeated later on French horn [1.07]. The band's choice of this material wasn't a case of delving into the obscure recent past of American pop; they were actually picking up on very recent developments by other artists. The Beach Boys had enjoyed a substantial worldwide hit in early 1966 with a revival of the Regents' "Barbara Ann," while Jan and Dean had released a single of "Batman" backed with "Bucket T" in June 1966, although the latter song was two years older.

Another song that was recorded for this project in August was a bizarre combination of "My Generation" and "Land of Hope and Glory"—a crude exercise in musical irony. A shortened version of "My Generation" (in a higher key than the original) begins with its familiar jolting anger, but during the chaotic feedback climax, "Land of Hope and Glory" abruptly appears [1.19] with Entwistle's trumpet prominent, giving an eerie effect. The tune from Elgar's *Pomp and Circumstance March No. 1*, with overbearingly patriotic lyrics by A. C. Benson, had become the unofficial second national anthem in England, and this recording is a bit of mischief-making in which the Establishment meets the anti–Establishment—musically and thematically—in a short two-minute duel. Inevitably, it sounds a little messy, and it might have been better if Pete Townshend had learned the words of "Land of Hope and Glory" properly! The fact that this recording was not released might be explained by Sir Edward Elgar's estate's having raised an objection, "Land of Hope and Glory" not being in the public domain at this time. Internally, it was thought that it was too bizarre even for the *Ready Steady Who!* concept and was shelved until the CD reissue of *A Quick One* in 1995. Probably because of the ungainly EP format, which didn't allow disc jockeys or juke boxes to focus on one song as singles did, *Ready Steady Who!* did not sell too well, only reaching the chart (at number 58) on its reissue in 1983. In America, where the *Ready Steady Go!* television show wasn't shown, it gained no release at all.

Throughout 1966, Kit Lambert and Chris Stamp had been hoping to form a record company specifically to release the Who's material. They had learned through bitter experience how the record industry in the U.K. worked and had laid out plans for a new label that would also feature other artists of an unconventional nature. It was announced in November 1966 that the Who had switched to Track Records, which was then described as "an independent outfit controlled by Robert Stigwood" (the Reaction boss). A spokesman for the Who said, "Reaction was a temporary measure. The Who are the first group on Track, but we will be expanding it."[11] It was also announced that the Who's new album—provisionally titled *Jigsaw Puzzle*—was to be released on Track on 1 December. This announcement proved to be premature, as problems were encountered with the new company, and Who recordings continued to appear for awhile on Reaction. When Track was finally launched, Lambert and Stamp solely managed it, and it operated through a distribution deal with Polydor Records—it cannot, therefore, be considered a truly independent record label.

Additional recording during October and November brought together all the tracks for the *Jigsaw Puzzle* LP, and a fan club newsletter announcement for November/December detailed the proposed track listing. This listed on side One "I'm a Boy," "Run Run Run," "Don't Look Away," "Circles," "I Need You," and "Showbiz Sonato," and on side two "In the City," "Boris the Spider," "Whiskey Man," "See My Way," "Heat Wave" and "Barbara Ann." The version of "I'm a Boy" was the aforementioned alternate version of the single. Also recorded at these sessions was "Happy Jack," which was scheduled as the next single with the moderate John Entwistle song "I've Been Away" on the B side. The only anomaly in this track listing was "Showbiz Sonato" (noted in the newsletter as being a Keith Moon composition), which is most likely an alternate title for the instrumental "Cobwebs and Strange," although Moon had already mentioned the correct title in October, and there is no explanation for the change. It remains possible (though highly unlikely) that "Showbiz Sonato"—an uninspiring title—is a song that was rejected and has since failed to resurface. This *Jigsaw Puzzle* version of the album was scrapped, and additional new material was added. As it stood, it would have offered only six new songs, with three of the titles ("Run Run Run," "Heat Wave" and "Barbara Ann") having been released by other artists, and three ("I'm A Boy," "Circles" and "In the City") having already appeared on Who records. This was obviously an unsatisfactory situation and was soon revised. Nick Jones of *Melody Maker* had been commissioned to write sleeve notes for the album, but these appeared only on the U.S. version.

For the revised album lineup, "So Sad About Us" was pressed into service, having been already made public via the Merseys' single and the Who's BBC session broadcast of September. This alone, however, did not complete the album. It was at this point that the *mini-opera* was conceived, a collection of six short song fragments with a cohesive narrative. This partly realized some of the ideas in extended form that Townshend and Lambert had proposed with the earlier *Quads*, and it conveniently filled a ten-minute gap in the album's playing time. "A Quick One While He's Away" was formed from six shorter segments, "Her Man's Been Gone," "Crying Town," "We Have a Remedy," "Ivor the Engine Driver," "Soon Be Home" and "You Are Forgiven."[12] Aside from any musical worth, "A Quick One While He's Away" had impact due to the sheer novelty of a mini-opera in a pop genre still rooted in self-contained two-minute singles. However, while the main point of interest seems to have come from the originality of the *form*, this now seems scarcely as radical as it did. In other genres, such a work would have been commonplace; the classical music tradition was rife with song cycles and operetta, and dramatic suites were also common on the Broadway/West End musical stage. Pete Townshend was well familiar, also, with Mose Allison's *Back Country Suite*, from which "Young Man Blues" had been extracted by the Who for live performances. A song of which the Who might not have been aware, however, was "What's Cooking," a six-minute saga by Freddie and the Dreamers, which was featured in the film *Every Day's a Holiday* (1964). Although it is hard to imagine a group more fundamentally divergent to the Who and the influence of such a song upon "A Quick One" must have been at best negligible, the comparison was nonetheless drawn by Alan Clayson in his expert chronicle of the 1960s U.K. pop scene *Beat Merchants*.[13]

"Happy Jack" was the song left off the album for exclusive single release in the U.K. (appearing in advance of the LP on 3 December), although in the U.S. it was reconstituted as the album's title track. Commercially, it fell only slightly short of "I'm a Boy" when it reached number 3 in the British charts on 21 January 1967, and maintained the dazzling run of Top Ten successes that was still unbroken since "I Can't Explain." However, "Happy Jack" was undoubtedly the weakest Who single thus far, a long way from the raw excitement of "My Generation" and in many ways a compromise of what the Who were playing on stage. This was another character song about a lonely but contented tramp on the Isle of Man who is unruffled by his social ostracism. The song is very simple, with a rudimentary verse and chorus punctuated by Moon's fierce drum riffs and some noisy chord strumming prior to each chorus. Yet its undeniable charm and innocent appeal, as well as its gimmicky "I saw you" yell from Townshend at the end, account for the success of the single. More important, however, "Happy Jack" made an impact in the U.S., despite its being unrepresentative of the Who. It reached number 24 in the U.S. singles chart in the spring of 1967—a modest but significant breakthrough.

A second version of "Happy Jack" has since emerged, played on an acoustic guitar and featuring a brief flourish of Spanish guitar picking toward the end [2.25]. The release of this track in 1995 was most welcome, although the sound quality is somewhat shallow and the guitar itself is a little thin in texture. However, it is most notable for the use—droning in the background—of a cello, which was played by Pete. This duplicated the arrangement of his demo recording but makes "Happy Jack" even more of a quirky comic novelty song and less rock and roll, which is most likely the reason why the tougher electric version was released as the single. Entwistle's solo composition "I've Been Away" found itself on the U.K. B side (the later American release used "Whiskey Man" from the album). "I've Been Away" is a plodding piano piece that lacks any guitar, a revenge saga about a man newly released from prison after being framed by his brother. A throwaway novelty tune, both the theme and musical feel of "I've Been Away" have an old-time music hall flavor that is at odds with the Who's basic rock-and-roll vocabulary.

Taking its title from the epic miniopera track, *A Quick One* was released on 10 December 1966. Although lacking any distinctive anthem as strong as "My Generation" or "Substitute," the album provides firm evidence of the Who's sound becoming rationalized and more flexible, with Daltrey's vocals blending more naturally with the other instruments. The song arrangements throughout are much less rigid than before, and the fluid subtlety of "I'm a Boy" is evident on many of the tracks. This was Kit Lambert's first sustained production work, and he applies a sober, if unambitious, approach, which has the effect of dampening down the fiery dramatic bursts of chaos of the Talmy–era recordings and allowing the instruments to level out without any domination. As a result, the record is more modest in scope (given the Who's voracity for radicalism and rule breaking) and arguably lacking in excitement, despite the enthusiasm of the performances.

What the LP does achieve, however, is an evenness and consistency of quality that was lacking from *My Generation*, and it introduces several fine songs. The fact that all the band members contributed material obviously shifts the creative power away from Pete Townshend somewhat and instills a much more democratic spirit on the album. It is clear that Townshend's songs were generally superior, although the record's purpose was to unify the band creatively—a beneficial exercise that sustained the Who's stability for the near future. If nothing else, *A Quick One* is the sound of a band enjoying themselves in the recording studio in a way that they had been unable to do with Shel Talmy. Some of the lighthearted fun of the *Ready Steady Who!* EP was carried over into these recording sessions.

The opening "Run Run Run" hits a dynamic, fast beat with a driving hard rock rhythm. This manic pace almost disguises the fact that "Run Run Run" is somewhat unmelodic and its most interesting feature is the spiralling, distorted guitar solo that runs into chaotic feedback—which momentarily suggests an atonal freak-out [1.36]—before returning to the thick riff texture and powerful beat. With double-tracked lead vocals and guitars, the band achieve a tremendously full sound, but ultimately the song doesn't really warrant such intensity. Lyrically, this is not the most intelligent Who song of this era, being an aggressive promise of revenge upon a woman whose luck is seen to be running out.

John Entwistle takes the lead vocal on the macabre "Boris the Spider," which soon became one of his most famous songs. This is a witty and perfectly conceived vignette that utilizes the deep, doomy resonances of both Entwistle's voice and his bass to form a classic, unique song with a darkly comic flavor. Although musically simple, the unusual riff and verse melody strike an instant campy feel that the band had previously approached only with the "Batman" theme. Detailing the grisly demise of an unwelcome domestic spider, the lyrics follow the sinister logic of a nursery rhyme. "Boris the Spider"—along with "Whiskey Man"—launched John Entwistle's status as the Who's second songwriter. In any other group, Entwistle would have come to the fore as a fine talent in his own right, but with the Who he would always be overshadowed by Pete Townshend. Luckily, John honed a dark, sinister strain of musical creation that was always in fine contrast to Townshend's more ascetic approach.

Although musically slight, Moon's first effort, "I Need You," is a moody, minor-key pop song that features Keith's tentative lead singing and thunderous drumming. It has a strangely haunting feel and concludes with a mock music hall harpsichord "outro." Given that expectations of Moon's songwriting powers were moderate, "I Need You" is refreshingly good and features a mock Liverpudlian spoken exchange, a brief snatch of dialogue [1.12] that seems to suggest that we are hearing a member of the Beatles being asked to move his car from outside of a nightclub![14] However, Keith later denied this, saying that it was "solely a musical illustration of a transport café.... We got our Liverpudlian road-manager to say a couple of things into the mike.... It was not a Lennon impression."[15] The second Entwistle song, "Whiskey Man," is almost as good as "Boris"; this is a character song, detailing the delirium tremens of an alcoholic whose life collapses when his liquor is taken from him by medical intervention—"life is very gloomy in this little padded cell." The haunting melody and echoey Phil Spector–ish production gives the song a ghostly feel and incorporates a very effective French horn counter melody [1.35] that follows through into a beautifully melancholy horn and guitar solo duet [1.53]. This concludes with a rare power chord [2.14] before the final refrain of what is a memorably downbeat composition.

The old favorite "Heat Wave" finally appears next on the disc after two years of being featured in the Who stage act. This is given a tight, agile treatment, much curtailed in length from the original, omitting a whole verse. A slick, smooth reading of the song, with very good vocal harmonies and a prominent bass melody, this recording of "Heat Wave" maintains the minor-key melancholic feel of "I Need You" and "Whiskey Man." An exceptionally short arrangement (1.54), this could easily have warranted the extended duration of the 1965 recording, which was nearly a minute longer. (However, some of the innovation of treating Tamla Motown songs to hard-edged British rock arrangements had now been lost: in 1965 the Birds had released "Leaving Here"—modeled after the unreleased Who version—and the Action had given a Who–type treatment to Martha and the Vandellas' "In My Lonely Room." The Who may now have seemed latecomers to a field they had pioneered, although they were aware that the inclusion of "Heat Wave" was a purely nostalgic gesture. Moon said that it was released "because it represents an era ... it provides a contrast to the newer stuff."[16])

Moon's "Cobwebs and Strange" is the oddest recording that the band had ever attempted. It is a bizarre instrumental, the surreal aural equivalent of a circus or carnival, a form of slapstick comedy in sound. The main purpose of the track is for Moon to rattle out four breakneck drum solos amid a chaotic melody line in which Entwistle's trumpet is featured heavily. One can imagine the theme accompanying a Buster Keaton comedy short; underneath the surface jollity lies a deranged element that threatens to overwhelm. It is, however, a novelty item first and last, and it is hard to argue that "Cobwebs and Strange" has any lasting musical worth.

With "Don't Look Away" on side two, we are presented with the softest song on the album, acoustic pop of perfect construction with a guitar solo very well played in a country & western style. Townshend seemed to have had an effortless ability to turn out such material at this time, despite its modest ambition and rudimentary treatment. The lyrics concern a sudden rejection and the pain of being jilted. In different circumstances, "Don't Look Away" would have been given away—like "Join My Gang" or "It's Alright"—for another group to try, but its function on *A Quick One* is mainly to diversify the range of songs.

Roger Daltrey's first solo composition is "See My Way"—a simplistic pop song of modest scope but considerable appeal. The vocal harmonies are good (as, indeed, they are throughout the album), but the arrangement lacks any kind of embellishment and the guitar is overmuted, leaving the bass to carry much of the musical force. The drum arrangement is similarly spartan, and Moon never seems to establish a hard beat. It has been stated—not least by Townshend—that Daltrey was here attempting to instigate a momentary return to the innocent pop values of Buddy Holly, and in this context "See My Way" works well enough. It is perhaps let down by the lack of color in the instrumentation—despite another horn embellishment, and at less than two minutes in length it tends to lack substance. Lyrically, the song advocates the dominance of the singer in a relationship through force of will. This seems to be an extension of the "Anyway Anyhow Anywhere" persona (Daltrey's earlier contribution) in less aggressive terms.

The best Townshend song on the record is probably "So Sad About Us," a classic bittersweet pop melody driven by a powerful beat from Moon and garnished with excellent vocal harmonies. This is confident, soaring music on which Daltrey gets exactly the right voice for the material—lacking all the mannerisms that blighted some of his singing on the first LP. Pete Townshend's trademark crashing chords, which aren't otherwise much featured on this album, are deployed to perfection on this song. The theme of "So Sad About Us" reflects a more mature attitude, lamenting the death of a relationship without blame or accusation, presented as a mutually tragic event.

The most discussed item, "A Quick One While He's Away," actually offers the least substantial music on the album, for here form is far more important than content. Detailing a somewhat farcical case of separation and neglect, infidelity, confession, forgiveness and reconciliation, none of the six themes rises above a kind of perfunctory functionality, as if the music is there merely to carry an already uninvolving plot through six movements. Yet, against all critical scrupulousness, the track somehow works—the appeal for the listener lies in the way in which the Who presents the material. The later description of the track as a "mini-opera" is rather grandiloquent for what is really a succession of undeveloped musical fragments, but the sheer novelty of the form was enough to make an impact.

The barbershop harmonies of "Her Man's Been Gone" are followed by "Crying Town" [0.22], a more conventional pop melody. "We Have a Remedy" [1.59] tends toward the bombastic, and John Entwistle's vocals on "Ivor the Engine Driver" [3.31] make this character alone come alive.[17] Keith Moon provides a few cymbal clashes to simulate a steam engine. "Soon Be Home" [5.14] is an innocent and gentle country & western pastiche, complete with a wobble-board and Townshend's "Come on, old horse" aside. Finally, the most forceful segment is the closing "You Are Forgiven" [6.40], which speeds up to a frenzy and uses a complex arrangement of vocal parts, dominated by Pete's gleefully emphatic voice, his only solo vocal on the record. Each of these six sections work well enough in themselves, but they inevitably don't fuse together quite so smoothly.

The cover of *A Quick One* featured a colorful painting of the band by Alan Aldridge in a pop art/psychedelic style that (like the cover artwork of the Kinks' *Face to Face* album) looks very much of its time and now seems somewhat dated. Once more, the Decca edition for the U.S. bore some changes on its release in May 1967. It was retitled *Happy Jack*, and "Heat Wave" was omitted in favor of "Happy Jack," although the front cover was the same. Decca also issued a stereo mix that, once again, hasn't found favor with subsequent reissues. One outtake that has now appeared is the band's version of the Everly Brothers' "Man with Money"—a masterly arrangement with muscular guitar work (both acoustic and electric) and a perfectly controlled central section [0.53]. The harmony singing is delightful, though Roger Daltrey particularly excels here. Finally, we are treated at the end to a traditional Who rave-up, with Pete throwing in a power chord/feedback solo. Although a very strong performance, one can understand why this was excluded from an album that was designed to promote the Who as indigenous songwriters all.

Reaching number 4 in the U.K. chart, *A Quick One* was a commercial success and was critically well received. *Melody Maker* splashed a front-page headline "WHO Great New LP" and Chris Welch wrote, "an incredible new album from The Who ... at last it fulfils the promise ... here is a collection of compositions and treatments that captures the Who essence, humour, cynicism, nervous drive, violence, and delicacy."[18] Penny Valentine concurred with Welch in *Disc*: "the most interesting LP ideas since the Beatles.... This LP is a milestone in The Who's career...."[19] Pete Townshend's reaction to *A Quick One* was somewhat cooler: "I call it our first LP. It's our most important record but it's also weak because the group haven't really got it together yet.... This is our first LP. Our first LP in reality was crap...."[20] The level of invention and variation on *A Quick One* is consistently high, and the colorful musical arrangements reveal a whole witty, fun-loving underside to the Who that the piously solemn *My Generation* image had hitherto obscured. In the canon of Who albums across the years, however, *A Quick One* does not rank so high, but this is because of the exceptional quality of what followed rather than any specific weakness endemic to this work.

The definitive CD version of *A Quick One* was released in 1995 and collected all the band's 1966 recordings apart from the three single A sides and "Circles." This release also made available for the first time the acoustic "Happy Jack," "Man with Money" and "My Generation/Land of Hope and Glory" (as well as "Doctor Doctor" from 1967). Unfortunately, the multitrack master tapes of the album could not be located, and Jon Astley was unable undertake a remix. (Rumor had it that the masters were stored in Kit Lambert's palazzo in Venice and destroyed in a fire, but more recent reports suggest that the tapes have been recovered, though obviously too late for Astley to use them). So the bulk of the CD presented remastered mono recordings with a few stereo mixes where these had survived. In terms of sound quality, this CD is the one most lacking in the Who catalog. A close listen reveals some distortion and dropouts on the masters, but it is still generally very acceptable for a recording from this era. The only other flaw is with the programming of the CD and the omission of the second version of "Circles," which would have fitted both thematically and in terms of running time.

At the close of 1966, the Who completed one more recording for the very last edition of *Ready Steady Go!* The band entered Ryemuse Studios in London on 16 December and completed a version of Johnny Kidd and the

Pirates' "Please Don't Touch," an eight-year-old rock-and-roll song that had been Kidd's first hit. After one broadcast on 23 December, this performance was archived and has yet to reemerge in any form. Johnny Kidd had been killed a few months earlier, and this choice of song can now be seen as a final gesture of allegiance to both the Who's roots and to *Ready Steady Go!* before the nature of rock changed completely in 1967. This change was in part due to the innovative and radical approach of groups such as the Who, and the new climate was one in which the band felt more comfortable.

As 1966 passed, rock music moved through a rapid upheaval that left many pop acts behind. *The Ready Steady Go!*/mod era ended, swallowed up and exploited within the whole Swinging London industry, and (in reaction) the underground was born. The underground scene in the U.K. was a radical movement centered around the magazines *Oz* and *International Times*, which advocated that rock and roll should play its part as a revolutionary tool rather than remain a mere commercial entertainment. The underground embraced drugs, sex and subversive politics and espoused communal living and multimedia happenings such as festivals. The newspapers generally categorized the people involved as hippies, and the movement wasn't just restricted to Britain and the United States. This new emergent scene gave the Who a new context in which to work, and rather than condemn the band for its chart success and commercial appeal, the underground actually championed the Who as visionaries, hailing "My Generation" as a battle cry two years before its time.

The Jimi Hendrix Experience and Pink Floyd were the new figureheads of the movement in the U.K.; the U.S. had Jefferson Airplane, Grateful Dead, Country Joe and the Fish. All these acts held in common a preoccupation with drugs, especially LSD. Hallucinogenic drugs were used as aids not only to listening to music, but to writing it and performing it as well. In general, this made rock music more loose, undisciplined and spaced-out often to the detriment of tight songwriting and compact, energetic playing (the established forte of bands like the Who). Pete Townshend took acid (along with pretty much everyone else at the time), but it influenced the Who in only very minor respects. It was around this time that the band had established within itself a permanent identity, and (unlike, say, the Beatles) they didn't feel they had to embrace all things hippie in order to become momentarily trendy.

The first recording work undertaken by the Who in 1967 was a session booking for BBC Radio's *Saturday Club* (21 January). On this occasion, the band reprised three songs from the last album and added a version of "Happy Jack" that duplicated the arrangement of the single and offered no great variation apart from John Entwistle's intoning the concluding "I saw you" line at the end in his gruff "Boris the Spider" voice. "Boris" itself lacked some of the menace of the album version and was more echoey, while "Run Run Run" had a longer distorted guitar solo. The main advantage of this session was to provide an improved "See My Way," which was given a superior guitar arrangement that brought out the R&B feel of the song as well as extended its length.

Kit Lambert and Chris Stamp finally launched Track Records, to which the Who were now signed, in early 1967. The Jimi Hendrix Experience were also on the label, and their "Purple Haze" became the first Track single release in March. The Who's next recording sessions in April yielded the single "Pictures of Lily" backed with Entwistle's "Doctor Doctor." All doubts that "Happy Jack" might have caused regarding the Who's capability to produce classic rock singles were immediately dispelled by this release, which reached number 4 in the chart on 20 May. "Pictures of Lily" vindicated the band's reputation with a triumphant return to a more aggressive instrumentation and a provocative lyrical theme. The single harnesses a powerful group sound—stripped down to basics and bristling with confidence yet supple and intricate. The structure of the song follows a complex but accessible pattern, with a descending chord motif and an emotive melody that is interrupted by the dramatic central section of the song. This is a startling highlight and packs a huge visceral punch with a gut-wrenching guitar riff [1.13], offset by Daltrey's delicately yearning intonation of the title line. Entwistle adds an eccentric horn overdub [1.28] that completes a masterly performance. The song has a raw, undetailed sound that lacks any surface flashiness and conceded nothing to contemporary notions of either pop or rock music—it stayed faithful only to a unified conception of the Who's music.

The theme of "Pictures of Lily" is masturbation, which was an unprecedented subject matter for a Top Five hit. Pete handled this bold theme with subtlety and insight, and Roger's singing was sensitive and clear. Despite the universality of masturbation, it has been given few opportunities for expression in song, which makes the achievement of "Pictures of Lily" all the greater.[21] The lyrical theme relates the sexual awakening of a teenager and the pain of unrequited love. The love here is based upon a pornographic image and not a real woman, and the song examines the relationship between the boy (whose only means of sexual expression is through masturbation) and Lily (who in one sense isn't a real person). The tragedy implicit in the theme comes when the young man yearns to develop his relationship with Lily and is told by his father that she has been "dead since 1929," and hence his world momentarily collapses. But the final lines, leaving the boy and his idealized female "together in ... dreams," offer a more mature position of acceptance and a coming to terms with the situation. (The title had been originally inspired by a postcard that Townshend had seen depicting Lilian Bayliss, the actress who was the theater manager of the Old Vic Company in London at the beginning of the twentieth century. However, the Lily of the song and the type of pictures Pete had in mind bore no other connection with this.)

The B side was also a treat: Entwistle's "Doctor Doctor" was by no means a throwaway effort, being a persistent hard rock song with a falsetto vocal. It is a frantic and funny hypochondriac's rant over an unrelenting and hypnotic riff, and the guitar is well submerged beneath John's thundering bass work. Entwistle's character is a paranoiac mulling over the imagined decay of his body (and mind) and pleading with his doctor to cure him. This is almost strong enough to have been a single A side, and certainly John Entwistle songs were never given the prominence or attention they deserved. (Townshend himself later admitted that "Boris the Spider" should have been a Who single in its own right.) Also recorded around the same time in April 1967 was "Glittering Girl" a simplistic pop song written (and sung) by Pete Townshend. This was based on a rising chord progression (E–G–A) that later found a fuller expression in the song "I'm Free." However, this conventional performance of an average composition, incorporating an upward key change, failed to gain a release at the time and was first issued in 1995 on the *Sell Out* CD.

The Who's concert career in the U.S. was effectively launched with their appearance at the Monterey Pop Festival on 18 June 1967. This short performance was filmed and recorded, and while "My Generation" appeared in the 1969 film *Monterey Pop*, the full concert tape was never considered good enough to release on record. However, during 1992 a CD boxed set of the whole festival was released, including the Who performance in full. This is the earliest Who concert material to appear on disk and it is wholly unrepresentative. Although the band played a tight, energetic set, they weren't using their usual amplification equipment and sounded underpowered and a little disjointed. The recording consists of "Substitute," "Summertime Blues," "Pictures of Lily," "A Quick One While He's Away," "Happy Jack" and "My Generation." This release is of historical interest only and was not authorized by the band members.

On returning to the U.K. from Monterey, the Who (minus John Entwistle, who was on his honeymoon) entered De Lane Lea Studios in London on 28 June 1967 to record a single in support of Mick Jagger and Keith Richard of the Rolling Stones, who had recently been given controversial sentences for drug offences. So thus two Rolling Stones' songs were given a unique Who treatment and rush-released within two days as a means of supporting Jagger and Richard's judicial appeal. The Who's arrangements of "The Last Time" and "Under My Thumb" copied the Stones' originals very closely, they lacked the swagger and exuberance of Mick Jagger's vocals but remained faithful to the structure of the two songs. Townshend played bass guitar as well as adding a fuzzed lead solo to each. An alternate take of "Under My Thumb"—which has a simplified bass arrangement and lacks the guitar solo—was discovered more recently and included on the 1998 CD *Odds and Sods*. The single reached number 44 in the U.K. charts but was not released in America, where its topicality was not so relevant. Further planned releases of Rolling Stones' material were abandoned when the appeal of Jagger and Richard was successful and they were able to resume their own careers.

From mid–1967, the Who recorded more extensively than ever before and developed a much more sophisticated approach to the recording studio. Although their output on record didn't tangibly increase during the year, a number of songs were set aside for future projects, often finally to be abandoned. Indeed, an album was provisionally expected in June called *Who's Lily*—obviously a reference to "Pictures of Lily" but otherwise undistinguished. The band members were excited about this work and envisaged an all-around creative effort. Pete Townshend told *Melody Maker*, "We learnt so much about each other on the last album ... the next one is going to be an absolute knockout to make. Every one of us is writing."[22] Shortly after Keith Moon confirmed this collaborative approach, saying, "All the material will be original, including some stuff I've been writing."[23] (Bear in mind that the Who's output of one album per year during the 1965–1967 era was much less than the average of the time, although it may now seem prolific.) It was evidence of the Who's innovative nature that they didn't rush out a straight LP of unconnected songs at this time, as *Who's Lily* would have been, but waited until they had produced ideas that far exceeded their previous album in both ambition and musical achievement. The Who had started to work in the U.S. from March 1967 and so now recorded material in a wider variety of locations than before. In general, 1967 saw the band's records reach a new level of sophistication, and two diverse factors were to shape the nature of their next album: one was pirate radio and the idea of advertisements in sound; the other was a new Townshend opera.

While in New York the Who were commissioned to produce an advertisement for Coca-Cola, which resulted in their recording two short but forceful themes, perfunctorily titled "Coke 1" and "Coke 2." "Coke 1" had the band singing "things go better with Coke" over a heavy riff, while the similar "Coke 2" boasted an even heavier riff and a vocal line of "Coke after Coke after Coca-Cola." These were fun excursions for the band, and John Entwistle's bass sound was every bit as distorted as Townshend's guitar. It is not known if these themes were ever used commercially.

Another commission of the same ilk was an instrumental theme for a documentary film apparently called *Live in London* (some references give the title as *Signal 30*). Whether this film ever emerged has not been established, but the Who's theme—which has at various times been called both "Signal 30" and "Instrumental—No Title" but which seems to have now acquired an official title of "Sodding About"—features a grinding heavy riff with horn overdubs and a furious bass guitar solo. This track has remained unreleased, although Jon Astley had remastered it for the *Odds and Sods* reissue of 1998, from which it was dropped at the last minute due to restrictions of space.

Some of this work suggested that the band should release an EP of purely instrumental themes, all of which would be more representative of their powerful stage sound. In fact, a whole series of such EPs were tentatively planned, and their imminent appearance was announced by Track Records in a press release to *New Musical Express* (18 March 1967). "Hall of the Mountain King" was conceived in the same vein (discussed later). Although his role in such an EP would be minimal, Roger Daltrey was surprisingly keen on the idea, saying, "The instrumental market is now pretty nil—and there's such a lot we do instrumentally anyway which we used to do a long time ago."[24] Unfortunately, what would have been one of the Who's more interesting diversions never materialized.

The idea of the Who performing ads inspired Townshend to write a glorious paean to the Jaguar E-type sports car (one of the most potent and iconoclastic artifacts of Britain in the 1960s) titled simply "Jaguar." This wasn't actually commissioned by Jaguar but it utilized the then current Jaguar sales slogan "Grace Space Pace" in a racy, spaced-out theme that was typical of the era. Although "Jaguar" was discarded, it convinced the band that a satirical development of advertising themes could provide a successful format for a pop art–influenced album. Also, no other group was offering a parody of commercials, though plenty of bands (including the Who) were recording the real things for pirate and commercial radio (Radio Luxembourg). (Remember that the U.K. at this time had no indigenous commercial radio network that carried advertisements or sponsorship, only the BBC and its three networks, the Home Service, Light Programme and Third Programme.) Pirate radio had been crucial to the success of many bands (including the Who) and ads, jingles and pop singles were inexorably bound in a barrage of sound that was vulgar, superficial and brash but also somehow exciting and vital, an essential part of the 1960s pop culture. As 1967 progressed, the pirate radio stations were forced off the airwaves, and the Who decided to program their next album to play like a radio show, with jingles, ads and songs interlinked. This was an ambitious format but one that seemed ideally suited to the band's current concerns.

Recording for the project began during the band's U.S. tour (playing backup for Herman's Hermits) in July and stretched into November. The band actually recorded a vast array of material through the latter half of the year, all of which was finally pulled together for the new album with many tracks to spare. During the first few months of 1967, Pete Townshend had begun to record (at his Wardour Street home) an opera in twenty-five scenes, set in 1999 and following the adventures of a man during a world takeover by the Chinese. "The hero goes through hundreds of different situations and there is music for each," Townshend explained. "He goes out in a boat and gets shipwrecked, he has a bad nightmare and so on. I have used sound effects for a lot of the situations with music over them."[25] Within a few months this was reworked as a shorter opera now titled *Rael*. "This may well have a full orchestra on it as I have written a fugue into it," Pete said. "The opera would last a good 20–30 minutes so I don't know if we could use it on the next LP. It would take up too much of the record."[26] For *Rael*, Pete produced several contrasting sections characterized by acoustic guitar and organ, starting with a folksy scene-setting song called "That Motherland Feeling" and concluding with a gentle (almost baroque) organ theme (the aforementioned fugue). Pete had learned to play piano and organ during the first part of 1967, and many of his new songs were keyboard-based. *Rael* was not considered immediately suitable for the Who, however, and it was initially developed as a concept piece for singer Arthur Brown, a psychedelic blues singer who had recently been signed to Track Records.

While in New York, Kit Lambert had listened through Pete's *Rael* demo tapes and the Who made an attempt at recording the work at Talent Masters Studios in July. A friend of the band who was present at the session was organist Al Kooper. Kooper recently recalled that the cleaning staff at Talent Masters had damaged the first few bars of the *Rael* master tape after it had been left out one night by mistake. When Townshend was informed that the beginning of the song would have to be rerecorded, he threw a chair in a temper through the control room's soundproof window causing thousands of dollars' worth of damage. (Although rerecorded and patched together with great skill, the join is still noticeable [0.24] to those who care to listen closely!)

Inevitably, *Rael* was whittled down from around thirty minutes in length to a shorter version with a single release in mind. This editing compressed the whole plot that Pete had written: the introductory "That Motherland Feeling" section was jettisoned entirely, and the lyrical theme became too obscure to easily discern. Nevertheless, "Rael" addressed the important ecological theme of world overpopulation and detailed the idealism of one character who wanted to colonise a Utopian island. More important, however, was the music: "Rael" included a dazzling instrumental theme that became one of Townshend's favorite works and was later incorporated into *Tommy* as "Sparks" and "Underture." The full version of *Rael* never materialized, as Pete explained: "Basically the story was running into about twenty scenes when Kit Lambert reminded me that while I was pretending to be Wagner, The Who needed a new single. What did I have? I had 'Rael.' Thus 'Rael' was edited down to four minutes (too long for a single in those days ironically) and recorded in New York for that purpose. It later appeared on an album. No one will ever know what it means, it has been squeezed up too tightly to make sense."[27]

In what was becoming a customary pattern, the Who's 1967 album was due for summer release but postponed. Due to their increasing concert commitments in the United States and the developing ideas for the concept of the record, the release was delayed and additional recording sessions were added where schedules would allow. While in the U.S. in July and September, they had recorded "Mary Anne with the Shaky Hand" (three versions), "Our Love Was," "I Can See for Miles," "I Can't Reach You," "Relax," "Rael" and "Someone's Coming." It is difficult to ascertain at which point the final conceptual framework of the album was finalized, and no single individual seems to have been credited with the idea. However, on returning to London in October, the Who recorded and mixed further material and devised the concept within which the new songs would be surrounded by advertisements and jingles in a close pastiche of pirate and commercial radio. This was a simple and highly effective idea for an album, and it was utilized to differentiate the new work as a very bold progression from *A Quick One*. Not only was the broad framework a stronger one, but the band had prepared a more formidable selection of songs than previously and had striven to produce something that would at least be as radically new as the title track from the previous album had been the year before.

More important, the band had now formulated a mature approach to recording. In the past the songs had been adapted to meet the overall band sound and usually given an arrangement that translated relatively easily to the demands of the concert format of three instruments and three voices (all of *My Generation* and some of *A Quick One* complies with this standard). The new material was approached in the opposite way: the band treated each song on its own terms and expanded the arrangements to obtain the best possible results, thus fully realizing the potential of each composition. This was largely achieved by the use of additional instruments. The basic guitar/bass/drums lineup was now augmented by additional guitars (Townshend tended to prefer both electric and acoustic on every song, rather than one or the other), organ and piano (again played by Townshend); brass and horn work (as on the previous album), and special tape effects. It is worth adding that at these sessions the band really got to grips with the technique of multitracking (that is, building up a sound scheme through many overdubs), and this breakthrough was in part the result of improving studio technology. (During this period, most recording studios were in the process of upgrading equipment from 4-track to 8-track, and mixing processes were increasingly geared toward working exclusively in stereo.)

The next Who single was an older song (written in 1966) for which Pete Townshend had high hopes. In fact, he believed it would be far and away the finest thing the band would ever release and a certainty for a number 1 hit. "I Can See for Miles" (released on 14 October) was undoubtedly the most powerful, complex and well achieved performance that the Who had ever recorded. It combines the sonic clarity of their earlier work with a new ethereal looseness and fluidity that is pitched with such consummate skill that it becomes transcendent. It isn't exactly psychedelia by definition, but it does encapsulate many of the heady, mystical qualities that were at the center of the best psychedelia, and it is accordingly embellished with flourishes of acid-tinged guitar. Thus, the single was perfectly in tune with the times and showed the Who to have mastered their music into the extreme limit of its potential.

Musically the song is a brooding, throbbing combination of inversions, drones and suspensions awash with distorted guitars filling all the spaces and unusual drum patterns moving in and out of the structure, and all built on a droning single-note bass line (the least demanding Who song that John Entwistle ever had to play—he was never overenthusiastic about the single.) The best aspect of the song is the immaculate, spine-chilling, multivoiced chorus that stands as evidence of a streak of pure genius that was becoming increasingly recognizable in the Who's music. The minimalist one-note guitar solo [2.11] again defies convention in accordance with a song that draws on power-chord density (two electrics and one acoustic guitar can be heard) and dynamics of a kind unapproached by any other act. Probably the only record of this era to achieve the same sublime and eerie quality of vocal harmony is another song with *miles* in the title: "Eight Miles High" by the Byrds.

At the center of "I Can See for Miles" is a magical, undefinable thrust of creativity, an unreproducible element of mystery that set out in clear terms the unique quality of the Who's music. Yet "I Can See for Miles" didn't alienate listeners (as did some psychedelia); it was accessible enough to become a hit in both Britain and the States. Climbing to number 9 in the U.S. charts was (and remains still) a record high for the Who, but its top position of number 10 in the U.K.—in other circumstances a respectable showing—was a profound disappointment for Townshend who (rightly) believed that only number 1 was good enough for his finest song. Chris Welch wrote of "I Can See for Miles" in *Melody Maker* that the song marked "the return of The Who as a major freak-out force ... filled with Townshend mystery and menace...."[28] Some listeners construed the meaning of the lyrics to indicate a heightened perception gained by drug use; Townshend later retorted with some sarcasm that it merely referred to "a jealous man with exceptionally good eyesight!"[29] A song of revenge, "I Can See for Miles" is about the use of a sixth sense—with a suggestion of magic—to reveal the truth by the character who has been deceived and betrayed. The lyrics here marvel at the use of the special power and celebrate doing someone one better, with the threatening promise "You're going to lose that smile."

The original mono single on Track was cut with such power and vitality that it almost sounds like a different (far superior) take in comparison to the subsequent stereo LP version. "The mono makes the stereo sound like the Carpenters," Townshend later wrote. "...The real production masterpiece in the Who/Lambert coalition ... I swoon when I hear the sound."[30] Although subsequent remixing and remastering has opened up the full, lush glory of stereo, collectors should be encouraged to investigate the original 45 rpm single to hear the song as it was preferred by Pete. An imaginative brass arrangement ushers in Entwistle's "Someone's Coming" on the B side, a fair pop song with a semi-romantic theme that was at odds with John's other, darker material. Fans in the States were deprived of this song in favor of another new Townshend work, "Mary Anne with the Shaky Hand," which was also scheduled for the forthcoming album. This was a different arrangement, featuring an electric guitar, and is laden with echo but lacks the appeal of the more Latin–flavored album track. (For the 1998 *Odds and Sods* CD, a fourth version of this song emerged that was essentially the original U.S. B side version with Al Kooper's prominent organ contribution.)

"I Can See for Miles" was premiered on the United States CBS television show *Smothers Brothers Comedy Hour* (17 September 1967), on which occasion the Who lip-synced to the recently completed recording. (In fact, the complexity of "I Can See for Miles" was such that the Who never managed to play it on stage until 1979). However, following this performance, they concluded with a version of "My Generation" that had been rerecorded especially for this show. This lacks some of the furious pace of the original and has an over-echoey lead vocal from Daltrey, but otherwise it is a pleasing remake of the song complete with twangy bass solo and an auto-destructive finale that concludes with a real explosion. Although in mono, the recording quality is immediate and clear, and this latter performance formed the opening sequence of both *The Kids Are Alright* film and soundtrack album.

Back in London, the Who's continuing relationship with BBC Radio reached a new development when they became the first act to gain clearance to present material for broadcast that was not recorded in a BBC studio. This meant that some of the material featured in radio sessions could now be merely remixed from the same master tapes that were used for Who records, although some songs were still rerecorded from scratch exclusively for broadcast. On *Saturday Club* (28 October), the Who presented a rerecording of "Pictures of Lily" with an organ part; "Summertime Blues," a fairly noncommittal version of the Eddie Cochran song that the Who played much better onstage; and "I Can See for Miles," which was identical to the single apart from the bass guitar, which played a different arrangement entirely.

A later session for *Top Gear* (16 November) premiered four of the tracks that had been recorded in the U.S. and that were due for inclusion on the new album: "Our Love Was" with Roger Daltrey on vocals; an alternative but similar take of "I Can't Reach You"; "Relax," which was an almost identical mix to that which appeared on the album; and, finally, a rerecording of "A Quick One While He's Away," more compact and shorter than the title track of the second album, reflecting the fact that this was now regularly included in the live act. Although they probably didn't realize it at the time, the Who were not to take up any further session bookings with the BBC for over two years—probably because they were spending an increasing amount of time in the U.S. and maybe because they seemed to have no great enthusiasm for such recordings.

The Who Sell Out, which appeared on 16 December 1967, is one of the most unusual albums ever released and an undisputed rock masterpiece. It is a concept album that offers an accurate pastiche of pirate radio—both a homage to and a parody of the semilegal offshore radio stations that had defined the sound of the mid–1960s in Britain, such as Radio Caroline and particularly Radio London.[31] Nothing was spared (good or bad) in the Who's satirical re-creation of Radio London: vulgarity of the commercials, the inane jingles that punctuated the music, and the thrill of the exciting new sounds that emanated through the airwaves. This is a radio station that plays constant Who music, of course, though to give the right impression, the band sequenced a selection of songs that reflected a wide range of styles and arrangements. Edited together as a huge sound package—an aural montage—the LP plays (on side one at least) like a continuous radio program with only one element missing, the disc jockey. For no apparent reason, however, this format ceases early into side two, although the expanded CD version of 1995 adds another chunk at the end. While the format continues, *Sell Out* forms a measured satire on commercial radio, with actual songs reflecting the themes of advertisements as well. Mixing with the songs are more serious rock numbers that reflect the Who's latest musical and lyrical developments. As indicated previously, the arrangements of the songs here are full and diverse with multitracked instruments, subtle and sophisticated playing, and a lush, sonorous production. The idea of simulating a radio program was a simple but highly original idea and ensured that the Who would again be credited as innovators.

The ads and jingles are a mixture of band originals and items taken from Radio London, and although many of the products were real, the music wasn't sponsored. A strong strain of good humor runs through the whole album, confirming an often-overlooked aspect of their work: The Who could be a first-class comedy act, and they had much in common with the then emerging Bonzo Dog Doo-Dah Band, the Fugs, and the Mothers of Invention—three groups who blended pop music with the 1960s vogue for satire and parody. The sleeve was also memorable and funny, featuring four individual shots of the band members each promoting a "product" (and related song). The satire, therefore, was evident visually as well as musically, and the record sleeve worked very much within the genre of pop art. It was designed by Track Records art directors David King and Roger Law (later a cocreator of the merciless U.K. television satire show *Spitting Image*), with photographs by David Montgomery. The lack of song titles on the sleeve was a notable first, and the band must have been the only act at this time who would have agreed to be photographed in such unflattering poses and seeming to suffer from such personal deficiencies as body odor, underdeveloped muscles, acne, and an inability to eat baked beans without their dribbling from the mouth. With the Who there was never a pretense that the band was any different from the average person who suffered from such commonplace problems.

Like the music on many albums from 1967, the opening song here is a thinly disguised celebration of drug use, and the title "Armenia City in the Sky" is merely a euphemism for the "destination" of an acid trip. Surprisingly, the song was written by John "Speedy" Keene (then working for Townshend as a driver), and the basic hard rock performance is laden with overdubs: backwards guitars (that is, guitars recorded as normal, then dubbed onto the track played in reverse), raga drones, feedback and even backward horns. Beneath this dazzling array of effects lies a pleasant but average song in an impossibly high key for Roger Daltrey's voice. The arrangements and stereo panning are reminiscent of the most successful of the Beatles' psychedelic experiments, "Tomorrow Never Knows" (1966); although coming a year later, this track sounds much less radical. However, "Armenia City in the Sky" could be taken as a *parody* of a song by psychedelic group, especially when toward the end we can hear chanted "freak out, freak out" in a silly voice. Musically, this is the weakest song on the album, but it adds much atmosphere in terms of creating the feel of an ultrahip radio show.

John Entwistle's "Heinz Baked Beans" is based on the earlier "Cobwebs and Strange" and features a suitably inane horn melody backed up by Townshend's banjo. It is a ludicrous but amusing sales pitch—a snapshot of "average" family life, according to the consumer society—and the highlight is Entwistle's "grandfather" voice on the line "What's for tea, Daughter?" The following, "Mary Anne with the Shaky Hand," is a delightful pop song in the Everly Brothers' mold, with a three-part vocal harmony, ridiculous lyrics, Latinate acoustic guitars, and very sparse drumming. Although ostensibly an innocent recitation of Mary Anne's advantages over the attributes of three other females, Chris Charlesworth boldly described this as "Pete's second great song about masturbation—the first was 'Pictures of Lily'—or a tasteless ode to an afflicted unfortunate?"[32] Keith Moon's pounding and persuasive ad for Premier drums fades in and out again before the record moves into "Odorono," sung by Pete, and featuring dual lead and rhythm guitar parts. This is the first narrative song, a cautionary tale of personal hygiene, and the attractive music is entirely appropriate for the amusing melodramatic lyrics. Although unambitious, "Odorono" is musically substantial and plays an important part in shaping the character of the LP. (The implausibly named deodorant Odorono was in fact a real product sometime in the past!)

Possibly the best song of all on the collection (after "I Can See for Miles") is the masterly "Tattoo," a sensitive exposition of the commonplace and universal truths of incipient manhood that could only have been matched in either theme or performance (if at all) by the Kinks. This beautiful and moving song is characterized by a brilliant vocal from Roger Daltrey and a thrilling sequence of arpeggio chord figures double-tracked on both electric and acoustic guitars. A sure production touch was to have the electric guitar play exclusively through the left stereo channel and the acoustic through the right—an effective system that would often be used on future work. The vocal harmonies are immaculate, the instrumentation is imaginative and the theme is handled with considerable insight, humor and warmth: "Tattoo" is a song of absolute inspiration.

It examines the pressures exerted by society on individuals to conform, one result of which is that men tattoo their bodies to enhance their manliness. This is expressed with irony and insight. The song clearly delineates the consequences of insecurity, showing how the doubt in the young men can prompt such an outwardly aggressive and spontaneous defacement of their skin in pursuit of a macho myth. Society makes that myth the most important goal, the boys will do anything to become "real men." The two brothers are here anxious to achieve an identity and are confused by the pressing issue, "What makes a man a man?" Of course, they don't see that there is no definitive answer to this question, although they suggest a few. We see the final capitulation and conformity in their inevitable trip to the tattooist. They emerge as figures of ridicule, no manlier than before and somewhat less as human beings. "Tattoo," however, is a warm, sympathetic song, and the characters aren't unduly criticized for their momentary weakness.

Pete Townshend again takes the lead vocals on the lively and capacious "Our Love Was," a mature love song with an intricate but energetic arrangement. The deep echo of the production here contributes to the overall beauty of the song, which also has an effective key change and raga-style guitar solo [2.09]. Pete's vocals are pitched high but the result is pure and true. An interesting contribution from Entwistle is the descending brass riff [1.49] during the chorus in the latter half of the song. Although undramatic on first listening, "Our Love Was" is short, catchy and sharp. This is a celebration of love—that rare thing in the Who canon—but love in the past tense, so it could easily have become a lament for what was, a eulogy in sound. An initial crisis, when love is "famine, frustration," is soon resolved to reveal the full splendor of the relationship, "shining like a summer morning." The character describes the relationship in superlatives and the song becomes almost too self-congratulatory. Following the ads and jingles is "I Can See for Miles," sounding more muted than the single and probably included to reinforce the stature of the song in general, though obviously most Who fans would already have the single. Whatever, it fits perfectly and chimes in straight after Entwistle's Rotosound strings advertisement.

The mock country & western ad for the Charles Atlas course is one of the more amusing fillers with vocals provided by Pete (the "before" part) and

John (the "after"). "I Can't Reach You" immediately follows, being an attractive piano-based uptempo pop song with an infectious chorus. Townshend again takes the lead vocals as well as the piano arrangement and acoustic rhythm guitar. Toward the end of the song the electric guitar lines become more prominent. Lyrically the song is a classical example of expressed frustration in which the unattainable is yearned for. The main problem is that the character doesn't realize the (emotional) distance between himself and the object of his desire, and the distance is expressed in physical terms. Entwistle's short piece about acne, "Medac," is a mildly amusing and purely functional advertisement, marking the end of the radio show format.

One of the most radical tracks is "Relax," which has a complex structure based on raga guitar drones and organ fills. It is the least Who–like song on the record, although it boasts strong melodies, changes in mood and pace, extensive vocal harmonies and a loud organ played by Pete. "Relax" is another drug-influenced song complete with a prime, manic and pounding psychedelic freak-out [1.32], just to prove that the Who could fly as high as Pink Floyd's "Interstellar Overdrive" if they wanted. Mercifully this improvised solo on the record is relatively brief (thirty seconds). (Onstage, the solo in "Relax" would be up to ten minutes long). "Relax" is an unequivocal endorsement for hedonism, through whatever turns you on—most obviously drugs.

The simple and effective character song "Silas Stingy" is John Entwistle's strongest contribution to the album and is sung as a round between John and Roger. This brilliant approximation of a folk ballad, concerning a Dickensian reclusive miser, is catchy, melodic and amusing, and once again Pete adds an organ part [0.41] that is suitably malevolent (in the style of Boëllmann's *Suite Gothique*). Silas spends so much money protecting his fortune that he finds he's spent it all. This sorry little tale encompasses a simple moral: Don't worry about money—it isn't that important; and if you do want to hoard quantities of mammon, use a bank! (Dave Marsh's sleeve notes for the 1995 CD reissue of *Sell Out* identified George Eliot's Silas Marner as a likely progenitor of Entwistle's Mr. Stingy.)

The most unexpected track is "Sunrise," a solo acoustic work bathed in echo. This is an emotional song of wonder with complex and delicate guitar figures, a sparse arrangement, and Moon, Daltrey and Entwistle made temporarily redundant. The melody reveals a jazz influence with a touch of bossa nova. Built around pleasingly poetic lyrics, this is a pure romance with no hint of discord but more than a suggestion of abstinence. Pete Townshend takes lead vocals on a total of four songs on *Sell Out*, which might have seemed disproportionate, especially as Pete contributed prominent backing vocals to most of the remaining songs as well. In fact, despite this seeming disparity, all the vocals on the album are consistently superb.

A fitting conclusion to a fine album is "Rael (1 and 2)," the previously discussed concept work. Certainly from a lyrical and thematic point of view this is edited and compressed, but enough of the theme comes through for it to be thought-provoking and philosophical. "Rael" is a political fable that addresses the issue of overpopulation and concerns the discovery of new lands and the idealism of an explorer. The explorer is later betrayed by his crew, who don't return to pick him up (he might not want to stay). A similar theme (possibly influenced) is "Wooden Ships" by David Crosby, which was recorded in 1969 by both Jefferson Airplane and Crosby, Stills and Nash. In Townshend's song, Rael is the Holy Grail of the character's quest, the Utopia he seeks. We, like the crew, don't hear whether or not he finds his nirvana.

Musically, "Rael" begins as a joyous carnival of melody: gripping, ambitious, complex and intense. This is music full of optimism and clarity, with heavy organ lines enriching the sound. The second part of the song [commencing at 3.41] adds a dramatic and finally despairing edge as the idealistic explorer of the first section is betrayed. This instrumental passage is a fine, jagged composition of almost baroque neatness and was later featured heavily in *Tommy*. The riff here is mostly carried by the reverbed bass guitar, and it gives Keith Moon a chance to display his expansive, flamboyant yet disciplined style. The piece concludes with the ghostly words of the narrative's abandoned hero. The album then ends with the crackling, scratchy gramophone advertisement for Track Records.

The various ads and jingles are atmospheric and authentic. They range from pompous items taken from the pirate stations ("Radio London reminds you: go to the church of your choice") to tongue-in-cheek originals ("Speakeasy, drink-easy, pull-easy"—Moon and Entwistle were regular patrons of the Speakeasy Club in London). The best ads, however, are Moon's "Premier Drums" and Entwistle's "Rotosound Strings," in which they both endorse products of which they were users. Many critics of the album were disappointed that the ads and jingles weren't included through at the second side. Enough material was available, and one cannot help but think that the album would have been stronger if the concept were carried right through. No adequate explanation was ever forwarded for this inconsistency, though the issue is not so much a problem now that the revised CD version of the album does continue the concept after the end of "Rael" with a further sequence of songs and ads that were left off the original LP.

In terms of recording quality and production, *Sell Out* is superlative. The crisp, resonant sound is echoey and spacious and remarkably consistent when one considers that it was recorded in several different studios in two countries over a four-month period. Kit Lambert was often criticized for allegedly lacking technical recording knowledge, but this record entirely refutes that theory. It is an album that luxuriates beautiful sounds. Obviously some of the jingles (being in mono) lack the depth of sound and clarity of the actual songs, but the overall result is superb. In short, the LP was the Who's finest achievement to date and a landmark album of the late 1960s.

Not as famous as the Beatles' *Sgt Pepper's Lonely Hearts Club Band* or notorious as the Rolling Stones' *Their Satanic Majesties Request*, *Sell Out* is arguably the finest rock-and-roll album to hail from 1967 and stands ahead of that year's other great releases such as *Something Else* (the Kinks), *Disraeli Gears* (Cream), *Piper at the Gates of Dawn* (Pink Floyd), *Axis: Bold as Love* (Jimi Hendrix) and *Younger Than Yesterday* (the Byrds).

Implicit in the overall thematic scheme of *Sell Out*—and, indeed, sardonically echoed in the very title of the album—is a critique of the forces of commerce that had created and sustained the whole pop industry of the 1950s and 1960s. By implication, the record also forms a wider critique of capitalism and the consumer society it has created in the late twentieth century. Because the Who were functioning as satirists (as opposed to socio-economists, sociologists or political agitators), they could enjoy biting the music industry hands that fed them without having to take any responsibility for suggesting an alternative or a solution.

The irony of the title was part of the critique—they were willing to count themselves as part of the industry that they mercilessly lampooned. Musically and economically, the Who had not sold out, of course. It was because their satire came from within that their commentary was all the more valid. Many numbers of idealistic folk singers protested in song and action throughout this era at the vile corporate commercialism of the music and entertainments industry. But their worthy deeds and sincere music would be unlikely to communicate as much as does *The Who Sell Out* about what was objectionable and risible in contemporary society. The Who album does not just talk about the issue, it *shows* the listener what's wrong. The only contemporary artists who worked in a similar manner during this era were the aforementioned Bonzo Dog Doo-Dah Band (in the U.K.) and Frank Zappa and the Mothers of Invention (in the U.S.). In fact, during 1968 Zappa's group released *We're Only in It for the Money*, the title of which was a very clear echo of the sardonic sentiment implied in the title *The Who Sell Out*.

On its release, Townshend explained how originally the band had a collection of fairly strong songs but felt that "There was nothing really to differentiate it from our last LP.... It needed something to make it stand out ... then we thought 'why not do a whole side of adverts?' As things progressed we realized the whole album could be built around this aspect of commercial advertising."[33] Chris Welch of *Melody Maker* was deeply impressed, saying that the album "easily surpassed anything The Who have done before."[34] In *Beat Instrumental,* John Ford described it as "a well thought out album, full of good Pete Townshend ideas, and songs."[35] U.S. critic Don Dornan also praised the album in *Time*: "The album is The Who's imaginative antidote to the greatest danger they see in rock today: its solemnity. The album also proves that the group has genuine musical impact even when deprived of its visual flair."[36]

Although well received by the critics, *Sell Out* did not prove to be much bigger commercially than either *My Generation* or *A Quick One*. The album reached number 13 in the U.K. charts, U.S. release followed on 6 January 1968 but surprisingly failed to capitalize on the success of "I Can See for Miles" and did not reach the chart. For the first time, the stereo mix of the album was considered definitive, although a mono mix was also offered. The mono versions of "Odorono" and "Our Love Was" had completely different lead guitar parts added, and these make interesting listening today but have never appeared on CD. In fact, the mono mix of "Our Love Was" was identical to that which had been featured on the BBC radio broadcast of 16 November, although it had Townshend on lead vocals. This version of the song is easily distinguished from the stereo mix as it had no horn arrangement and the fuzz-tone guitar solo is replaced by country & western pedal steel–type guitar sound. "Mary Anne with the Shaky Hand" in mono also features a fluttered tremolo effect on the vocals at the end of final line. The U.S. version offered (for the first time) an identical song listing to the U.K. Track release, although "Medac" was retitled "Spotted Henry," suggesting that Medac might have been a registered trade name in the States.

With all the master tapes being retained in the Who's archives, Jon Astley was able to lovingly remix and remaster every track to perfection, and the CD version of *Sell Out* is superlative. This reissue also collected the two aforementioned Coke ads, a drum-based jingle for BBC Radio's *Top Gear*, and ads for John Mason Cars and Bag O'Nails (a London nightclub). Otherwise uncollected tracks were sequenced in with these adverts: "Glittering Girl" (appearing for the first time), "Someone's Coming," an excised final chorus of "Odorono," an extra section of "Rael," and two songs from 1968 (to be discussed later), "Melancholia" and " Glow Girl." Outtakes from the *Sell Out* sessions were also incorporated into the CD: "Jaguar," "Hall of the Mountain King," "Early Morning Cold Taxi," "Girl's Eyes" and an alternate version of "Mary Anne with the Shaky Hand." Two Eddie Cochran songs "Summertime Blues" and "My Way" had also been recorded at this time but remained too routine to release on *Sell Out*, lacking the manic energy that made them (especially the former) highlights of the live act. Both finally gained a release on *Odds and Sods* in 1998, the former being the same master that had been broadcast on the BBC in September.

Written by Roger Daltrey and a member of the Who's road crew named Cyrano Langston, "Early Morning Cold Taxi" is more a series of unexpected and dramatic chord changes than a strong melody, though the electric and acoustic guitar parts offer a buoyant, full-bodied sound. "Girl's Eyes" is Keith Moon's attempt at a conventional pop melody and features some fine acoustic guitar work from Townshend. However, it was too slight—both lyrically and musically—to warrant release at the time. "Jaguar," as previously mentioned, is a pounding, mostly instrumental work that generates a specific atmosphere of its time. A captivating romp through "Hall of the Mountain King" gives Grieg's memorable theme a powerful shake-up with both the guitar and bass cranked up to distortion pitch; a succession of screams in the background representing the trolls, witches and goblins suggests that the Who had more than an inkling of what Ibsen's *Peer Gynt* was about. The Who cannot take credit for the idea of a rock version of this work, however, as it had already been a minor hit in 1961 for a U.K. group called Nero and the Gladiators.

An early electric version of "Mary Anne with the Shaky Hand" (the third to be released), featuring Al Kooper on organ, is a valuable addition; it gives the song a harder, more conventional rock sound. This version does much to invite comparison with the Byrds' 1965 cover of Bob Dylan's "All I Really Want to Do," the melody line of the verses of these two songs being very similar. The short coda to "Rael" here becomes "Rael 2" (although it should correctly be "Rael 3") and is an expressive passage emotively sung by Pete to a stark organ and drum accompaniment with a haunting feel. "Melancholia" and "Glow Girl" look forward to 1968, a year in which—against all efforts and expectations—the Who failed to release an album at all.

The eclecticism of rock and the dominance of psychedelia had actually thrown rock and roll into some confusion during 1967. When the Beatles released *Sgt Pepper's Lonely Hearts Club Band* in June, it seemed that the musical values of the underground had swamped even the most commercial forces in the pop industry, yet beneath the studio trickery on the Beatles' album lay a return to a Music hall charm and innocence but precious little fidelity to the roots of rock and roll. Almost every band flirted with some superficial aspects of psychedelia and exploited the genre for the short time that it dominated the music scene. Its worst influence, perhaps, was to dilute the vital energy of the street that rock and roll had always held at its core. The Who sensed this at the time and managed to keep a clear focus for their work—as *Sell Out* admirably proved. The energy and expansiveness of their music retained a quality of its own that had matured through the year without any overt concessions being made to psychedelia at all. Ultimately, the Who provided all the ingredients required in the psychedelic age, but their music—certainly onstage—began to conform to what we would now describe as a unique form of high-energy rock and roll, an imaginative and individual music that avoided the recognition of any limitations but stayed equally faithful to the basic excitement of the form.

4

High Energy, Deep Mysticism (1968–1970)

In general, 1968 was a year in which the Who seemed to lose some momentum. They initially had difficulty producing a studio album that would surpass *Sell Out*. Although they recorded patchily through the first part of the year, no substantial work resulted, and their run of Top Ten hit singles seemed to have dried up. The band worked throughout the year at their usual pace, making a deep impact in the United States but gaining less tangible success in Britain than in the previous few years. For the first time in three years, they made no radio appearances and undertook only a bare minimum of television work in the U.K. where their concerts continued to attract the hard-core fans.

It might have seemed that the Who's run of success had begun to stall, but in retrospect they were in the process of shedding any remaining vestiges of their pop image, further cultivating an underground audience at their gigs and talking to both the underground and mainstream music press in grandiose terms about a powerful new direction for their music. It was in reality a breathing space that paid off in dividends, but at the time the group was undoubtedly at a low ebb.

The singles released in the U.K. and U.S. during the first part of the year—"Dogs" and "Call Me Lightning"—almost entirely contradicted the gravity of their new aspirations (and true inspiration), seeming to be ostensibly lightweight, throwaway pop records. Thus the musical direction of the band seemed to have become confused, and their economic situation showed little improvement. But this was also a time when the band's live act was brought up to scratch and attempts were made to translate this onto record in the way of a live album. The band members knew that if they could successfully record one of their best live performances, it would make an exciting and memorable LP (in an era when live albums were generally notorious for cashing in on revamped previous hits). However, they had difficulty capturing a definitive performance, as their act was very visually oriented and didn't translate to tape so easily. Townshend claimed that attempts had been made to record Who concerts before but the results had always been disappointing, and the taped performance without any visual counterpart always sounded chaotic and imprecise.[1]

The Who's recording projects for the early part of the year worked vaguely toward several different aims: singles, a live album, a studio album in the middle of the year, an EP of cover versions that had featured in the live act, a commission from the American Cancer Society, and finally—always a goal of Pete Townshend and Kit Lambert—a fully realized opera project. Kit Lambert had ideas of putting out an album called *Who's for Tennis* to coincide with the Wimbledon tennis tournament in July. This must have been one of his more superficial and less inspired plans, and it fortunately came to nothing. Nevertheless, a studio album by the band in 1968 might have contained some fine music, but the climate of the time was such that the Who needed to adopt a more serious approach rather than continue to trade on frivolous ideas that used the group's name as a pun.

An Australasian tour in January was followed by an extensive U.S. tour from February to April and a further trip to the States between June and August. British concerts were slotted in between these tours, and ideas were also floated for a Who television series, provisionally titled *Sound and Picture City*. The series was to culminate in an album of songs that had been played in each episode of the show, and although this was for a while taken seriously, it was ultimately rejected as being the wrong direction in which to go. The Who, despite a streak of zaniness and a penchant for elaborate jokes, were not (and could never be) a British version of the Monkees—which is most likely what the producers of *Sound and Picture City* were hoping for. When plans for an album release had failed to materialize in the middle of the year, it appeared—in Britain at least—that the Who's era had passed and that the band might break up. Economically, they were in debt, and their constant live work was essential for a basic level of subsistence. The question was whether or not they could find a workable means of keeping ahead of the new directions being taken in rock music. Pete Townshend began to talk about a big opera project midway through 1968, but this obviously didn't materialize on schedule. As Townshend had talked of such grandiose schemes many times before without their coming into being, there was little reason for anyone to think that this time his aspiration would become reality.

One of the most significant events to occur in early 1968, however, was not musical at all. Townshend had been introduced to the mystical teachings of the Indian guru Meher Baba. It was trendy for awhile for various celebrities to claim an affinity with assorted Eastern spiritual teachers, but Townshend's interest in Baba was much different from the momentary craze that swept across Western society in the wake of the Beatles' relationship with Maharishi Yogi in 1967. First, Baba was not part of the flamboyant yoga-and-meditation school of gurus who epitomized the incense-clouded era of teach-ins and communal gatherings. Second, Townshend immersed himself fully in the teachings of Baba in what was to become a lifelong devotion. Baba essentially offered, through prayer and faith, a means of self-realization and closeness to God.

This spiritual discipline had a profound influence on the work of Townshend (and, therefore, on the Who), although Pete often had difficulty reconciling his lifestyle as a rock star (and its material rewards) with his religious convictions. Baba was specifically antipathetic towards the use of drugs, which jolted Pete uneasily out of a habit (smoking dope and taking hallucinogenics) that had been consistent for at least six years. Baba didn't, however, cause Pete to abstain from alcohol or nicotine. Keith Moon, Roger Daltrey and John Entwistle—while remaining tactfully silent on the subject in public—cannot be expected to have had any degree of sympathy with Pete's preoccupation with Meher Baba. However, since Townshend's devotion to Baba ultimately enriched and inspired greater music for the band, they would have little cause to complain.

In January 1968, in both London and Los Angeles, the Who began recording work for their next single. The contenders were "Call Me Lightning" (which had been written as long ago as 1965), "Glow Girl," "Faith in Something Bigger," and John Entwistle's latest effort, "Dr. Jekyll & Mr. Hyde." The Who were also due to deliver an antismoking song to the American Cancer Society and had been approached for a commercial from Great Shakes, an American milk shake firm. Additionally, several concerts on the U.S. tour had been slated for recording for a live album. There seemed to be no burning urgency or enthusiasm for any of these project, and no obsessive inspiration to create a new masterpiece—the recordings were largely to satiate the demands of a pop industry that was a treadmill where artists were judged to be only as good as their last hit.

The most significant song of this batch was "Glow Girl" (not to be confused with the earlier "Glittering Girl"). This is rich in both melody and ideas and was to have influential repercussions, but after initial consideration as a single, it was abandoned. In this moving tale of a plane crash, a taut performance incorporates some superb examples of Entwistle's characteristic bass and suggests some of the musical themes that would become *Tommy*. A great deal happens in a short duration in "Glow Girl," and the song encompasses Townshend's patent ringing guitar chords on the intro and an uptempo verse pattern with a sure beat from Moon before a simulated plane crash effect [1.24] gives way to a more placid coda in which the victim is reborn. Townshend considered "Glow Girl" to be "particularly interesting.... I tried to write an archetypal rock single, the reincarnation song. You know, the Shangri-Las type thing, the Jan & Dean type thing, the car crashes, the motorcycle goes over the cliff."[2] This was released for the first time on *Odds and Sods* in 1974, but it would have undoubtedly made a splendid single in 1968—that is if the listening public of the time could handle an unsentimental and optimistic vision of death followed by a cheerful rebirth.

In its place, at least in the United States, the band released "Call Me Lightning" on 16 March 1968. Withheld from European release, this marketing ploy was a further recognition that the stature and reputation of the Who differed in America and Britain, although their music was the same the world over. No contemporary single release for the U.K. was planned at this stage, and "Call Me Lightning" (for a while at least) was exclusively pitched to American listeners. The band must have had strong reservations about the single, as it was undoubtedly the weakest Who release thus far. Given the vastly superior quality of "Glow Girl" (and, indeed, the B side "Dr. Jekyll & Mr. Hyde"), it is unfathomable as to why it appeared at all. We can now view the release of this single as a mistake that didn't even redeem itself in commercial terms, climbing no higher than number 40 in the charts. To long-term fans of the band, it seemed like a betrayal of all the standards that had been set in live performance and on *Sell Out*.

The song had already been rejected once, in 1965, and was in reality even less suitable for a Who release three years later. It is an uptempo surf-influenced rocker that has the listener sit through a repetitive and mediocre verse in wait for a chorus hook that never arrives. The only unpredictable moment is a bass solo [1.13] that sounds like a self-conscious reference to "My Generation." The band's musical performance is nothing better than routine, and no element in the sound engages interest. The title of the song refers to a character's reputation with women and his peers, and an enshrined sexist attitude of a man, surrounded by ego props and status symbols such as the E-type Jaguar car that we are told is "shining brightly." The lyrics form a poor, failed attempt to legitimize an offensive attitude (male domination and female subjugation) and are completely unconvincing—a formulaic song without any of the characteristic Townshend warmth and humanism. In all, the single was most undistinguished and a lapse of judgement.

A brave defense of "Call Me Lightning" was attempted by Nancy Lewis in *Disc and Music Echo*, who claimed—in an article titled "Who Bring Back Rock!"—that the single caught a prevailing mood on American radio which she described as "a great leap backwards. Roger Daltrey sings out at the top of his lungs over a banjo and bass drum backing. And the song is even complete with a nonsense chorus.... It's so uncool that it's cool ... and it wouldn't surprise me if it sells a cool million copies!"[3] Even taking this most charitable view of "Call Me Lightning" fails to make any sense of the release, and British fans must have wondered what they were missing on the strength of Lewis's overstated praise.

It was in unfortunate adherence to a Who tradition that John Entwistle's

"Dr. Jekyll & Mr. Hyde" was to play B side to "Call Me Lightning." Although not necessarily ideal as a single in itself (being a macabre tribute to Keith Moon), the suitably spooky vocals and strongly inventive melody built on a grinding bass riff made it vastly superior. The aural equivalent of a Hammer horror film, this is one of the best of Entwistle's songs, and the music and performance combine to create a perfectly chilling horror-comic Gothic mood piece. The well-established theme concerns the two different dimensions of one character (good and evil), from the famous story by Robert Louis Stevenson. Two versions of "Dr. Jekyll & Mr. Hyde" were recorded; both sound very similar. A slightly longer version, later released in the U.K. on the B side of "Magic Bus," is distinguished by different guitar phrases and a demented ghoulish cackle during the final few bars.

Townshend's introduction to Meher Baba's teachings had followed the completion of a song called "Faith in Something Bigger," which addressed the spiritual vacuum that he felt in his life. It is an attempt, therefore, at a devotional song, but it sounds rather clumsy and leaden, despite a good conventional pop performance that relies on elaborate vocal harmonies. Melodically, the song just falls short of the accepted Who standard. "Faith in Something Bigger" is the first Who song to approximate a religious (or spiritual) message, but it lacks the necessary subtlety to assimilate the theme in a subtext that would allow for a more universal identification. In the end, the title says it all, although in general the song implores mankind to develop a spiritual relationship beyond materialism. The song was rejected and only released on *Odds and Sods*, at which appearance Townshend was still obviously embarrassed at the naivety of the sentiment.

One of the more unusual occurrences of the time was that the American Cancer Society commissioned an antismoking song from the Who specifically aimed at discouraging young people from developing the habit. Townshend offered them two songs, "Little Billy" and "Do You Want Kids, Kids?", of which the former was chosen and duly recorded. That all the members of the Who were at the time heavy smokers seemed not to worry anyone, and the hypocrisy of the situation in those less politically correct days was obviously not a problem. In the event, the American Cancer Society rejected "Little Billy," probably because it failed to deliver an easily palatable and overtly didactic message that could be thrown at the masses. The band members were simply told, however, that the song was too long—though at just over two minutes in length, it must rank as one of their least prolix tracks.

As a Who record, however, "Little Billy" was perfect, a delightfully controlled narrative song with a catchy melody, superb drumming and a theme that develops with an effective and chilling logic. The electric and acoustic guitars are finely balanced in the stereo mix, and a bridge section [1.01] is beautifully understated and crucial to the plot, although the bass guitar lines meander a little too widely during some of the verses. Obviously enshrining a strong antismoking message, in which the most unlikely kid in the class outlives his peers because they smoked and he didn't, the song expounds a simple moral. However, as a character we can also see Billy as representing the integrity of the individual in the face of peer pressure to conform. This was a classic Who character sketch with a moral, and good enough for the band to play in concert and consider as a potential single (where, again, it would have far outclassed "Call Me Lightning").

From the point of view of the American Cancer Society, it may have been too complex and unspecific for their purposes, but as a statement on the harmfulness of tobacco (as much as can be conveyed in one short song) it is masterful, ranking as a companion piece to the Kinks' gloriously ambivalent summation of the smoking habit "Harry Rag" from their album *Something Else* (1967). The second song, "Do You Want Kids, Kids?" has not emerged in any form since. "Little Billy" was never used by the American Cancer Society, but they retained the rights and thus prevented the Who from releasing the song for five years, until *Odds and Sods* (1974) was put together. Townshend commented on this project a few years later, saying, "We were told we had as much time as we liked and we could write a song opposing cigarette smoking.... I always wished that they used it as a commercial, I think it would have stopped a lot of people smoking."[4]

More conventionally, around this time the band also accepted a commission for a commercial for Great Shakes Milkshakes, narrated by Keith Moon. The Who's original song is a lively but functional rocker that seems derivative of both "Summertime Blues" and "Mary Anne with the Shaky Hand" and sounds like it was taken straight from *The Who Sell Out*. Although in many ways harmless and entertaining, advertisements such as this represented the more vulgar side of the pop business (exactly the criticism offered by *Sell Out*) and thankfully the Who fairly quickly abandoned all such commissions. However, this was not before Pete Townshend had recorded a commercial urging young men to join the United States Air Force—a lapse in judgement that ran against all the ideals of the counterculture and pacifist activity that had emerged as a result of opposition to the Vietnam War. If Pete's political convictions were not being compromised by this action, it can be assumed (as Dave Marsh has pointed out) that his adherence to Baba's teachings were.

Kit Lambert flew to the United States especially to supervise the recording of what was to be the Who's first live album. Before Lambert had left London, Track Records had announced the proposed recording of the album at the Who's concert at the Fillmore West, San Francisco, on 22 February 1968, to be titled *Live at the Fillmore*. For various reasons, this show was never recorded, and the plan was postponed for a few weeks. The recording did finally take place at Fillmore East, New York, on 4 and 5 April. Over the two nights the band played "Substitute," "Pictures of Lily," "Fortune Teller," "Tattoo," "Little Billy," "I Can't Explain," "Happy Jack," "Relax," "I'm a Boy," "A Quick One While He's Away," "My Way," "Summertime Blues," "C'mon Everybody," "Shakin' All Over," "Boris the Spider," and "My Generation." Although the range and quality of this material was abundant, the tapes were finally rejected. Despite the high-energy attack of the band's live sound and the expansive soloing on "Relax," "Shakin' All Over" and "My Generation," some of the performances were technically flawed and suffered from some guitar tuning problems—the curse of any live performance recording. The Who did not consider this material good enough to release, and the live album was postponed indefinitely. "It came out pretty badly," Townshend later admitted, without expressing any imminent intention to try such a recording again.[5] The master tapes from the two Fillmore East concerts have remained in the Who archives and, despite being plundered mercilessly by bootleggers over the years, have yet to gain any official release.

Further recording sessions in May 1968 at Advision studios in London produced "Dogs," "Melancholia" and two cover versions then being featured in the live act: "Shakin' All Over" and "Fortune Teller." The failure to glean a live album from the Fillmore East tapes had prompted the band to consider an EP of cover versions, for which these latter two songs were intended. It is rumored that a version of Bo Diddley's "Road Runner" was also to be part of this project, with "Summertime Blues" or "My Way" likely making up the quartet. It was clear that Pete had not managed to come up with a substantial album's worth of material at this time, although other excellent songs that he had written that might have added to the weight, such as the insidious hard rocking "Politician" and the lyrically soulful "I Always Say," were, sadly, not attempted by the band. (One cannot, however, imagine the Who making anything of "Goin' Fishing" or "Cookin'," two other quirky songs Pete had written).

The fact is that by this time Townshend was engrossed in the idea of an album-length opera for the Who that had been tentatively titled *Amazing Journey*, after another new song. (The first direct reference to the *Amazing Journey* opera as a work-in-progress seems to have been an article by Chris Welch in *Melody Maker* on 4 May 1968—a full year before its final realization.) The band decided to take a gamble and not attempt an album release until this bigger project was completed and to issue in the meantime a couple of unrelated singles to keep the market active. The fact that another U.S. tour had been booked through July and August meant that the new work wouldn't be completed until the end of the year at the earliest. In the meantime, new songs that Townshend was writing from mid–1968 such as "She's a Sensation," "We're Not Gonna Take It" and "I'm Free" were incorporated into the project after a few title or lyric changes. Other songs, such as "Now I'm a Farmer," were projected for the new project but finally discarded.

Seven months after "I Can See for Miles," a new single finally appeared in the U.K. with the release of "Dogs" on 15 June 1968. This marked the band's lowest point in their British career, and the single made a very modest chart showing at number 25, a fact that seemed to suggest that they had lost touch with the hit-making capability that they effortlessly maintained until then since January 1965. "Call Me Lightning" was consigned to the B side—evidence of their realization that this song would be unacceptable as a U.K. single (it was barely acceptable in the U.S., anyway). It is questionable whether "Dogs" should now be considered a charmingly innocent final attempt to glorify the 1960s pop orthodoxy or an embarrassing and unmitigated disaster; the record buying public at the time tended towards the latter conclusion. In strict career terms it undoubtedly showed the band to be flagging and seemingly out of touch with the latest developments in rock. But beneath the surface, the band's outlook was as innovative and forward-thinking as any group's, as evidenced by their live shows and some of the material they did record at this time but declined to release, such as the magnificent brooding "Melancholia." "Dogs" was never really meant to represent what the Who were capable of, it just happened to be a song that Pete Townshend had written that seemed suitable material for the chart—and had it been a huge hit, the question of its release would not have been raised. BBC Radio 1 was likely to play such an inoffensive single; Pete later explained, "To an extent that was why we released 'Dogs'—because we knew [the BBC] would pass it as fit for human consumption."[6]

The main problem with "Dogs" is that it is a light, breezy, amusing song that does not sit comfortably alongside "I Can See for Miles" (which preceded it) or the *Tommy* project to come. Certainly, in 1968, it sounded a little dated—redolent maybe of 1965 or 1966—and its release seemed to be a deliberate ploy to score a hit single, utilizing a kind of lowest common denominator, sing-along pop formula. It can only really be understood in the light of the Small Faces, whose "Lazy Sunday" had reached number 2 in April. "Lazy Sunday" was a novelty distillation of Lionel Bart, music hall and Cockney "knees-up" that had somehow found an enthusiastic ear with the pop audience, and its success must have influenced the decision to release "Dogs" a few weeks later. (It may be significant that Townshend's demo of "Dogs" featured an electric piano, an instrument also very prominent on "Lazy Sunday.") The subject matter of "Dogs" was the working-class pastimes of greyhound racing, gambling and beer drinking, and they are dealt with in an affectionate—if gently mocking—manner. An element of pastiche is heightened by the overemphasized cockney lilt of Roger Daltrey's delivery.[7] (This latter factor alone may account for the nonappearance of this song in the U.S.).

Examined out of context, however, and with clear objectivity, "Dogs" can be seen as a masterpiece of 1960s pop. It has soaring melodies, interesting chord changes and irresistible hook lines throughout and one really tremendous descending melody near the end [2.28]. A snatch of spoken dialogue "in character" by Townshend and Entwistle also compared with similar touches in "Lazy Sunday." It concerns the courtship of a young couple keen on greyhound racing (and beer!) and their marriage, raising of children and old age, which brings a stale familiarity between them. The song is constructed with great skill and craftsmanship and achieves the urgency of feel that characterized much Tamla Motown music (although, of course, one cannot imagine Marvin Gaye or Diana Ross singing of the delights of the White City dog track!). It is probably the most underrated song ever released by the Who, and it stands up to repeated contemporary listening in a way that probably wasn't envisaged in 1968.

In contrast in almost every way was "Melancholia," which was recorded at Advision a week after "Dogs." This is a powerful, moody, persuasive song about depression. It features much brooding guitar work that ranges from delicate diminished arpeggios to blasting power chords, all held together with a gripping melody and a superb chorus sequence. The middle-eight is a skillful, descending guitar figure [1.25] full of despair and turmoil, and imaginative use is made of piano. The only questionable moment in the song comes toward the end when Daltrey sings a repeat of the first verse in a higher octave than previously and loses a little of his vocal command. Townshend's demo of "Melancholia" is prime psychedelia, bathed in phasing effects, and while the Who's version fails to capture quite the emotional effect of the demo, it turns an introspective song into an angry, bitter one, emphasized with the tortured guitar soloing toward the end. It is tragic that "Melancholia" was not released at this time, being a first-rate song and a worthy successor to the best of the *Sell Out* material. The only explanation of its being shelved came with Pete's belated observation that it was "totally wrong for the band at a time we had just failed to get a hit with the glorious 'I Can See for Miles.'"[8] Townshend's judgement can hardly retain credibility if we are to take his comment as implying that "Call Me Lightning" was totally right. However, the objectivity of hindsight is easy now to assert.

Also notable lyrically, "Melancholia" employs two triple rhymes in each verse as it details the pit of despair into which its protagonist has fallen. The song charts the emotional and domestic decline of a man after the defection of his woman. The lyrics are sparse and tightly evocative and describe the depression in terms of a physiological sickness, a "virus." The despair is eloquently expressed and the only ray of hope is swiftly deflected: "The sun is shining, but not for me...." The song may have been too dark in tone to endear itself to the popular mass of listeners, but nevertheless "Melancholia" could have been a powerful single—its suppression remains one of the more unfathomable occurrences in Who history. Pragmatically, we can safely assume that if a Who album had been issued at this point in 1968, then

"Melancholia" would have been included. As it was, the song was first released in 1994 on *30 Years of Maximum R&B*. However, the point should be made that the Who were occasionally extremely blasé about discarding material of very great worth, a contention that can as well be applied to "Glow Girl."

A studio version of "Fortune Teller" (first performed by Benny Spellman but more recently popularized by Elmore James and the Rolling Stones) was recorded at the same session as "Melancholia" on 29 May, having been introduced to the live act in April. This was also unreleased, though with greater reason. The Who's arrangement attempted to add some variation of pace by slowing down the first two verses of the song (more noticeable onstage), and the studio recording also added some striking piano overdubs. This is a solid—if slightly dull—performance, with smooth vocal harmonies and a very restrained guitar arrangement. The master tape (as recently released) reveals a shaky transition between the slow verse and the faster section, including an actual guitar mistake [1.07] and the drums drifting off the beat [1.20], both of which would have been corrected if "Fortune Teller" were released. In 1994, however, these human lapses were deemed less significant when the song was mixed for its premier airing on *30 Years of Maximum R&B*. (A version of Johnny Kidd and the Pirates' "Shakin' All Over" recorded on the same date has yet to gain any release.)

The coordination between Europe and America over Who single releases was still out of sync, and the U.S. was the first market to hear "Magic Bus," which Decca released on 27 July 1968, backed with the older Entwistle song "Someone's Coming." The British version was finally unleashed on 18 September, coupled with a second version of "Dr. Jekyll & Mr. Hyde." Reaching number 25 in the U.S. and number 26 in the U.K., this single did not much improve the Who's commercial standing, although the song became justly famous because of its being prominently featured in the live act. The recording date of "Magic Bus" remains a mystery. The song was at least two years old by the time of its issue and had already been released by a group called Pudding in April 1967, who had failed to make the charts with it. According to Pete it was "recorded at a time when we had just returned from our first trip to America."[9] This also suggests April 1967. It was odd that the Who should have considered reviving it, being a simple novelty song, cashing in on the fact that red London double-decker buses had been a dominant part of Swinging London imagery a couple of years earlier.

The performance is all with "Magic Bus": based on a throbbing, percussive wood-block beat and a one-note bass line repeating a shuffling Bo Diddley–inspired rhythm, it becomes repetitive and insidious. Townshend provides fat, heavy acoustic strums with his customary dexterity, and the repeated response vocal ("too much, the magic bus") becomes catchy and melodic. It is a nonsense song about the sale of a bus, but it works well because of its odd sound texture, all murky and dark. Pete even manages *acoustic* power chords [1.39] in a sequence of vocal and guitar-chord exchanges similar to those on "Pictures of Lily." Electric guitar [2.02] is finally introduced and drums before fading out on a fittingly explosive climax—"She goes like thunder..." Townshend explained, "We all got absolutely paralytic drunk one lunch time and by the time we arrived at the studio no one cared what we did. 'Magic Bus' was just a lot of fun.... We were just all enjoying ourselves."[10]

The mono sound of "Magic Bus" is very compressed, and the backing vocals are rather overloaded, giving a tense, claustrophobic atmosphere. Jess Roden can be heard as a backing singer, adding a somewhat manic voice in a high pitch, and shrieking "Ah no..." as the song fades away. A second version of the song emerged on *Meaty Beaty Big & Bouncy* in 1971, and this was over a minute longer but not significantly different in any other respect. However, this single was merely the starting point for what became a hypnotic boogie "vehicle" on the stage, often stretching out in excess of 10 minutes. It was the loosest number in the Who canon—flexible in length, adaptable in arrangement and capable of maintaining an infinite degree of improvisation—and the fans loved it.

While working on the *Tommy* project toward the end of the year, the Who made one television appearance that has since been released. This was for the Rolling Stones' *Rock and Roll Circus* project, an all-star special that was ultimately scrapped and not fully screened until 1996. At InterTel Studios in London on 11 December 1968, the Who contributed a version of "A Quick One While He's Away." Two takes were recorded of the band playing live in the TV studio, and one was incorporated into *The Kids Are Alright* (film and soundtrack album), while some bits of the alternate take were used on the *30 Years of Maximum R&B* boxed set. This is a very good clear mono recording and sounds both exuberant and fresh, with the band's high-energy live sound going at full tilt. It was more compact than the 1966 album version, although some of the earlier passages are rough: Townshend's guitar is slightly out of tune and an error can be heard [0.49]. However, the final "You Are Forgiven" section is marvelously raucous, an explosion of energy and vitality that redeems some of the ungainliness of the suite.

As 1968 was drawing to a close, both Decca and Track had become frustrated at the lack of a new Who album, and both plundered the back catalog to produce hastily assembled greatest hits packages. Americans were treated to *Magic Bus—The Who on Tour* (released in September 1968) while Britain was offered *Direct Hits* (12 October 1968). Neither album was a definitive compilation, both lacking the Brunswick material. The Decca album had some rationale, as it offered "Disguises" and "Bucket T" for the first time in the States, but the remaining tracks were all readily available on single or album. The quality of the mastering and the sleeve was very poor, however, and the band members were disgusted with it. Unfortunately, utilizing the ambiguous subtitle *The Who on Tour*, it superficially resembled the live album that had been talked about earlier in the year and looked like the Who were trying to deceive the fans. *Direct Hits* was equally exploitative and likewise lacked the first three hits, although it managed to gather all the A sides of the other Who singles apart from "Magic Bus." Townshend and Daltrey agreed that the cover of this effort was even worse than *Magic Bus*'s. Neither album sold well, and both represented an anathema to the idealism of the underground.

The work-in-progress to which many interviews with the band of mid–1968 had referred was initially called (in May) *The Amazing Journey*. By September it had become *Deaf, Dumb and Blind Boy*, and as late as February 1969 this was given by *Melody Maker* as the album title. In March 1969, it had been amended to *Tommy, 1914–1984*, and finally plain *Tommy* in May 1969. Along the way it had also been called *The Brain Opera* and *Journey into Space*. Recording had actually commenced (mostly at IBC Studios) in October 1968, and plans to have the record out by Christmas were abandoned as work continued without an end in sight. Townshend's ideas had developed over the preceding few months, and he hoped to be able to go one step further than previous attempts at concept albums.

During 1968, the rock scene in general had witnessed the release of the first fruits of the post–*Sgt. Pepper* breakthrough. These were albums like the famous Beatles work that collected songs of a related nature and formed a song cycle, with tracks linked or designed to be played in a specific order. The lyrics of these sequences of song had related themes, and some involved characters. The most notable albums of this kind were *The Village Green Preservation Society* (the Kinks), *S. F. Sorrow* (the Pretty Things), and *Ogden's Nut Gone Flake* (the Small Faces). These albums had a common theme of some kind running through them, but they didn't always involve any sustained plot or character interaction. Keith West (singer of the British psychedelic group Tomorrow) had also worked on one titled *Teenage Opera* in 1967, from which two singles, "Excerpt from a Teenage Opera" and "Sam," had been taken. These were delightful but very superficial character vignettes of no real musical weight, and the full opera was never released. In the States, the ever exploratory Frank Zappa was similarly attempting to redefine the album format by introducing fictitious characters and scenarios across a wider canvas. Townshend intended the Who's work to be a complete, extended concept, carried by a continuous succession of short rock-and-roll songs (the "acts"), all based on or relating to the perceptions and experiences of one central character.

During the American tour in mid–August 1968, Townshend had explained in detail to Jann Wenner of *Rolling Stone* magazine his ideas and intentions for the new work. This interview revealed that the theme of *Tommy* was fully developed with much of the material prepared well in advance of the commencement of recording. The song lyrics had been sketched out, but Pete wanted the plot to evolve in the music as well as in the words. He told Wenner of the lyrics he had completed thus far, "great poetry, but so much depends on the music.... The lyrics are going to be okay, but every pitfall of what we are trying to say lies in the music, lies in the way we play the music, the way we interpret, the way things are going during the opera."[11]

Behind all the theorizing about the rock opera (Townshend was wary of using the term *rock opera* but he eventually succumbed in absence of any other appropriate description) lay a spiritual fidelity to Meher Baba's concept of devotional love. Townshend felt that he had been spiritually awakened by Baba, much in the same way that he envisaged his character (Tommy Walker) being suddenly liberated from years of sensory darkness. But Baba's work was difficult to reflect in song without sounding trite or condescending, so Townshend was careful to not proselytize his faith and merely reflected certain aspects of spiritual elation that were central to his work. In fact, Townshend was against any kind of proselytism in rock music, be it for political, religious or philosophical ends.

The concept of *Tommy*, then, had been fully considered by Pete, and the story line—which was functional and contrived—was paced to develop certain preconceived ideas. As the conception of the work coincided with Townshend's first immersion into the teachings of Meher Baba, he used a philosophical framework as a background to the themes developed in the songs. The Baba influence was not as integral to the record as some have claimed, and Baba's teachings are more clearly identifiable in later Who work.

The story of Tommy was basically a parable of a twentieth-century Christ figure. The work wasn't an opera at all, and the tag is misleading, but it was a sufficiently unusual name to grab the attention of the general public. A strong influence on the writing and structure of the work was Kit Lambert (who had a vast knowledge of classical opera), although Townshend simply wrote individual rock songs as only he knew how. He didn't attempt to create recitative operatic music or intend *Tommy* to function as conventional opera, he said, "The ingredients of the songs aren't there to put across a mood, or a feeling of an age, or a feeling of society—they're meant to tell a direct story in a literary manner."[12] The emphasis on plot led to the composition of a number of purely narrative link items, which were the only real structural deviations from the accepted length of the rock-and-roll song, some being only a few seconds in length.

"Amazing Journey" had been the germination song from which *Tommy* had sprung. The pattern that the songs were to fit was established only after laborious recording, rerecording and restructuring. Once the conception was clear, Townshend restructured some existing songs to fit into the new pattern; some merely needed slight changes to the lyrics. Although the work wasn't originally envisaged as a double album, the expansion to a two-record set finally gave the necessary breadth of canvas for the final work to take its true shape. Two of the more unsavory characters to be introduced to the story were Uncle Ernie and Cousin Kevin, and Townshend felt unable to do justice to such unpleasant people, so John Entwistle took on the task of supplying two suitably grisly key songs.

Pete Townshend's demo recordings for *Tommy* had a lighter, less solemn feel and a more prominent use of the organ than the treatment they was ultimately given by the Who. The group realization was built on chord progressions of acoustic guitar with embellishments of electric guitar and occasional organ. (The organ was a voguish sound element in rock music during 1967 to 1970, and much of the work of groups such as Procol Harum, the Band, the Crazy World of Arthur Brown, the Doors, Julie Driscoll, Brian Auger and the Trinity, and the Nice was notable for its electric organ sound—not to mention Al Kooper's work with Bob Dylan. However, it was a sound that was to date quickly, as the synthesizer took over its role in the early 1970s). On the final version of *Tommy*, the organ was used sparingly, which gave the sound of the album a more universal appeal.

Using many of the sounds successfully established on *Sell Out*, the recordings were based on guitar, bass and drums with three-part vocal arrangements. The acoustic guitar was Townshend's essential tool on *Tommy*, and it is this instrument that gives the work much of its distinctive flavor. Occasionally, electric guitar was added with piano and organ, and also John Entwistle added his customary horn and brass parts. The acoustic guitar sound was outstanding, energetic and vibrant, and *Tommy* arguably remains the best deployment of acoustic guitar in rock and roll.[13] Acoustic guitar was the central instrument upon which *Tommy* was developed, and it remained crucial to the structure of the sound, even in the final mixes. The drumming from Keith Moon was typically imaginative, sounding deep and spacious, and the bass guitar (although a little muted) was agile and expressive. No attempt was made to reproduce the live sound of the band (although "Young Man Blues" and "Dogs Part Two," an unrelated instrumental, both recorded at the same sessions, came close). Owing to the need for different character voices, Townshend and Entwistle sang more lead vocal parts than they had done before.

The introduction of "Pinball Wizard" late in the recording cycle—the most dynamic, catchy, exciting and concise song from *Tommy*—gave an unexpected turn to the plot by introducing a pinball champion (an idea influenced by writer and Who fan Nik Cohn). Up to this point the work had encapsulated two main themes: sensory deprivation of an individual and the access this can give to an infinite inner world of the spirit, and the status of gurus, holy leaders and messiahs in modern society. The theme was a strange one for an anarchic high-energy rock-and-roll band to expound, and it was as ambitious as anything any other rock act had attempted. It was mystical, sordid, obscure and melodramatic by turns, but it was thought-provoking and turned out (in the spiritual vacuum of the post–hippy era) to be eminently commercial. The concept was further disseminated by an elaborate sleeve design and accompanying booklet that contained the libretto and illustrations by leading underground artist and Baba–loving friend of Pete's, Mike McInnerney.

When all the basic tracks had been completed, much debate occurred between the members of the band and Kit Lambert about the final presentation of the work. It had been proposed to orchestrate some of the songs with overdubbed string arrangements, and a final running order had to be decided. The plot as developed in the song lyrics was not so rigidly sequential or chronologically detailed that it could not be changed around somewhat. However, the double-album format gave more scope for the programming and enabled the band to clearly visualize the final form of the work. (Double studio albums were not so common in the mid–1960s, but Bob Dylan's double album *Blonde on Blonde* and the Mothers of Invention's double album *Freak Out* had in 1966 prompted a trend that had seen the release in 1968 and 1969 of double albums *The Beatles* (White Album), Jimi Hendrix's *Electric Ladyland*, Cream's *Wheels of Fire*, Chicago's *Chicago Transit Authority* and Frank Zappa's *Uncle Meat*. This was a format that was to prove most suitable for the Who's expansive ideas, although the double album was certainly a lavish mode of presentation that was available only to the rock-and-roll elite.) Kit Lambert saw from an early stage a potential feature film in *Tommy*, and he produced a script based on Townshend's notes and the song lyrics. This script in turn apparently enabled the band to decide upon a final sequence to the plot, and McInnerney's illustrations reflected various aspects of the plot development.

Even with the extra running time provided by two disks (roughly 80 minutes), some of the material had to be excluded. Three jazz/blues standards had been considered: Mercy Dee's "One Room Country Shack" and Mose Allison's "Young Man Blues" and "Eyesight to the Blind" (although this latter song was originally by Sonny Boy Williamson, Townshend knew the song better in its version by Allison.) It seems Pete felt some strong affinity with Allison's 1957 album *Back Country Suite*, which was a jazz song cycle and from which "Young Man Blues" originated. What is surprising is that these nonoriginal songs were considered to fit into the plot without any of their original lyrics being changed. "The Hawker" was the title given by the Who to their arrangement of "Eyesight to the Blind." The recording of "One Room Country Shack" was abandoned and has since remained unheard. Four further songs were excluded from the final work: Entwistle's "Cousin Kevin Model Child," a short and catchy but routine rocker on which Keith Moon sings lead vocals in character (finally released on *Odds and Sods* in 1998); the short, purely expository "Success" and "Beat Up"; and "Girl from Lincoln

County," about which no information can be gleaned.¹⁴ "Cousin Kevin Model Child" was to have formed the introduction of the Kevin character in which he is seen as a goody-goody whom his parents can trust to look after Tommy and who at this stage shows no hint of the sadism that is to follow. Maybe the Who felt this contrast (between what Kevin was like with his parents and when they were away) was too difficult to project and would present an unnecessary complication.

Various sound effects were considered and (largely) rejected. These were to include battle sounds following "Overture" and pinball sounds during one of several tracks that had been provisionally titled "Dream Sequence." These were linking pieces of music that interspersed the narrative. Townshend's notes revealed that they were intended to reflect Tommy's states of mind regarding pinball, the erotic, school and the lost chord. The musical content of "Dream Sequences" was largely that used in "Sparks" and "Underture," which in turn were first used in "Rael." In fact, some early editions of *Tommy* that were issued to the press gave the titles of "Sparks" and "Underture" as "Dream Sequence" and "Dream Sequence (Underture)" respectively. In the end, commercial deadlines prompted the album to be assembled in a state that the Who considered in some ways unfinished. However, the notion of the intended orchestral overdubs is highly dubious, and if strings had been added, the basic rock-and-roll purity of *Tommy* would have been compromised.

Released two months in advance of the *Tommy* LP on 7 March 1969 was "Pinball Wizard," which, music aside, did much to confuse the expectations of the Who's audience. As an excerpt from an "opera," it was bizarre to say the least—a profoundly disabled boy becoming a champion pinball player was as odd a subject matter for a song as could be imagined. The fact that Tommy (although his name isn't mentioned in the song) was "deaf, dumb and blind" caused some concern among a minority of would-be moralists (particularly Tony Blackburn on BBC Radio 1) who considered the use of such a character to be sensationalistic and in very bad taste. The band was at pains to point out that the single didn't give a full enough picture of Tommy's character and that premature judgements would ultimately prove to be inaccurate. Townshend, anxious that his motives in utilizing a disabled character weren't misunderstood, sent a press release to various influential people in London requesting that they reserve judgment until the full album was released.

Without a doubt, "Pinball Wizard" was the finest Who single since "I Can See for Miles" and a work of unfaltering inspiration and originality. Built upon highly unusual descending suspended chord patterns, dextrously strummed with razor-edged precision on an acoustic guitar, the interplay between the rhythm and lead guitar is superb. The dramatic and urgent introduction of the electric riff, which reverberates with a jolt [0.24] against the two-chord strumming, is a towering and spine-chilling musical effect, comparable to the opening phrases of Richard Strauss's *Also Sprach Zarathustra* (1896), which had been prominently featured in one of Townshend's favorite films of the era, *2001: A Space Odyssey*. Rock and roll rarely provides such moments of sheer and overwhelming *musical* power. "Pinball Wizard" is a startlingly effective combination of melody and guitar dynamics, and the electric guitar chord sequence (B–A–D–E) that concludes each verse achieves a deeply resonant, crisply distorted tone, with the bottom E-major chord [0.50] really throwing a sonic punch that seems to hit the listener's solar plexus. John Entwistle plays a bouncing bass line that makes a contribution of its own without diminishing the guitar lines, and Roger Daltrey sings with great clarity and power. Overall, the acoustic guitar work—building from a quiet but forceful progression of chord figures—remains arguably the greatest use of its kind ever recorded in rock history.

Since its release in 1969, the song has become a standard of sorts and has been subject of many cover versions, orchestral treatments and misinterpretations, all of which have worked to insinuate the melody of this song into the parts of our consciousness labeled the *over-familiar*.[15] For this reason the mystery and power of the song may no longer be as apparent as they once were. Remember that on its first release "Pinball Wizard" showed the Who working at such a strong creative pitch that 99 percent of their contemporaries were left foundering in their wake. All the elements of the song were conventional enough in themselves, but the combination of these elements was startling and shifted rock and roll (or at least the rock and roll of the Who) onto a kind of celestial plane that proved that after one bad year the Who were back with a vengeance. The single reached number 4 in the U.K. charts but was only a modest hit in the States (number 19). The single's function was primarily to turn listeners onto *Tommy*. "It is a work of pure genius," wrote Penny Valentine. "It also shows that The Who, brilliant bunch that they are, improve all the time...."[16]

On the B side of the single—and with the kind of extreme contrast that characterized the Who—was "Dogs Part Two," an instrumental based on the phenomenal drumming of Keith Moon. This has no connection with the previous "Dogs" single other than that it included the barking of two dogs, Towser (Townshend's spaniel) and Jason (Entwistle's wolfhound). The dogs almost upstage the Who in a frantic, spaced-out, heavy metal thrash that updated the 1960s instrumental genre and bore some resemblance to "The Ox" from 1965. While Daltrey might have been concerned about his place being taken by two enthusiastic dogs, the three instrumentalists in the band let rip here with great verve and abandon, each taking turns to play a solo in a spontaneously agreeable and irreverent performance. "Dogs Part Two" is an unusual throwaway track that just happens to be wildly entertaining.

4. High Energy, Deep Mysticism (1968–1970)

When the double album *Tommy* was released on 23 May 1969 (and one week later in the States), it looked and sounded every bit as epic as Townshend had been promising during the preceding year. It was sufficiently large (in concept, duration and ideas) to fulfill all expectations, and it was an immediate success with the listening public. However, the very length and nature of the work meant that some of the material was not as consistent as it might have been, with a moderate quantity of functional makeweight items—several undeveloped short links that attempt to give continuity to the plot. The theme of the work shifts between the mystical and the fantastical (with an odd touch of melodrama), and viewed in synopsis the plot is almost tenuous and often ludicrous. However, the spiritual overtones, although obscure, in combination with the rock-and-roll essence of the sound render *Tommy* persuasive enough to justify the whole conceit of the rock opera idea. Certainly, at the time it marked a dramatic and exciting development in the Who's music and was the first example of the band's full maturity. (Remember, this was only the Who's fourth album. If we consider the music offered on the respective fourth albums of the Beatles, the Kinks, Bob Dylan, and the Rolling Stones, then it becomes clear just how much the Who had advanced in a short time).

It opens with the grand, ominous yet understated chords of "Overture." This piece is a dramatic contraction of riffs, themes and melodies from the main body of the work (notably "We're Not Gonna Take It," "Go to the Mirror," "See Me, Feel Me," and "Pinball Wizard") and was (for a rock record) an innovative step. John Entwistle's horn work on this track is particularly good, Moon's drumming, remarkably versatile; and the differing themes are neatly integrated (including several shifts of key), adding to the anticipation and cohesion of the whole record. The first entry of the organ [2.20] is arresting, and the drumming throughout is particularly expressive and skillful. "Overture" was probably the most ambitious work the band had attempted at the time. After several of the (musical) themes have been established, the music moves into a stark passage of Pete Townshend alone on the acoustic guitar and vocals, introducing the context of the story with "Captain Walker didn't come home...." The guitar moves to the center of the stereo picture for an imaginative and completely spontaneous solo [4.28] that rates as one of the most exciting and accomplished Townshend guitar performances on record. Despite its complexity, the music of "Overture" flows with a simplicity and strength: it is never overblown or cluttered by overarrangement. Signaled by a memorable three-note French horn phrase, the short "It's a Boy" refrain is sung by Pete in an almost impossibly high key.

The next song, "1921," is perhaps a little too strained, although it features some gentle melodies and expressive passages that convey the key incident in Tommy's life, the traumatic experience (witnessing his mother's lover being murdered by his father) that plunges him into an autistic state of sensory deprivation. The singing is fine, especially Pete's painfully emotive solo verses. "Amazing Journey" is the first major song on the record, unusual in structure and sound and forming a powerful introduction to Tommy's inner world. To enhance the chord progression, backwards tapes (which are beautifully restrained) are added to achieve a wispy mystical quality. The entry here of the drums [0.44] is extraordinary, and Roger Daltrey employs a very effective softer voice, which is double-tracked. The musical journey into Tommy's unconscious starts with a linking riff (incorporating a seamless edit [1.02] into a different take) that shifts the music into "Sparks," the potent and urgent instrumental developed from "Rael 2." The connection of the two tracks represents a shift of perspective from the objective narrative of "Amazing Journey" and into Tommy's subjectivity with "Sparks."

The band's bombastic run-through of "Eyesight to the Blind" (also named "The Hawker" after the character invented to deliver the lines) is a more puzzling choice because it is a blues standard. It seems that the references in the lyrics to a woman who can cure deafness and blindness gave rise to the creation of the gypsy featured in "Acid Queen," a kind of sequel. In fact, this song is intended to presage the later introduction of the Acid Queen, whose virtues are extolled here by the Hawker. An unconventional guitar solo brightens up what is otherwise a mundane track, interesting mostly for the bass/drum riff that crashes in over the guitar rhythm. Two different versions of "Eyesight to the Blind" have emerged on various pressings of *Tommy* since 1969. These are distinguishable only through Daltrey's vocals, one performance of which is in a higher octave than the other.

"Christmas" is a more conventional rock-and-roll song and is perhaps a little too forceful a performance for what is a somewhat laborious melody. However, the vivid and stark "Tommy, can you hear me?" passage [1.53] sets Pete's urgent voice against a thunderous drum roll, and Daltrey's "See me, feel me" section is quite beautiful. The first of John Entwistle's contributions is the morbid and sadistic "Cousin Kevin," which deceptively begins with a mock innocence that quickly turns into sheer malevolence and rampant sadism as each verse chillingly catalogs Tommy's fate. It is an effective and powerful composition, in a style only John Entwistle could approximate. The three-part vocals by John render with great conviction and relish the essence of Kevin the bully, a study in terror no less. "Cousin Kevin" is all the more effective for not being overstated or hysterical. "Acid Queen" is a distinctive and fully matured song in which Pete's vocals give a fine sense of urgency, suggesting that a sexual as well as drug initiation is being offered by the character. The arrangement is modest, but the electric piano phrases give it a sultry feel, and the overall effect is stark and strong.

The longest piece on the record is "Underture," an elongated version of "Sparks," which takes the guitar motifs of that instrumental to their furthest extent, with the addition of some wordless vocals. Although it could be argued that this is unnecessarily repetitive after "Sparks," it is difficult to tire of such a spellbinding piece of music. It features some fine guitar work, and some echoey arpeggios [6.38] usher in a different mood of mystery and wonder, culminating in a moody chord sequence [7.12]. A second riff theme emerges [8.01] with a forceful acoustic guitar part, and the ten-minute track brings the second side of the record to a close.

The third side of the original album commences with "Do You Think It's Alright?" which begins a varied but powerful sequence of songs. The very short "Do You Think It's Alright?" is actually brimming with melody, and the vocal harmonies are finely wrought. It leads into the sinister and sordid "Fiddle About," an introduction to the evil child molester, Uncle Ernie. This song is a masterpiece, and Entwistle's jolly vocal delivery makes it all the more disturbing, with a gruesome melody underpinned by a tuba riff along with the guitar and bass. There is no excess or dwelling upon the act of sexual abuse in "Fiddle About," and John has managed to pitch just the right degree of variation and lurid detail for the song to stand firm in its place. "Pinball Wizard" follows and as mentioned previously is a classic, definitive, individual composition of major proportions, standing as the one undisputed masterpiece on *Tommy*. The next link is the short, slight, jaunty piano and vocal filler "There's a Doctor," which seems rather full of Gilbert and Sullivan bombast.

As driving hard rock songs are in the minority on *Tommy*, "Go to the Mirror" adds a welcome shot of Who rock-and-roll orthodoxy and is one of the strongest songs on the set. However, even here the fast beat is punctuated by the delicate "see me, feel me" phrases until the central dramatic passage [2.04] where the line "Go to the mirror, boy!" is sung against a forceful guitar-and-drum phrase to back up the command. The moment where the verse breaks into the "listening to you..." section is exciting and moving. "Tommy Can You Hear Me?" is possibly the most resistible song on the collection, although despite its lack of substance it has some appealing guitar strumming and perfect harmony vocals. The bluesy "Smash the Mirror" is understated and kept deliberately concise, yet it has an unusual feel and some agreeably loose guitar figures from Townshend. It remains undeveloped musically (less than two minutes) and functions merely to head the critical part of the plot where Tommy smashes the mirror and becomes free of his affliction.

"Sensation" is a different kind of music, and deliberately so, reflecting Tommy's new freedom. It is a pure Townshend pop song of the 1960s, with a sweeping melody, rippling piano and horn fills and a catchy chorus. The song creates a carefree, joyous atmosphere with its trouble-free pace and clarity. "Miracle Cure" is another short narrative link presaging "Sally Simpson," which is the weakest song offered. This sounds uninspired and out of place with the remainder of the material; the lumpen melody sits uneasily alongside the more inspired tracks. This lapse into the banal is thankfully rescued by the brilliantly inventive "I'm Free," which combines an exciting riff, a lilting chorus and a brilliant acoustic guitar solo [1.20]. Other noteworthy detail in the song is the fine, three-note piano phrase [0.43] and the terse integration of guitar and piano alternating on and off the beat, and a reprise of the "Pinball Wizard" chord pattern [2.05] takes the song to its conclusion. "I'm Free" is one of the major songs on *Tommy* and has endured as a rock classic on its own considerable merits. "Welcome" begins with a gentle nursery rhyme melody and develops into an interesting if ungainly experiment at a radical song structure, with contrasting sections and a fast passage [1.37] that is led by some jazzy piano lines, reminiscent of the Dave Brubeck Quartet's "Take Five" (1961), and a harmonica blast. "Welcome" is almost a miniopera in itself, unorthodox and perhaps not entirely successful, and concludes with some random piano notes and the phrase "Welcome." The breezy "Tommy's Holiday Camp" is a seaside barrel organ music hall ditty sung for comic effect by Pete accompanied also by banjo. It is a shard of light relief (credited to Keith Moon) in a work that becomes increasingly solemn after "I'm Free."

The finale is suitably strong, with the two numbers linked under one title, "We're Not Gonna Take It." It has been since acknowledged that the second part of this is called "See Me, Feel Me." "We're Not Gonna Take It" is another fully developed song rich in melody and insistent of delivery, with good vocal harmonies, a solid structure and inspired chord changes. However, it is overshadowed by the delicate "See Me, Feel Me" passage and the concluding "Listening to you" chorus, a brilliantly written and performed song where the band's vocal harmonies—using all the skills developed on "I Can See for Miles"—produce a spine-chilling and haunting theme that is so uniquely fashioned that one cannot imagine it being realized by any act other than the Who. Thrilling and moving, this is a wonderfully evocative ending to a story, a universal prayer to greater things beyond.

Kit Lambert's production has been often criticized, although the sound scheme of *Tommy* is warm, clear and entirely appropriate for the story. Lambert was pleased with his work and came to realize that his role as a producer had reached its zenith. The band members eventually came to the same realization, and Lambert never again acted as a producer on Who records. *Tommy* compounded a trend in progressive music that resulted in many other acts' attempting to use the same format. A host of overblown concept albums followed in the 1970s, but nothing directly inspired by *Tommy* can match it for ideas, musical power or intelligence (except, of course, for *Quadrophenia*). On a more sensory level, however, one can simply appreciate the actual sound of the record and the deep, resounding guitars and drums and the innocent, optimistic singing. The record was remixed and remastered onto one CD in 1996 by Jon Astley, and the original sound enhanced and improved and previously submerged elements brought to the fore, such as the lead electric guitar lines on "Christmas" and the organ on "We're Not Gonna Take It." (As with *Sell Out*, Astley was able to access original 8-track masters). The enduring success of *Tommy* was not as an opera or a concept work, but purely as a rock-and-roll sound.

Despite the surface modesty in the playing and in the musical arrangements, *Tommy* was pitched high, but because of the unshakeable confidence of the band (and Townshend in particular) that permeated the whole project, the album avoided all charges of being overblown and trite. It had a calmness, holding a direct simplicity and a clear intellectual cohesiveness that very few comparable works in rock had achieved. "The general theme of the album," Pete Townshend said, "is a direct result of me getting involved with Baba, getting involved in a powerful spiritual move forward. I think [*Tommy*] is more powerful because of that very reason, because the project has got a very high ideal to it."[17] But ultimately it triumphed because it pushed rock and roll to the limit of what the form could do and still remained, in its pure essence, rock and roll.

In *Tommy* the concept never engulfed the songs; the production never put dramatic development above precision fidelity in the sound; the lyrics never lapsed into an indulgent, self-conscious simulation of artiness or poetry. The Who just presented their songs (some spectacular, others less so) with forthright vigor. *Tommy* wasn't supposed to be high art, real opera, a musical or a new breakthrough in rock form. It was simply a work that evoked a response in the consciousness of the rock audience of the time—its mystical flavor of spiritual yearning, the uniqueness of its themes and the originality of its characters gave it an appeal quite unlike any other work in rock music.

The plot of *Tommy* was never explicitly published by Pete Townshend or given on the album sleeve or accompanying lyric booklet, although concert programs used in the U.K. in early 1970 carried a detailed synopsis of the "story." Kit Lambert might well have written this text, and it certainly includes detail and elucidation that is not apparent from the song lyrics. The artwork and graphics of the album sleeve reflected only abstract themes, and Michael McInnerney's color illustrations had more than a touch of Magritte–inspired surrealism about them, not to mention a suggestion of the eye-puzzling graphics of Escher—they avoided specifics in favor of a heavy symbolism, as was appropriate. The sober three-panel blue sleeve illustration for *Tommy*, it should be noted, is a fine example of postpsychedelic artwork that complements the music rather than distracts.

The following synopsis of the plot is based upon the text given in the concert program.[18] Mrs. Walker gives birth to Tommy during the First World War after receiving word that her husband is missing in action ("It's a Boy"). She later takes a lover, and when Captain Walker unexpectedly returns after the war, he murders the man—a scene witnessed by young Tommy. "Tommy's mother beats and brainwashes the child.... She succeeds in shutting down all of Tommy's senses of speech, hearing and sight completely" ("1921"). Plunged into an autistic world, Tommy can now rely only on his sense of touch and the power of his imagination ("Amazing Journey"). He develops a fantastic inner world of vibration ("Sparks"). A traveling quack called the Hawker claims that his gypsy wife can cure Tommy with magical powers ("Eyesight to the Blind"), but in the meantime Tommy drives his parents to despair and frustration with his disabilities ("Christmas"). Out of neglect, his parents leave Tommy with Cousin Kevin, a vicious bully. In the meantime the Hawker's gypsy wife administers her "medicine," which is LSD ("Acid Queen"). Tommy's "trip" is portrayed musically ("Undertures"). Left with Uncle Ernie, Tommy is sexually assaulted ("Fiddle About").

As Tommy grows older, two factors become apparent: first, that he can feel vibrations to the extent that he can become a pinball champion ("Pinball Wizard"); and second, that he is aware of some degree of communication when looking at his reflection in the mirror ("Go to the Mirror"). A conventional doctor or psychologist fails to effect a cure. When his mother smashes the mirror in frustration, Tommy's inner block is broken ("Smash the Mirror"), and his senses return. "Tommy realises the enormous powers he now has and becomes aware of his destiny as a great popular religious leader" ("Sensation"). He starts an evangelical religious movement ("Sally Simpson"), which establishes a holiday camp where followers can worship ("Welcome"). However, the followers eventually rebel against Tommy's order and the camp is destroyed ("We're Not Gonna Take It"). The work concludes ("See Me, Feel Me") with "Tommy's continuing statement of wonder at that which encompasses him."

In many ways, *Tommy* was as radical in its lyrical themes as it was in its musical form. Within the whole work was a mixture of narrative and reflective songs, which varied between an objective and a subjective view of the events in the plot. The point of view shifts between various characters and alternates between the inner thoughts of Tommy, an objective narration, and the external reported speech and "thinking aloud" in song of the characters around him. The plot is a fable beginning in the first year of the First World War and stretching into the future (the early subtitle of Tommy's birth and death "1914–1984" seems accurate) and concerns the issues that confront individuals in modern society. The specific circumstances that trigger the action are entirely contrived to give a context for the expression of ideas. No attempt is made, therefore, at realism or even an adherence to convention—the ending, for example, is untidy, and we do not learn of Tommy's fate, or whether he lives or dies.

Although heavily influenced by Meher Baba, the themes of *Tommy* do not directly reflect Baba's philosophy, although the inner breakthrough experienced by Tommy is comparable to feelings gained by one coming to Baba for the first time. Throughout the work, it is emphasized that the spiritual world is much more tangible, life-enhancing and important than the organic world, so Tommy's sensory deprivation is a disability only in terms of the physical world, which superficially pities him ("Christmas"), abuses him mentally and physically ("Cousin Kevin") and exploits him both sexually ("Fiddle About") and commercially ("Pinball Wizard"). Within this context, Tommy can feel vibrations (the root of musical sounds), and he finally gains an insight into a spirituality that is denied so-called normal, able-bodied people. Pete later emphasized that Tommy's journey is "symbolic of what we all go through between birth and death, that we mistake what we're seeing and feeling for reality when in a way it's not; reality is what we end up with, reality is what we cause, reality is what we kind of build up."[19] Where Baba's teachings can be most clearly identified in *Tommy* are simply in the assertion of the importance and immortality of the metaphysical over and above the biological reality of existence.

The obvious parallel for Tommy in terms of the story line is that of Christ (and other prophets) and also the phony religious leaders who have exploited the masses to gain power or wealth, although Tommy doesn't set out with this intention. Although the lyrics to the work are printed in a booklet included with the LP (and CD), indicating which character is speaking which lines, the plot is not entirely clear throughout. This is of little consequence, as the action of the plot has no bearing on the integrity of the work. This latter factor is significant in explaining the overwhelming success of *Tommy* onstage, where some songs were omitted and it was not possible to differentiate character voices. The emotional force of the work was carried in the music and lyrics, and not in any elements of plot. It is clear that during the writing of the songs, Townshend had in mind all the philosophical themes he wanted to explore *before* the story line was firmly established, so the plot is disjointed, illogical and often exists purely to allow specific ideas to be developed.

So listeners who come to *Tommy* expecting a strong plot would be either baffled or disappointed. Townshend was at pains to point out, correctly, that if one were to look at the narrative structure of grand classical opera then one would discover equal weaknesses of plot. Even the band members themselves were doubtful and sometimes ambiguous in their accounts of what was supposed to be happening. Although one can presume that Pete had tabs on everything throughout, he wasn't necessarily able to explain it with sufficient clarity to those around him. John Entwistle recalled, "When we were recording the damn thing, nobody knew what it was all about or how the hell it was going to end.... I had absolutely no idea what the story was, who the characters were or what they did."[20]

A dominant motif in the work is the mirror that forms a strong subtext of the Narcissus complex, although Tommy's attraction to the mirror is not for the purpose of self-love, but self-realization and also what Townshend termed *God-realisation*. While the unconscious development of the character takes the form of mental journeys, very little justification is given for his only outward achievement at playing pinball, and the connection between a heightened spiritual awareness and pinball is extremely tenuous. It can be argued that the introduction of pinball into the work (about which Townshend himself had reservations) trivializes the nature of Tommy's plight and takes the plot of the whole work one step further into the realms of incredulity.

For Pete, *Tommy* was never envisaged as a means of expressing a personal credo, and he fully accepted that personal interpretation by the listener was inevitable: "It works on so many different levels," he explained, "and with something this big you just can't control it…. What really should happen is for me to entertain, and illustrate something which is going to make their lives more pleasant."[21] The element of originality of form and the luridness of some of the content ensured that *Tommy* would become controversial and inspire fervent loyalties and adverse criticisms in equal part. *Tommy* is a work that—if nothing else—prompts a strong response, if not always the one for which Pete might have hoped. But as *Tommy* sold in huge quantities, the record-buying public had made an affirmation that ultimately overcame any divergent interpretation.

Although in some cases written outside of the larger concept, the songs generally don't stand up as self-contained lyrics in terms of meaning; they lack the constrained pungency of argument of, say, "Substitute" or "Tattoo." They function as separate works adequately as pop lyrics (that is, not having to have any significant meaning beyond a few hook lines), but the concept as a whole is constructed from the many different angles, opinions, perspectives and characters that surround the plot. Many of the lyrics flow with an appealing poetic simplicity, and Tommy's repeated inner plea, "See me, feel me, touch me, heal me," is also memorably vivid in its simplicity. John Entwistle's songs, "Cousin Kevin" and "Fiddle About," are sung by the characters in the first person and provide a luminous contrast by describing their actions with such a gleeful directness. Although the amorality of Cousin Kevin and Uncle Ernie is abundantly clear, and despite some dramatic exaggeration, the characters are recognizably human and represent all-too-familiar persons from real life.

Tommy's spiritual insight is unspecific and obscure, and necessarily so, as the world of the metaphysical has no specific laws or principles. Meditation, prayer, drugs, reading, learning, physiological sensation or any tangible or defined route does not alone achieve the spiritual empathy that enables Tommy to encompass a larger psychological world. What happens to him is an entirely personal process, and although presented as a genuine spiritual odyssey for Tommy, it is not readily communicable to others. Tommy urges his followers to take the path he has traveled, but they cannot and so grow discontented, despite the fact that some of Tommy's state of enhancement rubs off on those around him. The breakthrough that Tommy gains is a direct result of his disability, and the idea of recreating a simulated disability in others for the same gain—in "We're Not Gonna Take It"—is shown to be substantially flawed.

The basis of *Tommy*'s originality (aside of its length and format) lies in its concern with the duality of perception—seeing the world differently from both the inside and the outside, the objective and subjective, the conscious and unconscious, first person and third person. This gives an uneven perspective of the whole, but it does ensure a depth of vision that enhances the events in terms of presenting a complete picture, so Tommy's plight becomes a more complex and multifaceted matter. It's worth a comparison with *Arthur* by the Kinks, a concept album released a few months after *Tommy*. In *Arthur*, one detached observer sings all the songs as an objective narrator, and subsequently Arthur as a character never comes alive and remains merely a vehicle for the observations of that narrator. (It should be mentioned, however, that *Arthur* is probably the only concept album comparable to *Tommy* that didn't disgrace the extended format or take pretentiousness to extreme and unpalatable limits).

Like much artistic creation, the meaning of *Tommy* comes down to individual interpretation based on one's response to the work as it stands, and Townshend's intentions—however often they have been stated—should not be considered as the key to understanding. Bear in mind the premise of the intentional fallacy school of literary criticism, which disassociates the work entirely from its creator and his or her conscious pronouncements upon it, if only because Townshend's ideas about *Tommy* have constantly changed through the years. Christians, Freudians, Baba-lovers, psychoanalysts, Jungians, psychologists and sociologists can read *Tommy* in a different though equally valid way. As the years passed, *Tommy* itself changed, and later adaptations for the cinema and musical theater each placed differing emphases on the action and consequently consciously altered the meaning of the work. It is always more rewarding, however, to return to the original Who format and be reminded of its strengths and weaknesses at the source.

In terms of adhering to a strict rock-and-roll idealism, *Tommy* is in many ways a betrayal. It is pretentious in its aspirations but has a powerful simplicity in its meaning and a direct punchiness in its sound that saves it from bathos and renders it seemingly immortal. But, as the Who would readily admit, *Tommy* is no great rock-and-roll album (it has too few classic tracks for that), and its meaning doesn't attempt to change the world as directly as was attempted with "My Generation." Its significance is that it represented the break from one narrow subculture (the pop world) into the wider creative field of art within society, and therefore helped legitimize rock and roll as an artistic form. Many would argue that this was an unnecessary and retrograde step, especially in the light of some of the art-rock and concept albums of the 1970s, which enhanced all of the pretentiousness and inherent banality of the form without the innocent vitality. In the case of *Tommy*, this criticism applied to the *work* but not to the Who themselves, as each time they stepped onstage they did as much as anyone to return rock back to its rebellious, primeval, cacophonous, violent, disrespectful and untamed roots.

Tommy was the Who's first million-selling album, reaching number 2 in the U.K. and number 4 in the U.S., where it stayed in the charts for a year. Initial critical opinion was split. It was dismissed in some quarters as sick and flawed, most notably by Richard Green in his *New Musical Express* article "Who's Sick Opera." Green said of the album, "A disappointment ... pretentious is too strong a word; maybe over-ambitious is the right term, but sick certainly does apply."[22] The majority of critics, however, considered it to be a masterpiece, first among whom was Chris Welch of *Melody Maker*, who answered Green a week later with a rave review billed "An Extremely Tasteful Opera."[23] In *Disc and Music Echo*, the reviewer said of *Tommy*, "A masterpiece ... the Who, as a magnificent group, project the story brilliantly in music."[24] *It* was ecstatic: "It is impossible to praise this album too highly," wrote Miles, a leading British underground figure. He went on to say, "The Who ... have pulled together the threads of Rock & Roll, progressive pop, social comment and present philosophical developments till they have crystallised into this one project—a massive undertaking.... The Who are ahead of everyone!"[25] Lavish praise was also given by Albert Goldman in the *New York Times*, who was among a handful of critics who felt the work was a breakthrough for opera as well as for rock and roll.[26]

It is often said that the release of *Tommy* changed the Who overnight into superstars (especially in America) and earned them vast quantities of money, setting them up for a long-term career. This is ostensibly true. At the start of 1969 the Who thought *Tommy* would be moderately successful but not quite as huge as it turned out to be. Their tour of the U.S. in May and June of 1969 took them to the same venues at which they had played during the preceding two years, and although anticipation for the new LP was high, the band didn't take its success for granted. The album was promoted at every opportunity, and Townshend in particular was keen to be interviewed as often as possible in the U.S. amid fears that Decca would promote the record badly.

It was onstage, however, that *Tommy* had the greatest impact. The Who's concerts were already very good, but *Tommy* transformed the act into a legendary event. Who concerts doubled in duration and brought consistent unanimous acclaim that surpassed every other act in rock. The stage show had become more focused and carefully paced, and the Who's playing was tighter, more disciplined and charged with excitement. The band members were now fully respected as serious artists, considered the most mature, intelligent and thought-provoking of all the British rock acts of the time. Through 1969 and 1970 *Tommy* achieved something that the Beatles and Bob Dylan had only tentatively broached: it had managed to spearhead a breakthrough from the derided and trivialized camp of popular culture into the higher arts mainstream in both Europe and America. *Tommy* was listened to by people who would never otherwise have heard a pop record; it was presented by the Who in concert halls and opera houses that would previously have embraced nothing more recent than Wagner; it was written about by critics and musicologists who hitherto would have considered modern jazz to be the farthest trajectory of the musical avant-garde.

A new generation of progressive rock bands were emerging in Britain at the time who employed very eclectic musical styles, often directly eschewing traditional rock-and-roll roots in favor of a jazz- or folk-based approach that had developed into an obsession with instrumental virtuosity and form at the expense of melody and the disciplines of song. The main exponents of this form were King Crimson, Pink Floyd, Van Der Graaf Generator, Genesis and Yes, and even more straightforward hard rock acts (Led Zeppelin, Family, Jethro Tull) tended in the same direction. What all these performers had in common was the rejection of the pop single as their *raison d'être* and an almost exclusive emphasis on the LP and concert format. These groups sought to attract a new, mature rock audience who took the music seriously and who were influenced (to a greater or lesser degree) by the counterculture and hippie movement of the late 1960s. *Tommy* and the Who were at the forefront of this movement by default. The Who didn't adopt a more technical mode of playing, yet *Tommy* was able to surpass any of the conceits of the welter of progressive concept albums. Nor were the Who a heavy metal band, but they could easily rival at that level the energy and power of Led Zeppelin or Black Sabbath in terms of sonic muscle. The Who produced a unique and precious kind of music that displayed the highest level of integrity and dynamism. *Tommy* was considered to be art, yet at the same time the band never lost touch with the roots of rock and the basic emotive power that it could harness.

This latter point was significant in relation to the band's next step on record. While much of the remainder of 1969 and 1970 were taken up with European and American tours and a projected feature film version of *Tommy*, the band members felt the time was right to finally nail down their concert act and issue a live album. Recordings commenced on the U.S. tour of October and November 1969, but prior to this a Who concert had been filmed and recorded at the Woodstock festival on 17 August. Woodstock had been a mediocre experience for the band, although their performance was reasonably good. A shortened version of their *Tommy* set was captured on tape, and several tracks have since emerged as soundtrack material. The documentary film *Woodstock* was accompanied by a soundtrack album (released in August 1970) that included a decent version of "See Me, Feel Me" (under its generic title, "We're Not Gonna Take It"). Further Woodstock tracks were incorporated into *The Kids Are Alright* (film and soundtrack) in 1979: a repeat of "See Me, Feel Me," a lively and frenetic "Sparks" and a slightly ragged but nonetheless electric reading of "Pinball Wizard." (MCA had hoped to issue a twenty-fifth anniversary CD of the Who's complete Woodstock set in 1994, but Townshend blocked the release.)

Prior to Woodstock, Track had released in July 1969 a compilation album, *The House That Track Built*, which included the Who's version of Mose Allison's "Young Man Blues," which had been recorded for and then omitted from *Tommy*. Allison's cool jazz sounds had been transformed into an angry and powerful free-form rock-and-roll workout, and this recording was laden with echo and sounds a little tentative in comparison with how the band played it onstage. The lyrics offered a succinct and subtle variation on the philosophy of "My Generation," which is the main reason the band were so attracted to it. *The House That Track Built* (released in the U.K. only) was quickly deleted, and this studio version of "Young Man Blues" has been unavailable for many years and is not available on CD. However, a very similar alternate take of the song recorded at the same sessions was included on the 1998 CD *Odds and Sods*. The original *House That Track Built* version is the faster of the two, with a double-tracked Daltrey vocal. This has a breezier feel than the more brooding alternate version, which is slower, earthier and in a lower key. Also, a live recording of "Young Man Blues" was made at a concert at the Coliseum in London on 14 December 1969 and issued on *The Kids Are Alright* LP in 1979. This agreeably noisy mono recording bathes the song in plenty of dissipated energy but lacks some of band's precision and drive. The long solo tends to meander to little purpose, despite some lyrical flourishes from Pete [1.35], and generally this is overshadowed in both performance and recording quality by the later *Live at Leeds* version.

It is clear that during this period a rift had developed between Kit Lambert and the members of the Who, and his close relationship with Pete Townshend in particular was beginning to deteriorate. So when the band returned to the recording studio in January 1970, Lambert was not present. Recording sessions at IBC Studios produced "The Seeker," which became the band's next single, released on 21 March (although Decca had issued "I'm Free" in the U.S. in July 1969, reaching number 37). This was not quite up to the standard of the celebrated *Tommy* hit "Pinball Wizard," reaching only number 19 in the U.K. and number 44 in the States. "The Seeker" is a serviceable hard rock song that reflected Pete Townshend's increasing mystical concerns. It is an unpretentious, unspectacular, back-to-basics record that served to confirm that the band was no longer to pander to the pop singles market, "The Seeker" was the first Who single without any overt commercial potential. Musically, it is a solid, heavy-chord workout—stripped-down hard rock with a compactness that harks back to "Pictures of Lily."

4. High Energy, Deep Mysticism (1968–1970)   129

The lyrics provide a thoughtful analysis of the spiritual restlessness of modern man and woman, all enhanced by Roger Daltrey's penetrating delivery—frustrated, unsettled and increasingly desperate. Not only does "The Seeker" ask suitably searching questions, but it is a song *about* the asking of questions. It reflects Townshend's perennial spiritual quest and voices a rejection of the values of the pop world (Beatles, Dylan) and some aspects of the counterculture (Timothy Leary). The only fulfillment, it is implied, is death—the one certainty of life. Townshend's character encapsulates the frustration and aggression of his earlier "My Generation" voice but now accepts a lack of fulfillment as being endemic of life itself, and not just a result of social or political conditions.

The song also features a very quirky ragtime guitar solo [1.43] above a backing track that has real drive and pace—the electric guitar being a prime example of Townshend's distinctive rhythmic chord work. The production, presumably by Pete Townshend, is a trifle dull for such a strong, uncompromising song. "The Seeker" was featured in a radical remix for the *30 Years* boxed set in 1994 and remains an underrated Who single. Roger Daltrey's second (and last) solo composition, "Here for More," forms the country & western–influenced B side. This is a pleasant though routine song and is barely suitable as Who material, with just one redeeming moment in an arresting slide guitar solo [1.09].

The Who recorded two concerts, at Leeds University (14 February 1970) and Hull City Hall (15 February 1970), on the 8-track Pye mobile unit after an accumulation of tapes from the U.S. and U.K. tours in late 1969 was deemed too laborious to sift through. Leeds was judged the better show, and Townshend mixed the tapes with the intention of producing a double album. However, the resulting *Live at Leeds* was a single LP, with the material pared down to just six titles. Released on 23 May 1970, *Live at Leeds* is one of the most difficult Who records to adequately describe, being an intensely aural experience. It is a record purely dedicated to presenting sound in its most undiluted sense, and it communicates meaning in exclusively visceral terms, without any concessions to pop accessibility. Its purpose is to preserve the live Who sound with absolute authenticity, which it admirably achieves.

The record is loud, brash, vibrant, thunderous, raw and immensely exciting—rock and roll in its purest form. In short, it captures almost all the best qualities of a Who performance (allowing for some sensory loss in not being there and witnessing the event in person) and sounds like an all-out assault on the senses with a white-hot level of energy; it's rock music with sweat dripping from its brow and blood pumping through its veins. It is a truism in the rock world that live albums tend to promise more than they can deliver; memories of concerts often exceed the reality of hearing the music on cold vinyl months afterwards. But *Live at Leeds* delivers the goods in better shape than could be expected. "It turned out to be one of the best and most enjoyable gigs we've ever done," said Townshend, although he had reservations about the recording quality.[27]

The Who's only electric blues interpretation is the aforementioned "Young Man Blues," which opens the album in fine form, with the unaccompanied vocal line getting a response from the driving riff before all the instruments break off into a simultaneous and spontaneous free-form workout [1.31] that forms a breathtaking jam free of any indulgences. No one part of the band dominates here, and this stands as firm evidence of the Who's sixth sense, the musical telepathy between the members that transcends notions of rehearsal and arrangement. The guitar, drums and bass each seem to thrash out at random but amazingly manage to lock together with a harmonious empathy that encapsulates the special ensemble magic of the Who on stage. Many bands were reworking blues material like this at the time, but very few achieved such an inspired and vital result. The Who didn't overwork this theme either: "Young Man Blues" was the only interpretation of this kind that they offered.

In contrast, "Substitute" is short and sharp (in an arrangement that omits the latter third of the original single), sounding up to date and fresh. Daltrey gleefully amends the lyric ("I look *bloody* young"), and the sheer power of Entwistle's bass lines are very evident on the intro [0.06], where he almost overpowers the guitar. "Summertime Blues" is a complete reconstruction of Eddie Cochran's classic expression of teenage discontent, here rendered in terms of absolute sonic power, with Townshend's block power chords and Entwistle's chugging bass lines building the song's stature beyond the thinner rockabilly framework of the original. An upward change of key [2.19] lifts the excitement to an even higher pitch. The humor of the lyric and the anger of the delivery are compounded by John's deep-voiced parody of the authority figure ("I'd like to help you, son, but you're too young to vote"). This is a pure celebration of an early era of rock brought joyously up to date with an overdose of electricity and adrenalin.

Signaled by the famous descending guitar figure, "Shakin' All Over" gets a similar treatment until breaking off into a frantic solo and morass of power chords and improvised variations. The harmony vocals of the title line are slowed down from Johnny Kidd's original, but Townshend renders that classic guitar figure with vivid fidelity. Perhaps "Shakin' All Over" stretches out a little too long for its own best interests and is the one song on the album that could have benefited from some discreet trimming. (The album had already been improved by the excision of "Spoonful", where Daltrey's voice had drifted too far off key.)

The second side of the album presents the end of the Who's concert set in its best and most adventurous form, highlighted by the "My Generation" medley, which offers the nearest the album comes to new material. It begins with a powerful run-through of "My Generation," moves into a couple of verses of "See Me, Feel Me," and then presents a sequence of improvisations connected with delicate passages of solo guitar. The first section [4.01] (on which Daltrey sings "So Very Long") later formed part of "Naked Eye," and is followed by a three-chord riff [6.59] over which Daltrey intones, "baba baba." "Coming out to get you" is one of the best of these impromptu themes [8.43]: a blistering, driving riff (good enough to have formed a complete song for a less ambitious heavy rock band!) that displays a mastery of the high-energy musical approach. A frantic reading of "Sparks" from *Tommy* follows, and the medley is closed with a purely instrumental theme [12.57], featuring a tight riff pattern and a prolonged ear-rending feedback climax. The medley functions to present a composite history of the Who and remains compelling despite being almost fifteen minutes long.

By the closing "Magic Bus," the pace slackens somewhat, and Daltrey and Townshend's vocals indulge in some playful banter before the song erupts into an explosive climax with Daltrey playing harmonica. Even at the end of this, Townshend cannot resist plowing straight into yet another improvised riff [6.26] that just churns out of his guitar, firmly backed up by the bass and drums after two bars. As with most of the songs here, the final bars are rendered grandiose and overblown. The Who often stretched out the endings to songs in a dramatic manner, and while this worked onstage as an accompaniment to jumps and theatrical movements, it could be wearisome on record where the visuals were missing. It is palatable here as an appropriately hysterical climax to the album, an orgy of decibels, drums and distortion.

The radicalism of *Live at Leeds* as a Who record is in its overall sound scheme, which was vastly different to the Who's studio work and in marked contrast to *Tommy*. It reaffirmed the fact that the Who hadn't grown out of their rebellious and uncompromising early stance and were more immersed in the germinal roots of their music than would ever have been thought judging from their recent studio recordings. Although the band had presented the rough, distorted and explosive sound on stage for several years, this was the first time that sound had been captured on record in a sustained manner. *Live at Leeds* can, therefore, be given unqualified consideration as the extreme example of high-energy rock and roll. It would possibly be accurate in some ways to classify this music as heavy metal or heavy rock if definitions must be applied, but this is undesirable for fear of diminishing the record's value through association with a genre that has rarely managed to rise above a turgid level of conformity and limited musical scope.

Central to the sheer sensuality of the sound of the Who's live recording is the extreme range of tone offered by Townshend's guitar. Without the aid of gimmicks, effect pedals or studio trickery, the guitar work—delivered exclusively through the right-hand stereo channel—is breathtaking. As with many of the Who's strengths, it is the subversion of orthodoxy that gives

Townshend's playing its essential genius, a fact sometimes misunderstood by those "guitar connoisseurs" who seek to dismiss Townshend's playing because it doesn't sound like Jeff Beck's, Alvin Lee's or Eric Clapton's. Townshend's primary musical vocabulary of the fuzzed power chord is supplemented by lyrical solo playing, feedback, gentle echoey arpeggios, Morse-code variations via the pick-up selector switch and clean, rhythmic strumming—often all within the scope of a single song—through the simple manipulation of the guitar volume control. The saturated distortion level from Pete's Hi-Watt amplifiers is phenomenal: it provides the real "dirt" sound that all heavy guitarists require but offers a refinement that allows for rich harmonics within that sound.

Live at Leeds is the Who's blueprint of the primal vitality of rock-and-roll music in its purest and most unadulterated form. It belongs to a tradition exemplified by acts starting with groups contemporaneous with the album's first release such as the Stooges (led by Iggy Pop) and the MC5, a tradition that has been rediscovered by successive generations via punk rock in the late 1970s and a great many forms of music in the 1980s and 1990s (Sonic Youth, Nirvana, Manic Street Preachers, Spin Doctors, Jesus and Mary Chain, hardcore acts and garage revivalists). The grunge movement of the early 1990s was only the latest tag to be attached to this long-running and self-perpetuating spirit of rock and roll. Some observers have fixed *Live at Leeds* as a seminal work within a distinct heavy metal tradition, as if the album is comparable with Black Sabbath, Grand Funk Railroad, Uriah Heep, Led Zeppelin or Deep Purple. This connection is tenuous and superficial and is best disregarded. In many ways, *Live at Leeds* is the first evidence of the Who as they really were (and everything that *Tommy* was not) unrestrained by convention, undiminished by studio technology and untrammeled by producers and accepted ideas of good taste, pop, musicianship and style. This release saw the Who communicating by means of sheer musical volume and electricity—an instinctive gesture of their true selves.

A preview was gained by Nik Cohn, who in the *New York Times* could hardly contain his excitement, saying, "[It is] the definitive hard-rock holocaust. It is the best live rock album ever made."[28] The album followed *Tommy* up the charts, reaching number 3 in the U.K. and number 4 in the U.S., and the critics praised it uniformly. Richard Green, capitulating his condemnation of *Tommy*, wrote in *New Musical Express* of it, "brilliant album.... It stands up as a perfect example of just what makes The Who as big as they are ... a beautiful album that is going to be an absolute monster without a doubt."[29] *Melody Maker*'s Chris Welch concluded, "the band play brilliantly and the recording sound is excellent with their special echo PA system.... It's exciting, violent, musical, and alive. And what's more, by golly it does you good!"[30] In the new underground paper *Friends*, Charles Radcliffe and Charles Weatherley noted, "the recording is excellent, crisp, clean, and clear, even capturing that explosive backdrop of feedback harmonics, static and splutter which hangs about The Who's sound like an aura ... a classic, an unmissable treat."[31] *Live at Leeds* is "the best thing The Who have done," wrote Graham Charnock in *Oz*, who went on to say, "'My Generation' is the best battle hymn for the revolution (for this kind of revolution, anyway) that I've ever heard."[32] Even the stark functionalism of the minimalist brown-paper packaging of *Live at Leeds* was much admired, containing a selection of Who memorabilia that gave a random scattering of the band's history and reminded fans of their more modest beginnings.

In exhuming the original Leeds master tape in 1993, Jon Astley was able to reconstruct a longer version for CD by including a devastatingly forceful "Heaven and Hell" that incorporates a fevered guitar solo; short, faithful and enthusiastic versions of "I Can't Explain," "Happy Jack," and "I'm a Boy"; a fine version of "Fortune Teller" that merges into an affectionate reading of "Tattoo"; and a hard, dynamic performance of "A Quick One While He's Away." A few excerpts of a full performance of *Tommy* that was played at the show have been released. A fine version of "See Me, Feel Me" appeared in *30 Years of Maximum R&B;* a brilliantly performed "Amazing Journey" and "Sparks" formed one of the highlights of the remixed CD (released in 1995) and; finally, "Pinball Wizard" gained a belated airing on the B side of a 1996 reissue of "My Generation" (in the U.K. only). This latter performance is delivered at a less frantic pace than usual (clocking in at 12 seconds longer than the version from Woodstock) but is clear and well executed. Only a slight detuning of the guitar, noticeable on the chord [0.52] could be called a flaw. Who fans have expressed considerable desire for the release of a the full live performance of *Tommy* from this show, but thus far Pete Townshend has declined to give his approval.

Prior to the release of *Live at Leeds*, the band had recorded a studio session for the BBC, in a return to radio work after a two-year lull. Recorded at IBC Studios on 13 April 1970, the songs were aired on the Dave Lee Travis show of 19 April. Recordings of "Shakin' All Over" (incorporating "Spoonful"), "Heaven and Hell" and an acoustic version of the most recent single, "The Seeker" alongside fine reworkings of "Pinball Wizard," "I'm Free," and "Substitute." Although this formed a fascinating broadcast, it did not include new material. "Heaven and Hell" had been recorded here for the first time, but the song was already a stage favorite of over a year's standing. Still working in mono, the BBC tapes sound a little compressed and shallow for the era, but their appearance was a welcome bonus for the fans. (This was the band's final session for the BBC for which material was exclusively recorded. Further sessions that were broadcast in 1970 and 1971 featured remixed versions of their regular record releases and so are of no specific interest from this point onwards).

A studio album was scheduled for mid–1970 release as a kind of interim measure. Pete wanted to embark upon another opera project but had yet to hit upon a worthwhile theme. The songs that the band were to gather for this album did not really form a strong enough whole to release. The album was to be recorded quickly (and cheaply) at Pete's Eel Pie Sound Studios at his home in Twickenham, England, where the pressures and constraints of a commercial studio could be avoided. It was originally believed that Pete's studio (at this point being upgraded from 8-track to 16-track) would be good enough, and recording work took place here intermittently between March and May of 1970. The band left for a highly successful U.S. tour in June and July (grossing over one million dollars), and at these shows they promised that their new album would be completed in August and September. However, on returning home, they didn't resume the recording.

The mixed bag of new songs that were intended for this album had considerable points of interest but taken together lacked a clear focus and sense of direction. They ranged from the reflective "I Don't Even Know Myself"; the comical "Now I'm a Farmer," a *Tommy* reject from 1968; the dynamic and philosophical "Naked Eye," which had become a memorable live number; an interesting but unmelodic power chord workout called "Water"; the jaunty "Postcard," a lightweight Entwistle song; "There's a Fortune in Those Hills," a slow country-blues effort; and "Heaven and Hell" (Entwistle's all-out rocker that was a long-standing live favorite). In reality, the failure to release these tracks (and to record others) was probably because the band were waiting for Pete to come up with some better material. Pete admitted to suffering a writer's block during this time and simply waiting for it to pass. While artistic temperaments could accommodate such blocks, the hardheaded commerce of the record industry was less sympathetic. The Who needed to release a new record.

Individually, however, the members of the band were more prolific. In late 1970 John Entwistle set about recording a solo album, a collection of his songs that the Who had found little space for on their records. Released in May 1971 and titled *Smash Your Head Against the Wall*, this is a well-crafted hard rock album with a few outstanding songs. Pete Townshend was more reticent about launching a solo career, however; and he limited his work to the soundtracks of two short art films, Richard Stanley's *The Lone Ranger* (1968) and Dick Fontaine's *Double Pisces* (1970), and to limited-edition albums for devotees of Meher Baba. The first of these albums emerged in February 1970, titled *Happy Birthday*. This included Townshend's songs "Day of Silence," "The Love Man," the demo of "The Seeker," a collaboration of "Mary Jane" and "Content" and a touching version of Cole Porter's "Begin the Beguine." This is attractive, plaintive music, unpretentious and benign, showed a folksy and acoustic Pete Townshend very different from the guitar-smashing noise anarchist.

Who records still emerged, however. On single, "Summertime Blues" was plucked from *Live at Leeds* to find only a moderate response in the charts: number 38 in the U.K. and number 27 in the U.S. It was a performance too raw at the edges to become a big hit, although the song had come to mean a great deal to the band. The single (released on 10 July) was significant because it offered on the B side John Entwistle's "Heaven and Hell," a tame studio version of the hard rock song that for the past year had been the tremendous opening salvo of the Who live set. In fact, this version sounds so tentative and halfhearted that it could be taken for a demo or rehearsal, and it was the same take that had already been aired on the BBC on 25 May. One of the main criticisms of the studio version of "Heaven and Hell" is that it is in mono, forcing the dual acoustic and electric guitars to mingle in the center of a muddy sound picture, despite some gusto in the playing. It is a song that lacks a strong melody but which succeeds through an accumulation of unusual chord changes and fluid bass variations. It also features a conventional guitar solo—rare for a Who studio recording—that concludes with a characteristic open G chord thrash [2.40] from Townshend. The definitive "Heaven and Hell" was the version recorded at Leeds, and fans had to wait twenty-five years for that to emerge.

Toward the end of 1970 Track Records thought that in lieu of an album four of the recently recorded songs would form an acceptable EP. Indeed, on several occasions up to February 1971, Track announced the imminent release of this EP (which was to comprise of "I Don't Even Know Myself," "Water," "Postcard" and "Naked Eye") and each time postponed it. Both the record companies had been waiting for new studio material for nearly two years (apart from the aforementioned "The Seeker") and had shown some degree of impatience by continuing to release *Tommy* material. A group called the Assembled Multitude had actually gained a U.S. hit with a version of "Overture," prompting MCA in August to release "See Me, Feel Me," backed with "Overture," which reached number 12 in the singles charts. In Britain, Track followed suit with a *Tommy* EP. As Who fans would already have the *Tommy* LP, all these releases were an opportunistic cashing in and of marginal significance. It may have been, however, that Lambert had wanted to keep *Tommy* on the boil pending completion of his abortive film project.

Regarding the EP of new material, no firm explanation has emerged as to why it wasn't released. The band have claimed that Track Records (or their distributors, Polydor) didn't like the extended play format and blocked its release, but as Track *did* release the aforesaid *Tommy* EP, this sounds unconvincing. The real problem may have been with Decca in the U.S., where the record industry had always been antipathetic to the EP format. More likely, as Townshend later admitted, the technical quality of the masters from Eel Pie was not good enough. Roger Daltrey claimed the songs were too long to fit on an EP and couldn't easily be edited, which may also have been true.

It is arguable whether this EP would have been worthwhile anyway. The material to be included was somewhat uneven, and the actual recordings lack depth and dynamism. The band knew that "Water" and "Naked Eye" were much stronger onstage. All four songs are interesting, especially "Naked Eye," but none would have upheld the standards of *Tommy* or *Live at Leeds*. Apart from Entwistle's "Postcard," all were long, meandering and somewhat underproduced and flat sounding. They did, however, show some progression from *Tommy*, being more mature compositions, and all possessed strong lyrics. Their main function, however, was to add some new material to the stage act, replacing older songs such as "Fortune Teller" and "Tattoo." "Water," "Naked Eye" and "I Don't Even Know Myself" (which will be discussed in greater detail in later chapters) were carried forward into 1971 to play their part in Pete Townshend's next big project, which was finally called *Lifehouse*.

The most significant trend of the band's 1970 studio recordings is the influence of country music. "Here for More," "I Don't Even Know Myself," "Now I'm a Farmer" and the unreleased "There's a Fortune in Those Hills" all bore in the delivery and stylistic aspects of the playing touches of country & western. This influence (which also saw a more fulfilling expression in the later songs "Time Is Passing" and "Going Mobile") was indicative of a general move to country and folk influences that permeated the rock scene in general. Bob Dylan and the Byrds had embraced the country & western style in 1968, and through 1969 many rising artists such as James Taylor; Crosby, Stills, Nash and Young, the Flying Burrito Brothers and others had helped define a style that became known as country rock.

One final artifact that has since emerged from 1970 is a lovingly restored complete recording of the Who's entire set from the Isle of Wight Festival, 29 August 1970. This was originally recorded as a soundtrack to a documentary film of the whole event, but the film did not materialize until 1995, and a video of the band's set (incomplete) followed in June 1996. The double CD set *Live at the Isle of Wight Festival 1970* was released in October 1996 and for the first time presented an entire Who concert on one release and a belated complete performance of *Tommy* (minus "Cousin Kevin", "Underture," "Sally Simpson" and "Welcome," which weren't performed). This set forms a counterpart to *Live at Leeds*, and despite the near proximity of recording dates and considerable overlap of material, the two sets sound markedly different. Playing before 600,000 fans in the open air in the early hours of a Sunday morning, the Who performed a long set which cannot be expected to have sustained the tight dynamics of the Leeds show. The recording quality is less fulsome than *Leeds* and tends toward a dullness, but Jon Astley and Andy Macpherson prepared a dazzling digital remaster that delivers the Who's performance in all its ragged glory.

Live at the Isle of Wight Festival 1970, then, is a faithful reproduction of a less than perfect but typically forthright Who set. It has a roughness about it that is appealing, but it doesn't attempt to disguise the flaws: the guitar sometimes isn't as loud or as distorted as it should be, and the backing vocals can be a little wayward. It lacks the sharp concentration of sound that was captured at Leeds, and the performances tend to be loose and prolix, as evident in the track durations: "Water," 8.46; "Young Man Blues," 5.28; "I Don't Even Know Myself," 5.03; and "Naked Eye," 6.33. When mixing this material, Jon Astley had obviously overcome any urge to trim and tighten, and mistakes are apparent: lines' being missing from "Substitute," the untogetherness of "Do You Think It's Alright?," Moon's wayward beat during parts of "Pinball Wizard" and the bass's being in the wrong key at the start of "Overture." There are also great moments: the ear-rending torrent of sustained feedback from Townshend during "Young Man Blues" [3.30], the sheer power of "Naked Eye," the improvisatory link between "Amazing Journey" and "Sparks," and the controlled chaos of the latter. Sandwiched into a medley with "Shakin' All Over" is the band's only officially released version of Howlin' Wolf's "Spoonful," followed by a knockabout performance of "Twist and Shout" with John Entwistle on lead vocal. The two CDs taken as a whole give exactly the right effect of the Who leviathan in full flow, like an unstoppable runaway train—it takes in the jokes, the feedback, the unsanitized noises, the ramshackle but frantic *Tommy*, and the reckless improvisations toward the end. It also features some exquisite guitar work from Pete. The release of this set is welcome and elucidating, although it fails to quite provide the volcanic heat of *Live at Leeds*.

Much of 1970 was spent touring with the devastating *Tommy* concert act, and the public reaction to the band was overwhelming. The Who had now joined the higher echelon of the world's rock-and-roll hierarchy, and they enjoyed the devoted support of millions of loyal fans and the lavish praise of the critics. By the end of 1970 they had become much more stable financially and felt some of the pressure to work was easing off. The Who were now the kind of band that did not need to release three singles aimed at the chart in each year. They did not need to appear on television. In a much improved climate, Pete Townshend could now take his time and plan the Who's next project without the worry of the band falling from popular favor. *Tommy, Live at Leeds* and the many concerts that they had played during 1969 and 1970 had earned the band a permanent niche, a status that was sustained through periods of inactivity. Internal problems still abounded, however, and certainly the band's ideas regarding their future direction significantly diverged from those of Kit Lambert. Lambert wanted to film *Tommy*: he undertook protracted negotiations with Universal Pictures and had written a script. Ultimately, Pete Townshend blocked this move. The Who were now satiated with *Tommy* and Townshend had a new project in mind, something that would redefine everything that the Who and rock-and-roll music were all about. *Tommy* had given them great power—musical, financial and social—but the Who had other music to play. The ground had been laid for Pete Townshend's real magnum opus, his true work of art, the very essence of his creative thinking, his composing and playing: *Lifehouse*.

5

To the Lifehouse (1971–1972)

For the Who's fans waiting for their next record of new material, 1970 was a long and frustrating year. Discounting *Live at Leeds*, only "The Seeker" had given any public indication of what musical direction the group might be taking. Since the actual sound of *Tommy* was very different from *Live at Leeds*, it was by no means clear at this stage how their new material would sound. "The Seeker" suggested that the band were ready to forgo the overt pop sensibilities of their 1960s work in the search for a purer rock aesthetic. Since they no longer needed hit singles, there was no reason to record overtly commercial songs. And fans had by now come to expect something exploratory with each Who album. At the very least, their audience would have wondered whether the new material would attempt to encapsulate the raw power of the stage act in the studio (something the band had so far meticulously avoided) or simply go one step further than *Tommy* into ornateness and sophistication.

The issue was not made any clearer by what Townshend was saying in interviews during 1970. He talked about the band's future direction and sound on two occasions and almost contradicted himself. "Pete Townshend Hopes to Soften the Who Sound" ran the title of an interview with Richard Green. "I'm trying to sophisticate our sound a little," Townshend said, "make it a little less ear-rending. If we try and do anything clever-clever it could be a mistake."[1] Yet later in the year, Pete affirmed to Green that the Who would "continue writing and playing hard rock".[2] Since Pete didn't specify in either of the interviews whether he was referring to the band's stage or studio sound—or indeed, whether in the future these would homogenize more—it would have been difficult to know quite what to expect.

The situation was later further complicated by Townshend's historic but tangential announcement (in January 1971) that the Who's new work would include extensive use of synthesizers and electronics. Many people at the time had never knowingly heard a synthesizer, and what *was* known about them seemed incompatible with the guitar dynamite that was *Live at Leeds*. But somewhere during 1970 Townshend had sniffed out the then obscure idea that synthesizers would somehow prove very important to rock's and the Who's future and had followed his instincts in believing that electronic experimentation would yield the sound of tomorrow. Townshend saw the future of the Who's music being linked more fully with the new technology, in both studio and live settings, and he explored every facet of the synthesizer in order to ascertain what could and would be possible within an existing rock sound, leaving the integrity of the traditional instruments intact. Also, he explored the new sound terrain that could be part of what rock and roll might become in the future. Synthesizers have been variously used and abused in rock since this time, but we should not overlook just how futuristic and unusual they sounded in 1970.

Townshend's interest in mysticism and the relationship between sounds, vibrations and the human soul also led him to believe that the synthesizer was *the* tool with which to realize an accurate musical expression of a human individual—not a conscious form of music produced by *playing*, but a bespoke form of composition gathered from physiological and psychological data. Any recordable information (such as heart rates, brain patterns, and pulses) could be processed through a computer and transformed into sound programs that a synthesizer would play. This suggested to Pete that for the first time the audience could truly participate in the *creation* of music and the barriers that had hitherto separated performer and listener could be diminished. For his part, Townshend saw the synthesizer as a means of boundless musical expression, akin to his earlier experiments with feedback. Electronics hadn't much yet found a place in rock and roll, although there were some avant-garde artists working loosely within the rock field. Pete's admiration for Terry Riley and Ron Geesin was well known, and they must have provided some inspiration for his experiments.

A possible difficulty that troubled him in introducing electronics was the danger of altering the Who's sound too much. He had proved that he could create the most undisciplined free-form music (such as his film soundtrack compositions and the freak-out section of the demo version of "Amazing Journey") when recording for his own noncommercial purposes. However, it is doubtful that he would have wished to plunge the Who into a similarly esoteric direction. The synthesizers, therefore, would have to be carefully dovetailed into the chord structures, rhythms and voices of a well-established rock-and-roll sound. Townshend also recognized that the timbre of the synthesizer—being infinitely variable—was very different to that of the guitar (unlike the piano and organ, which in the context of rock and roll had often merged with the guitar to the extent of superfluity resulting in aural clutter). The challenge that Townshend took upon his own and the Who's shoulders was to legitimize the synthesizer as an integral component of the rock-and-roll sound, a task which had yet to be convincingly achieved by anyone.

In late 1970, after plans for a conventional format album had been abandoned, Pete Townshend set about drawing together his dissonant ideas for a new project over a gestation period of a couple of months. Although the project was sometimes referred to as a rock opera, Pete was formulating something very different to *Tommy*, a musical event and film that was later titled *Lifehouse*. Townshend's demos had always been his blueprint for how the material would sound when played by the Who. However, on this occasion he intended his new songs to be a mere starting point, to be superseded if possible by music that was spontaneously created in a live situation and reflecting a creative contribution from an audience. So Townshend was torn between working out every detail (which he tried to do) or leaving things sufficiently tentative to allow for the material to evolve *in situ*. Also during this time, he had developed a theoretical framework for his songs and for the concept behind the film scenario. He began to mention his new ideas in interviews and in his occasional published writings, and the earliest reference to his current preoccupations came in September 1970 in a regular column he was contributing to *Melody Maker*.[3]

The theme was very esoteric and abstracted at this stage, and it probably didn't seem too connected with the solid earthy vigor of the Who's recent concerts. The basic notion was to be an exploration of a universal note or chord—a sound expressed musically—that would have positive effects upon the listener and musician alike. It was rooted in an idea that each individual human being had within him or her a personal musical note that would harmonize or produce discord depending upon how it combined with other people's notes. The combination of notes would produce a musical chord that would act as a metaphor for other kinds of harmony—social, spiritual and political. This was a starting point for a whole theory and concept and remained the central coda for the entire work. It related to the familiar legend of the Lost Chord.

It was long thought that within the Western harmonic system there lay concealed a sublime undiscovered chord. The idea of this Lost Chord formed a mythological legend in which the symbolic combination of notes held the power to restore the listener to an Arcadian innocence and harmony. Where a musical chord is a combination of different notes that combine in harmony when simultaneously struck, the symbolic chord of mankind reflects each individual as a component of the whole experience of life that—if combined as a communion of souls—would produce a vibrant, omnipotent chord of life. It represented (like the Holy Grail or the Philosopher's Stone) mankind's passionate quest for an idyll and a consummate knowledge of human existence and as such has remained unattainable. References to this idea are abundant.[4] Townshend was merely refining and updating a long-established musical legend. He was working within a mystical genre of musical theory; music as a root form of communication, a philosophical tool and a means of attaining spiritual enlightenment. He was also drawing upon ideas expressed in the writings of Inayat Khan on mysticism and music.[5]

Following this initial broaching of new ideas, the first extensive outline of what was coming together in Pete's head was relayed in an interview with Roy Shipston, resulting in a feature titled "Who's Future in a World of Science Fantasy."[6] The phrase "science fantasy" suggested a wide field of possibilities and probably wouldn't have surprised anyone familiar with *Tommy* (or indeed, Pete's earlier suite "Rael" from the *Sell Out* album.) At this point, Townshend had written three new songs that he felt would form the genesis of a new work. He referred back to how *Tommy* had begun from a handful of key songs and felt that the whole cycle would soon follow. The titles of the three songs were given as "The Note," later "Pure and Easy," "We're Moving," possibly an early version of "Going Mobile"; and finally, "The Two of Us," which song this developed into is unclear, possibly "Bargain," although it might well have been discarded as better songs came along. Although these titles give little indication of what later appeared, the concept of *Lifehouse* was clearly taking shape.

Townshend said that his plot would be based upon mystical ideas about vibrations in music and feature a rock band (played by the Who) and a roadie who was "trying to discover the note that is everything, the essence … a musical sort of infinity…. This group find a note which basically creates complete devastation … only the true note that they have been looking for is left."[7] This rough sketch of plot was somewhat ethereal, but it did mention the central character, the roadie later to be called Bobby. It seemed to show Townshend attempting to combine mystical ideas with practical dramatic reality. The work was to utilize a collision of two complementary ideas: the (real) emotional high generated between audience and performer at Who concerts, and the (fictitious) quest within mankind for a spiritual and physical high that could be discovered within a celestial and pure form of music.

The plot of *Lifehouse* was set in the near future and concerned a totalitarian society devoid of rock music, in which the oppressed youth discover that rock has a purifying, liberating effect upon themselves. The *lifehouse* here was the place where the music was played and where the young people collected to discover rock and roll as a powerful, almost religious, cult. Within this setting, Townshend had characters interacting and the repressive forces of society closing in until one day "a concert emerges that is so incredible that the whole audience disappears. I started off writing a series of songs about music, about the power of music and the mysticism of music."[8]

Essentially, Townshend's new songs celebrated music as a rejuvenating and cohesive force that could create a spiritual uplift in the musicians and listeners. In the plot, he finally had this spiritual unity pervading physical reality, with the band and audience literally moving onto a higher spiritual plane. He had taken the essentials of rock music and the relationship between performer and audience to a heightened level of fantasy, projecting the spiritual relationship that exists at a rock concert into literal terms in the film. The inner space of psychological impulses created by musical sensation and vibration was being explored. The audience and performers would "join together," sharing the same psychological state. Further plot detail was to be expounded in the film script with the interaction between various characters.

The plot is as follows. In a pollution-ridden future, where most of the remaining population of the world has retreated indoors or underground, the script broadly concerns the Establishment as represented by a technology-wielding security force who control the media and indoctrinate the populace through television and computer programs. In reaction, a number of rebels utilize "free" music and rock and roll and find it to be a liberating force, under the guidance of Bobby, a technical wizard and mystic visionary who believes that all the diverse threads of life could be drawn together with a musical event at which a Universal Note would be sounded. At a disused theater, renamed the Lifehouse, Bobby sets about creating an alternative society based upon harmony—musical, social and spiritual. A rock-and-roll band lead the music making, to which one by one members of the audience make an individual contribution. The Establishment seeks to repress the subversive activities at the Lifehouse, and after a violent confrontation, the rebels transcend their physical bodies as the music sounds a sublime, ultimate chord.

The finale of *Lifehouse* was to represent a means of overthrowing an oppressive regime through the use of sounds, vibrations and music—the combination of which has the power to strike a meaningful, omnipresent chord of life. The social framework of Townshend's story falls within the established literary genre of the dystopia (opposite of utopia) and speculative fiction rather than science fiction per se. The most obvious tradition from which *Lifehouse* follows is that of H. G. Wells's *When the Sleeper Wakes* (1899), Jack London's *The Iron Heel* (1907), Yevgeny Zamyatin's *We* (1923), Aldous Huxley's *Brave New World* (1932), Rex Warner's *The Aerodrome* (1941), George Orwell's *1984* (1949), Ray Bradbury's *Fahrenheit 451* (1953), and Anthony Burgess's *A Clockwork Orange* and *The Wanting Seed* (both 1963). The use of technology as a tool of repression stems most clearly from *Brave New World*, the novel to which *Lifehouse* bears the closest resemblance. The then current film *THX 1138* (1970) may have also been in Townshend's mind.

Although a film was the ultimate objective, Pete had doubts at this early stage as to whether the plot he had sketched in his script would be sufficiently strong in terms of narrative. Initially he was thinking only in terms of an album. But even the material for the album was far from prepared. However, *Lifehouse* was envisaged as an *event* first, even if not yet a film, and Pete wanted to utilize a new way of developing the music and revising the script with some audience collaboration. He thought that his lack of confidence in his first draft of the screenplay could be overcome by its being reshaped in the light of audience contact. So to fully explore the relationship between musician and audience, before the film production was finalized, Pete expressed a desire to play some small experimental shows in front of a regular audience.

The close of 1970 sealed a year in which the lack of a new studio album by the Who was conspicuous. Since the release of the *Tommy* LP, the talk of new projects, records and films had been incessant. Who fans had been given a morass of information from both official and unofficial sources over a period of eighteen months, some of which was contradictory and all of which subsequently proved to be unfounded. It had kept the Who in the news, however, and if nothing else it proved that Track Records really did have the most imaginative and energetic public relations team in the business. But the faith of the fans had been sustained throughout 1970 by constant gigging and a commitment that the Who (unlike many bands) was worth waiting for. Lack of activity or follow-through had been the deathblow for many artists, but the Who were one of the first groups to retain their fans and commercial potency through long periods of inactivity.

When a more firm announcement was made in December 1970 about the new project, it was a cause for some degree of excitement and anticipation for all Who followers. However, that the Who were now actually working on something new didn't instantly alleviate the frustration of the fans worldwide. They had begun to realise that anything the band now did would take a long time. It was becoming clear that the nineteen months that had elapsed between the release of *Sell Out* and *Tommy* wasn't just an unfortunately long gap between recording. It was the precedent for the pattern to which the fans must become accustomed. Who albums now took between two and three years to make; that had become the norm. (Led Zeppelin, Pink Floyd and the Rolling Stones all soon settled into an equally lethargic approach.) Even at this point in December the wait wasn't over yet.

The specific information that gave the fans cause to increase their expectations first appeared in *New Musical Express*, which carried a news item titled "Who: 2 Big Movies."[9] This stated that two Who films (one *Tommy* and another a new project) were to appear in 1971. In the U.S. on the same date, *Billboard* reported the same news in a piece by Mike Gross titled "Who Move to What (Films), How (As Indie Producers)."[10] Gross gave the new project two alternative working titles: *Your Turn in the Barrel* and *Barrel One, Barrel Two*. These strange, unspecific titles were not further explained but must surely have come from a Who press release or statement by the Who's New York office. The only connection they have to the completed work is in the reference to a double-barrelled shotgun, an image used in the song "Won't Get Fooled Again" and also touched upon by Townshend in some interviews. However, the titles here bear no apparent connection with the Universal Note theory that Pete had already discussed. The article also stated that the Who were to have starring roles in the new film.

Further confusion might have arisen in the U.S. by a simultaneous report in *Creem* titled "No *Tommy* Film."[11] This contradicted the two previous announcements by saying that the proposed film of *Tommy* had been postponed in favor of a new work. Pete was quoted briefly describing the futuristic plot, but no title was mentioned. During the last few days of 1970, Townshend held a conversation with Penny Valentine, a long-standing Who fan sympathetic to Pete's objectives. He confirmed in this interview, published in *Sounds*, that the film was definitely going ahead, with production starting on 1 February 1971: "We've got the place worked out ... the whole thing is welding together."[12] The filming was expected to take three months, to the end of April. Not only were the Who intending to encapsulate all their latent ability and power to produce "the finest music we're capable of," but Townshend saw the band as acting on behalf of rock music in general as "efficient catalysts" to lift it out of a rut: "it's not dead by any means but it's definitely stuck."[13] He emphasized the fact that hardware, equipment, machinery and technology were often disregarded as components of rock and roll and that they were vital tools in any effort to push rock music into a newer, more fulfilling epoch.

Amid the more grandiose plans for a film, Townshend was also aware of the more basic need for a new album. He felt it would be given a lower priority than usual because, in part, the Who were attempting to subvert (or at least circumvent) the routine annual single-album–tour cycle that had started to envelop and frustrate the bigger groups. The *Lifehouse* project was, in part, a concerted effort to not do things in the conventional way. Instead of mapping out the whole work precisely in song, Townshend wanted *Lifehouse* to absorb the influence of the audience and for the music to change and evolve as a theatrical event developed. This is why no *Lifehouse* songs were introduced into the Who's live act in late 1970. But obviously at some stage *Lifehouse* would involve recording activity, as Pete confirmed, saying, "The new album's tied up with the film, so we've kind of started on the film first."[14]

Despite an early suggestion of collaboration, *Lifehouse* was written entirely by Pete Townshend and was conceived as a genuine multimedia event that encompassed live performance, records, and finally, the film. The songs reflected a general theme, but the plot was entirely rooted in the script and the theatrical/concert event, which in itself would provide action for the film. The theater or concert hall (the Lifehouse of the script) would provide an environment for the film and music to develop. At its least the work would provide a new double album by the Who, and at its best a big-budget feature film. Undaunted by the magnitude of the concept or the vastness of the new medium of film, Townshend was extremely confident in the quality of his new songs and the soundness of his grand plan and had complete faith that the Who could make *Lifehouse* a monumental rock-and-roll (and film) event.

The Young Vic Theatre in London had been launched in September 1970, and its director Frank Dunlop had expressed an interest in staging a production of *Tommy*. After meetings between Dunlop and Townshend, it was decided that this theater would be the ideal place to develop the music, establish a dramatic scenario and to film the central concert scenes of *Lifehouse*. Commencing on 15 February 1971 and continuing on several successive Monday evenings, Townshend intended to use the workshop environment of the Young Vic to create new music in collaboration with the audience, involving a quadrophonic sound system, prerecorded tapes and electronics. As previously mentioned, the musical and spiritual climax of the film was to be a concert at which the symbolic Universal Chord was struck—a combination of notes that would represent each person present as part of a greater whole. Townshend hoped that a Who performance at the theater could provide the simulation of the sublime communication between audience and musicians for which the script called. He spoke at a press conference to launch *Lifehouse* on 13 January 1971 describing the work rather vaguely as "a fiction, or a play, or an opera ... a completely different kind of performance in rock."[15] And *The Times* also reported that the Who were intending to base their performance "on elements of rock music and new electronic sounds."[16]

The film and concert performance elements of *Lifehouse* here become a separate story: although integral to a whole understanding of *Lifehouse*, they constitute a complicated and protracted saga in themselves and are therefore beyond the scope of this book. It is necessary only to note that the Young Vic performances failed to achieve the breakthough in audience participation for which the Who had hoped, and Universal Pictures—which was ostensibly backing the film—failed to commit any funds to the production. Throughout this period, Kit Lambert—whose guidance and inspiration Townshend had previously relied upon—was in New York, seemingly oblivious to the problems Pete was encountering. Lambert felt snubbed by the Who's lack of commitment to his idea for the *Tommy* film and, although Pete had come to question Lambert's role as a record producer, he still felt his erstwhile mentor had some contribution to make. The failure to make any progress at the Young Vic came as a shattering blow to Townshend, who felt demoralized, confused and frustrated to the point of a breakdown. The Who very nearly disintegrated in March 1971 when Townshend's master plan was seen to be substantially flawed.

Note, alas, that despite a plethora of good ideas and an irrefutably brilliant collection of songs, *Lifehouse*—as it was envisaged at this point by Townshend—was hopelessly esoteric and too ethereal to make any practical progress as an event or film. The methods of development chosen by the Who were lacking the sufficient pragmatism to ever succeed. Despite the prominence of the idea of the auteur (especially in the cinema), Townshend could never have managed to bring to fruition so many dissonant elements singlehandedly, and his collaborators (the members of the band, Kit Lambert, Frank Dunlop) were equally unable to gather together and nail down any kind of foundations upon which the ideas could be developed.

What *Lifehouse* did achieve, however, was to furnish the Who with an outstanding collection of new songs. These were culled from Townshend's writings throughout 1970 and early 1971, and some were not written with the project in mind but later incorporated into the work if appropriate. The plot of *Lifehouse* was never to be conveyed in the song lyrics, and therefore no "narrative" songs were contrived. Since *Lifehouse* was never presented as a dramatic recorded work, it is not known exactly where each song was to fall in the plot; the song lyrics didn't form a libretto and lacked any interactive dialogue and reported speech. Even in terms of character development or thematic continuity, they lacked any discernible chronology. Where *Tommy* had focused on one character's subjectivity and contrasted it with the observations of those around that character, no comparable single viewpoint emerges from any of the *Lifehouse* songs, despite all of their being written in the first person singular. Obviously the lyrics were to reflect pertinent aspects of the theme, but when the concept fell away, the lyrics still retained an independent meaning and significance.

As far as can be ascertained, Pete Townshend had prepared around twenty completed songs and also had in hand a large number of synthesizer pieces. (Of the older songs that remained unreleased, "I Don't Even Know Myself" and John Entwistle's "Postcard" were not included in the *Lifehouse* concept, but "Water" and "Naked Eye" might well have found a niche in the new masterwork). However, some old favorites might also have been intended as part of the project in some way: at the Young Vic the Who had played versions of "Baby Don't You Do It" (resurrected from 1964), Bo Diddley's "Road Runner" and Larry Williams's "Bony Moronie." These songs had no obvious part in the development of the concept, but oddly enough Townshend was always keen to incorporate other artists' material into his work. John Entwistle also contributed the obviously non–*Lifehouse* songs "My Wife" and "When I Was a Boy" to the Who repertoire at this time. The central essence of *Lifehouse* is to be found in three of the new songs: "Pure and Easy," "Song Is Over" and "Getting in Tune." These reflect the central idea of music as a source of social and spiritual power and are the songs tied in most closely to the heart (but not the action) of the *Lifehouse* script. Even so, they stand independent, successfully disengaged from the concept. The remaining songs are less closely focused in theme and therefore are more able to stand alone. Rather than carry the plot themselves, the *Lifehouse* songs were to function more on the level of a Greek chorus in their relation to what was to happen in the film.

The standard of the *Lifehouse* songs was exemplary, even for someone with Townshend's own impeccable reputation. The compositions were the backbone of *Lifehouse* and in this sphere, if not in any other, the project was a triumph. As ever, Pete was grappling with a context in which these songs were to be presented in the belief that a form of unity and cohesion would give an extra resonance and dimension to the musical whole. For all the changes and rewriting of the script, the songs were fully formed, matured and already brought to fruition while all else was modified and changed. The songs are what Townshend started with, and they remained the most resilient part of the entire work. Several years into the future, the songs alone remain.

With the three Young Vic workshop sessions ending in disarray and the film schedule no nearer to becoming a reality, the Who seemed to be foundering. In the midst of this period of despondency, Kit Lambert appeared to be taking an interest in *Lifehouse* after all. He phoned Pete from New York and offered an olive branch, which Townshend and the rest of the band grasped as a lifeline. It came none too soon for Pete: "I was not suicidally depressed or anything, but I was very humbled and drinking more heavily than usual."[17] Lambert had been doing some production work in New York with the soul group LaBelle at the Record Plant, a newly upgraded state-of-the-art studio. Lambert found himself in a position to offer the Who studio time. It may not have been a very exciting proposal for the band after the expectations of the Young Vic, but it was enough. Townshend was in a poor mental state and seemed willing to go along with any remotely unifying idea where Kit might finally salvage *Lifehouse* and bring out its essential qualities. The circumstances may not have seemed favorable for any successful recording work, but the band utilized a collective reserve and relied on their musical abilities alone to get through the sessions.

By mid–March, then, the Who were in New York and for the first time having to think about recording some of Pete Townshend's new *Lifehouse* songs. Away from London and the British press they found a degree of freedom that the confines of the Young Vic had denied them, and something of this spirit seemed to come through in their recordings. At the Young Vic, Pete would have been very conscious of the fact that the legitimate cultural establishment (people like Frank Dunlop) were looking to him to prove that rock and roll could take its place among the higher artistic echelons. One cannot imagine Entwistle, Daltrey or Moon giving a damn about it, but Pete *was* conscious of rock and roll's need to demand its space in the cultural pantheon, and he was sensitive to rock's being dismissed as trivial juvenilia or drug-addled cacophony.

Whatever Townshend felt about the band and however deep his spirits had plummeted, he was invigorated by the music the Who recorded in New York and recalled the sessions as being "great fun ... it was a great experience but very stressful."[18] Pete's stress resulted in his intake of brandy considerably increasing. But Lambert, as Townshend suspected, wasn't ready to immerse himself in *Lifehouse* and snatch belated victory from the humiliating jaws of defeat; he was neither willing nor capable. Lambert had developed a heroin habit that had become his overriding priority. But his gesture meant *something* to Townshend, even if it didn't signal the resumption of their previous relationship.

The Record Plant had recently been refurbished and upgraded to Eastlake specifications, and its Studio 1 was thought to offer the ultimate in recording quality and acoustic ambience. The Who became the first group to record in Studio 1, although they also worked in Studio 2, engineered by Jack Adams and assisted by Felix Papparlardi (who had produced Cream's later work and was a member of the U.S. heavy rock group Mountain). The 16-track equipment and the Eastlake–designed room were enough to encourage Townshend to sink himself into the process of recording. Particularly tempting was the suggestion that the recordings could be mixed into quadrophonic (in keeping with one of the original *Lifehouse* aims) and also into what was called "3D stereo" (an early three-way attempt at "surround sound" that presaged the quadrophonic system). Realistically, Townshend expected at the very least a single to ensue from the sessions to act as a taster for the forthcoming film.

Between 16 and 18 March 1971, the Who recorded six songs: "Pure and Easy," "Getting in Tune," "Behind Blue Eyes," "Won't Get Fooled Again," "Love Ain't for Keeping" and "Baby Don't You Do It." This last song, as mentioned above, had been recorded in 1964. On the evidence of existing tapes of these sessions, no other songs were recorded. In the spirit of a loose jam session, the band were joined by Leslie West (guitarist of Mountain) and Al Kooper (the session keyboard played who had worked with the Who in 1967). The Who didn't need Kooper or West's particular talents for any purpose; they just happened to be working in the studio at the time and they joined in for the fun of it. A more recent comment on the sessions by Pete gives a more explicit account of the high conditions: "Jack Adams at or under the desk, Kit on the bathroom ceiling and me in the Remy Martin bottle."[19] But, amazingly enough, work progressed: songs were recorded and overdubs were completed to a high level of finish.

One of the strongest new songs was "Won't Get Fooled Again," a distillation of power chords, catchy melody and hypnotic synthesizer drone. The structure of this early recording of the song is still fairly loose, and it lacks the precision of the more familiar final version. The synthesizer track was newly scored in the studio and is inferior to that which Pete had incorporated into his demo version. On "Won't Get Fooled Again," "Love Ain't for Keeping" and "Baby Don't You Do It," Leslie West plays lead guitar. His style was steeped in the blues-based heavy rock tradition with a number of "virtuoso" finger harmonics and vibrato thrown in (which wasn't necessarily appropriate for the Who), and his contributions—thought technically faultless—add little more than flashy bluster to the songs.

"Behind Blue Eyes" is a beautiful acoustic ballad that closely follows Pete's demo version, with gorgeous vocal harmonies and Al Kooper's organ backing. Pete takes the lead vocal of "Love Ain't for Keeping," a medium-paced power chord rocker with an underlying synthesizer pattern. This highly attractive though simple song was drastically rearranged before its final release. Al Kooper's organ takes a more dominant part in "Getting in Tune," which extends beyond the structure of the song into some spontaneous jamming. What sounds like the most enjoyable studio jam, however, comes with the lengthy version of "Baby Don't You Do It," essentially a drum and vocal showpiece that Daltrey and Moon exploit to the full, making for a thrilling overall performance. The guitars of Townshend and Leslie West intertwine in solos, and Pete had added a three-chord variation [1.02] since the band had last played this song in 1965. The relentless rhythm all but swamps Al Kooper's organ work, but Roger's vocal performance is immensely thrilling.

Perhaps the most fully matured and successful recording is "Pure and Easy" (still logged as "The Note"), which was undoubtedly one of the best songs Townshend had ever written. This recording is definitive: acoustic and electric guitars blend to form a rich layer of moving chord work over the brisk beat, and great energy and invention seem to wash out of the band to form a joyous and emotionally involving performance. Finally, all the detail of the guitar work and bass runs is overwhelmed by pure melodicism, culminating in a final power chord sequence at the end [3.27]. "Pure and Easy"—over and above all the other songs at this stage—sounds like a masterpiece. In general, the theme of the song is a celebration of music as a triumphant rejuvenating power, passing through stages of innocence to omnipotence; the coda may well be a plea to mankind to recognize the Universal Note in themselves. However, the song has a very wide application and may just be a central affirmation of the basic themes. Townshend described the song as the "central pivot" of *Lifehouse*.[20]

An indication that the band's spirits weren't irrevocably dampened is provided by a comic interlude that preceded the recording of "Behind Blue Eyes" on 18 March. Just as the basic track was about to be recorded, Daltrey caught the backside of his jeans on something in the studio and looked over his shoulder into a reflective screen to see if they had ripped. "Roger's admiring his arse in the mirror as we start—very symbolic!" quipped Pete, to the general mirth of the band and technicians. There then followed a false start during which the group collectively attempted to clear its throat in a surreal Monty Python–esque manner. Townshend's stammering over the line "But my dreams…" caused him to repeat, "But, but, but, but … shut up, man, you sound like a motorboat!" in the manner of one of his comic heroes, Spike Milligan. (This amusing episode was included on the *30 Years of Maximum R&B* boxed set.)

5. To the Lifehouse (1971–1972)

The New York trip was personally devastating for Townshend, and tensions came to a head at the Navarro Hotel. A group meeting with Lambert resulted in Townshend's nearly jumping from a tenth-story window after Kit's personal rejection of him and *Lifehouse* finally came to the surface. Bewildered and frustrated, the Who returned to London with the tapes and thoughts of releasing "Behind Blue Eyes" from the sessions as a single, not least because it was the shortest and most melodic of the songs. However, when they played back the Record Plant masters in London they felt the music was somehow lacking the joyous spirit of the occasion. The tapes did prove, however, that some of the new material was exceptionally strong and would stand up lyrically as well as musically outside of the larger *Lifehouse* concept.

In many ways, these six songs were technically the highest-quality recordings the band had ever done, and the 16-track masters sounded exceptionally clean, vivid and up to date. The band initially had every intention of using them (and even attempted an experimental quadrophonic mix), but when the mixing came to be completed at Olympic Studios in London a month later, the band didn't think the tapes sounded good enough. By this time Glyn Johns had been engaged as producer, and he favored rerecording from scratch rather than mixing, never having had a high opinion of Kit Lambert's work in the studio. "Behind Blue Eyes," "Pure and Easy," and a shortened "Baby Don't You Do It" finally gained an official release on the revised *Who's Next* CD in 1995, and "Love Ain't for Keeping" followed on *Odds and Sods* in 1998. The New York versions of "Won't Get Fooled Again" and "Getting in Tune" are unreleased and are likely to so remain.

Back in London by the end of March, the next phase of *Lifehouse* was reluctantly considered. Whether Townshend felt himself able to make a constructive decision about where next to go is debatable. He must have felt so inexorably entangled with his divine creation that any objectivity was impossible. The Who could only fall back on the prospect of recording the *Lifehouse* material—which, taken song for song, formed the most substantial asset to hand. Pete began to realize that he would need to restrict his ambitions to something more manageable as a simple means of survival for the band. The film hadn't been abandoned entirely but had been postponed in the hope that it would come together at a later date.

After the New York debacle, and with the film slowly receding from their grasp, the group had to seek a more viable option for progress. It was decided that some performances could be recorded at the Young Vic and released on record; this would possibly capture some of the theatrical spirit of the original, without resorting to a conventional format studio album. A date was available at the theater on Monday, 26 April, and arrangements were made to use the Rolling Stones' mobile studio. Glyn Johns was duly invited to produce the session, assisted by his younger brother Andy. This was now the most logical move to make in order to get things moving along some kind of positive trajectory and one which introduced new blood into the team.

Before installing the Rolling Stones' mobile unit at the Young Vic, the Who decided to test the new equipment, which was parked at Mick Jagger's home, Stargroves, in Berkshire, England. This session was also a trial run for Glyn Johns as producer and took place in either late March or early April. Some of the happy-go-lucky desperation of the Record Plant seems to have been carried into this session, which Townshend referred to simply as "boozy."[21] They decided to start with the song that had turned out least well in New York, "Won't Get Fooled Again." Glyn Johns had heard Pete's demos and was hugely impressed with the music, but he was confused from the outset about the concept that surrounded the songs.

Mick Jagger's hall was used as the studio floor, and cables were run outside to the mobile, a crude but effective method that caught the band at an inspired point. The recordings were felt to be outstandingly successful. The atmosphere at Stargroves found favor with the band and restored some of Townshend's confidence. As using the Rolling Stones' mobile studio was by no means a permanent arrangement, Johns urged the Who to move into Olympic Studios in Barnes to continue working. That Johns and the Who had established a working relationship that produced the goods was a relief. "Won't Get Fooled Again" turned out so well that the band were delighted. What was intended as a test demo turned out to be a finished master. It received a few later overdubs at Olympic Studios and was mixed at Island Studios, but this epic song was captured at Stargroves in its definitive form, far surpassing the version recorded in New York. Other material was allegedly recorded at Stargroves at the same time, but there is no hard evidence to identify what this might be. Roger Daltrey recently stated that "quite a lot of other stuff" was recorded but didn't specify what, and John Entwistle recalled that "Pure and Easy" (usually credited as being recorded at Olympic) was in fact recorded at Stargroves.[22] As the 16-track master tape is missing from the Who's tape archive, this question may never be answered.

To record "Won't Get Fooled Again," the original synthesizer track from Townshend's demo was used on the master recording. It was obviously considered pointless rerecording what was perfectly played and recorded by Pete alone in the first place. As mentioned previously, the version recorded in New York in March used a rearranged synthesizer track that was softer and less focused. The band played over the synthesizer track with the regular guitar, bass and drums (Keith Moon had to very carefully synchronize with the synth) and Townshend later overdubbed an acoustic rhythm guitar, although this was finally mixed very low (so low, in fact, that many people were unaware of its being there until they heard it years later on CD). Pete playing through two amp set-ups simultaneously with his prized Gretsch guitar produced the electric guitar sound. In effect, "Won't Get Fooled Again" gave the band a new sound, but one with enough of the old characteristics to identify it as classic Who rock and roll.

Glyn Johns foresaw that the *Lifehouse* songs formed a very substantial musical achievement. "Won't Get Fooled Again" was merely the starting point. At Olympic, he was confident he would get the best out of the band. However, the Who were still unsure of their next step. Johns must have had little confidence in Townshend's hopes for *Lifehouse* being salvaged as a film, but he knew the Who had something special in their grasp and seemed to sense that he could coax out of the group the most remarkable performances and music of their career. Pete had made painstaking efforts to involve Glyn Johns in the full extent of the ideas behind *Lifehouse* as well as the music and had supplied him with a copy of the script along with his demo tapes. But Johns responded only to the music.

With "Won't Get Fooled Again" now in the can, time was booked at Olympic Studios to finish the job. However, the final date at the Young Vic on 26 April loomed before the band settled down to any serious work in the studio. A live recording was made of this show as planned, but it was approached in a casual manner and certainly didn't belatedly fulfill any of Townshend's early hopes. The band ran through a tentative running order of old and new songs, with the few recently revived cover versions from the past. The resulting tape, while technically excellent, was not considered good enough to be of immediate use, although a reassessment many years later meant that a number of tracks have now officially appeared. "Bony Moronie" is a knockabout rocker given a truly inspired though ramshackle treatment. It sounds barely rehearsed but tests the band's primal instincts to perfection. Daltrey's singing is extremely powerful, and the initial release of the song on a 1988 B side was a hugely entertaining bonus because the song wasn't ever attempted again. "Naked Eye" first appeared on *30 Years of Maximum R&B* in 1994 and encapsulates all the latent power of this complex, serious song in a performance that moves through delicate arpeggio verses, a power chord chorus riff and some flat-out solo work in its latter stages. "Water" (first released on the *Who's Next* CD in 1995) is less satisfying as a song but scores here in an inspired performance that develops into a lengthy solo. Both these performances far surpass the studio versions that were to have been issued on the 1970 EP.

Recording sessions began in earnest at Olympic Studios, Barnes, London, from April and stretched into June 1971. Using the Stargroves master of "Won't Get Fooled Again" as a blueprint for a working method and a sound scheme, the band set about recording the bulk of the songs Townshend had written for *Lifehouse*, along with at least two of John Entwistle's most recent compositions. Glyn Johns was able to gain a sound more detailed and clear than any previous Who recordings with multilayered instruments such as keyboards and brass in addition to the lead and rhythm guitars, bass and drums. Although the arrangements are rich and lush, they weren't overly ornate, and they have a robustness that maintained all of the band's basic rock power.

The synthesizer parts on "Baba O'Riley" and "Bargain" were, like "Won't Get Fooled Again," taken directly from Townshend's hypnotic demo recordings. "Baba O'Riley" was edited and restructured by the band, and it forms one of the most experimental rock works ever recorded. As Townshend recalled, "Glyn actually brought fresh energy and fresh spirit to the songs and he was also at his peak."[23] None of the songs had necessarily been designed as a single, but "Behind Blue Eyes," whether the New York version or the take newly captured at Olympic on a startlingly perfect recording, was still the favorite despite being for the most part a drumless ballad. Tentative plans were made to issue this with "I Don't Even Know Myself" on the B side. "Love Ain't for Keeping" was rearranged as a purely acoustic song without its original synthesizer backing, and "Going Mobile" used a guitar synthesizer effect called an *envelope follower* on the solo. Heavy use of synthesizer was made on "Song Is Over," mixing comfortably with a traditional piano sound and—just as extensively but less noticeably—on "Bargain."

The acoustic guitars were generally overdubbed after the electric lead guitar parts were in place, all played with Townshend's customary vigor and inspiration. The lead and backing vocals were the best the band had ever done, and the singing throughout these sessions was exemplary. Roger Daltrey showed a command and clarity of which he had only hinted on previous Who recordings. Moon's drumming was perfectly controlled and measured, and Entwistle got into the heart of the songs with his clear, agile bass lines. The band made no attempt to reproduce their combustible stage sound, opting for a much more multidimensional approach that suited the current need for rock music to be expansive rather than reductive. Expansiveness for the Who, however, did not mean an increased instrumentation or complexity of arrangement: it meant a fidelity and commitment to the limitless potential of song and melody.

Nicky Hopkins (with whom the band had last played in 1965) contributed piano to the songs that required a more complicated arrangement than Pete could handle, but all other keyboards were played by Townshend, except for "My Wife," on which John Entwistle played the piano. The tapes (apart from "Won't Get Fooled Again") were all mixed by Glyn Johns at Olympic, though the final tracks were produced by the Who with Johns as associate producer. Taken en bloc, these recordings represent the absolute creative peak of the Who's powers and are the most potent, mature, and innovative collection of songs they ever produced. Even within the wider rock field, they arguably surpass the best of their contemporaries. Throughout the recording, the band still assumed they were working on a double concept album called *Lifehouse*, but Glyn Johns had become less convinced that this would work. Without an accompanying film or stage show, the album would now have to stand alone. With a complete lack of narrative songs, a clear shape to the concept was not indicated. Pete Townshend may have worked out a rough chronological sequence of songs as related to the film script, but this was meaningless when merely presented on an LP. Johns found that any adherence to chronology put restrictions on his ability to satisfactorily sequence an album.

The band, for their part, were happy with the double album idea. It followed well in a tradition of Who grandiosity. They felt that expansive ideas needed, correspondingly, a big format in which to be presented. Halfway through the recording sessions, Roger spoke of the band's decision to release a double record set and was enthusiastic about its quality, saying, "I think we're making the best record we've ever made for a start.... We've got enough material recorded for a single album ... but we'll go on to make it a double.... It's got a theme because it works best for The Who. It builds where just a series of songs never seems to."[24] However, sometime between May and June, the double album idea was reconsidered and vetoed, with Townshend's reluctant agreement. Glyn Johns had instigated this change, primarily because he didn't see any cohesive unity in the concept and felt it would have been too obscure, despite Pete's best efforts to explain it to him. Feeling Johns's objectivity and judgement were likely to be more trustworthy than their own instincts, the Who allowed him to prepare the material he wanted for a single album, and all *Lifehouse* connotations were finally jettisoned.

At the time the band were obviously pleased (even relieved) to see a solid piece of work finally take shape before their eyes, but there were losses as well as gains. The overall quality of the available songs could have easily justified a double album, even if not sequenced as if forming a concept. Johns had selected nine songs that he presumably considered as offering the best representation of the whole: "Baba O'Riley," "Bargain," "Love Ain't for Keeping," "My Wife," "Song Is Over," "Getting in Tune," "Going Mobile," "Behind Blue Eyes" and "Won't Get Fooled Again." The leftovers included some awesome songs, including the aforementioned "Pure and Easy," the confident and compelling "Mary," and "Time Is Passing," a song of considerable beauty and charm. Townshend later said, "We could have put together a really tight concept album I think. Roger thought so too at the time."[25] In retrospect, and looking at the range of superb material that had now been completed, it is clear that the Who *should* have made *Who's Next* a double album. They were working at a white-hot level of intense creativity that was never again quite equalled—and the fact that some of the material created at this moment of absolute inspiration was discarded remains a tragedy that later reissues and archive releases have only been able to partially redress.

The release of "Won't Get Fooled Again" was heralded as a significant event on the contemporary rock scene, and the American Decca pressing of the single rather ironically (and anachronistically) stated on the label "from the motion picture *Lifehouse*." Decca was clearly some months out of date with its information. But the losses seemed to matter less with a tangible Who record materializing after months of delay. For the purpose of this single, "Won't Get Fooled Again" was edited down to just over a third of its true length. This necessary compromise emphasized the more dramatic parts of the song and omitted the second verse, some of the guitar solos and the sparse synthesizer passage that leads up to the drum solo. When heard initially, the strengths of the composition are apparent, but after listening to the full version on *Who's Next*, this abridged edit sounds unnaturally compressed and disjointed. Apart from the synthesizer backing (which in many ways resembles a standard electric organ) the song is fairly conventional, following a verse-and-chorus structure built on simple block guitar chords. The keyboards add a bouncy melodicism to the chord structure and the interplay between the two different melodic instruments (especially prior to the beginning of the first verse [0.39], where the guitar cuts out to allow the synth pattern to carry through for several bars on its own with the drums) is exceptionally good—being both ingenious and innovative as well as remarkably catchy.

Overall, "Won't Get Fooled Again" is a tight performance of sharp-edged rock and roll; the song simultaneously generates the Who's visceral guitar power (which is never leaden, dull or heavy-handed) and the new departure of the floating, meandering synthesizer drone. With Daltrey's strong vocal and definitive rock screams, the lyrics—detailing a revolution betrayed—stand out much more than on some previous Who singles and include a clever denouement ("Meet the new boss, same as the old boss"), although the edits to the single version rob it of the sense of pace and dramatic buildup toward the glorious final scream. The single was so strong that it was inevitably seen to represent a renaissance for the Who after months of apparent inactivity. By no means a blatantly commercial song—it was selected as a single at the last minute—"Won't Get Fooled Again" reached a respectable number 9 in the charts in the U.K. (on 14 August) and number 15 in the United States.

The B side was "I Don't Even Know Myself," written over a year earlier, but recently rerecorded and extensively featured in the live act. This is a soft rocker with a spartan production and has touches of a country influence in the beat and guitar arrangements. Despite a strong message against overinterpretation, the song lacks any real power in its melody, and it remains merely pleasant and interesting. By putting this song on the B side—where it belonged—the band had at least realized its merits for what they were, although perversely (the band was now flush with superb new songs) it remained in the live set for some time to come.

Soon after the release of "Won't Get Fooled Again," and after the critics had a chance to assimilate the message in the lyrics, Townshend took an opportunity to clarify its meaning, writing in a letter to *It* that "Won't Get Fooled Again" was "partly a personal song but mainly a song which screams defiance at those who feel that any cause is better than no cause, that death in a sick society is better than putting up with it, or resigning themselves to wait for change."[26] In typical fashion, Townshend, in this letter, turns an explanation of his lyrical theme in one song into a polemic on the role of the rock star in society and the kind of internal struggles that the Who have to accommodate to merely exist. This letter was written to dispel some ill-considered criticism that "Won't Get Fooled Again" was toying with revolutionary rhetoric to overall negative effect. Maybe Townshend overstated his case in response.

In general, however, the reception given to "Won't Get Fooled Again" was wholly encouraging. Peter Jones noted the "sundry changes of direction" and "predictably excellent guitar work from Pete Townshend, perhaps more of a front-running talent now than before. What certainly is there is that old-fashioned Who power and bite, which stems very largely from Keith Moon."[27] Jones also mentioned that further Who releases would feature material from sessions recorded in London and in New York, so rumors had obviously circulated about the Record Plant jaunt. The singles reviewer in *Melody Maker* said of it, "explosion of drums and guitars—and The Who blast back! It's so good to hear those Townshend chords flailing again ... a welcome burst of energy."[28]

The major event of the Who's year followed six weeks after the release of "Won't Get Fooled Again" when the album *Who's Next* appeared. With the issue of this LP, the Who entered a mature new phase, occupying a celestial level where they were judged only within their own elevated criteria. They no longer ranked alongside other acts and had moved above the realm of normal appreciation and appraisal. They were a rock group's rock group—not as individual musicians, but as the epitome of a *real* group in terms of musical cohesion and unity. They had grown for the past few years without the shackles of record company marketing and exploitation, without any group member leaving and being replaced, and yet with such continued positive affirmation from their fans that they found themselves with ample commercial power to (arguably) remain *outside* of the rock industry's norms and conventions.

The Rolling Stones and Led Zeppelin are generally cited as being the Who's only peers during the early 1970s, but in truth the Who were a band far apart from even these two colossal acts, both musically and sociologically. Zeppelin and the Stones outsold the Who in both album units and concert tickets (and therefore made much more money), but the Who held a precious quality that no other group came near to matching. It is impossible to define that quality further than to note the magical combination of personality, musicianship, individuality, style, eccentricity and passion for intelligence, integrity and truth. At times that combination seem to hold together only tenuously, but during 1970–1971 more than any other stage in their career, it worked miraculously well. And what was most important about the Who wasn't the different aspects and qualities noted above in themselves, but the way in which they combined.

As mentioned previously, *Who's Next* was issued devoid of any tangible connections with *Lifehouse* and was presented as a straightforward album. From the very first note of "Baba O'Riley" it surpasses the standards set by previous Who records: beautifully recorded, vigorously and imaginatively played, richly layered and full of confidence and ambition. It was the Who's most *musical* work to date, yet it lost none of the raw, guttural power and lithe energy that was at the heart of the group's essence. The experimental and innovative song structures were entirely successful within the disciplined strictures Townshend had imposed upon them, being incorporated into the Who sound without compromise, overcomplication or dilution of their central drive. Although the songs vary in style and texture, all are equally essential to the work as a whole and none could be written off as filler or inferior. If anything jars on the ear in stylistic and thematic terms, it is John Entwistle's "My Wife," where such an aesthetic divergence is unavoidable.

Although the format of the album is conventional, the music has such a radical edge that once more the Who were seen to be taking a stride forward beyond anything that had been achieved in rock music. The most prominent breakthrough was the use of the synthesizer as an integral rock instrument, a profound innovation. On "Baba O'Riley" and "Won't Get Fooled Again" the synthesizers provide a structural base on which the songs are built. No other rock musicians had taken the potential of the synthesizer this far before. Despite such complexities and technology, the Who didn't dilute their established energy. *Who's Next* was a triumph of primal rock-and-roll power in the spirit of "My Generation." It wasn't progressive rock or experimental to the extent that it sacrificed melodic strength merely for effect. A new Who sound had been established without any of the old sound being lost, and much of what was recorded formed a blueprint for the band to draw from for the next decade.

The remarkable "Baba O'Riley" formed the peak of the new innovation. The musical textures and components build a masterly sound scheme that consists of many disparate elements—basic power chord hard rock, avant-garde structures, evocative and poetically obtuse lyrics, a folksy atmosphere, skilled musicianship and compositional genius—all combining in perfect unison. It is a miraculous patchwork of integrated elements. The layers of sound simultaneously generate gut-wrenching guitar-based rock and the airy jig of a folk song in the rhythm, capped with Dave Arbus's violin finale. Roger Daltrey's vocal performance is masterful, far exceeding what he had done before in terms of power *and* subtlety. Lyrically, "Baba O'Riley" adopts a mystical and detached view of modern life that is both intellectually coherent and evocative, based around the key phrase "teenage wasteland"—an appropriate play upon T. S. Eliot's groundbreaking modernist epic poem "The Waste Land" (1922). This functions as a statement of a lost generation attempting to find a new direction amid the "teenage wasteland."

A more conventional rock framework is pushed to a sublime limit in "Bargain." This song has great strength and melody but lifts itself into the realms of euphoria by the inspiration of the performance. "Bargain" radiates sheer dynamism and excitement, and the brilliance of the playing turns the song into a masterpiece. The ensemble empathy and tautness between the guitar, bass and drums is remarkable, and Daltrey's vocals soar effortlessly. The lead guitar lines are charged with excitement, with Townshend playing so enthusiastically on his Gretsch Chet Atkins guitar and making use of a volume pedal to create a soft, warm swell over the two-chord introduction. (Townshend claimed his playing sounded like Neil Young on this song, but he actually sounds very characteristically like himself throughout.) With a beautiful bridge section [1.47] giving a contrast in mood, "Bargain" sounds spontaneous and fresh. Only when listened to closely is it apparent that (like "Baba O'Riley") the song has an underpinning synthesizer pattern running throughout, not merely on the more prominent bridge section and later toward the end. This was never used on a backing tape for live performances as the song hardly needs it from a structural point of view. Its theme is the duality of the human psyche, the delicate balance between ego and id. It generally addresses issues of individual identity and the perpetual striving toward self-realization. These are typically abstruse Townshend concerns, but they're shot through with terse, memorable couplets.

The less frantic "Love Ain't for Keeping" presents a lush acoustic guitar sound and a pleasingly buoyant beat, though still suffused with a rock-and-roll purity and chordal strength. This proved that relatively simple songs still had a valid place alongside the ARP synthesizer workouts. The synthesizer pattern of "Love Ain't for Keeping" was ditched along with the electric guitars, and what remains is a short, modest song full of delightful guitar work. The lyrics took a theme not developed elsewhere on *Who's Next*: an idyll of physical love and the forces of nature pervading an oppressive industrial environment, despite the odd appealing pastoral image such as "newly mown grass." The song concludes with a characteristic signing-off guitar phrase [2.05] that is sequenced directly into the opening riff of "My Wife."

"My Wife," in fact, is the sole area of contention on the album. *Lifehouse* was written by Townshend, but a sensible long-standing convention of Who albums meant that John Entwistle contributed a song or two as well. This had previously been beneficial both politically and musically. However, in the case of *Who's Next*, not only was "My Wife" stylistically at odds with

Townshend's songs, but it also lacked the homogeneity of lyrical feel. Generally, Entwistle's songs weren't the Who's weakest, and at times he was underrepresented in the Who canon. "My Wife" was one of his best songs, but the performance of it here leaves much room for improvement. The sound quality on this one song is noticeably inferior to the remainder of the record: it sounds too leaden, too one-dimensional, and it lacks the freshness and subtle qualities of the material surrounding it.

Whether this is down to the mixing or whether it was recorded under different circumstances from those of the other material is hard to say. The vocals in particular are too indistinct, despite being double-tracked, and the instrumental texture lacks color and airiness. All these factors combine to rob "My Wife" of its rightful power and stature. Everything is there to enhance it (piano, brass, wry lyrics, drumming), but they somehow fail to reach the pitch of excitement that could so easily have been maintained. If this performance was the best the band could muster in the studio, then maybe the song should have been left off *Who's Next* in favor of "Pure and Easy," "Mary" or "Time Is Passing"—three exemplary songs left by the wayside. (Some of what is missing from "My Wife" certainly does come down to the mixing. The 1995 CD reissue of *Who's Next* rectified this problem somewhat by making the guitar and piano parts much more distinct. A lot of fills and melodic flourishes had simply been buried in the mix.)

Most of the other material gains depth and subtlety because Townshend double-tracked both acoustic and electric guitars—but not, alas, on "My Wife," where this approach might have greatly helped. (Following the release of the album, a cult of John Entwistle fans in the United States, where Entwistle's early solo albums were particularly successful, claimed that "My Wife" was the best song on the album and accounted for its unsympathetic production by suggesting Townshend had taken a deliberately negative approach because he hadn't written it or that Townshend had deliberately "fixed" the production to make it sound weaker than his own songs! This conspiracy theory is best disregarded.) However, good as "My Wife" is, and despite the familiarity of its place on *Who's Next*, it remains the weakest song on the collection for the reasons indicated above.

The intricate ballad "Song Is Over" moves through plaintive verses into a dramatic and passionate chorus, and the contrasting voices of Pete and Roger work wonderfully well on what is a mature composition, structured with an almost baroque tidiness and order. The clean, uncluttered sound and the rich synthesizer patterns rendered "Song Is Over" too grandiose for live performances. It has the epic stature and sincerity of the organic conclusion to the *Lifehouse* cycle, addressing the personification of the concept of *song*. The drumming is superbly controlled and dramatic, and the bass is very expressive. Roger Daltrey's singing, however, is probably the strongest single element, allowing the lyrical sentiment to flow without being forced, even incorporating the theme of "Pure and Easy" in its last echoey refrain [5.27]. The fluid, classy musicianship was achieved in part by the presence of Nicky Hopkins, but even his piano work is overwhelmed by the beautiful, rich synthesizer chords on the verses, which showed what could be done with the instrument away from the extravagance of "Baba O'Riley." "Song Is Over" was intended as the film's final statement about the power of song being finally harnessed as a unifying strength.

As the song fades, the quotation from "Pure and Easy" ("The song is over, excepting one note / Pure and easy, playing so free like a breath rippling by") serves to give an indication of the cyclic continuum that *Lifehouse* would have formed. This provides some evidence that "Pure and Easy" was the starting point of the *Lifehouse* theme (almost like "Once upon a time...") and that "Song Is Over" was the natural ending, with a reintroduction of the beginning as a coda to suggest an organic, evolutionary process (a note into notes, notes into chords, chords into melody and song, songs into a musical cycle and finally returning to the note), and this in turn becomes symbolic of rebirth, reincarnation, and transmigration.

A direct continuation of both theme and sound scheme of "Song Is Over" (but without the synthesizer) follows with "Getting in Tune": a forceful and compelling performance that passes through simple melodic verses into a twisting, gripping chorus with brilliant backing voices before a rocking jam takes off toward the end. (This and "My Wife" are the only songs on *Who's Next* that fade out; all the others reach a precise final climax.) Again, "Getting in Tune" communicates with vivid clarity without utilizing an all-out aural attack of electric guitars or synthesizers. The singing really makes the song, and the themes are clearly articulated by Daltrey on the key subject of harmony—both musical and social. Lyrically, this is a restatement of the "Pure and Easy" theme about harmony and the central coda that the power of music can provide a key to the universal truths of mankind. Nicky Hopkins provides his most raucous piano performance as the song fades away into an increasingly more boisterous jam.

A breezy, uptempo acoustic guitar provides a foundation for "Going Mobile," with Pete's joyous celebration of life as perceived from within a motor home. This is a fast country-rock song that is kept light and energetic with some beautiful chord changes and a brisk, irreverent attitude. The synthesizer provides some substance during the few lulls in the melody and beat, and finally the guitar solo dominates the sound [1.57]—a curious effect that gives a wet, "wah-wah" texture. In short, "Going Mobile" is a fine, understated song. Its lively arrangement tends to undermine its musical value. This forms a carefree evocation of gypsy life that represents a freedom through a lack of urban conformity. This song holds a great deal of relevance today in the light of New Age travelers, although one line in the song ("I don't care about pollution") would not sit well with the New Age eco-warrior ideology of the 1990s.

Matchless in its beauty is "Behind Blue Eyes," the most gentle and precise song that the Who ever attempted. This plaintive, minor-key epic holds an inner strength that takes a grip of the listener's imagination—partly due to the compelling melody and partly because the character singing the most profoundly subjective of words seems so real and vivid that the listener really feels they are being party to a chilling confession. For once the *I* sounds convincingly like a real person—Townshend, Daltrey or otherwise. It is a song specifically expressing the self-doubt of a character taking stock and coming close to self-realization by embracing his failings and inadequacies, related in many ways to "The Seeker." The song doesn't use synthesizers or musical grandiosity to gain its force and sense of drama; it is conventional enough in structure and becomes overwhelmingly dynamic when it explodes into the fast third verse [2.18], which climaxes with an exquisite power chord sequence [3.06]. The performances—especially the singing—achieve a state of perfection that encapsulates more than does anything else the Who's latent genius. Most bands would have thrown a banal love ballad into the record here, but the Who give us an undiluted and uncompromising sound of pristine rock and roll charged with emotional dynamite. "Behind Blue Eyes" is an unforgettable experience.

Finally, "Won't Get Fooled Again" makes much more sense in its full length, being better paced and with the dramatics of the key change intact and the final denouement falling naturally within the full scope of the song. This is the quintessential *Who's Next* song, but not necessarily the best. In its full length, this stands as more of a warning against revolution and leaders who may turn out not to be what they appear. As good as "Won't Get Fooled Again" undoubtedly is, it perhaps meanders a little too much in the middle, but very few other groups at the time could produce a nine-minute song that doesn't rely upon extraneous solos or needless repetition. "Won't Get Fooled Again" stays taut and energetic, and Moon's drumming is brilliantly paced, this being one of his showcase performances.

A stark and haunting synthesizer passage [6.37] is shattered by Keith's drumroll [7.31] which prepares the way for an overwhelmingly forceful reprise of the power chord sequence [7.45] over which Daltrey gives a definitive scream. This is a brilliant microcosm of the Who's statement of pure anger and musical rage, and it remains one of the most distinctive moments that the Who ever committed to record. "Won't Get Fooled Again" is a song that simultaneously reaffirms the Who's commitment to both future technology *and* basic rock and roll, at a time when most groups were choosing one or the other. The Who proved that the two values were not only compatible and workable but essential factors if rock was to avoid stagnation or a descent into banality.

The overall cohesiveness and unity of the LP is such that no individual song could be excluded as substandard (notwithstanding the special circumstances surrounding "My Wife"). However, changes could have improved the record, even without the obvious desirability of the double album format. Could not "Pure and Easy" have been squeezed on as well? And what about "Mary" and "Time Is Passing"? It wasn't as if any of these songs had been earmarked for future single release, which would have changed the situation—but this speculation is to exercise the received wisdom of hindsight. Ultimately, all such reservations are irrelevant, and twenty-five years into the future *Who's Next* began to resemble something more of the double album originally planned thanks to the CD reissue of November 1995, which incorporated seven additional tracks.

The sleeve design for *Who's Next* was stunning. On a stark, wasted landscape, a single concrete pillar rises from the dead ground like the lone component of an ugly modern-day Stonehenge, onto which the members of the Who have just urinated. The band shrewdly eschewed interpretation, but the possibility remains that this is a visual suggestion of Townshend's teenage wasteland, or merely the earlier one poetically evoked by T. S. Eliot. Whatever, it perfectly suited the music and bore a suggestion of the futuristic surrealism of *Lifehouse* while retaining the earthy humor of *Sell Out*. More importantly, it connected with the whole *Zeitgeist* of the early 1970s as a potent symbol of alienation and urban decay—it looked like one of the desolate, dehumanized urban landscapes depicted in Stanley Kubrick's film *A Clockwork Orange* (1971), which had used actual locations in England rather than sets. The sleeve also suggests the black monolith of Kubrick's earlier film *2001: A Space Odyssey* (1968).

Far from being the contrived and meaningless art house shot that often adorned album covers of this era (of which a design team called Hipgnosis were the main offenders), this photograph by Ethan A. Russell was derived in a much more spontaneous way: all courtesy, it would appear, of Britain's National Coal Board. Russell was returning to London with the band from Sunderland after their show there on 5 May, and the concrete pillar was spotted near Sheffield on a slagheap. The sky was superimposed later from a different shot. The members of the band don't look like superstars on this photograph: they resemble tramps, lost souls alienated by the world, the kind of people who urinate in public. It is an image that enhanced the Who's aura of mystique but also stressed their basic human qualities. If nothing else, the pillar served to diminish the individuals in the band to four equally insignificant figures at the foot of something bigger than them all.[29]

The first public hearing of *Who's Next* came when Keith Moon threw a garden party at his new house, Tara, in Chertsey, England, on Wednesday, 14 July 1971. The rock press was present en masse, along with most of the Who's friends and associates. Two speaker stacks were set up in the garden, and *Who's Next* was blasted out for the first time to an excited (and inebriated) throng. Several photographs were taken of the band at this event, and Pete got into a heated discussion with Mick Farren and his colleagues from *It*. A massive commercial success, the album reached number 1 in the U.K. (the only Who album to achieve this feat) and number 4 in the States. The FM radio network in the U.S.—which very much supported album-based rock music—immediately seized upon *Who's Next* and to this day have never quite let it go, with "Won't Get Fooled Again," "Behind Blue Eyes" and "Baba O'Riley" in particular becoming programming staples.

Who's Next gained predictably glowing notices. Roy Carr of *Melody Maker* was not disappointed; he said of the album, "The studio concentration has been heavy in recent months, but now they've come up with a phenomenally good record. For uncomplicated sheer rock, it may turn out to be The Who's biggest recording triumph yet, for there isn't a duff track.... A superb Who album...."[30] In *Sounds*, Billy Walker wrote, "The fact that they settled for a straight-forward album rather than an extension of their rock opera says much for their courage and inventiveness.... Superb ... as much vintage Who as anything, tough, rocking music with that very distinctive pulsing sound."[31] The British underground press, by now often critical of very big groups, had some reservations about the Who's attitude to the "revolution," but Mick Farren couldn't deny the musical power, saying, "The music is brilliant (predictably brilliant), Pete's mania for electronics pays off."[32] In the U.S., John Mendelsohn offered a long and praiseworthy assessment of the album in *Rolling Stone*, while Dave Marsh found that any weak points were easily overcome by "Won't Get Fooled Again," in a review in *Creem*.[33] A similarly titled U.K. magazine, *Cream*, carried a review by Ray Tolliday in which he said, "Britain's greatest rock group at their best. A near masterpiece. Seventy five per cent of the tracks are brilliant ... a mature rock album."[34]

Kit Lambert's absence from the production credits—he received a token and somewhat meaningless mention as executive producer—did prompt a number of questions about his future with the Who. Journalists picked up on this, and Townshend was questioned about it in interviews. Pete took pains to explain what had happened with tact and diplomacy and without passing any overtly critical comment on Kit's behavior at all. "I think when Kit realised we were unhappy with him he was hurt and opted out completely rather than take a downward slide," Pete told Nick Logan at the *New Musical Express*. "We just generally moved apart. We think completely differently now."[35] And for Kit, "thinking differently" meant being pretty much oblivious to almost everything the band did from this point onwards.

By the time of its release, no one (apart from Pete) was talking about *Lifehouse* anymore. People were just glad to have the Who still together, releasing records and playing concerts. Amid the euphoria of the fans and critics, members of the band harbored doubts about the merits of their album, still disoriented by the experience of *Lifehouse*. Internally, a sense of anticlimax prevailed, and this often led to contradictory opinions in the press. Townshend, for instance, initially said, "I think the new album is a high-point musically for the group. There is a lot of exciting stuff on it.... I think The Who have actually gone through an incredible hump in their career. A lot of other groups would have split."[36] But soon afterward he seemed more disappointed. A year later he summed up his feelings about *Who's Next* as follows: "It was a compromise album. I felt [*Who's Next*] was making the best of what we had at the time—the whole theatre project, the film idea—all those new numbers were part of a bigger scheme."[37] And around the same time Roger Daltrey offered a different assessment of the album's merits (or otherwise): "The *Who's Next* album was very good, but it was too thought out.... Really, *Who's Next* was a bit airy-fairy for The Who. I think we left too much up to Glyn Johns and Pete and got a bit lost."[38] Since this time, Pete has come to regard it rather more warmly: "It has tremendous merit. It's a wonderful record. It's probably the best *record* record that The Who ever made."[39] John Entwistle also came to share this view he said, "I guess the time that [*Who's Next*] was recorded was the time we were happiest. We'd sorted out most of our problems by then and we were still being creative."[40]

The songs that would have formed the other half of the rejected double album aren't known in any exact order but included "Too Much of Anything," "Pure and Easy," "Time Is Passing," "Mary," "Naked Eye," "Water," "Join Together," "Let's See Action," "Relay," and "Put the Money Down." Other songs that weren't part of the concept but that could have been used were "I Don't Even Know Myself" (already consigned to the B side of "Won't Get Fooled Again") and John Entwistle's "When I Was a Boy" (due for a similar fate on the next single). Obviously, not all the extraneous material was consigned to the dustbin: "Let's See Action" had been selected for a future single, but the remainder found no immediate niche on record. The majority of these songs did subsequently appear on record releases over the next four years, but "Mary" officially appeared only as a Pete Townshend demo (ditto "Time Is Passing" until the Who's version was finally released in 1998). Indeed, "Time Is Passing," "Too Much of Anything," and "Pure and Easy" had all been played onstage during the early months of 1971, and announcements had suggested that they were to be released on the album.

"Time Is Passing" is laid back, philosophical and confident, with a melody of growing appeal, a commanding Daltrey vocal and a bouncy acoustic guitar arrangement. It has a distinct country flavor and makes use of pedal steel guitar and electric piano, overlaid by a whimsical synthesizer melody. This is a song of philosophical reflectiveness and has a tranquil Meher Baba perspective but restates an important *Lifehouse* credo: "It's only through the music we'll be free." The most evocative line in the song—the conclusion to a fine contrasting middle section—relates how "an empire of dead men leave their graves." The multitrack master tape of the song is absent from the Who's archives, and the only extant version remaining in the vaults is a one-quarter-inch mix that had deteriorated too much to allow any consistency between the two stereo channels: one side of the stereo picture was riddled with dropouts. For the 1998 *Odds and Sods* release, Jon Astley had little choice but to mix it into mono. This has the effect of removing much of the pedal steel guitar, electric piano and synthesizer from the track, although the fine qualities of the song still overcome such technical blights. "Time Is Passing" is one of the finest of the Who's latter-day archive releases.

Consciously echoing Bob Dylan's "Too Much of Nothing," "Too Much of Anything" stands as an overview of any society in a terminal state and the wearying effects of an excess of life. The theme seems to act as a comment on the excesses of the rock-and-roll lifestyle, however, with specific reference to the overblown hedonism related to Who tours. This song was written just at the point where Townshend had begun to grow weary of Who tours and his hell-raising superstar persona. Musically, this is a pleasant and soundly constructed soft rocker on which Nicky Hopkins's piano plays a prominent role, but it lacks the arresting edge of much of the other *Lifehouse* material. It was first released on *Odds and Sods* in 1974, then in an alternate mix on the *Who's Next* CD.

A much less orthodox Who song than "Too Much of Anything" is "Mary," which begins as a melodic folksy lament that is cut short by a jagged, descending acoustic guitar figure that forms an effective contrast in the dramatic second section of the song. A specific character song from a romantic subplot of *Lifehouse*, this seems to be sung by Mary's lover and addressed to Mary, detailing past experiences and lives. Only the demo of "Mary" has emerged on Pete Townshend's *Scoop* LP, and although there remains a strong possibility that the Who recorded a version of this at Olympic, such a tape has yet to be unearthed. (It is worth mentioning here that many of the Who's master tapes recorded at Olympic Studios during these sessions in 1971 are missing.)

A longer, second version of "Pure and Easy" was also recorded during the London sessions, a slower, more graceful, and less densely textured performance, which includes a heartfelt guitar solo [3.06]. This version retains all the fine melodic qualities and emotive changes of mood of the composition and merely reinforces the conviction that a song of such profound strength and vigor should have been included on *Who's Next*. It was first released on *Odds and Sods* in 1974. Townshend's weaker, less forthright demo version had appeared on his solo album *Who Came First* in 1972. It is less easy, however, to imagine the Who working on the synthesizer experiments titled "Meher Baba." These had been sequentially numbered by Pete as "M1," "M2" and so on, and three were released in 1993 on Townshend's *PsychoDerelict*, though the extent to which these had been subsequently worked on makes it difficult to tell how much of what remains belongs to 1971.

An older song that roughly fitted into the scheme of the new concept, "Water" found only a temporary home with *Lifehouse*, depicting a society without direction or spiritual nourishment. The lyrics are reminiscent of the wasteland approach taken in "Baba O'Riley." It also uses the image of a worldwide drought and the River Thames running dry, which reflects an extreme form of environmental decay. "Water" may have been abandoned from the final concept because it was musically of secondary importance, but it would have fitted in very well lyrically. The studio version (released in 1973) lacked the bite and apocalyptic force of the stage version, and "Water" is to be experienced in its definitive form in the live version from the Young Vic, 26 April 1971, first released on the *Who's Next* CD in 1995.

The fate of its companion piece, "Naked Eye," was similar. This remained a highlight of the live act between 1970 and 1974, during which time the recording went unreleased. Its potency as a carefully paced and startlingly powerful closer to the live act rendered the studio version somewhat innocuous. However, when released on *Odds and Sods* in 1974, the song still retained interest in a version that featured an electric piano arrangement. Lyrically, this dwells on territory similar to "Water" and surveys a world where appearance and illusion are greatly at odds with truth and reality. The shared vocal lines between Daltrey and Townshend are very effective, and the finest version of the song can be found on the *Who's Next* CD in a live version from the Young Vic. The contrast here between the gentle arpeggio guitar figures of the verse and fast riff of the chorus provides the main substance of the work.

For the CD reissue of *Who's Next* in 1995, Jon Astley was able to draw from this material to present a very satisfactory extended collection of *Lifehouse* tracks, with enlightening booklet notes by Pete Townshend. The additions included the first release of three songs from the New York sessions, "Baby Don't You Do It," "Pure and Easy" and "Behind Blue Eyes," all mixed and mastered from the original 16-track tape; "Naked Eye," repeated in a slightly more tidy form from the boxed set, and "Water," both live at the Young Vic; and "I Don't Even Know Myself" and "Too Much of Anything", both newly remastered. Unfortunately, due to the master tapes having been lost, Astley could only remix five of the album's original tracks. The remaining four, "Getting in Tune," "Bargain," "Won't Get Fooled Again" and "Song Is Over" were remastered from one-quarter-inch tapes that contained Glyn Johns's original stereo mixes. The extremely high quality of these original mixes meant that these tracks could be reassembled side by side without any greatly noticeable variation in sound quality, forming a superb sequence of prime Who material.

It is unclear whether the band initially or partially recorded "Join Together," "Relay" and "Put the Money Down" in 1971. The versions that finally emerged were completed in mid–1972. It is also quite likely that additional songs were to be part of the concept, and the band may have worked on these during the sessions. Pete Townshend's CD *PsychoDerelict* presented a return to the theme and some of the music of *Lifehouse*, prompting Pete to make new references to other songs that were part of the concept. A press release supporting *PsychoDerelict* clearly stated that many songs first intended for *Lifehouse* were later used on the following albums: *Rough Mix* (1977), *Who Are You* (1978) and *Empty Glass* (1980). Unfortunately, the press release didn't identify which were the relevant songs from these albums. It has been suggested but not confirmed that "Guitar and Pen" from *Who Are You* was originally a *Lifehouse* song, as was the synthesizer base of "Who Are You" itself, and also "Greyhound Girl," which was the B side of Pete Townshend's solo single "Let My Love Open the Door" (1980). Only a complete investigation of Pete Townshend's personal demo recordings would reveal the full extent of what was intended for *Lifehouse* and what was discarded along the way.

The latter half of 1971 was a busy period for the Who. Following the release of *Who's Next* they undertook a tour of the United States (East Coast and Midwest), a tour of Britain, and then another tour of the States (West Coast and the South) which took them to the end of the year. A big London charity concert at the Oval cricket ground was held on 18 September, and the Who topped the bill of several groups including the Faces and Mott the Hoople. This whole event was recorded in the hope of a multiartist live set being released, but the idea was eventually abandoned. It had apparently been proposed that a double album could be culled from the tapes, of which the Who were to have featured on one side. The master tapes of this recording from the Pye mobile unit were not retained in the Who archive, and a private owner of the tapes offered them to the band in 1994. However, the technical quality of the tape was too poor for any use to be made of them despite the brilliance of the Who's performance.

In October, further *Lifehouse* material appeared on record in the shape of "Let's See Action." This had been specifically held for single release, having a thematic connection with "Won't Get Fooled Again," and excluded from the album. Pete described it as "a planned pre-determined follow up."[41] However, he also later thought the release was unexpectedly early; he said, "The tracks were recorded at the tail end of the sessions for the last album, but I didn't realise it was going to be released so soon. We might have a bash at it on stage but we haven't rehearsed it yet. It's a very relaxed number for us."[42] For no clear reason, it was passed over for a U.S. release by Decca, who instead rather pointlessly selected for single issue "Behind Blue Eyes" (which reached number 34). The idea of releasing songs on single that *weren't* taken from forthcoming or existing albums was a continuation of the band's 1960s policy of giving value for money and was perhaps a little untidy for the more corporate American approach, where singles were considered to be either tasters or trailers for albums, or albums were collections of previous singles. The British attitude was certainly more sensible and appealing to the record buyer.

The strident and positive lyrical theme of "Let's See Action" provided an apt counterpoint to "Won't Get Fooled Again," which (as previously mentioned) had brought criticism of negativity and cynicism from some quarters. The message of "Let's See Action," although superficially unequivocal, isn't merely a straightforward call to arms. It encompasses assimilated Meher Baba ideas on soul searching and the utilization of positive impulses from within. In short, the theme was comparatively demanding for a pop single. It wasn't a big hit, reaching only number 16, but it remains a very worthwhile release.

"Let's See Action" is a fine song—a revolutionary pub sing-along, no less—that is perhaps let down by a murky production and an unappetizing barroom piano (courtesy of Nicky Hopkins). If sharpened up, this could have sounded much more like a masterpiece than it does, although the early rhythmic guitar solo cuts through with some definition. The ragtime easygoing feel is somewhat at odds with the uncompromising lyrics. The melodic bridge [2.00] sung by Pete—so typical of his *Lifehouse* songs—introduces a flourish of synthesizer before a masterly return to the verse pattern, [2.40] and the end refrain is inventive and memorable [3.30]. Ultimately, however, all this detail in the playing has to fight against a poor sound presentation that lacks a necessary edge and clarity. Jon Astley and Andy Macpherson remixed "Let's See Action" for the *30 Years of Maximum R&B* CD boxed set in 1994. This improved the sound considerably, but some listeners could justly complain about Daltrey's echo-repeated lead vocals still being set too far back in the mix. "Let's See Action" can finally stand as a straightforward appeal for change in society and how this can be achieved through cooperation and collaboration.

John Entwistle's "When I Was a Boy" on the B side is another good song hampered by a leaden, plodding arrangement and a similarly unflattering production, which repeated the problems of both "My Wife" and "Let's See Action." It offered some very attractive brass arrangements and Nicky Hopkins's piano, but (like "My Wife") the guitar sounds rudimentary to the point of apathy. Although lacking a dynamic thrust, the melody achieves a haunting and melancholy feel, enhanced by the brass section that is introduced on the chorus. Entwistle's song is a nostalgic lament for the short-lived optimism of childhood as contrasted with the unpleasant onset of adulthood, where heavy responsibilities and shattered dreams abound. The downbeat ending strikes an inconclusive but poignant note devoid of hope, as Entwistle asks, "I wonder what went wrong?" The sound quality of both sides of the single certainly falls far short of *Who's Next*, which suggests that neither song received the attention in the recording studio at the postproduction stage that it deserved. This is a lamentable situation, resulting in the impression that these songs were somehow rushed, though later CD issues have improved this fault somewhat.

A second important Who album of 1971 appeared in October when both Track and Decca released *Meaty Beaty Big & Bouncy*, a near-definitive collection of the Who's singles from the 1965–1970 period. This was prompted by the fact that many of the band's new (post–*Tommy*) fans did not have the early work (now deleted) and also that five years had elapsed making the Brunswick material available to release without Talmy's consent (although he still collected royalties on Who works, including *Who's Next*). The album is a fine, well-considered compilation, and the cover took an overtly nostalgic approach—a process tentatively begun with the packaging of *Live at Leeds* but which was to have much greater resonance for the upcoming *Quadrophenia* project. An element of revisionism had crept into the track selection, however: all the Who's singles were represented with the exception of "Dogs," the Rolling Stones support disk, and the *Ready Steady Who* material. In place of "Dogs" (which seemed to have been quietly disowned), however, was "Boris the Spider," the Who single that never was but maybe should have been, as Townshend readily admitted. "I'm a Boy" and "Magic Bus" were "new recordings and not previously released," as Track informed *Melody Maker*.[43] Such a collection of singles could hardly fail to form a dazzling album, although the sound varied between mono, stereo, and an unappetizing "mono enhanced into stereo."

The cover of *Meaty Beaty Big & Bouncy* utilizes the brilliant idea of depicting the Who as bedraggled youngsters outside a terraced house, presumably in the mid–1950s (and before they had in reality met each other), bathed in a sepia glow, with their latter-day selves watching (in color) from the window. The young Pete Townshend clutches an acoustic guitar (left-handed!), innocent but determined. The present-day Who look slightly cynical and faded. The inner gatefold sleeve carries a photograph of the Harrow and Wealdstone Railway Hotel (where they often played circa 1964) with the Who on a poster as an upcoming attraction, overshadowing a clutch of fading 1950s rock 'n' roll bands. There is some quality about this photograph that should strike a chord with anyone who is familiar with British working-class social habits in the 1960s; dingy and derelict as this public house looks, it is an absolutely true representation of the kind of establishment that can still be found throughout Britain. American fans should particularly note that this photograph is not a mythmaking construct of "lowlife" Britain. This is how it was (and is still).

Reaching number 9 in the U.K. and number 11 in the U.S., *Meaty Beaty Big & Bouncy* was considered in some quarters to be the finest Who record of them all, an assessment compounded by Pete Townshend, who wrote a long "review" of the album for *Rolling Stone* in which he classed the work as the "greatest of Who albums."[44] Chris Charlesworth noted that real Who fans would already have all the tracks but said "buy it anyway, 'cos it really represents yer 'Oos contribution to rock in one meaty album."[45] *Record Mirror*'s Lon Goddard said of it, "...terrific packaging and excellent sound reproduction from the oldest to the newest. Quite simply a mandatory inclusion in every collection...."[46] Peter Nikcol concluded in *Gramophone* that the album was a "truly classic collection."[47]

As the year concluded with a flourish of superb concert performances, the question of releasing a live album was once more breached when a show was recorded at San Francisco Civic Center on 13 December. Predictably, the album was scrapped, though not for reasons of deficiency in recording or performance. In fact, the handful of tracks that have since been released are brilliant, easily the match for anything on *Live at Leeds*. Only "Baby Don't You Do It" was issued at the time, but more recently "Bargain," "My Wife" and "Going Down," an impromptu version of a recent Freddie King blues song, have been released in pristine sound quality. "Bargain" is full-powered and tightly strung and includes an additional improvised riff coda [5.29] toward the end. This emerged on *Who's Missing* in 1985. The version of "My Wife" holds a relentless energy and drive and is much more satisfactory than the *Who's Next* version. "Going Down" starts as a guitar pyrotechnic exercise by Townshend but forms a spontaneous jam in the manner of the "My Generation" improvisations, based upon a descending riff pattern. The latter two songs were a highlight of 1987's *Two's Missing* LP.

The Who's 1972 output on record totaled no more that two singles, though they had intended it to be much more than this. In the wake of *Lifehouse*, the Who still thought their next album would be tied in with a film, a sort of *Lifehouse* once or twice removed. Feeling the momentum of the *Lifehouse* recording sessions could be resurrected a year later (along with some leftover material), they had booked time at Olympic Studios in May and June 1972 to once more work with Glyn Johns. Townshend's songs were *Lifehouse* and post–*Lifehouse* compositions. Some had been recorded in early 1971; others were fairly new. It is not known what the album resulting from these sessions would have contained in detail, but the following fourteen songs are likely contenders: "Pure and Easy," "Relay," "Join Together," "Too Much of Anything," "Naked Eye," "Water," "Time Is Passing," "Mary," "Put the Money Down," "Love Reign o'er Me," "Long Live Rock," "Is It in My Head?," "Why Can't You See I'm Easy" and "Riot in the Female Jail." The last five songs were the newest, and all but the last two are known to have been completed. "Wasp Man," also completed at these sessions, cannot be taken as a likely album track.

When recording work was nearing completion, the feeling that the album wouldn't achieve a consistent level of quality led to its being scrapped. Prior to this decision, however, Townshend had already settled upon the Who's recording another concept album or rock opera and had earmarked "Love Reign o'er Me" for this new work. Pete said, "We thought we needed an intermediary album, but [it] wouldn't have done anything new, added any coal to the Who fire."[48] Ultimately, the 1972 sessions simply didn't generate any positive response from Pete, as he recollected a year later, "We put a rough assembly together, and it sounded like a shadow, if this is possible, of *Who's Next*."[49] The band decided to release a couple of singles from these sessions while Pete worked up his new concept idea and composed additional songs.

"Join Together" appeared in June 1972 and was a wise choice as a single, being both catchy pop and complex rock and roll, full of unusual sounds and rhythms. The backing vocals are exemplary and carry the main force of a melody that is ingenious and infectious—the song has no chorus as such and delivers a forceful sound through the conviction of hypnotic repetition. The guitar solo signals in a repeated riff pattern that underlies the whole melody, and the harmonica and mouth-harp sounds merge into a drone that carries a repeated single note through the whole performance. The title of "Join Together" forms a simple and forceful message: a plea for the audience and performer to combine, to reach mutual harmony.

The reviews of "Join Together" were mixed. It was ostensibly well received, and *New Musical Express* said, "...a great record.... When it comes to making definitive rock group singles, the 'Oo are peers and proven masters of their Art ... the best music available. Hail, Hail, Rock 'n' Roll."[50] Chris Welch of *Melody Maker* found an element of blandness creeping in but felt the record would sound stronger in time.[51] *It*, however, raised an uncomfortable point: "Join Together could mean we all get to write cheques for ourselves from a joint 'Who & Us Joined Together' bank account, or maybe go and drink Moony's hotel dry. But thoughts of this nature ... no way."[52] A well-deserved number 9 hit in the U.K., the U.S. release made a respectable number 17 in the charts. On the B side is the live recording of "Baby Don't You Do It" from San Francisco (13 December 1971), a rough-edged hard rocker. This is not quite the most inspired version of the song that they played at concerts around this time, but it is well worth the release despite a somewhat dull mastering.

At the very end of 1972 came "Relay," a less commercial song than "Join Together" but equally strong. Despite conforming as a high-paced rock-and-roll outing, this is a more experimental sound, full of phasing and wah-wah, with interesting twists and turns throughout over what (for the Who) approximates a funky beat. It has a raw edge to it despite the layers of frantic acoustic rhythm guitar, angry electric lead guitar and the electronically treated guitar spitting and spluttering in the background. Unsurprisingly, the song climbed no higher than number 21 in the U.K. charts and a miserable number 39 in the States. The song relates a theme similar to that of "Let's See Action," a comment on the importance of the continuity of radical ideas between individuals, generations, nations and global communities. It suggests a rallying call of the revolutionaries, although it does imply that revolution itself can be bereft of meaning if undertaken dogmatically. *Melody Maker* was typically impressed, heading the review "The Who's next monster," perhaps thinking "Relay" would take the charts by storm.[53]

Two alternate studio versions of "Relay" cropped up in early 1973 on television programs. First, on *Russell Harty Plus* (broadcast on 6 January 1973) Daltrey sang a live vocal over the regular backing track from the single. More significant, however, was an appearance on the *Old Grey Whistle Test* (broadcast 30 January 1973), which also featured live vocals but was nearly a minute longer than the single, including some interesting variations in the guitar-synth backing. This appearance also featured a version of "Long Live Rock" (discussed below) complete with botched live vocals from Pete Townshend! These two isolated appearances were almost the last gasp of the Who's playing in television studios; after this time the band made only two further appearances on *Top of the Pops*, one in 1973, the other in 1981.

"Wasp Man" on the B side was Keith Moon's last composition to be recorded by the Who, a zany ode to a wasp (much in the tradition of "Dogs Part Two"), complete with various buzzing sound effects from Moon and with Townshend and Entwistle singing the title line (the only lyric in the song apart from Moon's "Sting!" rant). Roger Daltrey is busy on harmonica, wailing over a three-chord riff that is familiar from various live improvisations. "Wasp Man" is a one-take throwaway joke song that holds its own amid Pete Townshend's loftier musical concerns. "Put the Money Down" is an outtake from the 1972 sessions that falls slightly below the quality of the band's best 1971–1972 output. A swaggering rocker with a delicate synthesizer pattern, it has some interesting moments but tends to be too self-conscious, both musically and lyrically. "Put the Money Down" is a lament upon the relationship between the performer and the audience and an examination of the trust one instills in the other. There remain two songs that it would appear the Who did not get round to recording: "Riot in the Female Jail," an interesting funk-influenced male wish–fulfilment fantasy that was obviously written tongue-in-cheek, and "Why Can't You See I'm Easy," a song about a peacemaker delivered as a Crosby, Stills, Nash & Young soft rocker. Both could have been notable Who tracks but would have perhaps necessitated too drastic a departure from Who orthodoxy.

Of the remaining songs, "Love Reign o'er Me" and "Is It in My Head?" were incorporated into *Quadrophenia* and are discussed in the next chapter, leaving "Long Live Rock"—which was the germination of *Quadrophenia* itself. Musically, "Long Live Rock" is a self-conscious reiteration of the roots of the Who, in the style of a Chuck Berry song. It is essentially a novelty item, a specific recreation of the 1950s rock 'n' roll ethic, with some guttural guitar riffing and energetic piano playing in the background. The bridge section ("Landslide, rock's a falling...") shifts the song into a style—lyrically and musically—that reflects Townshend's more current concerns, as if pontificating upon rock music and its current state. Lyrically, the songs plays on the ritualized statement of succession of the British monarchy—"the King is dead / long live the King"—suggesting a succession within rock and roll itself, a self-perpetuating continuum. Drawing upon the real roots of rock 'n' roll, this song pitched the origins of the Who to a period even earlier than the mod era and served its purpose in giving Pete a starting point for an idea of a musical history of the Who. The song was played onstage during 1972, but the band resisted releasing it as a single. It first emerged on *Odds and Sods* in 1974. Where the residual ideas of *Lifehouse* were represented in the *Who's Next* tailpieces of "Join Together" and "Relay," "Long Live Rock," from the same sessions, represents the harbinger of the Who's immediate future and *Quadrophenia*.

Although 1972 now may seem a sparse year for the group, it formed the link between *Lifehouse* and *Quadrophenia*, the twin peaks of the Who's mature inspiration. During the year John Entwistle had released *Whistle Rhymes*, his second solo album, which collected more of his delightfully odd songwriting gems, and Pete Townshend put together *Who Came First*, ostensibly a selection of *Lifehouse* demos and songs reprised from a second Baba LP titled *I Am*. The band's touring policy was drastically revised for 1972 (they played one European tour during the year), and their workload was much reduced from this point onward. Firmly established within the rock-and-roll elite, the Who now worked when they pleased, took long breaks, enjoyed the comforts of their earnings, pursued solo projects and regrouped only when work had to be done. Singles were now commercially irrelevant to the band; the record companies still released singles, of course, but all remaining Who singles (and their B sides, apart from "Water" in 1973) were culled from albums. Such was the changing face of the rock-and-roll market place.

The failure of *Lifehouse* had taken its toll on Pete Townshend's faith, and through 1971 and into 1972 the Who's credibility as rock and roll's most honest, decent, hardworking and unpretentious band seemed to be called into question, hence the previously quoted review of "Join Together" in *It*. It could be argued that the band were still closer to their audience than 99 percent of other successful groups at the time and just as close as the selfproclaimed "people's bands," such as the Faces (who offered a loutish beery camaraderie), Hawkwind (free festival/drug culture hippies turned space rockers), and the Pink Fairies (underground antiheroes and hard rockers who evolved from a more politically motivated group, the Deviants) or indeed any group who were currently claiming to have climbed out of the gutter with long hair, battered guitars in their hands and a vision of the truth.

5. To the Lifehouse (1971–1972)

It is difficult to contrive a genuine form of "music for the people"; ultimately, mass popularity may provide a yardstick that cannot be challenged. In the pop world, history may—on this issue alone—judge most favorably the groups who enjoyed genuine popular appeal and offered the least pretentious and most directly communicable rock and roll possible. This is a criterion that edges close to a musical lowest common denominator and might well show groups from this era such as Slade, Status Quo, or T. Rex winning out over groups like the Who. In any case, by the early 1970s, the "people's band" idea was becoming less revered. A new generation of rock artists such as Roxy Music, Cockney Rebel, Rod Stewart, 10cc, Elton John, David Bowie, Genesis and Yes never pretended to represent anyone or even attempted to encapsulate in their music any part of the life experience of their audiences; on the contrary, they packaged their appeal as being escapist, elitist, and in some cases (particularly Bowie) almost other-worldly. The fantasy, camp glamour, aspiration toward a jet-set lifestyle, nouveau riche pseudoaristocratic posturing and unashamedly privileged persona of the 1970s rock star was something that the Who (as a collective body) sought to refute and debunk. (Though it must be said that Keith Moon played up to this stereotype with enthusiasm, sometimes—and maybe deliberately—to the point of parody.)

The Who *were* a people's band (past tense), but several successful years down the road, the distinctly esoteric trimmings their music and lives had accumulated—such as Meher Baba—had left them in an uneasy middle ground. In many ways, more than, say, the Rolling Stones, they held true to certain ideals of their formative years. At the same time, they couldn't avoid that fact that they were inevitably shielded from the harsher realities of life by their wealth. And it is these harsh realities that often shape and dominate the lives of young people and give vitality to the formative work of artists before compromise is liable to blunt their initial vision. At least the Who understood this and never pretended the situation was otherwise. Indeed, Townshend (almost alone among his peers) actively considered this to be a problem and arguably worried about it too much.

In terms of their music, it could be argued that the Who were more in touch with the realities of life and the situation of their audience than any other pre-punk group. This is certainly the case compared to the aforementioned Hawkwind and the Pink Fairies, both of whose music (however good) was often inaccessible and escapist by the very nature of its spaced-out credibility. (The prefix *pre-punk* is a necessary qualification because in 1976, groups such as the Clash and the Jam changed the ground rules very much for the better in terms of how rock groups were supposed to communicate with and relate to their audiences.) Because the Who didn't patronize, generalize, preach or condescend musically—even in their most mystical and obtuse moments—they managed to keep a level-headed and empathic focus on the emotions of their audience. As glib as it may now sound, Townshend's perception of himself as a rock *fan* (and a Who *fan*) as well as a musician and composer enabled him to function with the self-effacement and honesty sufficient to gain the unique confidence and respect of many people.

So when Pete claimed, as he had with *Lifehouse*, that his songs would "represent" his audience, in one sense he wasn't bluffing or contriving to pull off a conceit, as many rock musicians of the era did. Indeed, his past record speaks for itself. Has any song represented its audience more fully than "My Generation"? Prior to the first album by the Clash, in 1977, probably very few have. However, the *Lifehouse* songs weren't "My Generation"; they didn't voice any *direct* social insight into the practicalities of working-class life in Britain in 1971. Maybe the question of communication with the audience can only be answered by the sheer numbers of people who attended Who concerts and on the evidence of the massive worldwide sales of *Who's Next*. Maybe this is evidence enough that the Who's music evoked a spark of genuine empathy with an audience on a global scale. (Commercial success alone, of course, is a poor signifier of worth. However, there was never any element of sycophancy, dogma, trend following or fashion slavery about Who fans' response to the band's music; and likewise, there was no manipulation, pandering or lowering of standards from the band members themselves.) The issue of *audience* was to become one of Townshend's obsessions and was to form a vital element in what he hoped to explore in *Quadrophenia*.

6

Rockers and Mods (1973–1974)

Despite the fact that both *Tommy* and *Lifehouse* had failed to reach fruition as big-budget feature films, the Who continued to consider a variety of cinema projects during 1971 and 1972, all of which were belated attempts to in some way rework *Lifehouse*. During the latter few months of 1971, Nik Cohn had accompanied the band on their U.S. tour to gather material for a film script that would reflect the essential aspects of the band's performance art. This project was given the tentative titles *Rock Farm* or *Guitar Farm*. Needless to say, the film never got made: It was the perpetual Who problem in this era of ideas and ambition surpassing practical reality. But the artistic frustrations of *not* making a film inspired for Pete the form that *Quadrophenia* would ultimately take. He felt that if the band could not make a real film, then the next best thing would be to develop "a kind of movie without pictures," as he put it. This led to his thinking about the role of the four members of the Who and the idea of "casting the four guys in the band as four facets of an archetypal mod kid's personality."[1] Townshend had admired Frank Zappa's practice of envisaging a whole dramatic concept in music as if he were making a film and then either doing the film himself cheaply or it in sound form on record. The impressionistic sound-picture that *Quadrophenia* was to become was far removed from *Tommy* in terms of technique, and this difference really makes descriptions of *Quadrophenia* as a rock opera inaccurate and misleading. (Yet in the absence of a better term of description, rock opera prevailed—applied here even less appropriately than it had been to *Tommy*.)

The clearest account of *Quadrophenia*'s inception came in an interview Pete gave in August 1972, before the Who embarked on a European tour. Michael Watts reported in the resulting article "The Eternal Mod" that Townshend's new work dealt with "adolescence, a four-way caricature of The Who from their inception to the present day." Watts summarized Pete's intentions as being "an historical retrospective of the four people involved in The

Who." The band members' characteristics were identified with Moon dubbed insane, Entwistle as romantic, Daltrey as bad and Townshend as good. "They join together," Pete said, "and become one piece of music."[2] Despite the title of Watts's article, no mention was made of mod—Pete's interests here were with the consciousness of the teenager in general, a sort of universal youth. Strongly emphasized throughout this interview, indeed, was Pete's commitment to the ethic of the three-minute rock-and-roll single, which he held to be the most ideal and direct form of communication with and about youth. By this line of argument, double concept albums would be derided as passé and flatulent, yet this is the format that Pete would ultimately end up not only using but also defending. This dichotomy needs to be understood in the light of the Who's commitment to the single during the early 1970s. For a serious "album" act, as the Who now were, the series of non-album singles through this period—"Let's See Action," "Join Together" and "Relay"—was unprecedented. No other comparable act in rock retained such a fidelity to the single as an art form in itself during a time when the industry worked to diminish its status for all but the most obviously commercial of acts. Indeed, Led Zeppelin never released any singles in the U.K., and Pink Floyd had at this stage managed for several years without them. (It took the punk movement of 1976 to reestablish the vitality of the 45 rpm single ethic.)

A few weeks later during 1972, Townshend chatted to Robin Mackie of *Record Mirror*. He talked of merging the material that had been recorded in May and June with some of his newer songs around the concept on which he was now working. Mackie noted that such a quantity of material would stretch to double album proportions, which Pete confirmed. The plan at this stage was to use the material from the earlier sessions to form the first side of the double album, while the remaining three sides would form "a mini opera, which is now put together with 14 or 15 songs. I'd like to see this one recorded rather more loosely.... We might put out a super-condensed single called 'Joker James,' which I wrote at the same time as 'I'm a Boy.'"[3] A concept work that was to occupy three-quarters of a double LP set sounds somewhat untidy, and it is hardly surprising that it was expanded to cover the fourth side as well.

The "super-condensed single" mentioned by Townshend here as "Joker James" is also an unlikely idea. The history of this song is strange: "Joker James" was at least written by 1968, and if Pete's comment is accurate it dates from as early as 1965–1966. The lyrics had been printed in the American magazine *Eye* of 7 September 1968. Again, this early publication is something of an unusual occurrence, as Townshend never liked printing lyrics aside from the music, and this example—a lightweight character study of the "Happy Jack" ilk—hardly seemed worth the effort. As to the Who issuing this song in 1972, again this seems implausible, and its ultimate nonappearance bears out the nature of its unsuitability. The song has no real connection with *Quadrophenia* apart from the name of the character, in this case depicted merely as a practical joker. It was finally released as part of the soundtrack of the *Quadrophenia* film in 1979, and even there it seemed out of place. "James" doesn't seem to be the same person as Jimmy other than that he anticipates some of the prankster elements of Keith Moon's character.

Later still in October 1972, Townshend talked to Brian Southall of *Disc* about the work-in-progress, which he said was at this stage half finished (which we should take to mean half written). Pete described, with typically boundless ambition, what he wanted the work to be: "Big.... We are after something for the main body of the stage act—something like *Tommy* but not an opera—just a theme to run through it.... I am working on this LP and I want to push The Who and rock music into an area that has never been covered before."[4] So Pete's concerns here were also to produce a *stage work* that would challenge and extend the Who's capabilities. It is important to note that he specifically emphasized that it would not be an opera, in the sense that *Tommy* was, although *opera*, as mentioned above, is in any case an inappropriate description. *Quadrophenia* was planned as a stage work, that is, a work that the Who could play on stage. Pete obviously didn't think that imposing such a specific discipline would be incompatible with his expanding musical ideas and evolving multiinstrumental arrangements. "Baba O'Riley" and "Won't Get Fooled Again"—despite the initial *Lifehouse* teething troubles—had worked out very much to Townshend's satisfaction with the use of synchronized tapes, and he felt that this was still an area to be more fully explored by the band.

Kit Lambert had not been too dominant an influence on Townshend since they ended their creative partnership after failing to collaborate on *Lifehouse*. But Kit was asked to work on the new album, it being thought of (despite Pete's denial) as an opera and therefore more Lambert's kind of thing. In December 1972, the band began some recordings with Lambert, but predictably things fell apart fairly quickly and nothing from these sessions was ultimately used. (Indeed, it is not known which songs, if any, were attempted on this occasion). If nothing else, however, this aborted attempt at recording at least cemented the form the record would take. Roger Daltrey felt confident enough to speak to the press about it before the end of the year, saying, "There will definitely be another *Tommy*. We said we never would, but we will, and it will be about one person with quadrophenia, and will probably form one-half of a double album."[5]

The "14 or 15" songs that had been written by the end of 1972 were the latest phase of the development of the concept that had started with the single song "Long Live Rock" and then been expanded to the mini-opera length (one side of an LP) titled *Rock Is Dead: Long Live Rock*, finally growing to three album sides in length. A television special was also being considered to tie in with this work, but the form this would have taken is unknown. "Cut

My Hair" was noted as one of the new songs, and Roger Daltrey told the press in late 1972 that this would be the title of the work, the ideas here obviously being fairly well developed at this early stage. From the speedy writing and recording of "Long Live Rock" (demoed by Townshend on 2 May 1972 and recorded by the Who on 6 June) to the release of the double album constituted a period of eighteen months. This was about the average for the band.

Despite the spate of television exposure in early 1973 with *Russell Harty Plus* and the *Old Grey Whistle Test*, no new Who album was imminent, and people had started to question whether the band would manage to get their new work together. Such speculation was also fueled by the success of Roger Daltrey's first solo album, *Daltrey* (released April 1973), and his hit single "Giving It All Away," which had proved far more commercial than the solo work of either Entwistle or Townshend. However, Entwistle was still prolific as a solo artist, forming a group called Rigor Mortis for an album titled *Rigor Mortis Sets In* (released June 1973), which revisited the spirit of 1950s rock 'n' roll in the same manner as had "Long Live Rock." Mark Plummer of *Melody Maker* visited Townshend in early in 1973 and observed Pete in the middle of a period of creative stasis. Townshend was feeling frustrated and dejected that the work was taking so long to finalize: "I've got to get a new act together for The Who," Pete told Plummer with a hint of exasperation, "and I don't care if it takes me two years before you see The Who again. We've got to get something fresh."[6] But Pete was despondent because he couldn't "write a strong plot," as he admitted, and he even gave the impression to Plummer that it was unlikely that the Who would get the project together at all. Townshend also expressed his frustrations with the existing recording studios in London and mentioned that in recompense a Who studio was under construction.

Other interviews Pete gave during the early months of 1973 told a more confident story, however. More specific detail about the as-yet-unrecorded work was unveiled. Michelle Hush reported for the U.S. magazine *Rock* that the new project was "tentatively titled *Quadraphrenia* [sic]."[7]

This is the first indication of the title of the work and understandably used an *a* rather than an *o* (in the second syllable), and the use of an *r* as in *schizophrenia*. However, Daltrey had already mentioned *quadrophenia* in its correct spelling in *Record Mirror* (as quoted above), though not as the title. Pete later explained that as a coined word *quadrophrenia* was more correct but difficult to pronounce, so the *r* was dropped. This same interview saw Pete's thumbnail sketch of the work. He said, "I suppose what I'm really trying to do is a kind of *Clockwork Orange* musically.... There are so many tragic things involved with the Mods ... it's got this incredible triumph in that this kid's an individual in the midst of a world where the individual doesn't exist."[8]

Townshend's writing of *Quadrophenia* commenced toward the end of 1972 and stretched as far as mid–1973 when recording was due to start. One reason for the delay was that the Who did not feel comfortable in any of the existing London recording studios and had decided to build their own. For this purpose, they purchased a disused church at 115 Thessally Road in Battersea in London. Although it wasn't finished on schedule, recording began at this location with Ronnie Lane's mobile unit lending a hand. Initially known as the Kitchen, the studio in Thessally Road was later officially named Ramport and is still operating commercially as Townhouse Three. As usual, all the material was prepared in demo form (with the possible exception of the two lengthy instrumentals "Quadrophenia" and "The Rock"). That is, they all were apart from one key song, "5.15," which was worked on directly in the studio by the band. Townshend had written some lyrics while hanging around in Oxford Street ("magically bored on a quiet street corner") and, against the established custom, the music was put together by Pete in the studio just prior to recording. Townshend has stated that his original conception of *Quadrophenia* was much bigger and longer. He claimed to have written around "fifty songs" and that the band had "really creamed off the best."[9] If this is not an exaggeration (which it sounds like), then the thirty-odd rejects must have been kept well concealed from bootleggers and avid fans. Only one outtake from the sessions, "We Close Tonight," has ever been released (on *Odds and Sods* in 1998), along with two demo items on *Scoop*—a solo piano piece that duplicated some of the chords of "The Dirty Jobs," and "Recorders," a nonmusical sound-effects experiment. The titles "Bank Holiday" and "Wizardry" have been identified as outtakes but remain unreleased. We might add to this list "Joker James" and the two songs that were resurrected for the film soundtrack in 1979, "Get Out and Stay Out" and "Four Faces," but this would still leave over twenty songs unaccounted for.

For the recordings, the band required a pianist. The use of a session player had evolved from the *Lifehouse* sessions where both Al Kooper and Nicky Hopkins had been used to great effect. Pete had begun to compose more material on the piano and needed the discipline and technical ability of a high-calibre keyboard player to bring out the best in the piano parts. Hopkins's solid formality had added considerably to "Song Is Over" and "Getting in Tune," and Pete assumed Hopkins would be able to make a similar contribution to *Quadrophenia*. But, Hopkins was unavailable (he was in the United States with the Rolling Stones) when the sessions came along. Pete, unperturbed by this absence, chanced upon a replacement in Chris Stainton, who had played most notably with Joe Cocker. It happened that the piano part of one of the new compositions, "Drowned," bore a resemblance to a Joe Cocker song called "Hitchcock Railway," on which Stainton had made a distinctive contribution. Stainton's piano work confirmed the manic blues-like potential of "Drowned" and added a specific flavor to the final take.

The recording of "Drowned" led to the (possibly apocryphal) story—told by Pete a few years later—of Chris Stainton recording the take that appeared on the album on a rainy day while playing in a booth that was steadily filling up with water due to the uncompleted state of the roof of Ramport. Whatever, the feel achieved on "Drowned" was fluid and effortlessly buoyant (to sustain a watery metaphor!) and gave the Who a sound that they had not ever achieved before. It is arguable whether Nicky Hopkins could have made the same contribution. A similar atmosphere is lent to "5.15" thanks to Stainton's presence, although his work on a third song, "The Dirty Jobs," is more structured and less abandoned. Pete (with considerable skill) played all other piano parts, notably "Quadrophenia" and "Love Reign o'er Me."

With Pete having written *all* the songs (the only Who album to have this distinction), the contributions of Roger Daltrey, Keith Moon and John Entwistle were entirely as musicians, a fact for which Pete made special leeway by keeping his demo recordings as "rough sketches.... This was an approach that was designed to allow everybody to breathe.... I gained more strength as a composer than I've ever had by trying to keep everything under my thumb."[10] Pete's direction brought about a musical breakthrough for the whole band; he said he felt that *Quadrophenia* was "the first album where The Who have used each other's capabilities as musicians to the full."[11] After recording, however, came the biggest task of all: editing, mixing and pulling all the materials together to form a coherent whole. During this period, Townshend had also made many location stereo recordings of the sea, weather, and other naturalistic sounds. Pete claimed that *Quadrophenia* took six months to mix, with sound effects and tracks merging into one another, though in fact he was at work on it from July to partway into October—less than four months. Within the title of *Quadrophenia* was an allusion to the quadrophonic sound reproduction system that had been developed by the record industry as the logical four-way advance beyond stereo. It had been intended that the album would be made available in this format, and although successful quad mixes were prepared of the work, it proved too difficult to master down onto vinyl and was never released.

Not mentioned at the time, however, was a factor that proved an additional burden for Pete. He had invited Kit Lambert to produce the album in a gesture of faith and goodwill. Lambert had remained absent from the recording sessions. Pete hoped Kit would return to supervise the mixing and apply his instinctive overview of the work to fashion a masterpiece. But Lambert failed to show up, leaving the whole work to Pete. Roger Daltrey had already lost faith in Lambert (and was pushing for legal action to oust him from the band's management), but Pete was hoping to revive their earlier fruitful relationship. Needless to say, it all went wrong. This situation suggests that Pete was feeling in need of some objective input in the final shaping of a work by which one could imagine he was in danger—as with *Lifehouse*—of becoming overwhelmed. Thankfully, Pete kept his bearings and pulled it off alone. The final mixing was perfectly serviceable, and it is doubtful that any contribution that Lambert might have made would have resulted in a significantly better end product. There were criticisms made of Townshend's mixing, but they tended to be nit-pickings. It is true that Daltrey expressed considerable dissatisfaction with his vocal mixes, but this grievance was uttered a couple of years afterward.

Implicit in the way a great many people lived in the early 1960s was the universal situation that gave *Quadrophenia* its social background: the generation gap, the psychological schism between parents and teenagers that rock and roll had helped to illustrate, if not elucidate. Mod was a British youth response to that crisis, quirky, cultist and obsessive and riddled with contradictions and hesitancy. But it came about with a forthright effervescence and a healthy lack of overt predetermination. It was the product of its age and a harbinger of the youth of the future. Mod offered reassurance where it was most needed. Mod alleviated teenage anxieties and insecurities and offered an identity—at least that was the feeling of the time. As much as any allegiance to a peer group can give a sense of purpose, mod created—out of deprived circumstances—a whole person, or so insecure youths felt. Of course, this was an illusion, as Townshend knew, and the relationship between that illusion and its antithesis in reality formed the core of what *Quadrophenia* was about.

Quadrophenia is an examination of a Who fan called Jimmy, a West London mod circa 1964. A symbolic composite of the four personalities of the members of the Who, Jimmy is deemed to be "quadrophenic," suffering an imaginary mental illness that allows such a split personality. Jimmy's life is in crisis, and rock and roll (represented by the Who) may or may not be able to redeem him from his troubles. The situation at the start of the album is so bad that Jimmy is in the process of killing himself. The Who were under no illusions that the past, the golden era of the 1960s and rock and roll itself were things to be celebrated without objectivity. So the depiction of Jimmy's life was no blind exercise in nostalgia and had none of the happy-go-lucky romanticized recreation of an era that characterised so many West End and Broadway musicals, such as *Grease*. The past—as much as the present and the future—could be harsh and unyielding. The fact that much of the mythology surrounding mod concerns violence and mob rule was just one reason why such a roseate approach was inappropriate, the precedent of *West Side Story* notwithstanding.

Two basic realities of British (and maybe all) life shaped the issues that *Quadrophenia* would address. The first was the sheer material deprivation and levels of poverty that still existed after the war for so many people. Maybe Americans in particular cannot easily comprehend just how small was the amount of money upon which the majority of British working-class families had to exist or the extent of the poor quality of rented slum housing. And opportunities to change the situation, to gain social advancement, were almost nonexistent. Jimmy's father, for instance, would very likely have done the same skilled or semiskilled manual job all his working life (apart, maybe, from a spell in the armed forces) and would likely harbor no realistic hopes or aspirations to do anything else. This fact alone began to incense the younger generation, who emphatically did not want to end up like their parents but who ultimately fared little better.

The photography of Ethan A. Russell (who was in charge of the artwork and the photo-booklet that accompanies the album) is remarkably accurate in capturing an era. The terrace of four tiny houses might seem a quaint anachronism if it were not for the fact that many people in Britain still live in such houses. The problem for Jimmy's generation is not simply lack of money, however. It is also tied up with the nature of the class system in Britain. This is another alienating factor in Jimmy's life that Americans might find puzzling but about which many British people might reasonably have cause to complain. Because Jimmy is working-class he will never be taken seriously or given an opportunity for advancement. Little will be expected of him, and prejudice will prevail throughout his life. He belongs to a generation of people who were not called upon to fight a war or even to survive a depression and mass unemployment. Jimmy and his peers have no unifying social crisis around which to rally and find an identity.

Like his namesake Jimmy Porter (the lead character in John Osborne's groundbreaking 1956 play *Look Back in Anger*), Jimmy may have reason to lament that the world no longer offers a "just cause" for which to fight. The rebellion of such "angry young men" (as the media of the time dubbed them) was vehement but unfocused. Their motivation was largely apolitical and somewhat nihilistic—very much akin to what the Who were ten years earlier. Jimmy is very much of the same mold, although he has more in common with Alan Sillitoe's fictional characters Smith from *The Loneliness of the Long-Distance Runner* (1959) and Arthur Seaton in *Saturday Night and Sunday Morning* (1958), both of which were more famous as films. These characters fought the system without the cause of rock and roll on their side, however, and it is unclear in *Quadrophenia* whether Jimmy's faith in the Who and in rock music in general is misplaced or not. Townshend shrewdly leaves open the question of the validity of rock and roll.

The second crucial reality of life for Jimmy (and perhaps the root of his problems) is the fact that he, along with many of the British postwar generation, had discovered one devastating truth about life that cut across all class divides: that your parents could often be (at best) a stifling, irritating, intractable influence in your life and could be (at worst) downright damaging and antagonistic. Young people were stuck with them in the most uncomfortably intimate way for maybe over twenty formative years, and the hostility, lack of understanding and pressure to conform they offered often resulted in a level of alienation that is now identified as one of the great sociological crises of our age. (Contemporaneous with the creation of *Quadrophenia*, the British poet Philip Larkin—twenty-three years older than Townshend—summed up this situation with admirable brevity: "They fuck you up, your mum and dad / They may not mean to, but they do."[12])

The *generation gap* (as the problem was called before sociologists coined the term *dysfunctional family*) influenced such widespread disillusionment among young people that it could be said to have fueled the whole rock 'n' roll movement in the 1950s. For the Who, "My Generation" was an early but definitive response to the problem. A few years later *Tommy* examined the damage caused to a boy by parental strife, abuse, cruelty and general neglect at the hands of the adult world. *Quadrophenia* examines the damage caused to another young man by parents who were absolutely normal, typical and utterly recognizable. The caricature authority figures of *Tommy* are replaced in *Quadrophenia* with utterly plausible realistic archetypes. Not only that, but Jimmy fares worse than Tommy at the hands of such adversaries!

If *Tommy*'s theme is the notion that self-realization and inner harmony can overcome outward disability and restriction, then *Quadrophenia*'s theme can only be that outward disillusionment can lead—via an extremely painful route—to self-discovery and a balanced self-consciousness. But for Jimmy it is close run thing, so close, in fact, that we leave him still pondering his existence at the end of "Love Reign o'er Me"; there is no valedictory "listening to you" chorus to round things off here. For Jimmy's consciousness to make that vital leap is a bigger step than the scope of the album can allow. Jimmy's reemergence from his crisis (or not, as the case may be) is the profound issue that the listener is invited to consider at the album's close.

So much of *Quadrophenia* is an evocation of a specific social milieu—yet also a universal situation—that proved that Townshend had really gotten back to grappling with the basics of life on the street after the mystical, overly cerebral theories that had formed the thematic frameworks of both *Tommy* and *Lifehouse*. This social situation is not so much rooted in the early 1960s (which just happens to tie in with Townshend's personal experience) but is more fixed in that period of *every* young person's life when he or she is at the mercy of parents. These young people suffer from the lack of money, influence, strength of character and confidence enough to rise above everyday problems; they feel isolated, exposed and frustrated with life. By 1973 Townshend was both mature and confident enough to attempt a dissection of teenage problems from a less confrontational angle than "My Generation" did. At the age of twenty-eight—when most people have already begun to see the problems of youth from the other side as parents and are often dismissive of the foibles of those who are younger—Pete Townshend plunged himself back into the consciousness of a teenager. In any other walk of life he might never have needed to bother. It just happened that as a rock musician (and, indeed, rock spokesman) his audience was very largely in that age group.

For Pete, the concept of *audience* was often merged into a personification upon which he fixed. In Pete's case, this composite was formed from a small number of people that he had known in 1964–1965, prominent among whom was a man named Irish Jack Lyons, who became the first symbol of what a Who fan was. While the passage of time can render such people mere abstractions, Jack was no symbol at all and was very much a part of Townshend's present. He is a real person who was a mod and who was intimately involved with the group that started playing at the Goldhawk Social Club and progressed to greater things. But he came to represent for Pete exactly what mods were and how they responded to his songs. Jack holds an important part in the creation of *Quadrophenia* because he has been identified as an obvious real-life model for Jimmy. He was still in touch with Pete during the 1970s, although he had returned to Ireland, but Pete wanted to partly enshrine in his new work the kind of person Jack had been ten years earlier. (In many ways, Irish Jack should be the single dedicatee of *Quadrophenia*; as it is, he is mentioned by name only in "Long Live Rock" as "selling tickets made in Hong Kong," hardly a flattering allusion. However, Pete has identified the importance of Jack in numerous interviews over the years.) The formal dedication of *Quadrophenia* (printed on the back cover) was to "the kids of Goldhawk Road, Carpenders Park, Forest Hill, Stevenage New Town and to all the people we played to at the Marquee and Brighton Aquarium in the Summer of '65."

So Jimmy is a mod because Who fans (typified by Irish Jack) in 1964 were often mods. Pete Townshend spent much time among mods. He liked them, admired their iconoclastic style and was accepted by them as a leader. He also saw their faults. Mod gives a very specific background detail to *Quadrophenia*; it fixes the work chronologically because, by 1973, mod was regarded very much as part of a more innocent phase of 1960s juvenilia. Mod gives *Quadrophenia* an extra level of interest and allows for part of an era that might otherwise have been forgotten to be recorded for posterity. But essentially, mod is peripheral to the essence of *Quadrophenia*. In truth, Jimmy need not be a mod. He could have been anybody or nobody. (It may come as a surprise to many listeners and even to people well aware of *Quadrophenia* to learn that specific mod references come into the lyrics of only *four* songs from the work—"Cut My Hair," "I've Had Enough," "Sea and Sand" and "Bell Boy"—although the printed text in the album packaging is more explicit). Townshend explained that the final work had "come out looking more like the story of Mods per se than it really is ... it could really be the story of anybody ... it's a series of songs about the frustrations that come with growing up and those most commonly associated with rock, and the morality of the rock audience."[13]

But, of course, by intent Jimmy *is* a mod, and another dimension is gained because of him so being (even if this dimension is less substantial than may be first thought). Pete said that apart from the Who's historical involvement he felt that "Mod was [a] self-contained archetypal youthful image."[14] Mod forms the background to the work because obviously that was the social scene from which the Who had emerged, and *Quadrophenia* will always be, in one sense at least, an album that commemorates and enshrines that scene. Whether it accurately captures the era is for people who were there to assess for themselves. The framework of mod in the work is an historical construct, based in the large part on that most fickle of cerebral faculties, the memory. The majority of listeners since 1973 obviously can have no firsthand connection with the original mod movement of 1963–1965 (we should discount any periodic revivals of the cult, such as that which occurred in 1979), and the fact that *Quadrophenia* means so much to so many people is a testament to how successful the Who have been at creating a work that holds a genuinely universal significance. *Quadrophenia* transcends its historical antecedent with ease.

Townshend's faith in Meher Baba must also be recognized as a component in the work, and many of the songs can be read—as Pete has stated—as prayers to God. All the references to rain, water, storms, rivers, the sea, the ocean and the beach—and there are many—are images that connect directly to Baba's philosophy. In many ways, the pacifying, purifying, soul-cleansing sentiment of songs such as "Drowned" and "Love Reign o'er Me" is a long way from Jimmy's angst-ridden mod consciousness. Pete manages to make these two disparate elements become compatible by utilizing a brilliantly contrived coincidence: the sea and water are major Baba symbols of God and love, and much real-life mod activity, as well as all of Jimmy's fictitious formative experiences, took place at the seaside, on the beach, in the English Channel. These two elements merge seamlessly in the work and give it greater depth, although it could be argued that the aggressiveness of mod and the peaceful devotions of Baba could never really coalesce. Townshend implies, of course (probably unconsciously), that one is the antidote to the other and that Jimmy's fulfilment is to be found at the end of his spiritual quest.

The germination of *Quadrophenia* can be examined in more specific detail without dwelling too heavily on mod at all. Another antecedent is to be found in a British film called *Bronco Bullfrog* (1970), which might seem an unlikely place to start an examination of *Quadrophenia*'s roots, but its significance should become apparent. First, *Bronco Bullfrog* (directed by Barney Platts-Mills) is one of the most obscure and little-seen British films of its era, so it is no surprise that it hasn't been cited as being relevant to the genesis of *Quadrophenia*. Second, it is one of the very few films of its time that attempted to capture with authenticity the sheer hopelessness and frustration of young working-class people in the poorer districts of London without applying to them a sheen of romanticized gloss, and it remains a difficult and bleak piece of work. It offers no happy ending, no well-wrought plot, no color or optimism—just scenes of desultory confrontation and grimy, dreary, monochrome images of youthful angst, culminating in an unresolved crisis.

The antihero of *Bronco Bullfrog* is Del, a sixteen-year-old apprentice in a welder's shop and prominent member of a gang who indulges in petty crime and grasps no greater opportunities from life than to make a few extra quid from burglary, fight members of another gang, and to make out with his girl. He isn't a mod or a rocker or a hippie or a skinhead; rather an Everyman combination of all four. He dresses in a mod-type suit, has quite long hair and rides a motorbike, which is a prized totem of his individuality and superiority over his peers. We know nothing of his musical tastes, and his entire angst is driven by antagonism from his parents, the harsh brutality of his immediate environment with its ghastly tower-block architecture and omnipresent police force, and a general antipathy towards a society that offers him none of the material or emotional rewards in life. His relationship with his girl is constantly threatened by parental condemnation from both sides, mutual doubt and lack of articulation and dearth of money and the opportunity even to be alone together. They attempt to run away to a more rural environment but end up coming back because they haven't a clue how to survive outside their inner-city community.

Toward the end of the film, Del loses his motorbike. He leaves it parked by the curb, and a truck smashes into it. He watches this from afar. When he returns, all he can do is look at the shattered machine that had once been his symbol of freedom and rebellion. The same thing happens, of course, to Jimmy (depicted on page 26 of the CD booklet), whose scooter holds a similar significance. Unlike Jimmy, however, Del doesn't sit on the pavement looking distraught. When a policeman approaches him looking at the wreckage, asking if it is his bike, Del simply replies "no" and walks away. It is soon after this that the most obvious visual point of comparison with *Quadrophenia* occurs. In a very striking shot, we see Del—alone and isolated—walking along an Underground railway tunnel, which stretches to infinity behind him. This looks identical to the shot of Jimmy in the CD booklet (on page 11). So similar is it, in fact, that it is difficult to imagine either Townshend or Ethan A. Russell not having it in mind when putting together the *Quadrophenia* booklet.

Running against the grain of the times, *Bronco Bullfrog* took a vastly different approach to the concept of youth in the late 1960s than almost every other work of this era, *Tommy* among them. It may have inspired Townshend's move back toward naturalism after the fable-and-fantasy period of the late 1960s and early 1970s.[15] Just as *Bronco Bullfrog* seemed a singular and uncomfortably realistic film alongside the more popular Swinging London fantasies (such as *Smashing Time* or *The Knack*), so *Quadrophenia* shared the same fate among other "concept" releases of 1973. In the early 1960s, realism (naturalism) was still a new and exciting vogue in British film (*Saturday Night and Sunday Morning*, *This Sporting Life*, *A Taste of Honey*), but by 1965 fantasy, surrealism, escapism and picaresque satire had become more dominant—a situation still prevalent but less relevant in 1973. Indeed, this was an era when the concept album vogue—not started by the Who, but certainly crystallized by *Tommy*—was in full flood (and terminal decline). In the album charts during the year, *Quadrophenia* rubbed shoulders with *Tales from Topographic Oceans* by Yes, *Dark Side of the Moon* by Pink Floyd, *A Passion Play* by Jethro Tull, *Space Ritual* by Hawkwind and *Preservation Act 1* by the Kinks. In all these works, naturalism is eschewed in favor of fantasy, mock-fable, escapism, science fiction or downright muddleheaded pretentiousness. Even Bowie's *Pin-Ups*, a concept album of sorts, gave a collection of mid–1960s hits (including the first two Who singles) a sheen of glittery revisionism that painted a rather different and more glamorous kind of nostalgia than did *Quadrophenia*. (Ironically, David Bowie knew better than most the world in which Jimmy moved, having himself emerged from the same London mod scene).

The aforementioned *A Clockwork Orange* (which opened in the U.K. in early 1972) should perhaps also be mentioned here. Stanley Kubrick's adaptation of Anthony Burgess's novel was a much more glossy and stylized film than *Bronco Bullfrog*, although it examined broadly the same subject with much less warmth and compassion. The film had a profound influence on Britain in general and on rock and roll in particular, although it depicted a future British society were no rock music is heard, its hero favoring Beethoven. Similarities may be apparent between Jimmy and Alex (leader of *A Clockwork Orange*'s Droogs), but essentially it is the nature of gang fights and youth cults that prompts the comparison. In fact, there is only one gang fight (that is, a fight between two rival gangs) in *A Clockwork Orange*, but it is significant because the adversaries of Alex's Droogs, the gang led by Billyboy, are clearly rockers (albeit a more Nazi regalia–adorned Hell's Angels type of rocker). The Droogs are clean-cut, in white with black hats, compared with the rockers, but they do not really resemble mods and only slightly resemble skinheads (often wrongly identified as the subcultural heirs to the mod). *Lifehouse* had more in common with *A Clockwork Orange*, and if gang fights alone are to be identified as a point of comparison, then why not start with *West Side Story* (or indeed *Romeo and Juliet*)?

The element of mindless violence that is common to *Quadrophenia*, *Bronco Bullfrog*, and *A Clockwork Orange* is reflective of one of the harsher realities of our era. There is a danger—which moralists are always ready to shout about—that when utilizing a semisympathetic character who becomes involved in senseless violence one is *condoning* that violence rather than merely observing or portraying. *A Clockwork Orange*, in particular, became highly controversial because of this, and the same criticism was leveled at the *Quadrophenia* film of 1979, which likewise spared no niceties in its graphic portrayal of violence. Because the element of violence in the album of *Quadrophenia* is relayed secondhand by Jimmy, it does not linger over any detail. The attitude that Jimmy and his fellow mods embody displays a blind mob hatred: "There's nothing uglier than a rocker" Jimmy tells us. But Townshend has Jimmy's mindless aggression toward rockers tempered by reticence. The incident where Jimmy recalls three rockers' being chased down Brighton Pier is used not to show any brute power inherent in the numerically greater mod gang but in the implied cowardice of individuals hiding behind the front of safety in numbers. The mods—greatly outnumbering the rockers—back down from a fight because no individual is ultimately prepared to risk being beaten. Jimmy implies that leadership from the tougher Ace Face would have given the mods the sense of glory and physical supremacy they strive for, but Ace Face, as Jimmy later discovers, is not all he appears.

This incident is used to show that Jimmy's brainless prejudice against rockers is not followed through into actual physical brutality and therefore Jimmy feels something lacking in the invincible facade of mod. But Jimmy's hatred of rockers is simply an accurate depiction of a dominant mod attitude. In fact, this part of the work is based on an actual incident, about which Townshend obviously felt uncomfortable, where three rockers had been cornered at a Who concert in Brighton. So Pete's concern about his responsibility regarding the reverence he received at the Who's early Brighton concerts from potentially violent mods is finally assuaged ten years later by a main theme of a work that explicitly debunks the idea of leadership and hero worship.

Another film that went into production in 1972 of which Townshend was aware was *That'll Be the Day* (directed by Claude Whatham), which starred David Essex and featured not only Keith Moon as a drummer but also Billy Fury as a 1950s rocker singing Townshend's "Long Live Rock." As "Long Live Rock" itself was the starting point for *Quadrophenia*, some connection between this film and the Who must be made. *That'll Be the Day* is unavowedly nostalgic but has that mundane, gritty sharp-edged feel of many British films. It charted the impact that certain aspects of British society felt at the first coming of rock 'n' roll and the rebellion of youth that it inspired. The theme of the film can be seen as part of a trend that also bore fruit in America with *The Last Picture Show* (1971) and *American Graffiti* (1973)—the result of a new generation of writers and filmmakers who had become old enough to look back on their teenage years with affection.

Quite how *That'll Be the Day* came to use "Long Live Rock" is not clear, other than that Keith Moon had been cast in a minor role in the film and its producer David Puttnam had acknowledged an admiration for Pete Townshend. Despite this, however, Pete was unaware that it bore any comparison with his own incubating ideas, as he had not seen Ray Connolly's script. *That'll Be the Day* is a tale of youth disaffection among the rockers of 1958, and much of it is set in a seaside resort on the south coast of England. The simple facts are that Townshend was definitely thinking about working on *Quadrophenia* well before the release of *That'll Be the Day*, and "Long Live Rock" had most likely been written before Connolly's script was completed. However, *That'll Be the Day* was released in April 1973—before *Quadrophenia* was recorded but after "Long Live Rock," a song that was musically rooted in the late 1950s. (In its musical style, "Long Live Rock" is very much Rocker rather than mod.) In the final comparison, however, *Quadrophenia* shares much more with *Bronco Bullfrog* than with *That'll Be the Day* or *American Graffiti*, although Roy Baird, coproducer of *That'll Be the Day*, was later to work in the same capacity on the 1979 film of *Quadrophenia*. With this in mind *That'll Be the Day* and the *Quadrophenia* film do have some superficial similarities.

Another comparison that was made at the time was with David Bowie's *Ziggy Stardust and the Spiders from Mars*. This album had been released in June 1972 and followed a very loose concept. However, Bowie's work here bore more comparison with *Tommy* and *Lifehouse*, being a dissection of stardom and its pitfalls in a futuristic setting. Some observers actually saw more connection between *Quadrophenia* and Bowie's next-but-one album, the aforementioned *Pin-Ups* (October 1973), presumably because both works were, in vastly different ways, comments on specific aspects of the 1960s. But as a concept *Quadrophenia* has few peers. If *Ziggy Stardust* had been set in the past, then the connection would be more tangible, but it was set in the future and its concerns only slightly overlap with the areas of *Quadrophenia* covered in "Punk and the Godfather" and "I'm One."

The recording sessions for *Quadrophenia* began in May and ran through June and July. August and September were taken up with mixing and other postproduction tasks, and the record was scheduled for release in October. Following completion of the recording sessions, an excited Roger Daltrey told Tony Stewart of *New Musical Express* that *Quadrophenia* was "phenomenal. It really is. It really is amazing ... this one's really got the old Who back. It's got the clarity and good recording of *Who's Next* ... but it's got the old 'My Generation' Who there."[16] However, anticipation was quelled by forces beyond the band's or even the record industry's control: the worldwide fuel crisis of 1973 delayed the pressing process by a few weeks, and the album first appeared in the U.S. on 3 November and in the U.K. on 16 November. In both markets, the album rose to number 2 in the charts, hampered slightly by a high price tag on account of the thick, heavy-gauge-paper photo-booklet. A single preceded the album in each country: "5.15" in the U.K. and "Love Reign o'er Me" in the U.S. This was The Who's first release on MCA Records in the United States, a subsidiary of Decca that was more attuned to the rock marketplace (though Who releases retained a Track logo). Both singles were very much seen as trailers for the album rather than entities in their own right, although it must be said that both songs stood up well as detached from the story.

With a gloriously chaotic television benediction on *Top of the Pops* (4 October 1973) "5.15" erupted into the ether with a vengeance to prove that the Who's layoff had not blunted their abrasive edge. One of their toughest rockers with all the best elements that the band could muster behind it, "5.15" was headed by a glorious bludgeoning riff (reinforced by Entwistle's hard-edged brass), a lilting melody and a thoughtful chorus. Despite giving a fully representative taste of what was in store with *Quadrophenia*, "5.15" was too raw to get beyond number 20 in the charts, and the lyrical references to both drugs and underage sex did little to endear the single to the radio station playlists. The music press in Britain stayed faithful through changing trends and quiet periods, and writers had even begun to regard the Who as an utterly dependable institution. Roy Carr of *New Musical Express* said of "5.15," "...without a doubt the most dynamic single released by anyone so far this year. The Who just seem to get better and better."[17]

Predictably faring less well, "Love Reign o'er Me" (in an edited version) performed disastrously in the U.S. charts. It gained a top placing of number 76, which in no way did justice to its merits. The song was too demanding for a single, and its full weight was best felt coming as the climax of the whole work. On the B side of both versions of the single was the 1970 recording "Water," which the band had last played onstage in 1971. It sounded rather lame in comparison with the newer material but nevertheless was a sensible release of an otherwise unissued song that Who fans might well have remembered from the earlier concert performances. Ironically, the title "Water"— though not the whole song—sits very comfortably among the sea and water imagery in the titles of many of the *Quadrophenia* songs, all of which, of course, involve Meher Baba connotations.

With *Quadrophenia*, Townshend established a concept and situation (Jimmy sitting on a rock and thinking about how his life had culminated in such a crisis) and then allowed a succession of songs to illuminate different aspects of the character's persona and experience. It is clear from the sleeve that Jimmy is a mod. Listeners can learn from the lyrics and text that he is supposed to suffer from a personality split into four parts, which are aligned to character traits of the four members of the Who (each with a separate musical theme). A recurring coda is Jimmy's overindulgence in amphetamine drugs ("blues" or "leapers"), which brings out in him mood changes, from the keyed-up, edgy violence of the high to the lugubrious lethargy of the comedown. The "story" was represented only by a column of text on the album sleeve and a succession of photographs in the booklet. By excluding a great deal of surface action, Townshend achieved a deeper character penetration. The scene begins with Jimmy's reflections while sitting on a rock ("I am the Sea"), and the sequence of songs accounts for how he came to be there in the first place. He then reveals that his doctor, mother, girlfriend and clergyman have all failed to understand him and consider him to be mad ("The Real Me"). He feels the pressure to conform in order to impress his peers but incurs the anger of his parents ("Cut My Hair") and even questions the balance of power that prevails between rock star and fan ("Punk and the Godfather"). Jimmy despairs at the meaningless elements of his life despite his assertion that he is an individual ("I'm One"). Jobs available to him are poorly paid and unpleasant—he works as a garbageman ("The Dirty Jobs")—and political activism seems to offer no solution ("Helpless Dancer"). He resigns himself to his fate and feels his frustrations are insurmountable ("Is It in My Head" and "I've Had Enough").

In a desperate effort to regain some meaning in his life, Jimmy gets high on drugs and travels to Brighton, in the south of England, on the train ("5.15"), the scene of mod glories from his recent past ("Sea and Sand"). However, all he initially finds there is the unwelcoming sea ("Drowned") and finally the degrading spectacle of seeing his erstwhile mod hero Ace Face working in a demeaning job in a hotel ("Bell Boy"). His anger rises at this situation, and the aggressive and arrogant side to his character comes to the fore, as if he possesses a Jekyll and Hyde split personality ("Doctor Jimmy"). After a large intake of gin, he takes a boat out to the rock with thoughts of suicide. However, his reflections on the rock finally seem to give him a greater understanding of himself and his mortality ("Love Reign o'er Me"). "I don't really know how I imagine the boy walks away from the rock," Pete confessed, "or whether he drowns, or whether he wins or loses, or whatever. I haven't really made up my mind what happens."[18]

The opening sound effects tone poem, "I Am the Sea," is pure atmosphere, achieved with restraint and control. Rain, wind, voices, a cat, whispers, gentle synthesizer drones and thunder form the backdrop behind which the four themes are intoned (three by stray vocal lines and the fourth by a trumpet phrase) as voices from the past. The bold title "I Am the Sea" really presages the important subtext, because here at the very beginning, Townshend's main concern is stated: the personification of the sea, with its tides and changing moods, and Jimmy himself allowing his soul to flow with the tide and become one with the vast, ever changing enormity of the ocean. The wind blows and the thunder cracks around him; he is engulfed by an inhospitable storm. "I am the Sea" also presents the kind of struggle between humanity and the elements that reminds one of Joseph Conrad (significantly enough one of Pete's favorite authors). By turns calm and angry, the introduction is an imaginative sound-picture and is obviously completely unlike anything the Who (or anyone else) had done before. But the listener's potential bewilderment and confusion on first hearing are reassuringly laid to rest when Daltrey's angry question, "Can you see the real me? Can you? Can you?" drifts from left to right across the stereo picture and Townshend's slashing guitar chord rips from the speakers to form the startling and breathtaking link into the first song proper. Then the listener knows that the Who at their most arrestingly unhinged are with them on this journey.

A slice of pure, timeless rock and roll, "The Real Me" is a fully charged assault on the senses built from visceral razor-sharp guitar chords over a typically idiosyncratic drum pattern that gives an impression of wild, exciting spontaneity but simultaneously conveys the sound of a band in perfect synchronization and control. An intense but sparse sound, this is the Who stripped down to scintillating basics: one guitar, one bass, drums and one voice (with an ascending brass progression to back up the uplifting chorus). Daltrey's singing is powerful, a manic tirade of frustration that must rank as one of his best performances. One of the most effective moments is the classic third verse [1.30] in which the crisply distorted guitar cuts out completely to remind us just how potent is the Who rhythm section. A variation on the rhythm [2.09] for the last verse is another imaginative touch, bringing the song to natural climax.

The terseness of the verses of "The Real Me" thrusts the listener straight into Jimmy's consciousness, frustration and jaundiced perception of a society that simply doesn't recognize him for who he is. The trouble is he doesn't really know who he is himself. He wants his real self to be apparent and understood by others, but he is unable to make much sense of his own formless thoughts. His lack of identity turns into paranoia. Jimmy is all questions—questions to the doctor, mother, girlfriend and preacher. And all go unanswered. The questions to himself find a similar fate. Communication with his girl breaks down entirely—she simply passes him by. But somewhere in Jimmy's life is rock and roll. Maybe he feels rock and roll should be his salvation, and if so he is probably even more concerned that *it too* seems to be failing him.

But "The Real Me" offers in each of its four verses an examination of Jimmy's quad-divided consciousness. These occur in the Roger-Keith-John-Pete order imposed on them through the sequencing of the album (though not the order of "I Am the Sea" or "Quadrophenia.") The four-way split—the device dreamed up by Pete to correlate with the personalities of the Who members—is here given a four-way challenge: each facet of Jimmy's personality is given a counterpoint with the four external characters (and four verses) of "The Real Me." The doctor in the first verse evokes a response from the angry Daltrey persona, the mother in the second verse from the crazy Moon persona, the girl in the third verse from the romantic Entwistle persona, and finally the preacher in the last verse with the soul-seeking Townshend persona. In Townshend's demo, an additional verse was included about rock music itself, beginning with the line "Rock and roll's going to do me an evil wrong," but Pete may have realized just how self-conscious this was—it was Pete speaking rather than Jimmy, in whose mouth it would have sounded out of character. The analysis of rock and roll within *Quadrophenia* is perhaps more Pete than Jimmy, anyway—a point to be raised later apropos "The Punk and the Godfather."

The contrast between the stark, raw intensity of "The Real Me," where on a musical level each member of the band is so characteristically himself, and the opulence and symphonic grandeur of the following "Quadrophenia" displays the startling breadth of the Who's musical capabilities. Maybe "Quadrophenia" isn't by definition *rock and roll*, but its sheer musicality—strong melodies, tight structure and lush, layered soundscape—make it equally as compelling a Who performance as their customary high-energy attack. The bass and drums are solid and expressive, but the substance of the instrumental work lies within Pete's orchestral synthesizer score and the acoustic and electric guitars, which interweave the melody. The suite is formed from the four major musical themes of the work, beginning with the chord progressions of "Bell Boy," embellished with a solo guitar over some frantic piano and acoustic strums. The first synthesizer passage shimmers in for the slow, melancholic "Is It Me?" section, which in turn develops into the "Helpless Dancer" melody, which is perhaps a little too intricate and tricky. However, the fading in of the towering and mighty "Love Reign o'er Me" theme provides a compelling climax. Pete marvelled at having pulled off such a contrasting pair of opening tracks—the old blood-and-guts Who followed by a new smooth and sophisticated Who—before "Cut My Hair" and "Punk and the Godfather" established a stable rationale between the two musical extremes that would be reflected by all the remaining tracks.

Jimmy, we are told, is receiving psychiatric treatment. Perhaps this is legitimizing his mental schism too much, because the only evidence of the nature of his illness is that he "changed like the weather," which is somewhat insubstantial. To be sure, he's angry, unsure of himself, moody and prone to self-destructive depression. But so are great numbers of people (including many teenagers) whose problems do not warrant medical attention. Significantly, Jimmy makes little progress as a medical case. He fights through his mental block in the only way he knows how: escape, mental through drinking and drugs, and physical via his flight back to Brighton and his boat trip to the rock.

The bedrock of his feeling of enclosure is the domestic environment of his home. His parents drink, remain indifferent, and pressure him to conform and to act more responsibly. But—like Arthur Seaton's parents in *Saturday Night and Sunday Morning*—the pair here are so downtrodden and enmeshed by their own failure and are so trapped in such a tedious and predictable domestic routine that Jimmy *knows* that their attitude to life is wrong. "Cut

My Hair" indicates the two sets of pressures on Jimmy from both his parents and from his peers. The pressures are at odds, and Jimmy feels caught in the middle. Of course, he wants to be a mod—to rebel against his parents—but he feels that this fails to establish a real identity for him either. The changeability of mod fashion suggests its ephemeral nature. How can he stake his identity on something so facile?

The first two plaintive ballad verses of "Cut My Hair" give substance to Jimmy's wistful musing on what is and what might have been, rendered in Pete's voice, cynical and vulnerable but not really rebellious at all. The dramatic chorus chant (Daltrey's voice) is Jimmy's amphetamined harder self, and the double tracking is very effective, suggesting the divergent voices in Jimmy's head. But the buoyed-up energy and aggression is soon quelled into the nagging (then overwhelming) doubt of the "uncertain feeling ... still here in my brain." Pete's final two verses plunge Jimmy (in his sorry postamphetamine state of withdrawal) into downright antipathy towards the pressures of being a mod, and the final verse encapsulates the stark reality of Jimmy's life in the midst of his comedown from the drugs, where nothing really changes. The melody drifts into a minor key note of despair as the song ends [2.58], with Pete's emotive vocals above a stark synthesizer pattern.

"Cut My Hair" has strengths untypical of the Who, few guitars, a brass arrangement, and (like "The Dirty Jobs" to come) a well-crafted, keyboard-based structure and strong melody. Nowhere has the contrast between Pete's pure emotive voice and Roger's gritty power vocals on the vigorous chorus been so effective and appealing. The success of "Cut My Hair" is in no small way related to the fully integrated musical contrast between the two voices and the lyrical contrast of mood and expression of the character's state of mind that the song seeks to amplify. The dichotomy between conformism and individuality—both of which Jimmy wants—is clearly expounded for the first time in this song. The parents versus mods antinomy clashes almost with hammer blows to Jimmy's psyche. In "Cut My Hair" we realize that Jimmy responds both to his parents' point of view and position *and* to the mod ideal, but he cannot go all the way with either ethos, feeling maybe that his real self lies somewhere else again. But where? The song ends on a poignant, problematic note that is interrupted by a news item on the wireless about mod–rocker clashes in Brighton. (John Curle, who at the time was a BBC Radio 3 announcer, reads this fictitious bulletin.)

The placing of "The Punk and the Godfather" straight after "Cut My Hair" seems to suggest that rock and roll—a third factor influencing Jimmy's consciousness—may prove to be good and true, a genuinely liberating force that could save him from oblivion. Jimmy had responded to the Who—"They were alright," he recalls—and maybe, it is suggested, rock and roll would be enough to pull him through. But *Quadrophenia* doesn't proselytize on behalf of rock itself. In fact, the opposite emerges. The positive effect of Jimmy's listening to the Who at the Marquee may be equated with the contemporary audience listening to the *Quadrophenia* album. But Townshend avoids falling into the trap of assuming that his music can solve problems, ease pain, or give purpose and meaning to life. We know from interviews that he would *hope* his music might bring such values to his audience, but it would be pompous, conceited and egotistical for any rock artist to make such claims. The modest and humble side to Pete here prevailed. In *Quadrophenia*, rock and roll is seen to fail Jimmy, to abandon him even, during his time of need. And the fictitious encounter with the Who is astutely used as an ego-deflating exposé of the foibles and flaccidities of all rock-and-roll stars, *all* icons of power and fame.

"The Punk and the Godfather" is one of the strongest and ultimately most moving of Who songs, a sublime fusion of slash chord adrenalin and rock solid melody, fused with the twisting, tormented "guy in the sky" lines sung by Daltrey and Townshend's plaintive "It all belongs to me" verse. The three chords of the main riff are an inspiration, doubled up with acoustic and electric guitars, and the same three chords (played with less concentration) build the foundation of the verse pattern before the onset of the loquacious chorus that concludes with a sardonic quotation of the title line of "My Generation" complete with stuttering. The third verse [2.50] takes a different mood and is simply beautiful, with Pete's heartfelt ruminations on the rock-and-roll status quo. An effective return to the main riff is heralded by the cheers and whistles of a real rock audience [3.24] in the ecstasy of the rock-and-roll experience. The sound of this audience seems to be rendered with more than a little irony, as if in illustration of the hollow and sycophantic nature of manipulated adulation.

Despite its almost overwhelming strengths, "The Punk and the Godfather" is slightly out of place lyrically, working on a different level than do "Cut My Hair" and "I'm One," which surround it. Here we pass from Jimmy's consciousness into a wider field and possibly into a realm of communication that jars with the pitch of the whole work. The reason for this is quite simple: the dialogue between the fan and the star would come *outside* of Jimmy's experience. (In the narrative, the exchange is much more plausible and likely: a brief, banal conversation outside the Marquee, the Who member disinterested and finally offering the insensitive inquiry about whether Jimmy is working.)

The imagined exchange in the song is too much a product of Townshend's consciousness, unlikely to figure largely in Jimmy's scheme of things. Surely, only in Townshend's mind could the punk/godfather exchange have occurred. It is the star's version of what the fan would think about the star. Of course, being Townshend, he considerably amplifies on one hand the simple dignity of the fan and on the other hand the foibles and egomania of the star. This is pure Townshend–speak as opposed to Townshend-as-Jimmy–speak.

All that is implied in the narrative about the relationship between the fan and the star is explicitly expounded in the lyrics of the song, giving this most mysterious and tenuous of relationships a rationale and level of explanation that Jimmy would be unlikely to propagate himself.

Yet "The Punk and the Godfather" is utterly crucial to the whole scheme of *Quadrophenia* and serves a very important function. At the center of Jimmy's breakdown is his lack of faith in rock and roll and maybe the realization that the Who are not the paradigms of integrity that they might *appear* and that in many ways they are just as screwed up as he is. The power politics of the song are extremely pertinent and prescient, because the two voices transcend their immediate roles and assume a wider significance that echoes the hierarchies that prevail through different strata of capitalist society. The punk charges the godfather with being nothing more than a fraud, a fabricated leader who is empowered only by the wealth and influence that is given to him and who privately shirks responsibility and commitment. The punk knows of the truth that the godfather has hitherto managed to conceal or maybe even avoided facing himself. Confronted with the punk's exposing gaze, he knows the game is up. He owns up that he himself is "the punk in the gutter." But who controls whom? Who has the upper hand? The punk may have the truth, but the godfather can fall back on more tangible assets; "It all belongs" to him.

Pete's dialogue serves to remind the star (indeed, himself) that he is nothing more than what the fans made him. His power and wealth are in many ways illusory. He also assumes (with an obvious feeling of guilt and self-effacement) that he has let the fans down, failed to live up to an ideal, bamboozled and cajoled an audience and offered music that was insincere and hollow. Along with stardom — and being considered a leader, a spokesman — comes responsibility and insecurity, the insecurity that everything might just fall apart, that fans might find new allegiances. Leaders, of course, can be toppled by insurrection. And then, with this in mind, the listener begins to realize that "The Punk and the Godfather" is not just about music fans and pop stars at all but about how society is itself a balance of power between rulers and ruled and the subtle distinction of the values held between the two.

In 1977, the British punk group the Clash released a fine single called "Complete Control." This was ostensibly a tirade against record company control over artists and CBS's betrayal of the Clash (CBS had earlier released an unauthorized Clash single called "Remote Control"). Midway through the suitably angry performance, the Clash shift the focus of their song from their own immediate concerns and draw the parallel that control is applied to everyone throughout society and that the populace is controlled by the Establishment. When Joe Strummer sings that he is "Joe Public," it should be immediately apparent that this song expressed sentiments very similar to "The Punk and the Godfather," in which the music industry is used as a metaphor for society at large. However, the Who song actually penetrates the situation more deeply. The Clash simply raise an objection to the notion of control and argue in favor of freedom for the individual, which is all well and good. But Townshend (unlike the Clash) does not evade his own part in the problem. The Clash disassociate themselves as stars and assume they are speaking on behalf of the fans against the capitalist machine (or CBS Records) or any kind of corporate control. Townshend would typically not engage in such hypocrisy, which makes the Who song a constantly shifting dialogue of uncertainties in which even the names *punk* and *godfather* become reversible.

A wistful, acoustic folksy atmosphere is evoked with the first verse of "I'm One": the mood here is melancholic drifting into frustration and anger. Jimmy's acceptance of his lot and the ragged shapelessness of his life is just about vindicated by his assertion of "oneness." Where his mood grows more combustible, the sharp shards of electric guitar, explosive drums and bass enter [0.52], with a feeling of spontaneity and ensemble unity. "I'm One" is a fully realized song, simple and effective and sounding very much like a live performance, despite the fact that the electric guitar is overdubbed. Part gentle ballad and part all-out rocker, "I'm One" has an appealing rough-hewn quality that is lacking from much of the surrounding material. This is the only song on the work where Pete handles all the vocals, and his winsome yet yearning voice has rarely conveyed with such success so many changing moods within one song. It begins the second side of the album where Jimmy's concerns (noted by Townshend as pathos and anger) are explored in five contrasting songs. The focus of Jimmy's consciousness is here rendered at a deeper level than on side 1, which deals mostly with the surface of Jimmy's life.

However, in probing a deeper level, the following "The Dirty Jobs" and "Helpless Dancer" move into areas where Jimmy's experience and worldview would not be quite so formed or as forthright as the words that Townshend give him suggest (a similar out-of-character situation as in "The Punk and the Godfather"). Jimmy has only had one job, as a garbageman, and he only sticks with it for just two days, yet the two songs take in (or reflect) a fairly wide point of view. He is undergoing (unsuccessful) psychiatric treatment; he is at the point of being chucked out of home by his parents; his girlfriend has dumped him; and despite his best efforts he isn't quite as accepted as a mod as he would like. And yet in spite of all this the listener finds him taking on the inherent problems of capitalism and industrial relations like a veteran activist.

Musically, however, "The Dirty Jobs" gives a clean, bouncy line of melody. It is heavily synthesized, uptempo of beat, and features a jaunty rhythmic string pattern that achieves an infectious light breeziness that is somewhat at odds with Jimmy's mordant musings. The echo effects on Daltrey's voice during the final chorus [3.00] are very notable, and the optimism of the melody belies a sophisticated and radical musical arrangement. In contrast, the short "Helpless Dancer" offers a stark Wagnerian power, over three sparse piano chords pounded in a relentless fashion by Pete. Signaled by the sounding of an ominous horn phrase, the stirring theme is meted out with Roger's voice at its emotive and unflinching best, supported on the second verse by Pete's quite excellent acoustic guitar strumming. This performance achieves a texture comparable to the work of Kurt Weill and Bertolt Brecht—demanding, lyrically stinging and uncomfortable. Both "The Dirty Jobs" and "Helpless Dancer" are remarkable songs that succeed outside of the Who's customary musical framework, and both are realized with consummate skill.

"The Dirty Jobs" is really about apathy, the kind of apathy that makes exploitation and oppression possible in the workplace and beyond. Jimmy is clearly frustrated at his inability to make fellow workers stand up for their rights rather than be "put down" and "pushed round" all their lives. Of course, Jimmy has less to lose than some of the others, but his naiveté strikes a simple note of truth, and he seems to acknowledge that. Jimmy seems to be saying individuals must take responsibility for their own situations. However, his definition of the problem doesn't naturally lead to a solution. To simply quit the job—as Jimmy does—doesn't explain how the rest of us get our rubbish disposed of or how unskilled workers improve their social conditions.

It is not clear that the listener is to take the dialogue of "Helpless Dancer" as being a direct communication from Jimmy or an expression of Jimmy's feelings. The double quotes around the two verses as printed on the album (foolishly omitted on the recent CD version) make this *quoted* speech. So this may be what Jimmy is hearing from someone else. Additionally, this is Roger Daltrey's designated theme, reflecting his tough, pragmatic, no-nonsense characteristics. A dissection of society's ills within the metaphor of a dance, the two verses are about oppression: human lives controlled from above and the reality of life for those out of step (old people, gays, ethnic minorities, the poor) with the dominant archetype. Individuals dance to a tune forced upon them by the Establishment, the song asserts; and the final line suggests defiance as the only hope: "You stop dancing." The dance metaphor is from an established tradition (Delius's composition *A Life's Dance* and Anthony Powell's novel sequence *A Dance to the Music of Time* are two twentieth-century works that spring to mind). However, the predominance of dance amongst mods ("I Gotta Dance to Keep from Crying" was a Miracles single played onstage by the Who in 1964) makes this image very appropriate.

Best described as a power ballad, "Is It in My Head?" has a lethargic verse and a more uptempo chorus and is a delineation of Jimmy's uncertainty in the world. In fact, the song—written before the concept was devised—functions as a general-purpose expression of an individual's alienation in the face of an inhumane society. With a fierce, dependable sound, this mixes a piano melody, one-note synthesizer drones, and sparse heavy guitar chording and a vocal interplay between Daltrey (verse) and Townshend/Entwistle (chorus). By a hardly perceptible margin this may be the weakest part of the album. The crux of the matter is the last verse, a speeded-up bridge section [2.30], which seems to merely coast on straightforward Who rock-and-roll instinct. The inspirational drive of *Quadrophenia* just doesn't flow through this passage—the only one on the album—despite the beautiful guitar soloing that follows [2.57].

Any residual lethargy that "Is It in My Head?" leaves with its final coda is promptly kicked into touch by Keith Moon's thunderous drum intro to "I've Had Enough." The drive and intensity of this track have made it a *Quad* favorite, although one might have minor reservations about the constant shifting of mood and pace. But the Who's ability to achieve such color and contrast should be praised, even if some melodic unity is sacrificed in the process. Tough and uncompromising, "I've Had Enough" is best dealt with as another four-way split song, with four distinct musical and lyrical moods. This first is the frenetic guitar thrash (and one of Townshend's classic repeated root-note progressions similar to "Substitute" and "I Can See for Miles") with Roger's vocal range stretched on an ascending melody line from the low "You were…" [0.19] to the high "…that simple" [0.33] at which point the power chord sequence strikes in. Second, a slower beat power chord (in fact a well-established Who three-chord variation) with Pete's vocals [1.01]. Third, the plaintive synthesizer-based "Love Reign o'er Me" interlude [1.22]. And finally the jolly banjo sing-along cum suicide rap. How well these hang together is up to the listener. It's all musically interesting, and the guitars are breathtaking in their ear-razing edge; but the song is fragmented to the point where it could be accurately described as a miniopera, something like "A Quick One While He's Away." Yet the epic proportions and grandiose feel are well accommodated within the overall framework of *Quadrophenia*.

It may be that the four sections of "I've Had Enough" could be lyrically aligned with the four different Who personas in a way similar to on "The Real Me," but the listener should once more bear in mind that the first two verses of the first section are quoted speech, like "Helpless Dancer." They form the comment of someone speaking to Jimmy, maybe his own conscience, telling him how he's been manipulated and fooled (By society at large? By fellow mods?). Jimmy's response to criticism and scrutiny at the hands of other observers is to conform more readily and to adhere even more strongly to mod strictures. The second two verses delivered by the "observer" put Jimmy into the wider picture of society and point to his insignificant place within a hierarchy that is steeped against him and in which only some untapped inner strength can help him to survive. Jimmy's ultimate response is typically weak-willed: his litany of grievances and discontent form a suicide note that overwhelms in its negativity. But in the plot, the immediate response is not suicide, but a desperate flight away from home, from London, from the mod epicentres where he feels he is being judged a failure.

Somewhere during "I've Had Enough" Jimmy loses his scooter. He crashes it through carelessness in the foul weather. This important point is not reflected in the lyrics but is notable, as it dictates what happens next. In losing his scooter Jimmy loses a good deal of his status as a mod and much self-esteem, not to mention his mode of transport. Walking along the railway tracks offers an obvious but drastic opportunity for self-destruction, though in the end his overindulgence in "leapers" (amphetamine drugs) blunts the pain. Following the railway tracks he ends up at the station and finds before him an opportunity to return to Brighton.

At the start of the third side (or second CD), things really get moving (literally) with Jimmy's desperate pilgrimage to Brighton on the "5.15." From the deceptive calm of the railway station, a mournful sequence of guitar figures allows Pete to intone Jimmy's perennial question to himself and the world, "Why should I care?" before the frantic pace commences. The train—the 5:15—and the ensuing journey assume nightmare proportions due to Jimmy's restless state of mind and his overindulgence in pills, The stuffy City clerks whose scrutiny of him in "their" compartment (Jimmy is travelling first class no less!) only serves to increase his paranoia and isolation. The musical impetus of "5.15," propelled by Keith Moon's relentless drum beat and John Entwistle's wall-of-brass horn riff, suggests a force in motion that is careening out of control and is unstoppable, taking Jimmy to his doom. The driving and relentless piano from Chris Stainton and Townshend's abandoned but fully integrated guitar solo push this musical white-knuckle ride to its thrilling conclusion. (There is a tradition of such apocalyptic last rides, notably Mark Gertler's painting *The Merry-Go-Round* of 1916, presently in the Tate Gallery, London, which shows soldiers and sailors and their girlfriends on an ever turning, ever descending carousel ride into hell.)

The images evoked in "5.15" are almost phantasmagorical and inchoate. They are the thoughts of a mind drifting wildly in the midst of a crazy, irrational impulse (the return to Brighton), and they do not focus on any level of reality aside of the awareness of subjectivity versus objectivity ("Inside, outside") as Jimmy imagines seeing himself from both perspectives. The only controlled statement ("I'm out of my brain") confirms Jimmy's true state: overwrought by his intake of drink and amphetamines, beneath which he is overwhelmed by life's tribulations. "5.15" is a blowout, a kind of scream for help. It is Jimmy's crucial journey and the apocalyptic imagery reflects just how revelatory this unpremeditated trip has become. His journey's end is Brighton, however. Brighton holds the key to his life (or so Jimmy thinks) and maybe the pathway to the future (if there *is* a future, of course). "5.15" certainly makes more sense in the context of the album than it did as a single. It is the *Quadrophenia* song that "rocks" the most, and Daltrey is here on top of his powers with controlled frustration and rage echoed by John and Pete's harmonization of every second line. Keith Moon's awesome attack on the drums even simulates the train slowing down toward the end as Jimmy is delivered to face his destiny. The same sequence of chords as began the song and the "Why should I care?" refrain serve to slow down the tempo and finally bring the momentum to a halt.

Calming arpeggios that introduce the reflective mood of "Sea and Sand" suggest the nostalgia of Jimmy's return to Brighton. However, the song almost immediately relays Jimmy's disdain with his home life, mingling with his memories of his halcyon moment of glory, the time when he looked right, impressed his fellow mods and got the girl. But the reverie of the moment proves short-lived, and Jimmy's confidence in his looks and dress is immediately tempered by self-doubt (everyone else looks better). The gentle and ethereal texture of the arpeggios match the dreamy passages of reflection, and contrasting power chords back up the uneasiness of the more bitter lines. A well-constructed and neatly arranged song, this never settles to a fixed beat and incorporates a false ending [3.29]. "Sea and Sand," more than any other song here, painstakingly chronicles the perennial mod obsession: appearance, image, fashion adherence and looking cool. Yet the more Jimmy aspires to being a Face—a pacesetter, a leader—the more conscious he becomes of his inadequacy. The further he strives to raise his profile and impress his girl, the more he loses the comfort that anonymity brings.

In order to remind the listener of the ultimate mod obsession, the title line is sung by Pete from the High Numbers' single "I'm the Face" [3.47]. Along with "Zoot Suit," this song serves to remind us that in Jimmy's world, appearance is everything. This is also compounded by a repeat of the verse from "I've Had Enough," where Townshend expounds exacting detail of how a mod should look. But for Jimmy, the superficiality of mod and the fact that he finds nothing beyond the image is crisis enough. The discovery itself is the result of the facile values of his peer group disintegrating under his distraught scrutiny. The mod values, therefore, only hold true when Jimmy is up (that is, looking right, dressing cool, dancing well, keeping his scooter on the road, being seen in all the right places, impressing his girl). When he's down, no one values him at all or will speak to him. Of course, Jimmy initially blames himself rather than others and thinks the inadequacy is *his alone* rather than something inherent in his particular subculture.

The point of his realization that human crisis is inevitable and not attributable to his own failing comes somewhere within "Drowned" and "Bell Boy." The former seems to show Jimmy adopting a wider philosophy than mod conformism, while the latter teaches him a valuable lesson about the very nature of peer group hierarchy, myth versus reality, and the important fact that other individuals (when seen merely as individuals and not demigods or personifications of the ultimate antihero) are just as riddled with self-doubt and full of contradictions as himself. Like most lessons that really make an impact on one's life, Jimmy's discovery about the truth of the hero Ace Face is painful, almost unbearable.

There is such a purity of essence about "Drowned" that it can be seen as the quintessential *Quadrophenia* performance. It is comparatively simple and direct and encapsulates the actual feel of the album within one song, a remarkably "live" performance that is synthesizer-free. "Drowned" has none of the cleverness of the other songs, no dramatic musical effects or complex arrangements, and does not rely on the Who's abilities as individual musicians as much as on their collective ensemble sound—with the important addition of the aforementioned piano. The keynote to "Drowned," musically and lyrically, is freedom—not freedom as a vague and ethereal concept or cerebral ideal, but the joyous freedom that is given by *release*. Jimmy glimpses a freedom where his soul (either in metaphor or in spirit) can float and be tossed by the waves, where he can be buoyant (this is very much a Meher Baba–inspired symbol). And the music directly reflects this mood. The quiet and sensitive bridge section [1.49] concludes with the important line "I am in the water as far as I can see" at which point his self-realization is almost absolute. For Jimmy, however, the freedom remains a glimpse because he cannot transcend the limitations of his physical body and its flaws.

The contrasting "Bell Boy" is tightly structured with no loose free-form playing and no chaff, being memorably introduced with a confident, pounding drum roll. It is a beautiful set piece, with a dazzlingly original synthesizer score, and reflects a specific encounter through which Jimmy has to pass, his moment of great enlightenment. Additionally, this is Keith Moon's theme, reflecting a reckless, devil-may-care attitude but also delineating a vulnerable character full of contradictions. The freedom and release of the beach and the sea (evoked by the rich and atmospheric quality of the composition and arrangement) evaporate when he sees the "face coming through the haze." The "newly born" Ace Face is world-weary and spinning the cracked philosophy of an old-timer who has seen it all but is still at the bottom of life's pile. Ace Face's wistful passage [2.03] evokes a genuine note of pathos—partly due to Moon's sad-clown vocals, but largely because Ace Face has fallen so far from grace in Jimmy's eyes that to hear him attempt to salvage some dignity from life when his situation is so obviously demeaning and servile is extremely sad. But something in "Bell Boy" rings so true to life that the song cannot be reduced to being solely about Jimmy and Ace Face. Whereas Ace Face was the top dog in the little enclosed world of mod, the real world (which sooner or later engulfs us all) shows him up for what he is: not fit to do anything better than to scurry after the guests at a hotel, be at their constant beck and call and wallow in self-pity.

The dialogue between Jimmy's musing and Ace Face's melancholy "That's life, mate" stance is remarkably effective and undoubtedly presents a highlight of the whole record. And the dialogue is no less a highlight because it side-steps the whole Who musical orthodoxy inherent in, say, "Punk and the Godfather." These inversions here simply add to the charm of "Bell Boy":

the main guitar riff (a lovely sequence of power chords) coming between the verse and chorus [1.01] rather than at the very beginning and, of course, the strangely affecting singing of Keith (a little bit Lionel Bart, as Townshend admitted, but not without its power to bring a character to life). It is therefore one of the most unusual Who songs ever recorded. The only reservation I might raise is that the chorus exchange of "Bell boy!" and Keith's caught-on-the-hop response is a little bit too melodramatic and staccato, maybe *too* Lionel Bart, for a rock-and-roll song. But the breezy, confident vocals of the return of Roger's verse [2.32] with "A beach is a place…" gives the song a greatly uplifting quality that belies the effect of the situation on Jimmy.

The full-blown swagger and overwhelming urgency of "Doctor Jimmy" takes little analysis because here, unlike some other songs, Jimmy is laid bare. This is Jimmy as he wants us to think he is: the big, macho, seen it all–done everything tough guy, full of threat and aggressive intent. The music is solid and melodic, following an unrelenting path onward, with the brass riffs toughening up the first part of the chorus and the rough but shimmering string sounds enlivening the verses. This is a massive song that threatens to bludgeon all in its path with its verve and stature. Cast in the huge, grandiose style that only the Who could pull off without sounding pretentious or pompous, this is *Quadrophenia*'s magnum opus, with thrilling chord changes, gripping verses and a sweeping synthesizer score. And on the song goes with Jimmy's falsely bolstered self-confidence amply embodied by Daltrey's full-blooded vocals. Described by Townshend as "Wagnerian," this is a big production number, pulling all the stops and sparing no extravagance. One final reiteration of the chorus after a more sparse string pattern has Daltrey's voice backed up by a very effective lone piano [5.42]. Of course, the lapses into "Is It Me?" [3.18 and 6.25] change the mood to such an extent that they really represent Jimmy torn apart almost into two separate identities (Dr. Jimmy and Mr. Jim), as the title reference to Robert Louis Stevenson's *The Strange Case of Dr. Jekyll and Mr. Hyde* suggests. And here it could be argued that throwing in Entwistle's theme (the romantic dreamer) as a song within a song is a little glib. It follows smoothly enough musically, as Pete's craftsmanship makes sure, but it seems to diminish John's theme below the other three, each of whom has a whole song to himself.

"Is It Me?" is a strong and moving melody, full of passion and drama. It is arguable that this would have worked better as a self-contained song, a separate track falling between "Doctor Jimmy" and "The Rock." It is short but beautiful, and perhaps it would have needed a bit of an intro as well. For John's theme—an equal and valid one-quarter of Jimmy's makeup—it is maybe a little too buried at the end of the leviathan of "Doctor Jimmy." However, its being interpolated within "Doctor Jimmy" is obviously to give a real contrast to the other part of the Jekyll/Hyde duality. But since the whole album attempts to give substance to the idea of the split personality anyway, such a contrast within one song is hardly necessary. The effect of the combination is to make "Doctor Jimmy" a little unwieldy and "Is It Me?" something of a throwaway, a fate which neither track deserves.

The anger and frustration of "Doctor Jimmy" falls away as the placid calm of "The Rock" fades in. This is a minor-key variation on the four musical themes (in the order of "Bell Boy," "Is It Me?," "Helpless Dancer," and "Love Reign o'er Me") and strikes a more melancholic and reflective note than "Quadrophenia," its more strident counterpart. Variations on a theme of "Helpless Dancer" are rendered in a number of contrasting keys. A musical combination of the themes is here attempted, and the effect is striking but demanding. This is musicianship that fully realizes the potential of the composition yet echews all notion of solo virtuosity. It is not really the Who ensemble sound either, more a remarkable product of multitracking, dominated by Pete's guitars and keyboards but giving important space to Entwistle's bass and Moon's drums. A few inchoate voices can be heard intoning "stars are falling" as the piece reaches its complex but firmly focused climax. A dense and atmospheric texture, this track demands attention through all its variations and repetitions, and it remains (instrumentally) the most ambitious and intricate music that the group ever undertook.

After the preceding two tracks, the climactic "Love Reign o'er Me" is almost too much to take in. Taken alone, it is a powerful statement, musically weighty, passionate and flawless in conception. And Roger gives his all (as indeed does Jimmy!) This major song is a powerful ballad, with a fascinating contrapuntal synthesizer figure, a cyclic musical evocation of the tide and waves. The stirring rhythm is all set in motion by Pete's delicate piano tinkering (a full minute in duration) and concludes with a noisy finale in a traditional Who manner. A thrilling, swaggering, emotionally shattering song, the despair in "Love Reign o'er Me" is broken only by a revelatory third verse [2.57], which musically and lyrically takes a more optimistic line in which Jimmy pledges to hit the "dry and dusty road" home. A cool bottom-note-range guitar solo [3.58] is beautifully handled. This is Pete's theme and reflects the eternal mystical quest and restlessness of the human soul.

How else could *Quadrophenia* end? In despair, in tears, in hope, in death or life? "Love Reign o'er Me" could be all or either. The listener can take it as signifying Jimmy's redemption, his reconciliation and consummation with forces greater than those which his mod-consciousness has hitherto known. But this consummation could be the point at which Jimmy undergoes death and rebirth, or it could signify a continued thrust into life with a different insight into the human soul. It does not really matter whether Jimmy lives or dies because he has new understanding and a change has taken place within him. One could simply say that Jimmy has finally grown up—even in death.

Although not always appreciated as such, *Quadrophenia* must be accepted as the Who's finest achievement. It is their magnum opus: a work so rich in ideas, so suffused with musical inspiration, and so loaded with classic rock-and-roll moments that it is difficult to assimilate at once. It is an exemplary album on a scale so grand that it has occasionally deterred listeners with its sheer intensity and vigor. It represents a magnificent distillation of the Who in all their idiosyncratic and full-bodied glory. Some critics have found the concept or "story" either pretentious, baffling or alienating, though this pronouncement would not detract from the raw drive and melodic power of the individual songs. Even the lyrics stand alone as fine dissections of perennial rock-and-roll concerns, expressed with a consummate mastery of phrase and aptness of image. Intellectually, *Quadrophenia* is both coherent and cogent without the utilization of a detailed or chronological story line. That forms of fiction needed to harness a traditionally structured story or plot was one of the conventions that the modernist movement of the arts during the early twentieth century had managed to dispel. *Women in Love, Ulysses, Citizen Kane* and *Nostromo* all function without recourse to any formal narrative. And so too does *Quadrophenia*. Pete, however, never intended it to be judged merely as a story, and he readily admitted this.

There has lingered, nonetheless, an aurora of respectful distance between *Quadrophenia* and the general rock-listening public. Many people possess the album—it sold millions of copies—but a real intimacy with its contents can be found with rather fewer persons. It is a daunting, lengthy epic and is not readily sequenced in palatable chunks for the FM radio diet. Unlike many albums, it does not possess one or two standout tracks that facilitate easy listener access. Like the rock-and-roll equivalent of James Joyce's *Ulysses*, it is a title prominently displayed on the shelf often but explored and penetrated only rarely.

After the album had been on release for a couple of months and Pete had lived with his character for even longer, he analyzed Jimmy's problems and came to a conclusion that he thought went some way to explaining his crisis: "He feels a failure because he thinks these Ace Faces, these Mods he admired ... were really demi-gods because they had the things he wished he had.... But actually ... they were a few years older and more experienced.... In a sense he's a failed Mod, because he's made the ultimate Mod mistake, bad timing."[19] This plausible explanation shows a little too much retrospective interpretation, because the album does not define any chronology. Townshend implies that Jimmy missed being a top mod in 1963 or 1964 because he was too young and that by 1965 the mod movement was in decline. Although this is the essence of what happens, the album very much points to Jimmy's problems as being inherent in his character, rather than being immaturity per se.

Taken poetically, the words and music of *Quadrophenia* are not so much about mod or the concept of youth as about the sea—a metaphor for the changing nature of humanity—a timeless muse that has inspired both poetry and music. A recurring motif in Townshend's writings and seemingly a universal Meher Baba symbol of God's love, the sea is the predominant image that runs throughout *Quadrophenia*, and the splashing swell of the waves is heard between some of the tracks. The sea represents the ever-changing, restless omnipotence of the human soul, reflecting multiple dimensions of mood, emotion, will, imagination and enlightenment; the ghosts of Joseph Conrad and Walt Whitman seem to linger around many of the themes. David M. Barling, an American Who fan, has detected a very clear influence of Herman Hesse's *Siddhartha* (1922) and especially Joseph Conrad upon *Quadrophenia*. "*Lord Jim* is all over this album," Barling wrote. "Pete, in my opinion, was greatly influenced by Conrad.... The central character is named Jim who has an idealized viewpoint of himself in order to escape the reality of his vulnerability (an alternative reality).... *Nostromo* is all over this album as well.... *Quadrophenia* gives one a reason to live. We all at some point in our life climb onto The Rock. Pete captured that moment we all go through perfectly."[20]

Literary parallels aside, it might not be taking things too far to see the work in terms of the many other sea-inspired musical works, such as Debussy's *La Mer* (1905), Vaughan Williams's *A Sea Symphony* (1910), Elgar's *Sea Pictures* (1899), Sibelius's *The Oceanides* (1914), Britten's *Peter Grimes* (1946) and *Billy Budd* (1951), Bridge's *The Sea* (1913), Delius's *Sea Drift* (1903), Ravel's *Une Barque sur l'Ocean* (1905) and Bax's *Garden of Fand* (1920)—except, of course, that despite its symphonic trimmings *Quadrophenia* is rock and roll. But the unity is there, even as the recurring pulsing synthesizer melody of the "Love Reign o'er Me" theme evokes the rolling, endless tide. *Quadrophenia*, in many ways, *is* Pete Townshend's sea symphony.

The lavish packaging of *Quadrophenia* adopted a uniform grayness that might well have seriously disheartened the marketing executives within the record companies. The cover shot (by Graham Hughes) is murky and indistinct and doesn't even mention the band's name, apart from the logo chalked onto Jimmy's back. The only photographs of the band to appear are the four small reflections in the scooter's offside mirrors. Overall, the cover shot looks like a ghostly conclusion to the tale, with Jimmy traveling beyond the perimeters of life and death. The stark reality of his life, on the rear sleeve, is symbolized by the wrecked and "drowned" scooter lying in the sea. The booklet contains a further thirty-three photographs (with Jimmy personified by a "model" named Chad), along with an inner sleeve photograph of the seashore. In general the booklet is a sobering account of Jimmy's odyssey with the grainy monochrome finish catching the gritty realism of the events.

As an event, the release of *Quadrophenia* gained a very high profile in *Melody Maker* (20 October 1973) with an alliterative banner headline "Townshend Tops *Tommy*!" Chris Welch could hardly contain his reaction on the front page, exclaiming about *Quadrophenia,* [It] "sets new standards for British rock music, and will undoubtedly prove as big a world wide success as the famed 'rock opera.' In a series of brilliant performances, The Who capture the aggression, frustration and inherent romanticism of youth."[21] The idea that *Quadrophenia* was received coolly or with a feeling of bewilderment is almost utterly groundless. The Who gained some of the best reviews of their career. Rob Mackie in *Sounds* wrote, "If this isn't the album that will come to represent 1973 music in years to come, then someone is going to have to pull some genius-laden fingers out very speedily and lay down a highly ambitious master work to total perfection.... The results have to be heard to be believed.... Wow."[22] Charles Shaar Murray in *New Musical Express* described it as the "most rewarding musical experience of the year."[23] Chris Welch wrote in his review, "*Quadrophenia* is the kind of project that progressive British rock is all about. All the facilities, imagination and talent have been there, but rarely have a group succeeded in distilling their essence and embracing a motif as convincingly as The Who on this record."[24] Even the mainstream press in the U.K. offered an appreciation that exceeded the normal rock coverage when Tony Palmer wrote, "I doubt if there is another pop group extant who could have conceived, let alone realised, such an ambitious undertaking.... This double album can only reinforce the belief that The Who are the best group we have."[25]

The good reviews weren't limited to the U.K. either. The American press responded warmly, with very enthusiastic reviews from Les Daniels (*Fusion*, March 1974), Janis Schacht (*Circus*, April 1974), Hubert Saal (*Newsweek*, 12 November 1973), Arthur Levy (*Zoo World*, 6 December 1973), Lester Bangs (*Stereo Review*, February 1974) and John Roundtree (*Records and Recording*, December 1973). Significantly enough, the greatest reservations came from Dave Marsh, who reviewed the work twice (*Creem*, January 1974 and again in March 1974) and on neither occasion found much that was positive about it, a prejudice later enshrined in the much-read biography of the Who, *Before I Get Old* (1983). These few negative reviews propagated a myth that *Quadrophenia* was impenetrable to non–English ears. The seeming perpetual worry that U.S. audiences would fail to understand the social background and context of *Quadrophenia* is somewhat puzzling. The average intelligent American can surely understand the kind of conditions that British working-class people have to put up with. It cannot be much different to British people's understanding of the (equally remote) Chuck Berry/Beach Boys world of *American Graffiti*—a big hit in the U.K. at the same time as *Quadrophenia*.

The remixed CD reissue of *Quadrophenia* came in June 1996, heralded by Pete Townshend's comment that the new mix was "mind-blowingly wonderful."[26] With the complete album carefully preserved on 16-track master tapes, Jon Astley and Andy Macpherson managed to present a tremendous sound with all the raucous guts of the original intact. The clarity and range of each component in the sound-picture has been increased in tone and depth, sounding pure and clear. The only criticism that Who fans might have felt over the reissue is the fact that no additional tracks were added. While peripheral songs might well have spoiled the impact of such a complete and unified work, it meant that the two-CD set—the whole work being a few minutes too long to fit onto one CD—abounded with unutilized space. More important, no significant outtakes could be located at the time to expand the playing duration, "We Close Tonight" being discovered after the CD release.

Listened to as extracted from the concept, "We Close Tonight" is an amusing uptempo rocker with verses sung by John Entwistle and a theatrical "in character" chorus by Keith Moon. Melodically, this falls short of the remainder of the album and hardly adds anything to what we know of the character, detailing Jimmy's insecurity and reticence in approaching a girl and a meeting with a somewhat boastful jazz musician. Entwistle adds a typically dissonant jazzy bass run in illustration. The feel of the song is also at odds with the tone of *Quadrophenia*, and one can understand its deletion. It sounds very much like a John Entwistle song, in fact, so much so that during preparations for its first release on *Odds and Sods* in 1998, Chris Charlesworth meticulously checked its origins; but it was confirmed that it had been written by Townshend. However, the discovery of the song is a delightful bonus, and it makes for very entertaining listening.

The history of *Quadrophenia* continued beyond the release of the album, of course, with the somewhat shaky concert performances of 1973 and 1974, the film of 1979, and more recently the Who's onstage revival of the work in 1996 and 1997. But the album stands as the definitive reading of the work (as opposed to the situation with *Tommy*, where the live performances outshone the record). While the CD remains in production then the Who's major statement about these crazy times will be preserved. But who really knows if people will be able to make sense of anything thrown up by the rock culture of our era in two or three hundred years' time. If a work of genius has ever been produced by the rock-and-roll culture, then this album is surely it. And like most works of genius, it stimulates the listener, enriches the soul, elevates the consciousness and gives the kind of sustenance that is needed to avoid falling into a lethargy of mental stagnation that is threatened by the very tedium and superficiality of contemporary life. This is what the Who, at their best, were all about.

As 1974 unfolded, the band members began to think of *Quadrophenia* as something of a disappointment. This was not a direct judgement of its musical worth but more the result of its failure to come together onstage and maybe the undeniable fact that it was sometimes compared unfavorably with *Tommy*. "It's ironic—a rather bitter irony, actually. I wrote *Quadrophenia* to replace the old stage act," Townshend told John Rockwell in mid-1974. "But it didn't work and we're back to playing our old hits. Do I enjoy performing anymore? Not very much."[27] The concerts played in Britain and the U.S. between October and December of 1973 and in France in February 1974 were fraught with technical difficulties and fell short of the Who's impeccable onstage standards. Live recordings were made of *Quadrophenia* concerts in Philadelphia (4 December 1973) and Landover, Maryland, (6 December 1973), but these tapes have been deemed too poor for release on record (although the Philadelphia show was given a *King Biscuit Flower Hour* radio broadcast in the U.S. in 1974).[28] MCA issued an edited version of "The Real Me," backed with "I'm One" on single in the States in January 1974, which reached the unspectacular chart position of number 92.

In fact, *Tommy* had been back in the news around the time of *Quadrophenia*'s release, as a film deal had been negotiated in mid–1973 with producer Robert Stigwood, director Ken Russell and Columbia Pictures. Kit Lambert had no creative input to this production, and Ken Russell very much dominated the nonmusical aspects of the work. Russell was undoubtedly one of the most talented and controversial of British film directors and had specialized in off-beat and esoteric subjects, usually of a musical nature. He had filmed imaginative portraits (among others) of Debussy, Elgar, Bartok, Gaudier-Brzeska, Rossetti, Delius, Strauss, Tchaikovsky and Mahler, as well as powerful drama with *Women in Love* (1969) and *The Devils* (1971). Although he had encompassed popular music per se with *The Boyfriend* (1971), he had yet to approach rock and roll. Russell was given a crash course in the Who, attending concerts and familiarizing himself with all things related to *Tommy*, which he was happy to proclaim a masterpiece. For Pete Townshend, the film production entailed the arduous task of preparing an all-star rerecording of the work as a film soundtrack. These sessions commenced in early 1974 after the last of the *Quadrophenia* concerts had been played in France in February. This soundtrack recording was not finally credited to the Who and so falls outside of the scope of this book. But the four band members were heavily involved in many aspects of the sessions, and Roger Daltrey sang a significant portion of the songs in the role of Tommy.

The original plan, however, was rather different. The soundtrack was planned as being entirely a Who recording with guest vocalists singing the parts they had been cast. Unfortunately, when the sessions were about to commence, Keith Moon was taken ill and Townshend had to make expedient arrangements. "It was a blessing in disguise," said Pete. "...We were terrified as to how it was going to work out without him.... So I thought rather than try and replace him with *a* drummer, I'd choose an ideal bunch of musicians for each song."[29] Obviously, an exclusively Who soundtrack for the *Tommy* film would have turned out different from what was finally used, but the necessity of incorporating as vocalists the varied actors as cast suggests that the results would not necessarily have kept the film any closer to the original album.

In the event, this rerecording moved *Tommy* much more into the mainstream of popular music and away from rock and roll, with glossy and expansive arrangements featuring a heavy use of synthesizer. Pete contributed two additional songs, "Champagne" and "Mother and Son," neither of which would form essential listening for Who fans. The singing of Oliver Reed, Ann-Margret and Jack Nicholson was far away from the rock tradition. Polydor (in both the U.S. and U.K.) released a double album *Tommy (Original Soundtrack Recording)* in March 1975. As musical director of the film, Pete found the whole experience simply exhausting and depressing, but for the Who in general the prestige and commercial power of the production was reason enough to plunge into this challenging new genre.

The Who played a few concerts during 1974. For the band members, concerts were becoming increasingly unsatisfactory. An open-air concert at Charlton football ground in London and a run of four shows at Madison Square Garden, New York, in June 1974 marked a low point in the band's spirits. The Charlton concert (18 May) was recorded and broadcast both on television and radio, but the question of any of this live material being issued on record was firmly dismissed by the band. During the long periods of inactivity between studio albums in the 1970s, it was standard for a rock group to release a live album. Almost all the major groups succumbed to this trend, and despite record company pressure, the Who always resisted. (Further pressure to issue a second live album also prevailed during the Who release lull of 1976–1977.)

Yet during the short season in New York, during which Townshend was drinking heavily and feeling very pessimistic about the Who, plans were revealed for the band's next project in an interview with John Rockwell of the *New York Times*. This was to be an album and television special, a much more lightweight work than *Quadrophenia*, and the featured songs were to have the unusual and distinctive aspect of being commissioned from songwriters outside of the group. Pete had it in mind to approach Ray Davies, Frank Zappa, and Nicky Chinn and Mike Chapman (a songwriting duo who were responsible for many glam/glitter hits of the time by U.K. acts such as Mud, the Sweet, Suzi Quatro and Smokie)—all of whom he admired. The album was to be recorded in August and September 1974, and Townshend described the tie-in television show as "scenes with The Who and 100 topless lady accordionists, and other Zappa-esque things."[30] For this scene alone, Pete had written an appropriate new song called "Squeeze Box," about a female accordionist. This unusual and unlikely project—which also suggests a strong Ken Russell influence—was finally abandoned, though it was still being considered in a slightly amended form in early 1975.

As strange and as fascinating as it sounds, it is difficult to imagine the intended surrealistic visuals of this television film being a suitable vehicle for the Who's talents, and certainly the use of other songwriters' material would be little more than a pleasant diversion. The main reason most people listened to the Who in the first place was because of the songwriting of Pete Townshend (and John Entwistle). There was a trend at the time, however, for established artists to diversify into the realm of cover versions as a kind of harmless exercise for the space of one album to rediscover their roots or recharge their creative energies: David Bowie's *Pin-Ups* (1973), Bryan Ferry's *These Foolish Things* (1973), and John Lennon's *Rock 'n' Roll* (1975) are all examples of such albums. The proposed Who work was not quite in this category, consisting as it would of specially commissioned new songs, but it seems to generally belong to the same tradition.

Before the end of the year, however, the question of the Who's next album was already answered with the preparation (by John Entwistle) of *Odds and Sods*, which was a collection of songs that had been discarded from recording sessions over the previous six years, along with a reprise of the High Numbers "I'm the Face" that had been unavailable since 1965. Entwistle rooted out plenty of outtakes from which to choose, and two songs, "Postcard" and "Put the Money Down," needed some additional recording work to bring them up to an acceptable standard. The resulting album collected on side one "Postcard" (1970), "Now I'm a Farmer" (1970), "Put the Money Down," (1972), "Little Billy" (1968), "Too Much of Anything" (1971) and "Glow Girl" (1968) and on side two "Pure and Easy" (1971), "Faith in Something Bigger" (1968), "I'm the Face" (1964), "Naked Eye" (1970) and "Long Live Rock" (1972). The expanded CD version of 1998 added "Leaving Here" (1964), "Baby Don't You Do It" (1964), "Summertime Blues" (1967), "Under My Thumb" (1967), "Mary Anne with the Shaky Hand" (1967), "My Way" (1967), "Young Man Blues" (1968), "Cousin Kevin Model Child" (1968), "Love Ain't for Keeping" (1971), "Time Is Passing" (1971), "We Close Tonight" (1973) and "Water" (1970). As previously noted, the instrumental from 1967 called "Sodding About" was prepared by Jon Astley but omitted at the last minute due to space restrictions. (All these songs are discussed in earlier chapters in their correct chronological place.)

John Entwistle's production of *Odds and Sods* found favor with the whole group, and he was enthusiastic about the compilation. "We didn't realise there was so much unreleased stuff around that was good," John commented. "My particular favourite is 'Faith in Something Bigger'.... It's nostalgia for me."[31] Pete Townshend contributed notes for all the songs and specifically pointed to "Faith in Something Bigger" as one of his least notable achievements! In fact, Townshend's notes for the album took a cynical and derisory tone throughout, being very self-deprecatory even about some of the better tracks. "Little Billy" alone was hailed by Pete as a "masterpiece," and he also had a special fondness for "Glow Girl." However, for the printing of the album insert, some of Townshend's more cutting remarks were edited out. The full text appeared in *New Musical Express* and later in *Rolling Stone* and has now been restored to the CD booklet.[32]

Despite the fact that *Odds and Sods* contained no new material, it still managed to make an impact as an innovative album. Artist-endorsed albums of hitherto discarded material were very rare in 1974. Such collections only usually appeared after a performer had died, such as the Buddy Holly albums *Reminiscing* (1963) and *Showcase* (1964) and Jimi Hendrix's *Cry of Love* (1971), or had moved to another record label, such Bob Dylan's *Dylan* (1973) and the Rolling Stones' *Metamorphosis* (1975). Such albums often sounded like exactly what they were: thrown together with scant imagination, average-to-mediocre in content, with material hitherto discarded as leftovers and unfinished demos. Jefferson Airplane were perhaps the exception to this rule, endorsing an album of high-quality outtakes called *Early Flight* (1974), and the following year Bob Dylan released perhaps the most famous outtakes album of all with *The Basement Tapes*. Coming when it did, however, *Odds and Sods* itself was radical and distinctive after a fashion. It was well packaged, decently annotated (though full of inaccuracies as was later established) and formed a cohesive listening experience. The cohesion was not one of sound—which obviously reflected many different recording conditions, though still sounding remarkably unified—but of songwriting consistency.

What must have heartened the Who was the sheer enthusiasm displayed by the fans and critics for an album that they thought of as being aimed mainly at Who collectors and completists. Barbara Charone saw *Odds and Sods* as a "companion piece to the brilliant *Quadrophenia* ... an on the spot, you were there, documentary account of the coming of age of rock and roll. The Who's guide to Swinging London ... another chapter in the continuing history of The Who, one to be played and enjoyed forever."[33] In *Melody Maker*, the ever faithful Chris Welch commended the group for "laying bare their tortuous process of evolution.... If you have an archive, then this is an essential item for any Who fan."[34] The general response, indeed, was akin to that voiced by Roy Carr in *New Musical Express*, who argued that the Who's leftovers were better than most groups' best contemporary efforts. The album was released on 28 September in the U.K. (and reached number 10 in the charts) and 12 October in the States (where it reached number 15). MCA tried its luck with a single for the U.S. with "Postcard" backed by "Put the Money Down" in November, but it didn't take off.

By 1974, a crisis had enveloped the Who that would never be fully resolved. *Quadrophenia* had represented a consummation of so many currents of thought and musical quests that it formed the apex of the Who's vision. The magnitude of the Who's status worldwide, however, served to conceal the problems that the band members were facing. In breaking off their connections with Kit Lambert and Chris Stamp, they were able to get their business affairs in some kind of order, although the realization that they had been for some time fundamentally mismanaged and ill-treated financially was painful and was to cause many ongoing problems. The band opted to make

Bill Curbishley, from the ranks of Lambert and Stamp's company, their manager, and from 1976 to date Trinifold Management has handled the Who's affairs with remarkable success. Part of this process of change saw the band transferring their record deal directly to Polydor and away from Track, which dissolved as a company a couple of years later after failing to promote any new hit acts.

But musically, the Who found themselves at a turning point. As suggested by Barbara Charone (above), *Quadrophenia* and *Odds and Sods* represent two different responses to the past—to the 1960s and the history of the band, one very considered and self-conscious, the other more given to chance. They together represent the final culmination of Pete Townshend's obsessions with Who history and the mythology of mod that had surrounded it, an obsession that first gained expression within the packaging of *Live at Leeds* and with the *Meaty Beaty Big & Bouncy* LP. Pete wanted the band's past to be tied up once and for all with these releases, in order to start their future a clean slate and for preconceptions to be shattered. Pete told James Johnson that he hoped *Quadrophenia* would "end being tied down by the way The Who are and give it a grand, glorious send-off." But, he said that in some ways he felt "extremely old, worn, frustrated and tired of plodding along" and gave no clear indication of how the Who would survive, other than that his new songs would have to be "personal and direct because I really don't think it'd be honest anymore to pretend I knew what was in the heads of the young."[35] Despite Pete's self-doubt, the Who still had a future of sorts, although it cannot be denied that they had now lost some of the cutting edge of their genius. Beyond the glorious summit of their inspiration was a path that led— at first very gently and almost imperceptibly—in a downward direction; it took another eight years before they reached the end of the track.

7

Beating the Retreat (1975–1978)

The principal production of the *Tommy* film ran from April to August 1974, although Pete Townshend's responsibilities with the soundtrack occupied him almost for a full year. It was clear that the Who could not function as a band again until the film was completed, and during the latter months of 1974 a rumor had circulated throughout the music scene in London that the Who were on the verge of splitting up. Such rumors had been commonplace during the band's career. But on this occasion, Pete Townshend took action to dispel the false story by issuing a press release asserting that the Who would return with an album and concerts in 1975. More significant, however, in the same press release, he expressed his desire to record a solo album—a sentiment that he had not in the past felt the need to voice.

The Who were kept in the news with the release of the *Tommy* film in March 1975, and the band undertook publicity jaunts to promote it. The film was a very literal realization of the story without any dialogue, and Ken Russell's approach was to load visual imagery to excess, rather like a glossy television commercial. Daltrey and Moon made quite an impact as actors, but the film in general failed to present the essence of the Who or rock and roll in a shape that held any relevance other than as big-budget, mainstream entertainment. In terms of Ken Russell's oeuvre, *Tommy* fell far short of his superb earlier works such as *A Song of Summer* (1968), *The Devils* (1971) and *Savage Messiah* (1972), and he never again tackled a large-scale pop music subject. The film was a substantial commercial success with the general cinema-going public, but it enshrined too many of the consumer images of the 1970s to hold much continuing relevance. Viewed nowadays it looks very much like mid–1970s kitsch and for this reason has become a cult movie in the U.S. Coinciding with the release of the film came an unprecedented flurry of solo albums: *Mad Dog* by John Entwistle (March 1975), Keith Moon's *Two Sides of the Moon* (May 1975), and Roger Daltrey's *Ride a Rock Horse* (June 1975). Only Daltrey's album made the charts (both in the U.K. and U.S.), faring

7. Beating the Retreat (1975–1978)   217

better than his debut. Moon's was a pure celebrity novelty item, and Entwistle's lacked the songwriting excellence of his earlier solo works.

Roger Daltrey had felt the need for the Who to take a novel approach with their next project. One idea was quite fascinating: for the Who to record a live album of *new* songs. "I've always wanted to do an album onstage before it was recorded," said Roger. "Get some new tunes together as an act or part of an act and record them live for an album. I think we'd really come up with something good 'cause our live sound is getting quite good now."[1] This approach would have combined the vitality and freshness of the live sound, along with the stripped-down instrumentation, with new material. For various reasons, this idea never found favor and was left undeveloped. Maybe Townshend's new songs were not suitable for stage performances. In the end, only four songs from *The Who by Numbers* were played live, and only two with any regularity. It may also have been that the record industry disliked live albums of new material (or new material being recorded live). Very few artists ever took this step, with a few notable exceptions: Frank Zappa did quite regularly (although Zappa tended to function under special circumstances all around); the MC5's debut, *Kick Out the Jams*, (1969) was a rare example of such an approach; Jimi Hendrix had released *Band of Gypsies* (1970); and Neil Young was another maverick who released *Time Fades Away* (1973), the roughness of which seemed to come as a bit of a shock to his audience after the mellow sounds of his best-selling *Harvest* (1972).

Townshend's initial ideas for the next Who project were still along the lines of a television special and related album. However, by the spring of 1975 he had abandoned the idea of commissioning songs from other writers. In fact, he had gone to the opposite extreme, to considering having twelve different artists in the program performing specially written Townshend songs. The motivation involved was not so different; it was still a means of taking an unorthodox approach and thereby avoiding audience precognition and artistic stagnation. It was intended that Michael Lindsay-Hogg, who had worked with the band before on *Ready Steady Go!*, a promo film for "Happy Jack," and the Rolling Stones' *Rock and Roll Circus* would direct this film. The program was to have a comic and surreal flavor along the lines of *Monty Python's Flying Circus*, the cult BBC television show. The "Squeeze Box" scene was now envisaged by Pete as featuring the Dagenham Girl Pipers playing accordions in unison! Townshend said that the show was to be a "parody of the business as a whole and also of the group. It was a sort of comedy *Quadrophenia*, but with more accent on the group."[2] This idea came to nothing, and although envisaged as a lighter piece of work, it sounds a little bit too much like the Beatles' ill-fated *Magical Mystery Tour* (1967), that is, with television being used as a kind of box of toys rather than as a serious artistic medium. Townshend was also probably influenced in this idea by the Kinks, who had produced a television special, *Starmaker*, broadcast in September 1974.

Another new song, however, had a more serious intent. Townshend talked of a recent composition called "Imagine a Man" that he hoped would hold the "key to the way that rock could grow old."[3] The issue of how rock music could escape its perpetual adolescent framework and mature with dignity and grace had certainly become an abiding concern of Pete's ever since *Quadrophenia* had dispatched for good Pete's "universal youth." "Imagine a Man" addressed a midlife crisis, depicting a character losing direction and struggling to comprehend the changing values around him and suggesting the tragic situations that can ensue as a result. What the song confirmed for Townshend was that he could successfully broach middle-aged concerns (or the concerns of becoming middle-aged) and the problems that can occur as individuals enter their fourth decade of life. According to Pete, he wrote the song quite literally about an imaginary man, the type of man he had observed and perhaps in some ways disliked. When the song was finished, Pete realized that the song was about himself and his own crisis. "Imagine a Man" became the key song around which Townshend centered his lyrical concerns, and additional songs keyed into the same subject to form a very cohesive and sustained cycle. There can be little doubt that during the composition of this material, Townshend was going through a period of depression, was suffused with self-doubt and was feeling disconsolate towards the Who, their reverend status and the music business in general.

The relations between the group members were distant and meetings infrequent—indeed, Moon now lived in Los Angeles. When not working they would not see one another for months at a time, a situation of near estrangement that it was difficult to imagine prevailing with any other working band. An interview that Townshend gave to Roy Carr of *New Musical Express* in May (titled "The Punk as Godfather—If the Glove Fits...") was an outpouring of vitriol by Pete directed at the Who, his contemporaries and his situation in general. Very clear in this interview was his belief that the Who had to either change (which Pete felt the band couldn't do) or break up. He offered very little hope for any kind of survival. He thought his artistic future lay in solo projects, which he felt were hampered by the Who's demands for his best material, saying that "as long as The Who exists, I'll never get the pick of my own material ... and that's what I dream of.... They always rush up to me and insist that we've got to cut a new album and get back on the road."[4] Yet despite his despondency and with characteristic ambivalence, he emphasized to Carr that the Who's new album—which at this point was almost finished—was "the best thing we've ever done," which must have been about as strong a reason for optimism as could have been given.

Roger Daltrey, who had received much criticism in the Townshend interview, responded a couple of months later when he spoke to Tony Stewart. Countering some of Pete's more barbed charges, Daltrey also expressed some doubt as to how long the band could keep playing. He said, "I don't mind if the Who do finish, because we've done a helluva lot.... I'd hate to see anything mediocre come out by the Who." But like Pete he praised the forthcoming album, saying, "I'm really pleased with it," and added, also in concurrence with Pete, about "Imagine a Man," "...the best song Pete's ever written. There's a few mysteries in there, but it'll be a good album."[5] Daltrey and Townshend had a long history of disagreement, and at this point in their career, Roger seemed to need the Who somewhat less than his compatriots. His solo career had taken off with *Ride a Rock Horse*, and he had bagged another starring role, in Ken Russell's next film project, *Listzomania* during the first few months of 1975.

The onset of 1975 coincided with a low ebb within the music industry in general, and Pete's lack of faith was certainly exacerbated by the almost universal lethargy, dearth of new ideas, and lack of imagination in rock and roll. Pete had considered breaking up the band, but he didn't have the courage to carry it through. In any case, rock and roll needed him a little longer. If the Who ceased, he correctly reasoned, then rock would be left at the mercy of all the ascendant 1970s acts whose motivations and purpose and insincere and facile music Townshend felt to be a betrayal of what the 1960s had stood for. Certainly, this is a feeling that stands up to analysis in the light of the punk rock movement. During the 1974–1976 period, the top new rock acts were the likes of 10cc, Queen, Bad Company, Rainbow, Cockney Rebel, Fleetwood Mac (Americanized), Yes, and Genesis, not to mention the old faithfuls like Wings, Led Zeppelin, Rolling Stones, David Bowie, Pink Floyd, Peter Frampton and a myriad of nondescript hard rock bands like Boston, Kansas, Kiss, Nazareth, Uriah Heep, Foreigner, Rush, and UFO. The Who did attempt to actively support and encourage a healthier alternative in the immediate pre–punk period (Iggy and the Stooges, Kilburn and the High Roads, John Otway and Wild Willy Barrett and the Steve Gibbons Band), but none of these acts fulfilled their promise.

The first and most obvious response to the overblown state of rock and roll around this time was a move back to its roots and a partial rediscovery of 1960s values. In Britain, a new generation of bands embraced rhythm and blues, soul, rockabilly, and even country & western as reference points by which to escape the prevailing stasis of "stadium rock," "pomp rock," or whatever generic title could be applied to such music (exemplified by Pink Floyd and Emerson, Lake and Palmer). A rejection of the guitar hero pose and of the synthesizer and a return to the organ and piano were also apparent. The music played by the groups who congregated under this movement became known as *pub rock*, largely because the bands rarely rose to hit status but also reflecting the more modest and earthy quality of their music. Although their individual styles varied enormously, the bands who came to be gathered under this collective name included Dr. Feelgood, Brinsley Schwartz, Ducks Deluxe, Graham Parker and the Rumour, Kursaal Flyers, the 101-ers, Ace, and the Count Bishops. Although some of these groups produced enjoyable music, their back-to-basics approach ultimately proved too limiting in scope and failed to provide a new vision for rock and roll's future. The punk rock movement—which broke through in 1976 and 1977—was still bubbling under the surface in 1975. There can be no doubt, however, that punk rock did for the music industry everything that pub rock failed to do and by 1977 had become the genuine new voice of rock and roll.

Not only did Pete Townshend identify with great precision (and perception) exactly what was wrong with rock and roll in 1975 (including in his opinion the *Tommy* film), but he realized just how inappropriate the prevailing approach to rock was becoming. So when the Who gathered in late April to begin work on their new album at Shepperton Studios in London (with Ronnie Lane's mobile unit), they found a workable groove by partially tapping into the R&B roots that pub rock had rediscovered. Consequently, they jettisoned their synthesizers, and reunited themselves with Nicky Hopkins on piano. And a handful of the recordings displayed a very strong rhythm and blues feel, "However Much I Booze," "Squeeze Box," "Slip Kid" and "Success Story" in particular. Additionally, among the demos that Townshend had prepared was a very basic 12-bar boogie track (title unknown) that tapped into the roots of R&B more blatantly than anything the group had done since "Long Live Rock." (But the band did not record this song—perhaps it was *too* basic and visceral—and lack of information regarding the title has entailed its exclusion from Appendix 2 of this book.) The recordings commenced with a jam session to loosen up, and most of the tracks were completed during the last week of May 1975.

The Who by Numbers (the band name seemed to be included as part of the title) was the first album to be issued by the band on Polydor Records, on 18 October 1975. The album reached number 7 in the U.K. charts, and the MCA version in the States (released on 25 October) stalled at the number 8 spot. The commercial drive of the album was marginally less than it had been on the previous few albums, but this was hardly surprising given the uncompromising nature of the music and the lack of a single release (in the U.K.) to pave a route for the more casual record buyer to investigate. Having reached a secure plateau, the band's record sales could no longer be expected to increase with each release. The title of the album derived entirely from a partially completed connect-the-dots cartoon drawing of the band by John Entwistle. This unusual artwork gave the album an overtly comic slant that was perfectly in accordance with the sentiment of "Success Story," John's single contribution to the album, and with the bawdy jollity of "Squeeze Box" but which was maybe a little too flippant an image for some of the more mordant Townshend material. If nothing else, the unflattering nature of John's skillful and witty drawing once again displayed a lack of ego and absence of vanity rare in the superstar mentality.

The Who now held a secure and long-term market, but the other rock giants with whom they were generally bracketed at this time (Rolling Stones, Elton John, Pink Floyd, Wings, Led Zeppelin) all enjoyed greater record sales. Townshend reflected that if the Who had released an aggressive, uptempo, uncomplicated hard rock album—a kind of *Who's Next Part Two* with a glossy "rock super gods" cover photo (a release with which the rock marketplace would have been very comfortable)—then their record sales could have increased manyfold (especially in the U.S.). But such an album, he surmised, would have been dishonest and would have debased the Who's values and ideals.

Other artists fell back on such a lazy formula: the Rolling Stones' *It's Only Rock and Roll* (1974), Elton John's *Rock of the Westies* (1975), Rod Stewart's *Atlantic Crossing* (1975), and Wings' *At the Speed of Sound* (1976) all sold in enormous quantities by rehashing earlier established styles of the respective artists in a palatable form but failing to bring any new inspiration to bear. *The Who by Numbers*—whatever its shortcomings—was not such an album. Like Neil Young's earlier *Tonight's the Night* (1975), the work told the listener directly that the rock-and-roll dream, that hedonistic 1960s mythology and all that it entailed, was a fabrication that devalued the lives of those within it. Rock fans who routinely looked to superstar albums for affirmation and celebration of the dream had their preconceptions and faith shaken by such works. Pete Townshend—along with Neil Young and John Lennon—was foremost among a very small number of stars who were beginning to ask uncomfortable questions and who were prepared to shatter the illusions that prevailed at this time.

The music that is presented on *By Numbers* is sometimes prickly, sometimes deceptively smooth, very occasionally aggressive but generally most effective. It marked a few departures: it has no synthesizers, plenty of piano, few dramatic flourishes or dynamic instrumental interplay, and much acoustic guitar highlighted in the mix. What is overwhelming on *By Numbers*, however, is the pervading mood of the lyrics, which dominate much more than on previous albums. Since Townshend avoided his more esoteric and mystical subjects in favor of a kind of cathartic self-psychoanalysis, the lyrical attack—propelled by Roger Daltrey's scabrous delivery—is troubled, cynical and uncomfortable. This is the thirty-year-old Pete Townshend tackling (prematurely) the onset of middle-age head on and without sparing any niceties in the process. For the first time in years the listener heard Townshend's direct personal concerns, his unbridled analysis of his own life in crisis and, indeed, despair. What with the time devoted to three successive concept works, Townshend's last *personal* statement on record had been made years previously, and so *By Numbers* was a return, by implication, to "My Generation" territory. And significantly enough, the anger if not the musical style of that 1965 song permeated much of the material.

The dense and complex musical frameworks of *Who's Next* and *Quadrophenia* were here relaxed, allowing the songs to merge naturally into a more organic whole, with much of the music having an ensemble feel and a minimum of overdubbing. There is no stylistic musical innovation or experimentation, and the production smoothed down all the rougher edges of the sound into a homogenous unity. Little specific detail emerges from the sound, and few instruments are highlighted. The Who (and Nicky Hopkins, who plays on "Slip Kid," "Imagine a Man," "They Are All in Love" and "How Many Friends") combine into a well-balanced convergence of instruments and voices that is often earthy but not earth-shattering. *By Numbers* eschews overt technique and aural bravura in favor of the simple dignity and craftsmanship of the *song*. The material is not as overwhelming on the first hearing as the previous albums, and it takes many repeated plays for the finer qualities of the songs to emerge because the Who have here eliminated all surface thrills, all sensual effects. There are no lush seductive textures of guitars and synthesizers, few exciting power chords and no flashy playing.

Given the acrimony between Townshend and Daltrey during the recording, it is surprising to find that the musical cohesion on the album is so strong. The friction between the singer and the lyricist adds a *frisson* that becomes more potent than any dramatic effects. The listener is presented with Townshend's lyrics spewing forth his bile toward Daltrey and the other members of the band, yet the listener *hears* Roger Daltrey (on all but three songs) singing these lyrics back, like a mirror of truth almost *at* Townshend. Yet both Townshend as lyricist and Daltrey as vocalist sound like they mean business, and neither gives the listener (or each other) an easy ride. *By Numbers*, for this reason, is the stuff of artistic conjuncture, Pete Townshend's moment of truth. This obviously has repercussions for the other members of the Who, who are represented in different ways on the record. John Entwistle's song "Success Story" expresses a comic variant on the same theme—disillusionment—as had preoccupied Pete. Daltrey's vocals are the most obvious active expression of the same disillusionment. Only Moon is unable to add anything other than strictly musical input, but given the problems besetting Moon's private life by this time (alcoholism, drug addiction, marital breakdown, mental illness and chaotic finances) we can surmise that he might well (in a rare moment of sober reflection) have subscribed to Townshend's pessimism about the pitfalls of fame and stardom, if not to the doubts regarding the validity of the Who.

With the shuffling salsa beat of "Slip Kid," the album is ushered in with an unexpected and deceptively cheerful count-in. This seems to suggest that the listener is about to hear a laid-back and danceable piece of near-funk, but the sudden onslaught of the strident guitar and piano riff (beautifully interlocking with each instrument bearing a different part of the melody) immediately overwhelms with a song fully replete with traditional Who values of anger, energy and sardonic wit. This is undoubtedly one of the best songs on the album, with an anthemic quality and jagged-edged chord structure that forms an archetypal Who rocker. The cynicism and bitterness that had enveloped most of Townshend's writing at this time do not weigh it down. "Slip Kid" is a sustained shout of protest that is not unlike "My Generation" in its pungency: it's a mature and full-blooded song, with only a hint of the sophistication and diversity of the Who's later work. The music has a pure, undramatic quality that is offset by the razor-sharpness of the lyrics. The Who of "Slip Kid" are confident and seem to have nothing to prove; the music just spills out in fits and starts.

The beat is such that Keith Moon is forced to pace himself with a bit more discipline than usual, and, unlike almost every other Who song, it is possible to dance to the rhythm. The lyrics carry the cutting edge more than the music. This is a eulogy to the impossibility of attaining freedom (physical or psychological) and shedding responsibility. The character of the song is a rebel of uncertain age who concludes that the two universal truths in life are that "there's no easy way to be free" and that everyone else is in the same boat. The chorus has a fine, satisfying line of melody and is of perfect construction, the backing voices on the "slip kid, slip kid" lines being particularly effective.

Perhaps the biggest surprise is the guitar solo [2.05], which is of the conventional one-note wail variety usually avoided by Townshend. It works well enough here and moves into a few sparser moments with the introduction of some sustained feedback and the haunting use of a volume pedal [2.40] (a device that allows the sustain of a note or chord to be sounded without the initial attack on the strings being heard). This gives the effect of a bowed string sound and is quite beautiful. (A similar effect was previously employed on the opening bars of "Bargain"). A strong return of the verse and a final chorus move the track into a poignant fade-out over a yearning guitar solo, confirming the song's depressing main theme. And so ends a perfect performance that bridges a classical Who song structure with Townshend's revisionist lyrics and hints at a darker mood that becomes more evident as the album progresses.

A more lively sound is achieved with "However Much I Booze," where the acoustic guitars carry the full texture of the sound and rhythm, with R&B flourishes on the overdubbed lead guitar lines. Pete's lead vocals are strongly committed and (like "Slip Kid") reflect a bitter theme of being trapped that is handled with insight and a sardonic sense of self-criticism. Roger Daltrey apparently refused to sing the lyrics in which Townshend admitted in clear terms that he was caught fast in an alcoholic cycle of despair and self-vilification, a continued failure to conquer what he alone saw as the hypocrisy of his position. After a mad bout of lead guitar flourish, the song goes through a beautiful bridge section [2.44], which is moving and deeply felt. "However Much I Booze" is as repining as Townshend could get in a song that is, after all, presented for public consumption. Its success as a lyric overshadows its musical worth, though even here the mood is beset by a tendency toward self-pity. Pete regrettably falls into a contrite mood with the line "You at home can judge…," which is less effective because of its self-consciousness. Perhaps Pete's doglike howl toward the end [4.16] says it all.

In sound and intent "Squeeze Box" is the lightest song on the collection, almost a silly throwaway romp. Yet the enthusiasm of the performance renders it almost R&B *par excellence*. A trivial, daring, ludicrous song, it is achieved with such a positive feel that the listener can ignore its gross simplicities and just enjoy the exuberance and bounce. The quirky accordion and banjo confirm a music hall approach that employs a double entendre worthy of Max Miller or George Formby. Townshend's jokey sexual innuendo regarding the squeeze box runs through every possibility imaginable to sustain the tease. "Squeeze Box" is a rare throwback to the times when the band regularly recorded comic songs, only the humor here is rather more coarse than it was previously. Out of step with the remainder of the album (with the partial exception of "Success Story"), "Squeeze Box" was perhaps a bold inclusion, giving the only contrast with the more solemn material by which it is surrounded.

An undisputed masterpiece, however, is "Dreaming from the Waist," a surge of frustrated invective, detailing the tribulations of a man (assumed to be Townshend) caught between youth and middle age and feeling out of touch with either identity. A man out of control, as the original title "Control Myself" suggests, the character here can only dream of self-fulfillment. He finds himself torn between two sets of values, without any kind of reconciliation, and the only resignation is the acceptance of perpetual frustration. This builds from a gentle single-note figure into a massive texture of guitars, led by the acoustic rhythm but overlaid with a tortured electric guitar spitting vitriol into the proceedings. The chords, melody line and brilliantly paced chorus harmonies are stunning, and a beautiful chord sequence—with one root note running through—forms one of Townshend's most inspired moments. The structure and sense of dynamics that the whole band brings to the song confirms "Dreaming from the Waist" as the album's major achievement.

The much-vaunted "Imagine a Man" is a calm, profound ballad with gentle acoustic picked notes and muted bass and piano. This is a restrained though intense performance in which Daltrey takes the central position, his voice being the major melodic component. The song addresses a less focused theme of survival in the face of events, expressed in a series of eloquent and evocative poetic images. Townshend takes a rare position of detachment and looks at the world from the third-person perspective, examining some of the minutiae of everyday activity that form the whole of life's experience, concluding that come what may "you will see the end." There is a creditable lack of embellishment about "Imagine a Man" that retains its uncomfortable feel; many lesser acts would have added a string section to push through the emotional mood, but the Who leave the song as a stark, plaintive melody and forceful lyric. However, given both Townshend and Daltrey's assertion of the vast superiority of this song, it is difficult now to understand such lavish praise being heaped upon it. Few Who fans would agree that this was Townshend's all-time masterpiece. It invites comparison, inevitably, with "Behind Blue Eyes," but fails to match the sublime inspiration of that song.

The one contribution by John Entwistle sits surprisingly comfortably amid Townshend's tirades, at least in terms of theme. Musically, however, "Success Story" is the most basic of all the tracks, propelled by some incessant and catchy R&B riffing and a driving beat. Melody is sparing here, and John renders the sardonic lyrics with a double-tracked vocal performance (in differing octaves). The song features many humorous touches, including John's deep-voiced "I'm your fairy manager. You shall play at the Carnegie Hall." "Success Story" examines the dehumanizing effects of stardom and the lack of satisfaction to be found when "success" is achieved. It presents a similar sentiment as Townshend's songs, but like "Squeeze Box" has humor and warmth rather than bitterness at its center. In a characteristic mode, Entwistle adds a growling bass solo [2.11].

Nicky Hopkins gives perhaps his best keyboard performance on the album with "They Are All in Love," a beautiful piano/guitar ballad that has grace and almost baroque craftsmanship, capped by a lovely melodic vocal line. However, the sheer sarcasm and waspish vitriol of the lyrics undermine this placid and serene feeling. The deceptively pleasant evocation of mood in the first verse—where it sounds like butter wouldn't melt in Roger's mouth—shifts into a more angry vein by the final verse. The piano solo [1.22] is exquisite, and the gentle backing vocals on the title line belie what is a general repudiation of the world specifically from Townshend's personal perspective. The "they" of the title are those alongside whom Townshend has to live and who are oblivious to the decay, declining values and purposelessness of life that Townshend so acutely feels. But this isn't necessarily society in general being addressed, for Townshend's world was dominated by the music industry, and his bitterness was tempered by the poor shape of the Who's business affairs. The "punks" who are dismissed in the song are not necessarily younger musicians either, but could equally be any of the hangers-on or sycophants who abounded within the pop music community.

The most startlingly effective song (and the most sparsely arranged) is "Blue Red and Grey," which is a marvelous paean to the joys of nonconformism and eccentricity, advocating a life free from routine and tedium. This is not tainted by the cynicism of the bulk of the other material, and rather gives a refreshing alternative by advocating a mode of life as Townshend believes it should be. The stark ukulele backing is brilliantly effective, with a warm brass counterpoint by Entwistle [0.45]; otherwise it is Townshend's high-pitched and pure voice that carries the whole melody and stature of the song. "Blue Red and Grey" is an outstanding track, delightful in every way, but it is not a Who performance (a full band version was recorded and then rejected), nor is it rock and roll. That Townshend could produce a moving and poignant statement in so simple and unadorned a manner was partly an admission that the Who's blood-and-guts *Quadrophenia* approach (and indeed, Roger Daltrey's delivery) was becoming redundant and that Pete Townshend could communicate his own songs more effectively when left to his own instincts. (Also note that this performance confirmed for a lot of people that Townshend's songwriting skills could if necessary flourish not only without the Who but also outside of the rock genre.)

One of the more sharp-edged and acidic songs is "How Many Friends," a very strong, soundly constructed composition with a heavy piano texture intermingled with acoustic guitar chords, and with a high-register lead guitar soloing throughout the performance, giving an incessant tortured effect. Roger's vocals really stand out, and the changes of mood test his range to the full. He gets fully behind the sentiment of the song, as if he intuitively shares Townshend's point of view. This angry missive asks painful questions about sycophancy and the lack of sincerity with which those who are blessed with fame and power are faced. The three verses present set pieces where the motives of a male acquaintance in a bar are questioned, a woman (or groupie) is viewed with suspicion and, finally, associates in the band (or their managers) maintain a two-faced relationship pervaded by a lack of trust. In the first two verses, Pete does not merely dismiss the man and the woman involved in the two casual encounters; it is significant that he berates his own ego for its susceptibility to flattery and empty praise. The song bitterly concludes that Townshend's real friends could be counted "on one hand."

By Numbers closes with "In a Hand or a Face," which is the most conventional hard rock performance offered and is perhaps the weakest song. This sounds more one-dimensional than the other material, with a brittle all-electric guitar arrangement that trades on traditional power chords to less effect than is customary. The production on this one song sounds thinner and less translucent than the remainder of the album, and subsequently it lacks some of the magic. The highlight of "In a Hand or a Face" (a muddled and obscure title that replaced the more obvious "Round and Round") is the hypnotic chorus that is sung by Townshend and Entwistle. A prolonged drum roll forms a solo [1.58] before the number breaks into standard hard rock histrionics toward the end. The song is a kind of pessimistic rant, and the chorus line of "I am going round and round" sums up the hopelessness and directionlessness of life like a more cynical and depressing version of "Circles." Compared to the more fetid and prickly intimacies of the other songs, "In a Hand or a Face" is cold and remote, and it closes the album on a somewhat bitter note, both inconclusive and despondent.

The intrinsic qualities of *By Numbers* cannot be dismissed, for the Who had progressed once more and entered new terrain that was perhaps uncomfortable but did not ultimately lack any of their accustomed creativity. However, some of the surface excitement seemed to have been sacrificed in a single-minded thrust toward an entirely cerebral and emotional musical language. The dynamics, mysticism, and sensuality of the past is suppressed, as if the band members are forcing themselves to grow up, face reality and pass judgement on a world of decaying values. In the past much of the Who's belligerence and defiance was enshrined in a musical arrogance that defied established rules and conventions. With *By Numbers* Townshend in part reacts to and bemoans the expectation that such a defiance should *always* be part of his approach. He does not find himself isolated and cold, alienated from his audience, as might have happened, but rather relieved that he is understood (especially by the critics) and praised for the brutal honesty of his stance.

Roy Carr responded completely to the *The Who by Numbers* in *New Musical Express*, writing, "Against the underlying themes of frustration, isolation, cynicism, disillusionment and self-doubt, Townshend attempts to come to terms with Townshend ... a nihilistic attack: he lashes out in fury and frustration at The Who, severed business associates and himself ... an affirmation of four great, if somewhat idiosyncratic personalities. In short, this album is brilliant."[6] Chris Charlesworth was slightly less enthusiastic in his *Melody Maker* review "Townshend Gives It All Away," feeling the album lacked the rock-and-roll drive of earlier Who works, although Charlesworth certainly wasn't about to write off a band that he still considered to be the greatest in the world.[7] Dave Marsh saw the album as a concept work in a long review in *Rolling Stone* titled "Who's Ongoing Saga of Stardom and Failure," concluding that the record could prove to be the Who's best.[8] In *Trouser Press*, Ira Robbins considered it to be a "tremendous (albeit not their best) album."[9]

A couple of years later, Townshend looked back on the record with some objectivity, writing that the songs were "all negative in direction" reflecting "reality tinged with bitterness." He went on to say, "I knew as I was actually composing that what was happening to me was an exorcism.... Recording the album seemed to take me nowhere ... it's not a definitive Who album.... I felt detached from my own songs, from the whole record."[10] Despite this negativity, the catharsis of writing the songs certainly seemed to improve Pete's state of mind. He reflected that if the songs were taken as a suicide note, then the act of writing the note itself functioned to "flush out the trouble."[11] Roger

Daltrey later took the album to be a fairly straightforward assault on the perennial problems of aging, and especially turning thirty, and as such considered the album to be a brilliantly perceptive piece of work.

The Who by Numbers was remixed for its CD reissue in December 1996, and Jon Astley felt there was a need to brighten up the sound, saying of Glyn Johns's original production, "[It] sounded so dull. In fact, the multi-tracks are still dull—I mean there's not a lot of top end knocking around on that in the original recording, so rather than add it on at the cutting stage which is what happened last time, we tried to add it on at the mixing stage." The most noticeable change was with "Blue Red and Grey," where Entwistle's brass is made much more prominent. "We brought the brass up," said Astley, "because we thought Glyn Johns played it down too much. I think the brass is great, so why not feature it?"[12] Studio outtakes were thin on the ground from the original sessions, so three live tracks were added to the CD. These were "Squeeze Box," "Behind Blue Eyes" and "Dreaming from the Waist" from a concert performed in Swansea on 12 June 1976 (discussed below). Townshend's demos reveal a few additional tracks that were recorded around this time but which didn't coalesce lyrically with the theme of the album. These include the whimsical piano ballad "Girl in a Suitcase," a slick funky instrumental titled "Brrr" and "Keep Me Turning," which Townshend later recorded on his next solo project, a collaboration with Ronnie Lane (ex–Small Faces and Faces), who had enjoyed a solo career from 1973 by rejecting many of the superstar values of the times and reestablishing his roots in a way Townshend probably somewhat envied. Other rejected demos bore the titles "Ordinary Fella" and "Fight Until You're Mine."

In the U.S., a single was pulled from the album a month after its release. This matter was obviously a problem for the record companies, who in the past always put out a single in advance, as a taster for the album. The Who themselves were probably indifferent to this matter, but musically "Squeeze Box" was the most suitable and obvious choice. However, its lyrics were very risqué, and the record might easily have been banned from radio play. In the end, MCA took the plunge first and on 22 November "Squeeze Box," backed by "Success Story," was released. It seemed to avoid any controversy and reached number 16 in the charts. Polydor followed suit on 24 January 1976, having delayed the release until the U.S. reaction to the single could be assessed. The record did even better in Britain, reaching number 10. It did provoke a mild flurry of moralistic questioning in the tabloid press, but being such a carefully sustained double meaning, the record was only as "dirty" as the listener wanted it to be! Under analysis, the lyrics had a clean bill of moral health, and no bans prevailed. Later in 1976, MCA coupled a shortened version of "Slip Kid" with "Dreaming from the Waist" for a second single but found with this no chart success. Daltrey disliked tracks being plucked out as "instant singles" in this way. "Albums should be albums and singles should be singles," he protested on hearing of MCA's release of "Slip Kid." "They're completely different things; that's all ridiculous."[13]

Concert dates were booked from October until the end of 1975 and into 1976, and the Who hit the road with a vengeance, sounding harder, louder and more energetic than ever before. Amazingly enough, none of Townshend's doubts voiced on *By Numbers* were translated into his performances. Onstage, Pete was as good-humoured and captivating a performer as he had ever been. The raw power, drive and sparkling vitality of the band's live performances through 1975 and 1976 tended to somewhat disguise the fact that they were now offering an overtly retrospective live act. That the Who could play "I Can't Explain" and "My Generation" with such naked enthusiasm and freshness in many ways compensated fans for the fact that the live concert act had failed to progress much past *Who's Next*. Indeed, this torpidity would increasingly play on Pete's mind regarding his attitude toward the future of the group. As far as the *By Numbers* album went, only "Squeeze Box" and "Dreaming from the Waist" became regular features of the live set. "However Much I Booze" and "Slip Kid" were attempted on occasion but soon dropped.

The tours of 1975–1976 were more extensive than any since 1971, and the shows were a surefire commercial proposition at a time when the band's tangled business affairs limited their earnings from other sources. Another studio album was vaguely projected for late 1976, largely at the behest of Daltrey, who was determined for the band to work to a regular schedule. But as usual this was postponed, and it took Pete another year to get his new material together. He later commented on this phase, saying, "I didn't have any songs or any subject matter apart from the same old stuff that had brought forth all the dreary *Who by Numbers* material—alcoholic degradation."[14] In the absence of a studio LP and with a renewed onstage fire, the most obvious move during 1976 would have been to release a double live album of the current stage act, but the band did not favor this project. They seemed happier to allow *Live at Leeds* to remain the last word regarding live Who material. The double live album was by the mid–1970s a stopgap for many acts. Even at its most perfunctory (when rehashing a complete set of already-released material in all-but-identical versions), the double live album could be a moneymaker, as evidenced by Bob Dylan's *Before the Flood* (1974), Peter Frampton's *Frampton Comes Alive* (1975), Paul McCartney's *Wings over America* (1976) and the Rolling Stones' *Love You Live* (1977). Ironically, the Who had greater justification than most in releasing a live set, and such an album would have undoubtedly proved more than worthwhile. Who concerts were recorded, however, and a handful of tracks have since emerged from this period.

On 6 December 1975, the Who had played the premiere rock concert at the massive Silverdome stadium in Pontiac (Detroit), Michigan, and a sound recording was made to accompany a videotape that was taken from a back-of-stage projection screen. The Who were a little displeased with the vastness of the venue and the 76,000 fans before them but played a flawless set. This footage was drawn on for the *Kids Are Alright* film in 1979, and the soundtrack album featured an excerpt from a medley that started with "My Generation." The track faded in midway through "Join Together"—a vastly simplified jam based on the 1972 single—and followed with a fine version of Bo Diddley's "Road Runner" before concluding with a slower blues version of the main song titled "My Generation Blues." I must say that some of the lack of atmosphere and intimacy of such a remote venue is evident on these tracks. The music is well played and decently (if not spectacularly) recorded, but it seems a little bit too mechanical, lacking the Who's usual emotional force. "Road Runner" is the only officially released Who interpretation of the song and is an appealing knockabout blast of irreverence. The later CD release of *The Kids Are Alright* omits all three tracks as the result of the whittling down of a double album to one compact disc, and the songs are currently unrepresented in any CD catalogue.

A second large stadium show was recorded in Wales at Swansea City football ground on 12 June 1976 and has fared rather better than the Pontiac material. The venue still presented the problems of impersonality and detachment for the Who, but the sheer high quality of the 24-track recording on Ronnie Lane's mobile unit has compensated in some ways for the deficiency. The Who sound a little too cleanly recorded, and once more the tape lacks something in emotional heat and atmosphere, but ultimately the music is faultless and rigorous. The material was initially mixed by Glyn Johns for a radio broadcast in London and was under consideration for a live album release in late 1976, but this plan reflected much more the demands of the record company than the wishes of the Who, who resisted the urge to release it. (Unfortunately, in its place Polydor released a somewhat unnecessary compilation called *The Story of the Who*.)

The Swansea material was reassessed in 1993 for the boxed set, and its high technical quality and fine performances found favor with the compilers. The boxed set presented "Dreaming from the Waist" and "My Wife," and the reissue of *By Numbers* added "Behind Blue Eyes" and "Squeeze Box" (and repeated a slightly longer edit of "Dreaming from the Waist"). "My Wife" is the best of the live versions of this song, mostly on account of its being taken at a faster-than-usual pace. Pete's guitar solos are simply riotous, a manic display of unpredictable fluctuations between piercing lead lines and feedback powerchords. "Squeeze Box" is cheerful and incessant, with just the right degree of irreverence and jollity, and mostly enjoyable for the guitar work. A masterly run-through of "Dreaming from the Waist" adds power and visceral punch to the already towering stature of the song. The harmony vocals are effortlessly reproduced, and Townshend's power chords are exciting. The final word, however, must go to John Entwistle, whose bass work is breathtaking, especially toward the end, where he plays a blinding solo. "Behind Blue Eyes" is a more respectful reading of the song, lacking the absolute precision of the two studio versions but adding a more aggressive riff on the fast section. It is a worthy release, nonetheless, and this version is unlikely to be bettered.

As previously mentioned, Polydor put together a predictable compilation in *The Story of the Who*, which was released in October 1976. Backed by a promotional campaign on television, the album reached number 2 in the charts, and a reissue of "Substitute" on single reached number 7. MCA passed this set by and didn't attempt their own version of it. The album was flawed inasmuch as it entirely omitted all the 1965 material and *Quadrophenia* while overrepresenting *Tommy*. It included no previously unreleased songs and sported a garish cover photo of an exploding pinball machine. In general, *The Story of the Who* was an opportunist release by Polydor and showed a lapse in quality control on the band's part that would never have happened when they were with Track Records. As *Meaty Beaty Big & Bouncy* was still available at this time, *The Story of the Who* was largely redundant. The reissue of "Substitute," however, was prescient in other ways: during the latter half of 1976 it was featured in the act of the Sex Pistols, the British group who found themselves—within a year—at the forefront of the punk rock explosion.

The punk rock movement was perhaps the most exciting, most incandescent and least pretentious encapsulation of pure street-level rock-and-roll energy that ever occurred. In both Britain and America through 1976, groups like the Ramones, the Sex Pistols, the Clash, the Damned, the Jam, and the Buzzcocks proved themselves ready to carry the creative torch of rock and roll forward. Their music was direct, loud, fast and often exhilarating, while their ideologies were broadly subversive and nihilistic. By 1977, scores of these young bands were winning record contracts and edging the more established rock acts out of the critical favor of the music press. Many people cited the Who—especially in their early years—as a major influence on the punk acts, a comparison that was partially relevant but also misleading, as musically punk was very much establishing its own standards rather than updating the past. Punk is significant in the Who's story because it so much squared with Pete Townshend's hopes and beliefs that it changed his attitude and approach to his music.

In turn, we can now see more clearly what the Who meant to the punk bands. The Sex Pistols (apart from playing "Substitute") were characterized by a guitarist, Steve Jones, who very much drew from Townshend's onstage power chord sound. (When Steve Jones and Paul Cook, the Pistols' drummer, first met Townshend in January 1977, they were alarmed to hear that Pete wanted to quit playing with the band and told him that the Who were one of their favorite groups!) The Clash took "I Can't Explain" and distilled at least three songs from the chord pattern: "Capital Radio" (1977), "Clash City Rockers" (1978) and "Guns on the Roof" (1978). The Damned's drummer, Rat Scabies, very much modeled himself on Keith Moon (and, indeed, possessed some of Moon's talent), and bassist Captain Sensible was a longtime Who fan. The Jam were an overt mod–influenced group who self-consciously modeled themselves on the Who circa 1965–1966 (as well as on the Small Faces and the Kinks). Patti Smith, not quite a Punk artist herself but nonetheless a highly influential new wave performer, recorded a committed version of "My Generation" early in her career. However, although the Who were admired by younger musicians for what they had been and done in the past, as a contemporary group they were very much part of the rock music Establishment that the punk groups sought to nullify. Townshend accepted his position with dignity, championed the young bands and realized that the cutting edge of rock and roll no longer needed to reside with bands like the Who.

For the bulk of 1977, the Who undertook no work at all. Townshend had by now decided to abandon concert tours, frustrated with the lack of progression and the predictability of Who concert material and wearisome of long-haul travel and spells away from his home and family. The band members indulged in the expected solo work, even Townshend, who recorded a collaborative album with Ronnie Lane called *Rough Mix* (released in October). This work (to which Townshend contributed five new songs) was rooted in folk, R&B and country & western and so sidestepped his central creative drive as a rock and roller. But Townshend's satisfaction with *Rough Mix* was such that he began to seriously consider this as a way forward without the Who. Roger Daltrey had released *One of the Boys* earlier in the year, and both Daltrey and Keith Moon had film projects to occupy them.

Toward the end of the 1977, the Who settled on two projects for the immediate future: a new studio album and a film history of the band. But no live performances were scheduled. Work on both projects commenced around the same time, but both brought with them problems. The director of the film was Jeff Stein, and as well as assembling old footage from television shows and films, he wanted to obtain some high-quality contemporary concert material of the group. A concert was hastily scheduled for 15 December at the Gaumont State Cinema in Kilburn before an invited audience. The Who hadn't played together for over a year, during which time Keith Moon had deteriorated in health, and when the show came along the band were both underrehearsed and underenthusiastic. Although no footage from this concert was included in *The Kids Are Alright*, a version of "My Wife" was included on the soundtrack album. This performance was competently played and well recorded but was simply lacking any excitement; it did not do any justice to one of the band's greatest stage workouts. (Although this 1977 recording of "My Wife" was the first live version to be released, it has been now superseded by both the vastly superior renditions from San Francisco 1971 and Swansea, Wales, 1976.)

A second concert for filming was arranged at Shepperton Studios on 25 May 1978, and this proved more successful, with versions of "Baba O'Riley" and "Won't Get Fooled Again" making it onto both the film and soundtrack album. Certainly an improvement on "My Wife," these two performances are good and solid, with a fluid feel that does justice to the songs. "Won't Get Fooled Again" is the better of the two, with Pete enjoying himself immensely. However, both lack urgency and should be taken as representative rather than definitive live readings of the songs. It may well be that unreleased earlier live recordings could surpass them. By the time this material came to be released it held further significance, as it had become Keith Moon's final concert with the Who, and therefore its historical value outweighed all else.

The work on the studio album commenced in late 1977, an occasion for which Keith Moon returned from a prolonged and indulgent stay in Los Angeles. Glyn Johns had once more been invited to produce, this time assisted by Jon Astley (who had first worked with Pete on *Rough Mix* and was, in fact, the younger brother of Pete's wife, Karen). Sessions began, centered around a song that had been tentatively tested onstage as early as October 1976 called "Who Are You" and another titled "Sister Disco." However, as sessions dragged into 1978, Johns and the band made little progress in getting the album finished. Keith Moon's playing was erratic, and Daltrey and Johns came to blows at one point. In the end, Johns—with other commitments pending—left the sessions before the work was completed. "It was going too slowly for him," Jon Astley recalled. "...But he made it very obvious to Roger that he adored and loved Pete, and didn't think much of Roger."[15] Astley had to assume the production responsibilities alone, a daunting prospect for any young producer faced with the most notoriously temperamental rock band of them all. "They were at an all time low when I took over because things had been going very slowly and Keith was in no shape.... Pete was only coming in and working daytimes and Roger was coming in and working nights."[16] In the interest of expedience, the band had cast a wider-than-usual net in their recruitment of guest musicians, sharing Andy Fairweather-Low, Billy Nicholls, Nicholls's brother Michael and keyboardist Rod Argent. The sensitive matter of using a guest drummer was reluctantly considered as well in the light of Moon's declining capabilities.

Through overdubbing and rerecording, Astley painstakingly got the band to complete enough material for an album, with sessions stretching into May 1978. Moon managed to complete his drum tracks, making a Herculean effort to recapture his previous form. He didn't quite succeed. He had been disturbed by intimations from the other band members that if he didn't manage to regain his physical well-being and drumming ability, then the band would be looking to replace him. A further complication was that the group had rejected some of Glyn Johns' earlier mixes and instructed Astley to start remixing again from scratch. By 14 July 1978, the first material was ready for release on a single that took the shape of "Who Are You" and "Had Enough." In an unprecedented recognition of John Entwistle's songwriting talent, the record was pressed and promoted (in the U.K.) as being a double A side, with "Had Enough" being theoretically as important and prominent as "Who Are You." In practice, however, "Had Enough" was all but ignored, "Who Are You" was the song that was played on the radio, seen on television (the band had made a promotional film) and accepted as the Who's latest statement.

On single, "Who Are You" was shorn of a final verse but contains enough of the song to indicate a "classic" synthesizer-heavy Who sound. It is a clever, twisting, insidious song that seemed a little complex for a single, but one with enough melody and drive to stand its ground. However, Charles Shaar Murray, reviewing the disk for *New Musical Express*, found it a disappointment, saying of it, "...inconsequential twiddles for guitar and the ubiquitous synthesizer; pretty in places and twitchy in others." Murray went on to call "Had Enough" the "better track of the two and closer to the Who mainstream, being a simple song of rebellion."[17] Murray was critical of the Who for relying on a synthesizer (on both songs) rather than compensating with guitar, although this should be understood in the context of the time, when punk and new-wave groups were dominant, guitars were fashionable and synthesizers were out of favor. Murray did emphasize his continuing love of the Who and his still-unshaken faith in their future abilities, but the review can now be seen as the start of a critical backlash against the band, which continued with the reception of the *Who Are You* album. Despite its complexity, "Who Are You" performed decently well, reaching number 18 in the U.K. and number 14 in the U.S. Singles, however, were of little significance to the band; the album *Who Are You* was finally released a month later, arguably a year late.

Despite its slow, painful gestation and recording, *Who Are You* is very unified in sound, due to the extensive use of synthesizer, which forms the basis for every track on the album. This gives a high-tech sound that does not necessarily convince the listener that the material needs it; to reduce the musical compositions to such an automated pace tends to dampen the human elements that originally made the Who so characteristic and idiosyncratic. The songs are mostly complex, varying in pace, mood and character, usually within the space of one song. The arrangements are lush, multilayered and—in some cases—a little labored. Nothing on *Who Are You* sounds spontaneous or utilizes any ensemble group unity or instrumental empathy. All is overdubbed with antiseptic precision, to a high degree of musicianship. In short, the Who here fall back on recording technology and musical technique to shape the songs, rather than playing off each other as a "live" group.

The songs themselves—three by John Entwistle and six by Pete Townshend—are accomplished and well tailored. They are crafted rather than inspired, good rather than brilliant, interesting more than compulsive. In an attempt to instill drama and imagination, the band really push for a maximum exploration of each song's potential, but in the end the listener is more aware of the *process* of the band's attempt to make the material more interesting than the quality of the songs themselves. As a whole, *Who Are You* reveals the Who's impeccable standards wearing slightly thinner. The record lacks that extra special and undefinable quality that was still strong on *By Numbers*. Also, the lyrical thrust of the album is diverse and lacks any sustained cohesion of theme. In part, this is due to Entwistle's three songs—a higher quota of material than he had previously contributed to a Who album. Pete's pessimism had lessened since 1975, and his songs attempted to address real-life situations ("Sister Disco," "Who Are You") as well as indicating a more pragmatic approach to accommodating the subject of music itself and the process of making music ("New Song," "Music Must Change" and "Guitar and Pen"). Pete had tried to make his introspection accessible and universally applicable, but this did not always produce a palatable result.

It was, of course, heartening to have the first number on the record, "New Song," begin with a slash chord guitar phrase, but the pace and drive of the song (compared with, say, "The Real Me" or "Bargain") seems too sluggish. Where Keith Moon's drums used to almost forge ahead of the band, they here merely follow, and a resultant loss of vitality is noticeable. "New Song" has an exceptionally well constructed composite of guitar chords and synthesizer notes, but some of the fills and signatures seem to lamely plod along where once they would have smoothly flowed or spitted like molten lava. Roger Daltrey puts a lot of commanding singing into the performance, as if trying to keep up the energy level. That said, "New Song" is bright and lively, with a high-tech sound that eschews acoustic guitars for a high-profile synthesizer texture and jaunty stop-start rhythm. This sounds glossy and rich but ultimately results in a loss of intensity.

The theme is a very direct response by Townshend to the demands placed on him by the music industry, and he cynically suggests that his songwriting approach has become purely mechanical. "New Song" is about the making of music without inspiration, with the songwriter falling back on a force of habit, a craftsman's skills, which—it is implied—is not the way great music is created. The false self-pity, as in the line "My fingers kill me as I play my guitar," is amusing enough but slightly too heavy on irony to evoke sympathy. The line "new lamps for old" suggests the trading-in of musical ideas as a commodity that can be recycled to infinite effect, because the listener (Pete suggests) will never know. However, this also forms an admonishment to the audience who Pete feels will not allow him to progress beyond the "same old song." (The "same old song" idea is directly challenged by its later antidote

"Music Must Change," so it is perhaps unfair not to consider the themes of the two songs in tandem). Only the Baba–like suggestion of spiritual cleansing (in the metaphor of rain) hits a positive angle.

As the Who had already released a song called "I've Had Enough" (written by Townshend), John Entwistle's song dropped the (subjective) "I've" part of the title and focused on similar sentiments of frustration. The sound here is perhaps too slick, too technominded for the Who, more the kind of arrangement Genesis took into the charts after Phil Collins had become singer, or maybe comparable with the pristine emptiness of a song by Foreigner or Journey. Jon Astley's father, Ted (Edwin Astley had already enjoyed a fruitful career as a composer and arranger in the 1950s and 1960s), had added the string arrangement. Sumptuous and well orchestrated as they are, the strings are wholly unnecessary and incurred the wrath of Roger Daltrey, who thought the string overlay was setting a disastrous precedent for a rock-and-roll band. Many groups had succumbed to string settings before, but the Who had resisted, and Daltrey felt Glyn Johns was pushing the band into bland middle-of-the-road territory. The guitar seems too submerged in the mix, but this is a well-crafted song with an appealing melody, and an inspired touch comes with the brass break [2.59].

With an undeniable sense of ecological foresight, Entwistle complained that the world was "heavy" with humans—a conviction later amplified in the nightmare world of his song "905," where the human race self-perpetuates by mass production. In "Had Enough" the character expressing such sentiments does not want to be pushed around anymore and is vowing to change into an active protagonist rather than remain a passive victim. Crudely philosophical, the song concludes with the cheerfully apocalyptic "here comes the end of the world." Roger Daltrey sings the lead vocals rather than Entwistle, which John used as a ploy to get more of his songs onto the album. It evidently worked because the following "905" was also an Entwistle song, though this time sung by John. Completely in isolation, the lyric of this song is a self-contained sci-fi minidrama about a future embryo factory, very much from the tradition of *Brave New World*. The narrating character becomes conscious of his being and recognizes that all essential human qualities are missing from himself due to the automated method of his conception. The simple and forceful melody is heavily embellished with synthesizer in a very conscious attempt to sound futuristic. A somewhat sluggish pace robs the song of any dynamics, and it remains worthy rather than spectacular.

Even on "Sister Disco," which is structured very closely to a traditional Who sound and arrangement, an intricate synthesizer pattern is dominant and perhaps too ornate—"too many notes," as Salieri said to Mozart. "Sister Disco" is a song full of drama and drive but one in which the mock-baroque arrangement almost becomes too complicated too soon. It is very well sung by Roger Daltrey—at his most comfortable here—with the bridge section

[1.11] added by Pete. The terseness of the main verses and the four-chord chorus has a compacting effect that is weakened by four pompous-sounding, ungainly lines [2.07]. When the solid force of the melody is not swamped by the arrangement, some fine acoustic guitar work emerges [1.41], and the song concludes with a spurt of solo ragtime guitar. Superficially a song of street-level and nightlife experience, "Sister Disco," to whom or to which the character is saying goodbye, remains enigmatic. Is Sister Disco a woman, a place, a nightclub or the record industry in general? Or does he, she or it have some other tendentious connection with Townshend's psyche?

Smooth technology, a relaxed jazziness (or a cool blues, maybe) and high drama combine in the mercurial "Music Must Change" to provide the song with a radical edge and an intense, insidious atmosphere that is quite unlike anything else the Who ever recorded. It is highly melodramatic yet connects with another musical tradition—jazz-blues fusion—that gives it some degree of rationale. Compelling vocals from Roger reveal a passion and verve missing from much of the remaining material. "Music Must Change" is fine, inspired music and one of the most satisfying performances on *Who Are You*. The band members achieve here a new urgency, despite the fact that the song manages without Moon's drums—the 6/8 time signature caused him some difficulty. The jazz-tinged lead guitar work is masterly, and an almost discordant spontaneous phrase [3.45] is a touch of genius.[18] Lyrically, it is a poetic assertion, loaded with similes and metaphors, that music itself must be allowed to evolve and grow and that energy and spiritual impulses at any point in life can eventually find their natural expression in musical form.

Entwistle's third song is a characteristically thundering hard rock workout, "Trick of the Light," which boasts a muscular texture driven by a relentless eight-string bass riff that eventually breaks into a solo [1.24]. A fully realized song of strictly conventional form, this comes very close to the kind of orthodox heavy rock format that the Who were usually careful to avoid, though despite the bluster the tempo is medium-paced. The song is a reflection on a sexual experience with a prostitute in which the sex is a mere commodity. The narrator realizes that his motives and emotions are entirely different from the woman's. The client is anxious here to connect emotionally with the woman, but she cannot see him as anything but a dehumanized form or at best a man awash with sexual insecurity.

A dreamy jazz guitar and synthesizer passage leads into the mock operetta of "Guitar and Pen," which could have been either profound or amusing, but fails by getting stuck between the two. The song is simply too complicated, too overwrought, and too unwieldy to succeed. It tries to do too much and ends up somewhere between Andrew Lloyd Webber, Stephen Sondheim and Gilbert and Sullivan. Melodramatic to the point of bathos, this shows so much conceit and pure nerve that it almost gets away with it. The Gilbert and Sullivan chorus repeats are so irritating the listener might think that

"Guitar and Pen" is an elaborate joke. Some staccato guitar riffing is at times quite fierce but to no avail—the energy founders through lack of direction. Lyrically, the song is a straightforward and witty celebration of the creative impulse and its painful transition from aspiration to achievement: a return to a teenager's struggle to find a voice, the fight to find one's creativity.

Yet despite this seeming resurrection of earlier concerns, the Who here sound nothing less than a group out of touch with the basis of their original strengths; the arrangement is simply gross when compared with the fluid joyousness of "Song Is Over" or "Getting in Tune." The jolting, unsettled mood simply draws attention to what sounds like a song of flawed construction and an unsure sense of direction. Whatever Townshend's hopes or aspirations for "Guitar and Pen" might have been, the treatment simply condemns the song rather than redeems it. If Townshend intended a parody of Gilbert and Sullivan, he should perhaps have been reminded that the mock operetta of Gilbert and Sullivan often sounds like an ugly parody of itself in the first place.

For the first time on a Who album, Townshend self-consciously prepared a ballad, called "Love Is Coming Down," deliberately structured to provide a contrast in mood and pace. This is a song in a minor key, smooth and easy, with airy strings and Daltrey lifting his voice into a higher register. There is no grit or angst in the melody for Roger to seize upon, but the song is perfectly constructed and delivers drama and power through more subtle means. One of the highlights of "Love Is Coming Down" is the moving coda in G [3.04], but it must be said that the song lacks some pace and guts. In short, it is a fine composition and a heartfelt performance but not necessarily suitable as Who material. (A good alternative song, "Never Ask Me," was also considered and then dropped from the record. As if to confirm Townshend's "easy listening" intentions, he then sent the song to Frank Sinatra, who declined to use it.) "Love Is Coming Down" charts the highs and lows of emotional intimacy and sees Townshend in a mature and reflective mood. The title line draws from a Meher Baba metaphor of love falling as rain from the sky (this image also comes into play in the final verse of "Who Are You" itself). More than any other song on *Who Are You*, this sees the Who enter the domain of pure middle-of-the-road stodge: they sound eminently capable and listenable but a little too tasteful for comfort. Given that Roger Daltrey is not Andy Williams or Matt Monro, he tackles the song very well. One cannot imagine Townshend wanting to pave a way for the Who to break into the sequined-jacket, middle-aged Las Vegas circuit, yet "Love Is Coming Down" sounds like they are halfway there.

The title track of *Who Are You* is the most important and memorable item on the album, and it forms the last song of any longevity or enduring appeal that the Who ever produced. A pulsating, spitting, seething, fizzing rock song, "Who Are You" has a mesmeric synthesizer underlay and a block chord progression and strident melody. The carefully programmed synthesizer does tie the song down with a slightly sluggish structure, but this procures a strong beat that anchors the twisting and turning of the melody. It is a song that builds through masterly repetition, especially of the title line, and passes effectively through contrasting passages of calm and thunder. A delicate, jazzy acoustic guitar solo [2.30] is followed by a grandiose E–G–D power chord sequence [2.55] and Daltrey's "classic" yell, "*Who——are you.*" A haunting piano/guitar refrain is sounded [3.20]—suggesting an oddly Oriental flavor—before a final verse is worked in. Over six minutes of angst-ridden, red-blooded, gut-churning rock and roll assert the Who's old values on one final classic song. [It comes as little surprise to learn that the basis for "Who Are You" is to be found in the instrumental "Meher Baba M4 (Signal Box)," a *Lifehouse* demo from 1971.]

The words of "Who Are You" transgress the boundary between lurid naturalism and poetic ethereality. Much of the song is merely reassuringly functional rather than enlightening. "Who are you?" is a familiar enough everyday phrase, a question from any conversation, but it remains too open-ended and diverse here to imply a profound message. The first two verses refer to a few hours that Townshend spent in Soho, a neighborhood in London, renegotiating a publishing deal, receiving an check for unpaid royalties, drinking with the Sex Pistols at the Speakeasy, tearing up his check in disgust, fighting with a photographer and then collapsing drunk into a doorway before being prompted a few hours later to go home by the police or face arrest—all in a day's work for your average dysfunctional rock superstar. (Much of Townshend's working life was spent in Soho, London's bohemian quarter; the Who had offices in Wardour Street and London's music publishers were located in Denmark Street, known as Tin Pan Alley.) The conclusion drawn from this activity is that there's "got to be another way." The final verse, maybe suggesting a solution to the problem of dealing with the wretchedness of everyday life, is full of Baba's spiritual vibes of love. "Tell me, who are you?" remains the final question, however—and a question that saw the final phase of the Who's journey (almost) reach its conclusion.

There is much to enjoy on *Who Are You*, but the essence of the Who's vitality was clearly compromised to some extent by preconceptions and historical antecedents that demanded things to which the band members were now unequal. As musicians, their response was to be "musicianly," to revert to a utilization of technique and technology, where in the past they had barely been able to suppress an organic drive and energy surge that flowed from the strength of their collective personalities. When Keith Moon died shortly after the album's release, it could be more clearly seen as a closing chapter. But as a record in its own right, it marked a crisis point that the band would have needed to address in any case. Moon's death actually pointed a way beyond the crisis. What *The Who by Numbers* had succeeded in doing three years earlier was to give Pete Townshend a valid platform for his emotional strife. But *Who Are You* could not repeat the same process. *By Numbers* was a self-contained, oneshot statement, and Townshend now fluctuated between detachment, flippancy and self-consciousness. In writing with honesty and penetration about his own life's problems and concerns, Pete (perhaps for the first time) lost touch with the experience of his listeners. Life in the music industry—as Townshend himself has stated in interviews often enough—is manifestly not normal life, not the life of his audience and not universal experience. It can be significant and absorbing, to be sure, often offering a rich source of imagery and metaphor, and Townshend had the ability to render it fascinating and valid. But on "New Song," "Guitar and Pen," "Music Must Change" and "Who Are You," the lyrical focus lacked the real connection with everyday life that had initially made the Who so special. Even Townshend's low-life antics in Soho had about them the self-consciousness of the celebrity rocker with a mission at large in a possibly hostile and changing environment in which he was no longer sure of his purpose.

At the time of its release, Pete Townshend was pleased with *Who Are You*. He felt that the length of time that had been taken with the recording and mixing—despite the seeming lack of progress during many of the sessions—meant that the album was as near perfection as possible under the circumstances. The lack of impending concert dates following the recording period for the first time removed a lot of pressure from the band and allowed a more leisurely approach to be taken. From a musical point of view, Townshend was mostly satisfied with the unorthodox approach that had been achieved on "Music Must Change" and "Guitar and Pen." He felt he had been successful on the experimentation. He also felt "Who Are You" itself was a good slab of conventional Who music in the tradition of "Won't Get Fooled Again." But the jazzy diversions seemed to Pete to be the best indication of how the Who could survive and progress. With three successful songs, John Entwistle found himself responsible for a good proportion of the creative burden on *Who Are You*, a matter raised by Charles Shaar Murray, who seemed to expect Entwistle to step in at the point where Pete was beginning to ail. John just wished that the band would go out on tour, because he now gained very little *musically* from studio work. Daltrey felt that *Who Are You* contained some of the best music the group had ever played, but—ever the professional—he would be unlikely to say anything else.

Who Are You was released on 18 August 1978 in the U.K. (where it reached number 6 in the charts) and a week later in the U.S. (where it went to number 2). This was the first Who album to be released without the band's playing any concert dates to promote it, and it must have come as an enormous relief to Townshend that the sales of the album were so good, far better indeed than *By Numbers*, which had been heavily supported by extensive concert work. (A very prominent advertising campaign in the U.K. must have helped.) MCA tried its luck in December with a single release of "Trick of the Light" (backed with "905"); although unique in its coupling of two John Entwistle songs on one Who single, it gained no chart placement. The album sleeve—ostensibly devised by Keith Moon (the band members took turns)—was somewhat conventional: a posed color portrait of the four of them among a mass of old sound equipment and cables. It was a little disappointing because it seemed so superficially literal. In one of those fortuitous moments that later assume an implausible prescience, Keith Moon—two months ahead of his death—had been perched onto a chair that was labeled "Not to be taken away."

It was understandable that the critics were divided in their response, but in general the album gained more praise than might, in retrospect, seem reasonable. Charles Shaar Murray, in *New Musical Express*, recognized that the Who of "My Generation" had gone. He said, "There's no way that they can come on like The Voice Of The Kids any more and still remain honest. *Who Are You* is a testament to that honesty.... The theme of the album is rebirth ... a shedding of old responsibilities in order to shoulder new ones."[19] Murray felt the Who were at least being truthful about their situation and found most of the songs more than satisfactory—his reservations regarded "Sister Disco," "Love Is Coming Down" and "Guitar and Pen." Pete Silverton, writing in *Sounds*, found Townshend's lyrics to now be self-obsessive and tiresome. "Musically," he wrote, "it's impeccable middle of the road hard rock with a surfeit of synthesizers.... But, beyond that, there's an empty core."[20] In *Melody Maker*, Chris Welch's review titled "Boo Who" was not the condemnation it suggested, but he felt the album lacked the usual level of Who excitement.[21] Ira Robbins wrote in *Crawdaddy* that the record suffered from "over-production, underwriting, and lyrical obesity."[22] *Rolling Stone* (reviewer Greil Marcus) found *Who Are You* "strangely confident" but correctly pointed out that Moon had now "lost most of what he had."[23]

Because Jon Astley had been the coproducer of the original album, the CD reissue of *Who Are You* (in December 1996) was given an extra stamp of authority, as well as some unexpected bonus tracks. The most important outtake was "Empty Glass." Under the title "Choirboy," the band had attempted to pull this ambitious, complex song into shape. The version released on the CD shows that they had almost managed it. It is apparently a Townshend voice and guitar demo, to which Keith Moon and John Entwistle have overdubbed drums and bass. The weakest element in this recording is Pete's singing, which is tentative and rather low in the mix. Obviously, a finished version would have a more polished lead vocal, though probably not by Daltrey. The song has several contrasting sections, beginning stridently with a one-note guitar drone and then moving through several moody passages, including a truly beautiful falsetto section that is reprised three times [1.51,

3.52 and 5.43]. Despite a very personal crisis encapsulated in the lyrics, the song could have worked well enough to be included on the original album. (The loss of this song on *Who Are You* is lessened because Pete rerecorded the song with a very similar arrangement as the title track of his 1980 solo album *Empty Glass*).

A Townshend piano demo with a cool jazzy feel, "No Road Romance," was also included, a mature reflection on a touring life, very minor key, downtempo and introspective and more indicative of the kind of material that Townshend would explore on his later solo albums. (A similarly introspective guitar and vocal ballad, "Like It the Way It Is," was also rejected by the Who during these sessions.) It has been suggested, also, that the Who recorded a jolly sardonic sing-along called "Keep on Working," which was also to appear on *Empty Glass*, but, there seems to remain no evidence of this on tape. The remainder of the CD was made up of alternate mixes of "Guitar and Pen" (with a different guitar part), "Love Is Coming Down" subtitled "Work-in-Progress Mix" and "Who Are You," which had a completely different second verse and an alternate guitar track. Note that "Music Must Change" on this CD also uses a noticeably different guitar mix, with the original mix to be found on *30 Years of Maximum R&B*. One further anomaly from the sessions is a third mix of "Guitar and Pen," which only appeared in the U.S. on an earlier CD edition of *Who Are You* released by Mobile Fidelity Sound Labs (a specialist remastering company) in the early 1990s.

Midway through Thursday, 7 September 1978, Keith Moon died, having accidentally overdosed on prescribed drugs after a night out with his girlfriend. His death came, ironically, at a time when he had begun to curb his excessive lifestyle and was attempting to control his drinking and drug intake. While Moon's death seems to fall within an established rock-and-roll tradition of living fast and dying young, the genuine tragedy—which many obituary writers overlooked—was that Moon was a uniquely gifted and dazzlingly talented musician, both on record and on the stage. Whether his drumming ability would have continued to decline is arguable, but his achievements were utterly manifest. The world relished the eccentricity of the man, the "wild man of rock," "Moon-the-Loon" and hell-raiser reputation, the pranks that filled gossip columns and tabloid newspapers during his lifetime. But his position within the Who and their recorded history is that of a drummer of genius, and this fact first and foremost should be enshrined with his memory. That *Who Are You* contained Keith's weakest performances was lamentable, but a more balanced perspective of his whole oeuvre and technique can now be appreciated.

Although difficult to assess, Moon's drumming was a measured and balanced tension between control/precision and frenzy/assault. The sheer power and drive within him, that relentless pounding of limbs, was disciplined by a sense of pace, variation and color. His sense of rhythm—like his personality—was idiosyncratic. Because he didn't use the high-hat, he was able to add at an early stage an additional bass drum—very unusual in the mid-1960s—and he somehow managed to ride a cymbal almost constantly as well. The result sounded like he had an extra arm or was two standard drummers playing simultaneous complementary beats. His beat was irregular but true. His offbeats and downbeats were not explicitly stated. He would often play around an imaginary offbeat and downbeat, filling the spaces in between. John Entwistle has said that the bass often had to establish the beat. And Townshend's guitar often had to do this also.

But the beat was always there in what Moon did. His flamboyance sometimes led the listener to think that he had lost it, because he didn't always explicitly play it. In fact, Keith just loved variations. A good example is a heavy, drum-led song like "The Real Me," in which Moon establishes the beat with a characteristic phrase at the beginning but rarely repeats it. We know in our minds the beat is there, and we hear Keith filling in the spaces; the gaps become a challenge to him. Obviously, there are only a limited number of variations that can be fitted inside each tempo, but Moon makes the number sound infinite: he seems to never repeat himself. He doesn't rely upon the same few flashy riffs and rolls.

Lots of jazz drummers achieve variation, contrast and color through a more minimalist approach—playing less rather than more. Moon took the opposite approach: he achieved variation, contrast and color by playing *more*, because he had the energy, drive and imagination to make it work. After much listening—and the drums aren't always the most clear instrument on Who records—it becomes obvious that he did tackle each song as a separate item. Each song had a different drum arrangement, given Moon's overall consistency of style, and the overplaying never detracted or dominated a song. The drums would seem to fit perfectly, never being too harsh or crude. They had a subtlety, though subtlety might not apply to Keith so readily.

Some Who songs are obvious standouts in terms of the drumming: "I Can't Explain," "Leaving Here," "The Ox," "Bargain," "Won't Get Fooled Again," "Young Man Blues," "The Real Me," "The Rock," "Dogs Part Two," "Baby Don't You Do It" and dozens of others. Moon was consistent, especially live, at times when his character and personality might have led one to think otherwise. There are exceptions, of course, quite a few songs where the recording quality and production make the drums sound shallow and metallic (a lot of the early material) and not so many songs where Moon just didn't turn in a decent performance ("New Song" seems to be the most obvious, but, as previously stated, *Who Are You* in general lacks something from Keith). But generally what he offered was so consistently good, imaginative and powerful that it was taken for granted.

For the remaining members of the Who, taking Keith for granted was abruptly shattered on that Thursday, and obviously the whole future of the band was thrown into doubt. *Who Are You,* still riding high in the charts, was looked upon afresh. It no longer represented the Who's continuing struggle to find a mature voice to serve them into the future, but it very much started to resemble a last gasp, the closing phase of a glorious career. Keith Moon, despite the doubts about his health and continuing ability, was such an integral part of the Who that it was difficult to imagine the band without him. Surprisingly, they opted to continue with a new drummer, and toward the end of December 1978, Kenney Jones (ex–Small Faces and Faces) was named as his replacement. What the band members and their fans may not have realized at this time was that the true spirit of the Who was never to be recaptured. Moon had taken with him much more than the band first realized. No music played without him was ever the same again—The Who's magical and unique inspiration had now inevitably dissipated.

8

Second Generation (1979–1998)

Following Moon's funeral, John Entwistle, Roger Daltrey, Pete Townshend and Bill Curbishley held two meetings in late September 1978 to discuss the late drummer's estate. But no immediate decision was made regarding how or whether the Who would continue. Pete said that the band needed to find a workable solution, but "if we can't do it so that it will work, then we should knock it on the head."[1] *The Kids Are Alright* film was almost completed, and filming of *Quadrophenia* had begun in September. Lack of a drummer was not an immediate handicap because the band had no recording or touring commitments pending. Even so, many drummers felt they should offer their services to help the Who out on a temporary basis, among them Ginger Baker, Carmine Appice, Tony Newman, Carl Palmer, and Kenney Jones. By December the band had decided that Kenney Jones was the best choice as a permanent band member. A future of sorts was assured, although the Who's fans were split. A few were convinced that Moon's passing was a terminal blow, while many others were desperate to see the band reactivated and reborn.

The single most positive aspect of this tragic situation was that the band now felt themselves to be liberated from the four-piece lineup that had become enshrined inflexibly within tradition. It was now possible for additional musicians to be added. Although Jones was the only new shareholding member of the band, a keyboard player and a brass section were to be added for live shows. The band even talked of changing their name, although they probably never considered it seriously. The opportunity to play with additional musicians had the effect of renewing Pete Townshend's enthusiasm for live shows, and during the first couple of months of 1979, the band rehearsed with John "Rabbit" Bundrick on keyboards at Shepperton Studios. Some of these rehearsals were filmed and recorded by a BBC documentary film crew. But the resulting film, *Who Are You*, was later scrapped by the band under their right of veto and has not—apart from two clips—ever been publicly screened.

The band's projects for 1979 were considerable and diverse: the release of the two aforementioned films (each with a double soundtrack album and related singles); participation in a charity album project; selected concert performances in both Europe and the U.S.; the scheduled production for a further film about the notorious British criminal John McVicar; a revival of *Lifehouse* as a possible film project; and finally a new Who studio album. Additionally, Pete Townshend's solo career was activated with a record deal with Atco, and Pete had received a commission for a television musical work along the lines of a rock opera. Townshend had also developed a small publishing firm, Eel Pie, and had projected a collection of his own short stories on which he had been working for some time. This was a massive array of diverse activity and seemed to suggest a direction for the Who that would satisfy Daltrey's interest in film, Townshend's desire to try different forms of music and writing and Entwistle's preference to keep the Who as a working rock-and-roll band.

Record activity during 1979 was to be equally diverse. Two or more previously unreleased Who songs were scheduled for an all-star charity album that was to benefit the neuroelectrical therapy administered by Dr. Meg Patterson, which had cured Eric Clapton's heroin addiction and was later to help Townshend himself. This album never appeared, and the Who songs—tracks recorded with Keith Moon—remain unknown.

Also unrealized was the television special that Townshend was working on, intended for screening as part of London Weekend Television's *South Bank Show*, produced by Melvyn Bragg. The show was to have been a rock opera, an autobiographical piece based upon incidents from Pete's early life. (The plot was later reworked as a short story titled *Fish Shop*.[2]) The television project went uncompleted, though some of the music intended for this production may have comprised a series of orchestrated songs that Pete had been working on over the previous couple of years. On the *Rough Mix* album, Pete had added an experimental string arrangement (courtesy of Ted Astley) to his song "Street in the City," which was a remarkably effective crossover into the genre of the impressionistic orchestral song-setting. By September 1978, strings had been added with equal success to at least four other fine songs: "The Ferryman," "Brooklyn Kids," "Praying the Game," and "Football Fugue." This project was in fact Pete's final collaboration with Kit Lambert, but it was never resurrected after Keith's death. The four extant songs emerged for the first time in 1987 on *Another Scoop*, proving that the work would undoubtedly have been one of Pete's more productive solo ventures.

The Who's first recording work without Moon came in January 1979 and was an audition session for Kenney Jones at Ramport Studios. As a prelude to the release of the *Quadrophenia* film, the Who decided to rework "The Real Me," radically rearranged in a slower, looser interpretation.

Although interesting, this recording lacks the intensity of the original and tends to be a little indulgent. However, it hits an unusual funky beat, and John Entwistle is able to make a prominent contribution on bass. Its release in 1994 on the *30 Years of Maximum R&B* set was interesting rather than arresting, and it sounded as though the band were deliberately trying from the outset to avoid the kind of high-level attack that was characteristic during Moon's tenure with the band. Rehearsals at Shepperton were recorded and (as the soundtrack to the documentary film) included "Sister Disco" and "Who Are You." The latter two songs did not stray too much from the released versions, and footage was included in *30 Years of Maximum R&B Live* (1994). A later rehearsal at the Rainbow Theatre in London (where the band staged their comeback concert on 2 May) was also filmed by the BBC. Footage was shown (on the British program *Nationwide*) of "I Can't Explain" that was considerably rearranged into a less rigid shape, as if the band were at this stage attempting to shake off some of the long-standing conventions of their music.

In fact, the group devised a longer show with Kenney Jones and added a brass section to extend the range of sound available. Although they still presented the usual hits such as "Substitute," "My Generation," and "I Can't Explain" and the more celebrated bits of *Tommy* and *Who's Next*, the band made the center of their concert set more experimental with "Music Must Change," "Drowned," "5.15" and "Who Are You"—long songs on which the keyboards and brass came to the fore and an improvisatory spirit prevailed. In general, this version of the Who onstage offered a more conventional rock spectacle: it was evenly paced, with measured climaxes and a sustained level of enthusiasm. It lacked the unpredictability and explosive dynamics of the band of old, but it certainly convinced most fans that the Who would remain a creative force for another few years. However, despite the odd improvisatory jam instigated by Pete, through 1979 and into 1980 the band played it very safe and did not introduce any new songs into the live act.

On record and on film, the Who once again defined and celebrated their own past history with both *The Kids Are Alright* and *Quadrophenia*. The band's filmmaking urge had now come to fruition after years of false starts and aborted ideas. The wild, uncompromising dream of *Lifehouse* and the heavily compromised popularization of *Tommy* seemed to be the two extremes of approach to the Who on film, neither of which was necessarily desirable. The abilities of manager Bill Curbishley created a workable niche for the band that seemed, for a while at least, to show considerable promise. *The Kids Are Alright* (released in June 1979) was entirely a compilation of performance and interview footage, assembled with the correct degree of understanding and irreverence by director Jeff Stein to make it a classic of its kind. So entertaining and absorbing is it that the viewer can easily overlook that the film contains no footage from the definitive 1970–1974 era and nothing from

Quadrophenia. The film gained a warm critical response and performed decently well but was obviously of specialist appeal.

The film was initially promoted by the single release of "Long Live Rock," remixed from the *Odds and Sods* album and backed by both "I'm the Face," and a live version of "My Wife" from the upcoming soundtrack LP. This was a perfunctory release, as the song had no direct connection with the film other than that it was used to play over the closing credits. Understandably, the single reached only number 48 in the U.K. and number 54 in the States. The double soundtrack album, which was released in the U.K. on 9 June 1979 and two weeks later in the U.S., was of a rather different flavor from the film. Although mainly a genuine soundtrack collection of live and television performances (all previously noted), there was a slight tendency toward making the album another greatest hits collection. The inclusion of regular studio versions of "Magic Bus," "Tommy Can You Hear Me," "Long Live Rock" and "I Can See for Miles" is highly questionable, especially as the last did not even feature in the film. The remaining tracks were a cross section of live performances, ranging from the good ("Won't Get Fooled Again," "Baba O'Riley," "Pinball Wizard," "See Me, Feel Me" and "Sparks"), via the middling ("Young Man Blues" and "Road Runner"), to the mediocre ("My Wife" and "Join Together"). The novelty television performances were less solemn and more valuable: "Anyway Anyhow Anywhere," "My Generation," "A Quick One While He's Away" and "I Can't Explain"—all mono recordings of varying sound quality from the 1960s but well worth inclusion.

The film contained some moments that might have added to the value of the album—the "Barbara Ann" rehearsal and the version of "My Generation" from Monterey, California, 1967, for instance. The album begins with the Who's humorous encounter with the Smothers Brothers, and it might have gained from a few more snippets of the band's priceless comic dialogue (with which the film was gloriously awash). The main anomaly on the album was the version of "Happy Jack" from Leeds, England, 1970, which was well appreciated by the fans but somewhat out of place and miscaptioned in the glossy photo-booklet that came with the packaging. This album offered the first live Who material to be released since *Live at Leeds*, and as such was much anticipated by Who fans. In retrospect, it was slightly disappointing, as it seemed to close the vault on the Keith Moon era, from which more things might have been expected. The nature of a soundtrack album—as Led Zeppelin discovered with *The Song Remains the Same* (1976)—was that it tied the group down to releasing on record what was *heard* on the film, removing the selection process that inevitably contributes to the success of a live album. If the Who wanted to release a live version of "Pinball Wizard" on record, for instance, they would be unlikely to have selected the version that appears in the film. Yet the same version appears on record and therefore has to be judged separated from its visual elements.

Greil Marcus of *Rolling Stone* said of the album, "...a solid retrospective, very mainstream, with hardly a hint of the eccentricity that, at least in the early years, had as much to do with the group's identity as violence and noise. *The Kids Are Alright* lacks only excitement and surprise."[3] Charles Shaar Murray found the album to be an acutely endearing expression of nostalgia. "An embarrassment of riches," he declared in *New Musical Express*. "For me ... the continued survival of The Who is like a touchstone to my own: even without Moon, The Who still exist, and that's good enough."[4] Not all the critics were willing to concur with Murray by falling back on their memories, however. In *Sounds*, David Hepworth was unequivocally condemnatory, saying of the album, "[It's] a mess.... There is nothing anywhere that can't be found in better condition elsewhere.... It's time they either went forward with confidence or jacked the whole thing in."[5] An expensive package with a glossy color booklet, *The Kids Are Alright* retailed at a higher than usual price and reached number 26 in the U.K. and number 8 in the U.S.

The soundtrack for the film of *Quadrophenia* presented a number of problems. The film was specifically set (a few anachronisms accepted) in 1964 or 1965 and incorporated a number of contemporary soul and R&B tracks of this era. Mod purists questioned the validity of some of these selections (hits by the Cascades, the Crystals, and the Ronettes) but obviously the inclusions were dictated by licensing availability. Because *Quadrophenia* was a naturalistic film, the Who's music was used incidentally (and sparingly) at apposite points in the drama. However, the appropriateness of the music of an album of the early 1970s (especially one that used synthesizers) being matched up to a reconstructed social scene of ten years earlier was questionable. The real soundtrack to the mod era was R&B, soul, and Tamla Motown mingled with a few early Who and Small Faces singles. The music from a 1973 concept album had no place in an otherwise scrupulously authentic film taking place during 1964 or 1965 because it presented sounds from an entirely different milieu. The original album provided the basic framework of the film, but a more detailed script worked in a specific plot that provided an uncompromising insight into the sex, drugs, violence, gang rivalry and rebelliousness of British youth in the early 1960s. Very much in the tradition of gritty, working-class British naturalism, the film was exciting and unpretentious: a definitive and honest statement of youthful discontent at one crucial point in history. The film was criticized for its violence and lurid detail but was well received by most of the press. In America it was initially viewed much more as a novelty item but had by the early 1980s established itself as a bonafide cult film.

In presenting a soundtrack album, the Who clearly did not much fancy rerecording *Quadrophenia* in its entirety. Nor were they happy just applying the original music to the film. The compromise reached was to select the key tracks from the original double album and remix them. John Entwistle took charge of this task. He worked with "The Real Me," "I'm One," "5.15," "Love Reign o'er Me," "Bell Boy," "I've Had Enough," "Doctor Jimmy" and "Punk and the Godfather," giving them a punchier, harder sound. In all cases, Entwistle rerecorded his bass track, replacing the original with the more trebly and distorted sound that he used onstage. In some cases, additional instruments were added: an extra electric guitar on "Punk and the Godfather," a piano on "I'm One," and a flute on "Love Reign o'er Me." These two latter additions were superfluous and tended merely to add clutter to the arrangements. "Helpless Dancer" was merely a brief snatch of the final line of the song and "I am the Sea" was all but identical to the original.

The main point of interest was the inclusion of three new recordings of songs that Townshend had prepared specifically for the film (although it was suggested that these were leftovers from the 1973 sessions, and the aforementioned "Joker James" comes from even earlier.) Neither "Get Out and Stay Out," "Four Faces" or "Joker James" come anywhere near the standard of the original material, and none are really essential Who performances. "Get Out and Stay Out" has a catchy piano riff and a one-line vocal by Pete but is extended far beyond its melodic possibilities to become a tedious jam. It ties in directly to one scene in the film where Jimmy is thrown out of his parents' house. "Four Faces" is also based on piano with a Townshend vocal and has a complex but unwieldy arrangement. The lyrics give an overly literal exposition of Jimmy's psychological makeup, and the song fails to find any clear melodic focus. Potentially the most interesting of the songs on account of its age is "Joker James," which has a Daltrey lead vocal but ultimately suffers the same problem as "Four Faces." It meanders to little purpose and as mentioned in chapter 6 the practical joker element of Jimmy's character seems misplaced.

The resulting double album appeared on both sides of the Atlantic on 6 October 1979. The music included one new band (Cross Section), who had been commissioned in the film to play "Hi-Heeled Sneakers," an utterly routine R&B cover. A reprise of the High Numbers' "Zoot Suit" was obviously more authentic and acceptable. In general, the soundtrack was less gratifying to Who fans than had been *The Kids Are Alright*, and the *Quadrophenia* songs suffered by being presented in such a contracted manner. In *Melody Maker*, Richard Williams found the mixture of tracks most unsatisfactory and dismissed the Who songs as having "nothing whatsoever to do with the subject; their tone jars unacceptably against the luscious sleeve images of kids and coffee-bars and beaches and scooter-packs."[6] Tony Stewart of *New Musical Express* tended to agree with this adding that the album was "a timely anachronism: brutish early '70s rock 'n' roll aimed at the hard rock market of the time... As an album it is a failure."[7] In the States, the soundtrack album was more warmly received by John Swenson, who was enthusiastic about "Joker James," in his *Rolling Stone* review "Mod Quad."[8] British sales reflected the success of the film, and the album reached number 23. The American chart placement peaked at number 46, the album being on the Polydor label. In both countries "5.15" was selected as a single (backed by "I'm One"), but a number 45 placing in the States was the only chart showing of the disk.

More satisfactory for Who fans during 1979 was the return of the band to the concert stage in a kind of second coming—much less brilliant than the first coming but good enough under the circumstances to satiate all but the most purist of fans. After the live act had been tested with a number of concerts in Europe, and New York during the summer, the band played a short U.S. tour in December 1979. This tour is now mostly remembered for the tragic deaths of eleven members of the audience in Cincinnati on 3 December. However, many of the subsequent concerts on the tour were recorded, and a small glut of material was later released. A concert in Chicago on 8 December was filmed. One track from this concert was released in 1997 on the *Face Dances* CD. This was the jam "How Can You Do It Alone," which is an improvised Townshend rap over some power chord riffing. It forms a valuable memento of the improvisatory nature of the finale of Who shows of this era, and it has a spontaneity lacking in future studio work. Although it's repetitive and unmelodic, it is good to hear Pete's unrestrained guitar and John's bass sound being so raw and well recorded. Although it shares some lyrical ideas and a title line, this is ostensibly a different song from that which appeared later on the *Face Dances* album.

A few days later the Who played at the Spectrum in Philadelphia (11 December), and from this source was released "Dancing in the Street," on the 1988 U.K. EP reissue of "Won't Get Fooled Again." This is a tight, respectful performance, complete with full-bodied brass arrangement, and it moves into Townshend's improvisatory "Dance It Away" (uncredited on the label), which is worked into the same beat (though heavily edited for release). This track is also of high technical quality, although the pace is fairly moderate. Despite a contemporary (and now deleted) CD single release in 1988, the song has never been collected. Other concerts were also recorded (such as that played in New Haven, Connecticut, on 15 December) and it might have been that a live album was the sensible way to introduce Kenney Jones to the record-buying public, but all this material was consigned to the archives. (With hindsight, I can see that the 1979 concerts were the finest the band played with Kenney Jones, and a major live release from this period would have been infinitely more valuable than what emerged later from the 1982 tour.)

At the end of the year, the band played at London's Hammersmith Odeon in a benefit concert that was also televised. The accompanying live album, *Concerts for the People of Kampuchea* (released in March 1981) featured four Who songs recorded on 28 December: "Baba O'Riley," "Sister Disco,"

"Behind Blue Eyes" and "See Me, Feel Me." Considering that the Who played an excellent 150-minute set, some of the selections for the album were disappointing. "Baba O'Riley" is spoiled by an out-of-tune guitar (Townshend had banged the neck during the opening few bars of synthesizer). "Sister Disco" is decent, but an unspectacular reading of the song. "Behind Blue Eyes," on the other hand, is excellent, mixing delicate emotiveness with explosive power, and the showstopping "See Me, Feel Me," although it lacks some of the frenzy of the Moon–era performances, works its usual magic on the audience (despite Pete's out-of-tune solos). It is disappointing that such a poor version of "Baba O'Riley" should have been deemed fit for release while other excellent material from the concert such as "The Real Me," "My Wife," "Drowned" and "Punk and the Godfather" remained unheard.

New Who studio recordings were finally deferred until mid–1980, however. The members of the band were busy with a long tour of the United States in the spring of 1980, and Pete Townshend's long-awaited solo album, *Empty Glass,* appeared in April. This record was notable—in addition to for its intrinsic musical qualities—as being the first time that Townshend had selected the best of his recent songs and recorded them himself rather than have the Who work on them. *Empty Glass* offered ten songs of consistent quality and varied effect. Three high-energy rockers—"Rough Boys," "Gonna Get You" and "Jules and Jim" (and maybe even the joyous R&B workout "Cat's in the Cupboard")—might otherwise have become Who songs while the title track reworked the Who leftovers from 1978. Throughout the album, Townshend's sensitivity, subtlety and willingness to experiment seemed to exemplify a flexibility of approach that he could no longer attain with the band. The critical and commercial success of *Empty Glass* established Townshend as a more vital contemporary force on the music scene than the Who, who collectively seemed cautious of releasing new material despite maintaining their demand in the global rock marketplace and attracting many younger fans. (Note, however, that the band's recording contract with MCA had expired and negotiations were underway for a new deal. Finally, in March 1980, it was announced that the Who would sign to Warner Brothers for the North American market.)

The other important Who project of 1980 was the release of the film *McVicar* in June. The band's involvement was as executive producers and backing musicians on the soundtrack album. This was very much a vehicle for Roger Daltrey as actor. It had been planned that Pete Townshend would contribute material for the soundtrack, but finally songs and incidental music were commissioned from other artists—it may be that Townshend found the subject matter of the film uncongenial to his own songwriting concerns. The most memorable track from the film and album was a single, "Free Me," which was played in a style so similar to the Who's that many people confused it with the earlier "I'm Free." The film seemed to indicate a clear and successful new forte for the band, and for Daltrey in particular, and development deals were negotiated for two more films: a biography of London's East-End gangsters the Kray twins and a drama set in the trenches of the First World War. Neither film materialized.

In October 1980, Virgin Records negotiated with Shel Talmy to rerelease in Europe the Who's debut album, *My Generation*, which had been deleted for over ten years. This was a timely move, as many younger Who fans had not even heard the record and the mod revival that had gained ground in the U.K. during 1979 had alerted many people to the influential nature of the record. Welcomed by both fans and critics, sales of *My Generation* exceeded the usual reissue level and the LP reached number 20 in the U.K. charts. Pete Townshend attributed the success of this release to the preponderance (and curiosity) of fans of the Jam, a trio who had rapidly progressed from their mod roots to become one of Britain's top bands. Although the Jam's Paul Weller did not relate to latter-day Who music, he never refrained from singing the praises of *My Generation* and customarily cited this as his favorite album.

The reemergence of mod notwithstanding—which despite throwing up a handful of new bands was almost entirely a passing trend of fashion—the early 1980s were an unsettled time in which rock and roll drifted into many dissipated and indulgent byways. Since the Who had released *Who Are You* in 1978, punk had dissolved into New Wave, disco had dominated the charts, futurism and new romanticism had emerged, and reggae found a growing audience as a newly revitalized form. The most promising bands of the 1977–1978 era (and Townshend's favorites) were the Clash (characterized by anger, idealism and a ramshackle power base of political and musical invective) and the Jam (characterized by cynicism, upgraded mod rock tinged with passion in an aggressive reassertion of 1960s musical values refocused through punk). Yet, amazingly enough, three years later, when the Who came to release their next album, the Jam had almost turned into a Stax–influenced soul outfit and the Clash were more likely than not to be found playing disco, rap and reggae material. Amid the entrenched styles such as heavy metal and art rock, and a campy parade of pop theatricals such as Adam Ant and Duran Duran, the role of the rock dinosaurs was more questioned than ever. The Who, the Rolling Stones, David Bowie and a few others were always there, and they were as commercially potent as ever, but they had lost a little of their sense of purpose. Pete Townshend, more than most, must have known that the Who ritual could not continue for much longer. Other factors had begun to take their toll on the band—and Townshend in particular—and the momentum instigated by Kenney Jones's arrival was somewhat checked by the compounding effects of tragedy. Early mentor Pete Meaden had died (in August 1978) and was shortly followed, of course, by Moon, the eleven fans at Cincinnati (December 1979) and, finally, Kit Lambert (in April 1981).

The Who began recording at London's Odyssey Studios in June 1980, and American producer Bill Szymczyk had been invited to work with them on the album. Throughout the period of recording, Townshend was enveloped in a personal crisis, his descent into alcohol and narcotic dependency. While the recording sessions were in progress, the band probably did not perceive the problems that Townshend's new songs would raise. Some of the diverse flavor of *Empty Glass* was carried over into these compositions, but the new album ultimately dissipated into an unsatisfactory and unfocused piece of work. New values and new personnel (Jones, Szymczyk) had been incorporated in the band and Townshend's songs were markedly different in intent from previous Who material. But the attempt to define a new kind of Who music foundered, for reasons that were probably not apparent at the time.

It is an undeniable fact that the members of the band had grown apart musically since Keith Moon's death, and a three-way tension now persisted. Pete Townshend had demonstrated with *Empty Glass* that he could absorb some of the edgy energy of the new wave and hone songs of a quirky, intellectual and unpredictable nature. For his solo work, he had surrounded himself with younger backing musicians and enjoyed the lack of preconceptions for his music. More than anything, Townshend liked to take chances. His lyrics now tended toward a personal worldview that in some cases Roger Daltrey would be uncomfortable singing. Townshend later stated that if he had submitted "Rough Boys" for the Who, then Daltrey would have insisted on the gay allusions within the lyrics being toned down or eliminated, thus losing the carefully subtle inferences that Pete had intended. Ironically, Roger later said that he felt "Rough Boys" was the one song that the band *should* have recorded, although he was undoubtedly basing his comment on its musical rather than lyrical qualities. Other Townshend songs fell by the wayside: "Dirty Water" was a routine rockabilly workout that no one missed (it was later heard on *Scoop*); "Zelda" was a string-driven song, successful but too esoteric; "Boogie Friday" was a syncopated jazz-funk instrumental that showcased keyboards and harmonica; "Dance It Away" and "Face Dances"—more straightforward songs—were later released in solo Townshend versions; "You're So Clever" and "Body Language" were clever all-synthesizer pop songs; and finally, a magnificent and powerful song called "What Is Love," which found no outlet at all (and so far remains unreleased).

Roger Daltrey, for his part, was committed to keeping the Who a fresh, working unit that could evolve with the times and diversify. Musically, Daltrey wanted the band to retain its identity as a straightforward rock-and-roll band—encompassing a flexibility of styles and not being pinned down to any limited definition. Daltrey saw the Who as makers of music on a grand scale, defined by an anthemic musical power of the kind that was gaining Bruce Springsteen, U2, and Simple Minds stadiums full of fans. John Entwistle was committed to the slick hard rock approach that utilized the Who's musicianship to full advantage. He believed that the Who could outplay any of the contemporary hard rock and heavy metal acts and should exploit this strength. Kenney Jones had no discernible influence on musical policy other than that he enjoyed touring and found that the Who gave him a vast audience before which to perform.

Preceded by an uncharacteristically lengthy tour of Britain, during which a number of the new songs were highlighted, the Who's long-awaited post–Keith Moon album *Face Dances,* was finally released, two and a half years after the drummer's death. A single "You Better You Bet" backed with "The Quiet One" appeared first, on 27 February 1981 (and a week later in the States) and became a moderate hit in both countries (number 9 in Britain, number 18 in the U.S.). Both songs were taken from the album, although "You Better You Bet" had been shortened by one verse. It was perhaps a surprise that the Who could still reach the Top Ten in the U.K. with such an uncharacteristic single, and the sales of the *Face Dances* album likewise showed no slippage. Released on 21 March 1981, and well supported by the concert tour, *Face Dances* reached number 2 in the U.K. The American edition also earned an impressive number 4 placing.

One of the few positive things that can be said about *Face Dances* is that the Who managed to avoid the established musical conventions that they might have felt were played out on *Who Are You*: the block power-chords, the synthesizer patterns, Daltrey's screams and acoustic rhythm guitars. Townshend's guitar playing represented a major shift away from the sharp, crisply distorted thrashed chord work of their classic period, moving toward an arpeggio-based style that at times resembled the mid–1960s sound of the Byrds, even to the extent of Townshend using for the first time in fifteen years a Rickenbacker guitar. The characteristic doubling up of electric and acoustic guitars that had distinguished *Tommy, Who's Next* and *Quadrophenia* was entirely missing. Where Townshend does double-track the guitar—such as on the introduction to "You Better You Bet"—it is to form an intermingling mesh of arpeggios. The lack of aggressive, fiery guitar playing robbed the record of the most recognizable aspects of the Who sound.

Plenty of energy is in evidence, however, on the opening "You Better You Bet," but the lightness of touch makes the song and performance sound shallow. The melody twists and turns, and Daltrey delivers a plethora of words that tend to confuse the structure. The backing vocal harmonies on the title line gain acceptance through repetition, but the song is further damaged by an ugly staccato section [3.13]. The final few bars hit a minor key [5.05], and a mood of pathos prevails. The lyrics—like much of the album—chart emotional and sexual to-ing and fro-ing between the character and another individual in a kind of enclosed domestic deadlock. The same light airiness prevails on "Don't Let Go the Coat" but with a much lower level of energy. The melody here is sure, but the tendency toward blandness is unbroken.

Even the elegiac middle-eight [1.31]—hitherto one of the strongest elements of Townshend's songwriting—here seems lame and fails to deliver any sense of drama. "Don't Let Go the Coat"—titled after a Meher Baba reference too obscure to be of any value in the song, finds the Who dwelling in Cliff Richard territory and is altogether too easy on the ear. Pete's Spanish guitar solo [1.16] does little to redeem the song.

An uptempo three-chord rocker, "Cache Cache," follows, but even this lacks power and distinctive melody. The moralizing chorus takes an easier pace, and another minor-key finale is in evidence on the line "a hundred hours," which closes the song. The sheer esoteric nature of Townshend's lyric, which starts by asking, "Did you ever sleep in a bear pit?" (which apparently Townshend *did* during the band's 1980 European tour), displays how disconnected with real life Pete seemed to have become. Though it hardly reaches a profound conclusion, the song makes a comment on the nature of alienation and the need for security. "The Quiet One" had already appeared on the single B side, and John Entwistle's songs were by this time fairly predictable. John here offers a lumpen rocker with fierce guitar and bass work; it's heavy rock with a decent melody and cohesive (though one-dimensional) lyrical theme. His abrasive voice cuts the blandness to a minimum.

Idiosyncratic and quirky, "Did You Steal My Money?" is a genuine attempt to update the Who muse into an introspective, melancholic yet happy-go-lucky lament. Teasing backing vocals, rippling piano notes and good chord changes should form a memorable song, but once more the sheer lightness of tone detracts from any substance the song might have possessed. Performed somewhat tongue-in-cheek, Daltrey sings well, half-conscious of a stylistic divergence that seems unlikely of the Who, but retaining all the comic possibilities of the lyrics—which are little more than a number of variations on the question in the title. There is no aggression in Roger's reading of the song and more than a little affection.

The longest song on the album, at the start of the second side, is "How Can You Do It Alone," which genuinely builds on the new lightness of touch to form a strolling-paced rap addressing a real incident in which Pete Townshend innocently approached a flasher in the street and inadvertently discovered the stranger's secret. This is one song where Townshend's real-life observations retain a power to disturb, as the song develops into an examination of deviant and secretive sexual practices, with a second verse regarding a youth stealing pornography from a shop. The switch of focus in the third verse, however, moves into a more subjective view in which Townshend tries to see himself (and his own sexual relations) as part of the same picture, which seems somewhat unnecessary. The musical strengths of "How Can You Do It Alone" lie within Entwistle's great bass lines and a sound and solid structure that some may consider unintentionally funky. However, the bass lines and Daltrey's almost spoken verses (a world-weary swagger) work very well together, and a change of key [2.11] is most agreeable. This is marred, however, by a pompous synthesizer passage [2.45], which is accompanied by an almost military tattoo from Jones's drums.

The jangly guitar introduction to "Daily Records" is an undisguised retread of the Beach Boys' song "Sloop John B," but the wordiness of the song that follows offers such self-conceit that Townshend's intended humor sounds merely trite. A sardonic lament on the subject of recording music, this is merely cynical and forced. The melodic twist of the chorus, which builds in effect to the echoed title lines, is the single redeemable strength of the song. The irony of the Who's singing lines such as "Making records day in day out" (hardly commensurate with one album every three years!) or even worse, "My money keeps me poor" is difficult for the listener to take. Townshend's wit is in evidence, but the premise of this song seems just too implausible, despite Roger's appropriately comical delivery. The guitar during the last few bars adopts a country & western tinge.

John's second song, "You," is another slab of what is known as *AOR* music (which has variously been taken to stand for *album oriented radio* or *adult oriented rock*, both of which definitions amount to the same thing). Soundly constructed (as if using the musical equivalent of roughly cut blocks of concrete) the strength of the bass guitar lines holds up the whole song, and at one crucial point [3.25] the listener is treated to a lumbering double-tracked bass riff. It's as if this riff is supposed to assert John Entwistle's vision of rock-and-roll purity and maybe to say, "If Pete won't play power chords, then *I* will!" "You" has such a conventional hard rock feel and predictable lyrics that it perhaps provokes a lament for the times when John's songs added that quirky something special to Who records. However, the drama of the chord changes and some impassioned guitar phrases add a frisson of vitality to an album awash with hesitant and ethereal Townshend material. "You" is as heavy as Pete's songs are light.

Starting with the only traditional Who power chord of the album, "Another Tricky Day" includes both the good and bad points inherent in Townshend's songs of the time. It has an uneven beat, a jerky stop-start rhythm, a moralizing lyric and some delicious lines of melody ("just gotta get used to it"). Lyrically it strikes a mock winsome mood, as if the character is merrily resigned to a kind of impotence. A bass-driven second section [2.07] heralds a despairing descent into a self-pitying lament. The backing vocals become a little too intricate and rob Daltrey of some of the edge of his performance. This is the nearest *Face Dances* gets to providing the anthemic feel of the Who's classic period, and it simply sounds confused, a band going around in circles.

Empty Glass had established a new lyrical standard for Townshend; the same quality of introspection permeated *Face Dances*. Always capable of a witty line, cutting sarcasm and an unusual angle on his subjects, Townshend was now concerned with smaller-scale matters of emotional confusion and reproach, insecurities, the shifting values of lovers' relationships, and a jaundiced perception of getting from one day to the next in contemporary society without cracking up. The subjective *I* in these songs becomes much more aligned to Townshend alone, because we know the specific problems by which he was beset. The themes and lyrics that addressed the bigger musical, spiritual and societal matters that had obsessed him in the past were now superseded by songs that presented a cynical worldview on a more personal level. The songs were preoccupied with storms in teacups, domestic tiffs in which Townshend's approaching (or already having reached) middle age was taken for granted. There was no longer any teenage angst or rebellion, no undercurrent of nihilism. Townshend could no longer speak for youth, and often it was difficult to define exactly for whom he *was* speaking, other than for the more wayward aspects of his perennially insecure self-consciousness. (A couple of years later, Townshend stated that all the lyrics of the songs on *Face Dances* and *Chinese Eyes* concerned his own marital breakdown and the fact that he was living apart from his wife. They were later reunited.)

The net effect of *Face Dances* is that the world-weariness of Townshend's lyrics seems also to dominate the music, which lacks urgency, vitality and any sense of purpose. It seems confused, unfocussed and lacking in cogent ideas. Kenney Jones is professional and keen but lacks Keith Moon's imagination. The contrast with *Empty Glass* is marked, yet the feel of the material is not dissimilar. The lyrics seem to suffer for being sung by Roger Daltrey (Townshend took no lead vocals on the work—the only Who album to bear this distinction); and Roger's rather literal delivery misses some subtlety of nuance that Townshend would have retained as vocalist. That the album sold so well is a testament to the effect of a large-scale tour (in Britain), a hit single, a legendary reputation, and the dogged loyalty of fans (many of them young). Its success cannot be ascribed to any inherent musical inspiration or quality, even though its defects and flaws were not so apparent at the time either.

The British music press, which had somewhat changed allegiances in the past few years, could not be expected to be especially sympathetic to the Who's problems. The Who's loyal old friends Chris Welch, Chris Charlesworth, Roy Carr, Nik Cohn and Barbara Charone had by now all moved on from weekly rock journalism, and the band did not establish the same kind of rapport with any of the newer writers. Hugh Fielder in *Sounds* was ready to blame producer Bill Szymczyk for softening the Who's sound but still praised Pete's lyrics. He said, "Where Townshend starts getting contrived or overcomplicated—which he does on almost every album without fail—the production merely emphasizes the disruption.... Townshend's lyrical potency ... continues unabated."[9] However, Gavin Martin in *New Musical Express* was much less willing to give the band the benefit of the doubt, saying, "...vaguely depressing and directionless lyrics ... stodgy rehashed music ...

a hell of a shambles musically.... For Pete's sake, how much longer are we going to have to endure your irrelevant fantasies?"[10] Tom Carson was only slightly less condemnatory in *Rolling Stone*, commenting that Townshend and Daltrey "certainly do manage to bring out the worst in each other."[11] Ira Robbins (*Trouser Press*) and Richard C. Walls (*Creem*) both found *Face Dances* to be unexceptional.

Whatever the shortcomings with the music, the sleeve of *Face Dances* was truly memorable. Sixteen portraits of the four band members adorned the sleeve, all commissioned from leading artists, and coordinated by Peter Blake. The fact that so many notable artists—including David Hockney, Bill Jacklin, Richard Hamilton, Tom Phillips and David Tindle—had agreed to contribute was unusual in itself, although the real coup that Blake failed to bring off would have been to score portraits by Francis Bacon and Lucian Freud. The resulting collage of faces was most effective. This tied in with the title of the record, but the band had decided to reject Townshend's song "Face Dances," the absence of which rather weakened the idea. (Townshend released it as as "Face Dances Part Two" a year later). The diverse quality of the artwork was better appreciated on the large poster that was included with initial copies of the record.

This album was the first real full-scale disaster that the Who had ever released, and in the face of overwhelming criticism, the band were forced to consider the reasons why. They felt that on *Face Dances*, the first album with Kenney Jones, they were still finding their feet and were likely to complete a successful spate of recording only on a subsequent work. Also, a conscious effort had been made to change the Who's sound, to adapt to a new decade of rock and roll. Such change was not likely to be smooth or without its teething problems. Some felt that Bill Szymczyk was to blame and that his pedigree as producer of American soft rock acts such as the Eagles rendered him inappropriate; Townshend refuted this view, however, defending Szymczyk's work. Last, the suggestion was broached that Townshend had released all his best songs on *Empty Glass* and that *Face Dances* was made up of leftovers. This is perhaps a simplification, again denied by Pete. Whatever excuses were offered, Townshend did not think the album was defensible. A year after its release he said, "I was really frustrated with [*Face Dances*]. It didn't seem to do anything or go anywhere, and I couldn't quite work out why.... So my first reaction was to run like shit from The Who because they were confusing me more than ever."[12] A second single, "Don't Let Go the Coat" backed with "You," was released on 1 May 1981 and failed to emulate "You Better You Bet." It got no higher than number 47 in the U.K. and number 84 in the States.

In 1997, Jon Astley remixed *Face Dances* and added five bonus tracks, including three studio outtakes from the sessions. "I Like Nightmares" features a Townshend lead vocal, a funky beat, shimmering guitar and some barroom piano fills. The effect is moderately interesting, but the song has an unsure line of melody that tries to do a great deal all at once. It features some melodic quotations from "Time Is Passing" [0.41] and moves through some effective twists [2.00]. There are some notable lines along the way, but ultimately the song is unwieldy and structurally effete. "It's in You" is more robust, a solid boogie workout that has modest aspirations musically and is held together by John's and Pete's playing. Daltrey gets halfway to an angry vocal performance, in what is a curt reply to a letter from a fan named Virginia.

Later reworked by Townshend on his solo album *All the Best Cowboys Have Chinese Eyes*, "Somebody Saved Me" is thick with Pete's self-obsessed and painfully revealing confessional lyrical musings on his near brush with adultery. This is difficult to listen to because of the personal nature of the subject. The song is melodically strong and musically one of the best of Townshend's material of this era, but one can easily imagine why the band were reluctant to give it a release. (Incidentally, Townshend's solo version is very similar but slightly less effective.) The CD was made up with the aforementioned early live take of "How Can You Do It Alone" recorded in Chicago and a ferocious live performance of "The Quiet One" recorded in 1982 (and discussed below).

The final Who studio album, *It's Hard*, followed (in almost indecent haste, given the band's history) in September of 1982. It had been preceded by Townshend's third solo work, *All the Best Cowboys Have Chinese Eyes* three months earlier. *Chinese Eyes* followed the esoteric line established with *Empty Glass* and worked in a vague concept around the theme of stardom and disillusionment. However, despite a number of powerful songs, it seemed to strike too personal and indulgent a note for many people's tastes. Contemporary to its release, Townshend gave an extensive round of interviews in which he revealed for the first time the extent of his addiction to alcohol and heroin, from which he had recently been successfully cured, and the breakdown of his marriage. In the meantime MCA had consoled themselves for losing the Who to Warner Brothers by releasing in the States a double compilation album called *Hooligans*, which (apart from a few early hits) concentrated on the 1970s album material.

By mid–1982 the Who were in the studios once more with Glyn Johns, and hopes were running high, as Johns's track record with the band was so good. Also, Pete felt that the problems that had persisted with the *Face Dances* material—that is, the songs being too personal for the band as a whole to relate to—could be alleviated by his taking a different approach. A group meeting was called, and Pete asked Daltrey, Entwistle and Jones what kind of songs they wanted to record. Pete recalled that the band members were taken aback by this request, but a debate developed that managed to identify certain common areas of interest, such as fear of nuclear war. Pete felt that the discussion helped and immediately prior to recording declared that compared to the *Face Dances* songs, his new material had "come out much more successfully."[13] The band sailed through the recording sessions in June at Glyn Johns's Turn Up-Down Studios, in Surrey, England, knowing that a mammoth tour of the U.S. awaited them in September.

If the Who's newly found productivity in the studio—along with Pete's declared confidence in the quality of his songs—heightened the anticipation of the fans, then this only made the end result all the more disappointing. The Who needed an album that would redeem them after the debacle of *Face Dances*, but the resulting *It's Hard* saw their creative integrity plunge even lower. Although the subsequent concert tour broke box-office and earnings records, the realization that *It's Hard* marked a nadir from which there could be no easy escape gradually dawned upon the band members. To adapt the famous witticism of Oscar Wilde's Lady Bracknell, to lose one album may be regarded as a misfortune; to lose both looks like carelessness. Looking back at both albums, Townshend observed that they were made by a group who were feeling "very unsure about whether or not they wanted to be making a record."[14] Yet commercially *It's Hard* was a resounding success. It was released on 4 September 1982 and reached number 11 in the U.K. and number 8 in the U.S. Even the sleeve design was poor, reflecting the speed at which it the whole project seems to have been completed.

Glyn Johns, for his part, attempted to reestablish a more traditional Who sound, and much of the album avoided the eclecticism and airiness of its immediate predecessor. However, what was provided in its place was a welter of cliché and listener-friendly FM rock sludge: at its worst it sounded like the Who were falling back upon the debased values of dispassionate, mechanical, compromised music that in some misguided quarters passed for rock and roll and of which they had for so long (and sometimes single-handedly) been the embodied antithesis. There was no vigor or excitement in any of the songs on *It's Hard*, no spark in any of the performances and no feeling of commitment or urgency from the band. It was almost as if they were knocking off a "contractual obligation" album or collecting songs that had hitherto been rejected as substandard. Yet neither of these two suggestions was true: *It's Hard* was simply the best the Who could now manage, and it contained the music by which, in 1982, they had to be judged.

The problems become apparent from the very first gutless chord of "Athena." The song hits a funky beat and presents a catchy melody line, but this is repeated too often and the track becomes mundane rather quickly. A slower section that is sung by Townshend [2.33] suggests one spark of vitality, but this hardly redeems the song. John Entwistle's brass embellishments— once a great strength of the band—are here very routine. "Athena" is seemingly a very conventional song about a woman (it was originally entitled "Theresa") and thereby hits a subject almost untouched by Townshend since the 1960s.

A series of unusual and neurotic lines about Athena seem to use striking and extreme imagery for what we are later told is "just a girl." Townshend's verse "look into the face of a child" has a degree of beauty and forms one of the album's several allusions to childhood, with the character likely seeing himself in the child and evoking the momentary memory of innocence and youth.

The first of three John Entwistle songs, "It's Your Turn" is undoubtedly the weakest. A routine hard rocker with a melody even weaker than usual from John, this is predictable and turgid. Roger Daltrey offers a noncommittal lead vocal, and Andy Fairweather-Low plays guitar. Only the dramatic chord changes during the final few bars [3.27] offer anything memorable, recalling *Quadrophenia*. An interesting attempt at the unorthodox is made with "Cooks County," formed from an unusual mesh of insistent yet unspecific guitar and synthesizer lines. Daltrey's repeated phrases "People are suffering" and "People are lonely / I'll say it again" are delivered with such an inappropriately literal and clichéd style that his voice disarms the arrangement of most of its radical structure. The contrast with the upbeat section sung by Townshend [0.59] only serves to emphasize Daltrey's lack of feel for the song. Ultimately, this sounds like an uneasy collision of optimistic intent and lame performance, and it is hampered by the repetition. A few stabs of dramatic guitar chording [1.56] fail to transform the work into anything special. Lyrically, the song relates to the Cook County hospital in Chicago that offers free medical services to the community, although the listener could not know this from the song alone.

One expects title tracks of albums to be a little stronger than the norm, but "It's Hard" itself is nothing more than routine. Predictable, bland soft rock with weak chord work, this lacks any modicum of excitement or originality, and it is delivered with slick competence but with no discernible inspiration. The self-pity of the lyrics make the song even more unpalatable. That the Who had been reduced to offering what sounds like a rehash of the most inane and ineffective kind of pop is simply depressing. (Its forebear was a song called "Popular," which Townshend had recorded in 1980 and which was equally insipid.) "Dangerous" is the culmination of John Entwistle's high-tech rock approach that had first been taken with "Had Enough." It is very accomplished and melodic, with a sense of dramatic pace and a clear-cut role for Daltrey as singer. Constructed from thick, muscular bass guitar lines (surprisingly melodic) and interlocking synthesizer chords (played by Entwistle and Tim Gorman), the guitar here is purely nominal. Unfortunately, the Who once again sound like Genesis, Foreigner or Kansas, with added ecological strands in the lyrical theme.

Some of the same high-tech production values are brought to "Eminence Front," an off-the-wall, cool, insistent song that is undoubtedly the highlight of whole album. A naggingly captivating exercise in musical minimalism, this succeeds because it makes no attempt at a Who–like sound and has more in common with the material that Townshend performed on *Empty Glass* and *Chinese Eyes*. The only Who song that it partly resembles is "Music Must Change." Pete's vocal performance is very strong, and he makes the pared-down lyric work wonders, especially the repeated "People forget," which concludes each couplet. The song is a sharp observation on the cracks that are apparent in the facade of Western affluence, with specific reference to the burgeoning "cocaine-and-caviar" culture of the 1980s. "Eminence Front" is a strong composition and is treated with imagination and flexibility, and it benefits from the band's not succumbing to the temptation to overarrange or complicate. The electric piano and Entwistle's fine bass work offer a suggestion of a jazz-funk rationale, but the triumph of "Eminence Front" seemed to be Pete's alone—from the lengthy introductory guitar solo to his vocal performance, this is Townshend *par excellence*.

In the past, the Who had worked songs up from a root note (such as "Join Together"), and "I've Known No War" draws upon a similar approach. The song has some strengths that are noticeably lacking elsewhere on the album, but it is ultimately marred by a tendency toward the pompous, a situation exacerbated by Roger Daltrey's overwrought singing. The song is sound of construction, but at just under six minutes in duration is perhaps elongated beyond its possibilities. Entwistle's bass lines contribute a great deal of the musical body, and toward the end a string section drifts in and out without much purpose. The lyrics are a clear expression of Townshend's conviction that the lack of a World War in his lifetime has significantly shaped the attitudes of his and later generations, creating social conditions that were markedly different to those that prevailed for the war-torn generations that preceded.

It may have troubled the band to imagine quite where "One Life's Enough" should fit on a Who record. In the context of an album already struggling to find a consistent musical voice, "One Life's Enough" just adds to the general disarray, where in different circumstances it might have found a more comfortable niche. Going in the opposite direction of "Eminence Front," this piano-and-voice ballad sounds like it was lifted from one of the quiet, introspective interludes of a modern Broadway musical. It may have been difficult for Roger to adjust to material of this sort, which stretches his range and is not really suitable for his talents. The melody of the song is strong, supported by some fine piano work. The lyrics recall an Arcadian scene of consummated love and a memory that is vivid enough to make such a feeling of rapture last a lifetime. It took John Entwistle to prove that the Who could still make an attempt at humor, with "One at a Time." The jocular brass arrangement at the beginning is lighthearted, and the song continues in the same mode. A good-humored, unpretentious rocker, this thankfully relies on John's playing and singing rather than the synthesizer, which only emerges at the middle-eight. On this song Townshend supplies some suitably raucous guitar work. "One at a Time" is the jauntiest of John's three songs, with a theme of woman trouble that recalls "My Wife."

"Why Did I Fall for That" and "A Man Is a Man" are the two tracks that fall most blatantly into the AOR syndrome, and it is questionable whether or not the Who should have ever recorded them. Both songs are bland and inconsequential. The former sounds not dissimilar to an Elton John or Bruce Springsteen FM radio staple, and it never rises above a level of professional and slick competence. There is absolutely nothing in "Why Did I Fall for That" to arrest the imagination, and though holding a surface appeal, this is merely filler material (or perhaps a single B side). In one of those irritating little touches of which the band members were probably unaware, the fade-out sounds senselessly and annoyingly prolonged. "A Man Is a Man" is rather like a slower version of the same song. It is meandering and sentimental, and the lyrics fail to rise above the banal—the somewhat overworked theme debunking the macho traits of male behavior but asserting an essential masculine consciousness. Musically, the piano is once again dominant here, with weak, shimmering guitar lines (Townshend had begun to use the "chorus" effects pedal) that are simply too clean and watery. The concluding "be a man who's a man" line is very trite.

The final song, "Cry If You Want," is a good three-minute throwaway rocker stretched out too far; it is unmelodic but uses simple, strong chord changes and a Townshend guitar sound that has some of his old rhythm and bite. It is overly wordy, and the military tattoo drummed during the stop-start chorus soon becomes tiresome. As the song progresses, some more aggressive power chording [3.43] recalls the Who of old, a reminder that—alas—comes far too late. "Cry If You Want" sees a character looking back with embarrassment rather than anger, and it details the shortcomings of youth with humorous hindsight. The song is like a final exorcism of the Pete Townshend who wrote "My Generation," and the youthful arrogance and naïve cynicism is shown to have merely been ignorance and resentment. The song says that although this state of innocence is in some respects worth crying for, ultimately life is better in the state of maturity and experience.

We can't give *It's Hard* the benefit of the doubt; there were no mitigating circumstances. Who fans cannot pretend to see quality where it does not exist, whatever tale the global sales of the album might have told. The album closed the Who's recording career in a finite manner. One could even have excused a complete disorganized disaster of an album, but *It's Hard* is even worse than that: it is largely simply tedious, uninvolving and boring, the very things that true rock and roll should never be. "Eminence Front" alone has withstood the passage of time, and only then, ironically, because it is the least orthodox Who song on the set. All the charges of their critics—initially unkind and prejudicial—that the Who were passed it and too old to be taken seriously anymore could no longer be countered. The only semblance of vindication that can be offered is in the generally accepted view that the early 1980s was one of the most barren periods of rock history: 1982 was not awash with classic albums of any kind.

It's Hard was at best a passable shadow of what a good rock-and-roll record should be, but more important it was but a ghost of that which the Who were once capable. It is devoid of most of the quirky Englishness that gave *Face Dances* a vestige of remaining interest. If *Face Dances* was a conscious (albeit failed) response to the changing climate of the British rock scene, then *It's Hard* sounds like little more than an album clinically tailored to suit the less parochial demands of corporate America. It is a middle-ground, medium-core rock artifact that is the finely polished epitome of *Billboard*-friendly AOR rock, and which can be imagined lethargically drifting forth from FM radio sets across the States, all too comfortably intermingling with the sounds of the Eagles, REO Speedwagon, Fleetwood Mac, and James Taylor. It does not elucidate or reflect the psychology of the visionary rock-and-roll gestalt that "My Generation" had crystalized almost twenty years before: it neither challenges nor reassures.

Paul Du Noyer was one of the band's more sympathetic contemporary observers, but in his *New Musical Express* review of *It's Hard* he accurately stated, "This album sounds like it's struggling through a variety of difficulties—and overcomes none of them.... Townshend's songs are all but thrown away, tethered to a formula they've plainly outgrown."[15] In *Sounds* and *Melody Maker* (both 4 September 1982), Garry Bushell and Lynden Barber, respectively, savagely criticized the album, both stating in different ways that the Who were too old and should quit. In the States, the album fell much more comfortably within the U.S. rock mainstream and was generally accepted as a vast improvement on *Face Dances*. Two reviewers in particular, however, went further. Parke Puterbaugh in *Rolling Stone* considered the album to be the band's greatest since *Who's Next* and a fine piece of work on every level.[16] And in *Trouser Press*, Ira Robbins was equally impressed and saw the record as establishing the Who as a strong force for the 1980s.[17] It is extremely difficult to now reconcile these opinions with the record one actually hears, and Puterbaugh's implied belief that *It's Hard* is a superior album to *Quadrophenia* is one of the most perverse and risible examples of Who criticism imaginable.

The remixed version of *It's Hard* (released in June 1997) improved the album somewhat (it could hardly have made it worse), and listened to nowadays it sounds slightly less dire than it had originally. Glyn Johns's original production was as good as the material could expect, and unlike Szymczyk Johns emerged much better than did the band from the experience of making the album. In going back to the multitrack master tapes, Jon Astley had lengthened some of the tracks and brought many subtle changes into the sound-picture. A mistimed backing vocal on the first chorus of "Eminence

Front" was corrected, for example, and some parts of "It's Hard" used a different guitar track. None of this work, however, could ever save *It's Hard* from being the embarrassing end of the Who catalog. The addition of four live versions of *It's Hard* material give an opportunity to judge how the band presented these songs onstage: in all the cases the live versions are very similar to the originals and not played with any great enthusiasm. All the tracks were taken from a farewell concert in Toronto, Canada, on 17 December 1982.

Roger Daltrey had wanted "Cry If You Want" to be released as a single, but "Athena" was chosen. It could hardly have made any difference. "Athena" appeared after the album on 25 September 1982 and reached number 40 in the U.K. charts. In the U.S., however, it reached a number 28 slot, and over the subsequent months Warner Brothers also released on single "Eminence Front" (a number 68) and finally "It's Hard" itself. But the album was overshadowed by what was billed as the group's farewell tour of America. This signaled the band's intention to cease live performances, but they still planned to complete one final studio album in 1983. Opening in Landover on 22 September, the band played forty concerts in arena or stadium venues, closing the tour in Toronto in December. The tour was an overwhelming financial success. The band put on a highly professional, spectacular show that mixed new and old songs. It was predictable, well sustained, and—apart from a few impromptu moments—utterly sterile. A large number of these concerts were recorded, and the final show in Toronto, a live television broadcast, was released on video in 1983 as *The Who Rocks America*.

While the tour was in progress, a live album was planned, as if it had been contracted for in advance. However, it was November 1984 before the resulting *Who's Last* appeared. A double album, *Who's Last* was a predictable collection of songs taken mostly from the final Toronto concert. None of the albums after *Who Are You* were represented, and the material was cleanly mixed and offered no surprises. It was for the most part a rehash of the *Who Rocks America* video. The only "new" song to be added to the Who canon was "Twist and Shout," with Entwistle on lead vocals, released here for the first time (and also on single). Also, Townshend added a rockabilly reprise to "Long Live Rock." *Who's Last* was desperately lacking in imagination, despite the slightly audacious inclusion of an inferior version of "Doctor Jimmy." The packaging was banal (Union Jacks and glossy live onstage photos presumably selected to show how large the audiences were), and the album was understandably a disappointment saleswise, coming too late to catch the fervor that had greeted the tour. It was released in both the U.S. and U.K. by MCA, and it reached number 48 in Britain and number 81 in the States. The reviews of *Who's Last* were almost universally negative, and Townshend himself said of the record, "... embarrassing because it's competent. As a rule we would have said 'Stick it in the bin,' but we put it out because it was all we had."[18] (This statement does not account for the fact that much superior earlier live material could have been drawn upon, and MCA had at one point projected *Who's Last* as a compilation of live tracks stretching across ten years of Who concerts.)

A handful of further songs have also been issued from the 1982 tour. Included on *30 Years of Maximum R&B* is a version of "Twist and Shout" from Toronto, 9 October 1982 (a different and superior version to that on *Who's Last*). Although the sound quality is a little muddy, this performance injects some of the energy and irreverence of old into the song. The CD reissue of *Face Dances* added a fiery take of Entwistle's "The Quiet One," which is full of amazing guitar flourishes from Pete and easily surpasses the studio version, despite the fact that Entwistle's vocals tend to be slightly off key. Recorded at what was probably their best concert of the year, at Shea Stadium in New York on 13 October, this is the kind of off-the-wall blowout that was rare on the 1982 tour, with a dramatic shuffling beat. The *It's Hard* CD returned to the Toronto concert of 17 December with "It's Hard," "Eminence Front," "Dangerous" and "Cry If You Want" all lengthened beyond the studio versions and less focused in sound. However, Townshend plays some great solos across all the songs, although his guitar sound is much less abrasive than in the past. Entwistle's bass work is always arresting, but no one would wish to remember the live Who experience by these latter-day renditions.

In the meantime, Townshend had attempted through 1983 to gather material for the final studio album. It was tentatively called *Siege* and was a loose concept work, with songs gathered around a common theme. Townshend later said that *Siege* was based on the "idea that each of us is a soul in siege."[19] His 1985 solo album and film *White City* was most likely a development of this idea. The music that Townshend has released that related to *Siege* includes "Ask Yourself" and "Cat Snatch." Other material that had been written around this time included "Prelude: The Right to Write," "Prelude #556," "Baroque Ippanese" and "Holly Like Ivy." The common factor that characterizes all these demos is a multileveled use of synthesizers and sequencers and an almost complete lack of guitars. It must have soon become clear to Pete that this material was unsuitable for the Who. Roger Daltrey, with typical pugnacity and professionalism, wanted to have a go at recording the album, but Townshend knew when the game was up.

"I don't believe we would have made another record worth releasing," Pete later commented.[20] In the absence of any unified agreement on the matter, Townshend issued a press release in December 1983 declaring that from his point of view the Who were over. He cited as the main reason for the group's demise his own inability to produce suitable material for the final album. The only complication was that the Who were contracted with Warner Brothers to produce a further studio album of new material. In order to break the contract, the band had to repay several million dollars to the record company that they had received in advance. Townshend himself paid the bulk of this money, having the added advantage of songwriting royalties over and above his income from the group. The band's delivering a worthless, contract-fulfilling *Metal Machine Music* was considered far too irresponsible for the Who to contemplate, despite the glut of esoteric synthesizer material that Townshend had amassed.[21]

Polydor and MCA attempted to keep the commercial potential of the Who alive by releasing a succession of compilation albums. In the U.K. there was *Rarities Vol. 1: 1966–1968* and *Rarities Vol. 2: 1970–1973* (1983), both handy collections of non-album singles and B sides; *The Singles* (1984); *The Who Collection* (1985); and *Who's Better Who's Best* (1988) — all rehashing the hits and all making the charts. In the U.S., MCA released *Who's Greatest Hits* (1983), *Who's Missing* (1985), *Two's Missing* (1987) and *Who's Better Who's Best* (1988). Only *Who's Missing* and *Two's Missing* took chances and included previously unreleased material. The former gathered "Leaving Here" (1964), "Lubie (Come Back Home)" (1965) and the live "Bargain" (1971), all released for the first time. *Two's Missing* drew from the same sources "Heatwave," "Motoring" (both 1965), "My Wife" and "Going Down" (both live from 1971). In Britain, the only attempt at an archive release came when "Won't Get Fooled Again" was reissued in a twelve-inch EP format, and some enterprising soul at Polydor put the live "Bony Moronie" (1971) and "Dancing in the Street" (1979) onto the disk, along with the rare U.S. version of "Mary Anne with the Shaky Hand." For about a decade from the early 1980s onward, the Who's reputation and critical standing reached a nadir, particularly in Britain. The media remembered only the worst examples of Who music — the *Tommy* film, the band's reputation for so-called indulgent concept albums, recent solo work — and had all but forgotten what they had really achieved.

Townshend's next solo album (and short film) *White City* (1985) failed to make the kind of impact that was customary with the band. The same fate befell John Entwistle's solo album *Too Late the Hero* (1981) and Roger Daltrey's *Parting Should Be Painless* (1984), *Under a Raging Moon* (1985), *Can't Wait to See the Movie* (1987) and *Rocks in the Head* (1992). In fact, the only really memorable and vital solo releases during the 1980s came with Townshend's two collections of demo recordings from his own archives, *Scoop* (1983) and *Another Scoop* (1987). These albums — both of which contained used and unused material for the Who — covered a vast range of sounds and styles, and they gave a fascinating glimpse into the heart of Townshend's creative process. The failure of the members of the band to achieve consistent solo musical careers might have tempted them to reform on a more permanent basis, but the occasional reunion (such as that played at Live Aid on 13 July 1985 or at the BPI Awards ceremony in London on 8 February 1988) gave them little cause for optimism.

Later in 1988, there were stirrings of Who studio activity once more, and Pete Townshend's solo album *The Iron Man*—a projected musical based on the book by Ted Hughes—regrouped the Who for two songs. "Dig" is the most successful of the two performances, a song of medium tempo and solid melody that suits Daltrey's vocal style very well. The recording features a great power chord guitar solo, but otherwise it does not much improve upon the material from *It's Hard*. The second Who track was a revival of the Crazy World of Arthur Brown's "Fire," which was a number 1 hit produced by Kit Lambert and Pete Townshend in 1968. Unfortunately, much of the hysterical power of the original is dampened by a mechanical high-tech arrangement that lacks any feel or passion. Entwistle's bass playing sounds muted on both tracks. "Fire" is pretty much forgettable, and it lacks all of the fluid warmth that the Who seemed to have had at their disposal in the past. *The Iron Man*, released in June 1989, was an interesting collection of songs, but it did not find a mass audience and its proposed stage premier was delayed for four years.

This situation was made worse, rather than better, by the band's full-scale reunion tour of 1989. This was a purely financial exercise (and one of the most successful of all time) and saw the lineup expanded to major proportions with backing vocalists, a second guitarist, a keyboard player, a brass section and a percussionist. The professionalism of the 1982 tour was here recreated with consummate ease (along with the blandness), and the band's sound was now far removed from the concentrated fireworks of the past. Indeed, Townshend mostly played an acoustic guitar. It is difficult to accept this version of the Who as the real thing, and, alas, many old fans remained indifferent to the reunion. Predictably enough, another live album emerged titled *Join Together*, which took a staid but not *quite* so predictable path in its selection of material. During the tour the band had actually played a wide variety of songs (both their own and those of other artists), but the album did not reflect this diversity. It included four songs from Townshend's solo catalog and very deliberately avoided the 1960s hits. The main emphasis was a complete performance of *Tommy* and latter-day hits such as "Who Are You," "You Better You Bet," and "Won't Get Fooled Again." *Join Together* was released in March 1990 as a three–LP or two–CD set, and it was handled by Virgin in the U.K. and MCA in the States. It charted at number 180 in the U.S., was virtually ignored in the U.K., and attracted indifferent reviews. The boxed set of 1994 included one more token song from the tour, an amusing but ultimately tedious revival of "I'm a Man," a song the band hadn't played since 1965. (The only studio recordings undertaken by this lineup were "Join Together" and "I Can See for Miles," which were aired on a British television broadcast, *Aspel & Company*, on 10 March 1990.)

The final Who studio session took place in July 1991 in the form of a contribution to a tribute album to the songs of Elton John and Bernie Taupin. This unlikely project was supervised by Jon Astley, and the Who took on

Elton John's hardest rocker, "Saturday Night's Alright for Fighting." Despite the fact that Townshend, Entwistle and Daltrey were never in the studio at the same time, the result is surprisingly vibrant. The vicious guitar riff and synthesizer backdrop recall the classic Who sound of the early 1970s, and Daltrey really feels at home with the song, giving a great full-power performance. John Entwistle's trademark bass patterns remind listeners just how accomplished and unique is his style. Toward the end, Townshend sneaks in a few lines from another Elton John song, "Take Me to the Pilot." The song appeared on the album *Two Rooms: Celebrating the Songs of Elton John and Bernie Taupin* (Mercury) and was released in November 1991. More significant, the song was used to close the boxed set *30 Years of Maximum R&B*, sounding more like a "Who" song than anything on either *Face Dances* or *It's Hard*.

Although the Who's back-catalog had in various stages been mastered onto CD from the 1980s, their recorded legacy had been accorded no distinctive treatment or specialist attention. Both Polydor and MCA seemed indifferent to the band, but slowly interest grew in the Who once more, possibly because of the grunge movement, which reasserted the visceral qualities of pure rock and roll one more time. Later still, a collection of British acts—generically dubbed *Brit–pop* by the press—aggressively honed the rock values of the 1960s into a modern context. Several of these acts displayed an overt Who influence: Dodgy, Cast, Afghan Wigs and Swervedriver among them. Various protagonists within the grunge and Brit–pop movements named the Who as their spiritual godfathers, and once more it became fashionable to drop the Who's name rather than to deride them. Several factors combined to change the level of corporate apathy that had persisted in the 1980s. Younger fans were vocal about their needs, and they found fanzines such as *Relay* and *Generations* in which to indulge their enthusiasm. Pete Townshend released *PsychoDerelict* (1993), which not only reintroduced some themes and music from *Lifehouse* but also was Townshend's best collection of songs and most cogent concept work for years.

Many have long felt that the Who should be accorded the boxed set treatment, which would collect all their best tracks and unreleased rarities on one comprehensive high-quality CD collection. Polydor's first response to the boxed set format—that enduring product of late 1980s coffee table culture—was predictable and unimaginative, and it was rejected by Townshend. However, when Chris Charlesworth took up the cause in early 1993, Townshend's response was more favorable. Charlesworth didn't mince his words. He simply put Townshend on the spot, writing, "Enough is enough. Each month I read in *Q* magazine of yet another artist or group whose boxed set of three, four or five remastered CDs is now in the shops ... none of them worthy to lick the boots of The Who.... How come no-one at Polydor ... hasn't proposed and organised a decent Who boxed set.... Does nobody care any more? It's a fucking travesty.... Because I care, I hereby put myself forward as the coordinator of such a project."[22] Townshend called Charlesworth the following day and told him that the project was finally on.

After a considerable period of consultation and research regarding the boxed set's proposed contents, Polydor and MCA released *30 Years of Maximum R&B* in July 1994. The four CDs presented the hits, the best album tracks and a decent number of previously unreleased live and studio performances. While fans might quibble over the contents and the representation or absence of personal preferences, few could have not delighted in the sheer wealth of material. The sound quality had been enhanced on many tracks as well, as coproducer Jon Astley had undertaken to remix many of the original tapes to fully reflect the sound properties available with a state-of-the-art digital transfer. Interspersed with the music was a fascinating selection of dialogue interludes, announcements, jokes, comedy sketches, interviews and *verité* incidents. The set worked to reestablish the Who as one of Britain's most precious and vital groups, and the bad press of the last few years was all but erased. Leading the reviews was one in *Q* in which David Cavanagh described it as a "swaggering, bruising and damn near impeccable behemoth of a box set ... the best box set ever."[23]

The set performed well enough to set in motion a complete CD reissue program, tightly coordinated between Polydor and MCA, in which all the band's albums were remixed, remastered and expanded in length with the additional unreleased or uncollected tracks. Particular attention was given to the booklets, with expert sleeve notes being commissioned and previously unpublished photographs included. In general, each of these reissues looked and sounded magnificent; there was some overlap of tracks with the boxed set and a few lamentable omissions, but taken as a whole in terms of initiative and quality the CDs established a new standard for a major act reissue program. The first in the series, *Live at Leeds* (February 1995), was followed by *A Quick One* and *Sell Out* (both June 1995), *Who's Next* (November 1995), *Tommy* (March 1996), *Quadrophenia* (June 1996), *By Numbers* and *Who Are You* (both December 1996), *Face Dances* and *It's Hard* (both June 1997) and *Odds and Sods* (March 1998).

Sandwiched within this sequence came *Live at the Isle of Wight Festival 1970* (October 1996), which Polydor and MCA had declined to release due to its similarity to *Live at Leeds*, and a definitive compilation of the hit singles, *My Generation—The Very Best of the Who* (August 1996). With this sequence completed, very few studio tracks (apart from the BBC recordings) now remain unreleased, and it is unlikely that any further archive CDs will be released with studio material. However, a number of already released tracks have yet to be collected or mastered onto CD, and there is scope for such a collection (these tracks are indicated in Appendix 2). The band's studio recordings for the BBC are also long overdue for a CD collection in their own right, though licensing problems initially prevented Polydor's use of this material for the boxed set. The situation with live material is rather different. Hours of high quality concert material remain in the vaults, and both Jon Astley and Chris Charlesworth have long been planning an extensive CD collection of unreleased live material from 1968 through 1976. There is some question as to whether this project will ever emerge, due to record company reticence. If it goes through, it would undoubtedly be a very satisfactory way in which to complete the reissue program, and put into the market a substantial piece of work that would reflect the band at their very best.

The Who reactivated once more in 1996 with an expanded lineup to revive the neglected *Quadrophenia* as a concert piece, and this version of the band toured intermittently in 1996 and 1997. The show has been successful in itself, but it is unlikely that the Who will ever function again as a recording unit. If they did they would be unlikely to produce satisfactory results. The Who's essential qualities cannot be overemphasized, just as their deficiencies cannot be ignored. Yet the more enduring aspects of their music are the ones by which, finally, they will be judged. Young people will always be drawn to Who music, and two tribute CDs, *Who Covers Who* (1993) and *Whodunnit—Chicago Knows Who* (1997), demonstrate the affection and respect they engender among younger musicians such as Blur, Hyperhead, and Swervedriver. Who music also continues to appear in unlikely places, from high-profile advertisements for ice cream (Wall's Calippo), to the successful Hollywood film *Jerry Maguire* (1996).

Why should today's music fans retain an interest in or appreciation of the Who? The reason ultimately lies in their catalog of recorded music. The band were much less prolific than almost all their contemporaries, but a very high proportion of their music is of exemplary quality and will remain to be discovered, reinterpreted and enjoyed. Who music does not date and has already proved itself able to endure the stormy winds of changing fashion and trend. As long as recorded music remains, the Who will always be there and, more than any of their rock contemporaries, their work will enable us to understand the vagaries of life in the past, the present and the future. If rock and roll is an art, then the Who must be accepted as its supreme masters. To conclude this study I would like to reprise the very first piece of writing that I ever completed on the band over ten years ago and which I see no reason to modify:

> It is important to keep alive the kind of energy and communication the Who generated as a band. In comparison with the Who, very few rock-and-roll bands are worth writing about. But the Who were and are different—they encompassed so much with their music. They are loud, brash, hard, noisy, fast, and exciting but also subtle, complex, intelligent, imaginative and profound. It was a unique combination.[24]

Notes

Chapter 1: Art, Rock and Roll, and the Who

1. *Omnibus: All My Loving*, BBC-TV, broadcast 3 November 1968.
2. *Revolt Into Style* (Allen Lane, 1970).
3. *Melody Maker*, 5 June 1965.
4. Various accounts have rendered this name as either Metzker or Metzke. It is difficult to establish which is the correct spelling.
5. *The Who: Maximum R&B* (Eel Pie, 1982).
6. *Before I Get Old: The Story of the Who* (Plexus, 1983).
7. *The Who Concert File* (Omnibus, 1997).
8. *Sounds*, 18 October 1975.
9. The best extant examination of this phenomenon is *Mods!* (Eel Pie, 1979) by Richard Barnes.
10. One thing they had in common, however, was famous relatives: Lambert's father Constant had been a notable composer and musical director, and Stamp's brother Terence was an actor and voguish icon of the 1960s, star of *Billy Budd* (1962), *The Collector* (1965) and *Far from the Madding Crowd* (1967).
11. *Observer Colour Magazine*, 20 March 1966.
12. *Ibid.*
13. *Rock and Other Four Letter Words* (Bantam Books, 1968) by J. Marks and L. Eastham.
14. *New Musical Express*, 25 February 1965.
15. Constant Lambert (1905–1950) was a major figure in English music between the wars and is best known for his innovative and celebrated choral suite *The Rio Grande* (1927) and as author of *Music Ho!* (1934), an influential volume of music criticism.

Chapter 2: Maximum Reaction (1963–1965)

1. *Sounds*, 12 April 1975
2. *Before I Get Old: The Story of the Who* (Plexus, 1983).
3. *The Who: Maximum R&B* (Eel Pie, 1982).
4. "In Love with Meher Baba," *Rolling Stone*, 26 November 1970.
5. Press release, written by Peter Meaden, July 1964.
6. *Boyfriend*, 8 August 1964.
7. *Generations* 13, October 1994.

8. *A Whole Scene Going*, BBC-TV, broadcast 5 January 1966.
9. This silent 8-millimeter footage was included in the film *The Kids Are Alright*, released in June 1979.
10. Sleeve notes of *Another Scoop*, 1987.
11. "A Bargain—The Best You Ever Had!," *Crawdaddy!* (new) No. 18, late autumn 1997.
12. *Disc Weekly*, 27 February 1965.
13. *New Musical Express*, 23 April 1965.
14. *Saturday Club*, BBC Radio, broadcast 29 May 1965.
15. "First Album Completed," *Beat Instrumental*, July 1965.
16. *Melody Maker*, 17 July 1965.
17. *Record Mirror*, 6 November 1965.
18. *Melody Maker*, 11 December 1965.
19. *Naked Eye* No. 1, February 1996.
20. *Record Mirror*, 4 December 1965.
21. *New Musical Express*, 10 December 1965.
22. *Record Mirror*, 17 September 1966.
23. *Record Mirror*, 4 December 1965.
24. *Saturday Club*, BBC Radio, broadcast 27 November 1965.

Chapter 3: Art Pop (1966–1967)

1. "A Bargain—The Best You Ever Had!," *Crawdaddy* (new) No. 18, late autumn 1997.
2. *Record Mirror*, 2 April 1966.
3. *Who Fanclub Newsletter*, September/October 1966.
4. *Tommy* CD booklet notes, March 1996.
5. *Naked Eye* No. 1, February 1996.
6. *Zigzag* No. 43, July 1974.
7. *Eye* No. 1, 7 September 1968.
8. *Record Mirror*, 17 September 1966.
9. *New Musical Express*, 7 October 1966.
10. *Beat Instrumental*, November 1966.
11. *Record Mirror*, 5 November 1966.
12. These subtitles have not been listed on any of the LP or CD releases but have been included on printed scores of the music, primarily *A Decade of the Who* (Wise Publications, 1984).
13. *Beat Merchants* (Blandford, 1995), by Alan Clayson.
14. This was possibly influenced by the Yardbirds' single "Happenings Ten Years Time Ago," released in October 1966, which included a similar exchange of dialogue.
15. *Beat Instrumental*, January 1967.
16. *Ibid.*
17. An animated children's program on British television in the late–1960s was *Ivor the Engine*, which bears some similarity with this character.
18. *Melody Maker*, 10 December 1966.
19. *Disc*, 17 December 1966.
20. *The International Times* No. 8, 13–26 February 1967.
21. The only other rock song of note on this subject is "Orgasm Addict," a fine 1977 single by the British punk group the Buzzcocks, in which Howard Devoto treated the subject with a savage wit that was far less subtle but equally effective. "Orgasm

Addict" would have been banned and vilified in 1967, however, and the Who's song needed to be far less explicit to gain radio exposure.
22. *Melody Maker*, 29 April 1967.
23. *Melody Maker*, 20 May 1967.
24. *Record Mirror*, 6 May 1967.
25. *Beat Instrumental*, March 1967.
26. *Beat Instrumental*, August 1967.
27. *The Story of Tommy* (Eel Pie, 1977) by Richard Barnes and Pete Townshend.
28. *Melody Maker*, 14 October 1967.
29. *Rolling Stone*, 9 December 1971.
30. *Ibid.*
31. Radio London commenced broadcasting in December 1964 from a ship moored in the North Sea off Frinton on the east coast of England. It ceased operations when outlawed by a government act in August 1967. During its tenure on the air, it and other pirate stations were the only dedicated source of pop music available to U.K. listeners.
32. *The Complete Guide to the Music of the Who* (Omnibus Press, 1995).
33. *Melody Maker*, 16 December 1967.
34. *Ibid.*
35. *Beat Instrumental*, February 1968.
36. *Time Magazine*, 20 September 1968.

Chapter 4: High Energy, Deep Mysticism (1968–1970)

1. Despite Townshend's assertion, the only full concert recording that has survived from prior to 1968 is from Monterey, 18 June 1967, as discussed in the previous chapter.
2. *Your Mother Wouldn't Like It*, Capital Radio, broadcast October 1974.
3. *Disc and Music Echo*, 2 March 1968.
4. *Your Mother Wouldn't Like It*, Capital Radio, broadcast October 1974.
5. *Melody Maker*, 21 September 1968.
6. *New Musical Express*, 16 November 1968.
7. The 1960s had seen a succession of comic Cockney pop hits from artists such as Mike Sarne, Bernard Cribbins, Lonnie Donegan and Anthony Newley.
8. Sleeve notes of *Scoop* LP, 1983.
9. *New Musical Express*, 16 November 1968.
10. *Ibid.*
11. *Rolling Stone*, 28 September 1968.
12. Radio interview, WABC-FM, New York, broadcast 16 May 1969.
13. Some of the credit for this might well go to engineer Damon Lyon-Shaw, who soon afterward worked at the same studio with folk group Pentangle on their *Basket of Light* LP, also notable for its luscious acoustic guitar sounds.
14. Oddly enough, Dave Davies of the Kinks released a single titled "Lincoln County" in 1968. It is unknown whether there is any connection between the two songs.
15. More than twenty different versions of "Pinball Wizard" have been recorded by such diverse artists as the Shadows, James Last, the Portsmouth Sinfonia, the New Seekers, the LSO, Roger Ruskin Spear, and, of course, the unforgettable Harry Roche Constellation.
16. *Disc and Music Echo*, 8 March 1969.

17. *It* No. 58, 13–28 June 1969.
18. Program, prepared for the Who's concert at Hull City Hall, 15 February 1970.
19. *Los Angeles Times/Calendar*, 5 July 1992.
20. *New Musical Express*, 17 July 1976.
21. *Friends* No. 5, 14 April 1970.
22. *New Musical Express*, 24 May 1969.
23. *Melody Maker*, 31 May 1969.
24. *Disc and Music Echo*, 24 May 1969.
25. *It* No. 56, 9–22 May 1969.
26. "*Tommy*: The Red Dawn of Revolt?" *New York Times*, 30 November 1969.
27. *New Musical Express*, 18 April 1970.
28. *New York Times*, 8 March 1970.
29. *New Musical Express*, 23 May 1970.
30. *Melody Maker*, 23 May 1970.
31. *Friends*, 29 May 1970.
32. *Oz* No. 29, July 1970.

Chapter 5: To the Lifehouse (1971–1972)

1. *New Musical Express*, 18 April 1970.
2. *New Musical Express*, 14 November 1970.
3. "The Pete Townshend Page: Another Fight in the Playground," *Melody Maker*, 19 September 1970.
4. In the Victorian era, "The Lost Chord" (written in 1877) by Arthur Sullivan was a very popular drawing-room ballad, which in turn was a setting of an earlier poem by Adelaide Procter ("But I struck one chord of music / Like the sound of a great Amen").
5. Inayat Khan, Sufi music theorist and author of the essays "The Mysticism of Sound" and "Music." Townshend has acknowledged the influence of these works.
6. *Disc and Music Echo*, 24 October 1970.
7. *Ibid.*
8. *Zigzag* No. 43, July 1974, interviewed in October 1971.
9. *New Musical Express*, 19 December 1970.
10. *Billboard*, 19 December 1970.
11. *Creem*, December 1970.
12. *Sounds*, 2 January 1971.
13. *Ibid.*
14. *Ibid.*
15. *Melody Maker*, 23 January 1971.
16. *The Times*, 14 January 1971.
17. Notes for *Who's Next* CD booklet, written 7 May 1995.
18. *Ibid.*
19. Notes for *Who's Next* CD booklet, written 7 May 1995.
20. Sleeve notes for *Who Came First* LP, released October 1972.
21. Notes for *Who's Next* CD booklet, written 7 May 1995.
22. Daltrey's comment appeared in *Record Collector* No. 181, September 1994, and Entwistle's recollection was given verbally to Chris Charlesworth, early 1994.
23. *Classic Albums* (BBC Books, 1991), compiled by John Pidgeon, from a BBC radio interview broadcast 2 June 1990.

24. *Record Mirror*, 8 May 1971.
25. *Zigzag* No. 43, July 1974, interviewed in October 1971.
26. Letter to editor, *It* No. 112, 9–13 September 1971.
27. *Record Mirror*, 3 July 1971.
28. *Melody Maker*, 3 July 1971.
29. Similar symbolism was used later on *Quadrophenia*, with the use of the rock sticking out of the sea off the south coast of England.
30. *Melody Maker*, 21 August 1971.
31. *Sounds*, 28 August 1971.
32. *It* No.112, 9-23 September 1971.
33. *Rolling Stone*, 2 September 1971 and *Creem*, October 1971.
34. *Cream*, October 1971.
35. *New Musical Express*, 17 July 1971.
36. *Melody Maker*, 17 July 1971.
37. *Sounds*, 12 August 1972.
38. *Record Mirror*, 23 December 1972.
39. *Classic Albums* (BBC Books, 1991), compiled by John Pidgeon, from a BBC Radio interview broadcast 2 June 1990.
40. *Q*, September 1994.
41. *It* No. 112, 9–12 September 1971.
42. *Melody Maker*, 16 October 1971.
43. *Melody Maker*, 13 November 1971.
44. *Rolling Stone*, 9 December 1971.
45. *Melody Maker*, 4 December 1971.
46. *Record Mirror*, 4 December 1971.
47. *Gramophone* No.1443, February 1972.
48. *Sounds*, 27 October 1973.
49. *Melody Maker*, 27 October 1973.
50. *New Musical Express*, 17 June 1972.
51. *Melody Maker*, 17 June 1972.
52. *It* No. 134, 27 July–10 August 1972.
53. *Melody Maker*, 23 December 1972.

Chapter 6: Rockers and Mods (1973–1974)

1. *New Musical Express*, 3 November 1973.
2. *Melody Maker*, 19 August 1972.
3. *Record Mirror*, 23 September 1972.
4. *Disc*, 23 October 1972.
5. *Record Mirror*, 23 December 1972.
6. *Melody Maker*, 10 February 1973.
7. *Rock*, 9 April 1973.
8. *Ibid.*
9. *New Musical Express*, 3 November 1973.
10. *Sounds*, 28 October 1973.
11. *New Musical Express*, 3 November 1973.
12. "This Be the Verse," *High Windows* (Faber, 1974).
13. *Melody Maker*, 27 October 1973.
14. *Sounds*, 27 October 1973.
15. As far as I am aware, Pete Townshend has never acknowledged any influence

of *Bronco Bullfrog* on *Quadrophenia* and so may have been unaware of it. This is significant only because Townshend has otherwise always given due credit to those by whom he has been influenced.

16. *New Musical Express*, 6 October 1973.
17. *Ibid*.
18. *Rockspeak*, BBC Radio, broadcast 19 October 1973.
19. *Rolling Stone*, 3 January 1974.
20. Letter to author, 3 June 1997.
21. *Melody Maker*, 20 October 1973.
22. *Sounds*, 27 October 1973.
23. *New Musical Express*, 27 October 1973.
24. *Melody Maker*, 20 October 1973.
25. *The Observer*, November 1973.
26. *Mojo*, July 1996.
27. *New York Times*, 13 June 1974.
28. At the time of writing, *King Biscuit Flower Hour* is planning a commercial release of the full concert on a double CD.
29. *Rolling Stone*, 20 June 1974.
30. *New York Times*, 13 June 1974.
31. *Sounds*, 28 September 1974.
32. *New Musical Express*, 21 September 1974.
33. *Sounds*, 28 September 1974.
34. *Melody Maker*, 28 September 1974.
35. *New Musical Express*, 20 July 1974.

Chapter 7: Beating the Retreat (1975–1978)

1. *Sounds*, 28 December 1974.
2. *Sounds*, 12 April 1975.
3. *Ibid*.
4. *New Musical Express*, 31 May 1975.
5. *New Musical Express*, 9 August 1975.
6. *New Musical Express*, 4 October 1975.
7. *Melody Maker*, 4 October 1975.
8. *Rolling Stone*, 20 November 1975.
9. *Trouser Press*, November/December 1975.
10. "Pete Townshend's Back Pages," *New Musical Express*, 5 November 1977.
11. *Ibid*.
12. *Generations* No. 14, March 1995.
13. *Creem*, November 1976.
14. *Melody Maker*, 14 October 1978.
15. *Generations* No.14, March 1995.
16. *Ibid*.
17. *New Musical Express*, 15 July 1978.
18. This phrase is to be heard on the original mix only, to be found on *30 Years of Maximum R&B*. The 1996 reissue of *Who Are You* omits it.
19. *New Musical Express*, 19 August 1978.
20. *Sounds*, 19 August 1978.
21. *Melody Maker*, 19 August 1978.
22. *Crawdaddy*, October 1978.
23. *Rolling Stone*, 19 October 1978.

Chapter 8: Second Generation (1979–1998)

1. *Melody Maker*, 14 October 1978.
2. *Horse's Neck* (Faber, 1985) by Pete Townshend.
3. *Rolling Stone*, 23 August 1979.
4. *New Musical Express*, 9 June 1979.
5. *Sounds*, 9 June 1979.
6. *Melody Maker*, 13 October 1979.
7. *New Musical Express*, 22 September 1979.
8. *Rolling Stone*, 15 November 1979.
9. *Sounds*, 21 March 1981.
10. *New Musical Express*, 21 March 1981.
11. *Rolling Stone*, 14 May 1981.
12. *New Musical Express*, 12 June 1982.
13. *Ibid.*
14. *Jamming* No. 28, May 1985.
15. *New Musical Express*, 4 September 1982.
16. *Rolling Stone*, 30 September 1982.
17. *Trouser Press*, December 1982.
18. *Jamming* No. 28, May 1985.
19. Sleeve notes of *Another Scoop* LP, 1987.
20. *Jamming* No. 28, May 1985.
21. In 1974, Lou Reed had released a double album of "avant-garde electronics," *Metal Machine Music*, to fulfil a contract with RCA. By general consensus, Reed had duped his former company with a succession of worthless buzzes and static noises.
22. Letter from Chris Charlesworth to Pete Townshend, 24 February 1993.
23. *Q*, August 1994.
24. *Generations* No. 1, October 1988.

APPENDIX 1

Essential LP and CD Releases (1965–1998)

This is a chronological listing of essential Who albums. Albums that repeat already released material or that are reissued in a different form are not included. All the older compilation albums are omitted unless they contain items not otherwise available elsewhere. Catalog numbers for earlier CD releases by Polydor, MCA and Warner Bros. are not given where more recent upgraded editions have superseded such items. Pete Townshend's solo albums that contain Who demos or Who performances are also listed. (Single and EP releases are listed under the individual song entries in Appendix 2). Bootleg and underground LP and CD releases are not included.

LP and CD Releases by the Who

My Generation
U.K. LP: Brunswick (LAT 8616) [mono], 4 December 1965, reissued on Virgin (V2179), October 1980
Out in the Street/I Don't Mind/The Good's Gone/La-La-La-Lies/Much Too Much/My Generation/The Kids Are Alright/Please Please Please/It's Not True/I'm a Man/A Legal Matter/The Ox

The Who Sings My Generation
U.S. LP: Decca (DL 4664) [mono]/(DL 74664) [stereo], April 1966
U.S. CD: MCA (MCAD 31330) [mono mix]
Tracks as above but omits "I'm a Man" and adds "Circles" (titled "Instant Party") at the end of side 2.

A Quick One
U.K. LP: Reaction (593 002) [mono], 3 December 1966
U.K. CD: Polydor (527 758-2) [mono mix], June 1995
U.S.: CD MCA (MCAD 11268) [mono mix], June 1995
Run Run Run/Boris the Spider/I Need You/Whiskey Man/Heatwave/Cobwebs and Strange/Don't Look Away/See My Way/So Sad About Us/A Quick One While He's Away

Bonus CD tracks: Batman/Bucket T/Barbara Ann/Disguises/Doctor Doctor/I've Been Away/In the City/Happy Jack/Man with Money/My Generation—Land of Hope and Glory.

Happy Jack

U.S. LP: Decca (DL4892) [mono]/(DL74892) [stereo], May 1967.
U.S. CD: MCA (MCAD 31331) [mono mix]
Tracks as above LP but omits "Heatwave" and adds "Happy Jack" after "Cobwebs and Strange."

Sell Out

U.K. LP: Track (612 0020) [mono]/(613 002) [stereo], 16 December 1967
U.S. LP: Decca (DL4950) [mono]/(DL74950) [stereo], 6 January 1968
U.K. CD: Polydor (527 759-2) [stereo mix], June 1995
U.S. CD: MCA (MCAD 11268) [stereo mix], June 1995
Armenia City in the Sky/Heinz Baked Beans/Mary Anne with the Shaky Hand/Odorono/Tattoo/Our Love Was/I Can See for Miles/I Can't Reach You/Medac/Relax/Silas Stingy/Sunrise/Rael 1 & 2
Bonus CD tracks: Rael 2/Top Gear/Glittering Girl/Coke 2/Melancholia/Bag o' Nails/Someone's Coming/John Mason's Cars/Jaguar/John Mason's Cars (Reprise)/Early Morning Cold Taxi/Coke 1/Hall of the Mountain King/Radio 1 (Boris Mix)/Girl's Eyes/Odorono (Final Chorus)/Mary Anne with the Shaky Hand/Glow Girl/Track Records

The Magic Bus—The Who on Tour

U.S. LP: Decca (5064) [mono]/(75064) [stereo], September 1968
U.S. CD: MCA (MCAD 31333)
This compilation of previously released material is now notable only for the version (otherwise unavailable on LP or CD) of "Dr Jekyll & Mr Hyde."

Tommy

U.K. double LP: Track (613 013/4), 23 May 1969
U.S. double LP: Decca (DXSW 7205), 31 May 1969
U.K. CD: Polydor (531 043-2), March 1996
U.S. CD: Mobile Fidelity Sound Lab (UDCD 533) (earlier reissue)
U.S. CD: MCA (MCAD 11417), March 1996
Overture/It's a Boy/1921/Amazing Journey/Sparks/Eyesight to the Blind/Christmas/Cousin Kevin/The Acid Queen/Underture/Do You Think It's Alright/Fiddle About/Pinball Wizard/There's a Doctor/Go to the Mirror/Tommy Can You Hear Me?/Smash the Mirror/Sensation/Miracle Cure/Sally Simpson/I'm Free/Welcome/Tommy's Holiday Camp/We're Not Gonna Take It (including See Me, Feel Me)
Alternate CD track (MFSL version only): Eyesight to the Blind.

The House That Track Built (Various Artists)

U.K. LP: Track (613 016), July 1969
This compilation of previously released material is now only notable for the version (otherwise unavailable on LP or CD) of "Young Man Blues."

Live at Leeds

U.K. LP: Track (2406 001), 23 May 1970
U.S. LP: Decca (DL79175), 16 May 1970

U.K. CD: Polydor (527 169-2), February 1995
U.S. CD: MCA (MCAD 11215), February 1995
Young Man Blues/Substitute/Summertime Blues/Shakin' All Over/My Generation/Magic Bus
Bonus CD tracks: Heaven and Hell/I Can't Explain/Fortune Teller/Tattoo/Happy Jack/I'm a Boy/A Quick One While He's Away/Amazing Journey/Sparks

Who's Next
U.K. LP: Track (2408 102), 25 August 1971
U.S. LP: Decca (DL79182), 14 August 1971
U.K. CD: Polydor (527 760-2), November 1995
U.S. CD: MCA (MCAD 11269), November 1995
Baba O'Riley/Bargain/Love Ain't for Keeping/My Wife/Song Is Over/Getting in Tune/Going Mobile/Behind Blue Eyes/Won't Get Fooled Again
Bonus CD tracks: Pure and Easy/Baby Don't You Do It/Naked Eye/Water/Too Much of Anything/I Don't Even Know Myself/Behind Blue Eyes

Meaty Beaty Big & Bouncy
U.K. LP: Track (2406 006), 30 October 1971
U.S. LP: Decca (DL79184), 3 December 1971
U.S. CD: MCA (MCAD 37001)
This compilation of previously released material is now only notable for the versions (otherwise unavailable on LP or CD) of "I'm a Boy" and "Magic Bus."

Quadrophenia
U.K. double LP: Track (2657 013), 16 November 1973
U.S. double LP: MCA2 (10004), 3 November 1973
U.K. double CD: Polydor (531 971-2), June 1996
U.S. double CD: MCA (MCAD2 11463), June 1996
I Am the Sea/The Real Me/Quadrophenia/Cut My Hair/Punk and the Godfather/I'm One/The Dirty Jobs/Helpless Dancer/Is It in My Head?/I've Had Enough/5.15/Sea and Sand/Drowned/Bell Boy/Doctor Jimmy/The Rock/Love Reign o'er Me

Odds and Sods
U.K. LP: Track (2406 116), 28 September 1974
U.S. LP: MCA (2126), 12 October 1974
U.K. CD: Polydor (539 791-2), March 1998
U.S. CD: MCA (MCAD 11718), March 1998
Postcard/Now I'm a Farmer/Put the Money Down/Little Billy/Too Much of Anything/Glow Girl/Pure and Easy/Faith in Something Bigger/I'm The Face/Naked Eye/Long Live Rock
Bonus CD tracks: Leaving Here/Baby Don't You Do It/Under My Thumb/Mary Anne with the Shaky Hand/Summertime Blues/My Way/Young Man Blues/Cousin Kevin Model Child/Love Ain't for Keeping/Time Is Passing/We Close Tonight/Water

The Who by Numbers
U.K. LP: Polydor (2490 275), 18 October 1975
U.S. LP: MCA (2161), 25 October 1975
U.K. CD: Polydor (533 844-2), December 1996
U.S. CD: MCA (MCAD 11493), December 1996

Slip Kid/However Much I Booze/Squeeze Box/Dreaming from the Waist/ Imagine a Man/Success Story/They Are All in Love/Blue Red and Grey/How Many Friends/In a Hand or a Face

Bonus CD tracks: Squeeze Box/Behind Blue Eyes/Dreaming from the Waist

Who Are You

U.K. LP: Polydor (2683 084), 18 August 1978
U.S. LP: MCA (3050), 25 August 1978
U.K. CD: Polydor (533 845-2), December 1996
U.S. CD: Mobile Fidelity Sound Lab (UDCD 561), 1992 (earlier reissue)
U.S. CD: MCA (MCAD 11492), December 1996

New Song/Had Enough/905/Sister Disco/Music Must Change/Trick of the Light/Guitar and Pen/Love Is Coming Down/Who Are You

Bonus CD tracks: No Road Romance/Empty Glass/Guitar and Pen/Love Is Coming Down/Who Are You

Bonus CD track (MFSL version only): Guitar and Pen

The Kids Are Alright (Soundtrack)

U.K. double LP: Polydor (2675 179), 9 June 1979
U.S. double LP: MCA2 (11005), 23 June 1979
U.K. CD: Polydor (517 947-2)
U.S. CD: MCA (MCAD 6899)

Dialogue/My Generation/I Can't Explain/Happy Jack/I Can See for Miles/Magic Bus/Long Live Rock/Anyway Anyhow Anywhere/Young Man Blues/My Wife/Baba O'Riley/A Quick One While He's Away/Tommy Can You Hear Me?/Sparks/Pinball Wizard/See Me, Feel Me/Join Together*/Road Runner*/My Generation Blues*/Won't Get Fooled Again

Tracks marked (*) are omitted from both U.K. and U.S. CDs.

Quadrophenia (Soundtrack)

U.K. double LP: Polydor (2625 037), 6 October 1979
U.S. double LP: Polydor (PD2-6235), 6 October 1979
U.K. CD: Polydor (519 999-2)
U.S. CD: Polydor (314 519 999-2)

I Am the Sea/The Real Me/I'm One/5.15/Love Reign o'er Me/Bell Boy/I've Had Enough/Helpless Dancer/Doctor Jimmy/Zoot Suit/High Heeled Sneakers [Cross Section]*/Get Out and Stay Out/Four Faces/Joker James/Punk and the Godfather/Night Train [James Brown]*/Louie Louie [The Kingsmen]*/Green Onions [Booker T and the MGs]*/Be My Baby [The Ronettes]*/Da Doo Ron Ron [The Crystals]*/Rhythm of the Rain [The Cascades]*/He's So Fine [The Chiffons]*

Bonus CD track: I'm the Face. Tracks marked (*) are omitted from both U.K. and U.S. CDs.

Concerts for the People of Kampuchia (Various Artists)

U.K. double LP: Atlantic (K 60153), March 1981
U.S. double LP: Atlantic (SD-2 7005), March 1981
Includes Who tracks "Baba O'Riley," "Sister Disco," "Behind Blue Eyes" and "See Me, Feel Me."

Face Dances

U.K. LP: Polydor (2302 106), 21 March 1981

U.S. LP: Warner Brothers (WB HS3516), March 1981
U.K. CD: Polydor (537 695-2), June 1997
U.S. CD: MCA (MCAD 11634), June 1997
You Better You Bet/Don't Let Go the Coat/Cache Cache/The Quiet One/Did You Steal My Money?/How Can You Do It Alone/Daily Records/You/Another Tricky Day
Bonus CD tracks: I Like Nightmares/It's in You/Somebody Saved Me/How Can You Do It Alone/The Quiet One

It's Hard

U.K. LP: Polydor (WHOD 5066), 4 September 1982
U.S. LP: Warner Brothers (WB23731-1/2), 4 September 1982
U.K. CD: Polydor (537 696-2), June 1997
U.S. CD: MCA (MCAD 11635), June 1997
Athena/It's Your Turn/Cooks County/It's Hard/Dangerous/Eminence Front/I've Known No War/One Life's Enough/One at a Time/Why Did I Fall for That/A Man Is a Man/Cry If You Want
Bonus CD tracks: It's Hard/Eminence Front/Dangerous/Cry If You Want.

Rarities Vol. 1 1966–1968

U.K. LP: Polydor (SPELP9), September 1983
U.K. CD: Polydor (847 670-2), January 1991, coupled with LP below
This compilation of previously released material is now notable only for the version (otherwise unavailable on LP or CD) of "Dr Jekyll & Mr Hyde."

Rarities Vol. 2 1970–1973

U.K. LP: Polydor (SPELP10), September 1983
U.K. CD: Polydor (847 670-2), January 1991, coupled with LP above
This compilation of previously released material is now notable only for the version (otherwise unavailable on LP or CD) of "Baby Don't You Do It."

Who's Last

U.K. double LP: MCA (WHO1), 10 November 1984
U.S. double LP: MCA2 (8018), November 1984
U.K. CD: MCA (MCAD 19005), April 1992
U.S. double CD: MCA (MCAD 8018)
My Generation/I Can't Explain/Substitute/Behind Blue Eyes/Baba O'Riley/Boris the Spider/Who Are You/Pinball Wizard/See Me, Feel Me/Love Reign o'er Me/Long Live Rock/Long Live Rock (Reprise)/Won't Get Fooled Again/Doctor Jimmy/Magic Bus/Summertime Blues/Twist and Shout

The Singles

U.K. LP: Polydor (WHOD17), November 1984
U.K. CD: Polydor (815 965-2), 1985
This compilation of previously released material is now notable only for the version (otherwise unavailable on LP or CD) of "I Can See for Miles."

Who's Missing

U.K. LP: Polydor (837 557-1), October 1988
U.S.: LP MCA (5641), November 1985
U.K. CD: Polydor (SPECD 116), October 1988
U.S. CD: MCA (MCAD 31221)

Leaving Here/Lubie (Come Back Home)/Shout and Shimmy/Anytime You Want Me/Barbara Ann/I'm a Boy/Mary Anne with the Shaky Hand/Heaven and Hell/Here for More/I Don't Even Know Myself/When I Was a Boy/Bargain

Two's Missing

U.K. LP: Polydor (837 558-1), October 1988
U.S. LP: MCA (5712), April 1987
U.K. CD: Polydor (SPECD 117), October 1988
U.S. CD: MCA (MCAD 31222)
Bald Headed Woman/Under My Thumb/My Wife/I'm a Man/Dogs/Dogs Part Two/Circles/The Last Time/Water/Daddy Rolling Stone/Heatwave/Going Down/Motoring/Wasp Man

Join Together

U.K. triple LP: Virgin (VDT 102), March 1990
U.S. triple LP: MCA3 (19501), March 1990
U.K. double CD: Virgin (CDVDT 102), March 1990
U.S. double CD: MCA (MCAD 19501), March 1990
Overture/1921/Amazing Journey/Sparks/Eyesight to The Blind/Christmas/Cousin Kevin/The Acid Queen/Pinball Wizard/Do You Think It's Alright?/Fiddle About/There's a Doctor/Go to the Mirror/Smash the Mirror/Tommy Can You Hear Me?/I'm Free/Miracle Cure/Sally Simpson/Sensation/Tommy's Holiday Camp/We're Not Gonna Take It (including See Me, Feel Me)/Eminence Front/Face the Face/Dig/I Can See For Miles/A Little Is Enough/5.15/Love Reign o'er Me/Trick of the Light/Rough Boys/Join Together/You Better You Bet/Behind Blue Eyes/Won't Get Fooled Again

Monterey International Pop Festival (Various Artists)

U.K. 5-CD set: Castle Communications 1993, reissued Essential (ROK CD 102), December 1997
U.S. 5-CD set: Rhino (R270596), 9 October 1992
Includes Who tracks "Substitute," "Summertime Blues," "Pictures of Lily," "A Quick One While He's Away," "Happy Jack," and "My Generation."

30 Years of Maximum R&B

U.K. 4-CD set: Polydor (521 751-2), July 1994
U.S. 4-CD set: MCA (MCAD4 11020), July 1994
Pete Dialogue*/I'm the Face/Here 'Tis/Zoot Suit/Leaving Here/I Can't Explain/Anyway Anyhow Anywhere/Daddy Rolling Stone/My Generation/The Kids Are Alright/The Ox/A Legal Matter/Pete Dialogue*/Substitute/I'm a Boy/Disguises/Happy Jack/Boris the Spider/So Sad About Us/A Quick One While He's Away/Pictures of Lily/Early Morning Cold Taxi/Coke 2/The Last Time/I Can't Reach You/Girl's Eyes/Bag o'Nails/Call Me Lightning/Rotosound Strings/I Can See for Miles/Mary Anne with the Shaky Hand/Armenia City in the Sky/Tattoo/Our Love Was/Rael 1/Rael 2/Track Records/Premier Drums/Sunrise/Jaguar/Melancholia/Fortune Teller/Magic Bus/Little Billy/Russell Harty Dialogue*/Dogs/Overture/Acid Queen/Abbie Hoffman Incident*/Underture/Pinball Wizard/I'm Free/See Me, Feel Me/Heaven and Hell/Pete Dialogue*/Young Man Blues/Summertime Blues/Shakin' All Over/Baba O'Riley/Bargain/Pure and Easy/Song Is Over/Studio Dialogue*/Behind Blue Eyes/Won't Get Fooled Again/The Seeker/Bony Moronie/Let's See Action/Join Together/Relay/The Real Me/5.15/Bell Boy/Love Reign o'er Me/Long Live

Rock/Life with the Moons*/Naked Eye/University Challenge*/Slip Kid/Poetry Cornered*/Dreaming from the Waist/Blue Red and Grey/Life with The Moons 2*/Squeeze Box/My Wife/Who Are You/Music Must Change/Sister Disco/Guitar and Pen/You Better You Bet/Eminence Front/Twist and Shout/I'm a Man/Pete Dialogue*/Saturday Night's Alright for Fighting
Tracks marked (*) are dialogue items not included as song entries in Appendix 2.

Live at the Isle of Wight Festival 1970
U.K. double CD: Essential (EDF CD326), October 1996
U.S. double CD: Columbia/Legacy (65084), October 1996
Heaven and Hell/I Can't Explain/Young Man Blues/I Don't Even Know Myself/Water/Overture/It's a Boy/1921/Amazing Journey/Sparks/Eyesight to the Blind/Christmas/The Acid Queen/Pinball Wizard/Do You Think It's Alright/Fiddle About/Tommy Can You Hear Me?/There's a Doctor/Go to the Mirror/Smash The Mirror/Miracle Cure/I'm Free/Tommy's Holiday Camp/We're Not Gonna Take It (including See Me, Feel Me)/Summertime Blues/Shakin' All Over (including Spoonful and Twist and Shout)/Substitute/My Generation/Naked Eye/Magic Bus

My Generation—The Very Best of the Who
U.K. CD: Polydor (533 150-2), August 1996
U.S. CD: MCA (MCAD 11462), August 1996
I Can't Explain/Anyway Anyhow Anywhere/My Generation/Substitute/I'm a Boy/Boris the Spider/Happy Jack/Pictures of Lily/I Can See for Miles/Magic Bus/Pinball Wizard/The Seeker/Baba O'Riley/Won't Get Fooled Again/Let's See Action/5.15/Join Together/Squeeze Box/Who Are You/You Better You Bet
This CD is the current definitive "greatest hits" compilation and is the only CD where the newly remastered original version of "Substitute" can be found.

LP and CD Releases by Pete Townshend

This is a chronological listing of Pete Townshend solo releases that contain performances by the Who or demo material relating to the Who.

Glastonbury Fayre (Various Artists)
U.K. LP: Rev (3), June 1971
Includes demo of "Classified."

I Am (Various Artists)
U.S. LP: Universal Spiritual League (002), May 1972
Includes demo version of "Baba O'Riley."

Who Came First
U.K. LP: Track (2408 201), October 1972
U.S. LP: Decca (79189), October 1972
U.K./U.S. CD: Ryko (RCD 10246), October 1992
Pure and Easy/Evolution*/Forever's No Time at All*/Let's See Action/Time Is Passing/There's a Heartache Following Me*/Sheraton Gibson/Content*/Parvardigar*
Bonus CD tracks: His Hands*/The Seeker/Day of Silence*/Sleeping Dog*/The Love Man*/Lantern Cabin*

Tracks marked (*) are not included in Appendix 2 on the basis that they are highly unlikely to have been considered as demos for, or relating to, the Who.

Scoop

U.K. double LP: Atco (79-0063-1), March 1983
U.S. double LP: Atco (90063-1), March 1983
U.S. CD: Atco (90063-2)
So Sad About Us/Brrr/Squeeze Box/Zelda/Politician/Dirty Water/Circles/Piano: 'Tipperary'*/Unused Piano: 'Quadrophenia'/Melancholia/Bargain/Things Must Change/Popular/Behind Blue Eyes/Magic Bus/Cache Cache/Cookin'/Your So Clever/Body Language/Initial Machine Experiments/Mary/Recorders/Goin' Fishin'/To Barney Kessell*/You Came Back/Love Reign o'er Me
Tracks marked (*) are not included in Appendix 2 on the basis that they are highly unlikely to have been considered as demos for, or relating to, the Who.

Sometimes a Great Notion (Various Artists)

U.K. LP: EMI (TOPCAT 1), 1986
Includes demo version of "Relay."

Another Scoop

U.K. double LP: Polydor, 1989
U.S. double LP: Atco (90539-1-G), March 1987
U.S. double CD: Atco (90539-2)
You Better You Bet/Girl in a Suitcase/Brooklyn Kids/Pinball Wizard/Football Fugue/Happy Jack/Substitute/Long Live Rock/Call Me Lightning/Holly Like Ivy/Begin the Begine*/Vicious Interlude*/La-La-La-Lies/Cat Snatch/Prelude #556/Praying the Game/Driftin' Blues*/Christmas/Pictures of Lily/Don't Let Go the Coat/The Kids Are Alright/Prelude: The Right to Write/Never Ask Me/Ask Yourself/ The Ferryman/The Shout*
Tracks marked (*) are not included in Appendix 2 on the basis that they are highly unlikely to have been considered as demos for, or relating to, the Who.

The Iron Man

U.K. LP: Virgin (V2592), June 1989
U.S. LP: Atlantic (81996-1), June 1989
U.K. CD: Virgin (CDV 2592), June 1989
U.S. CD: Atlantic (81996-2), June 1989
Includes Who tracks "Dig" and "Fire."

Psychoderelict

U.K. CD: Atlantic (7567-82494-2), July 1993
U.S. CD: Atlantic (782494-2), July 1993
U.S. CD: Atlantic (782535-2) [music only], October 1993
Includes Who demos "Meher Baba M3," "Meher Baba M4 (Signal Box)," "Meher Baba M5 (Vivaldi)," and "Baba O'Riley" (excerpt).

APPENDIX 2

Index of Who Songs and Recorded Performances (1963–1991)

This is an A–Z listing of songs known to have been recorded by the Who, with variants and alternatives noted where relevant. The list also includes Pete Townshend songs that may have been considered as material for the Who but which were not subsequently recorded or released as such. However, in order to keep this list to manageable proportions, I have *excluded* songs and performances in the following categories:

(a) *Live material recorded by the Who that has not been released.* The number of live concerts held on tape by the band, especially from 1979 onward, is profuse and would add many hundreds of variants to many of the song entries. Therefore this list restricts itself only to the live material that has been officially released on record or CD. Rehearsal material, i.e., live recordings without an audience, has been included where this forms the soundtrack to film or video footage. Soundtrack recordings to other live concert material that exists on film or videotape have been omitted. Sound check and rehearsal recordings for live concerts are also excluded.

(b) *Pete Townshend demos and solo recordings that were clearly not intended for the Who.* It is often extremely difficult to differentiate among material that Townshend had intended for the Who, that which he had earmarked for other projects, and songs that floated for a while between the two. This listing basically omits songs which it can be confidently assumed would never have been worked on by the band. These are sometimes easy to identify (such as the Meher Baba material) or tracks for Townshend's later solo projects such as *White City* and *The Iron Man*. However, this list includes a number of demo recordings that Townshend never officially released on solo works and that could conceivably have become Who tracks (however unlikely). In many cases it is difficult to assess with any certainty.

(c) *Demo versions of songs by Pete Townshend or John Entwistle for which the Who subsequently recorded a group version.* However, in the cases where such demos have been officially released, the LP/CD title and duration are noted. These are not given a separate entry. All Townshend and Entwistle songs were originally recorded as home demo tapes.

(d) *Songs that were played onstage by the Who for which there remains no recorded evidence.* Many cover versions played live by the Who were never attempted in the recording studio.

The entries for each song adhere to the following format:

SONG TITLE with note in parenthesis to detail
- the composer(s), if other than Pete Townshend
- live concert recording (live)
- version number (2 or higher)
- radio broadcast recording (radio)
- TV or film soundtrack recording (TV) or (film)
- Pete Townshend demo recording (demo)

Song titles that are followed by an asterisk (*) are (at the date of writing) not officially available on CD. There then follows entries for some or all of the following data:

Original performer and release details of songs not original to the Who (where appropriate on first song entry only).

R: Recording location and date (if known).

P: Original producer of the session.

B: Broadcast details for television and radio recordings.

U.K./U.S: Format and date of original vinyl release on single or album title (see Appendix 1 for full data on LPs) in Britain (U.K.) and in the United States (U.S.).

CD: Title of most recent or best compact disc remaster that includes the track in question. (See Appendix 1 for full data on CDs).

N: Notes, including the format and length of track (if known) and any other relevant data, such as guest musicians and secondary releases on single. (Durations of tracks are mostly those as indexed on CDs. Note that CD track timings often include end gaps of a couple of seconds.) Guest musicians on later live work are omitted.

D: A demo recording by Pete Townshend may have been released. This entry notes on which CD or LP (on first entry only) it is to be found and the duration of demo track.

This index lists 544 main entries of which 120 (22 percent) are currently unavailable on CD.

The Acid Queen
R: IBC Studios, London, October 1968–March 1969. P: Kit Lambert. U.K./U.S.: *Tommy*. CD: *Tommy*. N: Stereo (3.35).

The Acid Queen (live)
R: Isle of Wight Festival, England, 29 August 1970. P: Jon Astley/Andy Macpherson. CD: *Live at the Isle of Wight Festival 1970*. N: Stereo (3.41). First released in 1996.

The Acid Queen (live) (2)
R: Radio City Music Hall, New York, or Universal Amphitheatre, Los Angeles, 27 June or 24 August 1989 (venue specified as one or the other). P: Billy Nicholls. U.K./U.S.: *Join Together*. CD: *Join Together*. N: Stereo (3.44).

Amazing Journey
R: IBC Studios, London, October 1968–March 1969. P: Kit Lambert. U.K./U.S.: *Tommy*. CD: *Tommy*. N: Stereo (3.25). Played as a medley with "Sparks."

Amazing Journey (live)
R: Leeds University, England, 14 February 1970. P: The Who (Pete Townshend). CD: *Live at Leeds*. N: Stereo (3.17). Played as medley with "Sparks." First released in 1995.

Amazing Journey (live) (2)
R: Isle of Wight Festival, England, 29 August 1970. P: Jon Astley/Andy Macpherson. CD: *Live at the Isle of Wight Festival 1970*. N: Stereo (3.19). First released in 1996.

Amazing Journey (live) (3)
R: Radio City Music Hall, New York, or Universal Amphitheatre, Los Angeles, 27 June or 24 August 1989 (venue specified as one or the other). P: Billy Nicholls. U.K./U.S.: *Join Together*. CD: *Join Together*. N: Stereo (3.07).

Another Tricky Day
R: Odyssey Studios, London, June–December 1980. P: Bill Szymczyk. U.K./U.S.: *Face Dances*. CD: *Face Dances*. N: Stereo (4.51).

Anytime You Want Me
 (Regovay/Mimms)
Originally performed by Garnet Mimms and the Enchanters and released as a single A side (United Artists), 1964. R: IBC Studios, London, 11 March 1965. P: Shel Talmy. U.S.: Single B side of "Anyway Anyhow Anywhere" (Decca 31801), May 1965. CD: *Who's Missing*. N: Mono (2.32). Featuring Nicky Hopkins (piano) and the Ivy League (backing vocals).

Anyway Anyhow Anywhere (Pete Townshend/Roger Daltrey)
R: IBC Studios, London, 13–14 April 1965. P: Shel Talmy. U.K.: Single A side (Brunswick 05935), 21 May 1965. U.S.: Single A-side (Decca 31801), May 1965 CD: *My Generation—The Very Best of the Who*. N: Mono (2.38). Featuring Nicky Hopkins (piano) and the Ivy League (backing vocals). The only Townshend/Daltrey songwriting collaboration in their forty-year partnership.

Anyway Anyhow Anywhere (2)*
R: IBC Studios, London, 13–14 April 1965. P: Shel Talmy. N: Mono (2.38). This version contains a mix with a different lead vocal track by Roger Daltrey, otherwise the performance is identical to above. Released on France–only EP (Brunswick 10668), July 1965.

Anyway Anyhow Anywhere (TV)
R: Associated-Rediffusion Studios, May 1965. B: *Ready Steady Goes Live!*, ITV TV, 21 May 1965. U.K./U.S.: *The Kids Are Alright*. CD: *The Kids Are Alright*. N: Mono (2.47).

Anyway Anyhow Anywhere (radio)*
R: BBC Studios, London, 24 May 1965 B: *Saturday Club*, BBC Light Programme, 29 May 1965. N: Mono (2.43)

Armenia City in the Sky (Speedy Keene)
R: IBC Studios, London, 20 October 1967. P: Kit Lambert. U.K./U.S.: *Sell Out*. CD: *Sell Out*. N: Mono/stereo (3.12).

Ask Yourself (demo)
R: Pete Townshend's home studio, London, 1982–1983. U.K./U.S.: *Another Scoop*. CD: *Another Scoop*. N: Stereo (4.30).

Athena
R: Turn Up-Down Studios, Surrey, June 1982. P: Glyn Johns. U.K./U.S.: *It's Hard*. CD: *It's Hard*. N: Stereo (3.46). Also released as a single A side in U.K. (Polydor WHO 6), 25 September 1982, and in U.S. (Warner Bros. WBS 7-29905), 4 September 1982.

Baba O'Riley
R: Olympic Studios, London, May 1971. P: The Who/Glyn Johns. U.K./U.S.: *Who's Next*. CD: *Who's Next*. N: Stereo (5.08). Featuring David Arbus (violin). D: *I Am* (LP only). Excerpts of this demo appear on *PsychoDerelict*.

Baba O'Riley (live)
R: Shepperton Sound Studio, London, 25 May 1978. P: John Entwistle. U.K./U.S.: *The Kids Are Alright*. CD: *The Kids Are Alright*. N: Stereo (5.29).

Baba O'Riley (live) (2)*
R: Hammersmith Odeon, London, 28 December 1979. P: Chris Thomas. U.K./U.S.: *Concerts for the People of Kampuchea*. N: Stereo (5.12).

Baba O'Riley (live) (3)
R: Venue unspecified, U.S. and Canada, December 1982. P: Not credited. Compiled by Cy Langston. U.K./U.S.: *Who's Last*. CD: *Who's Last*. N: Stereo (5.12). First released in 1984.

Baby Don't You Do It (Holland/Dozier/Holland)
Originally performed by Marvin Gaye as single A side (Motown 54101), 2 September 1964. R: Pye Studios, London, late 1964. CD: *Odds and Sods*. N: Mono (2.27). This is thought to hail from a test session recorded for Pye Records in London and exists only as a Pye acetate disk. In 1996 Jon Astley made a digital copy of this disk for its first release in 1998.

Baby Don't You Do It (TV)*
R: London, late 1965. B: *Ready Steady Go!* and *The New Year Starts Here!*, ITV TV, 24 and 31 December 1965. N: Mono. A live performance thought to hail from one of the above TV broadcasts.

Baby Don't You Do It (2)
R: Record Plant, New York, 16 March 1971. P: Kit Lambert/Felix Papparlardi. CD: *Who's Next*. N: Stereo (5.13). Featuring Al Kooper (organ) and Leslie West (guitar). Edited from longer master of (8.36). First released in 1995.

Baby Don't You Do It (live)
R: Civic Center, San Francisco, 13 December 1971. P: The Who. U.K.: Single B side of "Join Together" (Track 2094), 17 June 1972. U.S.: Single B side of "Join Together" (Decca 32983), 8 July 1972. CD: *Rarities 1 & 2*. N: Stereo (6.09).

Bald Headed Woman (Shel Talmy)
Originally performed by the Kinks on *The Kinks* LP (Pye NPL 18096), October 1964, and apparently adapted by Talmy from an unspecified blues song. R: Pye Studios, London, December 1964. P: Shel Talmy. U.K.: Single B side of "I Can't Explain" (Brunswick 05926), 15 January 1965. CD: *Two's Missing*. N: Mono (2.09). Featuring Jimmy Page (guitar).

Bank Holiday (demo)*
R: PT's home studio, London, 1972–1973. N: Unreleased. This is reported to be an outtake from *Quadrophenia*.

Barbara-Ann (Charles Fassert)
Originally performed by the Regents as single A side (Gee 1065), May 1961. R: IBC Studios, London, August 1966. P: Kit Lambert. U.K.: *Ready Steady Who* EP (Reaction 592001), 11 November 1966. CD: *A Quick One*. N: Mono (1.59).

Barbara-Ann (film)*
R: Shepperton Studios, London, December 1977. N: Stereo. A filmed

rehearsal sequence included in *The Kids Are Alright* film.

Bargain
R: Olympic Studios, London, April–June 1971. P: The Who/Glyn Johns. U.K./U.S.: *Who's Next*. CD: *Who's Next*. N: Stereo (5.32). D: *Scoop* (4.12).

Bargain (live)
R: Civic Center, San Francisco, 13 December 1971. P: The Who. U.K./U.S.: *Who's Missing*. CD: *Who's Missing/30 Years of Maximum R&B*. N: Stereo (6.22). Boxed set version is edited down to (4.54). First released in 1985.

Baroque Ippanese (demo)
R: PT's home studio, London, August 1982. U.K./U.S.: *Another Scoop*. CD: *Another Scoop*. N: Stereo (2.24).

Batman (Neal Hefti)
Originally performed by the Nelson Riddle Orchestra as "Batman Theme" and released as a single A side (Stateside SS 517), May 1966. R: IBC Studios, London, August 1966. P: Kit Lambert. U.K.: *Ready Steady Who* EP (Reaction 592001), 11 November 1966. CD: *A Quick One*. N: Mono/stereo (1.34). CD version features stereo vocal separation.

Batman (2)*
(aka *Caped Crusaders*). R: IBC Studios, London, August 1966. P: Kit Lambert. N: An instrumental version of above. Unreleased.

*Beat Up**
R: IBC Studios, London, October 1968–March 1969. P: Kit Lambert. N: Stereo. Unreleased short link piece from *Tommy*.

Behind Blue Eyes
R: Record Plant, New York, 18 March 1971. P: Kit Lambert/Felix Papparlardi. CD: *Who's Next*. N: Stereo (3.25). Projected as single release for May 1971 but withdrawn. First released in 1995. D: *Scoop* (3.25).

Behind Blue Eyes (2)
R: Olympic Studios, London, May 1971. P: The Who/Glyn Johns. U.K./U.S.: *Who's Next*. CD: *Who's Next*. N: Stereo (3.41). Also released as a single A side in U.S. (Decca 32888), 6 November 1971.

Behind Blue Eyes (live)
R: Football ground, Swansea, England, 12 June 1976. P: Jon Astley. CD: *By Numbers*. N: Stereo (3.37). First released in 1996.

Behind Blue Eyes (live) (2)*
R: Hammersmith Odeon, London, 28 December 1979. P: Chris Thomas. U.K./U.S.: *Concerts for the People of Kampuchea*. N: Stereo (3.36).

Behind Blue Eyes (live) (3)
R: Venue unspecified, U.S. and Canada, December 1982. P: Not credited. Compiled by Cy Langston. U.K./U.S.: *Who's Last*. CD: *Who's Last*. N: Stereo (3.30). First released in 1984.

Behind Blue Eyes (live) (4)
R: Universal Amphitheare, Los Angeles, 24 August 1989. P: Billy Nicholls. U.K./U.S.: *Join Together*. CD: *Join Together*. N: Stereo (3.38). Also released in U.K. as part of *Join Together* EP (Virgin VS 1259), March 1990.

Bell Boy
R: "The Kitchen", Ramport Studios, London, 1 June 1973. P: The Who (Pete Townshend). U.K./U.S.: *Quadrophenia*. CD: *Quadrophenia*. N: Stereo (4.55). Subtitled "Keith's Theme."

Bell Boy (2)
R: As above, with additional overdubs at Shepperton Studios, London, 1979. P: John Entwistle. U.K./U.S.: *Quadrophenia* (Soundtrack). CD: *Quadrophenia* (Soundtrack). N: Stereo (4.57). Remixed, with new bass guitar track.

Blue Red and Grey
R: Ronnie Lane's Mobile, Shepperton Sound Stage, London, May 1975. P:

Glyn Johns. U.K./U.S.: *By Numbers*. CD: *By Numbers*. N: Stereo (2.47).

Blue Red and Grey (2)*
R: Ronnie Lane's mobile unit, Shepperton Sound Stage, London, May 1975. P: Glyn Johns. N: Full group version of the above, the tapes of which have now been lost. Unreleased.

Body Language (demo)
R: Pete Townshend's home studio, London, 1981. U.K./U.S.: *Scoop*. CD: *Scoop*. N: Stereo (1.58).

Bony Moronie (Larry Williams) (live)
Originally performed by Larry Williams as a single A side (Speciality 615), October 1957. R: Young Vic Theatre, London, 26 April 1971. P: John Williams. U.K.: B side of reissue of "Won't Get Fooled Again" (Polydor POSPX917), June 1988. CD: *30 Years of Maximum R&B*. N: Stereo (3.18). CD is a different mix to 1988 single.

Boogie Friday (demo)*
R: PT's home studio, London, 1981. N: Stereo. Unreleased.

Boris the Spider (John Entwistle)
R: Pye Studios, London, October 1966. P: Kit Lambert. U.K.: *A Quick One*. U.S.: *Happy Jack*. CD: *A Quick One*. N: Mono (2.28).

Boris the Spider (radio)*
R: BBC Studios, London, 17 January 1967. B: *Saturday Club*, BBC Light Programme, 21 January 1967. N: Mono (2.14).

Boris the Spider (Radio 1) (radio)
(aka *Radio One* [Boris Mix]). R: BBC Studios, London, 10 October 1967. B: *Top Gear* and *Saturday Club*, BBC Radio 1, 15 and 28 October 1967. CD: *Sell Out*. N: Mono (0.05). Jingle.

Boris the Spider (live)
R: Venue unspecified, U.S. and Canada, December 1982. P: Not credited. Compiled by Cy Langston. U.K./U.S.: *Who's Last*. CD: *Who's Last*. N: Stereo (2.29). First released in 1984.

Brooklyn Kids (demo)
R: PT's home studio, London, September 1978. U.K./U.S.: *Another Scoop*. CD: *Another Scoop*. N: Stereo (4.45).

Brrr (demo)
R: Pete Townshend's home studio, London, 1975. U.K./U.S.: *Scoop*. CD: *Scoop*. N: Stereo (2.31).

Bucket T (Atfield/Christian/Torrence)
Originally performed by Jan and Dean on the LP *Dead Man's Curve/The New Girl in School* (Liberty LPP 3361), 1964. R: IBC Studios, London, August 1966. P: Kit Lambert. U.K.: *Ready Steady Who* EP (Reaction 592001), 11 November 1966. CD: *A Quick One*. N: Mono (2.07).

Cache Cache
R: Odyssey Studios, London, June–December 1980. P: Bill Szymczyk. U.K./U.S.: *Face Dances*. CD: *Face Dances*. N: Stereo (3.52). D: *Scoop* (3.42).

Call Me Lightning
R: Goldstar Studios, Los Angeles, U.S.A, 26 February 1968. P: Kit Lambert. U.K.: Single B side of "Dogs" (Track 604 023), 15 June 1968. U.S.: Single A side (Decca 32288), 16 March 1968. CD: *30 Years of Maximum R&B*. N: Mono (2.20). D: *Another Scoop* (2.12).

Can't You See I'm Easy? (see Why Can't You See I'm Easy?)

Caped Crusaders (see Batman)

Cat Snatch (demo)
R: Pete Townshend's home studio, London, 1982–1983. U.K./U.S.: *Another Scoop*. CD: *Another Scoop*. N: Stereo (3.18).

Choirboy (see Empty Glass)

Christmas
R: IBC Studios, London, October

1968–March 1969. P: Kit Lambert. U.K./U.S.: *Tommy*. CD: *Tommy*. N: Stereo (4.34). Also released in U.K. as part of *Tommy* EP (Track 2252 001), 7 November 1970. D: *Another Scoop* (1.55).

Christmas (live)
R: Isle of Wight Festival, England, 29 August 1970. P: Jon Astley/Andy Macpherson. CD: *Live at the Isle of Wight Festival 1970*. N: Stereo (3.16). First released in 1996.

Christmas (live) (2)
R: Radio City Music Hall, New York, or Universal Amphitheatre, Los Angeles, 27 June or 24 August 1989 (venue specified as one or the other). P: Billy Nicholls. U.K./U.S.: *Join Together*. CD: *Join Together*. N: Stereo (4.24). Also included as part of the CD version of the *Join Together* EP (Virgin VSCT 1259), March 1990.

Circles (aka *Instant Party*)
R: IBC Studios, London, November 1965. P: Shel Talmy. U.K.: Single B side of "A Legal Matter" (Brunswick 05956), 11 March 1966. U.S.: *The Who Sings My Generation*. CD: *The Who Sings My Generation*. N: Mono (3.05). Projected single release for January 1966. For legal reasons, the title of this was given on all releases as "Instant Party.". D: *Scoop* (2.09).

Circles (2) (aka *Instant Party*)
R: Olympic Studios, London, January 1966. P: The Who (Pete Townshend). U.K.: Single B side of "Substitute" (Reaction 591001), 4 March 1966. CD: *Who's Missing*. N: Mono (2.27). This was soon replaced on the B side of "Substitute" and later emerged on the *Ready Steady Who* EP (Reaction 592001), 11 November 1966 in U.K. only.

Circles (TV)*
R: Associated-Rediffusion Studios, London, January 1966. B: *Ready Steady Go!*, ITV TV, 28 January 1966. N: Mono. This was the public premier of "Circles," almost certainly performed live.

Classified (demo)*
R: Pete Townshend's home studio, London, 1971. U.K.: *Glastonbury Fair* LP (Rev 3), June 1971. N: Stereo. Also released as single B side of Pete Townshend's solo "Let My Love Open the Door" (Atco K11486), June 1980.

Cobwebs and Strange (Keith Moon)
R: Pye Studios, London, October 1966. P: Kit Lambert. U.K.: *A Quick One*. U.S.: *Happy Jack*. CD: *A Quick One*. N: Mono (2.29).

Coke After Coke (see *Coke No. 2*)

Coke No. 1 (aka *Things Go Better with Coke*)
R: London, late–1967. CD: *Sell Out*. N: Mono (0.30). Composer unknown. First released in 1995.

Coke No. 2 (aka *Coke After Coke*)
R: London, late–1967. CD: *Sell Out*. N: Stereo (1.03). Composer unknown. First released in 1994.

Cookin' (demo)
R: Pete Townshend's home studio, London, 1968. U.K./U.S.: *Scoop*. CD: *Scoop*. N: Stereo (3.18).

Cooks County
R: Turn Up-Down Studios, Surrey, England, June 1982. P: Glyn Johns. U.K./U.S.: *It's Hard*. CD: *It's Hard*. N: Stereo (3.52).

Cousin Kevin (John Entwistle)
R: IBC Studios, London, October 1968–March 1969. P: Kit Lambert. U.K./U.S.: *Tommy*. CD: *Tommy*. N: Stereo (4.07).

Cousin Kevin (live)
R: Radio City Music Hall, New York, or Universal Amphitheater, Los Angeles, 27 June or 24 August 1989 (venue specified as one or the other). P: Billy Nicholls. U.K./U.S.: *Join Together*. CD: *Join Together*. N: Stereo (3.56).

Cousin Kevin Model Child (John Entwistle)
R: IBC Studios, London, October 1968–March 1969. P: Kit Lambert. CD: *Odds and Sods*. N: Stereo (1.24). First released in 1998.

Cry If You Want
R: Turn Up-Down Studios, Surrey, England, June 1982. P: Glyn Johns. U.K./U.S.: *It's Hard*. CD: *It's Hard*. N: Stereo (5.18). CD version is 43 seconds longer than original album version.

Cry If You Want (live)
R: Maple Leaf Gardens, Toronto, 17 December 1982. P: Jon Astley. CD: *It's Hard*. N: Stereo (7.12). First released in 1997.

Cut My Hair
R: "The Kitchen," Ramport Studios, London, May–July 1973. P: The Who (Pete Townshend). U.K./U.S.: *Quadrophenia*. CD: *Quadrophenia*. N: Stereo (3.44). Featuring Chris Stainton (piano).

Cut My Hair (2)*
R: As above, with additional overdubs at Shepperton Studios, London, 1979. P: John Entwistle. N: Stereo. Excerpt used on *Quadrophenia* film soundtrack but not included on soundtrack album. Remixed with new bass guitar track.

Daddy Rolling Stone (Otis Blackwell)
Originally performed by Otis Blackwell, as a single A side (Vee Jay), 1953. R: IBC Studios, London, 13–14 April 1965. P: Shel Talmy. U.K.: Single B side of "Anyway Anyhow Anywhere" (Brunswick 05935), 21 May 1965. CD: *30 Years of Maximum R&B*. N: Mono/Stereo (2.48). Writing credit has sometimes been noted as Derek Martin, who also released a version in 1965.

Daily Records
R: Odyssey Studios, London, June–December 1980. P: Bill Szymczyk. U.K./U.S.: *Face Dances*. CD: *Face Dances*. N: Stereo (3.23).

Dance It Away (see *Dancing in the Street* [live])

Dancing in the Street (Stevenson/Gaye) (radio)*
Originally performed by Martha and the Vandellas as single A side (Gordy 7033), 31 July 1964. R: BBC Studios, London, 14 March 1966. B: *Saturday Club*, BBC Light Programme, 19 March 1966. N: Mono (2.20).

Dancing in the Street (live) (incorporating *Dance It Away*)
R: The Spectrum, Philadelphia, 11 December 1979. P: John Williams. U.K.: Single B side of "Won't Get Fooled Again" 12-inch EP reissue (Polydor POSPX917), June 1988. CD: CD single version of above (Polydor POCD 917), June 1988. N: Stereo (3.35). Edited from longer master.

Dangerous (John Entwistle)
R: Turn Up-Down Studios, Surrey, June 1982. P: Glyn Johns. U.K./U.S.: *It's Hard*. CD: *It's Hard*. N: Stereo (3.35). CD version is 20 seconds longer than original album version. Also available in U.S. as a single B side of "It's Hard" (Warner Bros. WB7-29731D) 1983.

Dangerous (live)
R: Maple Leaf Gardens, Toronto, Canada, 17 December 1982. P: Jon Astley. CD: *It's Hard*. N: Stereo (3.48). First released in 1997.

Did You Steal My Money?
R: Odyssey Studios, London, June–December 1980. P: Bill Szymczyk. U.K./U.S.: *Face Dances*. CD: *Face Dances*. N: Stereo (4.14).

Dig
R: Studio unknown, London, late 1988. P: Pete Townshend. U.K./U.S.: *The Iron Man*. CD: *The Iron Man*. N: Stereo (3.59).

Dig (live)
R: Universal Amphitheatre, Los Angeles, 24 August 1989. P: Billy Nicholls.

U.K./U.S.: *Join Together*. CD: *Join Together*. N: Stereo (3.46).

The Dirty Jobs
R: "The Kitchen," Ramport Studios, London, May–July 1973. P: The Who (Pete Townshend). U.K./U.S.: *Quadrophenia*. CD: *Quadrophenia*. N: Stereo (4.29).

Dirty Water (demo)
R: Pete Townshend's home studio, London, 1980. U.K./U.S.: *Scoop*. CD: *Scoop*. N: Stereo (2.06).

Disguises
R: Pye Studios, London, 14 June 1966. P: Kit Lambert. U.K.: *Ready Steady Who* EP (Reaction 592001), 11 November 1966. CD: *A Quick One*. N: Mono/Stereo (3.10).

Disguises (radio)*
R: BBC Studios, London, 13 September 1966. B: *Saturday Club*, BBC Light Programme, 17 September 1966. N: Mono (2.56).

Do the Strip (demo)*
R: Pete Townshend's home studio, London, 1965. N: Unreleased. A tongue-in-cheek dance-craze song.

Do You Think It's Alright?
R: IBC Studios, London, October 1968–March 1969. P: Kit Lambert. U.K./U.S.: *Tommy*. CD: *Tommy*. N: Stereo (0.24).

Do You Think It's Alright? (live)
R: Isle Of Wight Festival, England, 29 August 1970. P: Jon Astley/Andy Macpherson. CD: *Live at the Isle of Wight Festival 1970*. N: Stereo (0.21). First released in 1996.

Do You Think It's Alright? (live) (2)
R: Radio City Music Hall, New York, or Universal Amphitheatre, Los Angeles, 27 June or 24 August 1989 (venue specified as one or the other). P: Billy Nicholls. U.K./U.S.: *Join Together*. CD: *Join Together*. N: Stereo (0.23).

Do You Want Kids, Kids? (demo)*
R: Pete Townshend's home studio, London, 1968. N: Unreleased. An alternative song (see "Little Billy") for the American Cancer Society commission from early 1968. Although rumored, there has been no evidence that the Who ever completed a recording of this song.

Doctor Doctor (John Entwistle)
R: Ryemuse Studios, London, 7 April 1967. U.K.: Single B side of "Pictures of Lily" (Track 604 002), 22 April 1967. U.S.: Single B side of "Pictures Of Lily" (Decca 32156), June 1967. CD: *A Quick One*. N: Mono (2.59).

Dr. Jekyll and Mr. Hyde
R: Goldstar Studios, Los Angeles, U.S.A, 26 February 1968. P: Kit Lambert. U.S.: Single B side of "Call Me Lightning" (Decca 32288), 16 March 1968. CD: *Magic Bus—The Who on Tour*. N: Mono (2.24).

Dr. Jekyll and Mr. Hyde (2)
R: Goldstar Studios, Los Angeles, U.S.A, 26 February 1968. P: Kit Lambert. U.K.: Single B side of "Magic Bus" (Track 604 024), 18 September 1968. CD: *Rarities Vol. 1* and *Rarities Vol. 2*. N: Mono (2.35).

Doctor Jimmy (incorporating *Is It Me?*)
R: "The Kitchen," Ramport Studios, London, May–July 1973. P: The Who (Pete Townshend). U.K./U.S.: *Quadrophenia*. CD: *Quadrophenia*. N: Stereo (8.36). "Is It Me?" subtitled "John's Theme."

Doctor Jimmy (2) (incorporating *Is It Me?*)
R: As above, with additional overdubs at Shepperton Studios, London, 1979. P: John Entwistle. U.K./U.S.: *Quadrophenia* (Soundtrack). CD: *Quadrophenia* (Soundtrack). N: Stereo (7.32). Remixed, with new bass guitar track.

Doctor Jimmy (live)
R: Venue unspecified, U.S.A & Canada,

December 1982. P: Not credited. Compiled by Cy Langston. U.K./U.S.: *Who's Last*. CD: *Who's Last*. N: Stereo (4.35). First released in 1984.

Dogs
R: Advision Studio, London, 22 May 1968. P: Kit Lambert. U.K.: Single A side (Track 604 023), 15 June 1968. CD: *30 Years of Maximum R&B*. N: Mono/Stereo (3.01). Above set included the first stereo mix.

Dogs Part Two (Keith Moon/Towser/Jason)
R: IBC Studios, London, October 1968–March 1969. P: Kit Lambert. U.K.: Single B side of "Pinball Wizard" (Track 604 027), 7 March 1969. U.S.: Single B side of "Pinball Wizard" (Decca 732465) 22 March 1969. CD: *Two's Missing*. N: Stereo (2.26). U.S. Decca release credits this merely to Moon.

Don't Let Go the Coat
R: Odyssey Studios, London, June–December 1980. P: Bill Szymczyk. U.K./U.S.: *Face Dances*. CD: *Face Dances*. N: Stereo (3.45). D: *Another Scoop* (2.56).

Don't Look Away
R: IBC Studios, London, November 1966. P: Kit Lambert. U.K.: *A Quick One*. U.S.: *Happy Jack*. CD: *A Quick One*. N: Mono (2.51).

Double Pisces (Film Soundtrack) (demos)*
Main Theme. Bedroom Music. R: Pete Townshend's home studio, London, 1970. N: Mostly instrumental soundtrack music for the film directed by Dick Fontaine.

Dream Sequences (from *Tommy*)*
Pinball. Erotic. School. Lost Chord. N: Unreleased. These four instrumental links were originally scheduled for *Tommy*. It is likely that these were reconstituted as "Sparks" and "Underture."

Dreaming from the Waist
R: Ronnie Lane's mobile unit, Shepperton Studios, London, May 1975. P: Glyn Johns. U.K./U.S.: *By Numbers*. CD: *By Numbers*. N: Stereo (4.07). Originally titled "Control Myself." Also released as a single B side of "Slip Kid" in U.S. (MCA 40603), 7 August 1976.

Dreaming from the Waist (live)
R: Football ground, Swansea, 12 June 1976. P: Jon Astley. CD: *By Numbers*. N: Stereo (4.52). First released in 1994 on *30 Years of Maximum R&B* in a slightly shorter version.

Drowned
R: "The Kitchen," Ramport Studios, London, May–July 1973. P: The Who (Pete Townshend). U.K./U.S.: *Quadrophenia*. CD: *Quadrophenia*. N: Stereo (5.27). Featuring Chris Stainton (piano).

Early Morning Cold Taxi (Roger Daltrey/Cyrano Langston)
R: CBS Studios, London, 2 October 1967. P: Kit Lambert. CD: *Sell Out*. N: Stereo (2.55). First released in 1994.

Eel Pie Blues (demo)*
R: Pete Townshend's home studio, late 1960s. N: Unreleased R&B instrumental.

Electronic Tape Experiment (demo)*
R: Pete Townshend's home studio, London, 1970. N: Recorded during sessions for *Double Pisces* film.

Eminence Front
R: Turn Up-Down Studios, Surrey, England, June 1982. P: Glyn Johns. U.K./U.S.: *It's Hard*. CD: *It's Hard*. N: Stereo (5.39). Also released as a single in U.S. (Warner Bros. WB7-29814), December 1982.

Eminence Front (film)*
R: Rehearsal in U.S., September 1982. B: Promo film, October 1982. N: Stereo (5.25). Played live.

Eminence Front (live)
R: Maple Leaf Gardens, Toronto, 17

December 1982. P: Jon Astley. CD: *It's Hard*. N: Stereo (5.44). First released in 1997.

Eminence Front (live) (2)
R: Carter Finlay Stadium, Raleigh, North Carolina, 27 July 1989. P: Billy Nicholls. U.K./U.S.: *Join Together*. CD: *Join Together*. N: Stereo (5.43).

Empty Glass (originally titled *Choirboy*)
R: Ramport Studios, London, April 1978. P: Glyn Johns/Jon Astley. CD: *Who Are You*. N: Stereo (6.23). First released in 1996. Originally released on Pete Townshend's solo album *Empty Glass* (ATCO K50699), 14 April 1980.

Eyesight to the Blind (Sonny Boy Williamson) (aka *The Hawker*)
Originally performed by Sonny Boy Williamson as a single A side (Trumpet 129), 1951, though based on a later version by Mose Allison. R: IBC Studios, London, October 1968–March 1969. P: Kit Lambert. U.K./U.S.: *Tommy*. CD: *Tommy*. N: Stereo (2.14).

Eyesight to the Blind (2) (aka The Hawker)
R: IBC Studios, London, October 1968–March 1969. P: Kit Lambert. U.K./U.S.: *Tommy*. CD: *Tommy* (MFSL version). N: Stereo (2.14). This mix has an alternate lead vocal track from Roger Daltrey and was included on some pressings of the original album. This was also used on the earlier versions of the CD, but not on the definitive remixed version.

Eyesight to the Blind (live)
R: Isle of Wight Festival, England, 29 August 1970. P: Jon Astley/Andy Macpherson. CD: *Live at the Isle of Wight Festival 1970*. N: Stereo (1.59). First released in 1996.

Eyesight to the Blind (live) (2)
R: Radio City Music Hall, New York, or Universal Amphitheatre, Los Angeles, 27 June or 24 August 1989 (venue specified as one or the other). P: Billy Nicholls. U.K./U.S.: *Join Together*. CD: *Join Together*. N: Stereo (2.17).

Face the Face (live)
R: Jack Murphy Stadium, San Diego, 22 August 1989. P: Billy Nicholls. U.K./U.S.: *Join Together*. CD: *Join Together*. N: Stereo (6.03). Originally released on the Pete Townshend solo album *White City* (Atco 252 392-1), November 1985.

Faith in Something Bigger
R: CBS Studios, London, 4 January 1968. P: Kit Lambert. U.K./U.S.: *Odds And Sods*. CD: *Odds And Sods*. N: Stereo (2.59).

The Ferryman (Pete Townshend/Ted Astley) (demo)
R: Pete Townshend's home studio, London, September 1978. U.K./U.S.: *Another Scoop*. CD: *Another Scoop*. N: Stereo (5.40).

Fiddle About (John Entwistle)
R: IBC Studios, London, October 1968–March 1969. P: Kit Lambert. U.K./U.S.: *Tommy*. CD: *Tommy*. N: Stereo (1.30).

Fiddle About (live)
R: Isle of Wight Festival, England, 29 August 1970. P: Jon Astley/Andy Macpherson. CD: *Live at the Isle of Wight Festival 1970*. N: Stereo (1.14). First released in 1996.

Fiddle About (live) (2)
R: Radio City Music Hall, New York, or Universal Ampitheatre, Los Angeles, 27 June or 24 August 1989 (venue specified as one or the other). P: Billy Nicholls. U.K./U.S.: *Join Together*. CD: *Join Together*. N: Stereo (1.38).

Fight Until You're Mine (demo)*
R: Pete Townshend's home studio, London, 1974–1975. N: Stereo. Unrecorded by the Who, this was considered for the *By Numbers* album and rejected.

Fire (Arthur Brown/Vincent Crane)
Originally performed by the Crazy World of Arthur Brown as a single A side (Track 604 022), June 1968. R: Studio unknown, London, late 1988. P: Peter Wolf. U.K./U.S.: *The Iron Man*. CD: *The Iron Man*. N: Stereo (3.20).

5.15
R: "The Kitchen," Ramport Studios, London, 27 June 1973. P: The Who (Pete Townshend). U.K.: Single A side (Track 2094 115), 6 October 1973. U.S.: *Quadrophenia*. CD: *Quadrophenia*. N: Stereo (4.59). Featuring Chris Stainton (piano).

5.15 (2)
R: As above, with additional overdubs at Shepperton Studios, London, 1979. P: John Entwistle. U.K./U.S.: *Quadrophenia* (Soundtrack). CD: *Quadrophenia* (Soundtrack). N: Stereo (4.59). Remixed, with new bass guitar track. Also released as a single in U.K. (Polydor 2001 916), September 1979, and U.S. (Polydor 2022), September 1979.

5.15 (TV)*
R: BBC Television Studios, White City, London, 3 October 1973. B: *Top of the Pops*, BBC Television, 4 October 1973. N: Mono. Live performance mingled with backing tapes.

5.15 (live)
R: Carter Finlay Stadium, Raleigh, North Carolina, 27 July 1989. P: Billy Nicholls. U.K./U.S.: *Join Together*. CD: *Join Together*. N: Stereo (5.47).

Football Fugue (Pete Townshend/
Ted Astley) (demo)
R: Pete Townshend's home studio, London, September 1978. U.K./U.S.: *Another Scoop*. CD: *Another Scoop*. N: Stereo (3.25).

Fortune Teller (Naomi Neville)
Originally performed by Benny Spellman as single A side (London HLP 9570), 1962. R: Advision Studios, London, 29 May 1968. P: Kit Lambert. CD: *30 Years of Maximum R&B*. N: Stereo (2.18). First released in 1994.

Fortune Teller (live)
R: Leeds University, England, 14 February 1970. P: The Who (Pete Townshend). CD: *Live at Leeds*. N: Stereo (2.34). First released in 1995.

Four Faces
R: Shepperton Studios, London, 1979. P: John Entwistle. U.K./U.S.: *Quadrophenia* (Soundtrack). CD: *Quadrophenia* (Soundtrack). N: Stereo (3.21).

Get Out and Stay Out
R: Shepperton Studios, London, 1979. P: John Entwistle. U.K./U.S.: *Quadrophenia* (Soundtrack). CD: *Quadrophenia* (Soundtrack). N: Stereo (2.28).

*Getting in Tune**
R: Record Plant, New York, 18 March 1971. P: Kit Lambert/Felix Pappalardi. N: Stereo (7.04). Featuring Al Kooper (organ). Unreleased. Originally logged on tape box as "I'm in Tune."

Getting in Tune (2)
R: Olympic Studios, London, 7 June 1971. P: The Who/Glyn Johns. U.K./U.S.: *Who's Next*. CD: *Who's Next*. N: Stereo (4.50). Featuring Nicky Hopkins (piano).

*Girl from Lincoln County**
N: Unreleased. Composer unknown. Originally scheduled in 1968 as part of *Tommy*.

Girl in a Suitcase (demo)
R: Pete Townshend's home studio, London, 7 April 1975. U.K./U.S.: *Another Scoop*. CD: *Another Scoop*. N: Stereo (3.22).

Girl's Eyes (Keith Moon)
R: Sound Techniques Studios, London, October 1967. P: Kit Lambert. CD: *Sell Out*. N: Stereo (3.28). First released in 1994.

Glittering Girl
R: IBC Studios, London, April 1967.
CD: *Sell Out*. N: Mono (2.56) First released in 1995.

Glow Girl
R: De Lane Lea Studios, London, January 1968. P: Kit Lambert. U.K./U.S.: *Odds and Sods*. CD: *Odds and Sods*. N: Stereo (2.24).

Go to the Mirror!
R: IBC Studios, London, October 1968–March 1969. P: Kit Lambert. U.K./U.S.: *Tommy*. CD: *Tommy*. N: Stereo (3.50).

Go to the Mirror! (live)
R: Isle Of Wight Festival, England, 29 August 1970. P: Jon Astley/Andy Macpherson. CD: *Live at the Isle of Wight Festival 1970*. N: Stereo (3.29). First released in 1996.

Go to the Mirror! (live) (2).
R: Radio City Music Hall, New York, or Universal Amphitheatre, Los Angeles, 27 June or 24 August 1989 (venue specified as one or the other). P: Billy Nicholls. U.K./U.S.: *Join Together*. CD: *Join Together*. N: Stereo (3.21).

Goin' Fishin' (demo)
R: Pete Townshend's home studio, London, 1967. U.K./U.S.: *Scoop*. CD: *Scoop*. N: Stereo (2.53).

Going Down (Don Nix) (live)
Originally performed by Freddie King on the *Gettin' Ready* LP (Shelter SW-8905), 1971. R: Civic Center, San Francisco, 13 December 1971. U.K./U.S.: *Two's Missing*. CD: *Two Missing*. N: Stereo (3.41). First released in 1987. This title is sometimes given as "Goin' Down."

Going Mobile
R: Olympic Studios, London, May 1971. P: The Who/Glyn Johns. U.K./U.S.: *Who's Next*. CD: *Who's Next*. N: Stereo (3.42).

Good Lovin' (Clark/Resnick) (radio)*
Originally performed by the Olympics as single A side (Warner Bros. WB157), 1965. R: BBC Studios, London, 24 May 1965. B: *Saturday Club*, BBC Light Programme, 29 May 1965. N: Mono (1.50).

The Good's Gone
R: IBC Studios, London, October 1965. P: Shel Talmy. U.K.: *My Generation*. U.S.: *The Who Sings My Generation*. CD: *The Who Sings My Generation*. N: Mono (3.59). Also released as a single B side of "La-La-La-Lies" in U.K. (Brunswick 05968), 11 November 1966.

The Good's Gone (radio)*
R: BBC Studios, London, 22 November 1965. B: *Saturday Club*, BBC Light Programme, 27 November 1965. N: Mono (3.00).

Gratis Amatis (demo)*
R: Pete Townshend's home studio, London, April 1966. N: A ten-minute operatic parody. Unreleased.

*Great Shakes**
N: Advertisment from 1968. Composer unknown.

Greyhound Girl (demo)*
R: Pete Townshend's home studio, London, 1971. U.K.: Single B side of Pete Townshend's solo "Let My Love Open the Door" (Atco K11486), June 1980. N: Stereo.

Guitar and Pen
R: Ramport and RAK Studios, London, March 1978. P: Glyn Johns/Jon Astley. U.K./U.S.: *Who Are You*. CD: *Who Are You*. N: Stereo (5.57). Featuring Rod Argent (keyboards).

Guitar and Pen (2)
R: Ramport Studios, London, March 1978. P: Glyn Johns/Jon Astley. CD: *Who Are You* (MFSL version). N: Stereo (5.59). An alternative mix of the above with some different instrument parts. First released in 1992.

Guitar and Pen (Olympic '78 Mix) (3)
R: Ramport Studios, London, April

1978. P: Glyn Johns/Jon Astley. CD: *Who Are You*. N: Stereo (6.00). Alternate mix with different instrument parts. First released in 1996.

Had Enough (John Entwistle)
R: Olympic Studios, London, December 1977. P: Glyn Johns/Jon Astley. U.K.: Single B side "Who Are You" (Polydor 2121 361 WHO1), 14 July 1978. U.S.: Single B side "Who Are You" (MCA 40948), August 1978. CD: *Who Are You*. N: Stereo (4.30). Original single release of this song was cataloged as a "double" A side with "Who Are You."

Hall of the Mountain King (Edvard Grieg)
Adapted from "In the Hall of the Mountain King" from *Peer Gynt Suite No. 1* by Edvard Grieg. A pop arrangement had originally been released as "In the Hall of the Mountain King" by Nero and the Gladiators as a single A side (Decca F11367), July 1961. R: Kingsway Studio, London, October 1967. CD: *Sell Out*. N: Mono (4.14). Edited from a longer master.

Happy Jack
R: CBS Studios, London, 10 November 1966. P: Kit Lambert. U.K.: Single A side (Reaction 591010), 3 December 1966. U.S.: Single A side (Decca 32114), 18 March 1967. CD: *My Generation— The Very Best of the Who*. N: Mono (2.11). D: *Another Scoop* (2.04).

Happy Jack (2)
R: IBC Studios, London, November 1966. P: Kit Lambert. CD: *A Quick One*. N: Mono (2.51). Acoustic version. First released in 1995.

Happy Jack (radio)*
R: BBC Studios, London, 17 January 1967. B: *Saturday Club*, BBC Light Programme, 21 January 1967. N: Mono (2.10).

Happy Jack (live)
R: Monterey Pop Festival, U.S.A, 18 June 1967. CD: *The Monterey International Pop Festival*. N: Stereo. First released in 1992.

Happy Jack (Radio 1) (radio)
R: BBC Studios, London, 10 October 1967. B: *Top Gear* & *Saturday Club*, BBC Radio 1, 15 & 28 October 1967. CD: *30 Years Of Maximum R&B*. N: Mono (0.10). Jingle.

Happy Jack (live) (2)
R: Leeds University, 14 February 1970. P: The Who (Pete Townshend). U.K./U.S.: *The Kids Are Alright*. CD: *Live at Leeds*. N: Stereo (2.13). First released in 1979.

The Hawker (see *Eyesight to the Blind*)

Heat Wave (Holland/Dozier/Holland).
Originally performed by Martha and the Vandellas, single A side (Gordy 7022), 10 July 1963. R: IBC Studios, London, March 1965. P: Shel Talmy. CD: *Two's Missing*. N: Stereo (2.40). Featuring Nicky Hopkins (piano). This has been credited on Who releases as being one word, but on the original single it was separated into two, as above. Some later issues of this song by Martha and the Vandellas give the title as "(Love Is Like a) Heatwave." First released in 1985.

Heat Wave (2)
R: IBC Studios, London, August 1966. P: Kit Lambert. U.K.: *A Quick One*. CD: *A Quick One*. N: Mono (1.54). A shorter arrangement than above, omitting the last verse.

Heaven and Hell (John Entwistle) (live)
R: Leeds University, 14 February 1970. P: The Who (Pete Townshend). CD: *Live at Leeds*. N: Stereo (4.30). First released in 1995.

Heaven and Hell (radio)
R: IBC Studios, London, 13 April 1970.

B: *Dave Lee Travis Show*, BBC Radio 1, 19 April 1970. N: Mono (3.30).

Heaven and Hell
R: IBC Studios, London, 13 April 1970. P: The Who. U.K.: Single B side of "Summertime Blues" (Track 2094 002), 10 July 1970. U.S.: Single B side of "Summertime Blues" (Decca 32708), 11 July 1970. CD: *30 Years of Maximum R&B*. N: Mono (3.33). This is basically a slightly different mix to the broadcast version above.

Heaven and Hell (live) (2)
R: Isle of Wight Festival, England, 29 August 1970. P: Jon Astley/Andy Macpherson. CD: *Live at the Isle of Wight Festival 1970*. N: Stereo (4.43). First released in 1996.

Heinz Baked Beans (John Entwistle)
R: Kingsway Studios, London, 11 October 1967. P: Kit Lambert. U.K./U.S.: *Sell Out*. CD: *Sell Out*. N: Mono/Stereo (0.57).

Helpless Dancer
R: "The Kitchen," Ramport Studios, London, May–July 1973. P: The Who (Pete Townshend). U.K./U.S.: *Quadrophenia*. CD: *Quadrophenia*. N: Stereo (2.34). Subtitled "Roger's Theme."

Helpless Dancer (2)
R: As above, with additional overdubs at Shepperton Studios, London, 1979. P: John Entwistle. U.K./U.S.: *Quadrophenia* (Soundtrack). CD: *Quadrophenia* (Soundtrack). N: Stereo (0.23). Remixed, final segment of song only.

Here for More (Roger Daltrey)
R: IBC Studios, London, January 1970. P: The Who. U.K.: Single B side of "The Seeker" (Track 604 036), 21 March 1970. U.S.: Single B side of "The Seeker" (Decca 32670), April 1970. CD: *Who's Missing*. N: Stereo (2.25).

Here 'Tis (Ellas McDaniel)
Originally performed by Bo Diddley and released on the *Hey Bo Diddley* LP (Checker 860), 1960. R: Fontana Studios, London, June 1964. P: Chris Parmeinter/Peter Meaden. CD: *30 Years of Maximum R&B*. N: Stereo (2.08). This was mixed for the boxed set into stereo and edited from a longer master tape.

Holly Like Ivy (demo)
R: Pete Townshend's home studio, London, October 1982. U.K./U.S.: *Another Scoop*. CD: *Another Scoop*. N: Stereo (2.51).

How Can You Do It Alone (live)
R: International Amphitheatre, Chicago, 8 December 1979. P: Jon Astley. CD: *Face Dances*. N: Stereo (5.24). It should be noted that despite some lyrical similarities, this is an entirely different song from the entry below. First released in 1997.

How Can You Do It Alone
R: Odyssey Studios, London, June–December 1980. P: Bill Szymczyk. U.K./U.S.: *Face Dances*. CD: *Face Dances*. N: Stereo (5.24).

How Many Friends
R: Ronnie Lane's mobile unit, Shepperton Studios, London, 28 May 1975. P: Glyn Johns. U.K./U.S.: *By Numbers*. CD: *By Numbers*. N: Stereo (4.05). Featuring Nicky Hopkins (piano).

However Much I Booze
R: Ronnie Lane's mobile unit, Shepperton Studios, London, 7 May 1975. P: Glyn Johns. U.K./U.S.: *By Numbers*. CD: *By Numbers*. N: Stereo (5.02).

I Always Say (demo)*
R: Pete Townshend's home studio, London, circa 1967–1968. N: Rejected by the Who and described by Pete as a "Twickenham soul" song. Unreleased.

I Am the Sea
R: "The Kitchen," Ramport Studios, London, May–July 1973. P: The Who (Pete Townshend). U.K./U.S.: *Quadrophenia*. CD: *Quadrophenia*. N: Stereo (2.09).

I Am the Sea (2)
R: As above, with additional overdubs at Shepperton Studios, London, 1979. P: John Entwistle. U.K./U.S.: *Quadrophenia* (Soundtrack). CD: *Quadrophenia* (Soundtrack). N: Stereo (2.31). Remixed from the above master. Version featured in film is reedited.

I Can See for Miles
R: Talent Masters Studios, New York; Goldstar Studios, Los Angeles; CBS Studios, London; September 1967. P: Kit Lambert. U.K.: Single A side (Track 604 011), 14 October 1967. U.S.: Single A side (Decca 32206), 14 October 1967. CD: *Sell Out*. N: Stereo (4.18).

I Can See for Miles (radio)
R: BBC Studios, London, 10 October 1967. B: *Top Gear* and *Saturday Club*, BBC Radio 1, 15 and 28 October 1967. U.K.: *The Singles*. CD: *The Singles*. N: Mono/stereo (3.55). As version above but with different (much louder) bass track. Stereo version was probably included on the above compilation by mistake! First released in 1984.

I Can See for Miles (live)
R: Universal Amphitheatre, Los Angeles, 24 August 1989. P: Billy Nicholls. U.K./U.S.: *Join Together*. CD: *Join Together*. N: Stereo (3.42). Also released in U.K. as part of *Join Together* EP (Virgin VS 1259), March 1990.

I Can See for Miles (TV)*
R: South Bank Television Centre, London, March 1990. B: *Aspel & Company*, ITV TV, 10 March 1990. N: Stereo (3.36). Live vocals over a prerecorded backing track.

I Can't Explain
R: Pye Studios, London, December 1964. P: Shel Talmy. U.K.: Single A side (Brunswick 05926), 15 January 1965. U.S.: Single A side (Decca 31725), February 1965. CD: *My Generation—The Very Best of the Who*. N: Mono (2.03). Featuring the Ivy League (backing vocals). Jimmy Page was present at the session as second guitarist, but it has never been established whether or not he appears on the version here released.

I Can't Explain (live) (TV)
R: Fifth National Jazz and Blues Festival, Richmond, 6 August 1965. B: *Shindig*, U.S. TV, 6 October 1965 and 6 January 1966. U.K./U.S.: *The Kids Are Alright*. CD: *The Kids Are Alright*. N: Mono (2.01). This sound recording was made at the concert, had audience screams and applause added to it, and was later dubbed onto studio runthrough for final *Shindig* broadcast as above.

I Can't Explain (live)
R: Leeds University, 14 February 1970. P: The Who (Pete Townshend). CD: *Live at Leeds*. N: Stereo (2.16). First released in 1995.

I Can't Explain (live) (2)
R: Isle of Wight Festival, 29 August 1970. P: Jon Astley/Andy Macpherson. CD: *Live at the Isle of Wight Festival 1970*. N: Stereo (2.12). First released in 1996.

I Can't Explain (film)
R: Rehearsal, Rainbow Theatre, London, May 1979. B: *Nationwide*, BBC-TV, 11 May 1979. N: Mono (1.44). Excerpt.

I Can't Explain (live) (3)
R: Venue unspecified, U.S. and Canada, December 1982. P: Not credited. Compiled by Cy Langston. U.K./U.S.: *Who's Last*. CD: *Who's Last*. N: Stereo (2.27). First released in 1984. Also released in U.K. as single B side (MCA 927), November 1984.

I Can't Reach You
R: Talent Masters Studios, New York, July 1967. P: Kit Lambert. U.K./U.S.: *Sell Out*. CD: *Sell Out*. N: Mono/Stereo (3.03).

I Can't Reach You (radio)*
R: BBC Studios, London, 10 October 1967. B: *Top Gear* and *Saturday Club*, BBC Radio 1, 15 & 28 October 1967. N: Mono.

I Don't Even Know Myself
R: Eel Pie Studios, London, April–May 1970. P: The Who (Pete Townshend). N: Projected EP release. Unreleased.

I Don't Even Know Myself (TV)*
R: BBC Television Centre, 30 December 1970. B: *Into 71*, BBC-TV, 31 December 1970. N: Live vocals over a rerecorded backing track.

I Don't Even Know Myself (2)
R: Olympic Studios, London, May 1971. P: The Who/Glyn Johns. U.K.: Single B side of "Won't Get Fooled Again" (Track 2094 009), 25 June 1971. U.S.: Single B side of "Won't Get Fooled Again" (Decca 32846), July 1971. CD: *Who's Next*. N: Stereo (4.54). Title has been given variously as "I Don't Know Myself" and "Don't Even Know Myself" on different pressings.

I Don't Even Know Myself (live)
R: Isle of Wight Festival, England, 29 August 1970. P: Jon Astley/Andy Macpherson. CD: *Live at the Isle of Wight Festival 1970*. N: Stereo (5.03). First released in 1996.

I Don't Mind (James Brown)
Originally performed by James Brown and released as a single A side (King 5466), April 1961. R: IBC Studios, London, 11 March 1965. P: Shel Talmy. U.K.: *My Generation*. U.S.: *The Who Sings My Generation*. CD: *The Who Sings My Generation*. N: Mono (2.32). Features Nicky Hopkins (piano).

I Like Nightmares
R: Odyssey Studios, London, June–December 1980. P: Bill Szymczyk. CD: *Face Dances*. N: Stereo (3.09). First released in 1997.

I Saw Her Standing There (Lennon/McCartney) (film)*
Originally performed by the Beatles on the LP *Please Please Me* (Parlophone CDP7 46435 2), March 1963. R: Shepperton Studios rehearsal, London, late 1977. N: Stereo (3.21). Soundtrack for outtake footage from *The Kids Are Alright*. Unreleased.

I'm a Boy
R: IBC Studios, London, 1 August 1966. P: Kit Lambert. U.K.: Single A side (Reaction 591004), 26 August 1966. U.S.: Single A side (Decca 32058), December 1966. CD: *My Generation—The Very Best of the Who*. N: Mono (2.36).

I'm a Boy (2)
R: London, September 1966. P: Kit Lambert. U.K./U.S.: *Meaty Beaty Big & Bouncy*. CD: *Meaty Beaty Big & Bouncy*. N: Mono (3.42). First released in 1971.

I'm a Boy (3)*
R: London, late 1966. N: Instrumental version with elaborate brass arrangement. Unreleased.

I'm a Boy (radio)*
R: BBC Studios, London, 13 September 1966. B: *Saturday Club*, BBC Light Programme, 17 September 1966. N: Mono (2.37).

I'm a Boy (live)
R: Leeds University, 14 February 1970. P: The Who (Pete Townshend). CD: *Live at Leeds*. N: Stereo (2.40).

I'm a Man (Ellas McDaniel)
Originally performed by Bo Diddley and released with "Bo Diddley" as double A-sided single (Checker 814), July 1955. R: IBC Studios, London, 11 March 1965. P: Shel Talmy. U.K.: *My Generation*. CD: *Two's Missing*. N: Mono/stereo (3.09). Features Nicky Hopkins (piano). CD release included stereo mix.

I'm a Man (live)
R: Radio City Music Hall, New York, 27

June 1989. P: Jon Astley. CD: *30 Years of Maximum R&B*. N: Stereo (6.11).

I'm Free
R: IBC Studios, London, October 1968–March 1969. P: Kit Lambert. U.K./U.S.: *Tommy*. CD: *Tommy*. N: Stereo (2.40). Also released as single A side in U.S. (Decca 732519), 5 July 1969, and in U.K. as part of *Tommy* EP (Track 2252 001), 7 November 1970.

I'm Free (radio)*
R: IBC Studios, London, 13 April 1970. B: *Dave Lee Travis Show*, BBC Radio 1, 19 April 1970. N: Mono (2.25).

I'm Free (live)
R: Isle of Wight Festival, 29 August 1970. P: Jon Astley/Andy Macpherson. CD: *Live at the Isle of Wight Festival 1970*. N: Stereo (2.24). First released in 1996.

I'm Free (live) (2)
R: Radio City Music Hall, New York, or Universal Ampitheatre, Los Angeles, 27 June or 24 August 1989 (venue specified as one or the other). P: Billy Nicholls. U.K./U.S.: *Join Together*. CD: *Join Together*. N: Stereo (2.09).

I'm in Tune (see *Getting in Tune*)

I'm One
R: "The Kitchen," Ramport Studios, London, May–July 1973. P: The Who (Pete Townshend). U.K./U.S.: *Quadrophenia*. CD: *Quadrophenia*. N: Stereo (2.38).

I'm One (2)
R: As above, with additional overdubs at Shepperton Studios, London, 1979. P: John Entwistle. U.K./U.S.: *Quadrophenia* (Soundtrack). CD: *Quadrophenia* (Soundtrack). N: Stereo (2.40). Remixed, with new bass guitar track and piano. Also released as single B side in U.K. (Polydor 2001 916), and in U.S. (Polydor 2022), September 1979.

I'm the Face (Peter Meaden)
Based on "I've Got Love If You Want It," originally written and performed by Slim Harpo as single B side of "I'm a King Bee" (Excello 2113), 1957. R: Fontana Studios, London, June 1964. P: Chris Parmeinter, Peter Meaden. U.K.: Single A side (Fontana TF480), 3 July 1964. CD: *Odds and Sods*. N: Mono (2.32). Featuring an unidentified session piano player. This was remixed for boxed set into stereo (2.27), which fades out prematurely.

I Need You (Keith Moon)
R: Pye Studios, London, October 1966. P: Kit Lambert. U.K.: *A Quick One*. U.S.: *Happy Jack*. CD: *A Quick One*. N: Mono (2.14).

Imagine a Man
R: Ronnie Lane's mobile unit, Shepperton Studios, London, 29 May 1975. P: Glyn Johns. U.K./U.S.: *By Numbers*. CD: *By Numbers*. N: Stereo (4.00). Featuring Nicky Hopkins (piano).

In a Hand or a Face
R: Ronnie Lane's mobile unit, Shepperton Studios, London, 27 May 1975. P: Glyn Johns. U.K./U.S.: *By Numbers*. CD: *By Numbers*. N: Stereo (3.23). Originally titled "Round and Round."

In the City
R: IBC Studios, London, August 1966. P: Kit Lambert. U.K.: Single B side of "I'm a Boy" (Reaction 591004), 26 August 1966. U.S.: Single B side of "I'm a Boy" (Decca 32058), December 1966. CD: *A Quick One*. N: Mono (2.21).

Initial Machine Experiments (demo)
R: Pete Townshend's home studio, London, 1979. U.K./U.S.: *Scoop*. CD: *Scoop*. N: Stereo (1.51).

Instant Party (see *Circles*)

Is It in My Head?
R: Olympic Studios, London, May–July 1972. P: The Who/Glyn Johns. U.K./U.S.: *Quadrophenia*. CD: *Quadrophenia*. N: Stereo (3.43).

Is It in My Head? (2)*
R: As above, with additional overdubs at Shepperton Studios, London, 1979. P: John Entwistle. N: Stereo. Excerpt used on *Quadrophenia* film soundtrack but not included on soundtrack album. Remixed with new bass guitar track.

Is It Me? (see Doctor Jimmy)

*It Was You**
R: Barry Gray's studio, London, late 1963 or early 1964. N: Also rumored to exist as a demo acetate by the High Numbers recorded in 1964. First released by the Naturals as single A side (Parlophone R5202), November 1964.

It's a Boy
R: IBC Studios, London, October 1968–March 1969. P: Kit Lambert. U.K./U.S.: *Tommy*. CD: *Tommy*. N: Stereo (0.39).

It's a Boy (live)
R: Isle of Wight Festival, England, 29 August 1970. P: Jon Astley/Andy Macpherson. CD: *Live at the Isle of Wight Festival 1970*. N: Stereo (1.33). First released in 1996.

It's a Boy (live) (2)
R: Radio City Music Hall, New York, or Universal Ampitheatre, Los Angeles, 27 June or 24 August 1989 (venue specified as one or the other). P: Billy Nicholls. U.K./U.S.: *Join Together*. CD: *Join Together*. N: Stereo. Incorporated into track "Overture" and not separately indexed or timed.

It's Alright (demo)*
R: Pete Townshend's home studio, London, circa 1965 or early 1966. N: Unrecorded by the Who. Originally released as a single A side by the Rockin' Vicars (CBS 202051), March 1966. This is very much a derivation of "The Kids Are Alright."

It's Hard
R: Turn Up-Down Studios, Surrey, June 1982. P: Glyn Johns. U.K./U.S.: *It's Hard*. CD: *It's Hard*. N: Stereo (3.47). Also released as a single A side (Warner Bros. WB7-29731D), 1983.

It's Hard (live)
R: Maple Leaf Gardens, Toronto, Canada, 17 December 1982. P: Jon Astley. CD: *It's Hard*. N: Stereo (4.56). First released in 1997.

It's in You
R: Odyssey Studios, London, June–December 1980. P: Bill Szymczyk. CD: *Face Dances*. N: Stereo (4.59). Many of the initial pressings of this CD had a mastering error that caused this track to skip during the first verse. First released in 1997.

It's Not True
R: IBC Studios, London, October 1965. P: Shel Talmy. U.K.: *My Generation*. U.S.: *The Who Sings My Generation*. CD: *The Who Sings My Generation*. N: Mono (2.30). Features Nicky Hopkins (piano).

It's Your Turn (John Entwistle)
R: Turn Up-Down Studios, Surrey, England, June 1982. P: Glyn Johns. U.K./U.S.: *It's Hard*. CD: *It's Hard*. N: Stereo (3.39). Featuring Andy Fairweather-Low (rhythm guitar). Also released in U.S. as single B side of "Athena" (Warner Bros. WBS7-29905), 25 September 1982.

I've Been Away (John Entwistle)
R: Regent Sound Studios, London, September 1966. P: Kit Lambert. U.K.: Single B side of "Happy Jack" (Reaction 591010), 3 December 1966. CD: *A Quick One*. N: Mono/Stereo (2.07).

I've Had Enough
R: "The Kitchen," Ramport Studios, London, May–July 1973. P: The Who (Pete Townshend). U.K./U.S.: *Quadrophenia*. CD: *Quadrophenia*. N: Stereo (6.14).

I've Had Enough (2)
R: As above, with additional overdubs at Shepperton Studios, London, 1979. P: John Entwistle. U.K./U.S.: *Quadrophenia*

(Soundtrack). CD: *Quadrophenia* (Soundtrack). N: Stereo (6.12). Remixed, with new bass guitar track.

I've Known No War
R: Turn Up-Down Studios, Surrey, England, June 1982. P: Glyn Johns. U.K./U.S.: *It's Hard*. CD: *It's Hard*. N: Stereo (5.56). CD version is 13 seconds longer than original album version.

Jaguar
R: IBC Studios, London, November 1967. P: Kit Lambert. CD: *Sell Out*. N: Mono (2.51). First released in 1995 on boxed set in an edited version (2.03).

Jingle Bells (TV)*
R: London, late 1965. B: *Ready Steady Go!* and *The New Year Starts Here!* ITV TV, 24 and 31 December 1965. N: Mono. An ad-hoc instrumental tune with John Entwistle playing the French horn. Thought to come from one of the above TV broadcasts.

Join My Gang (demo)*
R: Pete Townshend's home studio, London, 1966. N: Unrecorded by the Who. Originally released by Oscar as a single A side (Reaction 591006), September 1966.

Join Together
R: Olympic Studios, London, 22 May 1972. P: The Who/Glyn Johns. U.K.: Single A side (Track 2094 102), 17 June 1972. U.S.: Single A side (Decca 32983), 8 July 1972. CD: *My Generation—The Very Best of the Who*. N: Stereo (4.22). Above CD is a remixed version. While compiling *Odds and Sods*, John Entwistle reported the existence of an unreleased version of "Join Together" that was significantly longer than the single. This has never emerged, and it may be that Entwistle was confusing it with "Relay," which does indeed exist in a longer alternate version.

Join Together (live)*
R: Pontiac Silverdome, Detroit, Michigan, 6 December 1975. U.K./U.S.: *The Kids Are Alright*. N: Stereo (4.09). First part of a medley with "Road Runner" and "My Generation Blues."

Join Together (live) (2)
R: Jack Murphy Stadium, San Diego, 22 August 1989. P: Billy Nicholls. U.K./U.S.: *Join Together*. CD: *Join Together*. N: Stereo (5.14). Also released as part of EP (Virgin VS 1259), March 1990.

Join Together (TV)*
R: South Bank Television Centre, London, March 1990. B: *Aspel & Company*, ITV TV, 10 March 1990. N: Stereo (4.35). Live vocals over a prerecorded backing track.

Joker James
R: Shepperton Studios, London, 1979. P: John Entwistle. U.K./U.S.: *Quadrophenia* (Soundtrack). CD: *Quadrophenia* (Soundtrack). N: Stereo (3.14). This song was written in the mid–1960s.

Just You and Me, Darling (James Brown) (radio)*
Originally performed by James Brown and released as B side of "I Love You, Yes I Do" (King 5547), September 1961. R: BBC Studios, London, 24 May 1965. B: *Saturday Club*, BBC Light Programme, 29 May 1965. N: Mono (2.00).

*Keep on Working**
R: Ramport Studios, London, 1977–1978. P: Glyn Johns/Jon Astley. N: Stereo. Unreleased. A version of this was reportedly completed for *Who Are You*. Originally released on Pete Townshend's solo album *Empty Glass* (ATCO K50699), 14 April 1980.

The Kids Are Alright
R: IBC Studios, London, 14 October 1965. P: Shel Talmy. U.K.: *My Generation*. U.S.: *The Who Sings My Generation*. CD: *30 Years of Maximum R&B*. N: Mono (3.05). Edited to (2.42) for U.S. release. Also released as single A side in U.K. (Brunswick 05965), 12 August 1966, and in U.S. (Decca 31988), July 1966. D: *Another Scoop* (2.54).

*The Kids Are Alright (TV)**
R: London, late 1965. B: *Ready Steady Go!* and *The New Year Starts Here!* ITV TV, 24 and 31 December 1965. N: Mono. A live performance thought to come from one of the above TV broadcasts.

Kill My Appetite (demo)*
R: Pete Townshend's home studio, London, circa 1965. N: Rejected by the Who. Remains unreleased.

Ladies in the Female Jail (see *Riot in the Female Jail*)

La-La-La-Lies
R: IBC Studios, London, October 1965. P: Shel Talmy. U.K.: *My Generation*. U.S.: *The Who Sings My Generation*. CD: *The Who Sings My Generation*. N: Mono (2.12) Features Nicky Hopkins (piano). Also released in U.K. as single A side (Brunswick 05968), 11 November 1966. D: *Another Scoop* (2.20)

La-La-La-Lies (radio)*
R: BBC Studios, London, 22 November 1965. B: *Saturday Club*, BBC Light Programme, 27 November 1965. N: Mono (2.12).

The Last Time (Mick Jagger/Keith Richard)
First performed by the Rolling Stones as single A side (Decca F12104), February 1965. R: De Lane Lea Studios, London, 29 June 1967. U.K.: Single A side (Track 604 006), 30 June 1967. CD: *30 Years of Maximum R&B*. N: Mono (2.59).

Lazy Fat People (demo)*
R: Pete Townshend's home studio, London, 1966. N: Unrecorded by the Who. First released by the Barron Knights as a single A side (Columbia DB 8161), April 1967.

Leaving Here
 (Holland/Dozier/Holland)
Originally performed by Eddie Holland and released as single A side (Motown 1052), 19 December 1963. R: Fontana Studios, London, June 1964. P: Chris Parmeinter/Peter Meaden. CD: *30 Years of Maximum R&B*. N: Stereo (2.46). Featuring an unidentified session piano player. First release in 1985 on *Who's Missing* that had a very severe and artificial stereo mix with the drums exclusively through the right channel. The boxed set presented a better stereo mix.

Leaving Here (2)
R: Pye Studios, London, late 1964. CD: *Odds and Sods*. N: Mono (2.12). This is thought to come from a test session recorded for Pye Records in London and exists only as a Pye acetate disk. In 1996 Jon Astley made a digital copy of this disk for its first release in 1998.

Leaving Here (radio)*
R: BBC Studios, London, 24 May 1965. B: *Saturday Club*, BBC Light Programme, 29 May 1965. N: Mono (2.35).

A Legal Matter
R: IBC Studios, London, October 1965. P: Shel Talmy. U.K.: *My Generation*. U.S.: *The Who Sings My Generation*. CD: *30 Years of Maximum R&B*. N: Mono (2.46). Featuring Nicky Hopkins (piano). Also released in U.K. as single A side (Brunswick 05956), 11 March 1966, and as B side of "The Kids Are Alright" in U.S. (Decca 31988), July 1966.

Let's See Action
R: Olympic Studios, London, 20 June 1971. P: The Who/Glyn Johns. U.K.: Single A side (Track 2094 012), 15 October 1971. CD: *My Generation—The Very Best of the Who*. N: Stereo (3.54). Featuring Nicky Hopkins (piano). D: *Who Came First* (6.21).

Like It the Way It Is (demo)*
R: Pete Townshend's home studio, London, 1977. N: Stereo. Unreleased.

Little Billy
R: IBC Studios, London, 11 February

1968. P: Kit Lambert. U.K./U.S.: *Odds and Sods*. CD: *Odds and Sods*. N: Stereo (2.17).

A Little Is Enough (live)
R: Silverdome, Pontiac, Detroit, Michigan, 25 July 1989. P: Billy Nicholls. U.K./U.S.: *Join Together*. CD: *Join Together*. N: Stereo (5.05). First released on the Pete Townshend solo album *Empty Glass* (Acto K50699), 14 April 1980.

The Lone Ranger (Film Soundtrack) (demo)*
(1) Main Theme (aka "Spanish Foot"). (2) Title Music. (3) Swimming Pool Sequence. (4) Frankenstein Sequence. R: Pete Townshend's home studio, London, 1968. N: Mostly instrumental soundtrack music for an experimental short 1968 film by Richard Stanley.

Long Live Rock
R: Olympic Studios, London, 5 June 1972. P: The Who/Glyn Johns. U.K./U.S.: *Odds and Sods*. CD: *Odds and Sods*. N: Stereo (3.56). First released in a version by Billy Fury on the soundtrack album of *That'll Be the Day* (Ronco MR2002/3), April 1973. D: *Another Scoop* (3.45).

Long Live Rock (TV)*
R: BBC Television Centre, London, January 1973. B: *Old Grey Whistle Test*, BBC-TV, 30 January 1973. N: Mono (3.52). Live vocals over a prerecorded backing track.

Long Live Rock (live) (incorporating *Long Live Rock* [Reprise])
R: Venue unspecified, U.S. and Canada, December 1982. P: Not credited. Compiled by Cy Langston. U.K./U.S.: *Who's Last*. CD: *Who's Last*. N: Stereo (3.35) and (1.30). First released in 1984.

Love Ain't for Keeping
R: Record Plant, New York, 17 March 1971. P: Kit Lambert/Felix Papparlardi. CD: *Odds and Sods*. N: Stereo (4.03). Featuring Leslie West (guitar). First released in 1998.

Love Ain't for Keeping (2)
R: Olympic Studios, London, May 1971. P: The Who/Glyn Johns. U.K./U.S.: *Who's Next*. CD: *Who's Next*. N: Stereo (2.10).

Love Is Coming Down
R: Ramport Studios, London, 18 October 1977. P: Glyn Johns/Jon Astley. U.K./U.S.: *Who Are You*. CD: *Who Are You*. N: Stereo (4.05). String arrangement by Ted Astley.

Love Is Coming Down (Work-in-Progress Mix) (2)
R: Ramport Studios, London, April 1978. P: Glyn Johns/Jon Astley. CD: *Who Are You*. N: Stereo (4.06). Alternate mix of above, with different piano, bass and vocal parts. First released in 1996.

Love Reign o'er Me
R: Olympic Studios, London, 8 June 1972. P: The Who/Glyn Johns. U.K.: *Quadrophenia*. U.S.: Single A side (MCA 40152), 27 October 1973. CD: *Quadrophenia*. N: Stereo (5.58). D: *Scoop* (4.56).

Love Reign o'er Me (2)
R: As above, with additional overdubs at Shepperton Studios, London, 1979. P: John Entwistle. U.K./U.S.: *Quadrophenia* (Soundtrack). CD: *Quadrophenia* (Soundtrack). N: Stereo (5.11). Remixed, with new bass guitar track.

Love Reign o'er Me (live)
R: Venue unspecified, U.S. and Canada, December 1982. P: Not credited. Compiled by Cy Langston. U.K./U.S.: *Who's Last*. CD: *Who's Last*. N: Stereo (4.39). First released in 1984.

Love Reign o'er Me (live) (2)
R: Universal Amphitheatre, Los Angeles, 24 August 1989. P: Billy Nicholls. U.K./U.S.: *Join Together*. CD: *Join Together*. N: Stereo (5.58).

Lubie (Come Back Home) (Paul Revere/Mark Lindsey)
Originally performed by Paul Revere and the Raiders (Columbia), further details unknown. R: IBC Studios, London, 11 March 1965. P: Shel Talmy. CD: *Who's Missing.* N: Stereo (3.36). Featuring Nicky Hopkins (piano). First released in 1985.

Magic Bus
R: IBC Studios, London, April 1967 (?). P: Kit Lambert. U.K.: Single A side (Track 604 024), 18 September 1968. U.S.: Single A side (Decca 32362), 27 July 1968. CD: *My Generation—The Very Best of the Who.* N: Mono/stereo (3.36). First released by Pudding as a single A side (Decca F12603), April 1967. Stereo version appeared on *Magic Bus—The Who on Tour* LP, while a version with an intro four seconds longer appeared on the LP/CD *The Singles.* Featuring Jess Roden (backing vocals). D: *Scoop* (4.20).

Magic Bus (2)
R: IBC Studios, London, April 1967 (?). P: Kit Lambert. U.K./U.S.: *Meaty Beaty Big & Bouncy.* CD: *Meaty Beaty Big & Bouncy.* N: Mono (4.28). Featuring Jess Roden (backing vocals). First released in 1971.

Magic Bus (live)
Magic Bus (6.25). Improvisation (0.58). R: Leeds University, England, 14 February 1970. P: The Who (Pete Townshend). U.K./U.S.: *Live at Leeds.* CD: *Live at Leeds.* N: Stereo (7.22).

Magic Bus (live) (2)
Magic Bus (3.30). Improvisation (0.39). R: Isle of Wight Festival, England, 29 August 1970. P: Jon Astley/Andy Macpherson. CD: *Live at the Isle of Wight Festival 1970.* N: Stereo (4.09). First released in 1996.

Magic Bus (live) (3)
R: Venue unspecified, U.S. and Canada, December 1982. P: Not credited. Compiled by Cy Langston. U.K./U.S.: *Who's Last.* CD: *Who's Last.* N: Stereo (6.49). First released in 1984.

Man with Money (Don & Phil Everly) (radio)*
Originally performed by the Everly Brothers and released on the LP *Beat and Soul* (Warner Bros. W1605), 1965. R: BBC Studios, London, 14 March 1966. B: *Saturday Club*, BBC Light Programme, 19 March 1966. N: Mono (2.35).

Man with Money
R: IBC Studios, London, August 1966. P: Kit Lambert. CD: *A Quick One.* N: Stereo (2.45). First released in 1995.

A Man Is a Man
R: Turn Up-Down Studios, Surrey, England, June 1982. P: Glyn Johns. U.K./U.S.: *It's Hard.* CD: *It's Hard.* N: Stereo (3.56). Also released in U.K. as single B side of "Athena" (Polydor WHO6), 25 September 1982.

*Mary**
R: Olympic Studios, London, May 1971. P: The Who/Glyn Johns. N: Stereo. Unreleased. D: *Scoop* (3.19). This is thought to have been recorded, but no tape remains in the Who archives.

Mary Anne with the Shaky Hand
R: Talent Masters Studios, New York, 6 August 1967. P: Kit Lambert. U.S.: Single B side of "I Can See for Miles" (Decca 32206), 14 October 1967. CD: *Two's Missing.* N: Mono (3.16).

Mary Anne with the Shaky Hand (2)
R: Talent Masters Studios, New York, 6 August 1967. P: Kit Lambert. CD: *Odds and Sods.* N: Stereo (3.21). Featuring Al Kooper (organ). Mix almost identical mix to above but with organ very prominent. First released in 1998.

Mary Anne with the Shaky Hand (3)
R: Talent Masters Studios, New York, 7 August 1967. P: Kit Lambert. CD: *Sell Out.* N: Mono (3.19). Featuring Al Kooper (organ). First released in 1995.

Mary Anne with the Shaky Hand (4)
R: De Lane Lea Studios, London, 24 October 1967. P: Kit Lambert. U.S./U.K.: *Sell Out*. CD: *Sell Out*. N: Mono/stereo (2.04). Mono mix has vocal flutter on final lines.

Medac
R: Kingsway Studios, London, October 1967. P: Kit Lambert. U.K./U.S.: *Sell Out*. CD: *Sell Out*. N: Stereo (0.57). Titled "Spotted Henry" on U.S. LP version.

Meher Baba M3 (demo)
R: Pete Townshend's home studio, London, 1970–1971. CD: *PsychoDerelict*. N: Stereo (3.32). Recorded as a *Lifehouse* demo and later reworked as Townshend solo track. This and the following two tracks are taken from a sequence of synthesizer pieces all titled "Meher Baba" and numbered.

Meher Baba M4 (Signal Box) (demo)
R: Pete Townshend's home studio, London, 1970–1971. CD: *PsychoDerelict*. N: Stereo (2.24). Recorded as a *Lifehouse* demo and later reworked as Townshend solo track.

Meher Baba M5 (Vivaldi) (demo)
R: Pete Townshend's home studio, London, 1970–1971. CD: *PsychoDerelict*. N: Stereo (2.40). Recorded as a *Lifehouse* demo and later reworked as Townshend solo track.

Melancholia
R: Advision Studios, London, 29 May 1968. P: Kit Lambert. CD: *Sell Out*. N: Stereo (3.17). First released in 1994. D: *Scoop* (3.19).

Miracle Cure
R: IBC Studios, London, October 1968–March 1969. P: Kit Lambert. U.K./U.S.: *Tommy*. CD: *Tommy*. N: Stereo (0.12).

Miracle Cure (live)
R: Isle of Wight Festival, 29 August 1970. P: Jon Astley/Andy Macpherson.
CD: *Live at the Isle of Wight Festival 1970*. N: Stereo (0.12). First released in 1996.

Miracle Cure (live) (2)
R: Radio City Music Hall, New York, or Universal Amphitheatre, Los Angeles, 27 June or 24 August 1989 (venue specified as one or the other). P: Billy Nicholls. U.K./U.S.: *Join Together*. CD: *Join Together*. N: Stereo (0.24).

Motoring (Holland/Dozier/Holland)
Originally performed by Martha and the Vandellas as single A side (Gordy 7039), 5 February 1965. R: IBC Studios, London, March 1965. P: Shel Talmy. CD: *Two's Missing*. N: Stereo (2.50). Featuring Nicky Hopkins (piano). The CD wrongly credits this song to Pete Townshend as composer. First released in 1987.

Much Too Much
R: IBC Studios, London, October 1965. P: Shel Talmy. U.K.: *My Generation*. U.S.: *The Who Sings My Generation*. CD: *The Who Sings My Generation*. N: Mono (2.45) Featuring Nicky Hopkins (piano).

Music Must Change
R: Pete Townshend's home studio and Goring-on-Thames and Ramport Studios, London, April and 2 May 1978. P: Glyn Johns/Jon Astley. U.K./U.S.: *Who Are You*. CD: *30 Years of Maximum R&B*. N: Stereo (4.36).

Music Must Change (2)
R: Pete Townshend's home studio and Goring-on-Thames and Ramport Studios, London, April and 2 May 1978. P: Glyn Johns/Jon Astley. CD: *Who Are You*. N: Stereo (4.38). Alternate mix featuring a different guitar part. First released in 1996.

My Favourite Station (see *My Generation* [Radio One])

My Generation
R: IBC Studios, London, 13 October 1965. P: Shel Talmy. U.K.: Single A side

(Brunswick 05944), 5 November 1965. U.S.: Single A side (Decca 31877), October 1965. CD: *My Generation—The Very Best of the Who*. N: Mono (3.17). D: Flexidisc (Eva-Tone 623827X5) included with original edition of book *The Who: Maximum R&B* by Richard Barnes (Eel Pie, 1982).

My Generation (radio)*
R: BBC Studios, London, 22 November 1965. B: *Saturday Club*, BBC Light Programme, 27 November 1965. N: Mono (3.23).

My Generation (live)
R: Monterey Pop Festival, California, 18 June 1967. CD: *The Monterey International Pop Festival*. N: Stereo. First released in 1992.

My Generation (TV)
R: CBS TV Studios, Los Angeles, 15 September 1967. B: *Smothers Brothers Comedy Hour*, CBS TV, 17 September 1967. U.K./U.S.: *The Kids Are Alright*. CD: *The Kids Are Alright*. N: Mono (2.52). Studio rerecording for U.S. TV show.

My Generation (live) (2)
My Generation (2.41). See Me, Feel Me (1.18). Improvisation (So Very Long) (1.50). Improvisation (Baba Baba) (2.07). Improvisation (Coming Out to Get You) (1.53). Sparks (2.47). Improvisation (Instrumental) (1.59). R: Leeds University, England, 14 February 1970. P: The Who (Pete Townshend). U.K./U.S.: *Live at Leeds*. CD: *Live at Leeds*. N: Stereo (14.45).

My Generation (live) (3)
My Generation (2.52). Improvisation (solo guitar) (1.33). Improvisation (same theme as [4] above) (1.01). Improvisation (Water) (0.30). Improvisation (1.15). R: Isle of Wight Festival, England, 29 August 1970. P: Jon Astley/Andy Macpherson. CD: *Live at the Isle of Wight Festival 1970*. N: Stereo (7.15). First released in 1996.

My Generation (live) (4)
R: Venue unspecified, U.S. and Canada, December 1982. P: Not credited. Compiled by Cy Langston. U.K./U.S.: *Who's Last*. CD: *Who's Last*. N: Stereo (2.40). First released in 1984.

My Generation Blues (live)*
R: Pontiac Silverdome, Detroit, Michigan, 6 December 1975. U.K./U.S.: *The Kids Are Alright*. N: Stereo (3.03). Third part of a medley of "Join Together" and "Road Runner."

My Generation (*Deep Love* Remix)
R: Leeds University, England, 14 February 1970, Tecnoir Studios, Manchester, England, mid–1996. P: Jon Astley/Love to Infinity. CD: CD single reissue of "My Generation" (Polydor 854 637-2), July 1996. N: Stereo (7.06). This is basically a new dance rhythm track (not by the Who) overlaid with a sampled edit of Roger Daltrey's lead vocals from "My Generation" recorded live at Leeds. This can only marginally be considered a Who track and is merely a novelty item: an attempt to redefine the Who's classic message of angst in terms of 1990s dance music. It is bland and repetitive.

My Generation/Land of Hope and Glory (Edward Elgar/A. C. Benson)
"Land of Hope and Glory" was originally an adaptation of Edward Elgar's *Pomp and Circumstance March No. 1*, with words by A. C. Benson. R: IBC Studios, London, August 1966. CD: *A Quick One*. N: Mono (2.03). First released in 1995.

My Generation (Radio 1) (radio)*
(aka *My Favourite Station*)
R: BBC Studios, London, 10 October 1967. B: *Top Gear* and *Saturday Club*, BBC Radio 1, 15 and 28 October 1967. N: Mono. Jingle.

My Way (Cochran/Capehart)
Originally performed by Eddie Cochran and released as a single A side (Liberty LIB 10088), 1963. R: De Lane

Lea Studios, London, 10 November 1967. P: Kit Lambert. CD: *Odds and Sods*. N: Stereo (2.26). First released in 1998.

My Wife (John Entwistle)
R: Olympic Studios, London, May 1971. P: The Who/Glyn Johns. U.K./U.S.: *Who's Next*. CD: *Who's Next*. N: Stereo (3.40). Also released in U.S. as single B side of "Behind Blue Eyes" (Decca 32888), 6 November 1971.

My Wife (live)
R: Civic Center, San Francisco, 13 December 1971. U.K./U.S.: *Two's Missing*. CD: *Two's Missing*. N: Stereo (6.38). First released in 1987.

My Wife (live) (2)
R: Football Ground, Swansea, Wales, 12 June 1976. P: Jon Astley. CD: *30 Years of Maximum R&B*. N: Stereo (4.14). First released in 1994.

My Wife (live) (3)
R: Gaumont State Theatre, Kilburn, London, 15 December 1977. P: John Entwistle. U.K./U.S.: *The Kids Are Alright*. CD: *The Kids Are Alright*. N: Stereo (6.08).

Naked Eye
R: Eel Pie Sound Studios, London, April–May 1970, Olympic Studios, London, 7 June 1971, and completed 16 August 1973. P: The Who/Glyn Johns. U.K./U.S.: *Odds and Sods*. CD: *Odds and Sods*. N: Stereo (5.26). First released in 1974. Olympic session noted above may have resulted in an alternate take. Original album release was shorter, timed at (5.10). CD remix is quite radical.

Naked Eye (live)
Naked Eye (4.47). Improvisation (1.46). R: Isle of Wight Festival, England, 29 August 1970. P: Jon Astley/Andy Macpherson. CD: *Live at the Isle of Wight Festival 1970*. N: Stereo (6.33). First released in 1996.

Naked Eye (TV)*
R: BBC Television Centre, 30 December 1970. B: *Into 71*, BBC-TV, 31 December 1970. N: Live vocals over a rerecorded backing track.

Naked Eye (live) (2)
R: Young Vic Theatre, London, 26 April 1971. P: The Who. CD: *Who's Next*. N: Stereo (5.22). First released on *30 Years of Maximum R&B* boxed set, this version has been tidied up a little.

Never Ask Me (demo)
R: Pete Townshend's home studio, London, 30 March 1977. U.K./U.S.: *Another Scoop*. CD: *Another Scoop*. N: Stereo (4.20).

New Song
R: Ramport Studios, 24 and 27 October 1977. P: Glyn Johns/Jon Astley. U.K./U.S.: *Who Are You*. CD: *Who Are You*. N: Stereo (4.13). Featuring Andy Fairweather-Low (backing vocals) and Billy Nicholls (backing vocals).

905 (John Entwistle)
R: Ramport and RAK Studios, London, March 1978. P: Glyn Johns/Jon Astley. U.K./U.S.: *Who Are You*. CD: *Who Are You*. N: Stereo (4.03). String arrangement by Ted Astley. Also released in U.S. as single B side of "Trick of the Light" (MCA 40978), 2 December 1978.

1921
R: IBC Studios, London, October 1968–March 1969. P: Kit Lambert. U.K./U.S.: *Tommy*. CD: *Tommy*. N: Stereo (2.50).

1921 (live)
R: Isle of Wight Festival, England, 29 August 1970. P: Jon Astley/Andy Macpherson. CD: *Live at the Isle of Wight Festival 1970*. N: Stereo (2.27). First released in 1996.

1921 (live) (2)
R: Radio City Music Hall, New York, or Universal Ampitheatre, Los Angeles, 27 June or 24 August 1989 (venue specified

as one or the other). P: Billy Nicholls. U.K./U.S.: *Join Together*. CD: *Join Together*. N: Stereo (2.52).

No Road Romance (demo)
R: Pete Townshend's home studio, London, April 1978. CD: *Who Are You*. N: Stereo (5.05). First released in 1996.

A Normal Day for Brian (A Man Who Died Every Day) (demo)*
R: Pete Townshend's home studio, London, June 1969. N: A tribute to Brian Jones, written on his death. Unreleased.

The Note (see *Pure and Easy*)

Now I'm a Farmer
R: Eel Pie Sound Studios, London, April–May 1970, completed 16 August 1973. P: The Who. U.K./U.S.: *Odds and Sods*. CD: *Odds and Sods*. N: Stereo (4.06).

Odorono
R: IBC Studios, London, 11 October 1967. P: Kit Lambert. U.K./U.S.: *Sell Out*. CD: *Sell Out*. N: Stereo (2.16).

Odorono (2)*
R: IBC Studios, London, 11 October 1967. P: Kit Lambert. U.K./U.S.: *Sell Out*. N: Mono (2.16). Alternate guitar arrangement to above.

Odorono (Final Chorus)
R: IBC Studios, London, 11 October 1967. P: Kit Lambert. CD: *Sell Out*. N: Stereo (0.23). Edited out off above master and first released in 1995.

One at a Time (John Entwistle)
R: Turn Up-Down Studios, Surrey, England, June 1982. P: Glyn Johns. U.K./U.S.: *It's Hard*. CD: *It's Hard*. N: Stereo (3.19). Featuring Tim Gorman (synthesizer). Also released in U.S. as single B side of "Eminence Front" (Warner Bros. WB7-29814), December 1982.

One Life's Enough
R: Turn Up-Down Studios, Surrey, England, June 1982. P: Glyn Johns. U.K./ U.S.: *It's Hard*. CD: *It's Hard*. N: Stereo (2.21). Featuring Tim Gorman (synthesizer).

One Room Country Shack (Mercy Dee Walton)*
Originally performed by Mercy Dee as a single A side (Speciality 458), 1953. N: Unreleased. This track was originally scheduled in 1968 for inclusion in *Tommy*. It is unconfirmed whether this recording was completed.

Ordinary Fella (demo)*
R: Pete Townshend's home studio, London, 1974–1975. N: Stereo. Unrecorded by the Who, this was considered for the *By Numbers* album and rejected.

Our Love Was
R: Columbia Studios, Los Angeles, September 1967. P: Kit Lambert. U.K./U.S.: *Sell Out*. CD: *Sell Out*. N: Stereo (3.06).

Our Love Was (2)*
R: Columbia Studios, Los Angeles, September 1967. P: Kit Lambert. U.K./U.S.: *Sell Out*. N: Mono (3.06). Alternate guitar arrangement to above.

Our Love Was (radio)*
R: BBC Studios, London, 10 October 1967. B: *Top Gear* and *Saturday Club*, BBC Radio 1, 15 and 28 October 1967. N: Mono (2.42). This was a version of the above mix but with Townshend's vocal replaced with Daltrey's.

Out in the Street
R: IBC Studios, London, 11 March 1965. P: Shel Talmy. U.K.: *My Generation*. U.S.: *The Who Sings My Generation*. CD: *The Who Sings My Generation*. N: Mono (2.30). Originally titled "You're Going to Know Me," the backing vocals sound like the Ivy League.

Overture
R: IBC Studios, London, October 1968–March 1969. P: Kit Lambert. U.K./U.S.: *Tommy*. CD: *Tommy*. N: Stereo (5.21). Also released as single B side in U.K. (Track 2094 004), 10 October 1970,

and on EP (Track 2252 001), 7 November 1970, and in U.S. (Decca 732729), August 1970.

Overture (live)
R: Isle of Wight Festival, 29 August 1970. P: Jon Astley/Andy Macpherson. CD: *Live at the Isle of Wight Festival 1970*. N: Stereo (5.07). First released in 1996.

Overture (live) (2)
R: Radio City Music Hall, New York, or Universal Ampitheatre, Los Angeles, 27 June or 24 August 1989 (venue specified as one or the other). P: Billy Nicholls. U.K./U.S.: *Join Together*. CD: *Join Together*. N: Stereo (5.24). Track duration includes "It's A Boy."

The Ox (Townshend/Entwistle/ Moon/Hopkins)
R: IBC Studios, London, October 1965. P: Shel Talmy. U.K.: *My Generation*. U.S.: *The Who Sings My Generation*. CD: *30 Years of Maximum R&B*. N: Mono (3.37). Features Nicky Hopkins (piano). Also released as a single B-side in U.K. (Brunswick 05965), 12 August 1966.

Pictures of Lily
R: IBC Studios, London, April 1967. U.K.: Single A side (Track 604 002), 22 April 1967. U.S.: Single A side (Decca 32156), June 1967. CD: *My Generation— The Very Best of the Who*. N: Mono (2.43). D: *Another Scoop* (2.50).

Pictures of Lily (live)
R: Monterey Pop Festival, California, 18 June 1967. CD: *The Monterey International Pop Festival*. N: Stereo. First released in 1992.

Pictures of Lily (radio)*
R: BBC Studios, London, 10 October 1967. B: *Top Gear* and *Saturday Club*, BBC Radio 1, 15 and 28 October 1967. N: Mono (2.35).

Pile Driver (demo)*
R: Pete Townshend's home studio, London, 1970. N: Instrumental recorded during sessions for *Double Pisces* film. Unreleased.

Pinball Wizard
R: Morgan Studios, London, 7 February 1969. P: Kit Lambert. U.K.: Single A side (Track 604 027), 7 March 1969. U.S.: Single A side (Decca 732465) 22 March 1969. CD: *Tommy*. N: Stereo (3.02). D: *Another Scoop* (2.45).

Pinball Wizard (TV)*
R: ATV Studios, London, 16 April 1969. B: *This Is Tom Jones*, ITV TV, 20 April 1969. N: Mono. A rerecorded electric version.

Pinball Wizard (live)
R: Woodstock Music and Arts Fair, New York, 17 August 1969. U.K./U.S.: *The Kids Are Alright*. CD: *The Kids Are Alright*. N: Stereo (2.48).

Pinball Wizard (radio)*
R: IBC Studios, London, 13 April 1970. B: *Dave Lee Travis Show*, BBC Radio 1, 19 April 1970. N: Mono (2.40).

Pinball Wizard (live) (2)
R: Leeds University, England, 14 February 1970. P: The Who (Pete Townshend). CD: CD single reissue of "My Generation" (Polydor 854 637-2), July 1996. N: Stereo (3.00). First released in 1996.

Pinball Wizard (live) (3)
R: Isle of Wight Festival, England, 29 August 1970. P: Jon Astley/Andy Macpherson. CD: *Live at the Isle of Wight Festival 1970*. N: Stereo (2.47). First released in 1996.

Pinball Wizard (live) (4)
R: Venue unspecified, U.S. and Canada, December 1982. P: Not credited. Compiled by Cy Langston. U.K./U.S.: *Who's Last*. CD: *Who's Last*. N: Stereo (2.50). First released in 1984.

Pinball Wizard (live) (5)
R: Radio City Music Hall, New York, or Universal Amphitheatre, Los Angeles, 27 June or 24 August 1989 (venue

specified as one or the other). P: Billy Nicholls. U.K./U.S.: *Join Together*. CD: *Join Together*. N: Stereo (4.20).

Please Don't Touch (Heath/Robinson) (TV)*
Originally performed by Johnny Kidd and the Pirates as single A side (HMV POP615), May 1959. R: Ryemuse Studios, London, 16 December 1966. B: *Ready Steady Goes!*, ITV TV, 23 December 1966. N: Mono.

Please, Please, Please (Brown/Terry)
Originally performed by James Brown and released as single A side (Federal 12258), March 1956. R: IBC Studios, London, 11 March 1965. P: Shel Talmy. U.K.: *My Generation*. U.S.: *The Who Sings My Generation*. CD: *The Who Sings My Generation*. N: Mono (2.45). Features Nicky Hopkins (piano).

Politician (demo)
R: Pete Townshend's home studio, London, 1967. U.K./U.S.: *Scoop*. CD: *Scoop*. N: Stereo (3.35).

Popular (demo)
R: Pete Townshend's home studio, London, 1980. U.K./U.S.: *Scoop*. CD: *Scoop*. N: Stereo (2.26).

Postcard (John Entwistle)
R: Eel Pie Sound Studios, London, April–May 1970, completed 14 August 1973. P: The Who. U.K./U.S.: *Odds and Sods*. CD: *Odds and Sods*. N: Stereo (3.30). First released in 1974. Also released as a single A side in U.S. (MCA 40330), November 1974.

Praying the Game (demo)
R: Pete Townshend's home studio, London, 1976–1978. U.K./U.S.: *Another Scoop*. CD: *Another Scoop*. N: Stereo (4.20).

Prelude #556 (demo)
R: Pete Townshend's home studio, London, 27 November 1982. U.K./U.S.: *Another Scoop*. CD: *Another Scoop*. N: Stereo (1.16).

Prelude: The Right to Write (demo)
R: Pete Townshend's home studio, London, January 1983. U.K./U.S.: *Another Scoop*. CD: *Another Scoop*. N: Stereo (1.32).

The Punk and the Godfather (aka *The Punk Meets the Godfather*)
R: "The Kitchen," Ramport Studios, London, May–July 1973. P: The Who (Pete Townshend). U.K./U.S.: *Quadrophenia*. CD: *Quadrophenia*. N: Stereo (5.11).

The Punk and the Godfather (2)
R: As above, with additional overdubs at Shepperton Studios, London, 1979. P: John Entwistle. U.K./U.S.: *Quadrophenia* (Soundtrack). CD: *Quadrophenia* (Soundtrack). N: Stereo (5.28). Remixed, with new bass guitar and guitar track.

The Punk and the Godfather (3)*
N: Stereo. Instrumental excerpt of above used on *Quadrophenia* film soundtrack but not included on soundtrack album. Remixed with new bass guitar track.

Pure and Easy
R: Record Plant, New York, 17 March 1971. P: Kit Lambert. CD: *Who's Next*. N: Stereo (4.19). First released in 1995. D: *Who Came First* (5.32). Originally referred to as "The Note."

Pure and Easy (2)
R: Rolling Stones mobile unit, Stargroves, Berkshire, England, April 1971. P: The Who/Glyn Johns. U.K./U.S.: *Odds and Sods*. CD: *Odds and Sods*. N: Stereo (5.21). First released in 1974. CD features a slightly longer fade-out.

Put the Money Down
R: Olympic Studios, London, 6 June 1972. P: The Who/Glyn Johns. U.K./U.S.: *Odds and Sods*. CD: *Odds and Sods*. N: Stereo (4.29). Original album version was faded out sooner, at [4.00]. Also released as a single B side of "Postcard" in U.S. (MCA 40330), November 1974.

Quadrophenia
Bell Boy. Is It Me?. Helpless Dancer.

Love Reign O'er Me. R: "The Kitchen," Ramport Studios, London, May–July 1973. P: The Who (Pete Townshend). U.K./U.S.: *Quadrophenia*. CD: *Quadrophenia*. N: Stereo (6.13).

Quadrophenia (2)*
R: As above, with additional overdubs at Shepperton Studios, London, 1979. P: John Entwistle. N: Stereo. Excerpt used on *Quadrophenia* film soundtrack but not included on soundtrack album. Remixed with new bass guitar track.

A Quick One While He's Away
Her Man's Been Gone (0.21). Crying Town (1.36). We Have a Remedy (1.31). Ivor the Engine Driver (1.42). Soon Be Home (1.25). You Are Forgiven (2.30). R: IBC, Pye and Regent Studios, London, November 1966. P: Kit Lambert. U.K.: *A Quick One*. U.S.: *Happy Jack*. CD: *A Quick One*. N: Mono (9.10). The breakdown of the six sections of this song are not noted on the LP or CD release, but have been detailed on the printed scores of the song.

A Quick One While He's Away (live)
Her Man's Been Gone. Crying Town. We Have a Remedy. Ivor the Engine Driver. Soon Be Home. You Are Forgiven. R: Monterey Pop Festival, California, 18 June 1967. CD: *The Monterey International Pop Festival*. N: Stereo. First released in 1992.

A Quick One While He's Away (radio)*
Her Man's Been Gone. Crying Town. We Have a Remedy. Ivor the Engine Driver. Soon Be Home. You Are Forgiven. R: BBC Studios, London, 10 October 1967. B: *Top Gear* and *Saturday Club*, BBC Radio 1, 15 and 28 October 1967. N: Mono (6.38).

A Quick One While He's Away (TV)
Her Man's Been Gone (0.19). Crying Town (1.12). We Have a Remedy (1.13). Ivor the Engine Driver (0.51). Soon Be Home (0.46). You Are Forgiven (2.53). R: InterTel Studios, London, 11 December 1968. P: Glyn Johns. U.K./U.S.: *The Kids Are Alright*. CD: *The Kids Are Alright*. N: Mono (7.19).

A Quick One While He's Away (TV) (2)
Her Man's Been Gone. Crying Town. We Have a Remedy. Ivor the Engine Driver. Soon Be Home. You Are Forgiven. R: InterTel Studios, London, 11 December 1968. P: Glyn Johns. CD: *30 Years of Maximum R&B*. N: Mono. Second take of above. Sections (1) and (6) of the above performance were incorporated into the edit of "A Quick One" featured on the boxed set.

A Quick One While He's Away (live) (2)
Her Man's Been Gone (0.21). Crying Town (1.36). We Have a Remedy (1.31). Ivor the Engine Driver (1.42). Soon Be Home (1.25). You Are Forgiven (2.30). R: Leeds University, England, 14 February 1970. P: The Who (Pete Townshend). CD: *Live at Leeds*. N: Stereo (8.25). First released in 1995.

The Quiet One (John Entwistle)
R: Odyssey Studios, London, June–December 1980. P: Bill Szymczyk. U.K.: Single B side of "You Better You Bet" (Polydor 2002 044 WHO4), 27 February 1981. U.S.: Single B side of "You Better You Bet" (Warner Bros. WBS 49698), March 1981. CD: *Face Dances*. N: Stereo (3.08).

The Quiet One (live)
R: Shea Stadium, New York, 13 October 1982. P: Jon Astley. CD: *Face Dances*. N: Stereo (4.28).

Radio London (see *Sell Out: Jingles and Adverts*)

Radio 1 (*Boris* Mix) (see *Boris the Spider* [Radio 1])

Rael (1 and 2)
R: Talent Masters Studios, New York,

July 1967. P: Kit Lambert. U.K./U.S.: *Sell Out*. CD: *Sell Out*. N: Mono/stereo (5.44). Part 1 duration (3.41) and part 2 duration (2.03). Title changed to "Rael 1" on CD with addition of below track as "Rael 2." The 1994 remix for the boxed set and *Sell Out* reissue restores a few lines in the first verse.

Rael 2
R: Talent Masters Studios, New York, July 1967. P: Kit Lambert. CD: *Sell Out*. N: Stereo (0.47). First released in 1994.

Rael: Organ Pieces & Fugue (demo)*
R: Pete Townshend's home studio, London, 1967. N: Unreleased.

Rael: That Motherland Feeling (demo)*
R: Pete Townshend's home studio, London, 1967. N: Unreleased.

The Real Me
R: "The Kitchen," Ramport Studios, London, May–July 1973. P: The Who (Pete Townshend). U.K./U.S.: *Quadrophenia*. CD: *Quadrophenia*. N: Stereo (3.21). Also released on single in the U.S. (MCA 40182), 12 January 1974. This single version has a lengthened instrumental ending that fades out.

The Real Me (2)
R: Ramport Studios, London, January 1979. P: Jon Astley. CD: *30 Years of Maximum R&B*. N: Stereo (3.29). Kenney Jones audition session.

The Real Me (3)
R: As original above, with additional overdubs at Shepperton Studios, London, 1979. P: John Entwistle. U.K./U.S.: *Quadrophenia* (Soundtrack). CD: *Quadrophenia* (Soundtrack). N: Stereo (3.30). Remixed, with new bass guitar track and longer ending.

Recorders (demo)
R: Pete Townshend's home studio, London, 1973. U.K./U.S.: *Scoop*. CD: *Scoop*. N: Stereo (1.17). Sound effects link excluded from *Quadrophenia*.

Relax
R: New York, August 1967. P: Kit Lambert. U.K./U.S.: *Sell Out*. CD: *Sell Out*. N: Stereo (2.38).

Relax (radio)*
R: BBC Studios, London, 10 October 1967. B: *Top Gear* and *Saturday Club*, BBC Radio 1, 15 and 28 October 1967. N: Mono (2.38). Alternate mix of above.

Relay
R: Olympic Studios, London, 26 May 1972. P: The Who/Glyn Johns. U.K.: Single A side (Track 2094 106), 16 December 1972. U.S.: Single A side (Decca 33041), 25 November 1972. CD: *30 Years of Maximum R&B*. N: Stereo (4.00). D: *Sometimes a Great Notion*.

Relay (TV)*.
R: South Bank Television Centre, London, January 1973. B: *Russell Harty Plus*, ITV TV, 6 January 1973. N: Mono (3.25). Live vocals mixed with a backing track that has a different guitar mix from above.

Relay (TV) (2)*
R: BBC Television Centre, London, January 1973. B: *Old Grey Whistle Test*, BBC-TV, 30 January 1973. N: Mono (4.50). Live vocals over a prerecorded backing track. This is nearly a minute longer that the release version above.

Riot in the Female Jail (demo)*
R: Pete Townshend's home studio, London, 1972. N: Stereo. Unreleased. Some sources list this title as "Ladies in the Female Jail.".

Road Runner (Ellas McDaniel) (live)*
Originally performed by Bo Diddley and released as a single A side (London HLM 9112), 1960. R: Pontiac Silverdome, Detroit, Michigan, 6 December 1975. U.K./U.S.: *The Kids Are Alright*. N: Stereo (2.22). Second part of a medley with "Join Together" and "My Generation Blues." It is reported that a studio

version of this song was recorded in 1968, but this remains unconfirmed.

The Rock
Bell Boy. Is It Me?. Helpless Dancer. Love Reign o'er Me. R: "The Kitchen," Ramport Studios, London, May–July 1973. P: The Who (Pete Townshend). U.K./U.S.: *Quadrophenia*. CD: *Quadrophenia*. N: Stereo (6.37).

The Rock (2)*
R: As above, with additional overdubs at Shepperton Studios, London, 1979. P: John Entwistle. N: Stereo. Excerpt used on *Quadrophenia* film soundtrack but not included on soundtrack album. Remixed with new bass guitar track.

Rough Boys (live)
R: Universal Amphitheatre, Los Angeles, 24 August 1989. P: Billy Nicholls. U.K./U.S.: *Join Together*. CD: *Join Together*. N: Stereo (4.35). First released on the Pete Townshend solo album *Empty Glass* (Acto K50699), 14 April 1980.

Run Run Run
R: IBC Studios, London, October 1966. P: Kit Lambert. U.K.: *A Quick One*. U.S.: *Happy Jack*. CD: *A Quick One*. N: Mono/stereo (2.43). Originally released as a single A side by Cat (Reaction 591003), May 1966.

Run Run Run (radio)*
R: BBC Studios, London, 17 January 1967. B: *Saturday Club*, BBC Light Programme, 21 January 1967. N: Mono (3.17).

Runaround Sue (DiMucci/Marseca) (TV)*
Originally performed by Dion and released as single A side (Laurie 3110), September 1961. R: London, late 1965. B: *Ready Steady Go!* and *The New Year Starts Here!* ITV TV, 24 and 31 December 1965. N: Mono. Thought to come from one of the above TV broadcasts.

Sally Simpson
R: IBC Studios, London, October 1968–March 1969. P: Kit Lambert. U.K./U.S.: *Tommy*. CD: *Tommy*. N: Stereo (4.12).

Sally Simpson (live)
R: Radio City Music Hall, New York, or Universal Amphitheatre, Los Angeles, 27 June or 24 August 1989 (venue specified as one or the other). P: Billy Nicholls. U.K./U.S.: *Join Together*. CD: *Join Together*. N: Stereo (4.18).

Saturday Night's Alright for Fighting (Elton John/Bernie Taupin)
Originally performed by Elton John on the *Goodbye Yellow Brick Road* album (DJM DJLPD 1001), 5 October 1973. R: Eel Pie Studios, London, and Revolution Studios, Manchester, England, July 1991. P: Jon Astley/Billy Nicholls. U.K./U.S.: *Two Rooms: Celebrating the Songs of Elton John and Bernie Taupin* (Mercury 845 749-1), November 1991. CD: *30 Years of Maximum R&B*. N: Stereo (4.33). Also features the refrain from Elton John and Bernie Taupin's "Take Me to the Pilot.".

Sea and Sand
R: "The Kitchen," Ramport Studios, London, May–July 1973. P: The Who (Pete Townshend). U.K./U.S.: *Quadrophenia*. CD: *Quadrophenia*. N: Stereo (5.01).

See Me, Feel Me (see also *We're Not Gonna Take It*)
R: IBC Studios, London, October 1968–March 1969. P: Kit Lambert. U.K./U.S.: *Tommy*. CD: *Tommy*. N: Stereo (3.39). Credited as a complete piece under the title "We're Not Gonna Take It." Also released as single A side in U.K. (Track 2094 004), 10 October 1970, and in U.S. (Decca 732729), August 1970. Also released in U.K. as part of *Tommy* EP (Track 2252 001), 7 November 1970.

See Me, Feel Me (live)
R: Woodstock Music and Arts Fair, New York, 17 August 1969. U.K./U.S.:

Woodstock (Atlantic 2663001), August 1970. CD: *The Kids Are Alright*. N: Stereo (5.25). Original *Woodstock* soundtrack version is slightly longer, including the last few bars of "We're Not Gonna Take It."

See Me, Feel Me (live) (2)
R: Leeds University, England, 14 February 1970. P: The Who (Pete Townshend). CD: *30 Years of Maximum R&B*. N: Stereo (3.31). First released in 1994.

See Me, Feel Me (live) (3)
R: Isle of Wight Festival, England, 29 August 1970. P: Jon Astley/Andy Macpherson. CD: *Live at the Isle of Wight Festival 1970*. N: Stereo (5.34). First released in 1996.

See Me, Feel Me (live) (4)*
R: Hammersmith Odeon, London, 28 December 1979. P: Chris Thomas. U.K./U.S.: *Concerts for the People of Kampuchea*. N: Stereo (5.49).

See Me, Feel Me (live) (5)
R: Venue unspecified, U.S. and Canada, December 1982. P: Not credited. Compiled by Cy Langston. U.K./U.S.: *Who's Last*. CD: *Who's Last*. N: Stereo (4.09). First released in 1984.

See Me, Feel Me (live) (6)
R: Radio City Music Hall, New York, or Universal Amphitheatre, Los Angeles, 27 June or 24 August 1989 (venue specified as one or the other). P: Billy Nicholls. U.K./U.S.: *Join Together*. CD: *Join Together*. N: Stereo. Incorporated into "We're Not Gonna Take It" and not separately indexed.

See My Way (Roger Daltrey)
R: IBC Studios, London, November 1966. P: Kit Lambert. U.K.: *A Quick One*. U.S.: *Happy Jack*. CD: *A Quick One*. N: Mono (1.52).

See My Way (radio)*
R: BBC Studios, London, 17 January 1967. B: *Saturday Club*, BBC Light Programme, 21 January 1967. N: Mono (1.50).

The Seeker
R: IBC Studios, London, 19 January 1970. P: The Who. U.K.: Single A side (Track 604 036), 21 March 1970. U.S.: Single A side (Decca 32670), April 1970. CD: *My Generation—The Very Best of the Who*. N: Stereo (3.21). CD version has a noticeably different mix. D: *Who Came First* (4.33).

The Seeker (radio)*
R: IBC Studios, London, 13 April 1970. B: *Dave Lee Travis Show*, BBC Radio 1, 19 April 1970. N: Mono (3.05).

Sell Out: Jingles and Adverts (aka *Radio London*)
Days Of The Week (0.28). Wonderful Radio London (0.09). More Music (0.03). Premier Drums (0.15). Instrumental Theme (0.09). Smooth Sailing (0.18). Go to the Church of Your Choice (0.09). Your Pussy Cat Knows Where It's At (0.07). Big L (0.01). Speakeasy Club (0.03). Rotosound Strings (0.05). Charles Atlas Course (0.26). Track Records (0.17). Loon at the Bag O'Nails (0.05). John Mason's Cars/John Mason's Cars (Rehearsal). Campers Are Here Again*. Radio London News Bulletin*. London England*. R: Various Studios, London, October–November 1967. U.K./U.S.: *Sell Out*. CD: *Sell Out*. N: All mono.

Sensation
R: IBC Studios, London, October 1968–March 1969. P: Kit Lambert. U.K./U.S.: *Tommy*. CD: *Tommy*. N: Stereo (2.28). Originally titled "She's a Sensation.".

Sensation (live)
R: Radio City Music Hall, New York, or Universal Amphitheatre, Los Angeles, 27 June or 24 August 1989 (venue specified as one or the other). P: Billy Nicholls. U.K./U.S.: *Join Together*. CD: *Join Together*. N: Stereo (2.21).

Shakin' All Over (Frederick Heath)*
Originally performed by Johnny Kidd and the Pirates as single A side (HMV POP 753), June 1960. R: Advision Studios, London, 29 May 1968. P: Kit Lambert. N: Stereo. Unreleased.

Shakin' All Over (live)
R: Leeds University, England, 14 February 1970. P: The Who (Pete Townshend). U.K./U.S.: *Live at Leeds*. CD: *Live at Leeds*. N: Stereo (4.15). Originally included "Spoonful" but edited from longer master (5.11) for release.

Shakin' All Over (radio)* (incorporating *Spoonful*)
R: IBC Studios, London, 13 April 1970. B: *Dave Lee Travis Show*, BBC Radio 1, 19 April 1970. N: Mono (3.40). Also includes "Spoonful" (see entry below).

Shakin' All Over (live) (2) (incorporating *Spoonful* and *Twist and Shout*)
Shakin' All Over (2.57). Spoonful (1.06). Twist And Shout (2.20). R: Isle of Wight Festival, England, 29 August 1970. P: Jon Astley/Andy Macpherson. CD: *Live at the Isle of Wight Festival 1970*. N: Stereo (6.25). Medley of three songs. See also individual entries. First released in 1996.

Sheraton Gibson (demo)
R: Pete Townshend's home studio, London, late 1971 or early 1972. U.K./U.S.: *Who Came First*. CD: *Who Came First*. N: Stereo (2.40).

Shout and Shimmy (James Brown)
Originally performed by James Brown, released as single A side (King 5657), June 1962. R: IBC Studios, London, March 1965. P: Shel Talmy. U.K.: Single B side of "My Generation" (Brunswick 05944), 5 November 1965. CD: *Who's Missing*. N: Mono (3.13).

Shout and Shimmy (TV)*
R: Associated-Rediffusion Studios, May 1965. B: *Ready Steady Goes Live!*, ITV TV, 21 May 1965. N: Mono (2.09).

Showbiz Sonato (Keith Moon)*
A song originally scheduled for *A Quick One* and assumed to be an alternate title of "Cobwebs and Strange."

*Signal 30** (see *Sodding About*)

Silas Stingy (John Entwistle)
R: Kingsway Studios, London, October 1967. P: Kit Lambert. U.K./U.S.: *Sell Out*. CD: *Sell Out*. N: Mono/Stereo (3.04).

Sister Disco
R: Ramport and Goring-on-Thames Studios, London, October 1977. P: Glyn Johns/Jon Astley. U.K./U.S.: *Who Are You*. CD: *Who Are You*. N: Stereo (4.22).

Sister Disco (film)*
R: Rehearsal, Shepperton Studios, London, April 1979. N: Mono (4.17). Included in *30 Years of Maximum R&B Live* video in 1994.

Sister Disco (live)*
R: Hammersmith Odeon, London, 28 December 1979. P: Chris Thomas. U.K./U.S.: *Concerts for the People of Kampuchea*. N: Stereo (5.16).

Slip Kid
R: Ronnie Lane's mobile unit, Shepperton Studios, London, 30 May 1975. P: Glyn Johns. U.K./U.S.: *By Numbers*. CD: *By Numbers*. N: Stereo (4.30). Featuring Nicky Hopkins (piano). Also released as a single A side in U.S. (MCA 40603), 7 August 1976.

Smash the Mirror
R: IBC Studios, London, October 1968–March 1969. P: Kit Lambert. U.K./U.S.: *Tommy*. CD: *Tommy*. N: Stereo (1.35).

Smash the Mirror (live)
R: Isle of Wight Festival, 29 August 1970. P: Jon Astley/Andy Macpherson. CD: *Live at the Isle of Wight Festival 1970*. N: Stereo (1.15). First released in 1996.

Smash the Mirror (live) (2)
R: Radio City Music Hall, New York, or Universal Amphitheatre, Los Angeles, 27 June or 24 August 1989 (venue specified as one or the other). P: Billy Nicholls. U.K./U.S.: *Join Together*. CD: *Join Together*. N: Stereo (1.09).

Smokestack Lightning (Chester Burnett)*
Originally performed by Howlin' Wolf as a single A side (Chess 1618), 1956. R: EMI Studios (Abbey Road), London, October 1964. P: John Burgess. N: The only song known to have been played at a High Numbers audition for EMI. This and other songs were pressed onto an acetate disk, but it is not known to have survived.

The Snail (demo)*
R: Pete Townshend's home studio, London, 1967–1968. N: Stereo. Instrumental. Unreleased.

So Sad About Us
R: IBC Studios, London, November 1966. P: Kit Lambert. U.K.: *A Quick One*. U.S.: *Happy Jack*. CD: *A Quick One*. N: Mono (3.01). Originally released as a single A side by the Merseys (Fontana TF732), July 1966. D: *Scoop* (1.45).

So Sad About Us (radio)*
R: BBC Studios, London, 13 September 1966. B: *Saturday Club*, BBC Light Programme, 17 September 1966. N: Mono (2.53).

*Sodding About** (aka *Signal 30* and *Instrumental—No Title*)
R: London, 1966 or 1967 (?). N: Stereo (2.50). Instrumental theme for film *Live in London*. Remixed for the *Odds and Sods* CD of 1998 but deleted from final version. Unreleased. The recording date of this item is questionable, largely because the band's archives date it as coming from the sessions in mid-1966 for *A Quick One*, but the actual sound of the track is very similar to that of "Hall of the Mountain King" from October 1967.

Somebody Saved Me
R: Odyssey Studios, London, June–December 1980. P: Bill Szymczyk. CD: *Face Dances*. N: Stereo (5.24). First released in 1997. Originally released in a solo version by Pete Townshend on *All the Best Cowboys Have Chinese Eyes* (Atco K50889), June 1982.

Someone's Coming (John Entwistle)
R: Talent Masters Studio, New York, and Bradley's Barn, Nashville, Tennessee, August 1967. P: Kit Lambert. U.K.: Single B side of "I Can See for Miles" (Track 604 011), 14 October 1967. U.S.: Single B side of "Magic Bus" (Decca 32362), July 1968. CD: *Sell Out*. N: Mono (2.29).

The Song Is Over
R: Olympic Studios, London, 11 May 1971. P: The Who/Glyn Johns. U.K./U.S.: *Who's Next*. CD: *Who's Next*. N: Stereo (6.13). Featuring Nicky Hopkins (piano).

Spanish Foot (demo)* (aka *Title Music from The Lone Ranger*)
R: Pete Townshend's home studio, London, 1968. N: Stereo. Unreleased.

Sparks
R: IBC Studios, London, October 1968–March 1969. P: Kit Lambert. U.K./U.S.: *Tommy*. CD: *Tommy*. N: Stereo (3.47).

Sparks (live)
R: Woodstock Music And Arts Fair, New York, 17 August 1969. U.K./U.S.: *The Kids Are Alright*. CD: *30 Years of Maximum R&B*. N: Stereo (3.01). CD version above is 52 seconds longer and titled "Underture."

Sparks (live) (2)
R: Leeds University, England, 14 February 1970. P: The Who (Pete Townshend). CD: *Live at Leeds*. N: Stereo (4.16). Second part of a medley with "Amazing Journey."

Sparks (live) (3)
R: Isle of Wight Festival, England, 29

August 1970. P: Jon Astley/Andy Macpherson. CD: *Live at the Isle of Wight Festival 1970.* N: Stereo (5.09). First released in 1996.

Sparks (live) (4)
R: Radio City Music Hall, New York, or Universal Amphitheatre, Los Angeles, 27 June or 24 August 1989 (venue specified as one or the other). P: Billy Nicholls. U.K./U.S.: *Join Together.* CD: *Join Together.* N: Stereo (4.35).

Spoonful (Willie Dixon) (live)
Originally performed by Howlin' Wolf as a single A side (Chess 1762), 1960. R: Isle of Wight Festival, England, 29 August 1970. P: Jon Astley/Andy Macpherson. CD: *Live at the Isle of Wight Festival 1970.* N: Stereo (1.06). Played as medley with "Shakin' All Over." First released in 1996.

Spotted Henry (see *Medac*)

Squeeze Box
R: Ronnie Lane's mobile Unit, Shepperton Studios, London, 30 May 1975. P: Glyn Johns. U.K./U.S.: *By Numbers.* CD: *By Numbers.* N: Stereo (2.41). Also released as a single A side in U.K. (Polydor 2121 275), 24 January 1976, and in the U.S. (MCA 2161), 22 November 1975. D: *Another Scoop* (2.53).

Squeeze Box (live)
R: Football Ground, Swansea, Wales, 12 June 1976. P: Jon Astley. CD: *By Numbers.* N: Stereo (3.11). First released in 1996.

Substitute
R: Olympic Studios, London, January 1966. P: The Who (Pete Townshend). U.K.: Single A side (Reaction 591001), 4 March 1966. CD: *My Generation—The Very Best of the Who.* N: Mono (3.47). It is rumored but unconfirmed that Shel Talmy recorded an earlier version of this song with the band that remains unreleased. D: *Another Scoop* (3.32).

Substitute (2)*
R: Olympic Studios, London, January 1966. P: The Who (Pete Townshend). U.S.: Single A side (Atco 45 6409), March 1966. N: Mono (3.47). As above but with amended lyrics for U.S. Atlantic. The line in the chorus "I look all white but my dad was black" is replaced with the less memorable "I try walking forward but my feet walk back.".

Substitute (radio)*
R: BBC Studios, London, 14 March 1966. B: *Saturday Club*, BBC Light Programme, 19 March 1966. N: Mono (3.30).

Substitute (TV)*
R: TV studios, Paris, France, March 1966. B: *Music Hall De France*, French TV, 30 March 1966. N: Mono. Played live in the studio.

Substitute (live)
R: Monterey Pop Festival, California, 18 June 1967. CD: *The Monterey International Pop Festival.* N: Stereo. First released in 1992.

Substitute (live) (2)
R: Leeds University, England, 14 February 1970. P: The Who (Pete Townshend). U.K./U.S.: *Live at Leeds.* CD: *Live at Leeds.* N: Stereo (2.07). Shortened arrangement.

Substitute (radio) (2)*
R: IBC Studios, London, 13 April 1970. B: *Dave Lee Travis Show*, BBC Radio 1, 19 April 1970. N: Mono (2.12).

Substitute (live) (3)
R: Isle of Wight Festival, England, 29 August 1970. P: Jon Astley/Andy Macpherson. CD: *Live at the Isle of Wight Festival 1970.* N: Stereo (2.10). First released in 1996.

Substitute (live) (4)
R: Venue unspecified, U.S. and Canada, December 1982. P: Not credited. Compiled by Cy Langston. U.K./U.S.: *Who's Last.* CD: *Who's Last.* N: Stereo (2.46). First released in 1984.

*Success**
R: IBC Studios, London, October 1968–March 1969. P: Kit Lambert. N: Stereo. Unreleased short link piece from *Tommy*.

Success Story (John Entwistle)
R: Ronnie Lane's mobile unit, Shepperton Studios, London, 23 May 1975. P: Glyn Johns. U.K./U.S.: *By Numbers*. CD: *By Numbers*. N: Stereo (3.20). Also released as a single B side of "Squeeze Box" in U.K. (Polydor 2121 275), 24 January 1976, and in U.S. (MCA 2161), 22 November 1975.

Summertime Blues (live)
R: Monterey Pop Festival, California, 18 June 1967. CD: *The Monterey International Pop Festival*. N: Stereo. First released in 1992.

Summertime Blues (Cochran/Capehart) (radio)
Originally performed by Eddie Cochran as single A side (Liberty 55144), July 1958. R: BBC Studios, London, 10 October 1967. B: *Top Gear* and *Saturday Club*, BBC Radio 1, 15 and 28 October 1967. CD: *Odds and Sods*. N: Mono/stereo (3.13). First released in 1998. Broadcast version and CD below are identical and undoubtedly come from the same master. CD version has very slight stereo separation.

Summertime Blues (live) (2)
R: Leeds University, England, 14 February 1970. P: The Who (Pete Townshend). U.K./U.S.: *Live at Leeds*. CD: *Live at Leeds*. N: Stereo (3.20). Also released as single A side in U.K. (Track 2094 002), 10 July 1970, and U.S. (Decca 32708), 11 July 1970.

Summertime Blues (live) (3)
R: Isle of Wight Festival, 29 August 1970. P: Jon Astley/Andy Macpherson. CD: *Live at the Isle of Wight Festival 1970*. N: Stereo (3.21). First released in 1996.

Summertime Blues (live) (4)
R: Venue unspecified, U.S. and Canada, December 1982. P: Not credited. Compiled by Cy Langston. U.K./U.S.: *Who's Last*. CD: *Who's Last*. N: Stereo (3.06). First released in 1984.

Sunrise
R: IBC Studios, London, 2 November 1967. P: Kit Lambert. U.K./U.S.: *Sell Out*. CD: *Sell Out*. N: Mono/Stereo (3.03).

Tattoo
R: IBC Studios, London, 12 October 1967. P: Kit Lambert. U.K./U.S.: *Sell Out*. CD: *Sell Out*. N: Mono/Stereo (2.42).

Tattoo (live)
R: Leeds University, England, 14 February 1970. P: The Who (Pete Townshend). CD: *Live at Leeds*. N: Stereo (2.51). First released in 1995.

*That Motherland Feeling** (see *Rael: That Motherland Feeling*)

There's a Doctor
R: IBC Studios, London, October 1968–March 1969. P: Kit Lambert. U.K./U.S.: *Tommy*. CD: *Tommy*. N: Stereo (0.24).

There's a Doctor (live)
R: Isle of Wight Festival, 29 August 1970. P: Jon Astley/Andy Macpherson. CD: *Live at the Isle of Wight Festival 1970*. N: Stereo (0.21). First released in 1996.

There's a Doctor (live) (2)
R: Radio City Music Hall, New York, or Universal Amphitheatre, Los Angeles, 27 June or 24 August 1989 (venue specified as one or the other). P: Billy Nicholls. U.K./U.S.: *Join Together*. CD: *Join Together*. N: Stereo (0.21).

There's a Fortune in Those Hills (demo)*
R: Pete Townshend's home studio,

London, 1969–1970. N: Described as a "slow, wailing country song." Unreleased.

They Are All in Love
R: Ronnie Lane's mobile unit, Shepperton Studios, London, 30 April 1975. P: Glyn Johns. U.K./U.S.: *By Numbers*. CD: *By Numbers*. N: Stereo (3.00). Originally titled "She Loves Everyone." Featuring Nicky Hopkins (piano).

Things Go Better with Coke (see *Coke No. 1*)

Things Have Changed (demo)
R: Pete Townshend's home studio, London, 1965. CD: *Scoop*. N: Mono (2.23). Unrecorded by the Who.

Time Is Passing
R: Olympic Studios, London, 12 April 1971. P: The Who/Glyn Johns. CD: *Odds and Sods*. N: Mono (3.29). First released in 1998. Damage to tape has resulted in a mono mix being released. D: *Who Came First* (3.25).

Time Waits for No Man (see *When I Was a Boy*)

To Barney Kessell (demo)
R: Pete Townshend's home studio, London, 1975. U.K./U.S.: *Scoop*. CD: *Scoop*. N: Stereo (1.58).

Tommy Can You Hear Me?
R: IBC Studios, London, October 1968–March 1969. P: Kit Lambert. U.K./U.S.: *Tommy*. CD: *Tommy*. N: Stereo (1.36).

Tommy Can You Hear Me? (live)
R: Isle of Wight Festival, England, 29 August 1970. P: Jon Astley/Andy Macpherson. CD: *Live at the Isle of Wight Festival 1970*. N: Stereo (0.57). First released in 1996.

Tommy Can You Hear Me? (live) (2)
R: Radio City Music Hall, New York, or Universal Amphitheatre, Los Angeles, 27 June or 24 August 1989 (venue specified as one or the other). P: Billy Nicholls. U.K./U.S.: *Join Together*. CD: *Join Together*. N: Stereo (0.57).

Tommy's Holiday Camp (Keith Moon)
R: IBC Studios, London, October 1968–March 1969. P: Kit Lambert. U.K./U.S.: *Tommy*. CD: *Tommy*. N: Stereo (0.57).

Tommy's Holiday Camp (live)
R: Isle of Wight Festival, England, 29 August 1970. P: Jon Astley/Andy Macpherson. CD: *Live at the Isle of Wight Festival 1970*. N: Stereo (1.01). First released in 1996.

Tommy's Holiday Camp (live) (2)
R: Radio City Music Hall, New York, or Universal Amphitheatre, Los Angeles, 27 June or 24 August 1989 (venue specified as one or the other). P: Billy Nicholls. U.K./U.S.: *Join Together*. CD: *Join Together*. N: Stereo (0.54).

Too Much of Anything
R: Olympic Studios, London, 12 April 1971. P: The Who/Glyn Johns. U.K./U.S.: *Odds and Sods*. CD: *Odds and Sods*. N: Stereo (4.21). Featuring Nicky Hopkins (piano). First released in 1974.

Too Much of Anything (2)
R: Olympic Studios, London, 12 April 1971. P: The Who/Glyn Johns. CD: *Who's Next*. N: Stereo (4.24). Featuring Nicky Hopkins (piano). First released in 1995. This alternate mix of the above track features some different instrumental parts.

Top Gear (Radio One) (radio)
R: BBC Studios, London, 10 October 1967. B: *Top Gear* and *Saturday Club*, BBC Radio 1, 15 and 28 October 1967. CD: *Sell Out*. N: Stereo (0.41).

Trick of the Light (John Entwistle)
R: RAK Studios, London, 13 and 14 March 1978. P: Glyn Johns/Jon Astley. U.K./U.S.: *Who Are You*. CD: *Who Are You*. N: Stereo (4.46). Also released as a

single A side in U.S. (MCA 40978), 2 December 1978.

Trick of the Light (live)
R: British Columbia Place Stadium, Vancouver, Canada, 19 August 1989. P: Billy Nicholls. U.K./U.S.: *Join Together*. CD: *Join Together*. N: Stereo (4.49).

Twist and Shout (Russell/Medley) (live)
Originally performed by the Top Notes circa early 1960s. R: Isle of Wight Festival, England, 29 August 1970. P: Jon Astley/Andy Macpherson. CD: *Live at the Isle of Wight Festival 1970*. N: Stereo (2.20). First released in 1996. Uncredited on disk, as this follows as part of a medley with "Shakin' All Over" and "Spoonful."

Twist and Shout (live) (2)
R: CNE Stadium, Toronto, Canada, 9 October 1982. P: Jon Astley. CD: *30 Years of Maximum R&B*. N: Stereo (3.01). First released in 1994.

Twist and Shout (live) (3)
R: Venue unspecified, U.S. and Canada, December 1982. P: Not credited. Compiled by Cy Langston. U.K./U.S.: *Who's Last*. CD: *Who's Last*. N: Stereo (3.49). First released in 1984. Also released as a single A side in U.K. (MCA 927), November 1984.

The Two of Us*
N: This song was noted as a *Lifehouse* demo in *Disc and Music Echo*, 24 October 1970. It could have subsequently been reworked under a different title (not confirmed).

Under My Thumb (Mick Jagger/Keith Richard)
Originally performed by the Rolling Stones on the LP *Aftermath* (Decca LK 4786), April 1966. R: De Lane Lea Studios, London, 28 June 1967. P: Kit Lambert. U.K.: Single B side of "The Last Time" (Track 604 006), 30 June 1967. CD: *Two's Missing*. N: Mono (2.35).

Under My Thumb (2)
R: De Lane Lea Studios, London, 28 June 1967. P: Kit Lambert. CD: *Odds and Sods*. N: Stereo (2.44). First released in 1998. This is essentially an earlier version of the above, with a simplified bass guitar track and lacking lead electric guitar overdubs. This mix has only very slight stereo separation.

Underture
R: IBC Studios, London, October 1968–March 1969. P: Kit Lambert. U.K./U.S.: *Tommy*. CD: *Tommy*. N: Stereo (10.09).

Underture (live) (see *Sparks* [live]).

Untitled Guitar Theme (demo)*
R: Pete Townshend's home studio, London, 1970. N: Recorded during sessions for *Double Pisces* film.

Unused Piano: Quadrophenia (demo)
R: Pete Townshend's home studio, London, 1973. U.K./U.S.: *Scoop*. CD: *Scoop*. N: Stereo (2.32).

Waltz for a Pig (Butcher)*
This song was credited to the Who Orchestra but is entirely the work of the Graham Bond Organisation and appeared on the B side of both the U.K. and U.S. versions of "Substitute," March 1966.

Wasp Man (Keith Moon)
R: Olympic Studios, London, May–June 1972. P: The Who/Glyn Johns. U.K.: Single B side of "Relay" (Track 2094 106), 16 December 1972. U.S.: Single B side of "Relay" (Decca 33041), 25 November 1972. CD: *Two's Missing*. N: Stereo (3.05).

Water
R: Eel Pie Sound Studios, London, April–May 1970, completed 16 August 1973. P: The Who. U.K.: Single B side "5.15" (Track 2094 115), 5 October 1973. CD: *Odds and Sods*. N: Stereo (4.32).

First released in 1973. Original single release was 7 seconds shorter than CD.

Water (live)
R: Isle of Wight Festival, England, 29 August 1970. P: Jon Astley/Andy Macpherson. CD: *Live at the Isle of Wight Festival 1970*. N: Stereo (8.56). First released in 1996.

Water (live) (2)
R: Young Vic Theatre, London, 26 April 1971. P: The Who. CD: *Who's Next*. N: Stereo (6.25). First released in 1995.

We Close Tonight
R: Ronnie Lane's mobile unit, Ramport Studios, London, 20 June 1973. P: The Who (Pete Townshend). CD: *Odds and Sods*. N: Stereo (2.56). First released in 1998.

Welcome
R: IBC Studios, London, October 1968–March 1969. P: Kit Lambert. U.K./U.S.: *Tommy*. CD: *Tommy*. N: Stereo (4.34).

*We're Moving**
N: This song was noted as a *Lifehouse* demo in *Disc and Music Echo*, 24 October 1970. It could subsequently have been reworked under a different title, probably "Going Mobile.".

We're Not Gonna Take It (incorporating *See Me, Feel Me*; also see separate entry)
R: IBC Studios, London, October 1968–March 1969. P: Kit Lambert. U.K./U.S.: *Tommy*. CD: *Tommy*. N: Stereo (7.09) comprising "We're Not Gonna Take It" (3.30) and "See Me, Feel Me" (3.39). Also released as single B side of "I'm Free" in U.S. (Decca 732519), 5 July 1969.

We're Not Gonna Take It (live)
R: Isle of Wight Festival, England, 29 August 1970. P: Jon Astley/Andy Macpherson. CD: *Live at the Isle of Wight Festival 1970*. N: Stereo (3.40). First released in 1996.

We're Not Gonna Take It (live) (2) (incorporating *See Me, Feel Me*; also see separate entry)
R: Radio City Music Hall, New York, or Universal Amphitheatre, Los Angeles, 27 June or 24 August 1989 (venue specified as one or the other). P: Billy Nicholls. U.K./U.S.: *Join Together*. CD: *Join Together*. N: Stereo (8.42). Timing and indexing incorporates "See Me, Feel Me."

What Is Love? (demo)*
R: Pete Townshend demo, Los Angeles, January 1980. N: Stereo. Unreleased.

When I Was a Boy (John Entwistle)
R: Olympic Studios, London, 7 June 1971. P: The Who/Glyn Johns. U.K.: Single B side of "Let's See Action" (Track 2094 012), 15 October 1971. CD: *Who's Missing*. N: Stereo (3.29). Featuring Nicky Hopkins (piano). Originally logged on tape box as "Time Waits for No Man."

Whiskey Man (John Entwistle)
R: IBC Studios, London, November 1966. P: Kit Lambert. U.K.: *A Quick One*. U.S.: *Happy Jack*. CD: *A Quick One*. N: Mono (2.57). Also released as a single B side of "Happy Jack" in U.S. (Decca 32114), 18 March 1967.

Who Are You
R: Ramport Studios, London, October 1977. P: Glyn Johns/Jon Astley. U.K.: Single A side (Polydor 2121 361 WHO1), 14 July 1978. U.S.: Single A side (MCA 40948), August 1978. CD: *Who Are You*. N: Stereo (6.17). Original single release was an edited version (5.00) of that which appeared as title track of the LP and CD. Promo copies for radio play (and soundtrack to promo film) replaced line "who the fuck are you?" with "who the hell are you?" Featuring Rod Argent (keyboards).

Who Are You (Lost Verse Mix) (2)
R: Ramport Studios, London, October 1977. P: Glyn Johns/Jon Astley. CD:

Who Are You. N: Stereo (6.21). An alternate mix of the above, with different instrument parts and an entirely different second verse. First released in 1996.

Who Are You (film)*
R: Shepperton Studios, London, late 1977. N: Stereo (4.53). This features an alternate take of the song on the soundtrack, released on the videodisc *Who's Better Who's Best* in 1988.

Who Are You (film) (2)*
R: Rehearsal, Shepperton Studios, London, April 1979. N: Mono (3.05). Excerpt included in *30 Years of Maximum R&B Live* video in 1994.

Who Are You (live)
R: Venue unspecified, U.S. and Canada, December 1982. P: Not credited. Compiled by Cy Langston. U.K./U.S.: *Who's Last*. CD: *Who's Last*. N: Stereo (6.28). First released in 1984.

Why Can't You See I'm Easy? (demo)*
R: Pete Townshend's home studio, London 1972. N: Stereo. Unreleased. A version of this song was listed as residing in Polygram's tape library in London, but Jon Astley found that the tape was missing when he attempted to retrieve it in 1995. This could have been a Who version of the song recorded during the May–June 1972 sessions. Some sources drop the "Why" from the title.

Why Did I Fall for That
R: Turn Up-Down Studios, Surrey, England, June 1982. P: Glyn Johns. U.K./U.S.: *It's Hard*. CD: *It's Hard*. N: Stereo (3.56). CD version is 38 seconds longer than original album version.

Wizardry (demo)*
R: Pete Townshend's home studio, London, 1972–1973. N: Unreleased. This is reported to be an outtake from *Quadrophenia*.

*Won't Get Fooled Again**
R: Record Plant, New York, 16 March 1971. P: Kit Lambert/Felix Pappalardi.

N: Stereo (8.56). Featuring Leslie West (guitar). Unreleased.

Won't Get Fooled Again (2)
R: Rolling Stones mobile unit, Stargroves, Berkshire, England, April 1971. P: The Who/Glyn Johns. U.K.: Single A side (Track 2094 009), 25 June 1971. U.S.: Single A side (Decca 32846), 17 July 1971. CD: *Who's Next*. N: Stereo (8.32). For single release a shorter version (3.35) was prepared.

Won't Get Fooled Again (live)
R: Shepperton Studios, London, 25 May 1978. P: John Entwistle. U.K./U.S.: *The Kids Are Alright*. CD: *The Kids Are Alright*. N: Stereo (9.48).

Won't Get Fooled Again (live) (2)
R: Venue unspecified, U.S. and Canada, December 1982. P: Not credited. Compiled by Cy Langston. U.K./U.S.: *Who's Last*. CD: *Who's Last*. N: Stereo (10.03). First released in 1984.

Won't Get Fooled Again (live) (3)
R: Universal Amphitheatre, Los Angeles, 24 August 1989. P: Billy Nicholls. U.K./U.S.: *Join Together*. CD: *Join Together*. N: Stereo (9.29).

You (John Entwistle)
R: Odyssey Studios, London, June–December 1980. P: Bill Szymczyk. U.K./U.S.: *Face Dances*. CD: *Face Dances*. N: Stereo (4.40). Also released as single B side of "Don't Let Go the Coat" in U.K. (Polydor WHO5), 1 May 1981, and in U.S. (Warner Bros. WBS 49743), May 1981.

You Better You Bet
R: Odyssey Studios, London, 4 November 1980. P: Bill Szymczyk. U.K.: A side of single (Polydor 2002 044 WHO4), 27 February 1981. U.S.: A side of single (Warner Bros. WBS 49698), March 1981. CD: *Face Dances*. N: Stereo (5.32). Original single release was an edited version. D: *Another Scoop* (5.16).

You Better You Bet (live)
R: Jack Murphy Stadium, San Diego, 22 August 1989. P: Billy Nicholls. U.K./U.S.: *Join Together*. CD: *Join Together*. N: Stereo (5.39).

You Came Back (demo)
R: Pete Townshend's home studio, London, circa 1974. U.K./U.S.: *Scoop*. CD: *Scoop*. N: Stereo (4.03).

You Don't Have to Jerk*
R: London, early 1965. P: Shel Talmy. N: It is reported that this song was recorded as a possible single A side for early 1965 but was soon abandoned. Pete Townshend definitely recorded a demo version, but a Who version remains unheard. "The Jerk" was a dance instigated by a song of the same name by the Larks single A side (Money 106), October 1964. This was followed by "Can You Jerk Like Me?," a single A side by the Contours (Gordy 7037), 16 November 1964, and "Come on Do the Jerk," a single A side by the Miracles (Tamla 54109), 20 November 1964. Only the Larks single reached the U.S. charts, but all three songs were popular on mod dance floors for a short while.

You Rang (TV)*
R: London, late 1965. B: *Ready Steady Go!* and *The New Year Starts Here!* ITV TV, 24 and 31 December 1965. N: Mono. A mainly instrumental work with John Entwistle's impersonation of Lurch from "The Addams Family" TV show. It is thought that the track actually originated from this show.

Young Man Blues (Mose Allison)*
Originally performed by Mose Allison as part of his *Back Country Suite* and called "Blues" (Prestige PRLP 7091), March 1957. Retitled by the Who and originally intended for *Tommy*. R: IBC Studios, London, October 1968. P: Kit Lambert. U.K.: *The House That Track Built*. N: Stereo (2.47).

Young Man Blues (2)
R: IBC Studios, London, October 1968. P: Kit Lambert. CD: *Odds and Sods*. N: Stereo (2.44). First released in 1998.

Young Man Blues (live)
R: Coliseum, London, 14 December 1969. U.K./U.S.: *The Kids Are Alright*. CD: *The Kids Are Alright*. N: Mono (5.46).

Young Man Blues (live) (2)
R: Leeds University, England, 14 February 1970. P: The Who (Pete Townshend). U.K./U.S.: *Live at Leeds*. CD: *Live at Leeds*. N: Stereo (4.56). The original LP version was edited down to (4.38), and the CD version restores some of this excision. The master tape runs to (5.13).

Young Man Blues (live) (3).
R: Isle of Wight Festival, 29 August 1970. P: Jon Astley/Andy Macpherson. CD: *Live at the Isle of Wight Festival 1970*. N: Stereo (5.28). First released in 1996.

You're Going to Know Me (see *Out in the Street*)

You're So Clever (demo)
R: Pete Townshend's home studio, London, 1979. U.K./U.S.: *Scoop*. CD: *Scoop*. N: Stereo (4.14).

Zelda (demo)
R: Pete Townshend's home studio, London, 1980. U.K./U.S.: *Scoop*. CD: *Scoop*. N: Stereo (2.23).

Zoot Suit (Peter Meaden)
Based on "Country Fool" by the Showmen, 1961. R: Fontana Studios, London, June 1964. P: Chris Parmeinter/Peter Meaden. U.K.: Single B side (Fontana TF480), 3 July 1964. CD: *30 Years of Maximum R&B*. N: Mono (1.57). This was remixed for the boxed set into stereo.

Index

Entries refer to names and titles to be found in the main text and notes only. For reasons of space I have omitted separate entries for The Who, Roger Daltrey, Keith Moon, Pete Townshend, John Entwistle and Kenney Jones.

Ace 220
"The Acid Queen" 118, 122
The Action 17, 50, 80
Adams, Jack 149
The Aerodrome (Rex Warner) 143
Aerosmith 9
Afghan Wigs 270
Aftermath (Rolling Stones) 64
"Albatross" (Fleetwood Mac) 58
Aldridge, Alan 82
Alexander, Arthur 12
"All I Really Want to Do" (Bob Dylan) 99
"All My Loving" (Beatles) 56
All the Best Cowboys Have Chinese Eyes (Pete Townshend) 28, 258, 260, 263
Allison, Mose 5, 12, 77, 114, 128
Also Sprach Zarathustra (Strauss) 116
Altham, Keith 30, 73
"Amazing Journey" 112, 118, 122, 133, 137
Amazing Journey (proposed album title) 106, 111
Amen Corner 8
American Graffiti (film) 190, 191, 209
The Animals 8, 18, 32, 34
Ann-Margret 212
Another Scoop (Pete Townshend) 35, 246, 268, 274
"Another Tricky Day" 257
Ant, Adam 253
Antonioni, Michelangelo 20
"Anytime You Want Me" 45, 47, 53
"Anyway Anyhow Anywhere" 20, 36, 40, 45–47, 49, 50, 53, 55, 65, 81, 248
Appice, Carmine 245

Arbus, Dave 158
Argent, Rod 233
"Armenia City in the Sky" 93
Arthur (Kinks) 125
"Ask Yourself" (Pete Townshend) 267
Aspel & Company (TV) 269
The Assembled Multitude 135
Astley, Edwin (Ted) 236, 246
Astley, Jon 3, 34, 36, 61, 82, 86, 98, 120–121, 133, 136, 137, 166, 167, 169, 209, 228, 233, 236, 241, 259, 265, 269, 271–272
At the Speed of Sound (Wings) 221
"Athena" 261–262, 266
Atlantic Crossing (Rod Stewart) 221
Auger, Brian 15, 113
Axis: Bold as Love (Jimi Hendrix) 97

Baba, Meher 24, 101–102, 104, 105, 112, 121, 122–123, 125, 134, 169, 175, 187, 192, 204, 208, 236, 238, 239, 256
"Baba O'Riley" 154, 155, 158–159, 161, 164, 167, 179, 233, 248, 251, 252
"Baby Don't You Do It" 35–36, 45, 147, 149, 150, 151, 167, 171, 172, 213, 243
Back Country Suite (Mose Allison) 77, 114
Bacon, Francis 259
Bad Company 219
"Bag O'Nails" 98
Baird, Roy 191
Baker, Ginger 245
"Bald Headed Woman" 42
The Band 113
Band of Gypsies (Jimi Hendrix) 217
Bangs, Lester 209
"Bank Holiday" 181

331

"Barbara Ann" 69, 72, 74, 75, 76, 248
Barber, Lynden 265
"Bargain" 142, 154, 155, 159, 167, 171, 223, 235, 243, 268
Barling, David M. 208
Barnes, Richard 3, 11, 13, 31, 32, 41, 72, 273, 275
"Baroque Ippanese" (Pete Townshend) 267
Barrel One, Barrel Two (proposed film title) 144
Barrett, Wild Willy 219
The Barron Knights 69
Bart, Lionel 107, 205
Bartok, Bela 211
The Basement Tapes (Bob Dylan) 214
Basket of Light (Pentangle) 275
"Batman" 74, 75, 79
Batman (TV) 75
Baverstock, Jack 32
Bax, Sir Arnold 208
Bayliss, Lilian 84
The Beach Boys 12, 25, 39, 69, 71, 75, 209, 257
The Beachcombers 58
Beat Club (TV) 21
Beat Merchants (Alan Clayson) 274
"Beat Up" 114
The Beatles 1, 6, 7, 8, 11, 12, 16, 18, 20, 21, 22, 24, 25, 30, 31, 34, 36, 38, 39, 41, 49, 56, 58, 64, 73, 79, 82, 83, 93, 97, 99, 111, 114, 117, 127, 129, 217
The Beatles (White Album) 114
"Beatnik Fly" (Tune Rockers) 58
Beck, Jeff 15, 16, 132
Before the Flood (Bob Dylan) 229
"Begin the Beguine" (Pete Townshend) 134
"Behind Blue Eyes" 149, 150, 151, 154, 155, 162, 164, 167, 168, 225, 228, 230, 231, 252
"Bell Boy" 186, 193, 195, 203–205, 206, 250
Benson, A.C. 75
Berry, Chuck 6, 12, 30, 58, 209
Billy Budd (Britten) 208
Billy Budd (film) 273
The Billy Cotton Band Show (TV) 21
The Birds 50, 80
Birtwistle, Sir Harrison 6
Black Sabbath 127, 132
Blackburn, Tony 115
Blackwell, Otis 12, 45
Blake, Peter 259

Blonde on Blonde (Bob Dylan) 114
Blow-Up (film) 20
"Blue Red and Grey" 225–226, 228
Blur 8, 9, 272
"Body Language" (Pete Townshend) 254
Boellmann, Léon 95
Bon Jovi 9
Bond, Graham 66
"Bony Moronie" 147, 153, 268
Bonzo Dog Doo–Dah Band 92, 97
"Boogie Friday" (Pete Townshend) 254
"Boris the Spider" 73, 76, 79, 83, 85, 106, 170
Boston 219
Bowie, David 175, 189, 191, 213, 219, 253
The Boyfriend (film) 211
Bradbury, Ray 143
Bragg, Melvyn 246
The Brain Opera (proposed album title) 111
Brave New World (Aldous Huxley) 143, 236
Brecht, Bertolt 200
Bridge, Frank 208
Brinsley Schwartz 220
Britten, Sir Benjamin 208
Bronco Bullfrog (film) 187–189, 191, 278
"Brooklyn Kids" (Pete Townshend) 246
Brown, Arthur 40, 88; see also Crazy World of Arthur Brown
Brown, James 12, 31, 45, 49, 53, 55, 57, 59
Brown, Joe 29
"Brrr" (Pete Townshend) 228
Brubeck, Dave 120
"Bucket T" 74, 75, 110
Bundrick, John "Rabbit" 27, 245
Burgess, Anthony 143, 189
Bushell, Garry 265
Buzzcocks 231, 274
By Numbers 26–27, 217, 218–228, 229, 235, 239–240, 271
The Byrds 3, 39, 60, 64, 69, 90, 97, 99, 136

"Cache Cache" 256
"Call Me Lightning" 41, 100, 102, 103, 104, 105, 107, 108
Can't Wait to See the Movie (Roger Daltrey) 268
"Capital Radio" (The Clash) 232
The Carpenters 90
Carr, Roy 164, 192, 214, 218, 227, 258
Carson, Tom 259

The Cascades 249
Cast 270
The Cat 69
"Cat Snatch" (Pete Townshend) 267
Catch Us If You Can (film) 21
"Cat's in the Cupboard" (Pete Townshend) 252
Cavanagh, David 271
Chad 208
"Champagne" (*Tommy* film soundtrack) 212
Chapman, Mike 212
"Charles Atlas Course" 94–95
Charlesworth, Chris 3, 28, 41, 67, 93, 171, 210, 227, 258, 270–272, 276, 279
Charnock, Graham 133
Charone, Barbara 214, 215, 258
Chicago 114
Chicago Transit Authority (Chicago) 114
Chinese Eyes see *All the Best Cowboys Have Chinese Eyes*
Chinn, Nicky 212
"Choirboy" (early title of "Empty Glass") 118, 121, 122, 123
"Christmas" 118, 121, 122, 123
"Circles" 51, 54, 59, 60–61, 64, 65–66, 67, 68, 71, 74, 76, 82, 227
Citizen Kane (film) 207
Clapton, Eric 6, 8, 15, 132, 246
The Clash 3, 8, 175, 176, 198–199, 231–232, 253
"Clash City Rockers" (The Clash) 232
Clayson, Alan 77, 274
A Clockwork Orange (Anthony Burgess) 143, 180
A Clockwork Orange (film) 163, 189–190
"C'mon Everybody" 106
"Cobwebs and Strange" 73, 76, 80, 93
Cochran, Eddie 12, 52, 98, 130
Cocker, Joe 181
Cockney Rebel 175, 219
Cohn, Nik 113, 132, 177, 258
"Coke 1" 86, 98
"Coke 2" 86, 98
The Collector (film) 273
Collins, Phil 236
Coltrane, John 60
"Come On" (Rolling Stones) 18
"Complete Control" (The Clash) 198
Comyns, Barbara 53
Concerts for the People of Kampuchea (Various Artists) 251–252
Connolly, Ray 191
Conrad, Joseph 193, 208

"Content" (Pete Townshend) 134
"Control Myself" (early title of "Dreaming from the Waist") 224
Cook, Paul 231
"Cookin'" (Pete Townshend) 106
"Cooks County" 262
Count Bishops 220
"Country Fool" (The Showmen) 32
Country Joe & the Fish 83
"Cousin Kevin" 118, 123, 124, 136
"Cousin Kevin Model Child" 114, 213
The Crazy World of Arthur Brown 39–40, 113, 269; *see also* Brown, Arthur
Cream 68, 97, 114, 149
The Creation 16, 50
Cribbins, Bernard 275
Crosby, David 96
Crosby, Stills and Nash 96
Crosby, Stills, Nash and Young 136, 173
Cross Section 250
"Cry If You Want" 264, 266, 267
Cry of Love (Jimi Hendrix) 214
"Crying Town" 77, 81
The Crystals 249
Curbishley, Bill 215, 245, 247
Curle, John 196
"Cut My Hair" 179–180, 186, 193, 195–196, 197

"Daddy Rolling Stone" 45, 53
"Daily Records" 257
Daltrey (Roger Daltrey) 180
The Damned 231, 232
"Dance It Away" 251, 254
A Dance to the Music of Time (Anthony Powell) 200
"Dancing in the Street" 66–67, 69, 251, 268
"Dangerous" 262, 267
Dark Side of the Moon (Pink Floyd) 189
The Dave Clark Five 8, 10, 21
Davies, Dave 14, 275
Davies, Ray 7, 41, 65, 212
Dawson, Colin 13
"Day of Silence" (Pete Townshend) 134
Dead Sea Fruit 69
Deaf, Dumb and Blind Boy (proposed album title) 111
Debussy, Claude 208, 211
Dee, Mercy 114
Deep Purple 132
Def Leppard 9
Delius, Frederick 200, 208, 211
De Seduoy, Alain 20

The Detours 11–15, 30–31
Deviants 174
The Devils (film) 211, 216
Devoto, Howard 274
"Did You Steal My Money?" 256
Diddley, Bo 12, 33, 45, 71, 109, 147, 230
"Dig" 269
Dion 69
Dire Straits 8
Direct Hits 110–111
"The Dirty Jobs" 181, 182, 193, 199–200
"Dirty Water" (Pete Townshend) 254
"Disguises" 69, 72, 74–75, 110
Disraeli Gears (Cream) 97
"Do the Strip" (Pete Townshend) 51
"Do You Think It's Alright?" 119, 137
"Do You Want Kids, Kids?" 104, 105
"Doctor Doctor" 82, 84, 85
Dr. Feelgood 220
"Dr. Jekyll & Mr. Hyde" 102, 103, 104, 109
Dr. Jekyll and Mr. Hyde see *The Strange Case of Dr. Jekyll and Mr. Hyde*
"Doctor Jimmy" 193, 205–206, 250, 266
Dodgy 270
"Dogs" 100, 106, 107–108, 170
"Dogs Part Two" 113, 116, 173, 243
Donegan, Lonnie 275
"Don't Let Go the Coat" 255–256, 259
"Don't Look Away" 76, 80
The Doors 113
Dornan, Don 97
Double Pisces (film) 134
"Drag City" (Jan and Dean) 71
"Dream Sequence" (early title of "Sparks") 115
"Dream Sequence (Underture)" (early title of "Underture") 115
"Dreaming from the Waist" 224, 228, 229, 230–231
"Drowned" 181–182, 187, 193, 203–204, 247, 252
Druce, Frank 13
Du Noyer, Paul 265
Ducks Deluxe 220
Dunlop, Frank 146, 147, 148
Duran Duran 253
Dylan (Bob Dylan) 214
Dylan, Bob 1, 22, 41, 65, 99, 113, 114, 117, 127, 129, 136, 166, 214, 229

The Eagles 259, 265
Early Flight (Jefferson Airplane) 214
"Early Morning Cold Taxi" 98
Eastham, Linda 273

Eddy, Duane 12
"Eight Miles High" (Byrds) 60, 69, 90
Electric Ladyland (Jimi Hendrix) 114
Elgar, Sir Edward 75, 208, 211
Eliot, George 95
Eliot, T.S. 159, 163
Emerson Lake and Palmer 219
Emery, John 47
"Eminence Front" 262–263, 264, 265–266, 267
"Empty Glass" 241–242, 252
Empty Glass (Pete Townshend) 28, 168, 242, 254, 257–258, 259, 260, 263
Escher, M.C. 121
Essex, David 190
The Everly Brothers 12, 54, 66, 68, 93
Every Day's a Holiday (film) 21, 77
"Excerpt from a Teenage Opera" (Keith West) 111
The Eyes 50
"Eyesight to the Blind" 114, 118, 122

Face Dances 27, 251, 254–260, 261, 265, 267, 270, 271
"Face Dances" ("Face Dances Part Two") 254, 259
Face to Face (Kinks) 64, 81
The Faces 168, 174, 228, 244
Fahrenheit 451 (Ray Bradbury) 143
Fairweather-Low, Andy 233, 262
"Faith in Something Bigger" 102, 104, 213
Family 127
Far from the Madding Crowd (film) 273
Farren, Mick 164
Ferry, Bryan 213
"The Ferryman" (Pete Townshend) 246
"Fiddle About" 119, 122, 123, 124
Fielder, Hugh 258
Fifth Dimension (Byrds) 64
"Fight Until You're Mine" 228
"Fire" 269
Fireball XL5 (TV) 30
The First Rays of the New Rising Sun (Jimi Hendrix) 25
Fish Shop (story by Pete Townshend) 246
"5.15" 181, 182, 191, 193, 202–203, 247, 250, 251
Fleetwood Mac 58, 219, 265
The Fleur-De-Lys 68, 69
Flying Burrito Brothers 136
Fontaine, Dick 134
"Football Fugue" (Pete Townshend) 246
Ford, John 97
Foreigner 219, 236, 262

Index

Formby, George 224
"Fortune Teller" 106, 109, 133, 136
"Four Faces" 181, 250
Frampton, Peter 219, 229
Frampton Comes Alive (Peter Frampton) 229
Freak Out (Mothers of Invention) 114
Freddie and the Dreamers 10, 77
"Free Me" (Roger Daltrey) 252
Freud, Lucian 259
The Fugs 92
Funeral Music for Queen Mary (Purcell) 70
Fury, Billy 30, 190

Garden of Fand (Bax) 208
Gaudier-Brzeska, Henri 211
Gaye, Marvin 12, 35, 108
Genesis 127, 175, 219, 236, 262
Gerry and the Pacemakers 8
Gertler, Mark 202
Get Back (Beatles) 25
"Get Out and Stay Out" 181, 250
"Getting in Tune" 147, 149, 150, 151, 155, 161, 167, 181, 238
Gilbert, William S. 72, 119, 237–238
"Girl from Lincoln County" 114–115
"Girl in a Suitcase" (Pete Townshend) 228
"Girl's Eyes" 98
"Giving It All Away" (Roger Daltrey) 180
"Glittering Girl" 85, 98, 102
"Glow Girl" 98, 99, 102–103, 109, 213
"Go to the Mirror" 117, 119, 122
Goddard, Lon 171
"Goin' Fishing" 106
"Going Down" 171, 268
"Going Mobile" 136, 142, 154, 155, 161
Goldman, Albert 126
Gonks Go Beat (film) 21
"Gonna Get You" (Pete Townshend) 252
"Good Lovin'" 49
"The Good's Gone" 51, 54, 55–56, 60
Gorden, Helmut 13, 16, 32, 37
Gorman, Tim 262
"Got Love If You Want It" (Slim Harpo) 32
Graham Parker and the Rumour 220
Grand Funk Railroad 132
Grateful Dead 83
"Gratis Amatis" 72
Gray, Barry 30
Grease (musical) 183
"Great Shakes" 102, 105
Green, Mick 14
Green, Richard 59, 68, 126, 132, 139

"The Green Mosquito" (Johnny & the Hurricanes) 58
"Greyhound Girl" (Pete Townshend) 168
Grieg, Edvard 99
Gross, Mike 144
"Guitar and Pen" 168, 235, 237–238, 240, 241, 242
Guitar Farm (proposed film title) 177
Guns n' Roses 9
"Guns on the Roof" (The Clash) 232

"Had Enough" 234, 236, 262
Haley, Bill 6
"Hall of the Mountain King" 87, 98, 99
Hamilton, Richard 259
"Happenings Ten Years Time Ago" (Yardbirds) 274
Happy Birthday (Various Artists) 134
"Happy Jack" 74, 76, 77–78, 81, 82, 83, 84, 85, 106, 133, 178, 217, 248
Happy Jack 81
"A Hard Day's Night" (Beatles) 34
A Hard Day's Night (film) 21
Harpo, Slim 32
"Harry Rag" (Kinks) 105
Harry Roche Constellation 275
Harvest (Neil Young) 217
Harvey, P.J. 8
"The Hawker" 114, 118
Hawkwind 174, 175, 189
"Heat Wave" 45, 47, 48, 59, 69, 72, 76, 79–80, 81, 268
"Heaven and Hell" 133, 134, 135
Heilpern, John 64
"Heinz Baked Beans" 93
"Helpless Dancer" 193, 195, 199–200, 206
Hendrix, Jimi 6, 16, 25, 68, 83, 84, 97, 114, 214, 217
Hepworth, David 249
"Her Man's Been Gone" 77, 81
"Here for More" 129, 136
"Here 'Tis" 33
Herman's Hermits 10, 23, 87
Hesse, Herman 208
"Hi-Heeled Sneakers" (Cross Section) 250
High Windows (Philip Larkin) 277
"Hitchcock Railway" (Joe Cocker) 181
Hockney, David 259
Hold On (film) 21
Holland, Eddie 33
The Hollies 8
Holly, Buddy 80, 214
"Holly Like Ivy" (Pete Townshend) 267
Hooligans 260

Hopkins, Nicky 45, 52, 54, 55, 57, 58, 59, 154, 161, 166, 181, 182, 220
Hopkins, Phil 3, 36
"House of the Rising Sun" (Animals) 34
The House That Track Built (Various Artists) 128
"How Can You Do It Alone" 251, 256–257, 260
"How Many Friends" 222, 226
"However Much I Booze" 220, 223–224, 229
Hughes, Graham 208
Hughes, Ted 269
Hush, Michelle 180
Huxley, Aldous 143
Hyperhead 272

"I Always Say" (Pete Townshend) 106
I Am (Various Artists) 174
"I Am the Sea" 193, 194
"I Can See for Miles" 89–91, 93, 94, 98, 107, 108, 115, 120, 201, 248, 269
"I Can't Explain" 19, 20, 31, 35, 40–41, 42–44, 45, 46, 56, 61, 65, 74, 77, 106, 133, 229, 231, 243, 247, 248
"I Can't Reach You" 89, 91, 95
"I Don't Even Know Myself" 134, 135, 136, 137, 147, 154, 156, 165, 167
"I Don't Mind" 44–45, 47, 54, 55, 57, 59
"I Feel Fine" (Beatles) 16
"I Gotta Dance to Keep from Crying" (Miracles) 200
"I Like Nightmares" 259
"I Need You" 73, 76, 79, 80
"I Need You (Like I Need a Hole in the Head)" (proposed early title) 73
Ibsen, Henrik 99
Iggy and the Stooges 219; *see also* Pop, Iggy
"I'm a Boy" 69, 70–72, 73, 78, 106, 133, 170, 178
"I'm a Man" 45, 47, 54, 57, 59, 60, 71, 76, 269
"I'm Free" 85, 106, 120, 128, 133, 252
"I'm One" 191, 193, 197, 199, 211, 250, 251
"I'm the Face" 18, 30, 32–34, 38, 203, 213, 248
"Imagine a Man" 218, 219, 222, 224–225
"In a Hand or a Face" 226–227
"In My Lonely Room" (The Action) 80
"In the City" 71, 74, 76
"In the City" (The Jam) 71
"Instant Party" 60, 61, 66, 67; *see also* "Circles"

Instant Party (Everly Brothers) 54
"Instrumental—No Title" 86
"Interstellar Overdrive" (Pink Floyd) 95
The Iron Heel (Jack London) 143
The Iron Man (Pete Townshend) 269
"Is It in My Head?" 171, 173, 193, 200–201
"Is It Me?" 195, 205–206
"It Was You" 30–31, 35, 41
"It's a Boy" 117, 121
"It's Alright" (Rockin' Vicars) 68, 80
"It's Hard" 262, 266, 267
It's Hard 27, 260–266, 267, 269, 270, 271
"It's in You" 260
"It's Not True" 51, 54, 57–58, 59
It's Only Rock and Roll (Rolling Stones) 221
"It's Your Turn" 262
"I've Been Away" 78
"I've Had Enough" 186, 193, 201–202, 203, 236, 250
"I've Known No War" 263
Ivor the Engine (TV) 274
"Ivor the Engine Driver" 77, 81
The Ivy League 42, 45

Jack the Barber 32
Jacklin, Bill 259
Jagger, Mick 85–86, 152
"Jaguar" 87, 98–99
The Jam 175, 231, 232, 253
James, Elmore 109
Jan and Dean 71, 75, 102
Jefferson Airplane 83, 96, 214
Jerry Maguire (film) 272
Jesus and Mary Chain 132
Jethro Tull 127, 189
Jigsaw Puzzle (proposed album title) 76
Joe Loss Pop Show (radio) 49
John, Elton 175, 221, 264, 269–270
"John Mason Cars" 98
Johnny & The Hurricanes 58
Johnny Kidd and the Pirates 12, 13, 14, 82–83, 109; *see also* Kidd, Johnny
Johns, Andy 152
Johns, Glyn 42, 151–152, 153–154, 155, 165, 167, 171, 228, 230, 233, 234, 236, 260, 261, 265
"Join My Gang" (Oscar) 72, 80
"Join Together" 165, 167, 171, 172, 174, 178, 230, 248, 263, 269
Join Together 269
"Joker James" 178–179, 181, 250
Jones, Brian 15

Jones, Colin 64
Jones, Nick 76
Jones, Peter 157
Jones, Steve 231
Jopling, Norman 72
Journey 236
Journey into Space (proposed album title) 111
Joyce, James 207
"Jules and Jim" (Pete Townshend) 252
Julie Driscoll, Brian Augur and the Trinity 113
"Just You and Me, Darling" 49

Kansas 219, 262
Keaton, Buster 80
Keene, John "Speedy" 93
"Keep Me Turning" (Pete Townshend and Ronnie Lane) 228
"Keep on Working" (Pete Townshend) 242
"Kensington High Street" (Dead Sea Fruit) 69
Khan, Inayat 142, 276
Kick Out the Jams (MC5) 217
Kidd, Johnny 30, 130; *see also* Johnny Kidd and the Pirates
"The Kids Are Alright" 35, 41, 54, 56–57, 60, 62, 67, 68
The Kids Are Alright (soundtrack) 46, 91, 110, 128, 230, 232–233, 245, 247–249, 250
The Kids Are Alright (film) 19, 46, 91, 110, 128, 230, 232–233, 247–248, 274
Kilburn and the High Roads 219
"Kill My Appetite" (Pete Townshend) 51
King, David 92
King, Freddie 171
King Biscuit Flower Hour (radio) 211, 278
King Crimson 127
The Kinks 1, 2, 3, 11, 12, 18, 22, 30, 32, 34, 36, 39, 40, 41, 42, 50, 52, 64, 69, 73, 81, 94, 97, 105, 111, 117, 125, 189, 217, 232, 275
Kiss 219
The Knack (film) 189
Kooper, Al 88, 91, 99, 113, 149, 150, 181
Kray, Ronald & Reginald 253
Kubrick, Stanley 163, 189
Kursaal Flyers 220

La Mer (Debussy) 208
"La-La-La-Lies" 51, 54, 56, 58, 60, 67
LaBelle 148

Lambert, Constant 23, 273
Lambert, Kit 18, 21, 22, 23, 30, 35, 37–38, 39, 40, 47, 48, 51, 54, 64, 69, 70, 72, 74, 76, 78, 82, 84, 88, 90, 96, 101, 105, 112, 114, 120, 121, 128, 135, 137, 146, 147, 148–149, 151, 164, 179, 182–183, 214–215, 246, 253, 269, 273
"Land of Hope and Glory" (Edward Elgar & AC Benson) 75
Lane, Ronnie 181, 220, 228, 230, 232
Langston, Cyrano 98
Larkin, Philip 185
Last, James 275
The Last Picture Show (film) 190
"The Last Time" 85
Law, Roger 92
"Lazy Fat People" (Barron Knights) 69
"Lazy Sunday" (Small Faces) 107–108
Leary, Timothy 129
"Leaving Here" 33, 35–36, 45, 47, 48, 49, 59, 80, 213, 243, 268
Led Zeppelin 39, 42, 127, 132, 144, 157, 178, 219, 221, 248
Lee, Alvin 132
Lee Lewis, Jerry 6, 30
"A Legal Matter" 51, 54, 57, 62, 67
Lennon, John 7, 79, 213, 221
"Let My Love Open the Door" (Pete Townshend) 168
"Let's See Action" 165, 168, 169–170, 172, 178
Levy, Arthur 209
Lewis, Nancy 103
Lifehouse (proposed film and album title) 22, 24, 25, 27, 136, 138, 141–155, 165, 166, 167, 168, 169, 171, 174, 176, 177, 179, 181, 185, 189, 191, 239, 246, 247, 270
A Life's Dance (Delius) 200
"Like It the Way It Is" (Pete Townshend) 242
Lindsay-Hogg, Michael 217
Listzomania (film) 219
"Little Billy" 104–105, 106, 213
Little Richard 6, 30
Live at Leeds 24, 28, 128, 129–133, 135, 136, 137, 139, 170, 171, 215, 229, 248, 271
Live at the Fillmore (proposed album title) 105–106
Live at the Isle of Wight Festival 1970 136–137, 271
Live in London (film) 86
Live It Up (film) 21

Lloyd Webber, Andrew 237
Logan, Nick 164
London, Jack 143
London Symphony Orchestra (L.S.O.) 275
The Lone Ranger (film) 134
The Loneliness of the Long-Distance Runner (Alan Sillitoe) 184
"Long Live Rock" 171, 173–174, 179, 180, 186, 190, 191, 213, 220, 248, 266
"Long Tall Sally" (Kinks) 18
Look Back in Anger (John Osborne) 184
Lord Jim (Joseph Conrad) 208
"The Lost Chord" (Arthur Sullivan) 276
"Love Ain't for Keeping" 149, 150, 151, 154, 155, 159, 213
"Love Hurts" 66, 68
"Love Is Coming Down" 238, 241, 242
"The Love Man" (Pete Townshend) 134
"Love Me Do" (Beatles) 18
"Love Reign O'er Me" 171, 172, 173, 182, 185, 187, 191, 192, 195, 201, 206, 208, 256
Love You Live (Rolling Stones) 229
Lovin' Spoonful 69
"Lubie (Come Back Home)" 45, 47, 48, 268
Lulu and the Luvvers 53
Lyons, Irish Jack 2, 3, 11, 17, 186
Lyon-Shaw, Damon 275

McCartney, Sir Paul 229
McInnerney, Michael 114, 121
Mackie, Robin 178, 209
McMichael, Joe 2, 3, 4, 11
Macpherson, Andy 4, 136, 169, 209
McVicar, John 246
McVicar (film) 252–253
Mad Dog (John Entwistle) 216
"Mad Goose" (Beachcombers) 58
"Magic Bus" 104, 109–110, 111, 131, 170, 248
Magic Bus — The Who on Tour 110–111
Magical Mystery Tour (TV) 217
Magritte, René 121
Mahler, Gustav 211
"A Man Is a Man" 264
"Man with Money" 66, 68, 74, 81–82
Manic Street Preachers 132
Mann, Manfred 15
Marcus, Greil 241, 249
Marsh, Dave 3, 11, 31, 95, 105, 164, 209, 227
Martha and the Vandellas 12, 45, 48, 66

Martin, Gavin 258
Marvin, Hank 14, 15
"Mary" 155, 160, 163, 165, 166, 171
"Mary Anne with the Shaky Hand" 89, 91, 98, 99, 105, 213, 268
"Mary Jane" (Pete Townshend) 134
Matthew, Brian 60
MC5 8, 132, 217
Meaden, Peter 16–18, 30, 31–33, 37–38, 253, 273
Meaty Beaty Big & Bouncy 71, 110, 170–171, 215, 231
"Medac" 95, 98
"Meher Baba M3" (Pete Townshend) 166
"Meher Baba M4 (Signal Box)" (Pete Townshend) 166, 239
"Meher Baba M5 (Vivaldi)" (Pete Townshend) 166
"Melancholia" 98, 99, 107, 108–109
Melly, George 7
"Memphis Tennessee" (Chuck Berry) 58
Mendelsohn, John 164
The Merry-Go-Round (Mark Gertler) 202
The Merseys 69, 77
Metal Machine Music (Lou Reed) 268, 279
Metallica 9
Metamorphosis (Rolling Stones) 214
Metzker (or Metzke), Gustav 10, 19, 38, 273
Miles 126
Miller, Max 224
Milligan, Spike 150
Mimms, Garnet 45
The Mindbenders 8
"Miracle Cure" 119
Miracles 200
Mods! (Richard Barnes) 273
Monkees 101
Monro, Matt 238
Monterey Pop (film) 21, 85
Montgomery, David 92
Monty Python's Flying Circus (TV) 150, 217
Morrissey 8
"Mother and Son" (*Tommy* film soundtrack) 212
Mothers of Invention 92, 97, 114; *see also* Zappa, Frank
"Motoring" 45, 47, 48, 268
Mott the Hoople 168
Mountain 149
Mozart, Wolfgang Amadeus 236

"Much Too Much" 51, 54, 56
Mud 212
Murray, Charles Shaar 209, 234, 240, 241, 249
"Music" (Inayat Khan) 276
Music Ho! (Constant Lambert) 273
"Music Must Change" 27, 235, 236, 237, 240, 242, 247, 263
"My Generation" 20, 38, 46, 51–53, 54, 55, 56, 57, 59, 60, 63, 64, 65, 68, 70, 77, 78, 83, 85, 91, 103, 106, 125, 128, 129, 130–131, 133, 158, 171, 176, 185, 191, 222, 223, 229, 230, 232, 241, 247, 248, 264, 265
My Generation 22, 53, 54–59, 61, 67, 68, 75, 78, 82, 89, 98, 253
"My Generation Blues" 230
"My Generation/Land of Hope and Glory" 74, 75, 82
My Generation—The Very Best of the Who 271
"My Way" 98, 106, 213
"My Wife" 147, 154, 155, 158, 159–160, 161, 163, 169, 171, 230, 232–233, 248, 252, 264, 268
"The Mysticism of Sound" (Inayat Khan) 276

"Naked Eye" 131, 134, 135, 136, 137, 147, 153, 165, 167, 171, 213
Nationwide (TV) 247
The Naturals 31
Nazareth 219
Nelson, Sandy 58
Nero & the Gladiators 99
"Never Ask Me" (Pete Townshend) 238
New Seekers 275
"New Song" 235–236, 240, 243
Newley, Anthony 275
Newman, Tony 245
The Nice 113
Nicholls, Billy 233
Nicholls, Michael 233
Nicholson, Jack 212
Nikcol, Peter 171
"905" 236, 241
Nineteen Eighty-Four (George Orwell) 143
"1921" 117–118, 122
Nirvana 8, 9, 132
"No Road Romance" (Pete Townshend) 242
Nostromo (Joseph Conrad) 207, 208

"The Note" (early title of "Pure and Easy") 142, 150
"Now I'm a Farmer" 106, 134, 136, 213

Oasis 8, 9
The Oceanides (Sibelius) 208
Odds and Sods 32, 34, 36, 85, 91, 98, 103, 104, 114, 128, 166, 167, 174, 181, 210, 213–214, 215, 248, 271
"Odorono" 93, 98
Ogden's Nut Gone Flake (Small Faces) 111
Old Grey Whistle Test (TV) 173, 180
Omnibus: All My Loving (TV) 273
"On the Road Again" (Lovin' Spoonful) 69
"One at a Time" 263–264
101-ers 220
"One Life's Enough" 263
One of the Boys (Roger Daltrey) 232
"One Room Country Shack" (Mercy Dee) 114
"Ordinary Fella" (Pete Townshend) 228
"Orgasm Addict" (Buzzcocks) 274–275
Orwell, George 143
Osborne, John 184
Oscar 72
Otway, John 219
"Our Love Was" 89, 91, 94, 98
"Out in the Street" 41, 45, 53, 54, 55
Out of Sight (film) 21
"Overture" 115, 117, 135, 137
"The Ox" 19, 54, 58, 59, 62, 116, 243

Page, Jimmy 42
Palmer, Carl 245
Palmer, Tony 209
Papparlardi, Felix 149
Parmeinter, Chris 32
Parting Should Be Painless (Roger Daltrey) 268
Passion Play (Jethro Tull) 189
Patterson, Dr Meg 246
Paul Revere And The Raiders 45
Peer Gynt (Ibsen) 99
Pentangle 275
Pet Sounds (Beach Boys) 64
Peter Grimes (Britten) 208
Phillips, Eddie 16
Phillips, Tom 259
"Pictures of Lily" 84, 85, 86, 91, 93, 106, 110, 128
Pidgeon, John 276, 277
"Pinball Wizard" 113, 115–116, 117, 119, 120, 122, 123, 128, 133, 137, 248

Pink Fairies 174, 175
Pink Floyd 8, 39, 68, 83, 95, 97, 127, 144, 178, 189, 219, 221
Pin-Ups (David Bowie) 189, 191, 213
Piper at the Gates of Dawn (Pink Floyd) 97
Platts-Mills, Barney 187
"Please Don't Touch" 13, 83
"Please Please Please" 45, 47, 54, 57, 59
"Plum Nellie" (Howlin' Wolf) 12, 31
Plummer, Mark 180
"Politician" (Pete Townshend) 106
Pomp and Circumstance March No.1 (Elgar) 75
Pop, Iggy 134; *see also* Iggy and the Stooges; The Stooges
"Popular" (Pete Townshend) 262
Porter, Cole 134
Portsmouth Sinfonia 275
"Postcard" 134, 135, 136, 147, 213, 214
Powell, Anthony 200
"Praying the Game" (Pete Townshend) 246
"Prelude: The Right to Write" (Pete Townshend) 267
"Prelude #556" (Pete Townshend) 267
"Premier Drums" 93, 96
Preservation Act 1 (The Kinks) 189
Presley, Elvis 6, 30
The Pretty Things 111
Procol Harum 113
Procter, Adelaide 276
PsychoDerelict (Pete Townshend) 166, 167, 270
The Pudding 109
"The Punk and the Godfather" 191, 193, 195, 196–199, 204, 250, 252
Purcell, Henry 70–71
"Pure and Easy" 142, 147, 149, 150, 151, 152, 155, 160, 161, 163, 165, 166, 167, 171, 213
"Purple Haze" (Jimi Hendrix Experience) 84
"Put the Money Down" 165, 167, 171, 173, 213, 214
Puterbaugh, Parke 265
Puttnam, David 190

Quadrophenia 17, 22, 26, 44, 120, 170, 173, 176, 177–210, 211, 212, 214, 215, 217, 218, 222, 226, 231, 248, 249–251, 255, 262, 265, 271, 272, 278
"Quadrophenia" 181, 182, 194, 195, 206
Quadrophenia (film) 245, 246, 249
Quadrophenia (soundtrack) 34, 249–251

Quads (proposed album title) 22, 72, 77
Quatro, Suzi 212
Queen 219
A Quick One 22, 64, 75, 76–82, 89, 98, 271
"A Quick One While He's Away" 22–23, 77, 81, 91, 106, 120, 133, 201, 248
"The Quiet One" 255, 256, 260, 267

Radcliffe, Charles 132
"Rael" 22, 23, 88–89, 95–96, 98, 99, 115, 118, 142
Rael (proposed album title) 88
Rainbow 219
The Ramones 8, 231
Rarities Vol 1: 1966–1968 268
Rarities Vol 2: 1970–1973 268
Ravel, Maurice 208
Ready Steady Go! (TV) 10, 21, 66, 74, 76, 82–83, 217
Ready Steady Goes Live! (TV) 46–47
Ready Steady Who! 74–76, 78, 170
"The Real Me" 193, 194–195, 201, 211, 235, 243, 246, 250, 252
"Recorders" (Pete Townshend) 181
Reed, Jimmy 5, 12, 31, 51
Reed, Lou 279
Reed, Oliver 212
The Regents 75
"Relax" 89, 91, 95, 106
"Relay" 165, 167, 171, 172–173, 174, 178
R.E.M. 3, 8, 9
"Remote Control" (The Clash) 198
Reminiscing (Buddy Holly) 265
REO Speedwagon 265
Revolt into Style (George Melly) 273
Revolver (Beatles) 7, 64
Richard, Cliff 10, 30, 33, 256
Richard, Keith 85–86
Ride a Rock Horse (Roger Daltrey) 216, 219
Rigor Mortis 180
Rigor Mortis Sets In (John Entwistle) 180
Riley, Terry 140
The Rio Grande (Constant Lambert) 273
"Riot in the Female Jail" (Pete Townshend) 171, 173
"Road Runner" 106, 147, 230, 248
Robbins, Ira 227, 241, 259, 265
"The Rock" 181, 206, 243
Rock and Other Four Letter Words (J. Marks & L. Eastham) 273
Rock and Roll Circus (TV) 110, 217
Rock Farm (proposed film title) 177
Rock of the Westies (Elton John) 221

Rock Is Dead: Long Live Rock (proposed album title) 179
Rock 'n' Roll (John Lennon) 213
The Rockin' Vicars 68, 69
Rock's in the Head (Roger Daltrey) 268
Rockspeak (radio) 278
Rockwell, John 210, 212
Roden, Jess 110
The Rolling Stones 1, 7, 8, 11, 12, 18, 20, 22, 30, 32, 41, 42, 57, 58, 64, 73, 85–86, 97, 109, 110, 117, 144, 152, 157, 170, 175, 181, 214, 217, 219, 221, 229, 253
Romeo and Juliet (Shakespeare) 189
The Ronettes 249
Ross, Diana 108
Rossetti, Dante Gabriel 211
"Rotosound Strings" 94, 96
"Rough Boys" (Pete Townshend) 252, 254
Rough Mix (Pete Townshend & Ronnie Lane) 168, 232, 233, 246
"Round and Round" (early title of "In a Hand or a Face") 226
Rountree, John 209
Roxy Music 175
Rubber Soul (Beatles) 7
"Run Run Run" 69, 76, 78–79, 83–84
"Runaround Sue" 69
Rush 219
Ruskin Spear, Roger 275
Russell, Bertrand 5
Russell, Ethan A. 163, 184, 188
Russell, Ken 211–212, 216, 219
Russell Harty Plus (TV) 173, 180

Saal, Hubert 209
Salieri, Antonio 236
"Sally Simpson" 119, 122, 136
"Sam" (Keith West) 111
Sandom, Doug 13, 30
Sarne, Mike 275
Saturday Club (radio) 49, 59, 66, 72, 83, 91, 274
Saturday Night and Sunday Morning (Alan Sillitoe) 184, 195
Saturday Night and Sunday Morning (film) 184, 189
"Saturday Night's Alright for Fighting" 270
Savage Messiah (film) 216
Scabies, Rat 232
Schacht, Janis 209
Scoop (Pete Townshend) 166, 181, 268, 275
The Sea (Frank Bridge) 208
"Sea and Sand" 186, 193, 203

Sea Drift (Delius) 208
Sea Pictures (Elgar) 208
A Sea Symphony (Vaughan Williams) 208
The Searchers 8
"See Me, Feel Me" 117, 120, 122, 128, 131, 133, 135, 248, 252
"See My Friend" (Kinks) 69
"See My Way" 76, 80–81, 84
"The Seeker" 128–129, 133, 134, 135, 139, 162
Sell Out 22, 85, 92–99, 100, 103, 105, 108, 113, 142, 144, 163, 271,
"Sensation" 119, 122
Sensible, Captain 232
Sgt Pepper's Lonely Hearts Club Band (Beatles) 25, 97, 99, 111
Sex Pistols 8, 231, 239
S. F. Sorrow (Pretty Things) 111
The Shadows 12, 33, 275
"Shakin' All Over" 13, 106, 109, 130, 133, 137
Shangri Las 102
"She's a Sensation" (early title of "Sensation") 106
Shindig (TV) 21
Shipston, Roy 142
"Shout" (Lulu and the Luvvers) 53
"Shout and Shimmy" 44, 47, 53, 54
"Showbiz Sonato" 76
Showcase (Buddy Holly) 214
The Showmen 32
Sibelius, Jean 6, 208
Siddhartha (Herman Hesse) 208
Siege (proposed album title) 267
"Signal 30" 86
"Silas Stingy" 95
Sillitoe, Alan 184
Silverton, Pete 241
Simple Minds 254
Sinatra, Frank 238
The Singles 268
"Sister Disco" 233, 235, 236–237, 241, 247, 251, 252
Sisters by a River (Barbara Comyns) 53
Slade 175
"Slip Kid" 220, 222–223, 228–229
"Sloop John B" (Beach Boys) 257
The Small Faces 8, 17, 22, 107, 111, 228, 232, 244, 249
"Smash the Mirror" 119, 122
Smash Your Head Against the Wall (John Entwistle) 134
Smashing Time (film) 189

Smile (Beach Boys) 25
Smith, Patti 8, 232
Smith, Reginald (Marty Wilde) 30
The Smiths 3
"Smokestack Lightning" (Howlin' Wolf) 12, 35, 47
Smokie 212
Smothers Brothers Comedy Hour (TV) 21, 91
"So Sad About Us" 69, 72, 76–77, 81
"So Very Long" 131
"Sodding About" 86, 213
The Soft Machine 68
"Somebody Saved Me" 260
"Someone's Coming" 89, 91, 98, 109
Something Else (Kinks) 97, 105
Sondheim, Stephen 237
"Song Is Over" 147, 154, 155, 160–161, 167, 181, 238
A Song of Summer (TV) 216
The Song Remains the Same (Led Zeppelin) 248
Sonic Youth 132
"Soon Be Home" 77, 81
Sound and Picture City (proposed TV title) 101
The South Bank Show (TV) 246
Southall, Brian 179
Space Ritual (Hawkwind) 189
"Sparks" 88, 115, 118, 119, 122, 128, 131, 133, 137, 248
Spector, Phil 79
Spellman, Benny 109
Spin Doctors 132
Spitting Image (TV) 92
"Spoonful" 12, 130, 133, 137
"Spotted Henry" 98
Springsteen, Bruce 8, 254, 264
"Squeeze Box" 217, 220, 224, 225, 228, 229, 230
Stainton, Chris 181–182, 202
Stamp, Chris 18, 21, 22, 30, 35, 37–38, 40, 48, 51, 64, 76, 84, 214–215, 273
Stamp, Terence 273
Stanley, Richard 134
Starmaker (TV) 217
Status Quo 175
Stein, Jeff 232, 247
Steve Gibbons Band 219
Stevenson, Robert Louis 104, 205
Stewart, Rod 15, 175, 221
Stewart, Tony 191, 218, 250
Stigwood, Robert 65, 66, 76, 211
Stingray (TV) 30

The Stooges 8, 132; *see also* Iggy and the Stooges
The Story of the Who 230, 231
The Story of Tommy (Richard Barnes & Pete Townshend) 275
The Strange Case of Dr. Jekyll and Mr. Hyde (Robert Louis Stevenson) 104, 205
Strauss, Richard 116, 211
Stravinsky, Igor 6
"Street in the City" (Pete Townshend & Ronnie Lane) 246
Strummer, Joe 198
"Substitute" 60, 61, 64–65, 66, 67, 68, 70, 74, 78, 85, 106, 124, 130, 133, 137, 201, 231, 247
"Success" 114
"Success Story" 220, 222, 224, 225, 228
Suite Gothique (Boellmann) 95
Sullivan, Arthur 72, 119, 237–238, 276
"Summertime Blues" 52, 85, 91, 98, 105, 106, 135, 213
Sunday Night at the London Palladium (TV) 21
"Sunrise" 95
"Surf City" (Jan And Dean) 71
The Sweet 212
Swenson, John 250
Swervedriver 270, 272
Szymczyk, Bill 254, 258, 259, 265

T. Rex 175
"Take Five" (Dave Brubeck Quartet) 120
"Take Me to the Pilot" 270
Tales from Topographic Oceans (Yes) 189
Talmy, Shel 22, 40, 42, 45, 48, 49, 52, 53, 54, 55, 59, 60, 61–62, 63, 64, 66, 67, 70, 78, 253
A Taste of Honey (film) 189
"Tattoo" 93–94, 106, 124, 133, 136
Taupin, Bernie 269–270
Taylor, James 136, 265
Tchaikovsky, Peter 211
Teenage Opera (Keith West) 111
10cc 175, 219
"That Motherland Feeling" 88
That'll Be the Day (film) 190–191
Their Satanic Majesties Request (Rolling Stones) 97
"There's a Doctor" 119
"There's a Fortune in Those Hills" 134, 136
These Foolish Things (Bryan Ferry) 213
"They Are All in Love" 222, 225

Index

"Things Have Changed" (Pete Townshend) 51
30 Years of Maximum R&B 28, 34, 62, 74, 109, 110, 129, 133, 150, 153, 169, 242, 247, 267, 270–271, 278
30 Years of Maximum R&B Live (video) 247
"This Be the Verse" (Philip Larkin) 277
This Sporting Life (film) 189
Thunderbirds (TV) 30
THX 1138 (film) 143
Time Fades Away (Neil Young) 217
"Time Is Passing" 136, 155, 160, 163, 165–166, 171, 213, 260,
Tindle, David 259
Tolliday, Ray 72, 164
Tommy 21, 22, 23, 24, 26, 88, 96, 102, 107, 110, 111–127, 128, 131, 132, 133, 134, 135, 136, 137, 139, 142, 144, 145, 146, 147, 170, 177, 179, 185, 188, 189, 191, 208, 210, 211–212, 231, 247, 255, 269, 271, 274
Tommy (film) 21, 211–212, 216, 220, 247, 268
"Tommy Can You Hear Me?" 119, 248
Tommy 1914–1984 (proposed album title) 111
Tommy (Original Soundtrack Recording) (Various Artists) 211–212
The Tommy Steele Story (film) 29
"Tommy's Holiday Camp" 120
Tomorrow 111
"Tomorrow Never Knows" (Beatles) 93
Tonight's the Night (Neil Young) 221
Too Late the Hero (John Entwistle) 28, 268
"Too Much of Anything" 165, 166, 167, 171, 213
"Too Much of Nothing" (Bob Dylan) 166
"Top Gear" 98
Top Gear (radio) 91, 98
Top of the Pops (TV) 10, 21, 192
Townshend, Cliff 30
Townshend, Karen 233
"Track Records" 96
Travis, Dave Lee 133
The Tremeloes 8
"Trick of the Light" 237, 241
The Tune Rockers 58
Twice a Fortnight (TV) 21
"Twist and Shout" 137, 266, 267
"The Two of Us" 142
Two Rooms (Various Artists) 270

Two Sides of the Moon (Keith Moon) 216
2001: A Space Odyssey (film) 116, 163
Two's Missing 48, 171, 268

UFO 219
Ulysses (James Joyce) 207
Uncle Meat (Frank Zappa) 114
Under a Raging Moon (Roger Daltrey) 28, 268
"Under My Thumb" 85, 213
"Underture" 88, 115, 118–119, 122, 136
Une Barque sur l'Ocean (Ravel) 208
Unit 4+2 8
"Uptight" (Stevie Wonder) 69
Uriah Heep 132, 219
U2 254

Valentine, Penny 82, 116, 145
Van Der Graaf Generator 127
Vaughan Williams, Ralph 208
Velvet Underground 8, 16
The Ventures 12, 58
The Village Green Preservation Society (Kinks) 111

Wagner, Richard 88, 127, 199, 205
Walker, Billy 164
Walls, Richard C. 259
"Waltz for a Pig" 66
The Wanting Seed (Anthony Burgess) 143
Warner, Rex 143
"Wasp Man" 171, 173
"The Waste Land" (T.S. Eliot) 159
"Water" 134, 135, 136, 137, 147, 153, 165, 167, 171, 174, 192, 213
Waters, Muddy 12
Watts, Michael 177–178
We (Yevgeny Zamyatin) 143
"We Close Tonight" 181, 210, 213
"We Have a Remedy" 77, 81
Weatherley, Charles 132
Wedgbury, David 58, 60
Weill, Kurt 200
Welch, Chris 82, 90, 97, 106, 126, 132, 172, 208–209, 214, 241, 258
"Welcome" 120, 122, 136
Weller, Paul 253
Wells, H.G. 143
Wenner, Jan 111
"We're Moving" 142
"We're Not Gonna Take It" 106, 117, 120, 121, 122, 125, 128
We're Only in It for the Money (Frank Zappa & the Mothers of Invention) 97

West, Keith 111
West, Leslie 149–150
West Side Story (musical) 183, 189
What a Crazy World (film) 29
"What Is Love?" (Pete Townshend) 254
Whatham, Claude 190
"What's Cooking" (Freddie and the Dreamers) 77
Wheels of Fire (Cream) 114
"When I Was a Boy" 147, 169–170
When the Sleeper Wakes (H.G. Wells) 143
"Whiskey Man" 73, 76, 78, 79, 80
Whistle Rhymes (John Entwistle) 174
White City (Pete Townshend) 267, 268
White Light/White Heat (Velvet Underground) 16
Whitman, Walt 208
"Who Are You" 27, 168, 233, 234, 235, 238–239, 240, 242, 247, 269
Who Are You 27, 168, 233–242, 243, 244, 253, 255, 266
Who Are You (proposed TV title) 245
The Who by Numbers see *By Numbers*
Who Came First (Pete Townshend) 166, 174
The Who Collection 268
Who Covers Who (Various Artists) 272
Who Dunnit – Chicago Knows Who (Various Artists) 272
The Who Orchestra 66
The Who Rocks America (video) 266
The Who Sell Out see *Sell Out*
The Who Sings My Generation 60–61
Who's Better Who's Best 268
Who's for Tennis (proposed album title) 101
Who's Greatest Hits 268
Who's Last 266–267
Who's Lily (proposed album title) 86
Who's Missing 48, 171, 268
Who's Next 24, 25, 26, 153–167, 168, 169, 170, 171, 172, 174, 176, 191, 222, 247, 255, 265, 271, 276
A Whole Scene Going (TV) 21, 69, 274
"Why" (Byrds) 60
"Why Can't You See I'm Easy" 171, 173
"Why Did I Fall for That" 264
Wilde, Marty 20
Wilde, Oscar 261
Williams, Andy 238

Williams, Larry 12, 147
Williams, Richard 250
Williamson, Sonny Boy 114
Wings 219, 221, 229
Wings Over America (Wings) 229
Wire 3
"Wizardry" 181
Wolf, Howlin' 12, 137
Women in Love (D. H. Lawrence) 207
Women in Love (film) 211
Wonder, Stevie 69
Wonderful Life (film) 21
"Won't Get Fooled Again" 144, 149, 152–153, 154, 155, 156–157, 158, 162, 164, 165, 167, 168, 169, 179, 233, 240, 243, 248, 251, 268, 269
"Wooden Ships" (David Crosby) 96
Woodstock (film) 21, 127–128
Woodstock (Original Soundtrack) (Various Artists) 127–128
Wray, Link 12, 14, 58
Wycherly, Ronald (Billy Fury) 30

The Yardbirds 8, 16, 18, 20, 22, 32, 33, 42, 64, 274
Yes 127, 175, 189, 219
Yogi, Maharishi 101
"You" 257, 259
"You Are Forgiven" 77, 81, 110
"You Better You Bet" 255, 269
"You Don't Have to Jerk" 41, 44, 47, 61
"You Really Got Me" (The Kinks) 34, 40
Young, Neil 159, 217, 221
"Young Man Blues" 77, 113, 114, 128, 130, 137, 213, 243, 248
Younger Than Yesterday (Byrds) 97
Your Turn in the Barrel (proposed film title) 144
"You're Going to Know Me" (early title of "Out in the Street") 41, 45, 47, 54
"You're So Clever" (Pete Townshend) 254

Zamyatin, Yevgeny 143
Zappa, Frank 6, 97, 111, 177, 212, 217
"Zelda" (Pete Townshend) 254
Ziggy Stardust and the Spiders from Mars (David Bowie) 191
"Zoot Suit" 18, 32–34, 203, 250